TEXTUAL

EDITING

AND

CRITICISM

An Introduction

Thomas Gray's "Elegy Written in a Country Churchyard" was first published with a variant title.

AN

ELEGY

WROTE IN A

Country Church Yard.

LONDON:

Printed for R. DODSLEY in *Pall-mall*;

And fold by M. COOPER in *Pater-nofter-Row*. 1751.

[Price Six-pence.]

A N
E L E G Y
WRITTEN IN A
Country Church Yard.

The THIRD EDITION, corrected.

L O N D O N:
Printed for R. DODSLEY in *Pall-mall*;
And sold by M. COOPER in *Pater-noster-Row.* 1751.
[Price Six-pence.]

TEXTUAL

EDITING

AND

CRITICISM

An Introduction

ERICK KELEMEN

FORDHAM UNIVERSITY

Foreword by

DONALD H. REIMAN

W. W. NORTON & COMPANY · NEW YORK · LONDON

W. W. Norton & Company has been independent since its founding in 1923, when William Warder Norton and Mary D. Herter Norton first published lectures delivered at the People's Institute, the adult education division of New York City's Cooper Union. The Nortons soon expanded their program beyond the Institute, publishing books by celebrated academics from America and abroad. By mid-century, the two major pillars of Norton's publishing program—trade books and college texts—were firmly established. In the 1950s, the Norton family transferred control of the company to its employees, and today—with a staff of four hundred and a comparable number of trade, college, and professional titles published each year—W. W. Norton & Company stands as the largest and oldest publishing house owned wholly by its employees.

The text of this book is composed in Bembo
with the display set in Bernhard Modern.
Book design by Jo Anne Metsch.
Composition by Binghamton Valley Composition.
Page layout by Carole Desnoes.
Manufacturing by the Courier Companies—Westford, MA.
Copy editor: Katharine Ings.
Production manager: Benjamin Reynolds.
Project editor: Lory A. Frenkel.

Library of Congress Cataloging-in-Publication Data

    Textual editing and criticism : an introduction / Erick Kelemen ; foreword by Donald H. Reiman.—1st ed.
        p. cm.

    Includes bibliographical references and index.
    ISBN 978-0-393-92942-3
    1. Criticism, Textual.   I. Kelemen, Erick.
    P47.T49 2008
    801'.959 — dc22   2008001785

W. W. Norton & Company, Inc., 500 Fifth Avenue, New York, N.Y. 10110-0017
www.wwnorton.com

W. W. Norton & Company Ltd., Castle House, 75/76 Wells Street, London W1T 3QT

1 2 3 4 5 6 7 8 9 0

FOR
KATHRINE
AND
HENRY

CONTENTS

PART THREE

Working with Editions

Working with Documents

Acknowledgments

UNLIKE MANY OTHER kinds of debts, the ones incurred in writing are pleasurable to remember. I wish to offer my thanks to the staffs of several libraries: Peter Neely, Lucia D'Agostino, Mary Batterson, and Janet Caruthers at Stafford Library of Columbia College, Columbia, Missouri; the staff of Ellis Library at the University of Missouri, Columbia, especially Cindy Cotner; the staff of the libraries at the University of Kentucky, Lexington, particularly Diane Brun at Young Library, Jim Birchfield, William Marshall, Gordon Hogg, and Mary Molinaro at King Library, and Paul Holbrook at the King Library Press; Olin Library, Washington University, St. Louis, specifically Sarah Patton; Bettina C. Smith at Folger Shakespeare Library, Washington, DC; Cambridge University Library; British Library, London; Margaret Thompson at the Cheshunt Foundation Archives, Westminster College, Cambridge; Richard Clement at the Spencer Research Library, University of Kansas, Lawrence; Greg Giuliano at the Rosenbach Museum and Library; Melissa Dalziel at the Bodleian, Oxford; Jayne Amat at the University of Nottingham Library; Phillipa Grimstone at Magdalene College Library, Cambridge; Stephen Tabor and Lita Garcia at Huntington Library, San Marino, California; Jaclyn Penny at the American Antiquarian Society, Worcester, Massachusetts; Christina Henshaw at Lambeth Palace Library, London; Jonathan Smith at Trinity College Library, Cambridge; Rachel Howarth at Harvard University's Houghton Library, Cambridge, Massachusetts. I wish to thank my students for submitting to field tests of

xi

many of the ideas in this book and for offering useful comments and encouragement: first and foremost, Brooke Taylor, who also did valuable research for me at the Olin Library, at Washington University; also Alicia Inman, Amanda Mueller, Austin Pickett, Rhonda Vitale, and Karissa Scott, who were tested more than perhaps any others; and, finally, Holly Osborn and Seth Holler, who read and commented on portions of this book while in my bibliography and methods of research class at the University of Kentucky. Thanks are also due to many colleagues, friends, and teachers for help and support: George Justice, Devoney Looser, John Evelev, Emma Lipton, Tom Quirk, Pamela McClure, John Bryant, Bill Harrison, Beth McCoy, Ann Hawkins, Leon Higdon, Catherine Carter, Scott Lightsey, Michael Winship, Mardi Marzek, Tom Berger, the late Thomas Calhoun, Ernest Sullivan, J. A. Leo Lemay, W. D. Snodgrass, Donald Mell, Charles Robinson, Peter Blayney, Jonathan Allison, and Walter Foreman. I owe perhaps the most profound debts to Lois Potter and to James M. Dean, whose teaching brought me to just this kind of book. The people at W. W. Norton have been remarkable: Rivka Genesen, Brian Baker, and especially Carol Bemis. Don Reiman has provided help and guidance from the beginning. I can't imagine a more kind or more gentle mentor than he has been. Most pleasant of all to remember are the debts I owe to my wife, Kathrine Varnes, my first and best editor, my source. What is good in this book, I owe to the generous people named above. Errors that remain are wholly mine—and are perhaps intentional.

ERICK KELEMEN
Lexington, Kentucky

FOREWORD

WHILE I WAS a member of the Modern Language Association's Committee on Scholarly Editions (CSE), I agreed to organize a program on editorial matters at the MLA's annual convention at Philadelphia in December 2004. The program's title, which alluded to the CSE's program for examining scholarly editions and awarding a Seal of Approval to volumes that conform to the Committee's standards, was "Seals and Walruses: What Can We Learn from Bad Editions?" That MLA panel featured papers by three senior scholars who examined problems in editions of Walt Whitman's manuscripts, Percy Bysshe Shelley's poetry, and Spanish dramas of the Golden Age. But it was the fourth speaker—a younger scholar named Erick Kelemen—whose response struck me as being the most original talk in the session. In it, Kelemen emphasized the usefulness of teaching the rudiments of textual analysis to students. He described how he had challenged a class of run-of-the-mill undergraduates, who had no experience with editing or textual criticism, to prepare a critical edition of Chaucer's "Truth." By working cooperatively with facsimiles of five manuscripts of that poem, the students selected a base text, discussed cruxes in textual and informational notes, and completed the assignment with an introduction that outlined their procedures and provided a brief critical discussion of Chaucer's poem. Even though both Kelemen and the class recognized that the jerry-built edition was a "walrus," rather than a seal, the students learned more about the various aspects of one poem than they had ever learned before.

Their involvement in the process of closely comparing the details of the primary documents alerted them to the subtle opportunities for error in the transmission of texts and also made them much better readers of poetry.

The next day Carol Bemis of W. W. Norton (also a member of the CSE who had heard Erick Kelemen's talk) and I agreed to encourage him to prepare a proposal for a textbook that could lead undergraduates, as well as graduate students, into the neglected study of textual analysis. Such a book, we agreed, could help teachers, students, and the reading public to become more critically aware of how editors and publishers develop the texts that are used in their classrooms and to sharpen their skills in the close reading of verbal details. The skills cultivated by those engaged in textual criticism can carry over into many other disciplines and professions. Analyzing and comparing the detailed evidence provided by less-than-perfect documents and reaching conclusions based on material evidence, an understanding of human behavior, and the laws of probability can not only serve the pragmatic needs of those who study literary documents, but can also be extremely useful to (among others) historians, attorneys, scientists, pharmacists, cartographers, detectives, financial analysts, and presidential aides.

So sure was I that Erick Kelemen would succeed in this effort that at the March 2005 conference of the Society for Textual Scholarship (STS) I added a paragraph to my presidential address that quoted from Kelemen's classroom work on Chaucer's "Truth"; I went on to suggest that it was an opportune time for STS to move beyond its discussions of theory and methods presented by and for experienced editors. Encouraging other programs that could teach textual criticism in the classrooms of colleges and universities and disseminating the central ideas of the discipline by engaging students in solving textual problems, I argued, would be good for the STS and for students in both their academic studies and their later careers.

As one who specializes in the study of English and American poetry, I take special delight in Kelemen's success in creating this well-thought-out and clearly presented approach to the spectrum of editorial methods and the principles of textual analysis because this training has been so important to my own life. Each of us has favorite texts, whether they are classic poems, the lyrics of popular songs or hymns, or historical documents such as the Declaration of Independence or Lincoln's Gettysburg Address, and each of us would like, if possible, to use our own words to communicate our feelings and ideas as clearly and effectively as possible. The study of textual criticism helps to preserve the integrity of texts written by authors who have achieved that goal and—as a bonus—it can also help us to understand how they succeeded, so that we can improve our own communication with others.

When I was about eleven years old, I was given a slim paperback entitled *One Hundred and One Famous Poems.* Reading those *Famous Poems* and the verse in a larger collection, *Best Loved Poems of the American People,* so stirred my imagination, that they became constant companions. At first, the poems that appealed to me might simply tell a story or make witty observations on human foibles. But as time passed, I fell in love with the richness of the English language and its prosody and delighted in literary images and rhetorical patterns. As the intense feelings of adolescence came upon me, I began to wonder why those poems had such power to amuse me or move me and how those combinations of simple words could link the poets' lives and experiences to mine, broadening and deepening my maturing thoughts and feelings. Most of my teachers in high school, college, and even graduate school taught the history of literature, or appreciation of literature, more than analysis of it, but they failed to explain to me how language can be magnetized to transmit Life across Time to produce good books that, as Milton wrote, become the precious life-blood of master-spirits, "embalmed and treasured up on purpose to a life beyond life."

When William Shakespeare, or William Wordsworth and other English romantic poets, or such novelists as Charles Dickens, Fëdor Dostoevski, and Joseph Conrad informed and comforted me in the midst of joys and woes far removed from their times and situations, these authors seemed to me like magicians who refused to share their secrets with us lesser beings. Our routine, everyday language fills us with information but often lacks the beauty, precision, and vitality that characterizes the very best writings that have given knowledge, comfort, and enjoyment for decades, or even centuries, after those authors were in their graves. While I was writing my dissertation on Shelley's "The Triumph of Life," I was forced for the first time to engage textual studies in a serious way and, after traveling to Oxford and immersing myself in the study of Shelley's manuscripts there, I began for the first time to understand the creative process at work. By spending many hours intensively analyzing primary documents, which reveal the craft of poets most clearly, I found that textual studies provide perhaps the best means to understand poetry. By following the growth of a poem from its inception, as revealed in the poet's letters or notes, through its various stages of composition to its published form, and finally by witnessing the reactions of the author's contemporaries after its publication, one can learn at least some of the magician's secrets. Textual scholarship thus provides a fruitful route to literary understanding—the ultimate goal of the study of literature. Literary understanding embodies at least two primary components: cognitive enlightenment and aesthetic appreciation—teaching and delighting, or sweetness and light. Writings that lack one of these two elements may be, as Samuel Taylor Coleridge noted, part of a *poem*, but they are not *poetry*.

Erick Kelemen's *Textual Editing and Criticism: An Introduction* will enable students to initiate—and empower many teachers to strengthen—their understanding of how to analyze texts, permitting all of them to distinguish well-prepared editions from careless ones and stimulating many to gain the skills to improve, or even to undertake their own editions of short texts, thereby preparing themselves to do whatever is necessary in the academy or in other professions based upon the accurate use of words and symbols. Professor Kelemen provides multiple paths to such understanding. He begins by presenting problems that readers have found in important texts and moves on to discuss the techniques used to cope with those problems and to outline the history of textual studies in many literary fields, ending his opening chapters with a survey of important perspectives on editing and textual analysis. In Part Two, he provides a generous selection of major statements on how to edit and theories of the text that have been—and are still being—debated by the leading theorists and practitioners of editing since the mid-twentieth century. Finally, he sets problems that have faced editors of complicated texts and, by providing alternate texts worked out by different editors, he invites readers to develop their own solutions and learn from hands-on experience (often the very best teacher) by attempting to cope with those or similar problems. Kelemen's accurate glossary of bibliographical and editorial terms recaps important historical issues and current points of disagreement, while the rich list in his bibliography provides the teacher with additional reading assignments on the topics of discussion in the field and enterprising students with additional sources for their knowledge of the subject.

One final word: It is important to remember that the field of editorial and textual theory is still vibrant and unsettled, as it has been since the 1980s. This means that many ideas propounded by those of us active in these discussions are not universally accepted and may be taken with a dash of salt. But it also means that younger teachers and students who find textual studies congenial and who choose to debate the issues at conferences of the Society for Textual Scholarship and other venues may join with senior scholars in shaping the future direction of this burgeoning discipline. Welcome to all!

DONALD H. REIMAN
Newark, Delaware

PART ONE

Why Study Textual Editing and Criticism

THE FOLLOWING IS the narrative of Jesus and the adulterous woman (the *pericope adulterae*—"the passage of the adulteress") as it appears in *The Oxford Study Bible*'s English translation:

[1]. . . Jesus went to the mount of Olives. [2]At daybreak he appeared again in the temple, and all the people gathered round him. He had taken his seat and was engaged in teaching them [3]when the scribes and the Pharisees brought in a woman caught committing adultery. Making her stand in the middle [4]they said to him, "Teacher, this woman was caught in the very act of adultery. [5]In the law Moses has laid down that such women are to be stoned. What do you say about it?" [6]They put the question as a test, hoping to frame a charge against him. Jesus bent down and wrote with his finger on the ground. [7]When they continued to press their question he sat up straight and said, "Let whichever of you is free from sin throw the first stone at her." [8]Then once again he bent down and wrote on the ground. [9]When they heard what he said, one by one they went away, the eldest first; and Jesus was left alone, with the woman still standing there. [10]Jesus again sat up and said to the woman, "Where are they? Has no one condemned you?" [11]She answered, "No one, sir." "Neither do I condemn you," Jesus said. "Go, do not sin again."[1]

---

1. M. Jack Suggs, Katharine Doob Sakenfeld, and James R. Mueller, eds., *The Oxford Study Bible, Revised English Bible with the Apocrypha* (New York: Oxford University Press, 1992), 1393.

3

In this compact and appealing story, Jesus protects a woman who is being used as a pawn and establishes an ethical principle about the power to judge. For many it encapsulates several primary themes of Christian doctrine, such as everybody's need for forgiveness since all people are imperfect.

Would it make any difference if we added or left out a few words?

This is not only a hypothetical question. Some early witnesses, the sources editors rely on, have a variant (or different) verse nine: "When they heard what he said, one by one they went away, *convicted by their conscience,* the eldest first, and Jesus was left alone, with the woman still standing there." Some might argue that in this story about sin and forgiveness, "convicted by their conscience" is implied by the context, so an editor might as well follow those witnesses without the phrase. Others might argue that the phrase is not a redundancy. Since the Scribes and Pharisees are trying to trap Jesus, a version of the story without the phrase might suggest that their departure stems from disappointment (rather than guilt or shame) when they see that Jesus will not respond directly to their question. For these readers, the variant emphasizes one of several interpretations, so its presence or absence is quite significant.

This passage has invited much controversy and commentary and is what is known as a textual problem or crux.[2] The editors of *The Oxford Study Bible* had to decide at this point not only which version of verse nine to print, but what to do with the whole passage, because the entire story is a variant. Some witnesses do not have the story at all. Some witnesses have the story in the Gospel of Luke, some in the Gospel of John. To further complicate the issue, when the passage appears in John, it appears in one of three different positions. Editors are faced with no fewer than six options in handling this tale. The first is to choose not to print the story at all. Because not all early witnesses contain it, and

---

2. The textual problem is actually even more complicated than is suggested here. The story contains more variants than any other portion of the Gospels. For a detailed technical discussion, see Wieland Willker, *A Textual Commentary on the Greek Gospels,* vol. 4b, The *Pericope de Adultera:* John 7.53–8.11 (Jesus and the Adultress), 3rd ed., 2005, http://www.-user.uni-bremen.de/~wie/TCG/TC-John-PA.pdf.

because it appears in different places in different witnesses, it may be that overzealous copyists years after the Gospels were composed inserted the passage on their own, an interpolation. The second through fifth options are to print the story in one of the four traditional places recorded in the various witnesses. The editors of *The Oxford Study Bible* select a sixth option, printing it as a separate piece at the end of John, with a note explaining the different places it might fit. Similarly, rather than print the phrase "convicted by their conscience" in verse nine, the Oxford editors put it in a note at the end of the tale, where they also explain that problem. Perhaps the *Oxford* editors felt that neither the story as a whole nor the phrase in particular had quite enough authority. That is, perhaps the editors were not convinced enough by the evidence to include the story as a genuine part of the early Gospels' text, but nevertheless wished to include it to give readers a sense of that text's history.

The Oxford Study Bible is an example of a scholarly or critical edition, a result of textual or critical editing. Like all varieties of editing, critical editing presents a text for readers, but unlike other varieties, it employs and includes textual criticism in its process and its results, generally making the editor's sources and decisions more open to readers. The traditional understanding of textual criticism is that it is the practice of identifying and correcting—emending—errors in the text. This definition of textual criticism may not itself serve to distinguish critical editing from, say, copy-editing, which also seeks to identify and correct errors. Textual criticism and critical editing also may attempt to identify for readers points of ambiguity or disagreement about a text, while copy-editing aims to resolve, eliminate, or conceal such points. But the more significant difference lies in textual criticism's concern with the history of a text, from its composition to the most current editions. Textual criticism makes critical editing, to borrow the words of D. C. Greetham, a kind of "archaeology of the text, . . . uncovering the layers of textual history as they accumulate one on another."[3] A major aspect

---

3. D. C. Greetham, "Introduction," *Scholarly Editing: a Guide to Research* (New York: The Modern Language Association, 1995), 1–7, see 2.

of these "layers of textual history" is the body of variants one finds in the witnesses, but these layers also include, among other things, the choices editors have made concerning the text over the years.

Textual criticism assumes that even small differences in texts can be significant, shaping different meanings as we read. If that premise is true, then a basic understanding of textual criticism and of editing can be useful for every reader. True, textual criticism and editing are the provinces of experts. But we need not become the editors of *The Oxford Study Bible* to benefit from learning to read and think somewhat as they do. We will all, however, require a basic introduction to the methods and aims of textual criticism and textual editing to begin to be aware of the issues that concern them. And doing for ourselves even a little of what they do teaches a great deal. Jerome McGann predicts that "[i]n the next fifty years the entirety of our inherited archive of cultural works will have to be reedited within a network of digital storage, access, and dissemination."[4] McGann, whose online archive of materials relating to the nineteenth-century painter and poet Dante Gabriel Rossetti has done perhaps as much as any other project to begin to realize the potential of this digital system, is himself aware that the monumental task he describes began in many ways decades ago (with projects like *The Dictionary of Old English* at the University of Toronto, which began in the 1970s by digitizing vast numbers of Old English texts for a microfiche concordance, which appeared in 1980)[5] and has seen phenomenal growth with the advent of the World Wide Web.[6] But for McGann, the prospect of his "prophecy" is a grim one:

> Just when we will be needing young people well-trained in the histo-
> ries of textual transmission and the theory and practice of scholarly
> method and editing, our universities are seriously unprepared to educate

4. Jerome McGann, "A Note on the Current State of Humanities Scholarship," *Critical Inquiry* 30.2 (2004): 409–13, see 410.

5. See *The Dictionary of Old English* website: http://www.doe.utoronto.ca/.

6. See the Rossetti archive: http://www.rossettiarchive.org/.

such persons. Electronic scholarship and editing necessarily draw their primary models from long-standing philological practices in language study, textual scholarship, and bibliography. As we know, these three core disciplines preserve but a ghostly presence in most of our Ph.D. programs. (410)

Digitized archives will likely be of little value for their users if their editors are unprepared for the work. For this reason, McGann sees "an educational emergency now grown acute with the proliferation of digital technology" (410). Crisis or no, one can certainly agree with McGann that instruction in his "core disciplines" will be fruitful, and not only because of potential job opportunities, but also because we are seeing the beginnings of an eruption of materials that previously have been unavailable to general readers. Some understanding of the issues in their digital publication will be valuable for consumers as well as for producers.

This volume offers undergraduate and beginning graduate students of English and American literature an introduction to textual criticism and critical editing, providing in addition both a sampling of major statements in the field and a broad variety of examples and materials for hands-on practice. Perhaps textual criticism is not taught at the graduate level as much as it ought to be, but for too long it has been treated as a subject fit only for specialists in training. This may be because textual criticism has been seen by many as having only practical applications in preparing editions, the work of a few college professors, while literary criticism, so the thinking goes, can be practiced by all and aims not to make texts better but to make students better people, preparing future citizens of the world. Whatever else one may think about this distinction, it certainly relies upon a wrong notion, too much fostered in the past by textual critics themselves, that interpretation is not a part of textual criticism, that textual criticism is a branch of study essential to but separate from literary criticism, as M. L. West seems to do:

Students have sometimes said to me that they recognize the necessity of textual criticism, but they are content to leave it to the editor of the text they are reading and to trust in his superior knowledge. Unfortunately editors are not always people who can be trusted, and critical apparatuses are provided so that readers are not dependent upon them. Though the reader lacks the editor's long acquaintance with the text and its problems, he may nevertheless surpass him in his feeling for the language or in ordinary common sense, and he should be prepared to consider the facts presented in the apparatus and exercise his own judgment on them. He *must* do so in places where the text is important to him for some further purpose.[7]

West's point is that in order for an interpretation of a work to be valid, the text on which the interpretation is based has to be an accurate representative of that work. West may be correct, but we undervalue textual criticism if we consider its role to be only a fact-checking precursor to interpretation. As should be clear from the story of Jesus and the adulteress, textual criticism involves interpretation in fundamental ways. In Greetham's words again, "the single most important characteristic of textual *criticism* . . . is that it is *critical*, it does involve a speculative, personal, and individual confrontation of one mind by another."[8] Textual criticism concerns itself with the text's transmission history, and since that history is the history of aesthetic and political choices, textual criticism goes hand in hand with other critical approaches. Seeing textual criticism as the "archaeology of the text" means that the two fields, textual criticism and literary criticism, cannot be kept separate, but that they are in fact interlinked aspects of the same activity.

More than a cursory fact-checking, textual criticism teaches attitudes and skills valuable to all readers. Many literary critics today insist that a work of literature must be understood as a product of historical conditions, and textual criticism teaches us that the specific manifestations of the work—the documents we hold in our hands—have affected our

7. M. L. West, *Textual Criticism and Editorial Technique Applicable to Greek and Latin Texts* (Stuttgart: Teubner, 1973), 8–9.

8. Greetham, *Textual Scholarship: an Introduction,* corr. repr. (New York: Garland, 1994), 295.

understanding of the work without our necessarily being aware of it. At a minimum, textual criticism cannot fail to instill a basic skepticism toward the text that is, for many, a prerequisite for all literature students. But more than that, textual criticism is something like the close reading that underlies nearly all contemporary critical approaches, relying on similar non-linear and recursive reading habits in order to draw the text's details into greater relief. To return to the *Oxford Study Bible* for an example, whatever the editorial reasoning behind their treatment of the story of Jesus and the adulteress (as a note at the end of John, explaining where it might go in the text of either John or Luke), the result for traditional readers is a mixed one. All the elements are present to be pieced together as a reader might choose, but the disjointed presentation results in a disjointed reading experience. Some assembly is required, encouraging if not necessitating several re-readings and some page flipping. Such interruptions may well frustrate those whose primary aim in reading is to gather information, that is, to read for the plot. But such frustrations are also useful in that they encourage closer attention to the text and may generate greater sensitivity to its subtleties and complexities and greater appreciation of its value. In some ways the tools of textual criticism may be more empowering for the student than traditional close reading, since a fundamental principle in textual criticism is that no text is ever truly final, so that each reader can participate in creating (or recovering) it.

WORKS, TEXTS, AND DOCUMENTS

That textual criticism and literary theory and criticism have competing definitions of the same words presents one obstacle to perceiving their integration. The most obvious of these words is *text,* which in textual criticism generally means an arrangement of words, but which in literary criticism usually has a much broader connotation, sometimes synonymous with the term *work.* Influential French literary theorist Roland Barthes attempts to distinguish the terms for literary criticism in his essay,

"From Work to Text."[9] The work, Barthes writes, is an object, "a fragment of substance, occupying a part of the space of books (in a library for
example)" (156–57). The text, on the other hand, is non-corporeal: "the
work can be held in the hand, the text is held in language" (156–57). In
Barthes's formulation, the term *work* signifies a way of thinking about
literature in which meaning resides in the piece itself, so that a reader's
task is to read properly in order to receive that meaning, while the term
text, on the other hand, signifies a way of thinking about literature in
which an indefinite number of meanings can emerge as a reader plays
the text in the way a musician might play a song, "ask[ing] of the reader
a practical collaboration" (163).

Barthes's formulations may not have been adopted by all literary critics, but at the least they offer an example of the expanding popularity of
the term *text* that G. Thomas Tanselle critiques from the perspective of a
textual critic in his essay, "Textual Criticism and Deconstruction."[10]
Tanselle points out that because the meaning of *text* has expanded for
most readers, "the term 'textual criticism' has become ambiguous, some
people regarding it as a synonym for 'literary criticism' " (203). Tanselle
would welcome "any development that brings 'textual critics' and 'literary critics' closer together" (203), but the blurring of *work* and *text* seems
to ignore for him the issues that textual criticism addresses. As for Barthes,
a work and a text for Tanselle are not the same. But Tanselle adds a third
term, *document*, which is essential to understanding what textual critics
mean by the first two terms. In Tanselle's view (and most textual critics
would agree with Tanselle here), a text is simply an arrangement of
words, something which both works and documents possess, just as they
might also possess a reputation or a history. While Barthes defines *work*
and *text* in opposition, the opposites for Tanselle are *work* and *document*.
The work, such as Shakespeare's *King Lear*, is an abstraction, reminiscent

9. Roland Barthes, "From Work to Text," *Image, Music, Text*, trans. Stephen Heath (New
York: Hill and Wang, 1977), 155–64.

10. G. Thomas Tanselle, "Textual Criticism and Deconstruction," *Literature and Artifacts*
(Charlottesville: Bibliographical Society of the University of Virginia, 1998), 203–35.

of Plato's ideal forms. A document, by contrast, is what Tanselle might agree to call "a fragment of substance," the actual object held before our eyes as we read, whether a manuscript, a printed book, or a file displayed on a computer screen. As an abstraction, an ideal, a work's text can always only be imperfectly realized in a document's text, and the role of textual criticism is, in this formulation, to attempt to reconstruct the ideal text from the imperfect versions in the various documents.

The situation with Shakespeare's *King Lear* provides a vivid illustration. The differences between the texts of the two earliest major printings of the play, the First Quarto (1608) and the First Folio (1623), are so great that one might reasonably ask, "Is *Lear* one work or two?" The answer is . . . "Yes"—at least according to *The Norton Shakespeare,* which presents three very different plays, one based on the 1608 quarto (known as *The History of King Lear*), another on the 1623 folio (called *The Tragedy of King Lear*), and a third that conflates the two.[11] Some might object to a conflated text, arguing that there is no early edition whose text looks like it, that this is an editor's creation, not Shakespeare's. But even the texts based on only one printing each are eclectic. The seventeenth-century printer's practices of correcting pages while they were being printed, of not rejecting pages known to contain errors, and of unintentionally mixing corrected and uncorrected pages, have made it likely that no two copies of one printing are identical. To construct the 1623 text, for instance, the Norton and Oxford editors have chosen among nonidentical copies of a single printing. What's more, they have emended the texts where they have seen fit. In other words, the Norton version of the 1623 text does not match exactly the text of any surviving copy of the

11. Unless otherwise indicated, all quotations of William Shakespeare's works are from *The Norton Shakespeare*, ed. Stephen Greenblatt, et al. (New York: W. W. Norton and Company, 1997). The *Norton Shakespeare* text is based on the Oxford edition: *William Shakespeare, The Complete Works*, ed. Stanley Wells and Gary Taylor (Oxford: The Clarendon Press, 1986). But the Oxford edition only presents two versions of *Lear*, while the Norton edition adds a conflation of the two. The reader may wish to note that the Oxford editors actually produced two editions in this year, one with modernized spelling and one that retains the old spelling. The Norton editors adopt the modernized.

1623 folio, nor perhaps any that ever existed, but presents an idealized form of it.

Each document (each copy) provides readers a concrete text (arrangement of words), but not one that is necessarily identical to the text of the work (the idea). This is true even if the work in question were to survive in only one document—the text of the document is never necessarily identical to the text of the work. Tanselle's insistence (and in general textual criticism's insistence) on the distinction between the text of a work and the text of a document is significant, because the document places its text in a specific context that contributes to its meaning. A text that is relatively unchanged from one document to another may nevertheless acquire wildly different meanings because of those contexts, an argument that McGann makes about Lord Byron's poem, "Fare Thee Well!" in "What Is Critical Editing?"[12] McGann writes that the poem appeared in three forms in 1816, when Byron wrote it, but that "the linguistic text of this work is quite stable." Nevertheless, the poem means radically different things in each of the three forms.

> The first (private) printing, in fifty copies, was carried out under Byron's instructions as a part of his effort to gain power (both psychologically and politically) over his wife during their 1816 marriage separation struggles. The unauthorized newspaper printing by *The Champion,* accompanied by an extensive editorial attack on Byron, used Byron's poem—which was meant for a weapon against his wife—as a weapon against him. The third version, the authorized book publication, was part of Byron's effort to regain some control over the situation. (59)

Surely something similar can be said about the story of Jesus and the adulteress. Imagine two documents, each containing the story, but one placing it in the Gospel of Luke, the other in the Gospel of John.

12. Jerome J. McGann, "What Is Critical Editing?" *The Textual Condition* (Princeton, NJ: Princeton University Press, 1991), 48–68.

Though the text of the story may not differ from one document to the next, its meanings might well be different in different documents, because the other texts in the documents are certainly different. For most textual critics, then, a document is a tangible thing whose text will always remain suspect, and a work is an abstraction whose text will never be perfectly recovered from these textually suspect documents. These formulations of *work* and *text* might seem a reversal of Barthes's, since for textual editors and critics, the work has a bodiless reality and texts may be variant but are always finite, while for Barthes, the work "can be held in the hand" while the text is uncontainable. One could hardly be faulted for thinking that textual critics and literary critics are speaking about different beasts altogether. Examining McGann's argument about Byron's poem, however, should suggest that the textual editor and textual critic have more in common with literary theorists and literary critics than might first appear. Both McGann and Barthes, after all, argue that the words of the poem alone do not generate the meanings one finds in the poem. In sum, even brief attention to the concerns that drive textual criticism will begin to challenge a reader's assumptions about important categories in literary criticism in ways that many literary theorists and literary critics would applaud.

READING FOR INSTABILITY

Once one knows how to look, one finds good examples for textual criticism are everywhere, not only tucked away in vaults in special collections libraries. All texts to one degree or another share the uncertainties enjoyed by the story of Jesus and the adulteress, because all texts are transmitted, and transmission affects texts. Between Shakespeare and modern readers and audiences stand uncountable people who might have altered the text by the time it was first printed: copyists, actors, theater managers, friends and fellow playwrights, publishers, printers and their employees, not to mention official censors. Making the situation even more complex is the fact that Shakespeare himself seems to have revised many of his plays after they first saw publication. Adding to these conditions that create textual uncertainty is a long history of publication, an army of printers and editors who come after Shakespeare's death and make changes in his works. The poet Alexander Pope was one, in 1725, whose solutions to cruxes are sometimes still adopted by editors today. Moreover, there is the history of preservation by owners and readers, librarians and collectors, any of whom can alter the text in individual copies, influencing later editions based on those copies. Shakespeare provides some of the more complex textual situations, while the student browsing literature published a century ago and not edited since is likely to encounter less textual complexity. But even were one to imagine the simplest of situations where as many variables of transmission have been eliminated as possible—even in such texts there is work for the textual critic.

And even the smallest of uncertainties provides an opportunity for textual study that can enrich our literary understanding and raise important theoretical questions of meaning and authorship. Below are two versions of the final stanza of Robert Frost's well-known poem, "Stopping by Woods on a Snowy Evening," the left-hand one as it appears in Frost's book *New Hampshire*, published in 1923, the right-hand one as it appears in the collection of Frost's poetry edited by Edward Lathem in 1969, six years after Frost's death.[13]

The woods are lovely, dark and deep.	The woods are lovely, dark, and deep,
But I have promises to keep	But I have promises to keep
And miles to go before I sleep,	And miles to go before I sleep,
And miles to go before I sleep.	And miles to go before I sleep.

Textual criticism calls close comparison of this sort *collation*, and it is one of the field's basic techniques for gathering data. It has the reputation of being as tedious a task as has ever been invented, especially when the

13. Robert Frost, "Stopping by Woods on a Snowy Evening," *New Hampshire* (New York: Holt, 1923), 87; and *The Poetry of Robert Frost*, ed. Edward Connery Lathem (New York: Holt, 1969), 24–25.

texts are long and the witnesses to collate are many. Nevertheless, it is an essential tool. Collation of the two versions of the stanza above discovers, for instance, that the stanzas differ in a comma after "dark" in the first line. Some might say that the difference reflects only the two standard ways of punctuating short lists and therefore is accidental and not substantive. *Accidental* and *substantive* are the terms that many textual critics use to categorize kinds of variation, borrowing them from medieval scholastic philosophy, especially the Realist camp. A thing's *substance* is its essence, its identity, while its *accidence* is its specific physical manifestation, and Realism holds that accidence can change while substance remains the same. Most textual critics are Realists, believing that a change in the physical appearance of the work—changing the typeface, for instance—does not change its substance, does not make it into a new work. Substantives, according to most textual critics, are variants that affect a text's substance, its meaning, while accidentals do not affect meaning. Traditionally, substantives are a text's words, while accidentals are such features as spelling, hyphenation, and punctuation, like this comma after "dark." But many of Frost's readers point out, as Richard Poirier and Donald Hall do, that the 1923 version of the stanza permits an interpretation not allowed by the 1969 version.[14] In the second version, the punctuation means that the adjectives all must modify "woods," so that the woods are lovely, they are dark, and they are also deep. But in the first version, without the comma, "dark and deep" might modify

14. Richard Poirier, *Robert Frost: The Work of Knowing* (New York: Oxford University Press, 1977), 181, and Donald Hall, "Robert Frost Corrupted," *The Weather for Poetry: Essays, Reviews, and Notes on Poetry, 1971–1981* (Ann Arbor: University of Michigan Press, 1982), 140–59. Both Poirier and Hall are passionate in preferring the punctuation of the earlier version. Poirier calls Lathem's emendation "obtuse" (181), and Hall concludes that "Lathem's edition should be allowed to go out of print," and that "a responsible literary scholar" should re-edit Frost's poems (159). As with the story of Jesus and the adulteress, the textual situation for Frost's poem is actually more complex than reported here, as is hinted by the fact that the first line of the stanza ends with a period in the 1923 version but a comma in the 1969 version, an emendation Lathem made but did not report in his notes. In fact, the poem's textual history reveals several variants, mostly involving punctuation, which are discussed by George Monteiro, "To Point or Not to Point: Frost's 'Stopping by Woods,'" *ANQ* 16.1 (Winter 2003): 38–40.

either "woods" or "lovely." More than simply being lovely *and* dark *and* deep woods, the woods may be lovely *because* they are dark and deep, an interpretation that the inserted comma denies to the second version. It is a slight difference, but it is significant because the poem juxtaposes the woods with the village and its business, juxtaposes the quiet isolation of the moment with the intrusions of society in the form of promises that encroach on the speaker, much as the horse does when, earlier in the poem, "He gives his harness bells a shake / To ask if there is some mistake" (9–10). The speaker who sees the woods as lovely because they are dark and deep will seem more in love with loneliness. In short, whether there is a comma after "dark" helps determine which feelings readers find in the speaker. Textual critics often employ the substantives/accidentals distinction when collations reveal too many variants to record in an economical set of notes. By silently emending accidentals (that is, emending the text without supplying a note for each instance), an editor can save the cost of printing them and save the reader time in sifting through them. An editor will usually supply an explanation of what kinds of emendations have been made silently. But, as one can see, whether one variant is substantive or accidental is a question of interpretation.

Once one has decided whether a variant is substantive, it is equally a matter of interpretation whether one variant is better than the others for any given crux. For much textual criticism, a basic assumption has been that each work has a single author who, in the genius of inspiration, had a single vision of the work. Working under these assumptions, textual critics have labored to recover an author's intentions (by which they mean not the intended meaning of the text, but the intended wording) by trying to recover the authorized (or authorial) version. The closer one can get to an authorized version, or the more authorized one can claim a version is, the more one can claim its unique or distinctive readings have authority. Even those who accept this definition of authorship have had disagreements about authorial intention, realizing of course that authors can have different intentions at different times. Some argue for recovering the author's last intentions for a text, while others argue that these last intentions are too often influenced by other people, and that the first moments of composition come closer to the author's true intentions. To further complicate matters, challenges to these Romantic age ideas of authorship have destabilized the idea of authorial intention. What happens if we understand the author of a work to be plural? A hypothetical novel might, for instance, have three major authors: 1) the named author; 2) the author's brother, who discusses the idea with her before her pen touches paper and then revises her first draft, inserting his own words here and there; 3) the publisher's editor, who cuts the manuscript by a third and reshapes many sentences in preparing the novel for publication, all changes implicitly approved by the author, who read and corrected proofs. In such a case, what kind of criterion is authorial intention? How does one disentangle the author from her brother, much less the author from her publisher's editor, whose work she approved? In place of authorial intention as the source for textual authority a textual editor might substitute history, choosing to print the text as it appeared at a specific moment or in a range of versions. Or an editor might substitute aesthetic principles, choosing to print what, in the editor's view, makes for the most beautiful version of the text. One should probably note here that modern reviewers and theorists have not been kind to editors who choose aesthetics over other authorities, but aesthetic principles are always part of an editor's concerns, and many editors openly consider the primary task in textual criticism and critical editing to be attuning the editor's sense of literary beauty with the author's, becoming something like a medium, channeling the author in order to follow the author's intentions. Before dismissing the editor-author relationship as wishful thinking, we should remember that editors typically rank among the foremost experts on an author's works and that their editions can take the better part of a career to prepare.

That the editor has spent a lifetime on one author's work does not mean that the beginner must refrain from questioning the editor's work. As M. L. West points out, the case is precisely the opposite. A critical editor indicates in the editorial apparatus (the *apparatus criticus*) the principles on which the edition is based, the evidence considered in making the edition, and the individual decisions that have been made, not only so that readers can verify the editor's choices, but so that the reader can begin to occupy the editor's position. Far from being an imposing warning to keep out, the textual notes are an invitation to join in the process, to test the hypothesis that is a critical edition. It is relatively easy to learn how to read the apparatus and, by so doing, to learn how to work backward from the notes toward the raw materials an editor employs. The apparatus is, loosely defined, everything except the text—the introductions and explanatory notes that surround the text—but it refers specifically to the explanation of the editorial procedures and to the textual notes, the notes that indicate emendations and usually record variant readings. Once one has learned to decipher the critical edition's codes, one can dip in and out of the apparatus at will, generating richer reading experiences by gaining access to an editor's decisions, which can be questioned and tested. Even if the reader agrees with the editor's choices, exploring the notes can reveal interesting details in the text's history. Using the notes and comparing them against the printed text, the reader can begin to reconstruct the features of the text of whichever document is of interest. For instance, one might determine how the English edition of a novel differs from its American counterpart. Of course, notes cannot provide everything, but they are a start.

Attentiveness to textual issues need not limit itself to an edition with a critical apparatus. Every work bears traces of the processes that brought it to its current state, and an attentive reader can, with a little care, begin to follow and decipher those traces. One way, of course, is to collate the text at hand with another edition of the same work. Often the differences between two competing editions of a book will be striking, but even when they are not, the similarities mean something about the work's textual history. And, as the Frost poem shows, even small differences might matter. Collation can be laborious. But after some time locating and thinking about textual issues, readers will develop an awareness of the almost invisible influence of the editorial processes without having to compare versions. The following passage, found in chapter seven of several electronic editions of James Fenimore Cooper's 1826 novel, *The Last of the Mohicans*, that are free for downloading on the World Wide Web, will help illustrate this skill:

> "It is extraordinary!" said Heyward, taking his pistols from the place where he had laid them on entering; "be it a sign of peach or a signal of war, it must be looked to. Lead the way, my friend; I follow."

Readers often unconsciously correct such simple misprints. If their correction is instead a conscious one, the phrase after the conjunction, "a signal of war," so quickly helps readers supply a correction for "sign of peach" that it might as well be unconscious. If textual criticism begins as the act of discovering and correcting errors, it quickly will lead readers to develop theories about how these errors arose, employing whatever knowledge they have—about the language, about the production of print and electronic books, and about the ways that humans or machines introduce changes to texts. One theory we might concoct is that whoever was responsible for "peach" reached this portion of the novel just before lunch, and that an overpowering hunger sabotaged the text. As theories go, though, the story of The Very Hungry Compositor doesn't take us very far. To work up a second theory, the first question one might ask is where in the text's history this variant originates. One cannot be sure without collating other editions or checking a critical edition of the novel, which might record a source for this error in its notes. But without doing so it is still possible to imagine the process by which the electronic text came to be and think about what technological realities might account for this variant's creation and preservation. The text of Cooper's novel was first published in the hand-press era, has been reprinted many, many times, and must have been entered into a computer file in one of two ways, either by scanner or by a typist, who likely was not paying any more attention to literal sense than would optical character recognition (OCR) software. This electronic edition either preserves a mistake in its printed exemplar, the document that the electronic edition copies from, or it originated the error itself. If the mistake originates with the electronic edition and if the text was scanned, it is entirely possible that the text was somehow obscured, by a mark or some dirt perhaps, so that the OCR software recognized an *h* rather than an *e*. If the text was keyed in by hand, it seems unlikely that the typist's finger accidentally struck the *h* key instead of the *e,* since these keys are too far apart on a typical computer keyboard. Perhaps the hungry compositor is not such a crazy idea. Just as likely these days, though, is the possibility that a typist struck a key other than the *h* or the *e*, or the OCR software recognized another letter, producing a word not in the word processor's dictionary, which was then mis-corrected to "peach," possibly automatically or by an inattentive technician. If the electronic texts' "peach" originates in the exemplar, it seems an error that is unlikely to have been caused by a keyboarder's mechanical inattentiveness, given the positions of the *h* and *e* on linotype and monotype keyboards. But "peach" was a more likely flub in the hand-press period, the period when Cooper's novel was first published, since the box in which the *e*'s were kept was directly above the box in which the *h*'s were stored in the type case. It could have been a slip of the hand in picking up the type or, more likely, a slip in putting the type away from a previous job, resulting in what is called a *foul case*. In other words, a compositor might have picked up an *h*, thinking he was picking up an *e* (see the chart on pp. 39–40). Whatever the source of the error, the fact that it is found in several free versions is itself instructive: these multiple free versions likely derive from a single electronic version, and this repeated error begins to discredit the distributors as sources for reliable electronic texts.[15] What other problems, one might reasonably wonder, have crept through unnoticed?

Like the word-processing software that automatically identifies and then occasionally corrects misspelled words, all readers already have a "theory of error" in place that allows them to identify many varieties of error, to make sense of them, and so to continue to read once they have encountered them. At the outset we might distinguish two kinds of errors, involving different aspects of the error-correction faculties built

15. The error is unrecorded in the 1983 edition, *The Last of the Mohicans; A Narrative of 1757*, ed. James Franklin Beard, James A. Sappenfield, and E. N. Feltskog (Albany: SUNY Press, 1983). I have not been able to locate the error in any of the printed editions I have checked.

into the language centers of our brains. Easiest to spot, and perhaps easiest to correct, are linguistic problems, the sorts in which rules of spalling or syntax are been broken. More difficult are semantic or logical problems, ones that result when the something violates the sense of a sentence, a passage, or a work as a whole. The sentence cited from Cooper's *The Last of the Mohicans* provides a good example of a local semantic error. While "peach" is a misprint, it remains a viable word and, moreover, does not violate grammatical rules, since "peace" and "peach" are both nouns. (Trying to substitute "peaty" will illustrate the grammatical acceptability of "peach.") But the word is practically nonsense as it stands, and the context suggests an easy solution. Some errors will only become obvious when a reader discovers that the sense of much larger sections of text are violated. Errors in narrative exposition in Alice Walker's *The Color Purple* cause characters to age at substantially different rates, the main charac-ter's children aging only a few years while she ages as much as thirty.[16] Most readers do not notice these problems right away, if ever, since they evolve slowly over the course of the entire novel. Textual criticism sharpens a reader's awareness of errors and reorients a reader's attitude toward them so that they are no longer noise or blanks in the message (that can be corrected or, alternatively, ignored) but meaningful evidence about the history of the text and therefore perhaps about the meanings of the text. Error correction is built into the brain's language centers, so that in fact practicing textual criticism (like proofreading and copy-editing) involves suppressing an automatic activity that is usual when one reads for sense, so one can pay closer attention to the text's surface fea-tures. Much like the non-linear techniques of close reading promulgated by the New Critics, textual criticism's approach to reading disrupts a reader's usual (or, at any rate, desired) linear path through a text, as one can see in collating the stanza from Frost's poem and in the page-flipping one must do with the *Oxford Study Bible*. The result is a defamiliarized text, out of which the reader can construct more complex meanings.

16. See Steven C. Weisenburger, "Errant Narrative and *The Color Purple*," *Journal of Nar-rative Technique* 19.3 (Fall 1989): 257–75. Errors of this magnitude would be impossible for an editor to correct, of course, and, as Weisenberger's essay suggests, a case can be made for narrative error being part of the novel's aesthetic.

Now, not all critical editors value the critical text's disruption of the comfortable ways that most people try to read. Those who do not might instead argue for a *clear text* edition, one that minimizes the evidence of an editor's intrusion by printing the text relatively unmarked and placing the textual notes and other parts of the apparatus at the end of the volume. This method reflects one of the primary goals of any editor, to make a text accessible. Another goal, however, complicates a critical editor's efforts to facilitate reading. The critical editor also aims to base the edition on a historical investigation of the text and to record the details of that investigation and the ways that its findings influenced editorial decisions. The clear text edition preserves the second goal but openly subordinates it to the first. Editions that print text and apparatus on the same page clearly take an opposing view. It is useful to consider how these sometimes conflicting aims of the critical editor might be reflected in the edition. The following passage is from the 1605 play, *The London Prodigal*, whose title page claims William Shakespeare as the author, an attribution now rejected.[16] Here Sir Lancelot Spurcock and his friend Weathercock discuss Spurcock's daughter, Delia, who has refused Weathercock's marriage proposal.

> *Lance.* Nay be not angry fyr, at her deniall,
> Shee hath refuf'de feauen of the worfhipfulft and worthyeft
> houf-keepers this day in *Kent*:
> Indeed fhe will not marry I fuppofe,
>   *Wea.* The more foole fhe,
>   *Lance.* What is it folly to loue Charitie?
>   *Wea.* No miftake me not fyr *Lancelot*,
> But tis an old prouerbe, and you know it well,
> That women dying maides, lead apes in hell.
>   *Lance.* Thats a foolifh prouerbe, and a falfe.

(B1r-v)

16. The title page attributes the play to Shakespeare, "as it was plaide by the Kings Maiesties seruants," Shakespeare's company. It was published by Nathaniel Butter, who would later publish *King Lear*. It also has echoes of and affinities with a number of Shakespeare plays. Despite this evidence, virtually no reader will think this play is by Shakespeare—unless we change our ideas about authors and authorship. Richard Proudfoot makes a subtle argument for Shakespeare to have had a hand in it in his essay, "Shakespeare's Most Neglected Play," *Textual Formations and Reformations*, edited by Laurie E. Maguire and Thomas L. Berger (Newark: University of Delaware Press, 1998), 149–57.

The uninitiated modern reader will balk at many unfamiliar aspects of the text that this transcript preserves:

- the letter form of the long-s, "ſ," which is easily confused with an "f," even more so when italicized, like so: "*ſ*" is not "*f*."
- the use of u as a vowel or consonant after the first letter of a word;[17]
- unexpected and missing punctuation;
- unexpected line-breaks;
- mixed italics and roman fonts (as in "L*auncelot*");
- old spellings.

These perplexing features become much easier to read with only a little experience and instruction, but that is not necessarily an argument in favor of an editor's preserving them, only an objection to anyone who would insist that the text must be modernized. Many readers might reject it as not worth the effort involved in learning to read such a text. On the other hand, one loses a sense of the text's history—especially of what it was like for early readers to encounter this play—if one utterly effaces its features. Moreover, some features, such as spelling, might help indicate authorship and are therefore valuable, since its authorship is doubtful. Charlton Hinman used spelling patterns to show how Shakespeare's First Folio was assembled, page by page, leading to interesting discoveries about the working conditions in the printing house that had a bearing on the text they printed. As writers do, editors consider what needs or limitations their readers will have and how they might put the text to use. The preservation or emendation of these unfamiliar features is a question of *normalization*. An editor who desires to make a reader's

---

17. u and v were actually two forms of the same letter in Shakespeare's day, just as ſ and s were: v was generally used only at the beginnings of words, with u used everywhere else, so that university would have been written vniuersity. As for ſ and s, generally the long-s was used initially and medially, while the short-s was used at the end of words. A similar rule obtained for i and j, with i used everywhere except as the last in a series of i's. The name John would be written Iohn, while the roman numeral three would be written iij. In short, these are not spelling rules so much as rules about the use of letter forms, like upper-case letters or italics.

experience with the text an easy one, favoring a clear text edition, will likely also favor substantial *regularization* and perhaps even *modernization*. Regularization means simply to emend the text to make it conform to a single set of rules, something early manuscripts and early printed editions did not necessarily do. In regularizing texts, editors might make the features conform to a rigid system acceptable in the period in which the text was composed, not bringing modern rules to bear on the text but reducing the variation, producing an old-spelling edition for example, or they might make the text conform to modern rules altogether. An editor might well mix and match when regularizing a text. If we choose to print "Nay, be not angry, syr, at her deniall" instead of "Nay be not angry ſyr, at her deniall," we have modernized the punctuation and letter-forms, but kept the old spelling.

Regularization sometimes extends beyond making spelling and punctuation conform to altering poetic lines in order to "improve" the scansion, though this is more frowned upon now than in the past. While the first and third lines of Lancelot's speech scan in fairly clean iambic pentameter, something seems to have gone wrong with the second line (from "Shee hath" to "in Kent"), which is lineated as prose:

> *Lance.* Nay be not angry ſyr, at her deniall,
> Shee hath refuſ'de ſeauen of the worſhipfulſt and worthyeſt
> houſ-keepers this day in *Kent:*
> Indeed ſhe will not marry I ſuppoſe.

It has an iambic feel, with eleven stresses in as many as twenty-two syllables, but these are more than enough for two lines of verse, and they will not break easily into either two or three lines. An editor more given to improving readability than to preserving the documentary evidence might search for emendations that will allow those lines to scan more smoothly, or might, on the other hand, deemphasize the verse lineation, so that more of the passage appeared as prose. These lines make sense as they are, however, and many editorial theorists insist that an editor may only emend in order to correct violations of sense, not violations of beauty standards. This stricture, however, raises a question for the fifth line, which would read as follows in a modernized edition: "What, is it foolish to love Charity?" The problem here, as some editors have noted, is that "Charity" isn't the best word, and they posit another of the cardinal virtues, "Chastity," as a better choice. Now, "Charity" does not violate the sense of the passage in the way that "peach" did in the sentence from Cooper's novel. But "Chastity" fits the context better. One is not necessarily at risk of dying a virgin if one pursues an enthusiasm for compassion, but too much chastity has been known to do the trick. Yet if the question is "which word fits the sense better," rather than "which one does not violate the sense," are we not making a judgment based on beauty? While a degree or two more difficult than the Cooper example above, the real complication for this passage is not in finding a solution, but in the theoretical issue it raises: once one has begun emending the text for sense, where and how does one draw the line?

THE PLAN OF THIS BOOK

Even simple textual problems lead to profound theoretical and practical questions about textual editing. It is a contention of this textbook that when students attend to textual problems such as these and when they begin to puzzle through such theoretical questions as the last, they begin to alter their reading styles, to the point that they need not always have notes or alternate editions to notice textual problems. There once was a tendency among textual critics, a tendency that seems at last to be dying out, to believe that textual criticism could not be taught. It required, so they felt, a special critical genius for detecting problems and discovering solutions, a natural talent that no amount of study could ever supply. This book aims not merely to abandon that old belief, but to turn it on its head. Textual criticism does not require a special sensitivity to the text as a precursor so much as it teaches that special sensitivity in its practice.

This book is divided into three parts. The remaining two chapters in Part One introduce the rudiments of textual criticism and editing, its concepts and controversies, not only so that students will feel comfortable deciphering the fine print tucked away in the dark corners of their textbooks and of their libraries, but so that they will see the interest, the value, and perhaps the beauty, in doing so. "Text Technologies and Textual Transmissions" outlines how the physical production of texts (like copying by hand or printing with movable types) matters in their transmission, and sketches those processes of transmission in order to suggest where variation or error can enter. "Textual Criticism and Kinds of Editions" presents a history of textual criticism, emphasizing the debates that have stirred the field since the mid-twentieth century, primarily by describing a variety of editorial methods and kinds of editions. That chapter emphasizes understanding how to decipher such editions and how each might differ from another, since understanding their assumptions is as important as learning how to read their texts and their specialized and abbreviated codes.

For those students who wish to explore the concepts and controversies in greater depth, Part Two of this book collects important statements by theorists and practitioners of textual criticism, some theoretical in nature, some more practical and on texts represented in the third part. Though textual criticism is one of the oldest humanistic activities, the writings here are drawn from the twentieth century. Earlier textual criticism, while still valuable to the student of literature in English (and other vernaculars), has primarily concerned itself with biblical and classical literature, and so has largely been excluded. For similar reasons, the essays are also limited primarily to the Anglo-American school of textual criticism, though other schools are discussed in Chapter Three of Part One, and students who wish to explore them can follow the references in the bibliography. Though focusing on textual scholarship since around 1950, this book has largely had to exclude the remarkable work done recently in digital textual scholarship. The issues and ideas addressed in this book should serve as a prolegomenon to students' explorations in that rapidly growing and more rapidly changing field.[18]

18. A good place to start is the Modern Language Association's collection of essays on the subject, *Electronic Textual Editing*, ed. Lou Burnard, Katherine O'Brien O'Keeffe, and John Unsworth (New York: MLA, 2006).

While one might easily fill a textbook twice this size with such essays, the soul of this book, Part Three, is given to example texts and editions with which students can engage in hands-on learning. It offers up these materials for exercise, texts as they have been treated in a variety of editions and texts (as much as possible) in facsimile. Few schools have been wealthy enough to collect and preserve a range of rare literary books and manuscripts on which the student may practice, and many also must do without the microfilm and digital resources whose aim is to share those riches around the world. More and more of these archives (the very ones that McGann worries about) are placing images of their holdings on the World Wide Web for free or are creating inexpensive digital editions that include high-quality digital scans of the original documents, and students should certainly celebrate and explore these resources. Some documents may in fact be better studied online or in a digital form than in person or in paper facsimile. Students should also be aware, however, that these digital archives are sometimes mere hints of the archive's actual holdings or are museum displays for literary tourism, not materials intended or always suitable for study. While the collections offered in this volume are of course limited by space, they have been chosen in an effort to represent as many historical periods and as many genres as possible, and they offer one distinct advantage in gathering together from far-flung institutions samples of all or most of the rare documents on which an edition would be based.

Text Technologies and
Textual Transmissions

WHETHER RECOVERING AN ideal form of the work or recording the work's textual history, the textual critic needs some understanding of the ways in which a work has been transmitted from author to reader, specifically the technologies used to transmit its text and the networks of people employing that technology. Texts are linguistic, and as such do not have a fixed physical form. That is, an arrangement of words might be expressed in many kinds of media: a text may be spoken or "read aloud" by a computer; it may be signed using a system such as Signed English; it may be handwritten, typed, printed, or displayed as letters on computer screen; in none of these is the form of the text the same. This volume will generally be concerned with written and printed texts. The omission of other text technologies does not mean to imply that their study is not important. Knowledge of the oral and digital composition and transmission of texts is valuable in its own right and can provide important insights for the literary scholar and textual critics alike. Those who are interested in *Beowulf*, for instance, must take into account the possibility that it may have a history as an oral text that predates its being copied into its unique manuscript, a history that might account for puzzling textual details. While some scholars doubt an oral composition for *Beowulf*, a textual critic of the poem might still wish to consider how oral transmission can affect the written form of a text, because the poem nevertheless has an oral aesthetic. Digital composition and transmission present similarly thorny issues for textual criticism and editing, since they alter the processes by which a text can be manipulated, stored, accessed, and understood.

Digital transmission matters for textual critics in another way, since a critical editor now has the option to present an electronic edition of a work, making available to readers new, more dynamic editions than are possible in print. Using various text-encoding techniques (such as Extensible Markup Language, or XML) and a bit of programming, editors are able now to present more than one kind of edition of a work simultaneously, and can even allow readers to construct other editions according to principles of their choosing, even switching back and forth between very different kinds of editions at will. Such flexibility does not eliminate the role of the textual critic, of the editor, or of the textual theorist, since the choices a reader can make will still be determined by the choices an editor offers and by the structure used to mark up the texts that comprise the edition. That is, if an electronic edition does not offer an eclectic text mode, it will take no small tinkering on the part of the reader to create one. It will be good to remember, too, that as new technologies are introduced, they do not entirely replace the old. Thousands of years after the advent of writing, oral poetry is still being produced and transmitted, though probably in less volume than before. Similarly, people still write by hand and circulate handwritten copies, despite the prevalence of the computer. In fact, for centuries after the arrival of print in Europe, the manuscript was still valued so highly that some readers would hire scriveners to copy printed books so that they might read them in the manuscript form they preferred. While no panacea, digital media certainly open up possibilities in presentation that used to be too time-consuming for readers to navigate and too expensive for publishers to produce.

So oral technologies and digital technologies are important, but they lie outside the compass of this book, largely because manuscript and print technologies are those with which textual criticism and editing have the longest histories and most activity. In fact, textual criticism is one of the oldest recorded scholarly activities, going back at least to early Greek attempts to establish a text of Homer's epics. Many changes in textual criticism in the last century have largely been driven by an interest in works from the age of print—primarily those of Shakespeare and his contemporaries. In addition, manuscript and print technologies overlap in ways that make them more immediately accessible in a textbook such as this. Oral and digital technologies are perhaps best represented by other media. For these reasons, this chapter will be concerned with the technologies of the book, whether hand-copied or printed. Detailed studies of these transmissions' physical forms belong to the fields of paleography and typography (the study of old handwriting and of typefaces), of codicology (the study of manuscript books), and of analytical bibliography (the study of printed books). Often these fields (and others) are lumped together under the single term, *bibliography*. Though these fields of study hold great significance to the textual critic, we cannot do justice to their complexities and keep this textbook to a reasonable length. The most this chapter can do is sketch out some of their terms and concerns in order to illustrate how they reflect on the work of the textual critic and editor.

PAPYRUS SCROLLS, WAX TABLETS, PARCHMENT, AND PAPER CODICES

Manuscripts as a means of publication in the West saw their heyday between the sixth century B.C.E. and the eighteenth century C.E., a span that saw significant shifts in manuscript technology. Of the three major manuscript technologies, scrolls, wax tablets, and codices, the student of literature in English is likely to encounter only the last. But knowledge about the first two can give us a base of comparison for understanding production and reading practices for literature produced in what we might call the age of the codex. Scrolls, usually made from papyrus and written with a reed pen and a soot-based ink, were the primary form for these manuscripts until around the third century C.E., after which time the codex, the ancestor of the modern book, generally written on parchment, became the medium of choice. At first, papyrus, made from a plant that grew along the Nile River, had an economic advantage over parchment in that the plant was cheaper to harvest and process than were animal skins. Papyrus is formed by soaking long and thin strips of the plant's fibrous and sticky inner tissue, then hammering a horizontal layer of strips over a similar vertical layer until the two are bonded together in a thin sheet, which is dried and then smoothed. Glued end-to-end, such sheets form a long band which can be rolled up with other papyrus sheets to form a scroll as much as one hundred feet wide. The text would then be written in multiple columns a few inches wide, so that dozens—even hundreds—of columns could be placed on a scroll. Readers would unroll the scroll with one hand while rolling it up with the other, exposing only a few columns at a time. It should be no surprise to learn that the English word that usually describes a book in a series, *volume,* ultimately derives from the Latin verb "to roll," *volvere.* While easy to use, it is not as practical as it might be, since one can really use only one side of the scroll. Perhaps just as significant is the fact that scrolls make it difficult to shuttle back and forth within a text and between several texts, because the scroll must be rolled and unrolled in order to locate a wanted passage. By contrast, the reader of a codex who wishes to compare two passages eighty columns apart merely needs to stick a thumb in to mark the page of the first passage, then to flip to another page in order to call up the second. It's a simple technological advantage in access that is actually quite revolutionary. For this and other reasons (sheep and goats will prosper in more climates than papyrus will and have more uses than providing writing surfaces), the papyrus scroll began to lose ground to the parchment codex in late antiquity. As digital texts proliferate and as interfaces are designed and redesigned, it may be valuable to remember this technological shift and its effects.

Alongside the papyrus scroll developed another technology, the wax tablet. Tablets were thin wooden boards, whose edges were higher than the somewhat recessed center, forming a kind of frame into which a dark wax was poured. Using a metal or bone stylus, the writer could inscribe text in the wax so that the lighter board beneath would show through. If he or she wished to make small corrections or to erase the whole tablet, the writer could use the broader end of the stylus to smooth over the wax. Two or more of these boards could be fastened together with thongs to form a diptych or triptych, that is, a small codex-like wax tablet book, with each page's frame keeping the book's other surfaces from marring what was written in the wax. Such tablets were common until as late as the nineteenth century. Though they were used for official documents as important as birth certificates in the ancient world, in the Middle Ages and Renaissance they were notebooks in which were kept items whose longevity was not essential.

The earliest English books are parchment codices. Parchment, or vellum, was made primarily from sheepskin or calfskin, although other sources were not unknown. A skin was soaked in a caustic solution, usually a lye bath, and then stretched on a frame, scraped with a broad, rounded knife, and rubbed with pumice. This process removed the fat and hair and made a parchment thin enough and smooth enough for writing. After its edges were trimmed away and the layout of the book had been planned, the parchment was ruled for writing and decorating. The parchment was then folded to form booklets, called quires, of four, eight, sixteen, or more leaves. Trimming all but one folded edge produced bifolia, or pairs of sheets joined at the spine—two bifolia for a four-leaf quire, four bifolia for an eight-leaf quire, and so on.

When several quires are sewn together at the untrimmed folds to form the spine of a book, the bifolia provide greater strength and less bulk than individually attached sheets. Moreover, folding the sheet of parchment assures that the hair-sides of each leaf, with their follicles and generally darker and more irregular appearance, will face other hair-sides, and that flesh-sides, which are smoother and lighter in color, will face other flesh-sides, producing a kind of uniformity for each opening in the quire and thus in the codex. Irregularities in this hair-and-flesh pattern are usually easily spotted, and they can indicate where material has been removed or lost, or where extra leaves or bifolia have been added in order to accommodate unexpected overruns in—or perhaps additions to—the text. Irregularities in the hair-and-flesh pattern might also mean that the manuscript has been disassembled and rearranged at some point in its history.

In the late Middle Ages, paper became more and more common in manuscript books and was nearly universal by the sixteenth century.

A single sheet folded twice to form quarto leaves and two bifolia. The top edge is not yet trimmed.

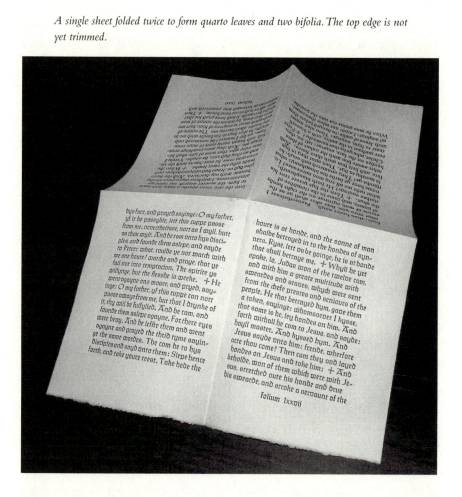

Paper was made by reducing linen rags—like cast-off clothing—to a pulp and suspending the fibers in water. Into vats of this slurry papermakers dipped rectangular wooden frames holding tight wire screens (called *moulds*) to collect thin layers of these fibers, letting the water drain away, then transferring the resulting sheet of paper to a piece of felt to dry. Turning sheets out of the moulds one after another, alternating each resulting sheet of paper with a layer of felt, one on top of another, the papermaker could make many such stacks of paper more quickly than the parchmenter could produce completely one skin. After excess water had been pressed out of the stack, the individual sheets were hung up to dry. Then the paper was coated in animal gelatin, known as *sizing*, so that any ink applied to the paper would remain on its surface and not be absorbed to form blots. Anyone who has tried to write a note on a paper napkin with loosely flowing ink knows the difficulty of writing on unsized paper. Paper moulds leave unique patterns on handmade paper, useful identifying markings for bibliographers. The wire screen in the mould consists of two gauges of wires, the heavier gauge and more widely spaced chains running parallel to the longer sides of the mould, and the lighter gauge and tightly packed wires running across (and attached to) the chains, parallel to the shorter sides of the mould. This screen left its trace in the paper itself, so that one can usually see its imprint in the paper fairly easily. Sewn onto the wire screen were watermarks, designs fashioned from wire which also would leave an impression in the paper. Because watermarks varied from region to region and from papermaker to papermaker, and even from batch to batch by a single papermaker, they can help to date and to locate the manufacture of the paper, which is useful information in trying to determine the origin of a manuscript or book. Some very clever bibliographic forgeries have failed because they have been executed on paper that is not as old as it ought to be. A few mills still make paper in this old-fashioned way, primarily for the book-arts world. But since the early nineteenth century, there have been three major changes in larger papermaking operations. First, papermakers switched from the moulds described above, which produced *laid paper*, to moulds made with woven screens, which produced paper that was much more uniform in texture, called *wove paper*. Before long, papermaking was mechanized, using a variety of kinds of machines, but each with a similar effect: larger-width paper of a more uniform quality, produced not in single sheets but in long rolls. Using a roller to emboss patterns on the still wet paper, these machines could—and still do today, since the technology has not much changed—imitate the look of laid paper, complete with watermark. But the most important change in papermaking, perhaps, is the most recent: the introduction of wood-pulp for the paper's fibers. Linen-rag paper is in some ways more durable than wood-pulp paper, because linen paper is free of the acid that makes untreated wood-pulp paper brown and become brittle, slowly turning itself into dust. The result is that most paper medieval manuscripts and early printed books are in remarkably good shape for their age, more supple and clear than many books printed in, say, the 1940s.

PENS, INKS, AND TYPE

Until about the sixth century, the manuscript would have been written with a pen made from a reed, cut so that its nib could be split to control better the ink and so that it could be sharpened frequently. The reed pen then lost popularity to the quill pen, the primary writing instrument for one thousand years, which was usually made from a goose's flight feather. The quill could be sharpened in a variety of ways, producing a myriad of calligraphic effects. Quills remain sharp longer than reed pens and are more flexible writing instruments, and they remained dominant until the metal-nib dip pen (of the sort still used by many artists and by calligraphers) took over in the early 1800s, soon to be followed by the fountain pen (which many swear is still the finest sort of writing instrument).

The basic recipe for ink in pens—a pigment (like soot) suspended in a solvent (usually water), mixed with an agent that causes the pigment to adhere to a surface (like shellac or gum arabic)—has remained unchanged, despite specific chemical substitutions, to this day. Iron-gall ink, used when carbon-based inks were discovered to be unsuitable for parchment, was made from iron sulfate (from iron treated with an acid) mixed with tannin (derived from powdered and boiled oak tree galls, which are caused by a parasitic wasp). This mixture was thickened with gum arabic or something similar, and mixed with water. Unlike carbon-based inks, which can be erased with a little water and a little rubbing, iron-gall inks oxidized when exposed to air, not only darkening on the parchment as it dried and soon after (though these inks also could fade with time from black to light brown) but also burning into the uppermost layers of parchment. To erase iron-gall ink from parchment one must scrape away the parchment's surface. Now, parchment was valuable, and rather than let unwanted books sit idle or dispose of them, many copyists reused old parchments, scraping away the old text and copying a new text over it, creating a *palimpsest.*

In this fifteenth-century palimpsest manuscript, the faint lines of a tenth-century text can be seen running vertically under the main text.

Often the old text of these palimpsests can still be read beneath the new text, sometimes with the unaided eye, sometimes under certain kinds of light or with special photographic equipment. Palimpsests occasionally provide us with the only known copy of a work, and they are therefore particularly exciting when discovered or finally rendered legible. Printer's ink is very different from writing ink. Normal writing ink is too fluid to remain on the type's surface, so printers developed an ink that was not as liquid. Printer's ink has the consistency of an artist's oil paints and something like its chemical content—an oil-based varnish with pigment, mainly soot for black.

It would be wrong to say that the invention of the printing press entirely replaced the manuscript as a technology for publication. But soon after its invention in the fifteenth century, the hand press replaced the manuscript as the way to publish to the widest possible audience, and it all but eliminated manuscript book production as a viable trade. Book historian Elizabeth Eisenstein argues that this publishing revolution had profound effects, shaping the Protestant Reformation, for example, whose successes were due in no small part to the press's ability to spread dissent quickly.[1] The hand press's advantage over scribal technologies came in achieving economies of scale. One could produce hundreds or

No matter the size, all type is the same height (height-to-paper).

1. Elizabeth Eisenstein, *The Printing Press as an Agent of Change*, 2 vols. (Cambridge: Cambridge University Press, 1979).

thousands of copies of a book in roughly the time it might take a scribe to write out just one by hand. Of course, the economics of printing were such that if only a few copies were required, copying by hand was still preferable. The key element in the invention of printing is not the press itself, but the movable type. Type pieces are small metal blocks all of the same height (called *type-high* or *height-to-paper*) no matter their other dimensions. When rows and rows of these are set next to one another, they will form a block that can be inked and that can leave on paper an impression of the letters and other marks that comprise the block's surface. In the hand-press era, a compositor would select and arrange by hand the individual pieces of type from the type-cases, not only the letters, punctuation, and other marks but also the non-printing spaces. Originally, there were two cases for type, one set on a stand above the other, giving us *uppercase* and *lowercase* letters.

Upper- and lowercase layout in the English style (from John Smith and Charles Stower, A Printer's Grammar, *1787). In the lower case, the "n" has accidentally been turned on its side. The italic "m" and "n" on the right-hand side are spaces the width of an "m" and of an "n." The "Qu." below them are larger spaces called "quads."*

A SCHEME of a Pair of Cafes.

UPPER CASE.

A	B	C	D	E	F	G	A	B	C	D	E	F	G
H	I	K	L	M	N	O	H	I	K	L	M	N	O
P	Q	R	S	T	V	W	P	Q	R	S	T	V	W
X	Y	Z	Æ	Œ	U	J	X	Y	Z	æ	Œ	U	J
1	2	3	4	5	6	7	â	ê	î	ô	û	¶	‡
8	9	0	ç	HS.	fb	fk	á	é	í	ó	ú	‖	†
ä	ë	ï	ö	ü	ft	k	à	è	ì	ò	ù	§	*

LOWER CASE.

ct	□	æ	œ	'	j		s	()	?	!	;	fl	fl
&							i					ff	ff
ffi	b	c	d	e				f	f	g	fh	fi	fi
ffi													
ffl	l	m	ᴚ	h			o	y	p	q	w	n	m
z										,	:		
	v	u	t	Spaces			a	r				Qu.
x										.	-		

Since the late nineteenth century, most hand-press printers (in the United States, at any rate) have used California job cases, where the two cases are combined into one as though laid out side-by-side, rather than one above the other. The compositor would assemble these pieces of type one at a time, word by word, phrase by phrase, into lines in a hand-held shelf, called a *compositor's stick*, that could be adjusted to a predetermined line-length and could hold several lines of type at a time.

A compositor's stick with type. Type was assembled upside-down and backward in the stick.

Before finishing each line and moving on to the next, the compositor would try to correct any typos and would justify the line (adding spaces between words to create an even right margin for prose). When the compositor had several lines finished in the stick, he would turn these lines out onto a table, assembling in time a page of these lines. Each page, tied tightly with string, was then arranged in relation to other pages to be printed on the same sheet, and, by using a frame and a combination of wedges and wooden blocks that could be adjusted to keep the type blocks in place, the compositor created a *forme*, which could be placed on the press and inked. Sheets could then be printed from this inked forme, one sheet at a time, each being hung up to dry as it came off the press. When the full run had been printed from a forme, the compositor disassembled it and returned the type, piece by piece, back to the cases from which they came. Naturally, in distributing the type, as it was called, compositors could make mistakes, dropping an *h* in the *e* compartment for instance, resulting in a foul case, which might lead to unintentional errors when setting the next set of pages. Once the other side of the sheet was printed—once the sheet had been *perfected*—it could be hung up to dry, then folded into quires and arranged and sewn with other quires to form a book.

In the nineteenth century, printers began to use plates for printing in place of the tied-up blocks of type of the earlier hand-press period. These plates were produced by a variety of means with a variety of metals, but always from a mould made of the hand-composed type pages. Using plates meant that type could be used more efficiently and that popular books could be reprinted from the same plates years later, without having to set an entirely new edition.[2] In the nineteenth century, printers

---

2. When the first edition of Cooper's *The Last of the Mohicans* sold well in 1826, Carey and Lea, the publishers, re-set the book for a second edition and created plates for it which were used for twenty-eight impressions, the last in 1864 by James G. Gregory. He had inherited the plates from W. Townsend & Co., who had purchased the plates from Carey and Lea in 1849. Cooper revised the novel for another publisher in 1831, but, of course, those changes are not reflected in editions using the 1826 plates. For full details, see James Fenimore Cooper, *The Last of the Mohicans; A Narrative of 1757*, ed. James Franklin Beard, James A. Sappenfield and E. N. Feltskog (Albany: SUNY Press, 1983).

also began developing mechanized printing presses that, in general, began to automate much of the movement involved in printing sheets of paper. These improvements called for similar improvements in the speed of setting type. The first step was to mechanize the delivery of the type from storage to the composed line in what is called a *cold-metal* machine. The compositor worked at a keyboard attached to type magazines that, something like a vending machine that drops soft drinks down a chute, delivered pre-cast (hence *cold*) individual pieces of type in a line so that they could be justified by hand and then assembled into pages. The trouble, of course, was that it was still time-consuming (and therefore expensive) to return this type to its storage magazines above the keyboard. Moreover, type itself was expensive, and this machine didn't reduce the amount of type on hand needed to set a book. The next advance was the *hot-metal* machine, casting a complete line of letters and spaces as a single piece of metal, called *slugs*. This was the Linotype. Corrections required re-setting the entire slug where a change was necessary. Like the Linotype, the Monotype created new type as it was needed, rather than pulling already formed type from a case as earlier machines did. Unlike the Linotype, the Monotype substituted an intermediary stage, a paper spool on which were punched holes by a compositor sitting at another keyboard; these holes encoded the characters and spacing for the lines of type. The paper spool with its encoded holes then was fed into a machine that cast and assembled entire pages of individual pieces of type—which could then be proofread and corrected as before in the hand-press era.

Just as machine presses began to replace hand presses in the nineteenth century, so too newer printing methods—first photographic, then xerographic—began to replace the machine press in the middle of the twentieth century. These methods do not impress letters into the paper but deposit them, adhering a pigment to the page either through heat or through a chemical process. The advent of the computer and especially of the personal computer has changed typesetting and proof correction substantially. Now an author's manuscript is often delivered to publishers as an electronic file rather than as a typescript, saving a step in which the typescript is keyed into the computer by a typesetter. The electronic text is next arranged in a page-layout program and printed directly from these computer files, reducing the kinds of compositor errors one is used to seeing in older books—though probably introducing (or preserving) other varieties of variation, and changing the kinds of evidence textual critics might employ to write textual histories of that work in the future.

TEXTUAL TRANSMISSIONS

To reconstruct the textual history of a work requires not only a sense of the physical materials that might affect the text but also of the human agencies involved in transferring the text from one document to another, since this transmission invites variation. The author is plainly the most significant and most widely regarded agent in textual production, but the authorship of any work is complex in that the author is rarely if ever singular. Despite Romantic claims to the contrary, few if any works are the result of a single moment of inspiration and creative activity. Dispersed among many moments of creation and many hands of transmission, even the simplest works can have complex textual histories. At the same time, a primary assumption for most textual critics is that transmission encourages the degeneration of a text. That is, each time a text is copied from one document to another, the process of copying will likely preserve variants in the exemplar (the version being copied) and introduce more variation of its own. While some have pointed out that copies can often improve or correct their exemplar's readings, the general principle still holds sway for most textual critics: the further removed from the author's copy, the less accuracy the text has. For this reason, textual critics are often very concerned with locating and evaluating the earliest versions of a text, particularly *holograph* manuscripts, that is, manuscripts written by the author, such as notes, but more especially either rough drafts or fair copies.

   Few authors work without taking notes, which often represent the first stage a textual critic can examine in constructing a history of the work. Notes were not always considered valuable beyond a certain stage in the composition process. During the Middle Ages and into the Renaissance, an author's earliest work would likely have been on a wax tablet's reusable surface, and so have not survived. At the end of Act 1 of *Hamlet*, the title character twice mentions tablets (which he calls his "tables").

> Remember thee?
> Yea, from the table of my memory
> I'll wipe away all trivial fond records,
> All saws of books, all forms, all pressures past,
> That youth and observation copied there,
> And thy commandment all alone shall live
> Within the book and volume of my brain. . . .
> My tables,
> My tables—meet it is I set it down,
> That one may smile and smile and be a villain. (1.5.97–109)

Hamlet first uses "tables" as a metaphor for his memory that, like a wax tablet, can be wiped blank, then, forgetting his promise to remember the ghost's "commandment all alone," seems to use his actual tablets as aid to his memory for a clever observation he wants to jot down. Parchment was always too valuable to be used for items considered to be private and unfinished, and wax tablets could be erased and reused when the material they contained was no longer needed, after a manuscript copy had been made, for instance. For this reason few if any notes or rough drafts survive from the medieval period. By Shakespeare's day, paper was beginning to become inexpensive enough for everyday use, so, although wax tablets were still very common, it is in this period that we begin to see paper replace tablets for commonplace books, notebooks like the one that Hamlet describes, in which one might record events, expenses, pithy sayings one finds in books (Hamlet's "saws of books"), anecdotes, and so on. Though his character seems to use wax tablets, it is clear from the manuscript of the play called *Sir Thomas More*, which contains a few pages of a relatively clean first rough draft in Shakespeare's own handwriting, that Shakespeare, in this case at any rate, drafted on paper. The

Sir Thomas More manuscript most likely survives because the play was never allowed to be performed, so the manuscript was never used and was allowed to sit. Otherwise, it, too, might have perished as have so many plays from the period. Not until the nineteenth century did rough drafts and journals begin to attain a status that encourages careful preservation after an author's death. These days, famous writers often contract with major archives during their own lifetimes (in return for what is sometimes a great deal of money) to deliver up all papers, no matter how minor or rough, when they are no longer needed. In the late 1980s, to take one example, actor and writer Steve Martin made such an arrangement with the Harry Ransom Humanities Research Center at the University of Texas in Austin. We can be fairly sure that Mr. Martin does not use wax tablets, but to what degree do his works germinate from notes in other media that have a degree of ephemeralness? Computer files, as any student working all night under a deadline knows, can be wiped away almost as if by black magic, never to be recovered. If Martin receives a text message on his mobile phone that sparks an idea for a novel, play, or film, and he records a quick voice memo about it for himself, we might never know. Though the care for evidence of composition and transmission may never have been greater than it is today, there will always be evidence a scholar might wish to have that no longer exists.

It is not impossible that the author might show his or her notes to others and invite comment. Generally, however, that activity is reserved for the draft stage. Rough drafts come in many shapes and sizes, often shading into the category of notes on the one hand or fair copy on the other, so that the application of the term is a matter of convention. Shakespeare's contemporaries used the term *foul papers* to denote rough drafts, a phrase that gives a good sense of the state in which we find most rough drafts in the age before typewriters—and even today for writers who prefer to compose by pen or pencil rather than at the keyboard. Even typewritten and word-processed drafts, however, can be quite unruly. In general, however, the category of rough draft is characterized not by how the document looks—since word processors can make drafts look very polished, and some authors can have very neat handwriting—

but by being somewhat more organized, more complete, and more public than notes and less organized, less complete, and less public than a fair copy. It is at this stage that an author is first likely to share his or her work with a few readers, seeking feedback for revision, and many works evolve through several such draft-and-revision cycles before being prepared as a fair copy (or clean typescript). Many people understand a new draft to be the result of substantial changes rather than of editing or proofing, but what constitutes a substantial change rather than mere proofing is not easily defined. To be strict, only an author may initiate the change from one draft to another, but since it is sometimes difficult to determine who is an author, each individual document prior to publication preserving a state of the text different from another should be considered a separate draft, no matter how little it differs from the others. Textual critics have disagreed about the relative importance of rough drafts, some arguing that the earliest complete drafts best preserve the author's intentions for a work, while others argue that authorial intention can encompass the revisions suggested or pressed by the author's pre-publication readers, such as a spouse or a publisher's editor. F. Scott Fitzgerald's last novel provides an interesting case study for the status of the rough draft and the ways in which others might contribute to the work at the draft stage. Fitzgerald died with only seventeen of thirty planned episodes of *The Love of the Last Tycoon* drafted. This highly acclaimed partial rough draft has twice been edited since Fitzgerald's death, the first by his friend, literary critic Edmund Wilson, under the title *The Last Tycoon*, the second in the 1990s, under the full title.[3] The change in title suggests the degree to which Wilson's editorial hand might be felt in that text.

A fair copy is also technically a draft, distinguished from foul papers or from a rough draft by being complete and prepared for wider circulation and perhaps publication. We might distinguish two kinds of fair copies, those prepared by the author (authorial fair copy) and those prepared by a scribe (scribal fair copy). Clean typescripts are sometimes

---

3. F. Scott Fitzgerald, *The Last Tycoon* (New York: Scribner, 1941). F. Scott Fitzgerald, *The Love of the Last Tycoon*, ed. Matthew J. Bruccoli (New York: Simon and Schuster, 1995).

more difficult to distinguish in this way—a document typed by the author might look much like one prepared by someone else working from the author's manuscript. So many authors now use word processors that this distinction is even harder to maintain today. Nevertheless, from the textual critic's point of view, the distinction is important, since it indicates at least one more hand involved in the transmission of the text. Whether to circulate for feedback or to submit for publication, any number of fair copies might be made—by hand, by typewriter and carbon paper or photocopier, or through electronic distribution. However it is done, multiple copies present a wrinkle for the textual critic, since those copies might contain significant differences, might have been shuffled with one another, and might contain different stages of authorial and non-authorial marginal or interlinear notations, which the author may or may not have incorporated in later versions.

There are occasions when authors are their own copyists, as is sometimes the case with poet and professional scribe Thomas Hoccleve, Chaucer's contemporary.[4] A few holographs survive from as early as the fourteenth century, more from the Renaissance, and still more after, but even for modern authors, holograph manuscripts are usually single copies and therefore very rare. More often another scribe has been at work, and that scribe's relationship to the author can range from one that is very close to one that is virtually non-existent. For years people have speculated about the identity of Chaucer's scribe, the "Adam" whom Chaucer names in a funny lyric that urges him to be more careful in copying:

> Adam, scriveyn, if ever it thee bifalle
> Boece or Troilus for to writen newe,
> Under thy long lokkes thou most have the scalle,
> But after my makyng thou wryte more trewe;

---

4. Durham University Library MS Cosin V. iii. 9 contains a holograph manuscript of a large portion of Thomas Hoccleve's five linked pieces collectively known as his *Series*, but even in the holograph portion, Hoccleve, a professional scribe, occasionally "miswrites," according to one recent editor: Thomas Hoccleve, *Thomas Hoccleve's Complaint and Dialogue*, ed. J. A. Burrow, Early English Text Society, O. S. 313 (Oxford: Oxford University Press, 1999), see ix–x.

So ofte adaye I mote thy werk renewe,

It to correcte and eke to rubbe and scrape,

And al is thorugh thy negligence and rape.[5]

Most scholars had given up on ever finding a historical Adam. Linne Mooney's paleographic research has found conclusive evidence that the scribe who copied what have long been acknowledged to be the best versions of *The Canterbury Tales*, the Hengwrt and Ellesmere manuscripts, was a man named Adam Pynkhurst.[6] Mooney's work makes it fairly clear, now, that Chaucer and Pynkhurst worked closely together for many years, and it suggests that, as she writes, "The readings in Hengwrt and Ellesmere, then, are likely the closest we can come in the surviving materials to Chaucer's own authorial version of the *Tales*" (105). Many manuscript copies of Chaucer's poems, however, date from at least fifty years after the poet's death, meaning that the scribe had very little connection to the poet and therefore to his best copies. This relationship to the author is a shorthand way of thinking about authority, one of the values we place on evidence in determining a text. Authority, for most textual critics, is the likelihood that a given element in the text can be ascribed to the author or conforms to the author's intentions or wishes. The greater the authority, for some editors, the more weight that evidence must receive. (Others would say it's the other way around: the greater the weight editors wish to give to a piece of evidence, the more authority they will claim it has.) The problem with equating proximity to the author (in date, geographical location, or social milieu) with textual authority is that even a holograph manuscript may be badly copied or may represent an early or rough version later revised by an author. Chaucer's poem to Adam scolds the scribe for introducing errors into what he copies, forcing Chaucer to correct them, but, no doubt, Chaucer was negligent, too (the poem loses some of its humor without that real-

5. Geoffrey Chaucer, "Chaucers Wordes unto Adam, His Owne Scriveyn," *The Riverside Chaucer*, ed. Larry D. Benson et al. (Boston: Houghton Mifflin, 1986), 650.

6. Linne R. Mooney, "Chaucer's Scribe," *Speculum* 81.1 (2006): 97–138.

ization). Even Hoccleve's holograph manuscripts are not without what seem to be problems. Theoretically, at least, a manuscript copied centuries after an author's death may derive from a copy with more authority than even the holograph that survives, as it might well represent a later stage of an author's work more exactly.

In the manuscript era, which overlapped with the first two centuries or so of printing, the fair copy was essentially the last authorized version of the work—the published version. More often in the manuscript era than in the print era, the author's fair copy might have circulated first in a coterie, a kind of limited publication that at first provides the author some degree of control over who may read the work. Coterie publication is much like privately printing a work, where the author assumes the cost of printing, for circulation only among friends. But with coterie publication as with private printings, these texts can and do begin to circulate outside the author's circle. Copies can be made and clearly often were. In the medieval period, when a scribe received a text from a patron who wished to have a copy made, that scribe would likely make two copies so that he might sell further copies to future customers. Since the evidence suggests that Chaucer worked closely with Adam Pynkhurst for many years, it may be that some medieval authors developed relationships with particular scribes as a way of publishing their works. Certainly some worked with professional scribes in order to prepare presentation copies, elaborate productions for the author's patrons.

Playscripts from the early modern period offer another set of problems. A playscript in Shakespeare's day was delivered to the acting company (who purchased the script from the author), either as a fair copy or as foul papers, in which case the company's scribe made a fair copy of it. The fair copy was then annotated by the company for use as a promptbook, noting entrances and exits, important stage directions, necessary props, and the like. The scribe would then prepare two further sorts of documents from this book, one a schedule of scenes with the names of the characters in them, called a *platt* or *plot*, and second, the *parts*, pages consisting only of a character's cues and lines. This system of breaking up the script into parts so that none of the actors had a complete script saved valuable resources, namely the time of the scribe. But it may also be responsible for some textual situations like the first printing of *Hamlet*. The First Quarto (Q1, 1603), as it is called, seems to be a memorial reconstruction that reports the speeches of some characters very well, specifically, those of the actor responsible for the reconstruction and of the characters who were onstage with him. But it positively butchers speeches that the actor could not hear clearly, since he was offstage. As though in response to the shoddy first printing, the Second Quarto (Q2, 1604) seems to have been printed from Shakespeare's foul papers, which would no longer have been useful to the company, and it explains why Q2 is much longer than Q1: the play would have been cut for performance, but no such need existed for printing. At least, so goes one theory.

Early printed editions are very valuable even for those textual critics who are primarily concerned with works preserved in manuscript. Though these texts may not have been proofed by the author, the printer may have had access to manuscripts that no longer exist, manuscripts that may be very valuable textually. Chaucer was dead some seventy years by the time William Caxton printed the first of his two editions of *The Canterbury Tales*. The manuscripts for these are now lost, but the texts Caxton preserves provide valuable evidence for the manuscript circulation of the work.

The copyist is, of course, almost never alone in the work of copying a text. Rather, we ought to think of several copyists, since scribes often shared labor and have often intervened over time in one another's work. Two hands shared copying *Beowulf*, one taking over for another midway through the poem, midway through a page, and midway through a sentence, in fact. Adam Pynkhurst's hand is not alone in the early Chaucer manuscripts: Linne Mooney has identified Thomas Hoccleve's hand correcting lines originally copied by Pynkhurst. In the middle of Shakespeare's portion of *Sir Thomas More*, a professional scribe has deleted two dozen syntactically tangled words by Shakespeare and written in their place four simple ones of his own. The last two examples illustrate not only the fact that copyists are not soloists, but also that they are not simply copyists. That is, far from mindlessly reproducing what is before them, scribes sometimes work as editors or collaborators, deleting, supplementing, and emending the text, sometimes glossing or annotating it along the way. We must also occasionally take into account the other workers besides scribes who help to create manuscripts—illuminators and other decorators, for instance, who fill in blanks left for illustration, decoration, and emphasis. While these aspects of manuscripts are often non-linguistic, they are nonetheless meaningful elements interacting with the texts and can have a physical effect on the text itself. Scribes might, for instance, begin to crowd letters or introduce more abbreviations as they near a planned illustration, making the words less legible and perhaps altering the actual words in order to fit the text to the available space.

Although the technology of book production changed substantially with the advent of printing, and those changes effected some differences from manuscript textual transmission, in some ways early printing textual transmission shares more in common with manuscript transmission than it does with later printing transmission. For most textual critics, the same principle of "proximity to the author" holds for early printed books as for manuscripts. With a few notable exceptions, like Ben Jonson, authors of the period did not have much oversight for the printing, much less the reprinting, of their works, though they might have been shown proofs. The first edition is generally favored as being likelier to contain fewer errors and likelier to preserve authorial readings. Though most textual critics have therefore granted greater authority to the first edition (when no authorial manuscript survives), this does not mean that later editions have no interest for the textual scholar. New books sold better than old books, so after a few years hand-press printers would sometimes remove (or *cancel*) old title pages and reissue old books with new title pages; these are not considered second editions. Genuine later editions were often printed directly from earlier editions and so may have little textual interest. But not infrequently there is evidence that the printer has used more than one source for the reprinting—checking the first edition against an author's rough draft for instance. Moreover, authors may have revised between printings, sometimes drastically, as many now

Formats from left to right: octavo, quarto, duodecimo (front), and folio.

think was the case with many of Shakespeare's major plays. Such corrections, revisions, and expansions are often advertised on the title pages of later editions, even if these advertisements are not always true.

In the hand-press period, the printer made a number of important decisions about the manuscript he was to print that are still made by publishers today, such as what sorts of typeface, illustrations, and other extra-textual features to include. But the most significant of these perhaps was determining the size and format of the book. The format of the book determined how compositors worked with a manuscript. Format is a shorthand way of speaking about how many pages there are per forme, how the type pages are laid out in the forme, and therefore how the paper is folded so as to form gatherings. A format's name indicates both the number of folds necessary and the rough size of the book, and it may be further modified to indicate how sheets were gathered together, affecting further how the type was laid out.

The basic major formats are, largest to smallest:

Folio (or 2°, indicating that each sheet has one fold, forming two leaves, four pages);

Quarto (or 4°, two folds, four leaves, eight pages);

Octavo (8°, three folds, eight leaves, sixteen pages);

Duodecimo (12°, twelve leaves, twenty-four pages); twelvemo, as it is often called, could come in several varieties, some involving cutting the page before folding and then folding the two sections in different patterns.

There were also several smaller formats, sextodecimo or sixteenmo (16°), octodecimo or eighteenmo (18°), and twenty-fourmo (24°).

In the larger formats, several sheets were sometimes nested inside another. The result is called a *quire* and is designated by how many leaves it contained. A 4° in 8s (quarto-in-eights), a fairly common format, consisted of two quarto sheets, one inside the other, making a quire of eight leaves and sixteen pages, so that on the first sheet was printed pages 1–4 and 13–16 of the quire, while the second sheet held pages 5–12.

Two quarto sheets, folded and nested.

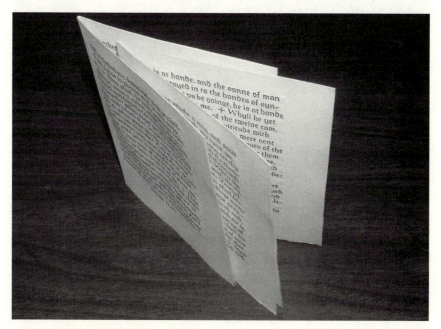

A quarto-in-eights, sewn but not yet covered. One sheet, folded twice to form quarto pages, has been nested within the center fold of another quarto sheet to form a single gathering. Many such gatherings are then sewn through their center folds to cloth strips to form the spine of the book. The top folds have not yet been trimmed.

It was not uncommon for a printer to lay out the pages in such a way that the same forme might serve for both the inner and outer part of the sheet, a system called "work and turn" or half-sheet imposition. After both sides had been printed, the page would be cut in half, resulting in two identical half-sheets. An 8° in 4s worked in half-sheet imposition will look like a quarto, but smaller and with the markings in the paper, such as the watermark and the chain lines, oriented differently than in a typical quarto volume.

For the first couple hundred years of printing, format helped determine how a compositor went about setting type. One option was to set the text seriatim, page by page, beginning with the first. A quick folding exercise with three sheets of paper will illustrate how inefficient setting a text seriatim is. Folding the sheets once and nesting them within one another creates a folio-in-sixes gathering, a fairly standard format, and the format for Shakespeare's First Folio (1623). Numbering the pages that result will show that the first sheet contains pages one and twelve on one side, the outer forme, with two and eleven on the other side, the inner forme. Set seriatim, the type in page one must wait, literally tied up, until ten more pages have been set, before it (and the finally set page twelve) can be printed. Type was expensive, and printers in the sixteenth century generally did not have enough type to keep up to seven full pages idle at a time. This changed over the years, as printers began keeping enough type on hand, well before mechanized typesetting. But up until the later seventeenth century, most manuscripts were therefore cast off and set out of order, even for a smaller format book, like quarto or octavo. Knowing the size of the page and size of type, one could estimate the average number of words per page, then rather quickly calculate how much manuscript would fit on a page and soon make rough marks in the manuscript to indicate where pages should begin and end. While more efficient in the use of type and the time of a compositor and of pressmen, setting by formes was not without trouble. If, in casting off, not enough text was allotted to a page, the compositor was faced with leaving blank space, an inefficient use of paper and something quite unattractive if it happens in the middle of a text. It was up to the compositor to determine how best to justify a line so that the margins would be neat on the page, and this meant that spelling was often a matter for the compositor's discretion —so that a compositor might set the word as *do* or *doe* depending partly on how the word was spelled in the manuscript, partly on the compositor's preferences, and partly on space requirements. If too much text was mistakenly assigned to a single page, a compositor was faced with disassembling other pages in order to adjust, or, if that were not possible, simply trying to make the text fit by resorting to cramped spacing, frequent abbreviations, shorter spellings, and perhaps even setting verse as prose. Might a desperate compositor resort to cutting or adding whole words and phrases? It may have been rare, but the evidence for this is sometimes very good.[7]

After a forme had been readied, there might be several iterations of the cycle of printing single sheets, proofreading these, and making corrections in the forme. Once the press began printing the forme in earnest, it was still not uncommon for one of the first sheets to be proofread again and for more changes to be required, resulting in stop-press corrections. Uncorrected early sheets were not thrown away, since they represented an investment of time and material by the printer, so stop-press changes by definition will appear in some copies of the edition in question and not in others. We know from surviving copies that even sheets with proofreader's marks could be returned to the pile of printed sheets and later folded and bound up in a copy of the edition. A forme might go through several such stop-press changes before the full number of sheets were printed from it. Because of the way that sheets were naturally shuffled in drying and perfecting (that is, printing the second side of the sheet), no copy of any large book in the hand-press era was likely to be made only from completely corrected sheets and no copy would be exactly identical to another copy. This is the case with Shakespeare's First Folio, each copy being in some senses as unique as a manuscript.

Mechanization for printing has meant not only greater numbers of books printed in shorter periods of time, but also, and maybe more importantly, greater bibliographic uniformity, so that, while important differences may still be found within single editions from the mechanical-press period, they will be fewer than in the hand-press. But part of this uniformity comes from procedural changes that largely predate mechanization and that seem to have grown out of changes in the finances of printing entrepreneurship and in the higher expectations coming from the rising status of authorship. When it comes to spelling, punctuation, capitalization, and other surface features of a text, it was not a case of anything goes, as some students seem to think when they first

---

7. For a more detailed account of the possible effects of setting by formes on the text, see Peter Blayney's article in Part Two of this volume.

confront early hand-press documents, though it is true that mechanical rules were not so rigid then as they seem to be now. In the early hand-press era, such rules were generally passed down from senior compositors to apprentices in the course of training. House styles, the rules governing the way the compositors for a certain printing house would convert idiosyncratic authorial manuscripts into print, arose around the end of the hand-press era. Later, house styles moved from the control of the printer to the publisher. It is no coincidence that *The Chicago Manual of Style*, one of the major published style guides, was first printed only in 1906, nor is it coincidental that it began as a simple list of rules drawn up by a proofreader at the University of Chicago's press in the 1890s.[8] The creation of such rules implies a growing group of employees at a press helping to prepare a manuscript for publication—the editorial department. Greater editorial oversight also comes with greater authorial oversight, so that in the mechanical-press period an author is more likely to have had more control over the printed version. Authors could often ask for several rounds of proofs (everything after the first proof was called *revises*), though there remains some question about how much control an author expected over such things as punctuation and spelling. These proofs sometimes survive, and when they do, they provide valuable evidence for textual critics.

The chart on the next page provides a brief example of the tortuous path a hypothetical work might take as it moves from notes, through successive rough drafts, to one fair manuscript copy, to three simultaneous typescript copies, each of which is annotated, to one clean revised typescript, and, finally, through two sets of proofs, to the printed edition. As each of these documents incorporates revisions suggested at various stages by a spouse, by friends, and by editors, and includes both accidental changes made by typists and intended changes urged by copy-editors, none of them is exactly like another. The reader is invited to imagine the involutions possible when one considers corrected subsequent editions printed from a corrected first edition.

---

8. Margaret D. F. Mahan, "Preface," *The Chicago Manual of Style*, 15th ed. (Chicago: University of Chicago Press, 2003), xiii.

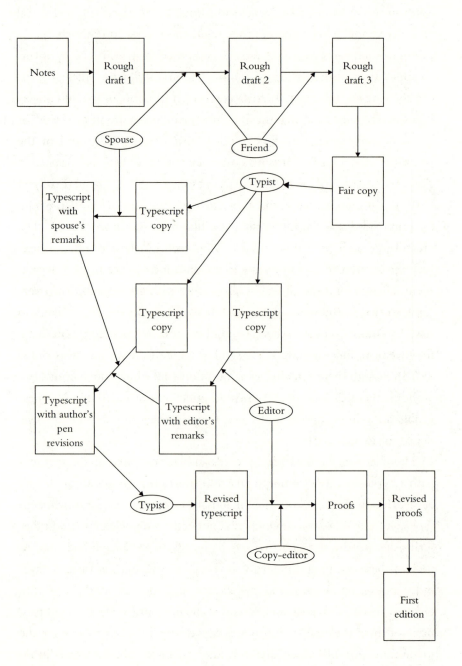

KINDS OF VARIATION

Transmitting a text from one document to another is often a laborious process that, even under the most careful practices, introduces changes in the text, many beneficial, some more noticeable than others. Often such changes become calcified, as it were, by later scribes or printers, who either reproduce them exactly, or, in trying to make sense of apparent nonsense in their exemplar, emend the text and thus produce yet another variant. By the same process an otherwise diligent person may mistakenly emend a correct reading that he does not understand or thinks to be in error. This possibility, that a well-intentioned scribe or compositor might edit the text he copies in order to make better sense for him has led textual critics to develop the principle *lectio dificilior potior*: the more difficult reading is the stronger. Faced with two or more possible readings, the textual critic will generally prefer the one that is the more obscure, since it is the likeliest to have been misunderstood and simplified by those reproducing the text. The impression we might get from this and from focusing so much upon perceived errors in a document is that scribes and compositors were hasty and unconcerned with the accuracy of their work. We should probably understand the reverse to be the case. Scribes who had doubts about the quality of their exemplar often sought out another and introduced readings from it or switched to it altogether. From the scribes' and their customers' perspectives, these emendations are improvements. In fact, it is clear that such scribes were motivated by the same desires that motivate many modern editors and that they employed methods and judgments very similar to those of modern editors. For the textual critic, however, the result is horizontal contamination, something that complicates efforts to trace a textual history and makes trouble for reconstructing the manuscript which provided copy to the scribe.

Some would refer to these differences as *variants*, some as *errors*. To the uninitiated, it may seem that textual criticism treats the terms *variant* and *error* like synonyms, and though some may in fact treat them as such, it can be valuable to distinguish them. The term *variant* carries no value judgment with it, implying a relative equality among possible readings, while the term *error* clearly indicates its allegiances. *Variation* allows for a range of possibilities, while *error* insists on a binary opposition: either a reading is right or it is wrong. Some might argue that a further distinction be made, that variation can exist only where there are two witnesses to a work, while an error may nevertheless be detected in the text of a work with a single authority. But to find an error in a single text is to find a theoretical variation, a variation between an actual and an ideal text. Without assuming the existence of an ideal text, one that is *not* identical to the witness, it would be impossible to find an error in that witness. For this reason, it is probably best to consider error a subcategory of variation, of which another subcategory would be revision. It is also valuable to consider the two categories, error and revision, to be non-exclusive. That is, there may be some revisions that are also errors. While oftentimes a feature of a text will seem easy to identify as an error, such determinations are usually never certain. For some, the determining characteristic of error is that it violates the sense of a text. But literature is replete with examples of purposefully nonsensical words, phrases, sentences, passages, even whole poems, which is as much as to say that sometimes, a violation of sense is intentional. And, sometimes, what is nonsense to one reader is sense to another.

Variation can be either authorial or non-authorial. Each of these branches may be further subdivided by intention. A variation that is authorial and intentional is a revision or a version. A variation that is authorial but unintentional is an error in composition. Variation that is non-authorial and intentional is an emendation, a case of editing no matter who does it, while non-authorial, unintentional variation is an error in transmission. Because textual criticism arose primarily from the study of classical and biblical literatures which do not preserve any authorial documents, errors in transmission have been the most studied and the most theorized.

Not all errors in transmission may be the result of an error in the act of reproducing the text. If, for instance, a page has been lost from a manuscript so that some text is missing, later copies of that manuscript will preserve that error, and this is not the result of an unthinking compositor

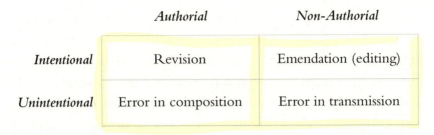

	Authorial	Non-Authorial
Intentional	Revision	Emendation (editing)
Unintentional	Error in composition	Error in transmission

or scribe. Some textual critics have carefully categorized what we might instead call mechanical errors, ones that can occur in reproducing the text, either in hand-copying or in setting the text in type, and while this careful categorization can seem like overkill to the novice, even briefly studying them can reveal much about the precariousness of textual transmission and can sharpen a reader's eyes for textual errors. Mechanical errors might be divided into those likely to have been caused by a scribe's or typesetter's inattentiveness, and those where the original being reproduced might have been confusing if not outright faulty.

The first sort of error produced by copyists and typesetters, transposition, is probably most common on the smaller scale, such as at the level of letters (perhaps the most common srot of typo) or of words (he said, said he). But it is not unknown for lines of verse to be reversed, and there is a very famous case of two entire chapters in Henry James's novel, *The Ambassadors*, having been switched, appearing in one order in the English edition, another in the American edition published a month later.[9] It may be useful to distinguish further among errors of transposition, especially between smaller and larger scales. It is probable that the flipping of chapters 28 and 29 in *The Ambassadors* resulted from

9. The textual situation is actually much more complex than described here. It is not certain how the two chapters came to be switched. The novel first appeared in serialized form in 1903. James revised this text for the American version, which appeared in November 1903. But before this edition appeared, James revised the novel again for the English version, which was published in September 1903. So the English edition, though published earlier, presents (for most) a better text than the American edition. Strangely, when James revised again a few years later for what is called The New York Edition of his collected works, published in 1909, he revised not the text of the English edition, but that of the faulty American one. For more details, see Henry James, *The Ambassadors*, 2nd ed., ed. S. P. Rosenbaum (New York: W. W. Norton & Company, 1994).

shuffling manuscript pages, or some other accident, but the scale of the transposition would make one think that someone did it intentionally. *The Canterbury Tales* manuscripts that are most complete suggest two major ways of ordering its contents, suggesting that Chaucer revised its order after it had begun to circulate. Transpositions of smaller elements, like individual letters, likely result from copyists and compositors who are inattentive, although in fairness it should be noted that if such transpositions persist, others involved in copying or printing are also being inattentive. Meanwhile, transposed words and even transposed lines of verse might suggest that the person copying the text has taken the text into memory imperfectly, perhaps taking in more than he or she can hold accurately. The compositor or copyist may have taken the sense into memory quite well, but not the exact wording, matching instead an expected pattern or coordinating with a memory of another text, resulting in what textual critics call a *conflation*. Such errors show that reading for wording and reading for sense are different activities. Copyists and compositors may not have paid attention to the meanings of the texts they copied or set into type. As we shall see with the next kind of error, there are mechanical reasons why this should be the case.

Omissions of repeated material from the text, a second sort of copyist error, can likewise vary in scale, from a few letters (called *haplography*: "philogist" for "philologist," or "this an example of haplography" for "this *is* an example of haplography") to several words and as much as whole lines of verse or prose, when it is called *eyeskip.* To see how eyeskip might occur, imagine someone copying the following passage from the Act 3 of *Hamlet*, as Hamlet asks his mother to compare the pictures of her first and second husbands, likening the second to a diseased ear of grain, infecting those around it:

This *was* your husband. Look you now what follows.
Here *is* your husband, like a mildewed ear
Blasting his wholesome brother. Have you eyes?
Could you on this fair mountain leave to feed,
And batten on this moor? Ha, have you eyes?

You cannot call it love, for at your age
The heyday in the blood is tame, it's humble. . . . (3.4.62–68)

The invention of the keyboard and touch typing has probably reduced omissions, since the typist does not need to—and in fact is trained *not* to—look back and forth between the exemplar and the typewriter or, now, the computer screen and keyboard. But the person copying a manuscript by hand or setting type by hand absolutely must look back and forth. The compositor or copyist first must read a section of the exemplar taking it into short-term memory. Then he or she must turn to the copy being produced or to the type cases in which the letters are held and must add the section of memorized text to what has already been copied or assembled in the composing stick. Then the scribe or compositor can return to the exemplar, find the place where he or she left off, and can take into memory the next piece.

1 ————→ 2   5 ————————→ 6
This was your husband. Look you, now, what follows:

9 ←———— 10   13 ————→ 14
Here is your husband, like a mildewed ear,

3 ————→ 4   7 ————————→ 8
This was your husband. Look you, now, what follows:

11 ————→ 12   15 ————→ 16
Here is your husband, like a mildewed ear,

The result, as the diagram shows, is a zig-zagging pattern for the eyes, back and forth between exemplar and copy, one that makes it difficult if not impossible to understand the senses of the text, since it is a disjunctive reading process, sometimes breaking up the text without regard to syntactical units. It is a pattern that copyists will fall into naturally, but it practically invites errors of omission. It is not impossible to imagine a copyist's eyes, already spinning from the first two-and-a-half acts of *Hamlet*, to reach point #4 in the process and then, in skipping back to the exemplar, to pick up "husband" not at #2 but at #10, and to continue copying not at the words "Look you, now" at #5 but with the words "like a mildewed ear" at #13—

1   → 2   5   6

This was your husband. Look you, now, what follows:

9   10   13   → 14

Here is your husband, like a mildewed ear,

                                3   → 4 7   → 8

                           This was your husband, like a mildewed ear,

—resulting in: "This was your husband, like a mildewed ear, / Blasting his wholesome brother. Have you eyes?" If a case of haplography or eye-skip in poetry does not disorder the meter or rhyme scheme, it will usually disrupt the sense. In this hypothetical case, the meter is preserved; the clue that two half-lines of poetry have been omitted is the peculiar verb tense, since the "mildewed ear" must refer to the man who *is* her husband, not the one who *was*. That this omission might occur is made more difficult by the fact that the two *husband*s occur in the middle of the poetic line and that the punctuation after the two *husband*s is not identical. It may be different altogether for another case of eyeskip that could occur with this passage. Imagine the tired or distracted copyist or typesetter, finishing copying the text from $1 \rightarrow 2$ as $3 \rightarrow 4$, ending with the first "Have you eyes?" Instead of coming back to the exemplar at position 2 in order to find "Could you on this . . ." at position 5, he or she comes back to the exemplar at position 6, two lines too low, and starts copying from 7, "You cannot call it love" at position 8 (see opposite page). This second example of eyeskip is more likely because ends of the lines look more alike than middles. A moment's reflection on our own reading practices should convince us how easy it is to make such a mistake. Few readers have not resorted at one time or another to using the long edge of a bookmark or the tip of a finger to mark a line in a dense text so that the eye does not skip too far ahead or repeat a line already read.

Scribes and typesetters might also mistakenly add to the text. It is called *dittography* when as much as a phrase is mistakenly repeated. It can happen that whole lines may be copied twice, but the longer the repetition, the more likely it is that a scribe or compositor will notice the error as it is being made and correct it. Other kinds of errors of addition

This was your husband. Look you, now, what follows:

Here is your husband, like a mildewed ear,

1 ⸻▶ 2

Blasting his wholesome brother. Have you eyes?

5   Could you on this fair mountain leave to feed,

And batten on this moor? Ha? Have you eyes?   6

7   You cannot call it love, for at your age

The hey-day in the blood is tame, it's humble. . . .

This was your husband. Look you, now, what follows:

Here is your husband, like a mildewed ear,

3 ⸻▶ 4

Blasting his wholesome brother. Have you eyes?

8   You cannot call it love, for at your age

The hey-day in the blood is tame, it's humble. . . .

occur when the scribe or the compositor does not understand extra-textual features, such as notes or interlinear comments, and includes them as part of the text. Such is one of the jokes that Vladimir Nabokov plays in the opening pages of his parody of critical editing, *Pale Fire*. In the false "Foreword," Nabokov's fictional critical editor describes some of the process he has undertaken with the publisher's editor, Frank, and a "professional proofreader":

> Frank has acknowledged the safe return of the galleys I had been sent here and has asked me to mention in my Preface—and this I willingly do—that I alone am responsible for any mistakes in my commentary. Insert before a professional. A professional proofreader has carefully rechecked the printed text of the poem against the phototype of the manuscript, and has found a few trivial misprints I had missed. . . . [10]

10. Vladimir Nabokov, *Pale Fire* (New York: Vintage, 1962), 18.

Erroneous additions such as these are easier to spot in formal poetry, because they disrupt the meter, but additions are occasionally discovered in prose when they violate the sense of the passage in question. This is the case with the passage from *Moll Flanders* discussed later in this volume, where the compositor apparently did not understand that one passage was inserted in the manuscript in order to replace another passage that had been marked for deletion, printing both passages, resulting in a confusing, somewhat contradictory duplication.

One might be forgiven for thinking from this catalogue of possible errors that these laborers were a lazy, corner-cutting lot. In fact, it is not remarkable that scribes and typesetters make errors as they do their work. What is remarkable is that there are not more errors. Textual critics have also developed extensive categories of errors caused not by scribal incompetence but by documents that are less than clear. The often-heard lament about the deterioration of the general public's handwriting skills may be correct, but it has also always been the case that there are generally two kinds of documents, formal and informal, employing different degrees of care and materials in presenting legible texts. It is often the job of scribes and typesetters to turn informal documents, meant for only a few eyes, into formal documents for many more to see. Even formal documents, however, are not always easily read. In fact, it is the nature of all writing systems that some of their elements can be confused with others. The situation is complicated by conventions of spelling or pronunciation that change over time or that vary from region to region. Given the conditions, scribes and typesetters have done remarkable work over the years.

The first sort of error that we ought not blame entirely on the copyist is the result of easily confused letterforms, something that was especially common in medieval and Renaissance scripts. Confusion between ſ (the long-s) and f, especially in italic type (*ſ* and *f*) and in cursive hands, often slows students who are just learning to read older documents, and sometimes produces a bit of anachronistic, gutter-minded fun:

> Marke but this flea, and marke in this,
>
> How little that which thou deny'ſt me is;
>
> It ſuck'd me first, and now ſucks thee. . . . [11]

A little practice clears up most difficulties like this, but the similarities between, say, c and t in some older scripts could confuse the very scribes who wrote them. The word *minim* describes the short vertical stroke that forms the main part of every letter in *minimum*, a word consisting of fifteen uninterrupted minims. In some scripts in the middle ages, the letters m, n, i, and u were written with very little to determine the differences among them, so that errors in words consisting of strings of three or four minims at a time are not unexpected.

English scribes borrowed a French script, called *Secretary*, during the fifteenth, sixteenth, and early seventeenth centuries. Mixed with the early English Gothic book hands, it evolved into a script called *English Secretary*, or sometimes *Elizabethan Secretary*, the style of writing used by Shakespeare and most of his contemporaries. Even when written by a professional scribe, *English Secretary* is much more difficult for students to begin to read than the Gothic hands of just a century or two prior and than the italic hands that enter England in the sixteenth century and begin to dominate in the seventeenth. By the middle of the seventeenth century, the italic hand taught in schools today as *cursive* is the standard in handwritten documents, making them easier for a modern reader to decipher. Nevertheless, an uncommonly cramped or poorly executed handwritten document from any period can be difficult to read and therefore to copy.

A second kind of error might result from inconsistent spacing between words. If the writing of a document has become cramped, because the first copyist had begun to run out of room on the page, then it may be difficult for the second copyist to tell the difference between *therapist* and *the rapist*, or *frees laughter* and *free slaughter*. Such errors are usually fairly easily discovered and corrected in context. Textual critics

---

11. John Donne, "The Flea," *Poems, by J.D. VVith elegies on the authors death*, 1633, Gg3ᵛ.

who work with classical languages are more likely to be interested in errors produced by inconsistent spacing and word division, since the earliest manuscripts were written in *scriptura continua,* meaning with no word division. Medieval and Renaissance manuscripts often employed an extensive system of abbreviations, but because these abbreviations could change from region to region and over the course of time, later scribes and printers might misunderstand them occasionally, producing another sort of error that isn't much seen in the modern era. Finally, linguistic changes, changes in spelling and pronunciation for instance, may help introduce errors in the text, where a copyist tries to make the best of a text that is confusing to him or her. For modern readers the past tense of *to eat* is *ate*. But as late as the eighteenth century, the past tense could be spelled *eat*, and pronounced, as it still is in some parts of the world, as *et*, and one can see how the form can cause some small confusion. The issue is greater when one is working with texts from the medieval or early modern periods, when spelling rules were not as firm or as standardized as they are now, when the grammar was different enough so as to be unfamiliar to today's novice, and when certain words that have since dropped out of the language were still in circulation.

Cataloguing the variety of changes that might be introduced, understanding the networks of people and institutions involved, and having an awareness of the physical natures of the documents that were printed or copied teaches us not only how better to look for variants in texts. It also teaches us how unstable texts are, how uncertain communication of any sort is, and how much every text is a collaborative product. It teaches us that texts have histories, that they did not appear on the bookstore shelf from nowhere, fully formed, nor did they emerge—poof—from the author's pen exactly as we have them. The task of textual criticism is to recover the text's history so that it might be employed in comprehending the work. We might reconstruct that history as part of an argument on the work, as do many of the writers in Part Two. Or we might reconstruct that history to make an edition of the work, which, as the next chapter will point out, is another sort of argument. Of course, reconstructing a history—even just a partial history—is also valuable as a strategy for the reader who wishes only to read, concerned only with the pleasure of taking in the text.

A student's first encounters with manuscripts from before the eighteenth century can be frustrating, not only because of the changes in the language but also because of the changes in the shapes (and kinds) of letters. Gothic English manuscripts—those written from, say, the twelfth to the sixteenth centuries, are famously difficult to read because of the high degree of biting in their scripts, that is, where letters touch and overlap, and because of their many unfamiliar abbreviations. But even the letterforms can confuse readers used to common roman and italic shapes. As the merest beginning for the study of paleography, this chart provides examples of letters from four manuscript facsimiles that appear in part three of this volume. The manuscripts vary in age from the early fifteenth century until the early sixteenth. We have attempted to highlight at least one example of the majuscule (i.e. capital) and miniscule (lowercase) of each letter in the context of an entire word. When a manuscript uses more than one form for a letter, and this occurs frequently in early manuscripts, we have attempted to give a sense of the variety. Italics are used to indicate expanded abbreviations.

	Add.10340, early 15th century (see p. 510)		Add.36983, before 1450 (see p. 512)		Harley 7333, after 1450 (see p. 516)		Arch. Seld B.24, early 16th century (see p. 519)	
	Majuscules	Miniscules	Majuscules	Miniscules	Majuscules	Miniscules	Majuscules	Miniscules
A, a	*And*	*schal*		*a falle*				
B, b	*Bywar*	*be*						
C, c	*Crie*	*clymbyng* / *crokke*				*clymbyng*		
D, d	*Daunte*	*drede*						

	Add.10340, early 15th century (see p. 510)		Add.36983, before 1450 (see p. 512)		Harley 7333, after 1450 (see p. 516)		Arch. Seld B.24, early 16th century (see p. 519)	
	Majuscules	Miniscules	Majuscules	Miniscules	Majuscules	Miniscules	Majuscules	Miniscules
E, e		receyue			Ebrue			ressaue
F, f	Fle	self		(doubled *f*) (single *f*)		(-ff)		
G, g		god			Grete		Grete	
H, h	Holde	byhove					Here	
I, i, J, j	In	hie	In	in is				
K, k	Knowe	croked						
L, l, ll		litel	Loke	(doubled *l*)				
M, m	Made	more						
N, n	Ne	þanne						
O, o	Out	horde						
P, p	Prees	pres						
Q, q							Quhat	

	Add.10340, early 15th century (see p. 510)		Add.36983, before 1450 (see p. 512)		Harley 7333, after 1450 (see p. 516)		Arch. Seld B.24, early 16th century (see p. 519)	
	Majuscules	Miniscules	Majuscules	Miniscules	Majuscules	Miniscules	Majuscules	Miniscules
R, r	Reule	þerfore / operes						redresse
S, s	Suffise	is sent		as				this is / is sent
T, t	Tempest	tourneþ		t		lete		t
U, u V, v	Unto / Vache	enuye / leue / out / unto				spurne / envy		
W, w	Were	worlde						
X, x		axeþ						
Y, y		a3eyns						
Þ, þ (thorn)	Þat, that	doÞe, dothe						
3, 3 (yogh)		nou3t, nought						

	Add.10340, early 15th century (see p. 510)		Add.36983, before 1450 (see p. 512)		Harley 7333, after 1450 (see p. 516)		Arch. Seld B.24, early 16th century (see p. 519)	
	Majuscules	Miniscules	Majuscules	Miniscules	Majuscules	Miniscules	Majuscules	Miniscules
and								
-er-ur		oueral				deliuer		wilderness
per, par, or pur		parson						
-n-m (nasal suspension)		buxhumnesse						bowsumness
wᵗ, þᵗ				with		that with		that with
-es								otheres

Textual Criticism and Kinds of Editions

THE USUAL (though by no means only or necessary) end product for textual criticism is the critical edition, employing the editor's discoveries about a work's textual history. A critical edition is, as Kane and Donaldson define it in the introduction to their edition of the *Piers Plowman* B-text, "a theoretical structure, a complex hypothesis designed to account for a body of phenomena in the light of knowledge about the circumstances which generated them."[1] Like an analytical essay, then, a critical edition is an argument that describes its data, sets forward its methods and reasoning, and presents its results—the text. "Like all hypotheses," Kane and Donaldson add, editions are "essentially presumptive, that is subject to modification by the emergence of new data, or to replacement by a superior hypothesis" (212). In a critical edition, in short, an editor makes an argument about what a text *should* be, based upon a critical analysis of the witnesses. By contrast, any edition that does not determine its text through textual criticism is an uncritical (or non-critical) edition. For scholars the distinction comes with a set of broad value judgments, with critical editions usually valued much more highly than non-critical ones. It is one of the traditional early (and sometimes more embarrassing) lessons of most graduate programs in literature that one cannot cite simply any edition of a work in a literary analysis.

---

1. William Langland, *Piers Plowman: The B Version*, ed. George Kane and E. Talbot Donaldson (London: Athlone Press, 1975), 212.

This is the case, for example, with Edgar Allan Poe's opinions of Nathaniel Hawthorne's *Twice-told Tales* and *Mosses from an Old Manse*, remarks that bear on Poe's much-discussed ideas about the short story. A reader of Edmund Stedman and George Woodberry's edition of Poe's works (first published in 1894, but reprinted as late as 1971) might be forgiven for thinking that Poe contradicts himself, flip-flopping in his estimation of Hawthorne's literary genius.[2] In section I of the essay, Poe writes,

> if Hawthorne were really original he could not fail of making himself felt by the public. But the fact is, he is not original in any sense. (25)

Not many paragraphs later, in section II, Poe seems to have forgotten what he just wrote:

> Mr. Hawthorne's distinctive trait is invention, creation, imagination, originality—a trait which, in the literature of fiction, is positively worth all the rest. But the nature of originality, so far as regards its manifestation in letters, is but imperfectly understood. The inventive or original mind as frequently displays itself in novelty of tone as in novelty of matter. Mr. Hawthorne is original in all points. (41–42)

In section III, Poe reverts to his first position, asserting that Hawthorne

> is peculiar and *not* original—unless in those detailed fancies and detached thoughts which in his want of general originality will deprive of the appreciation due to them, in preventing them from reaching the public eye. (46)

How can Hawthorne be "not original in any sense," then, "original in all points," and finally, "peculiar and not original," except in a few small points? Poe's contradiction may seem like a symptom, indicating that he

---

2. Edgar Allan Poe, *The Works of Edgar Allan Poe; Newly Collected and Edited, With a Memoir, Critical Introductions, and Notes*, ed. Edmund Clarence Stedman and George Edward Woodberry (1894).

was drunk, insane, or simply jealous, until one investigates the notes at the end of the volume and discovers the following:

> *Hawthorne's "Tales."* I. Published in "Godey's Lady's Book," November, 1847. II. Published in "Graham's Magazine," May, 1842. III. Published in "Godey's Lady's Book," November, 1847. (429)

Far from the single piece it appears to be, the review is really two reviews, the earlier sandwiched between parts of the later, making Poe's ideas seem muddled and obscuring the history of those ideas. In fact, Poe wrote three reviews of Hawthorne's work, only two of which are used in Stedman and Woodberry. The first two reviews, both positive, appeared a few months apart in 1842 in *Graham's Magazine*, and the third, this time quite negative, appeared five years later in *Godey's Lady's Book*. Though Stedman and Woodberry's note suggests that the periodicals provide the source for their text, in fact they are reprinting with few if any meaningful changes the text that appears in Rufus Wilmot Griswold's edition of Poe's works (published in 1856 but also reprinted many times).[3] Stedman and Woodberry add section numbers where Griswold's edition signals a section break with a horizontal rule (a short line or bar), but otherwise they repeat Griswold's rearrangement of the text and his omissions exactly. The fact that Stedman and Woodberry indicate sources at all suggests that they were aware of the problem but chose not to correct it. They were not alone in their recognition, nor in nevertheless perpetuating errors with these texts. Their edition was predated by John Ingram's edition (1874, but also reprinted many times),[4] which claims to correct Griswold's many errors:

> Many of the critiques contained in this volume, it may be remarked, differ considerably from those in the American collection of Poe's

3. Edgar Allan Poe, *The Works of the Late Edgar Allan Poe: With Notices of His Life and Genius*, ed. Rufus W. Griswold, N. P. Willis, and James Russell Lowell (1856).

4. Edgar Allan Poe, *The Works of Edgar Allan Poe*, ed. John Henry Ingram (1874).

works, edited by Mr. Griswold; in explanation of these discrepancies I
can but state the fact that they are now printed (with a few omissions
of quotations) as they appeared in the original publications. (iii)

Ingram disassembles Griswold's sandwich and prints material that Griswold eliminated from the reviews. But Ingram also gives no indication
that his text derives from more than one review, so that the negative
review of 1847 follows the 1842 review with only a paragraph break to
mark the transition. Griswold's biography of Poe spread the view that
his subject was a madman. His edition of Poe's reviews certainly does
not help dispel that notion. Ingram, on the other hand, did not hold such
negative views, but Poe's thinking seems as muddled in Ingram's edition
as in Griswold's. Other editions of these reviews (and there are several)
generally either print one or both of the positive reviews from 1842, or
they print the negative review from 1847. In that they tend not to combine the reviews, they are better editions, but they are generally not
complete, nor do they always indicate the fact that Poe held another
view at another time. James A. Harrison's 1902 edition was the first edition to straighten out the relationships among the three works, allowing
a reader to piece together more easily Poe's shifting ideas about
Hawthorne and the short story.[5]

This lengthy example from Poe's work suggests why the critical edition usually becomes the "definitive edition" or the "standard edition,"
the edition that the scholarly community generally agrees should be cited
when one publishes an essay or a book about that work. Non-critical editions are often viewed as suspect at best. They are likely to be defective,
incomplete, or corrupt, like Griswold's conflation. While the critical edition is often praised as a monument to the author's work and an achieve-
ment by the editor or editors, the non-critical edition is sometimes
viewed in the scholarly community as a form of opportunism, almost as a
legal form of piracy. This is because many of the "classic" works that are
taught at the college level, especially in inexpensive paperbacks and elec-

5. Edgar Allan Poe, *The Complete Works of Edgar Allan Poe*, ed. James A. Harrison (1902).

tronic editions available on the Internet, will reprint uncritically the text of another edition, usually an older one whose copyright has expired. Using such public domain texts can save publishers money, since they will not have to pay an another publisher for permission to publish that text. But doing so also means that the reprint edition will ignore the sometimes remarkable discoveries about the textual history made since the old edition's publication, or, worse, may reprint some rather remarkable and even reprehensible errors made by previous editors. The impulse that values the critical edition over the non-critical is plainly not without merit.

But these value judgments can be assailed in many ways, not the least of which is to accuse them of a kind of snobbery. Who cares if the Jane Austen novel I plan to read on vacation at the beach is the standard edition? More important to the vacationer, surely, is the price of the book and the amount of space it occupies in the carry-on bag. One might reply that even the budget-conscious vacationer shouldn't be forced to see an accurate text as a luxury. Beach-going readers might not know the difference, or much care, but that doesn't absolve the scholar from caring on their behalf. Errors shouldn't be perpetuated just because they're economical. The complaint by the textual critic, here, isn't against the uninformed consumer but the unscrupulous publisher. Even if the charge of snobbery can be defended, however, such value judgments sometimes turn out to be simply incorrect, and we should be wary of them just as we should any prejudice. The simple fact is that the difference between critical and non-critical editions is not scholarship or even editorial care. A scholarly editor of a non-critical edition might supply an extensive biography of the author, ample explanatory notes, a glossary, several indexes and an extensive bibliography, making for a very useful edition. Moreover, this non-critical editor might—and this is paramount— exercise great care to keep from introducing errors into the text chosen for reprinting. Though the reprinted text can't be much better, it probably will not be much worse than the original. In this case, if that original edition presented a reliable text, the reprint, too, will likely be a valuable edition. By contrast, not all critical editions are of the same quality; some are widely regarded by scholars as being positively terrible.

Neville Rogers's edition of Percy Bysshe Shelley's complete poetry was abandoned after only two of its projected four volumes appeared because the reviews complained about its poor editorial choices and substantial inconsistencies.[6] If prepared by an idiosyncratic and misguided editor, or simply an inconsistent, sloppy, or inattentive one, a critical edition might introduce all manner of changes that most of the scholarly community would reject. The result may well be that a non-critical edition presents a better, more reliable text than a corresponding critical edition. But because the text of the non-critical edition is not based on an investigation of its history, it is not a critical edition. In short, what matters in determining whether an edition is a critical one is not the quality of the text, nor even the presence of much of a critical apparatus (though usually a very good sign), but in the editor's having subjected the work to textual criticism in determining what to print.

Editions of Emily Dickinson's poetry provide another a vivid example of these distinctions. Searching for her poem that begins "Safe in their alabaster chambers" in an inexpensive copy of her poems at a bookstore or in an online database or website, one is more than likely to find a three-stanza poem. If this publication or website gives credit to the source of its text, it is very likely to be an early edition, deriving ultimately from the first edition of Dickinson's poetry, printed in the 1890s, edited by Mabel Loomis Todd and T. W. Higginson. The excerpts from editions of Dickinson's poetry contained here (see Part Three of this volume) should give a sense of how the poem printed in the paperback came to be a twelve-line poem instead of one of the several eight-line versions that Dickinson actually wrote. Comparing inexpensive reprints found in virtually any bookstore or online with the excerpts from the critical editions of the poem reprinted here should also give a sense of the different aims in a critical edition and a non-critical one. Any book that reprints the

6. Percy Bysshe Shelley, *The Complete Poetical Works of Percy Bysshe Shelley*, 2 vols., ed. Neville Rogers (Oxford: Clarendon Press, 1972). See Donald H. Reiman and Neil Fraistat, *The Complete Poetry of Percy Bysshe Shelley*, vol. 1 (Baltimore: Johns Hopkins University Press, 2000), xxvii–xxviii. For Donald Reiman's own review, see "Rogers's Oxford Shelley," *Romantic Texts and Contexts* (Columbia: University of Missouri Press, 1987), 41–54.

Todd and Higginson text likely either ignores or discounts the discoveries represented in the two critical editions printed since then, and some critics would argue that it ignores the artistic wishes of Dickinson herself. Now, some would point out that Todd and Higginson's edition is itself, in fact, a critical edition. Later editors may disagree with their methods, in regularizing spelling and in introducing punctuation—and especially in conflating versions of this poem to create one that is four lines longer than any version Dickinson herself produced. Todd and Higginson do not record the evidence they consulted nor do they explain any of their critical choices and emendations, providing, in other words, no critical apparatus. Nevertheless, they did examine Dickinson's manuscripts and the poems printed in the *Springfield Republican*, and then they selected and emended texts from among the many versions they found, sifting evidence and deciding what to print based on their interpretation of that evidence. In this sense, though it is doubtless a bad one, Todd and Higginson's is a critical edition. It would be difficult to maintain, however, when an inexpensive paperback reprints Todd and Higginson's text, that it is also therefore a critical edition, since its editors probably have not based their text on an investigation of the text's history. What, then, is the status of Ferguson, Salter, and Stallworthy's text of the poem in the *Norton Anthology of Poetry*? On the one hand, the editors have reprinted the text of another edition, not themselves edited the poem anew. Even though they have adopted the text of the latest critical edition, R. W. Franklin's, their edition should not be called a critical one. On the other hand, they print two versions of the poem, one from 1859, the other from 1862, a strategy that begins to represent some of Franklin's discoveries about the poem's textual history and encourages the reader to begin constructing a textual history for the poem. Perhaps we should call this an incomplete critical edition, perhaps call it *versioning* (see below). What it suggests is that rather than being binary opposites, critical editions and non-critical editions are rough designations on a continuum of editorial activity; editions can be more or less critical. Fredson Bowers's term, *practical editions*, in which the editor takes care to present as reliable a text as possible within the financial and scholarly limits that the markets for such books dictate, begins to describe some of the ground between the more and less critical ends of this scale.[7]

MANY KINDS OF EDITIONS

Within the category of critical editions there are several kinds, a diversity that arises from divergent purposes and theoretical grounds. A critical edition that aims to recover the text that an author intended to be published will very likely be different from one that aims to recover the text that saw widest circulation in one historical moment. Even in editorial approaches with similar aims there is variety. To reconstruct the author's intended text, for instance, one might need to decide at what point in the author's writing process one should gauge an author's intention. One editor might argue that an author's intentions are best represented by the first printed edition, while another might argue for the first fair-copy manuscript, while a third might argue that the second printed edition shows that the author revised the work, suggesting that text should best represent the author's mind. The disagreement over where in the process editors want to fix intention depends just as much on how we understand authorship as how we understand intention. People in the publishing house—editors, typesetters, and perhaps others, like official censors—will have altered the author's text in turning the manuscript into the first printed edition. One critical editor may wish to eliminate that external influence as much as possible, while another might argue that authors often expect and even count on that sort of intervention to clean up their text and make it presentable to readers. By one definition, the author is a single person with a single intention that others sometimes disrupt; by another, the author is not a single person but many, with multiple, overlapping, contradictory and complementary intentions. Editorial work is always interpretive, and, as with interpretive essays, those interpretations will be determined not only by the evidence (which will usually but not always be the same for one edi-

---

7. Fredson Bowers, "Definitive vs. Practical Editions," *CEAA Newsletter* 2 (July 1969): 14.

tor as another), nor only the interpretive contexts one applies to that evidence (like the definitions of *author* and *intention*, which might be shared by both editors), but by the editor's imaginative acts of interpretation (which are very likely to be individual). Precisely because editions depend upon decisions made by editors, no two editions will be alike.

That different editors will produce different editions may seem obvious, but it is worth saying because a major tendency in editorial theory since at least the mid-nineteenth century has been to try to eliminate this subjective character of editing by codifying its procedures and by spelling out the rules by which an editor makes choices in deciding what to print. The *Lachmannian* approach to editing is named for Karl Lachmann (1793–1851), a German scholar of classical and biblical texts, who is widely acknowledged to be the first to offer a scientific approach to textual criticism and editing. As E. Talbot Donaldson writes, Lachmannianism's appeal lies in its "attempt to devise a computing mechanism," a machine that runs the process of transmitting texts in reverse, practically automating the task of the editor.[8] From the 1960s on, this scientific urge in textual criticism has been exemplified best by the excitement over computer-assisted editorial practices, the latest of which is a revision of Lachmannian principles called *cladistics*. Not all textual critics have been happy with this scientific trend. A. E. Housman's objection to the Lachmannian editions being produced in the late nineteenth and early twentieth centuries is perhaps the most famous statement in opposition to this trend.[9] He writes that "textual criticism is a science, and, since it comprises recension and emendation, it is also an art. It is the science of discovering error in texts and the art of removing it" (123, this volume). But, he adds, it is not an exact science, like mathematics:

> A textual critic engaged upon his business is not at all like Newton investigating the motions of the planets: he is much more like a dog hunting for fleas. If a dog hunted for fleas on mathematical principles,

8. E. Talbot Donaldson, "The Psychology of Editors of Middle English Texts," *Speaking of Chaucer* (New York: W. W. Norton & Company, 1972), 102–18, see 112.

9. See A. E. Housman, "The Application of Thought to Textual Criticism," in Part Two of this volume.

basing his researches on statistics of area and population, he would never catch a flea except by accident. (124, this volume)

Even Housman wasn't opposed to developing rules, only to applying them unthinkingly, as the title of his essay indicates.

Predicating most approaches to textual criticism is the assumption that the true text is forever lost, and that all witnesses in which that lost true text finds expression are always imperfect. That all witnesses are imperfect holds true for some textual critics even when a holograph manuscript survives, as they frequently do for modern authors, since the ultimate lost archetype is the text that existed in the mind of the author, not one in a document that might have admitted a slip of the pen. Our scientific efforts to recover the lost archetype are therefore a paradoxical pursuit of something we acknowledge to be unattainable. Even though one might use stemmatic analysis to recover so much detail about that lost archetype as to know how many lines it had per page (and this is something that Lachmann in fact did), the archetype is still—and this is key—nothing more than the last manuscript from which all the surviving manuscripts ultimately derived, not an ideal version of the work, but a manuscript always at some incalculable remove from that ideal. The reconstructed archetype is always only a consolation prize, a text that is itself assumed to be imperfect and, what's more, always imperfectly reconstructed. The scientific impulse offers the dream that the more finely we can tune our instruments and the more technological advances we can apply, the closer we can come to this archetype, this Holy Grail, the ideal text. One might wish to oppose both the scientific and artistic approaches with a third, one that values the imperfections of the document and, rather than attempt to recover a lost original, seeks instead to make the document itself (as much as possible) available to readers. Such textual critics are more likely to favor diplomatic transcriptions, or facsimiles, or some variety of what Don Reiman calls versioning.[10] Even these documentary approaches, paradoxically, begin with the idea that the document is an imperfect realization of an ideal text.

10. Donald H. Reiman, " 'Versioning': The Presentation of Multiple Texts," *Romantic Texts and Contexts* (Columbia: University of Missouri Press, 1987), 167–80.

GENEALOGICAL EDITIONS

Lachmannian editions, also called stemmatic or genealogical editions, base their texts on an analysis of the witnesses as though they are progeny of other documents. The method arose for editing classical and biblical texts, but was soon applied to vernacular texts from the Middle Ages. The goal in a genealogical edition is to reconstruct a text closer to (if not quite synonymous with) the original by comparing and analyzing the surviving texts. Genealogical editions ought not be confused with genetic editions, which seek to reconstruct the development of a text over time, sometimes restricting the project to a single document, such as a writer's rough draft. The genealogical edition, on the other hand, is by definition interested in more than one document, and is particularly interested in the relation of one document to the next, but not in order to determine the process of composition. It instead aims to determine and fix (in the sense of *pinning down*, but also in the sense of *correcting*) the form of a text that no longer exists in any document—in other words, an ideal text. Lachmann was not alone in developing the methods associated with his name. In fact, many ideas we associate with him derive from other important editors, such as Desiderius Erasmus (1466?–1536) and Richard Bentley (1662–1742). And in truth, Lachmann never set out his "method" in a single, programmatic document. For that, one must turn to the twentieth-century German textual critic, Paul Maas. Nevertheless, it is Lachmann's name that is generally associated with the genealogical method.

However much or little we might owe to Lachmann himself for the approach that so often bears his name, we must acknowledge that its methods mark a sea change in textual criticism. Editions prior to those produced by these genealogists of the text generally reproduced the *textus receptus*, the received text, the version that had the widest circulation and so had become the standard, which usually but not always was the text printed in the *editio princeps*, the first edition. This is not to say that earlier textual criticism was without good practices. Early textual critics were often very good about spotting textual problems and more often than not used great care, good reasoning, and painstaking scholarship—

locating obscure and rare manuscripts—in their efforts to restore texts that they felt had been corrupted by much copying over time. The principle of following the *textus receptus*, however, meant that these editors respected the weight of tradition and of common use. This means that if there were an early printed edition, it was likely to become the received text, and therefore was the leading candidate for later editions. While some may want to fault earlier editors with a failure of imagination, we must acknowledge that when editors were faced with a corrupt text prior to Lachmann, they also faced limitations in resources to correct those corruptions. Traditional textual criticism is time-consuming and expensive in that it often requires substantial travel (though microfilm and, now, digital imaging are making travel less and less required). This is because textual criticism of the sort that Lachmann practiced requires access to a large number of often widely scattered and inaccessible documents. Leaving aside some now-lost and nearly mythical libraries, such as the library at Alexandria in Egypt, the great research libraries where these documents are now collected were founded only in the century or so before Lachmann's day—the Bibliothèque Nationale in France in 1720, the British Museum (now the British Library) in 1753, the Library of Congress in 1800. One could argue that modern textual criticism simply wasn't possible until after the monastic and private collections began to be drawn together and opened to the public with the advent of such libraries and—a point that cannot be stressed too heavily—with their published catalogues. More and more documents have made their way to research libraries' collections since then, and more and better catalogues have been produced, but even today a great many documents are still held in private collections and are therefore difficult to access. If textual criticism prior to Lachmann lacked a scientific approach, it lacked more the resources that made the development of such an approach possible than the intentions to produce reliable editions.

Once access to more witnesses became possible, Lachmannianism's essential advance over earlier methods of editing was to codify a systematic method for reconstructing the lost archetype. This systematic method divided the editor's activity into two ostensibly separate phases, the first (*recensio*) being the collection and evaluation of textual data resulting in a reconstructed text, the second (*emendatio*) the emendation of the text assembled in the first phase. No longer does the *textus receptus* hold inordinate sway, since the editor initially treats all witnesses as equals. Nor is the editor's unaided judgment left unchecked, since it must wait upon the evaluation of the available data. And that is perhaps the most important point: "corrections" to the texts are no longer permissible until after the relationships among the witnesses have been established and the reconstructed text found still to be lacking. This forestalls an editor's prejudice against witnesses whose readings are unfamiliar. In place of a system that largely relied on the individual genius of the editor to evaluate variants and make emendations, Lachmannianism installs an exhaustive method with rigorous step-by-step procedures.

recensio {

1. Construct a *stemma codicum* (Latin for "a family tree of books") as completely as possible by analyzing shared similarities and significant differences in the witnesses.
2. Use the stemma
   a. to eliminate from consideration any manuscripts which can be shown to derive only from existing manuscripts (since they therefore can contribute nothing to the reconstruction), and
   b. to guide the reconstruction of the hyparchetypes.
3. Reconstruct the archetype in stages, based primarily upon the application of a system, a "calculus of variants," as W. W. Greg has called it.[11]

emendatio {

4. Emend the reconstructed archetypal text where the testimony of the hyparchetypes and of the witnesses do not provide a clear or viable answer.

11. W. W. Greg, *The Calculus of Variants* (Oxford: Clarendon Press, 1927).

As the phrase "viable answer" should indicate, the final arbiter for any reconstruction is meaning. If the text produced by reconstruction is nonsensical, it must be emended. For a Lachmannian reconstruction, the process of determining readings, selecting among the readings attested in the witnesses, is therefore not thought of as an act of emendation. Emendation, rather, comes when the editor cannot resolve the readings by means of the pre-established rules and must resort to conjecture, that is, to educated guesses and reasoned arguments to arrive at an answer not found in the witnesses.

The Lachmannian method will be clearer with a simplified, fictional example. Imagine that we have eight manuscripts and printed editions of a nursery rhyme, none of them exactly like another, each also given an imaginary *siglum*. *Sigla* are abbreviations (often of the library or collection in which the witness can be found) that serve as a shorthand way of indicating which witness is which. These abbreviations are keyed to a list of the witnesses that are described, often in great detail, elsewhere in the edition, usually at the beginning of the discussion of the text.

Ad	C1
The Viscountess of Hearts,	The Countess of Hearts,
She made some tarts	She baked some tarts
All of a winter's day	All of a summer's day
The Knave of Hearts,	The Knave of Hearts,
He stole the tarts	He stole the tarts
And took them far away.	And took them all away.
The King of Hearts	The King of Hearts
Called for the tarts	Called for the tarts
And beat the Knave full sore.	And beat the Knave full sore.
The Knave of Hearts	
Brought back the tarts	
And vowed he'd steal no more.	

C2	Ca
The Viscountess of Hearts,	The Viscountess of Hearts,
She made the tarts	She made the tarts

All of a summer's day

Then stole the tarts,

That Knave of Hearts,

And took them clean away.

The King of Hearts

Called for the tarts

And beat the Knave full sore.

The Knave of Hearts

Brought home the tarts

And vowed he'd steal no more.

All of a summer's day.

Then stole the tarts,

That Knave of Hearts,

And took them clean away.

The King of Hearts

Called for the tarts

And beat the Knave full sore.

The Knave of Hearts

Brought home the tarts

And vowed he'd steal no more.

D

The Viscountess of Hearts,

She made the tarts

All of a summer's day.

Then stole the tarts,

That Knave of Hearts,

And took them clean away.

The King of Hearts

Called for the tarts

And beat the Knave full sore.

The Knave of Hearts

Brought back the tarts

And claimed he'd steal no more.

Hm

The Dame of Hearts,

She made some tarts

All of a winter's day.

The Knave of Hearts,

He stole the tarts

And took them far away.

The King of Hearts

Called for the tarts

And beat the Knave full sore.

The Knave of Hearts

Returned the tarts

And vowed he'd steal no more.

N

The Countess of Hearts,

She cooked up tarts

All of a summer's day.

The Knave of Hearts,

He stole the tarts

And took them clean away.

The King of Hearts

Called for the tarts

And beat the Knave full sore.

P

The Viscountess of Hearts,

She made some tarts

All of a winter's day.

The Knave of Hearts,

He stole the tarts

And took them far away.

The King of Hearts

Called for the hearts

And beat the Knave full sore.

The Knave of Hearts

Brought back the tarts

And swore he'd steal no more.

The first step is to collate the witnesses, strictly a data-gathering activity. Collation aids in an analysis meant to discover conjunction and disjunction, beginning to group witnesses by similarities and differences. It is important to stress that an analysis of variants will only begin to indicate groups. Convergent variation—coincidental agreement among witnesses—is always a possibility, so that the groupings that an editor arrives at are the result of an act of critical judgment, guided not only by the weight of accumulated similarity, but also by the editor's estimation of the quality of the individual variants. Because the testimony of the variants must be evaluated in the context of other variants, it is therefore important to collect all of the variants before making any judgments. Some will collate witnesses by selecting the one felt to be the best and comparing each to it, but, since one aims to record all variation, it is as well to begin with any manuscript, perhaps the longest, and to compare it to the next, recording any variation, line by line (this is more difficult with prose, but still possible). Manly and Rickert, editors of the first critical edition of *The Canterbury Tales* to be based on all the early witnesses (over eighty manuscripts), proceeded by using sets of note cards, at the top of which appears the section of text to be compared and the various identifiers that help editors order the cards.[12] On the lines beneath the header, one by one, are the variants, placed so as to show where the variant appears (to forestall re-copying text that isn't variant), each line keyed to the witness in which the variant is found. If no variant occurs in the witness, the sigla is struck through to indicate agreement with the text at the top and the line is left blank. If the witness does not contain the text at all, the collator records the omission with the abbreviation *om.*

It should be easy to see how this method might be adapted to a computer database or spreadsheet file, but even the collation tools in most word processors can aid in collating a small number of witnesses for, say, a lyric poem. So long as the text has been transcribed accurately, the computer is a much faster, much more accurate collator than any human. On the other hand, learning to collate by hand is a useful tool,

---

12. Geoffrey Chaucer, *The Text of the Canterbury Tales, Studied on the Basis of All Known Manuscripts*, 8 vols., ed. John M. Manly, Edith Rickert, et al. (Chicago: University of Chicago Press, 1940).

Line 12

Ad		And vowed he'd steal no more.
C1	*om.*	
~~C2~~		
~~Ca~~		
D		claimed
~~Hm~~		
N	*om.*	
P		swore

building a kind of discipline in close reading that is not often achieved in other ways.

Once each witness has thus been compared with each of the other manuscripts, one can build a list of variants. Collation of our witnesses will reveal the following variants:

1   Viscountess AdC2CaDP; Countess C1N; Dame Hm

2   made some AdHmP; made the C2CaD; baked some C1; cooked up N

3   summer's C1C2CaDN; winter's AdHmP

4–5   The Knave of Hearts, / He stole the tarts AdC1HmNP; Then stole the tarts, / That Knave of Hearts, C2CaD

6   far AdCaHmP; all C1; clean C2DN

10–12 The Knave . . . more. AdC2CaDHmP; *om.* C1N

11   Brought back AdDP; Returned Hm; Brought home C2Ca

12   vowed AdC2CaHm; swore P; claimed D

Collations are usually keyed by line numbers, as above, and will indicate a reading, followed by a list of sigla, each reading separated from the previous reading by a semicolon (though sometimes the separation is signaled by extra space). Comments by the editor will usually be in italics, as is "*om.*" in the collation for lines 10–12. Some collations will substitute a Σ for the long list of witnesses, when there is general agreement, so that we might have written the following instead:

10–12 The Knave . . . more. Σ; *om.* C1N

Once the variants have been recorded, the next task is to analyze them for conjunctive and disjunctive variation. Ad, Hm, and P, for instance, agree with one another against other witnesses in lines 2, 3, 4, and 6, sometimes being the only three to agree about a given reading. So they seem to form one group, we'll call α. Likewise, C2, Ca, and D seem to form another group (β), while C1 and N seem to form a third (γ). Important in drawing up these groups are variants such as those in lines 4–5, where C2, Ca, and D (i.e., β) transpose the lines as they appear in other witnesses, and those in lines 10–12, where C1 and N (i.e., γ) seem to be missing material. These sorts of variants, because they are more substantial, seem less likely to be coincidental than smaller variants such as "clean," "far," and "all" in line 6. In fact, if we assign the manuscripts to groups according to the variation in lines 2, 3, 4–5, and 10–12, then line 6 shows convergent variation, with Ca not with its usual group, C2 and D. Agreement between two manuscripts in transpositions or in missing material is less likely to be the result of coincidence than is the reading of a single word, and more likely the result of having a common ancestor with that trait.

In brief texts such as this one (with, therefore, few variants) and ones with only a few witnesses, simply forming groups may be as far as one can go, but with longer texts and more variants to classify, more detailed relationships can be discovered, and a full stemma might be worked out. In working out these relationships, one is likely to discover many useful things. If, for instance, one witness clearly derives directly from another, the editor usually eliminates that witness from consideration, in a process called *eliminatio codicum descriptorum.* So, if Lambeth MS 344 (p. 534) is a copy of Bodleian Hatton 73 (p. 524), as some argue, then Lambeth ought to be recorded but given no weight in an edition of Chaucer's poem "Truth." The reasoning for such elimination is that the copy will be further from the archetype and cannot, therefore, supply readings superior to those in its exemplar. It should be stressed that not all textual critics agree about this principle, arguing that it is often difficult to prove without a doubt and that scribes have been known to improve their exemplars, correcting errors as they copy. That a witness might be a copy of another witness is usual after printing becomes the dominant mode of publication. It is easier, after all, to set up type from another book than from manuscript. But that does not mean that the later copy is necessarily inferior. Caxton himself, the first English printer, for his second edition of the *Canterbury Tales*, collated his first edition with a better manuscript a disappointed reader had brought him. By the same token, authors will often use a printed edition rather than their own manuscript as a base when they sit to revise a work. Interestingly, it is not impossible that an early printed edition will also provide the exemplar for a manuscript. Such is generally accepted to be the case with Bodleian MS Arch. Selden B.10 (see pp. 519–20), which copies Wynkyn de Worde's early sixteenth-century edition (see pp. 545–46).[13]

The stemma is often given a graphic form so that readers can visualize the relationships one discovers in collating the witnesses. Stemma will generally look like inverted trees consisting of roughly three levels. At the highest level of the tree, the root, the editor will usually place the symbol for the archetype, sometimes given as ω, sometimes as *O* or *O'* (*O prime*). At the lowest level, the editor arranges the sigla that refer to witnesses. In the middle are the hyparchetypes, usually represented by Greek letters, as we have seen. This middle level might become quite complex, as when an editor can work out subgroups of major groups, and subgroups of those subgroups, and so on. Two hyparchtypes, each with their own dependencies, for example, might combine with the sigla of single witnesses to form a branch deriving from another hyparchetype, which in turn combines with other witnesses to form yet another hyparchetype. But the following stemma has been kept relatively simple for illustrative purposes, with three major hyparchetypes, each deriving from the archetype, from each of which radiate the sigla of the individual witnesses.

13. For the witnesses of Chaucer's poem, "Truth," see Part Three. For more about their relationships, see Geoffrey Chaucer, *A Variorum Edition of the Works of Geoffrey Chaucer, The Minor Poems*, vol. 5, pt. 1, ed. George B. Pace and Alfred David (Norman, OK: University of Oklahoma Press, 1982), 52–58.

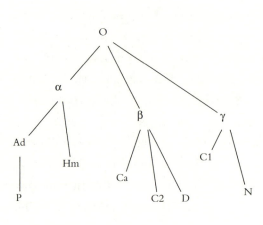

O = The archetype—the single, lost manuscript from which all surviving witnesses derive.

α, β, γ = Hyparchetypes.

Ad, Ca, N, etc. = The sigla.

Other stemmata might not indicate positions relative to the archetype, but many will look like this one, which indicates that hyparchetype α is closer to the archetype than either β or γ. The stemma indicates also that Ad is the best witness and that P has been determined to be a copy of Ad.

The editor's next task is to reconstruct the texts of the hyparchetypes (α, β, γ), the copies from which the witnesses of a particular group derive. This reconstruction proceeds by comparing readings and applying a "majority rules" approach: if two witnesses agree against the third, the reading of the two is adopted. If there are only two witnesses in a group, agreement with a witness from another group will trump the unique reading. So, in order to reconstruct γ's text, the editor will need to choose between "baked some" and "cooked up" in line 2, neither of which is attested in any other witness. But C1's "baked some" is certainly closer to α's "made some" than N's reading is to any other reading, so it is the likelier choice. Likewise in line 6, the editor must choose between C1's "all" and N's "clean." Here, however, N agrees with C2 and D, while C1 is unique. Thus N's reading is preferred. We may in this way reconstruct the γ text:

> The Countess of Hearts,
> She baked some tarts
> All of a summer's day.
> The Knave of Hearts,

He stole the tarts

And took them clean away.

The King of Hearts

Called for the tarts

And beat the Knave full sore.

When all three hyparchetypes have been reconstructed, they are treated as were the witnesses in the individual groups, so that the archetype itself can be reconstructed from the hyparchetypes. Reconstructing the archetype from the hyparchetypes and not directly from the individual manuscripts reduces the likelihood that a branch of the tree with many more witnesses than any other branch will automatically tip the scales in its favor. Line 6 of the reconstructed archetype, below, provides an example of this protection: "clean" is attested in only three manuscripts, while "far" is more numerous, with four. But reconstructions of γ (as we have seen) and β (as readers may do for themselves) both result in "clean," while only α reads "far." Majority rule at the level of the reconstructed hyparchetypes means that "clean" becomes the reading in the reconstructed archetype. Step by inexorable step, the genealogical editor slowly rebuilds the archetype from the testimony of unreliable witnesses, building an argument about a text from a rule-driven examination of individual readings from several witnesses.

The final edition, the reconstructed archetype:

The Queen of Hearts,

She made some tarts

All of a summer's day.

The Knave of Hearts,

He stole the tarts

And took them clean away.

The King of Hearts

Called for the tarts

And beat the Knave full sore.

The Knave of Hearts

> Brought back the tarts
>
> And vowed he'd steal no more.

The textual notes will record readings rejected either by recension or in favor of an emendation:

  1 *Queen] Viscountess* Σ; *Countess C1N; Dame Hm*
  2 *made some] made the CaC2D; baked some C1; cooked up N*
  3 *summer's] winter's HmAdP*
4–5 *The Knave . . . the tarts] Then stole the tarts, / That Knave of Hearts, CaC2D*
  6 *clean] far HmAdPCa; all C1*
10–12 *The Knave . . . more.] om. C1N*
  11 *Brought back] Returned Hm; Brought home CaC2*
  12 *vowed] swore P; claimed D*

Attentive readers will have noticed the emendation—"Queen"—in the first line. What ought an editor do about the title of the woman—is she a "Viscountess," a "Countess," or a "Dame"? Majority rule at the hyparchetype level and even at the level of the witnesses would suggest that "Viscountess" is the preferred reading. But an editor might reasonably demur. First of all, "Viscountess" ruins the scansion of the poetic line. A one-syllable or two-syllable word is clearly called for. The argument for "Dame" is therefore stronger than its single witness status would suggest. Would it be wrong for an editor to print a conjectural reading here, "Queen"? It is attested in none of the witnesses, but one might reason that it makes better sense with "King" than do the other titles. According to some practitioners, such emendations are permissible when recension does not solve problematic readings, such as readings that remain nonsensical or somehow clearly in error (unmetrical, in this case). Usually an editor will explain the reasons behind such emendations in the notes, which is valuable for readers interested in the passage in question; our editor has been unfortunately silent about his thinking. Conjectural emendation is not unheard of in genealogical editions; it even has a Latin tag or two, *emenda-*

tio and *divinatio*. But the trend in genealogical editions is away from conjecture except where absolutely necessary, and the very term *divinatio* ought to indicate the distrust genealogical theory holds for it.

As one might imagine, this aspect of the Lachmannian school has invited substantial critique. Housman objected to an editor's mindlessly adhering to hard-and-fast rules, as we have seen, as inappropriate to the task at hand, and Donaldson lamented this system's tendency to efface the editor's expertise, what Donaldson calls "his learning, his judgment, his taste, his experience, and his intelligence" (106). To be fair, even Paul Maas, whose book on textual criticism is now the *locus classicus* for an explanation of the Lachmannian method, ends his discussion of examples by saying that "the core of practically every problem in textual criticism is a problem of style. . . . there is the further danger that the editor in making his recension may fall into the habit of forgetting his responsibility for being continually alive to the author's style."[14] Maas is clearly alive to the objection.

Perhaps the approach still can be too scientific, but others theorists have critiqued it for not being scientific enough. Donaldson is, ironically, one of these theorists, too. One aspect of his critique of Lachmannianism is that its logic is circular and therefore dishonest. In order to edit by Lachmannian methods, he argues, one must first develop a stemma; but in order to draw a stemma, one must first edit the text, to decide what readings are errors and what readings are not. Anyway, he reasons, if one can determine which readings are errors and which are not, why not skip the stemma and simply correct the errors? Our example has few witnesses and few variants, and of course these are invented to throw light on what can seem an obscure process. But even with this example one can see how, if we were to start with a text different from Ad, we might not collate differently, but we might interpret that collation somewhat differently.

14. Paul Maas, *Textual Criticism*, trans. Barbara Fowler (Oxford: Clarendon Press, 1958), 40–41.

CLADISTICS

Borrowing methods from phylogenic systematics in the biological sciences, cladistics is a more modern form of *recensio*. A *clade* is a group of organisms with a modern ancestor; the word comes from the Greek word for *branch*.

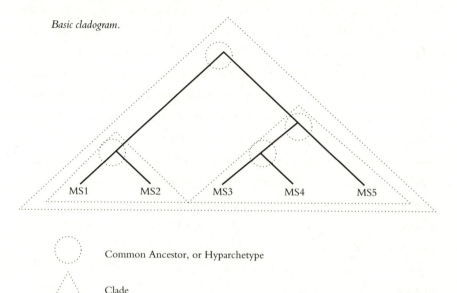

Basic cladogram.

○ Common Ancestor, or Hyparchetype

△ Clade

In cladistic analysis, witnesses' variants are analyzed with the aid of a computer, which derives the most parsimonious stemma, that is, the one with the fewest steps between archetype and witness. The advantage that cladistics has over the traditional Lachmannian approach is that though its analysis also draws trees that represent the relationships between and among witnesses, these trees are "unrooted." Perhaps a better way of saying this is that, unlike the Lachmannian approach, one does not need to decide which witnesses stand closer to the archetype than others (that is, which readings are errors and which true) in order to draw the tree; this begins to eliminate the charge of circular reasoning that Donaldson leveled at Lachmannianism. Treating all variants the same, as potentially ancestral and potentially convergent, cladistics draws many hypothetical trees and opts for the simplest one as the most likely. So, for instance, the following partial cladograms map out two possible paths of descent for the three fictional hyparchetypes of the nursery rhyme above, based on its bifurcations at lines 4–5 and at lines 10–12. One way to think about what a cladogram depicts is an evolutionary (or, since the assumption is that the copying process introduces errors, more properly, devolutionary) textual history. It describes which errors were introduced earlier, and which later. Another way to think about the meaning of a cladogram is as a chart of affinity. In the first cladogram, α and β are more like one another than either is like γ, because the first change differentiates γ from αβ, and only after that change did β and α split. The same data can be made to produce a different history, in which β splits from αγ first and α and γ differentiate after.

Two possible cladograms for divergence at lines 4–5 and 10–12.

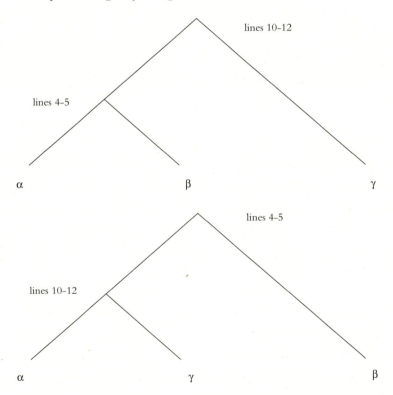

These are admittedly simple cladograms illustrating a rather simple conflict with a simple and small dataset. As the data for a cladistic editing project grows in size, so too will the conflicts grow more complex, resulting in very many possible trees, and it is there that the computer becomes essential in resolving them, working out which one is the most parsimonious. As one might imagine, the cladogram at right (one of several from the project) would be remarkably difficult to work out with pencil and paper.

To many editors, cladistic analysis offers the hope that the task of determining the text will be made even less subject to the judgment of the editor, even more scientific. Cladistics nevertheless has its limitations. As one can see from the cladograms above, cladistics generally assumes bifurcated structures, each clade having two branches, from which sub-clades may grow. This structure typical of traditional cladistics (not all cladistic theories agree, of course) poses a problem for its application to textual criticism, namely that any number of copies might be made from a hyparchetype, resulting in many more than two branches from a single node. Robinson's cladogram for the most part follows precisely a bifurcated structure, especially in the witnesses further from the archetype. In most cases each manuscript is paired either with one other manuscript or with one other branch of manuscripts. But one part of the cladogram is unusual. At the root of the tree, on the left-hand side, the node divides in three rather than two. One branch ends only in Hg (the Hengwrt manuscript, one we now know to have been copied by Adam Pynkhurst, Chaucer's longtime personal scribe); a second becomes the clade Bo2 and Ht; and the third contains all the other witnesses in the tree.

Peter Robinson's cladogram admits to a widely acknowledged general weakness in genealogical analysis. Stemmatics finds it difficult to account for convergent variation, where manuscripts have some readings that suggest it belongs to one family and other readings that suggest a different family. Transferring words from one page to another by pen or by type is not a purely mechanical exercise; the human judgment of the copyist comes into play, with the uncomfortable result that shared readings may not indicate a shared exemplar but perhaps a shared sensibility. That is, shared readings may be simply coincidental, resulting from a scribal adaptation. To draw an analogy from evolutionary biology, both

A cladogram of the fundamental witness groupings of the Wife of Bath's Prologue, from Peter Robinson, "A Stemmatic Analysis of the Fifteenth-Century Witnesses to the Wife of Bath's Prologue," The Canterbury Tales Project: Occasional Papers II, *ed. N. F. Blake and P. M. W. Robinson (Oxford: Office for Humanities Communication, 1997), 13.*

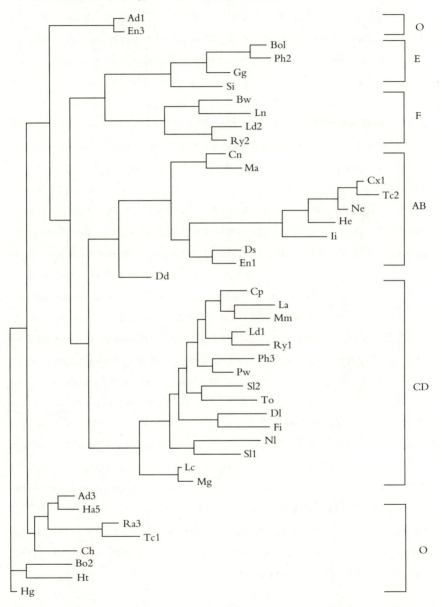

bats and birds have wings, but that characteristic does not allow us to group them on the same part of the evolutionary tree: wings are a convergent variation, not ancestral, a coincidental development responding to similar needs and environmental factors. These sorts of shared but unrelated readings can complicate a computer's attempts to draw the most parsimonious stemma. In order to do so, an editor may need to exercise judgment to eliminate witnesses with coincidental convergent variation or to deemphasize that variant in the analysis. Another way in which manuscripts might develop convergent variation is through a process called *contamination*, where a witness is not copied from a single exemplar, but adjusts some of its readings by referring to one or more secondary exemplars. The process is perhaps a bit like two varieties of snake interbreeding and maybe more like a scientist splicing a section of seaweed DNA into potato DNA. Contaminated manuscripts similarly resist classification in a classic stemma or in a cladogram such as this. Extensive contamination is why one of the more famous witnesses to *The Canterbury Tales* is not represented on this cladogram: the Ellesmere Manuscript, also copied by Adam Pynkhurst and used as the basis for one of the standard Chaucer textbooks, *The Riverside Chaucer*.[15] Elsewhere in his study Robinson attempts to account for its contamination by performing cladistic analyses on its text in sections, one hundred lines at a time. In this way he is able to show, in other cladograms, how Ellesmere (given the siglum El) shifts from one clade to another over the course of the Wife's Prologue. Robinson's method of sampling sections of text at a time is not foolproof, by any means, but it does offer intriguing results.

Stemmatic approaches have been faulted for pretending to scientific certainty. But even when someone like Maas writes that one can "demonstrate incontestably the interrelationship of all surviving witnesses," or "reconstruct with certainty the text of the archetype at all places" (3), his claims are qualified by strict assumptions and conditions, some rather unlikely in any manuscript tradition:

15. Geoffrey Chaucer, *The Riverside Chaucer*, ed. Larry D. Benson et al. (Boston: Houghton Mifflin, 1986). This edition retains Ellesmere as its base text, despite acknowledging Hengwrt often to be the superior version.

In what follows it is assumed (1) that the copies made since the primary split in the tradition each reproduce one exemplar only, i.e. that no scribe has combined several exemplars (contaminatio), (2) that each scribe consciously or unconsciously deviates from his exemplar, i.e. makes "peculiar errors." (3)

Assuming that each scribe makes "peculiar errors" means that no two scribes made the same mistake independently. Stemmatics, such as Lachmannianism and cladistics, attempts to reconstruct the lines of descent for a family of manuscripts and then work backward through this line of descent to reconstruct the archetype, the lost manuscript that is the last common ancestor for all of the surviving manuscripts. But stemmatics does not usually claim to go beyond the archetype to recover an author's intentions. And its rules cannot always determine what the right reading is, occasionally indicating with a gap an undecidable problem. In building its reconstruction, it acknowledges, moreover, that "no such work," as Tanselle puts it, "is ever definitive."[16] As monumental as the stemmatic edition usually is, it also tacitly imagines its own obsolescence. In these ways, it admits a kind of failure up front, and in a sense, this is part of its strength and part of its scientific character. Its scientific approach offers not the original text, nor what readers will henceforth always know the text to be, but a clear demarcation of the limits of our knowledge in this attempt at a historical reconstruction. Its admission of ignorance makes its discoveries extraordinarily valuable. But it is a frustrating shortcoming for many. Some, like Donaldson, wonder why one should stop at the archetype. Since stemmatics produces a reconstruction—a hypothesis—and relies upon an editor's subjective judgment to do so, why not apply that judgment further to arrive at something beyond that archetype, namely an author's intended text? Alternatively, if the reconstruction is by definition flawed, why not set the sights lower, and produce a text less conjectural than the archetype, a text about which one can be more certain. The

16. G. Thomas Tanselle, *A Rationale of Textual Criticism* (Philadelphia: University of Pennsylvania Press, 1989), 74.

former objection leads to an eclectic edition, the latter objection may lead to a best text edition or to another form of historical-critical approach, such as the parallel text edition.

DIRECT, DEEP, OR ECLECTIC EDITIONS

Eclectic editions provide composite texts in which readings from variant witnesses are combined to produce a text that approximates (so the editor hopes) the ideal (usually understood to be the author's intended) text but that is therefore unlike the text in any one of the witnesses. Eclecticism was not unheard of prior to the twentieth century. It is what medieval scribes did frequently when they were confronted with an exemplar that they felt was deficient—they turned to a second exemplar and adopted some of its readings. But the primary advocates of eclectic editions arrive in the twentieth century: Housman, W. W. Greg, Fredson Bowers, G. Thomas Tanselle, and Donaldson and Kane. Greg's ideas about copy-text editing, which he proposed for editions of Renaissance dramas, have been applied perhaps more widely than he expected, becoming very much a dominant mode in the last half of the twentieth century.[17] Greg's system distinguishes between *substantives,* or the words, and what he calls *accidentals,* the spelling, punctuation, and capitalization, and it introduces the concept of *copy-text,* the text on which the critical edition is based and which provides the chief authority for the readings of the accidentals but not necessarily the substantives. The copy-text, Greg argues, ought to come from an early version, usually the first printed edition, unless it is manifestly defective, like the first quarto of *Hamlet.* The earlier edition will better preserve certain features of an author's intentions, so the thinking goes, especially in its accidentals. Later editions, Greg argues, are more and more likely to introduce non-authorial readings in those accidentals, changing spelling and punctuation away from an author's usage. But the authority of the copy-text is not so strong when it comes to substantives. Greg argues

17. See W. W. Greg, "The Rationale of Copy-Text," in Part Three of this volume.

that the copy-text should govern (generally) in the matter of accidentals, but that the choice between substantive readings belongs to the general theory of textual criticism and lies altogether beyond the narrow principle of the copy-text. Thus it may happen that in a critical edition the text rightly chosen as copy may not by any means be the one that supplies most substantive readings in cases of variation. (143, this volume)

What this means is that Greg would have editors be strict in following the first edition of a work for the spelling, punctuation, and other "surface features" of the text, but be open in deciding what the words ought to be, choosing those readings from other witnesses which solve perceived problems in the copy-text. The following is a fabricated example of Greg's principles in action, based on one real variant and one invented in the final couplet of John Donne's "Holy Sonnet X," the poem that begins, "Death, be not proud." An editor might be faced with two witnesses, A and B, A the earlier edition, B the later.

A

One short sleepe past, we wake eternally,
And death shall be no more, death, thou shalt die.

B

One short sleep pass'd, we live eternally,
And Death shall be no more. Death, thou shalt die!

Following Greg's principles, we would choose A for our copy-text, because it is more likely to preserve the authorial surface features of Donne's text. These features are things like spellings such as "sleepe" and "past," capitalization, or lack of it, in "death," and (perhaps most famously, after Margaret Edson's Pulitzer Prize–winning drama, *W;t*) punctuation, namely the comma before and period after "death, thou shalt die," rather than the period and exclamation point, of witness B.[18]

18. Margaret Edson, *W;t: A Play* (New York: Faber and Faber, 1999). The title, using a semicolon in place of an *i*, is only one aspect of the play's interest in textual matters.

But we are also faced with a substantive variant (the invented one): *wake/live*. Most editors would probably choose "wake," since it makes more sense with "sleep." But if one could make a case for "live" instead, choosing to print it would result in an eclectic edition of the sort that Greg approves, sharing the features of two different texts:

> One short sleepe past, we live eternally,
> And death shall be no more, death, thou shalt die.

This is not to say that in an eclectic text, the whims of the editor are given free rein. Moreover, such emendations are often based on minute analysis of the kinds of errors that copyists are likely to make and on the tendencies of the author. These editorial methods and the reasoning behind the individual decisions are often spelled out in great detail either in the introduction or in the notes to the emendations themselves. Greg's own methods were genealogical, on the one hand, but in keeping with Housman's critique of Lachmannianism on the other hand. The copy-text should generally be the witness identified by *recensio* as the best witness, which, since Greg was dealing with a literature that survives primarily only in print, generally means the first edition, from which later editions usually derive. But Greg objects to the conservative tendency in editors, such as R. B. McKerrow, to feel that "it was an editor's duty to follow [the copy-text's] substantive readings with a minimum of interference" because doing so would cause less "harm" to the text than would "opening the door to individual choice among variants" (142, this volume). For Greg, as for those who follow him, the insights genealogical work provides are valuable, but he objects to the effort to rid textual criticism of subjective evaluation. Greg writes:

> It is impossible to exclude individual judgement from editorial procedure: it operates of necessity in the all-important matter of the choice of copy-text and in the minor one of deciding what readings are possible and what not; why, therefore, should the choice between possible readings be withdrawn from its competence? (142–43, this volume)

Some would go further and suggest that editors are uniquely qualified by their immersions in the texts to use conjecture to emend these texts, and they argue that conjecture is underutilized. Others challenge the idea, arguing that conjecture is based on an editor's sense of the author's style, which is determined in turn by an edited text, resulting in a circular logic.

Just as Housman, Greg, and Donaldson—eclectic editors—raised objections to the Lachmannian school, so too have others raised objections about the eclectic school and especially Greg's "Rationale." Philip Gaskell faults Greg's approach for misunderstanding the relationship between author and printer.[19] Greg sees as intrusive the changes that printers and publishers always effect in an author's text, whether to the substantives or, even more likely Greg asserts, to the accidentals, and he would attempt to recover the author's intentions from these intrusions. Gaskell writes that "most authors even today expect the printer to normalize their spelling and capitalization (and until late in the nineteenth century they expected the punctuation to be normalized as well)" (339). According to his thinking, then, it is a mistake to prefer evidence of an author's accidentals, since they are not evidence of how "the author wanted it to be read" (339). The issue here, as with many other challenges to Greg and his most prolific adherent, Bowers, is over how one gauges authorial intention. Greg's assumption is that there is but one author, and that author's text has been intruded upon by others, who are not the author. Gaskell suggests that an author might accept those intrusions as the nature of the business, or more, might even authorize them. Others, such as Jerome McGann, would challenge the idea of the single author, emphasizing the collective activity of literary production and reception. McGann argues that details many would consider external to a work affect its meaning: "It makes a difference if the poem we read is printed in *The New Yorker*, *The New York Review of Books*, or *The New Republic*."[20] To reprint that poem in another

19. Philip Gaskell, *A New Introduction to Bibliography* (Oxford: Oxford University Press, 1972).

20. Jerome McGann, "The Monks and the Giants: Textual and Bibliographical Studies and the Interpretation of Literary Works," *Textual Criticism and Literary Interpretation*, ed. Jerome McGann (Chicago: University of Chicago Press, 1982), 180–99, see 191.

context, say an anthology of poetry, is to lose some of that contextual meaning, a meaning not necessarily generated but quite possibly sought out by the author. How do we account for such intentional meanings in this category of "authorial intention"? Despite the many critiques of the Greg-Bowers school of textual criticism—too scientific for some, not scientific for others—it has been the dominant mode for editorial practice in English and American literature for the past half-century.

BEST TEXT EDITIONS

French scholar Joseph Bédier (1864–1938) is the person most closely associated with best-text editing, but he is certainly not alone, other important practitioners being the aforementioned Englishman Ronald Brunlees McKerrow (1872–1940) and Russian expatriate Eugène (Yevgeny Maksimovich) Vinaver (1899–1979), who studied under Bédier at the University of Paris. Bédier began as a Lachmannian, but in time concluded that its scientific methods were not, in fact, scientific. In particular, Bédier criticized *recensio*, especially the drawing of stemmata, deciding that they are too arbitrary and too much governed by what an editor wishes to see, by an editor's tastes, masked only by a veneer of science. If a stemma is itself a hypothesis that is by and large untestable, it cannot be used to reconstruct a lost archetype with any reliability. To attempt to do so only produces composite texts that, in Bédier's view, are truly collaborations between editors and authors. But an investigation of the textual history can be used to understand to a degree the relationships among the witnesses that survive; namely, to ascertain their relative quality, and from this understanding one might select a good text. Bédier's idea from there is to assure a kind of editorial conservatism. Once the best text has been selected, the editor presents a cleaned-up transcription of the text, not quite a diplomatic edition but with as little intrusion as possible, restricting emendations to corrections of obvious faults, and carefully documenting all such emendations. Conjectural emendations, Bédier argues, should be kept apart from the chosen text, listed perhaps in the notes or an appendix. This sort of edition is easier to arrive at when works survive in unique copies or in holographs, or when a work shows such profound variation between recensions that a composite text would be nearly untenable. Although it sounds like a very strict form, best-text editions do allow for significant variety, and not all editors are as strict about emendations as Bédier or Vinaver would have them be. Some best-text editions will provide something more like a composite text in their apparatuses. Others might report all the substantial variants of the major witnesses. Still others will print several best texts in parallel. The ultimate result from best-text editions is something like versioning: each witness has its own validity and its own uses. The logical end to such an argument is to suggest, with John Dagenais, that we "shift . . . the unit we study from 'text' to (for medievalists, at least) the individual, unique, concrete manuscript codex. This would mean, for example, that instead of studying the *Poema de mio Cid* we would study Madrid, Biblioteca Nacional, MS Vitrina 7–17."[21] There are problems, however, with best-text editing as well. First, how is one to determine which text is the best text? Bédier expresses some distrust of *recensio*, but is willing to accept it as an aid in choosing the best text. One might argue that if the recension isn't good enough to begin reconstructing hyparchetypes, it probably isn't good enough to determine the best text. In fact, Bédier's system will only reproduce a poor text if the editor chooses poorly. An editor might confuse the earliest witness with the best, when in fact, sometimes a much later witness provides a more reliable text than an earlier one. What's to stop an editor from choosing a best text based on which witness has the prettiest illustrations? While best-text editing has largely been applied to works that predate printing, it need not be restricted to pre-modern works.

21. John Dagenais, "That Bothersome Residue: Toward a Theory of the Physical Text," *Vox intexta: Orality and Textuality in the Middle Ages*, ed. A. N. Doane and Carol Braun Pasternack (Madison: University of Wisconsin Press, 1991), 246–59, see 252.

HISTORICAL-CRITICAL EDITIONS, GENETIC EDITIONS, DIPLOMATIC EDITIONS, AND FACSIMILES

The best-text model is especially useful (but by no means the only method) when an editor's aim is not to recover some lost ideal text, whether one means the author's final intentions or some other stage of the composition of the work, but to recover the text in a specific historical and cultural moment, such as a first printed edition, or the text of a work as it would have been circulating in a particular moment, or as a particular person or group would be familiar with it. The shift in editorial perspective is significant here. Whereas the ghost of the author haunts the Lachmannian, eclectic, and some best-text methods at every stage of their processes, in this new perspective, that ghost has been, if not exorcized then certainly fragmented, dispersed, and generally reduced in authority. In the author's place now sits History, whether understood as the history of the creation of a text or even a certain document's text (the genetic edition), or as the history of reception, which will govern the choice of which text to reproduce and how that text will be presented (diplomatic editions, facsimiles). So, when Jack Stillinger argues for at least seven authors for John Stuart Mill's *Autobiography*, writing, "We can for the most part recover Mill's original sentences in the Early Draft manuscript, but these clearly do not constitute an intended text," the implication is that neither a composite text based on printed editions checked against manuscripts, nor an archaeological project to sift Mill's own words from those of his co-authors will suffice to represent the work.[22] So defined, the work is scattered over not only two or seven (or more) authors, but also over several distinct textual moments—among them the Early Draft and its revisions in 1854, the second manuscript in 1861 and 1869–70, the transcript used as printer's copy made after Mill's death in 1873, the first edition in that year, and so

22. Jack Stillinger, "Who Wrote J. S. Mill's *Autobiography*?" *Victorian Studies* 27.1 (Autumn 1983): 7–23, 10.

on until the present moment. The questions one wishes to ask of the work will determine what kind of text one needs to print.

The diplomatic edition aims to report the text of a single, usually unique and usually notable document with as little editorial intrusion as possible. While the edition may report on extra-textual features, its emphasis is generally on preserving the exact words and punctuation of the text rather than the bibliographic codes of the document that carries it. Unlike other kinds of editions, the diplomatic edition will not clean up obvious errors in the text, or regularize spelling, punctuation, or capitalization. The facsimile goes one step further, aiming to reproduce the bibliographic codes—some go so far as to try to duplicate the color, weight, and feel of the paper or parchment of the original. Some editions, most notably the facsimile of T. S. Eliot's typescript of "The Waste Land" with manuscript revisions by Ezra Pound and Vivienne Eliot, combine photofacsimile images with diplomatic transcriptions in facing pages.[23] This is a common solution in facsimiles of hard-to-read manuscripts or typescripts. *The Riverside Shakespeare* contains photofacsimile pages of Shakespeare's handwriting in *The Book of Sir Thomas More*, preceded by a diplomatic transcription and facing-page modernized edition.[24] Shakespeare used a kind of script called *English secretary hand*, the norm in his day but generally unknown now, and his manuscript is cramped and somewhat smudged in appearance, making it difficult to read, even for many who do have some knowledge of secretary hand. What is it that separates the photofacsimile (or type facsimile) from the uncritical reprint? Nothing, if the act of reprinting the text in facsimile is unguided by a prior act of textual criticism. But in fact, facsimiles are usually just as much determined by editorial decisions as other critical editions are,

23. T. S. Eliot, *The Waste Land: A Facsimile and Transcript of the Original Drafts, Including the Annotations of Ezra Pound*, ed. Valerie Eliot (New York: Harcourt, Brace, Jovanovich, 1971).

24. William Shakespeare, *The Riverside Shakespeare*, 2nd ed., ed. G. Blakemore Evans (Boston: Houghton Mifflin, 1997), 1175–794.

even if these decisions are normally not as intrusive. Charlton Hinman's facsimile of Shakespeare's First Folio provides a striking example of the difference between an uncritical reprint and a photofacsimile critical edition.[25] Hinman's facsimile, the result of a painstaking analysis, which he carried out by collating each copy in the Folger Library, is not of any single copy of the First Folio but an amalgam of what Hinman decided were the best pages of the many copies in the Folger collection. In this respect, it is much like a traditional edition, except that Hinman's edition takes the smallest unit of variation not to be individual words but individual pages. It is possible in a facsimile—especially a type facsimile, in which the appearance of the original is mimicked in a completely new resetting of type—to correct errors one finds on the exemplar's page just as a traditional editor might, though this isn't often done, since the point of the facsimile would seem to be lost in such cases, the text's idiosyncrasies being as important to preserve as the unique bibliographic codes of the exemplar. Even when the facsimile is drawn from a single document, as it is with the Yale First Folio facsimile, it is unlikely that that document's choice' was uncritical: the Yale facsimile reproduces an important copy of the First Folio.[26] Often facsimiles will indicate where its text disagrees with other witnesses, as the Chaucer Variorum facsimile of the Hengwrt manuscript of the *Canterbury Tales* does in collating readings from the Ellesmere manuscript.[27] Ultimately, the decision to produce a facsimile is itself an indication that an investigation of the history of the text lies behind the edition. Facsimiles, after all, are more expensive than printing the text from a transcript. To produce a facsimile is to

25. William Shakespeare, *The First Folio of Shakespeare,* ed. Charlton Hinman (New York: W. W. Norton & Company, 1968).

26. William Shakespeare, *Mr. William Shakespeare's Comedies, Histories, & Tragedies: A photographic facsimile of the First Folio edition,* ed. Helge Kökeritz and Charles Tyler Prouty (New Haven: Yale University Press, 1954).

27. Geoffrey Chaucer, *The Canterbury Tales: A Facsimile and Transcription of the Hengwrt Manuscript with Variants from the Ellesmere Manuscript,* ed. Paul G. Ruggiers et al. (Norman: University of Oklahoma Press, 1979).

argue, if tacitly, that the text as it is presented in that document (or edition) is valuable enough in the textual history of that work for scholars to have a copy more accessible than the original, which is usually stored away in a private collection or a special collections library.

The genetic edition is similar to a diplomatic edition, but it sees the text less as a static entity than as a palimpsest, a record of a process, sometimes appearing as layers in a single document—a main text surrounded, interlined, and marked over by successive writings in the process of composition, for instance, in which case it actually is palimpsestic. Genetic criticism attempts to sift these layers of text in order to document and to chart this textual process. A typical genetic edition might attempt to present the text of a single document, such as a rough draft, in such a way that a reader can reconstruct any of several textual moments—first drafts, maybe, or subsequent revisions—at will. The same principle will work with a text's progress through several documents. Rather than relegate variants to the notes at the bottom of the page or end of the volume, the second and following layers of the text are encoded with the first layers in such a way that a reader (or a computer program) can switch from one version of the text to another. In practice, printed genetic editions can be difficult to read at first, marked as they are with symbols that indicate various layers:

Frank ↑ turned and↓ <exclaimed>↑shouted↓, "<Dang!> There goes the banjo player's Porsche!"

Once the reader has internalized the idea that arrows enclose interlinear insertions and that angle brackets enclose deletions, lines such as these become easier to read. But it does take some patience on the part of many readers. Printed genetic editions (in English at least) were not in production for very long before computerized encoding and display technologies were discovered to be almost ideally suited to the aims and requirements of genetic criticism. The codes that used to be for human readers can now be devised for a program like a web browser to display the text and allow the reader to "edit" the text interactively.

V E R S I O N I N G

A term coined by Donald Reiman to name a rather venerable idea, versioning is the simultaneous presentation of more than one version of a work. As Reiman points out, Origen's (185–253?) *Hexapla*, an edition of the Old Testament, has six parallel columns, one in Hebrew, the next a transliteration using the Greek alphabet, and then four independent Greek translations. For Reiman and others, versioning is an effort to bring the value of textual criticism home to a wider audience, but it is also an approach to critical editing aimed at encouraging and enabling the reader to engage in textual criticism alongside the editor. With a little coaching, it is not impossible to work backward through most textual notes to reconstruct the readings of witnesses (see below), but doing so results in a reconstruction (usually only in the reader's mind), and might very likely not bring to light some important feature of the text that would be more visible were the witness given an edition of its own. Moreover, notes and collations are as prone to error as any other text. Reiman argues that editors will often find it

> more useful and more efficient to provide critics and students with complete texts of two or more different stages of a literary work, each of which can be read as an integral whole, than to chop up all but one version into small pieces and then mix and sprinkle these dismembered fragments at the bottoms of pages, or shuffle them at the back of the book as tables of "variants" or "collations." (170)

Versioning is, in this sense, not one kind of edition in the way a stemmatic edition is. It is, rather, a philosophy about editions in opposition to traditional critical editions that are plagued by the theoretical questions of authorship, intention, and reconstruction. Critical editions by and large have been seen as the province of scholars who have dedicated decades to an author's works, but versioning imagines a much more democratic and fast-moving field. The primary documents that used to be reserved for the textual critic are from this perspective the very documents that ought to be provided to a more general readership. Rather than hide away the work of textual criticism in dusty books, Reiman imagines an abundance of less cumbersome editions—best-text editions, parallel-text editions, diplomatic editions, facsimiles, and even cleaned-up photo-offset reproductions, all with minimal editorial interference—so that the general reader can engage in at least part of the process of textual criticism. Versioning has close affinities with the "unediting" called for by Renaissance scholars like Leah Marcus, Randall McCleod (who sometimes publishes under pseudonyms like Random Cloud and Ana Mary Armygram), and David Scott Kastan, who claim that reading early modern works in their early printed editions opens up avenues for interpretation closed off by the encrustations of eighteenth- and nineteenth-century ideas about these texts that form the basis of modern editions. Versioning may also be seen as a part of a larger movement in textual criticism, exemplified also by D. F. McKenzie's and Jerome McGann's calls for understanding texts within their specific historical moments and their specific social environments. Such an approach would seem to need multiple versions (especially facsimiles) readily available if they are to translate well to the classroom.

Versioning is especially useful when a work appears in substantially different forms, either as the result of revision or for another reason, so that producing a composite text will change the nature of either, and in such cases the parallel-text edition is exceptionally valuable. Versioning is the theory behind the Oxford Shakespeare editions of *King Lear*. It presents two versions of the play: the *History of King Lear* (1608) and *Tragedy of King Lear* (1623). *The Norton Shakespeare* goes one (or two) better, printing parallel texts of the *History* and the *Tragedy* in facing pages, and adding a composite version after these two. How these versions are arrived at and how they are edited does not define the parallel-text edition. Rather, the parallel-text edition is a kind of book layout as much as a method of editing. At its root, it assumes that more than one version of the text ought to be provided to the reader, and it usually presents these texts in parallel columns or in facing pages. But the texts may themselves be prepared under any variety of editorial method. W. W. Skeat's edition of *Piers Plowman* prints the A-text on the top half of each page, with the B-text below it on the left-hand side of an opening opposite the C-text on the right.[28] Each of the three versions is presented in an eclectic text, but another editor might have chosen best texts.

Versioning should not be seen as a general rejection of Lachmannian or of eclectic critical editions, nor is it call for a flood of uncritical reprints. It does not release the editor from the responsibilities that other varieties of critical editing bestow. Versioning is more a call to reduce the scope of individual editorial projects. An editor will still be responsible for mastering and applying the textual history in choosing which texts to reproduce. And though the editorial intrusions will likely be fewer and less substantial, the editor will not disappear entirely from view. At the minimum, an editor might correct (or at least note) obvious and less obvious problems in a text, and might do more. But the goal of versioning is to begin to shift some of the duties, prerogatives, and pleasures of the editor to the readers, primarily the interpretive acts an editor engages in when determining what exactly the work is when faced with a multiplicity of varying documents.

READING THE APPARATUS

Reiman's call for versioning is in part a call for more inexpensive but higher quality textbooks. Since critical editions are often massive and expensive multi-volume works, they do not make good textbooks, but the quality of information they contain is precisely the sort many would wish to have enrich classroom discussion. What makes critical editions so bulky and so expensive are usually their paratextual features, namely, the apparatus. But, as I hope is already clear, the apparatus is what makes these editions so valuable. The apparatus can generally be divided into two parts, the textual introduction and the textual notes, but it will often

28. William Langland, *Piers the Plowman and Richard the Redeless*, 2 vols., ed. Walter W. Skeat (Oxford: Oxford University Press, 1886, repr. 2001).

also comprehend other elements that can help a reader understand the physical features of the texts on which the edition is based, elements such as a table of words that were hyphenated in a certain edition in order to break a line of prose. The apparatus is the reader's guide to the editor's presented text: how to read it, how it was constructed (or reconstructed), and what the bases were for the editor's decisions. The apparatus is, in other words, the evidence for this "complex hypothesis" that is an edition. Besides the expense in publishing it, and the time required to create it in the first place, the apparatus can be a menacing swamp of fine print and obscure abbreviations that might scare off most readers. But it is worth learning to navigate.

The textual introduction is the editor's discursive presentation of the evidence. It usually contains a description of witnesses with their sigla, date, provenance, quality, and so on. These descriptions of the documents can be very valuable to the literary critic, in that they will tie a disembodied text to a specific document, created and first read in a specific historical context. It will also help make sense of the editor's decision about what kind of edition has been selected and about which witness the edition is based on. These descriptions will be of most value in understanding the textual notes, and so they sometimes will immediately precede the notes rather than reside in the introduction proper. While a textual introduction may well contain answers to questions readers might have about the text or about the information in the textual notes, and while other features of the apparatus will very often refer the reader to the introduction for a discussion of elements that are too complicated to deal with in a note or a table, the textual introduction will sometimes, especially in a clear-text edition, be removed to a position after the text. Even editors who spend their lives working on the notes and on the introduction know that many readers will wish to skip the information provided, until and unless they need it for their own purposes.

Textual notes can be the most daunting aspect of a critical edition for students who are unaccustomed to seeing them. Often they are concealed in a section at the end of the book (or in a separate volume entirely), and so few will see them who are not actively looking for them. When they are printed at the bottom of the page, they can look like a forbiddingly strange code intruding on the smooth functioning of the text. In fact, they are relatively simple to learn to read. Perhaps the first thing to recognize is that, while sometimes combined, *textual notes* differ from and are sometimes kept separate from *explanatory notes*, which are intended to help readers make sense of the passage in question, providing definitions or explanations of arcana. Textual notes are instead concerned almost wholly with microhistories of the text, usually providing:

· the reading of the text that serves as the edition's basis when the editor has emended it;
· the authority for those emendations, if any; and
· variants in other witnesses (occasionally including emendations by other modern or important historical editors), sometimes even when the editor hasn't emended the text.

In other words, while the editor has elsewhere set out principles for editing the text and has indicated what sorts of changes were made without recording them (called *silent emendations*), the textual notes are a minute record of other choices an editor has made or has rejected.

Different editors will use different systems—sometimes the same editor will use different systems in different editions—but most are modeled on the suggestions codified by R. B. McKerrow in 1939.[29] Textual notes are generally divided in two parts: the *lemma* (Greek for *heading*; the plural is *lemmata*), or the reading in question, and the stemmatic readings, that is, the variants from the witnesses, from which evidence a *stemma*, or family tree, might be derived. In the following hypothetical textual note:

214.30 banjo . . . Porsche] Σ; fiddle ~ Porch T; fiddler's Maserati QSW; *om.* α and XYZ

29. R. B. McKerrow, *Prolegomena for the Oxford Shakespeare: A Study in Editorial Method* (Oxford: Clarendon Press, 1939).

- The closing square bracket "]" (there is no opening bracket) indicates the end of the lemma, and the beginning of the "stemmatic" readings.
- "214.30" is the location to which the note is keyed (either in the edition or in the document on which the edition is based). This is usually a line number for poetry. For longer prose works, as imagined here, the note might be keyed to a page and line number. In plays, such as those by Shakespeare, notes will often be keyed to act, scene, and line numbers (i.e., 4.3.156–82).
- "banjo . . . Porsche" is the lemma proper. Ellipses (. . .) are often employed to abbreviate longer lemmata, but lemmata are always understood to be inclusive.
- Capital letters are the *sigla*, or abbreviations, for the witnesses (whether manuscript, early print witness, or modern edition). Lowercase Greek letters (like α) indicate entire witness groups or the hyparchetype reading. Uppercase sigmas (Σ) indicate an agreement in witnesses that are not specified in the note. Some editors will instead use a "+" after the first witness listed, as in "H+," in order to indicate that the remaining witnesses are in agreement. The tilde or swung dash (~) is a shorthand way of indicating that the reading of the lemma remains unchanged except for the material indicated.
- Separate readings are divided by semicolons.

Translated into prose, this note might read:

The phrase, "banjo player's British racing-green Porsche," which appears on page 214 at line 30, did not appear this way in our copy-text, but in all forty-three of the witnesses not listed later in this note. It appears as "fiddle player's British racing-green Porch" in T, and as "fiddler's Maserati" in manuscripts Q, S, and W. The phrase doesn't appear at all in the fifteen alpha manuscripts or in manuscripts X, Y and Z.

Below is a genuine example, the first four lines from Kane and Donaldson's edition of the B-text of William Langland's *Piers Plowman*. This is the text as it appears in their edition:

IN a somer seson whan softe was þe sonne

I shoop me into [a] shrou[d] as I a sheep weere;

In habite as an heremite, vnholy of werkes,

Wente wide in þis world wondres to here. (227)

The square brackets in the second line of the text (around the first "a" and around the "d" in "shrou[d]"), indicate that the editors have emended the text of their basic manuscript (Trinity College Cambridge MS B.15.17), emendations that are detailed in the notes, but that might be clear from the brackets alone: in the case of these brackets, the editors have added material to and subtracted material from the reading of W. The notes that apply to these lines:

1–12   *over erasure another ink* Hm.

1   *a] om* F.   somer] someres HmG.   Softe] set HmCr.

2   into] in GYOC2CLMH (to *above line* M).   a shroud] a schroude H; shroudes WHmGYOC²CLMF; shroubes Cr.   a(2)] *om.* F.   sheep] schep H; shepe CrGYCL.

3   *line om* F.   In] In an H.   as] of HmH.

4   Wente] & wente FH; Wend Cr¹.   þis] þe H.

The method Kane and Donaldson have employed for separating lemmas within the same line, punctuating the end of each stemma as though it were the end of a sentence, then beginning the next lemma after a short space, makes for relatively easy reading. Other editors will occasionally simply use extra space with no punctuation between the end of a stemma and the beginning of the next lemma. Still others will simply provide new line numbers for each lemma. The notes detail substantive variations (that is, variants that might affect meaning), including omissions, and on two occasions they give a sense of corrections made to witnesses by earlier readers. In the first case, the note to lines 1–12 indicates that the manuscript Hm (Huntington Library MS 128, at the Huntington Library in San Marino, California) has had its opening erased and the first lines rewritten in a second ink (a *palimpsest*). In the note to line 2, the editors indicate that

someone added a "to" above the line to correct "in" to "into" in manuscript M (British Library MS Add. 35287), after the line was first copied.

Using these notes, one can theoretically reconstruct the readings of
one manuscript, say, H (British Library MS Harley 3954), with its variant
readings italicized:

> IN a somer seson whan softe was þe sonne
>
> I shoop me *in a schroude* as I a schep weere;
>
> In *an* habite *of* an heremite, vnholy of werkes,
>
> & wente wide in þe world wondres to here.

This may not be an exact transcription of H—in fact, it is almost certainly not, since there are probably spelling differences that Kane and
Donaldson consider to be non-substantive, and the punctuation is surely
modern and not medieval—but it is a beginning. Perhaps more interesting, given its omission of a whole line, is the version one can reconstruct
for F (Corpus Christi College, Oxford 201):

> IN somer seson whan softe was þe sonne
>
> I shoop me into *shroudes* as I sheep weere;
>
> *& wente* wide in þis world wondres to here.

Does the omission begin to blunt Langland's attack on monasticism as it
was practiced in his day? Perhaps. Using Kane and Donaldson's notes, an
interested reader can begin to piece together the unique features of F in
comparison to other manuscripts in addition to the reconstructed text
they provide. Reading the textual notes in this way, with an eye to
reconstructing individual witnesses, one can test what Kane and Donaldson call their "hypothesis," the text of their edition. In doing so, one
begins to engage in the sorts of inquiry that Reiman and others would
like to encourage. One becomes a textual critic alongside Donaldson
and Kane, beginning to experience the variety that is in the documents,
perhaps beginning to compose one's own hypotheses for short passages,
and, perhaps even, one day, the whole poem.

The next part of this book contains a menagerie of textual criticism and textual theory, meant to lead students toward fuller work from textual critics. Some of these essays and excerpts are major statements in the field, some have been selected because they speak to the samples in the third part of the textbook. Because of the diversity and size of the field, there is no hope of any textbook being truly representative or of even covering the scope. All that can be hoped for is a beginning. The bibliography at the end of the volume will point interested readers toward the riches that could not be included in this anthology. Part Three samples a few critical and non-critical editions, on which readers can begin to practice working. Simpler examples are followed by more complex ones. I have tried, where possible, to include facsimile pages of early witnesses for readers to compare with an edition's text and notes. Finally, in the belief that there is no better teacher than experience, the third part also includes several mini-archives, collections of witnesses of short texts and excerpts of longer ones for readers to examine and to begin to practice textual criticism and critical editing on their own.

PART TWO

from The Application of Thought
to Textual Criticism[†]

A. E. Housman

IN BEGINNING TO speak about the application of thought to textual criticism, I do not intend to define the term *thought*, because I hope that the sense which I attach to the word will emerge from what I say. But it is necessary at the outset to define *textual criticism*, because many people, and even some people who profess to teach it to others, do not know what it is. One sees books calling themselves introductions to textual criticism which contain nothing about textual criticism from beginning to end; which are all about palaeography and manuscripts and collation, and have no more to do with textual criticism than if they were all about accidence and syntax. Palaeography is one of the things with which a textual critic needs to acquaint himself, but grammar is another, and equally indispensable; and no amount either of grammar or of palaeography will teach a man one scrap of textual criticism.

Textual criticism is a science, and, since it comprises recension and emendation, it is also an art. It is the science of discovering error in texts and the art of removing it. That is its definition, that is what the name *denotes*. But I must also say something about what it does and does not *connote*, what attributes it does and does not imply; because here also there are false impressions abroad.

† From "The Application of Thought to Textual Criticism," in *The Classical Papers of A. E. Houseman*. Reprinted with the permission of Cambridge University Press.

First, then, it is not a sacred mystery. It is purely a matter of reason and of common sense. We exercise textual criticism whenever we notice and correct a misprint. A man who possesses common sense and the use of reason must not expect to learn from treatises or lectures on textual criticism anything that he could not, with leisure and industry, find out for himself. What the lectures and treatises can do for him is to save him time and trouble by presenting to him immediately considerations which would in any case occur to him sooner or later. And whatever he reads about textual criticism in books, or hears at lectures, he should test by reason and common sense, and reject everything which conflicts with either as mere hocus-pocus.

Secondly, textual criticism is not a branch of mathematics, nor indeed an exact science at all. It deals with a matter not rigid and constant, like lines and numbers, but fluid and variable; namely the frailties and aberrations of the human mind, and of its insubordinate servants, the human fingers. It therefore is not susceptible of hard-and-fast rules. It would be much easier if it were; and that is why people try to pretend that it is, or at least behave as if they thought so. Of course you can have hard-and-fast rules if you like, but then you will have false rules, and they will lead you wrong; because their simplicity will render them inapplicable to problems which are not simple, but complicated by the play of personality. A textual critic engaged upon his business is not at all like Newton investigating the motions of the planets: he is much more like a dog hunting for fleas. If a dog hunted for fleas on mathematical principles, basing his researches on statistics of area and population, he would never catch a flea except by accident. They require to be treated as individuals; and every problem which presents itself to the textual critic must be regarded as possibly unique.

Textual criticism therefore is neither mystery nor mathematics: it cannot be learnt either like the catechism or like the multiplication table. This science and this art require more in the learner than a simply receptive mind; and indeed the truth is that they cannot be taught at all: *criticus nascitur, non fit*. If a dog is to hunt for fleas successfully he must be quick and he must be sensitive. It is no good for a rhinoceros to hunt for fleas: he does not know where they are, and could not catch them if he did. It has sometimes been said that textual criticism is the crown and summit of all scholarship. This is not evidently or necessarily true; but it is true that the qualities which make a critic, whether they are thus transcendent or no, are rare, and that a good critic is a much less common thing than for instance a good grammarian. I have in my mind a paper by a well-known scholar on a certain Latin writer, half of which was concerned with grammar and half with criticism. The grammatical part was excellent; it showed wide reading and accurate observation, and contributed matter which was both new and valuable. In the textual part the author was like nothing so much as an ill-bred child interrupting the conversation of grown men. If it was possible to mistake the question at issue, he mistook it. If an opponent's arguments were contained in some book which was not at hand, he did not try to find the book, but he tried to guess the arguments; and he never succeeded. If the book was at hand, and he had read the arguments, he did not understand them; and represented his opponents as saying the opposite of what they had said. If another scholar had already removed a corruption by slightly altering the text, he proposed to remove it by altering the text violently. So possible is it to be a learned man, and admirable in other departments, and yet to have in you not even the makings of a critic.

But the application of thought to textual criticism is an action which ought to be within the power of anyone who can apply thought to anything. It is not, like the talent for textual criticism, a gift of nature, but it is a habit: and, like other habits, it can be formed. And, when formed, although it cannot fill the place of an absent talent, it can modify and minimise the ill effects of the talent's absence. Because a man is not a born critic, he need not therefore act like a born fool; but when he engages in textual criticism he often does. There are reasons for everything, and there are reasons for this; and I will now set forth the chief of them. The *fact* that thought is not sufficiently applied to the subject I shall show hereafter by examples; but at present I consider the causes which bring that result about.

First, then, not only is a natural aptitude for the study rare, but so also is a genuine interest in it. Most people, and many scholars among them, find it rather dry and rather dull. Now if a subject bores us, we are apt to avoid the trouble of thinking about it; but if we do that, we had better go further and avoid also the trouble of writing about it. And that is what

English scholars often did in the middle of the nineteenth century, when nobody in England wanted to hear about textual criticism. This was not an ideal condition of affairs, but it had its compensation. The less one says about a subject which one does not understand, the less one will say about it which is foolish; and on this subject editors were allowed by public opinion to be silent if they chose. But public opinion is now aware that textual criticism, however repulsive, is nevertheless indispensable, and editors find that some pretence of dealing with the subject is obligatory; and in these circumstances they apply, not thought, but words, to textual criticism. They get rules by rote without grasping the realities of which those rules are merely emblems, and recite them on inappropriate occasions instead of seriously thinking out each problem as it arises.

Secondly, it is only a minority of those who engage in this study who are sincerely bent upon the discovery of truth. We all know that the discovery of truth is seldom the sole object of political writers; and the world believes, justly or unjustly, that it is not always the sole object of theologians: but the amount of sub-conscious dishonesty which pervades the textual criticism of the Greek and Latin classics is little suspected except by those who have had occasion to analyse it. People come upon this field bringing with them prepossessions and preferences; they are not willing to look all facts in the face, nor to draw the most probable conclusion unless it is also the most agreeable conclusion. Most men are rather stupid, and most of those who are not stupid are, consequently, rather vain; and it is hardly possible to step aside from the pursuit of truth without falling a victim either to your stupidity or else to your vanity. Stupidity will then attach you to received opinions, and you will stick in the mud; or vanity will set you hunting for novelty, and you will find mare's-nests. Added to these snares and hindrances there are the various forms of partisanship: sectarianism, which handcuffs you to your own school and teachers and associates, and patriotism, which handcuffs you to your own country. Patriotism has a great name as a virtue, and in civic matters, at the present stage of the world's history, it possibly still does more good than harm; but in the sphere of intellect it is an unmitigated nuisance. I do not know which cuts the worse figure: a German scholar encouraging his countrymen to believe that 'wir Deutsche' have nothing to learn from foreigners, or an Englishman demonstrating the unity of Homer by sneers at 'Teutonic professors', who are supposed by his audience to have goggle eyes behind large spectacles, and ragged moustaches saturated in lager beer, and consequently to be incapable of forming literary judgments.

Thirdly, these internal causes of error and folly are subject to very little counteraction or correction from outside. The average reader knows hardly anything about textual criticism, and therefore cannot exercise a vigilant control over the writer: the addle-pate is at liberty to maunder and the impostor is at liberty to lie. And, what is worse, the reader often shares the writer's prejudices, and is far too well pleased with his conclusions to examine either his premises or his reasoning. Stand on a barrel in the streets of Bagdad, and say in a loud voice, 'Twice two is four, and ginger is hot in the mouth, therefore Mohammed is the prophet of God', and your logic will probably escape criticism; or, if anyone by chance should criticise it, you could easily silence him by calling him a Christian dog.

Fourthly, the things which the textual critic has to talk about are not things which present themselves clearly and sharply to the mind; and it is easy to say, and to fancy that you think, what you really do not think, and even what, if you seriously tried to think it, you would find to be unthinkable. Mistakes are therefore made which could not be made if the matter under discussion were any corporeal object, having qualities perceptible to the senses. The human senses have had a much longer history than the human intellect, and have been brought much nearer to perfection: they are far more acute, far less easy to deceive. The difference between an icicle and a red-hot poker is really much slighter than the difference between truth and falsehood or sense and nonsense; yet it is much more immediately noticeable and much more universally noticed, because the body is more sensitive than the mind. I find therefore that a good way of exposing the falsehood of a statement or the absurdity of an argument in textual criticism is to transpose it into sensuous terms and see what it looks like then. If the nouns which we use are the names of things which can be handled or tasted, differing from one another in being hot or cold, sweet or sour, then we realise what we are saying and take care what we say. But the terms of textual criticism are deplorably intellectual; and probably in no other field do men tell so many falsehoods in the idle hope that they are telling the truth, or talk so much nonsense in the vague belief that they are talking sense.

This is particularly unfortunate and particularly reprehensible, because there is no science in which it is more necessary to take precautions against error arising from internal causes. Those who follow the physical sciences enjoy the great advantage that they can constantly bring their opinions to the test of fact, and verify or falsify their theories by experiment. When a chemist has mixed sulphur and saltpetre and charcoal in certain proportions and wishes to ascertain if the mixture is explosive, he need only apply a match. When a doctor has compounded a new drug and desires to find out what diseases, if any, it is good for, he has only to give it to his patients all round and notice which die and which recover. Our conclusions regarding the truth or falsehood of a MS reading can never be confirmed or corrected by an equally decisive test; for the only equally decisive test would be the production of the author's autograph. The discovery merely of better and older MSS than were previously known to us is *not* equally decisive; and even this inadequate verification is not to be expected often, or on a large scale. It is therefore a matter of common prudence and common decency that we should neglect no safeguard lying within our reach; that we should look sharp after ourselves; that we should narrowly scrutinise our own proceedings and rigorously analyse our springs of action.

★ ★ ★

There are two MSS of a certain author, which we will call A and B. Of these two it is recognised that A is the more correct but the less sincere, and that B is the more corrupt but the less interpolated.[1] It is desired to know which MS, if either, is better than the other, or whether both are equal. One scholar tries to determine this question by the collection and comparison of examples. But another thinks that he knows a shorter way than that; and it consists in saying 'the more sincere MS is and must be for any critic who understands his business the better MS.'

This I cite as a specimen of the things which people may say if they do not think about the meaning of what they are saying, and especially as an example of the danger of dealing in generalisations. The best way to treat such pretentious inanities is to transfer them from the sphere of textual criticism, where the difference between truth and falsehood or between sense and nonsense is little regarded and seldom even perceived, into some sphere where men are obliged to use concrete and sensuous terms, which force them, however reluctantly, to think.

I ask this scholar, this critic who knows his business, and who says that the more sincere of two MSS is and must be the better—I ask him to tell me which weighs most, a tall man or a fat man. He cannot answer; nobody can; everybody sees in a moment that the question is absurd. *Tall* and *fat* are adjectives which transport even a textual critic from the world of humbug into the world of reality, a world inhabited by comparatively thoughtful people, such as butchers and grocers, who depend on their brains for their bread. There he begins to understand that to such general questions any answer must be false; that judgment can only be pronounced on individual specimens; that everything depends on the degree of tallness and the degree of fatness. It may well be that an inch of girth adds more weight than an inch of height, or vice versa; but that altitude is incomparably more ponderous than obesity, or obesity than altitude, and that an inch of one depresses the scale more than a yard of the other, has never been maintained. The way to find out whether this tall man weighs more

1. [Housman distinguishes two kinds of "error": corruption and interpolation. Corruption occurs when a scribe copies mistakenly, perhaps producing gibberish. Interpolation, on the other hand, occurs when a scribe consciously alters his source, usually to correct what he perceives to be an error. So manuscript A shows fewer errors (say, grammatical or metrical) but appears less "sincere," having been cleaned up by a scribe, while manuscript B shows more errors but appears to be more unadulterated —*Editor.*]

or less than that fat man is to weigh them; and the way to find out whether this corrupt MS is better or worse than that interpolated MS is to collect and compare their readings; not to ride easily off on the false and ridiculous generalisation that the more sincere MS is and must be the better.

When you call a MS *sincere* you instantly engage on its behalf the moral sympathy of the thoughtless: moral sympathy is a line in which they are very strong. I do not desire to exclude morality from textual criticism; I wish indeed that some moral qualities were commoner in textual criticism than they are; but let us not indulge our moral emotions out of season. It may be that a scribe who interpolates, who makes changes deliberately, is guilty of wickedness, while a scribe who makes changes accidentally, because he is sleepy or illiterate or drunk, is guilty of none; but that is a question which will be determined by a competent authority at the Day of Judgment, and is no concern of ours. Our concern is not with the eternal destiny of the scribe, but with the temporal utility of the MS; and a MS is useful or the reverse in proportion to the amount of truth which it discloses or conceals, no matter what may be the causes of the disclosure or concealment. It is a mistake to suppose that deliberate change is always or necessarily more destructive of truth than accidental change; and even if it were, the main question, as I have said already, is one of degree. A MS in which 1 per cent of the words have been viciously and intentionally altered and 99 per cent are right is not so bad as a MS in which only 1 per cent are right and 99 per cent have been altered virtuously and unintentionally; and if you go to a critic with any such vague inquiry as the question whether the 'more sincere' or the 'more correct' of two MSS is the better, he will reply, 'If I am to answer that question, you must show me the two MSS first; for aught that I know at present, from the terms of your query, either may be better than the other, or both may be equal.' But that is what the incompetent intruders into criticism can never admit. They *must* have a better MS, whether it exists or no; because they could never get along without one. If Providence permitted two MSS to be equal, the editor would have to choose between their readings by considerations of intrinsic merit, and in order to do that he would need to acquire intelligence and impartiality and willingness to take pains, and all sorts of things which he neither has nor wishes for; and he feels sure that God, who tempers the wind to the shorn lamb, can never have meant to lay upon his shoulders such a burden as this.

This is thoughtlessness in the sphere of recension: come now to the sphere of emendation. There is one foolish sort of conjecture which seems to be commoner in the British Isles than anywhere else, though it is also practised abroad, and of late years especially at Munich. The practice is, if you have persuaded yourself that a text is corrupt, to alter a letter or two and see what happens. If what happens is anything which the warmest good-will can mistake for sense and grammar, you call it an emendation; and you call this silly game the palaeographical method.

The palaeographical method has always been the delight of tiros and the scorn of critics. Haupt,[2] for example, used to warn his pupils against mistaking this sort of thing for emendation. 'The prime requisite of a good emendation', said he, 'is that it should start from the thought; it is only afterwards that other considerations, such as those of metre, or possibilities, such as the interchange of letters, are taken into account.' And again: 'If the sense requires it, I am prepared to write *Constantinopolitanus* where the MSS have the monosyllabic interjection *o*.' And again: 'From the requirement that one should always begin with the thought, there results, as is self-evident, the negative aspect of the case, that one should not, at the outset, consider what exchange of letters may possibly have brought about the corruption of the passage one is dealing with.' And further, in his oration on Lachmann as a critic: 'Some people, if they see that anything in an ancient text wants correcting, immediately betake themselves to the art of palaeography, investigate the shapes of letters and the forms of abbreviation, and try one dodge after another, as if it were a game, until they hit upon something which they think they can substitute for the corruption; as if forsooth truth were generally discovered by shots of that sort, or as if emendation could take its rise from anything but a careful consideration of the thought.'

But even when palaeography is kept in her proper place, as handmaid, and not allowed to give herself the airs of mistress, she is apt to be

2. [Moritz Haupt (1808–1874), German editor of classical and medieval literature. In 1853 he was chosen as the Chair for Latin literature at the University of Berlin after the death of the previous chair, his friend Karl Lachmann (1793–1851) —*Editor.*]

overworked. There is a preference for conjectures which call in the aid of palaeography, and which assume, as the cause of error, the accidental interchange of similar letters or similar words, although other causes of error are known to exist. One is presented, for instance, with the following maxim: 'Interpolation is, speaking generally, comparatively an uncommon source of alteration, and we should therefore be loth to assume it in a given case.'

Every case is a given case; so what this maxim really means is that we should always be loth to assume interpolation as a source of alteration. But it is certain, and admitted by this writer when he uses the phrase 'comparatively uncommon', that interpolation does occur; so he is telling us that we should be loth to assume interpolation even when that assumption is true. And the reason why we are to behave in this ridiculous manner is that interpolation is, speaking generally, comparatively an uncommon source of alteration.

Now to detect a *non sequitur*, unless it leads to an unwelcome conclusion, is as much beyond the power of the average reader as it is beyond the power of the average writer to attach ideas to his own words when those words are terms of textual criticism. I will therefore substitute other terms, terms to which ideas must be attached; and I invite consideration of this maxim and this ratiocination:

'A bullet-wound is, speaking generally, comparatively an uncommon cause of death, and we should therefore be loth to assume it in a given case.'

Should we? Should we be loth to assume a bullet-wound as the cause of death if the given case were death on a battlefield? and should we be loth to do so for the reason alleged, that a bullet-wound is, speaking generally, comparatively an uncommon cause of death? Ought we to assume instead the commonest cause of death, and assign death on a battlefield to tuberculosis? What would be thought of a counsellor who enjoined that method of procedure? Well, it would probably be thought that he was a textual critic strayed from home.

Why is interpolation comparatively uncommon? For the same reason that bullet-wounds are: because the opportunity for it is comparatively uncommon. Interpolation is provoked by real or supposed difficulties, and is not frequently volunteered where all is plain sailing; whereas accidental alteration may happen anywhere. Every letter of every word lies exposed to it, and that is the sole reason why accidental alteration is more common. In a given case where either assumption is possible, the assumption of interpolation is equally probable, nay more probable; because action with a motive is more probable than action without a motive. The truth therefore is that in such a case we should be loth to assume accident and should rather assume interpolation; and the circumstance that such cases are comparatively uncommon is no reason for behaving irrationally when they occur.

There is one special province of textual criticism, a large and important province, which is concerned with the establishment of rules of grammar and of metre. Those rules are in part traditional, and given us by the ancient grammarians; but in part they are formed by our own induction from what we find in the MSS of Greek and Latin authors; and even the traditional rules must of course be tested by comparison with the witness of the MSS. But every rule, whether traditional or framed from induction, is sometimes broken by the MSS; it may be by few, it may be by many; it may be seldom, it may be often; and critics may then say that the MSS are wrong, and may correct them in accordance with the rule. This state of affairs is apparently, nay evidently, paradoxical. The MSS are the material upon which we base our rule, and then, when we have got our rule, we turn round upon the MSS and say that the rule, based upon them, convicts them of error. We are thus working in a circle, that is a fact which there is no denying; but, as Lachmann says, the task of the critic is just this, to tread that circle deftly and warily; and that is precisely what elevates the critic's business above mere mechanical labour. The difficulty is one which lies in the nature of the case, and is inevitable; and the only way to surmount it is just to be a critic.

The paradox is more formidable in appearance than in reality, and has plenty of analogies in daily life. In a trial or lawsuit the jury's verdict is mainly based upon the evidence of the witnesses; but that does not prevent the jury from making up its mind, from the evidence in general, that one or more witnesses have been guilty of perjury and that their evidence is to be disregarded. It is quite possible to elicit from the general testimony of MSS a rule of sufficient certainty to convict of falsehood their exceptional testimony, or of sufficient probability to throw doubt upon it. But that exceptional testimony must in each case be considered. It must be recognised that there are two hypotheses between which we have to decide: the question is whether the exceptions come from the author, and so break down the rule, or whether they come from the scribe, and are to be corrected by it: and in order to decide this we must keep our eyes open for any peculiarity which may happen to characterise them.

★ ★ ★

It is supposed that there has been progress in the science of textual criticism, and the most frivolous pretender has learnt to talk superciliously about 'the old unscientific days'. The old unscientific days are everlasting; they are here and now; they are renewed perennially by the ear which takes formulas in, and the tongue which gives them out again, and the mind which meanwhile is empty of reflexion and stuffed with self-complacency. Progress there has been, but where? In superior intellects: the rabble do not share it. Such a man as Scaliger, living in our time, would be a better critic than Scaliger was; but we shall not be better critics than Scaliger by the simple act of living in our own time.[3] Textual criticism, like most other sciences, is an aristocratic affair, not communicable to all men, nor to most men. Not to be a textual critic is no reproach to anyone, unless he pretends to be what he is not. To *be* a textual critic requires aptitude for thinking and willingness to think; and though it also requires other things, those things are supplements and cannot be substitutes. Knowledge is good, method is good, but one thing beyond all others is necessary; and that is to have a head, not a pumpkin, on your shoulders, and brains, not pudding, in your head.

3. [Joseph Justice Scaliger (1540–1609), a French textual critic and editor —*Editor.*]

The Rationale of Copy-Text[†]

W. W. Greg

WHEN, IN HIS edition of Nashe, McKerrow[1] invented the term 'copy-text', he was merely giving a name to a conception already familiar, and he used it in a general sense to indicate that early text of a work which an editor selected as the basis of his own. Later, as we shall see, he gave it a somewhat different and more restricted meaning. It is this change in conception and its implications that I wish to consider.

The idea of treating some one text, usually of course a manuscript, as possessing over-riding authority originated among classical scholars, though something similar may no doubt be traced in the work of biblical critics. So long as purely eclectic methods prevailed, any preference for one manuscript over another, if it showed itself, was of course arbitrary; but when, towards the middle of last century, Lachmann and others introduced the genealogical classification of manuscripts as a principle of textual criticism, this appeared to provide at least some scientific basis for the conception of the most authoritative text. The genealogical method was the greatest advance ever made in this field, but its introduction was not unaccompanied by error. For lack of logical analysis, it led, at the hands of its less discriminating exponents, to an attempt to reduce textual criticism to a

---

† "The Rationale of Copy-Text," from *Studies in Bibliography* 3 (1950): 19–36. Reproduced by permission of *Studies in Bibliography* and the Rector and Visitors of the University of Virginia.

1. [Thomas Nashe, *The Works of Thomas Nashe, Edited from the Original Texts*, ed. R. B. McKerrow (London: A. H. Bullen, 1904–1910) —*Editor.*]

code of mechanical rules. There was just this much excuse, that the method did make it possible to sweep away mechanically a great deal of rubbish. What its more hasty devotees failed to understand, or at any rate sufficiently to bear in mind, was that authority is never absolute, but only relative. Thus a school arose, mainly in Germany, that taught that if a manuscript could be shown to be generally more correct than any other and to have descended from the archetype independently of other lines of transmission, it was 'scientific' to follow its readings whenever they were not manifestly impossible. It was this fallacy that Housman exposed with devastating sarcasm. He had only to point out that 'Chance and the common course of nature will not bring it to pass that the readings of a MS are right wherever they are possible and impossible wherever they are wrong'.[2] That if a scribe makes a mistake he will inevitably produce nonsense is the tacit and wholly unwarranted assumption of the school in question,[3] and it is one that naturally commends itself to those who believe themselves capable of distinguishing between sense and nonsense, but who know themselves incapable of distinguishing between right and wrong. Unfortunately the attractions of a mechanical method misled many who were capable of better things.

There is one important respect in which the editing of classical texts differs from that of English. In the former it is the common practice, for fairly obvious reasons, to normalize the spelling, so that (apart from emendation) the function of an editor is limited to choosing between those manuscript readings that offer significant variants. In English it is now usual to preserve the spelling of the earliest or it may be some other selected text. Thus it will be seen that the conception of 'copy-text' does not present itself to the classical and to the English editor in quite the same way; indeed, if I am right in the view I am about to put forward,

2. Introduction to Manilius, 1903, p. xxxii.

3. The more naive the scribe, the more often will the assumption prove correct; the more sophisticated, the less often. This, no doubt, is why critics of this school tend to reject 'the more correct but the less sincere' manuscript in favour of 'the more corrupt but the less interpolated', as Housman elsewhere observes ('The Application of Thought to Textual Criticism', *Proceedings of the Classical Association*, 1921, xviii. 75 [128–31 this volume —*Editor*]). Still, any reasonable critic will prefer the work of a naive to that of a sophisticated scribe, though he may not regard it as necessarily 'better'.

the classical theory of the 'best' or 'most authoritative' manuscript, whether it be held in a reasonable or in an obviously fallacious form, has really nothing to do with the English theory of 'copy-text' at all.

I do not wish to argue the case of 'old spelling' *versus* 'modern spelling'; I accept the view now prevalent among English scholars. But I cannot avoid some reference to the ground on which present practice is based, since it is intimately connected with my own views on copy-text. The former practice of modernizing the spelling of English works is no longer popular with editors, since spelling is now recognized as an essential characteristic of an author, or at least of his time and locality. So far as my knowledge goes, the alternative of normalization has not been seriously explored, but its philological difficulties are clearly considerable.[4] Whether, with the advance of linguistic science, it will some day be possible to establish a standard spelling for a particular period or district or author, or whether the historical circumstances in which our language has developed must always forbid any attempt of the sort (at any rate before comparatively recent times) I am not competent to say; but I agree with what appears to be the general opinion that such an attempt would at present only result in confusion and misrepresentation. It is therefore the modern editorial practice to choose whatever extant text may be supposed to represent most nearly what the author wrote and to follow it with the least possible alteration. But here we need to draw a distinction between the significant, or as I shall call them 'substantive', readings of the text, those namely that affect the author's meaning or the essence of his expression, and others, such in general as spelling, punctuation, word-division, and the like, affecting mainly its formal presentation, which may be regarded as the accidents, or as I shall call them 'accidentals', of the text.[5] The distinction is not arbitrary or theoretical, but

---

4. I believe that an attempt has been made in the case of certain Old and Middle English texts, but how consistently and with what success I cannot judge. In any case I am here concerned chiefly with works of the sixteenth and seventeenth centuries.

5. It will, no doubt, be objected that punctuation may very seriously 'affect' an author's meaning; still it remains properly a matter of presentation, as spelling does in spite of its use in distinguishing homonyms. The distinction I am trying to draw is practical, not philosophic. It is also true that between substantive readings and spellings there is an intermediate class of word-forms about the assignment of which opinions may differ and which may have to be treated differently in dealing with the work of different scribes.

has an immediate bearing on textual criticism, for scribes (or compositors) may in general be expected to react, and experience shows that they generally do react, differently to the two categories. As regards substantive readings their aim may be assumed to be to reproduce exactly those of their copy, though they will doubtless sometimes depart from them accidentally and may even, for one reason or another, do so intentionally: as regards accidentals they will normally follow their own habits or inclination, though they may, for various reasons and to varying degrees, be influenced by their copy. Thus a contemporary manuscript will at least preserve the spelling of the period, and may even retain some of the author's own, while it may at the same time depart frequently from the wording of the original: on the other hand a later transcript of the same original may reproduce the wording with essential accuracy while completely modernizing the spelling. Since, then it is only on grounds of expediency, and in consequence either of philological ignorance or of linguistic circumstances, that we select a particular original as our copy-text, I suggest that it is only in the matter of accidentals that we are bound (within reason) to follow it, and that in respect of substantive readings we have exactly the same liberty (and obligation) of choice as has a classical editor, or as we should have were it a modernized text that we were preparing.[6]

But the distinction has not been generally recognized, and has never, so far as I am aware, been explicitly drawn.[7] This is not surprising. The battle between 'old spelling' and 'modern spelling' was fought out over

6. For the sake of clearness in making the distinction I have above stressed the independence of scribes and compositors in the matter of accidentals: at the same time, when he selects his copy-text, an editor will naturally hope that it retains at least something of the character of the original. Experience, however, shows that while the distribution of substantive variants generally agrees with the genetic relation of the texts, that of accidental variants is comparatively arbitrary.

7. Some discussion bearing on it will be found in the Prolegomena to my lectures on *The Editorial Problem in Shakespeare: A Survey of the Foundations of the Text* ([Oxford: Clarendon Press,] 1942), 'Note on Accidental Characteristics of the Text' (pp. l–lv), particularly the paragraph on pp. liii–liv, and note 1. But at the time of writing I was still a long way from any consistent theory regarding copy-text.

works written for the most part between 1550 and 1650, and for which the original authorities are therefore as a rule printed editions. Now printed editions usually form an ancestral series, in which each is derived from its immediate predecessor; whereas the extant manuscripts of any work have usually only a collateral relationship, each being derived from the original independently, or more or less independently, of the others. Thus in the case of printed books, and in the absence of revision in a later edition, it is normally the first edition alone that can claim authority, and this authority naturally extends to substantive readings and accidentals alike. There was, therefore, little to force the distinction upon the notice of editors of works of the sixteenth and seventeenth centuries, and it apparently never occurred to them that some fundamental difference of editorial method might be called for in the rare cases in which a later edition had been revised by the author or in which there existed more than one 'substantive' edition of comparable authority.[8] Had they been more familiar with works transmitted in manuscript, they might possibly have reconsidered their methods and been led to draw the distinction I am suggesting. For although the underlying principles of textual criticism are, of course, the same in the case of works transmitted in manuscripts and in print, particular circumstances differ, and certain aspects of the common principles may emerge more clearly in the one case than in the other. However, since the idea of copy-text originated and has generally been applied in connexion with the editing of printed books, it is such that I shall mainly consider, and in what follows reference may be understood as confined to them unless manuscripts are specifically mentioned.

The distinction I am proposing between substantive readings and accidentals, or at any rate its relevance to the question of copy-text, was clearly

---

8. A 'substantive' edition is McKerrow's term for an edition that is not a reprint of any other. I shall use the term in this sense, since I do not think that there should be any danger of confusion between 'substantive editions' and 'substantive readings'.

I have above ignored the practice of some eccentric editors who took as copy-text for a work the latest edition printed in the author's lifetime, on the assumption, presumably, that he revised each edition as it appeared. The textual results were naturally deplorable.

not present to McKerrow's mind when in 1904 he published the second volume of his edition of the Works of Thomas Nashe, which included *The Unfortunate Traveller*. Collation of the early editions of this romance led him to the conclusion that the second, advertised on the title as 'Newly corrected and augmented', had in fact been revised by the author, but at the same time that not all the alterations could with certainty be ascribed to him.[9] He nevertheless proceeded to enunciate the rule that 'if an editor has reason to suppose that a certain text embodies later corrections than any other, and at the same time has no ground for disbelieving that these corrections, *or some of them at least*, are the work of the author, he has no choice but to make that text the basis of his reprint'.[10] The italics are mine.[11] This is applying with a vengeance the principle that I once approvingly described as 'maintaining the integrity of the copy-text'. But it must be pointed out that there are in fact two quite distinct principles involved. One, put in more general form, is that if, for whatever reason, a particular authority be on the whole preferred, an editor is bound to accept all its substantive readings (if not manifestly impossible). This is the old fallacy of the 'best text', and may be taken to be now generally rejected. The other principle, also put in general form, is that whatever particular authority be preferred, whether as being revised or as generally preserving the substantive readings more faithfully than any other, it must be taken as copy-text, that is to say that it must also be followed in the matter of accidentals. This is the principle that interests us at the moment, and it is one that McKerrow himself came, at least partly, to question.

9. He believed, or at least strongly suspected, that some were due to the printer's desire to save space, and that others were 'the work of some person who had not thoroughly considered the sense of the passage which he was altering' (ii.195).

10. Nashe, ii.197. The word 'reprint' really begs the question. If all an 'editor' aims at is an exact reprint, then obviously he will choose one early edition, on whatever grounds he considers relevant, and reproduce it as it stands. But McKerrow does emend his copy-text where necessary. It is symptomatic that he did not distinguish between a critical edition and a reprint.

11. Without the italicized phrase the statement would appear much more plausible (though I should still regard it as fallacious, and so would McKerrow himself have done later on) but it would not justify the procedure adopted.

In 1939 McKerrow published his *Prolegomena for the Oxford Shakespeare*, and he would not have been the critic he was if his views had not undergone some changes in the course of thirty-five years. One was in respect of revision. He had come to the opinion that to take a reprint, even a revised reprint, as copy-text was indefensible. Whatever may be the relation of a particular substantive edition to the author's manuscript (provided that there is any transcriptional link at all) it stands to reason that the relation of a reprint of that edition must be more remote. If then, putting aside all question of revision, a particular substantive edition has an over-riding claim to be taken as copy-text, to displace it in favour of a reprint, whether revised or not, means receding at least one step further from the author's original in so far as the general form of the text is concerned.[12] Some such considerations must have been in McKerrow's mind when he wrote (*Prolegomena*, pp. 17–18): 'Even if, however, we were to assure ourselves . . . that certain corrections found in a later edition of a play were of Shakespearian authority, it would not by any means follow that that edition should be used as the copy-text of a reprint.[13] It would undoubtedly be necessary to incorporate these corrections in our text, but . . . it seems evident that . . . this later edition will (except for the corrections) deviate more widely than the earliest print from the author's original manuscript. . . . [Thus] the nearest approach to our ideal . . . will be produced by using the earliest "good" print as copy-text and inserting into it, from the first edition which contains them, such corrections as appear to us to be derived from the author.' This is a clear statement of the position, and in it he draws exactly the distinction between substantive readings (in the form of corrections) and accidentals (or general texture) on which I am insisting. He then, however, relapsed into heresy in the matter of the substantive readings. Having spoken, as above, of the need to introduce 'such corrections as appear to us to be derived from the

---

12. This may, at any rate, be put forward as a general proposition, leaving possible exceptions to be considered later (pp. 33 ff. [pp. 150–52 this volume —*Editor*]).

13. Again he speaks of a 'reprint' where he evidently had in mind a critical edition on conservative lines.

author', he seems to have feared conceding too much to eclecticism, and he proceeded: 'We are not to regard the "goodness" of a reading in and by itself, or to consider whether it appeals to our aesthetic sensibilities or not; we are to consider whether a particular edition taken *as a whole* contains variants from the edition from which it was otherwise printed which could not reasonably be attributed to an ordinary press-corrector, but by reason of their style, point, and what we may call inner harmony with the spirit of the play as a whole, seem likely to be the work of the author: and once having decided this to our satisfaction we must accept *all* the alterations of that edition, saving any which seem obvious blunders or misprints.' We can see clearly enough what he had in mind, namely that the evidence of correction (under which head he presumably intended to include revision) must be considered *as a whole*; but he failed to add the equally important proviso that the alterations must also be *of a piece* (and not, as in *The Unfortunate Traveller*, of apparently disparate origin) before we can be called upon to accept them *all*. As he states it his canon is open to exactly the same objections as the 'most authoritative manuscript' theory in classical editing.

McKerrow was, therefore, in his later work quite conscious of the distinction between substantive readings and accidentals, in so far as the problem of revision is concerned. But he never applied the conception to cases in which we have more than one substantive text, as in *Hamlet* and perhaps in 2 *Henry IV, Troilus and Cressida*, and *Othello*. Presumably he would have argued that since faithfulness to the wording of the author was one of the criteria he laid down for determining the choice of the copy-text, it was an editor's duty to follow its substantive readings with a minimum of interference.

We may assume that neither McKerrow nor other editors of the conservative school imagined that such a procedure would always result in establishing the authentic text of the original; what they believed was that from it less harm would result than from opening the door to individual choice among variants, since it substituted an objective for a subjective method of determination. This is, I think, open to question. It is impossible to exclude individual judgement from editorial procedure: it operates of necessity in the all-important matter of the choice of copy-text and in the minor one of deciding what readings are possible and what not; why, therefore, should the choice between possible readings be withdrawn from its competence? Uniformity of result at the hands of different editors is worth little if it means only uniformity in error; and it may not be too optimistic a belief that the judgement of an editor, fallible as it must necessarily be, is likely to bring us closer to what the author wrote than the enforcement of an arbitrary rule.

The true theory is, I contend, that the copy-text should govern (generally) in the matter of accidentals, but that the choice between substantive readings belongs to the general theory of textual criticism and lies altogether beyond the narrow principle of the copy-text. Thus it may happen that in a critical edition the text rightly chosen as copy may not by any means be the one that supplies most substantive readings in cases of variation. The failure to make this distinction and to apply this principle has naturally led to too close and too general a reliance upon the text chosen as basis for an edition, and there has arisen what may be called the tyranny of the copy-text, a tyranny that has, in my opinion, vitiated much of the best editorial work of the past generation.

I will give a couple of examples of the sort of thing I mean that I have lately come across in the course of my own work. They are all the more suitable as illustrations since they occur in texts edited by scholars of recognized authority, neither of whom is particularly subject to the tyranny in question. One is from the edition of Marlowe's *Doctor Faustus* by Professor F. S. Boas (1932). The editor, rightly I think, took the so-called B-text (1616) as the basis of his own, correcting it where necessary by comparison with the A-text (1604).[14] Now a famous line in Faustus's opening soliloquy runs in 1604,

14. Boas's text is in fact modernized, so that my theory of copy-text does not strictly apply, but since he definitely accepts the B-text as his authority, the principle is the same. [Christopher Marlowe's celebrated play *Doctor Faustus* presents a notoriously difficult textual situation. See Christopher Marlowe, *Dr. Faustus*, ed. David Scott Kastan (New York: W. W. Norton & Company, 2004) —*Editor.*]

Bid *Oncaymaeon* farewell, *Galen* come

and in 1616,

Bid *Oeconomy* farewell; and *Galen* come . . .

Here *Oncaymaeon* is now recognized as standing for *on cay mae on* or ὄν
καὶ μὴ ὄν: but this was not understood at the time, and *Oeconomy* was
substituted in reprints of the A-text in 1609 and 1611, and thence taken
over by the B-text. The change, however, produced a rather awkward
line, and in 1616 the *and* was introduced as a metrical accommodation.
In the first half of the line Boas rightly restored the reading implied in
A; but in the second half he retained, out of deference to his copy-text,
the *and* whose only object was to accommodate the reading he had
rejected in the first. One could hardly find a better example of the
contradictions to which a mechanical following of the copy-text may
lead.[15]

My other instance is from *The Gipsies Metamorphosed* as edited by Dr.
Percy Simpson among the masques of Ben Jonson in 1941.[16] He took as
his copy-text the Huntington manuscript, and I entirely agree with his
choice. In this, and in Simpson's edition, a line of the ribald Cock Lorel
ballad runs (sir-reverence!),

All wch he blewe away with a fart

15. Or consider the following readings: 1604, 1609 'Consissylogismes', 1611 'subtile syl-
ogismes', 1616 'subtle Sillogismes'. Here 'subtile', an irresponsible guess by the printer of
1611 for a word he did not understand, was taken over in 1616. The correct reading is,
of course, 'concise syllogisms'. Boas's refusal to take account of the copy used in 1615
led him here and elsewhere to perpetuate some of its manifest errors. In this particular
instance he appears to have been unaware of the reading of 1611.

16. [The complete works of Ben Jonson (1572–1637) appeared in an eleven-volume edition that was fifty years in the making. Published by Oxford's Clarendon Press between
1925 and 1952, it was begun in 1902 by Charles Harold Herford, who was soon joined by
Percy Simpson, and then, after Herford's death in 1931, by Simpson's wife, the John Donne
scholar and editor, Evelyn Simpson (1885–1963). The phrase "sir-reverence," below, is an
Elizabethan exclamation to beg forgiveness for uttering something offensive —*Editor*.]

whereas for *blewe* other authorities have *flirted*. Now, the meaning of *flirted* is not immediately apparent, for no appropriate sense of the word is recorded. There is, however, a rare use of the substantive *flirt* for a sudden gust of wind, and it is impossible to doubt that this is what Jonson had in mind, for no scribe or compositor could have invented the reading *flirted*. It follows that in the manuscript *blewe* is nothing but the conjecture of a scribe who did not understand his original: only the mesmeric influence of the copy-text could obscure so obvious a fact.[17]

I give these examples merely to illustrate the kind of error that, in modern editions of English works, often results from undue deference to the copy-text. This reliance on one particular authority results from the desire for an objective theory of text-construction and a distrust, often no doubt justified, of the operation of individual judgement. The attitude may be explained historically as a natural and largely salutary reaction against the methods of earlier editors. Dissatisfied with the results of eclectic freedom and reliance on personal taste, critics sought to establish some sort of mechanical apparatus for dealing with textual problems that should lead to uniform results independent of the operator. Their efforts were not altogether unattended by success. One result was the recognition of the general worthlessness of reprints. And even in the more difficult field of manuscript transmission it is true that formal rules will carry us part of the way: they can at least effect a preliminary clearing of the ground. This I sought to show in my essay on *The Calculus of Variants* (1927); but in the course of investigation it became clear that there is a definite limit to the field over which formal rules are applicable. Between readings of equal extrinsic authority no rules of the sort can decide, since by their very nature it is only to extrinsic relations that they are relevant. The choice is necessarily a matter for editorial judgement, and an editor who declines or is unable to exercise his judgement and falls back on some arbitrary canon, such as the authority of the copy-text, is in fact

---

17. At another point two lines appear in an unnatural order in the manuscript. The genetic relation of the texts proves the inversion to be an error. But of this relation Simpson seems to have been ignorant. He was again content to rely on the copy-text.

abdicating his editorial function. Yet this is what has been frequently commended as 'scientific'—'streng wissenschaftlich'[18] in the prevalent idiom—and the result is that what many editors have done is to produce, not editions of their authors' works at all, but only editions of particular authorities for those works, a course that may be perfectly legitimate in itself, but was not the one they were professedly pursuing.

This by way, more or less, of digression. At the risk of repetition I should like to recapitulate my view of the position of copy-text in editorial procedure. The thesis I am arguing is that the historical circumstances of the English language make it necessary to adopt in formal matters the guidance of some particular early text. If the several extant texts of a work form an ancestral series, the earliest will naturally be selected, and since this will not only come nearest to the author's original in accidentals, but also (revision apart) most faithfully preserve the correct readings where substantive variants are in question, everything is straight-forward, and the conservative treatment of the copy-text is justified. But whenever there is more than one substantive text of comparable authority,[19] then although it will still be necessary to choose one of them as copy-text, and to follow it in accidentals, this copy-text can be allowed no over-riding or even preponderant authority so far as substantive readings are concerned. The choice between these, in cases of variation, will be determined partly by the opinion the editor may form respecting the nature of the copy from which each substantive edition was printed, which is a matter of external authority; partly by the intrinsic authority of the several texts as judged by the relative frequency of manifest errors therein; and partly by the editor's judgement of the intrinsic claims of individual readings to originality—in other words their intrinsic merit, so long as by 'merit' we mean the likelihood of their being what the author wrote rather than their appeal to the individual taste of the editor.

18. ["Strictly scientific" (German) —*Editor.*]

19. The proviso is inserted to meet the case of the so-called 'bad quartos' of Shakespearian and other Elizabethan plays and of the whole class of 'reported' texts, whose testimony can in general be neglected.

Such, as I see it, is the general theory of copy-text. But there remain a number of subsidiary questions that it may be worthwhile to discuss. One is the degree of faithfulness with which the copy-text should be reproduced. Since the adoption of a copy-text is a matter of convenience rather than of principle—being imposed on us either by linguistic circumstances or our own philological ignorance—it follows that there is no reason for treating it as sacrosanct, even apart from the question of substantive variation. Every editor aiming at a critical edition will, of course, correct scribal or typographical errors. He will also correct readings in accordance with any errata included in the edition taken as copy-text. I see no reason why he should not alter misleading or eccentric spellings which he is satisfied emanate from the scribe or compositor and not from the author. If the punctuation is persistently erroneous or defective an editor may prefer to discard it altogether to make way for one of his own. He is, I think, at liberty to do so, provided that he gives due weight to the original in deciding on his own, and that he records the alteration whenever the sense is appreciably affected. Much the same applies to the use of capitals and italics. I should favour expanding contractions (except perhaps when dealing with an author's holograph) so long as ambiguities and abnormalities are recorded. A critical edition does not seem to me a suitable place in which to record the graphic peculiarities of particular texts,[20] and in this respect the copy-text is only one among others. These, however, are all matters within the discretion of an editor: I am only concerned to uphold his liberty of judgement.

Some minor points arise when it becomes necessary to replace a reading of the copy-text by one derived from another source. It need not, I think, be copied in the exact form in which it there appears. Suppose that the copy-text follows the earlier convention in the use of *u* and *v*, and the source from which the reading is taken follows the later. Naturally in transferring the reading from the latter to the former it would be made to conform to the earlier convention. I would go further. Suppose

---

20. That is, certainly not in the text, and probably not in the general apparatus: they may appropriately form the subject of an appendix.

that the copy-text reads 'hazard', but that we have reason to believe that the correct reading is 'venture': suppose further that whenever this word occurs in the copy-text it is in the form 'venter': then 'venter', I maintain, is the form we should adopt. In like manner editorial emendations should be made to conform to the habitual spelling of the copy-text.

In the case of rival substantive editions the choice between substantive variants is, I have explained, generally independent of the copy-text. Perhaps one concession should be made. Suppose that the claims of two readings, one in the copy-text and one in some other authority, appear to be exactly balanced: what then should an editor do? In such a case, while there can be no logical reason for giving preference to the copy-text, in practice, if there is no reason for altering its reading, the obvious thing seems to be to let it stand.[21]

Much more important, and difficult, are the problems that arise in connexion with revision. McKerrow seems only to mention correction, but I think he must have intended to include revision, so long as this falls short of complete rewriting: in any case the principle is the same. I have already considered the practice he advocated (pp. 139–42, this volume)—namely that an editor should take the original edition as his copy-text and introduce into it all the substantive variants of the revised reprint, other than manifest errors—and have explained that I regard it as too sweeping and mechanical. The emendation that I proposed (p. 143,

---

21. This is the course I recommended in the Prolegomena to *The Editorial Problem in Shakespeare* (p. xxix), adding that it 'at least saves the trouble of tossing a coin'. What I actually wrote in 1942 was that in such circumstances an editor 'will naturally retain the reading of the copy-text, this being the text which he has already decided is *prima facie* the more correct'. This implies that correctness in respect of substantive readings is one of the criteria in the choice of the copy-text; and indeed I followed McKerrow in laying it down that an editor should select as copy-text the one that 'appears likely to have departed least in wording, spelling, and punctuation from the author's manuscript'. There is a good deal in my Prolegomena that I should now express differently, and on this particular point I have definitely changed my opinion. I should now say that the choice of the copy-text depends solely on its formal features (accidentals) and that fidelity as regards substantive readings is irrelevant—though fortunately in nine cases our of ten the choice will be the same whichever rule we adopt.

this volume) is, I think, theoretically sufficient, but from a practical point of view it lacks precision. In a case of revision or correction the normal procedure would be for the author to send the printer either a list of the alterations to be made or else a corrected copy of an earlier edition. In setting up the new edition we may suppose that the printer would incorporate the alterations thus indicated by the author; but it must be assumed that he would also introduce a normal amount of unauthorized variation of his own.[22] The problem that faces the editor is to distinguish between the two categories. I suggest the following frankly subjective procedure. Granting that the fact of revision (or correction) is established, an editor should in every case of variation ask himself (1) whether the original reading is one that can reasonably be attributed to the author, and (2) whether the later reading is one that the author can reasonably be supposed to have substituted for the former. If the answer to the first question is negative, then the later reading should be accepted as at least possibly an authoritative correction (unless, of course, it is itself incredible). If the answer to (1) is affirmative and the answer to (2) is negative, the original reading should be retained. If the answers to both questions are affirmative, then the later reading should be presumed to be due to revision and admitted into the text, whether the editor himself considers it an improvement or not. It will be observed that one implication of this procedure is that a later variant that is either completely indifferent or manifestly inferior, or for the substitution of which no motive can be suggested, should be treated as fortuitous and refused admission to the text—to the scandal of faithful followers of McKerrow. I do not, of course, pretend that my procedure will lead to consistently correct results, but I think that the results, if less uniform, will be on the whole preferable to those achieved through following any mechanical rule. I am, no doubt, presupposing an editor of reasonable competence; but if an editor is really incompetent, I doubt whether it much matters what procedure he adopts: he may indeed do less harm with some than with others, he will do little good with any. And in any case, I consider

---

22. I mean substantive variation, such as occurs in all but the most faithful reprints.

that it would be disastrous to curb the liberty of competent editors in the hope of preventing fools from behaving after their kind.

I will give one illustration of the procedure in operation, taken again from Jonson's *Masque of Gipsies*, a work that is known to have been extensively revised for a later performance. At one point the text of the original version runs as follows,

> a wise Gypsie . . . is as politicke a piece of Flesh, as most Iustices in the County where he maunds

whereas the texts of the revised version replace *maunds* by *stalkes*. Now, *maund* is a recognized canting term meaning to beg, and there is not the least doubt that it is what Jonson originally wrote. Further, it might well be argued that it is less likely that he should have displaced it in revision by a comparatively common-place alternative, than that a scribe should have altered a rather unusual word that he failed to understand—just as we know that, in a line already quoted (p. 144, this volume), a scribe altered *flirted* to *blewe*. I should myself incline to this view were it not that at another point Jonson in revision added the lines,

> And then ye may stalke
> The *Gypsies* walke

where *stalk*, in the sense of going stealthily, is used almost as a technical term. In view of this I do not think it unreasonable to suppose that Jonson himself substituted *stalkes* for *maunds* from a desire to avoid the implication that his aristocratic Gipsies were beggars, and I conclude that it must be allowed to pass as (at least possibly) a correction, though no reasonable critic would *prefer* it to the original.

With McKerrow's view that in all normal cases of correction or revision the original edition should still be taken as the copy-text, I am in complete agreement. But not all cases are normal, as McKerrow himself recognized. While advocating, in the passage already quoted (p. 141, this volume), that the earliest 'good' edition should be taken as copy-text and corrections incorporated in it, he added the proviso, 'unless we could show that the [revised] edition in question (or the copy from which it had been printed) had been gone over and corrected *throughout* by' the author (my italics). This proviso is not in fact very explicit, but it clearly assumes that there are (or at least may be) cases in which an editor would be justified in taking a revised reprint as his copy-text, and it may be worth inquiring what these supposed cases are. If a work has been entirely rewritten, and is printed from a new manuscript, the question does not arise, since the revised edition will be a substantive one, and as such will presumably be chosen by the editor as his copy-text. But short of this, an author, wishing to make corrections or alterations in his work, may not merely hand the printer a revised copy of an earlier edition, but himself supervise the printing of the new edition and correct the proofs as the sheets go through the press. In such a case it may be argued that even though the earlier edition, if printed from his own manuscript, will preserve the author's individual peculiarities more faithfully than the revised reprint, he must nevertheless be assumed to have taken responsibility for the latter in respect of accidentals no less than substantive readings, and that it is therefore the revised reprint that should be taken as copy-text.

The classical example is afforded by the plays in the 1616 folio of Ben Jonson's Works. In this it appears that even the largely recast *Every Man in his Humour* was not set up from an independent manuscript but from a much corrected copy of the quarto of 1601. That Jonson revised the proofs of the folio has indeed been disputed, but Simpson is most likely correct in supposing that he did so, and he was almost certainly responsible for the numerous corrections made while the sheets were in process of printing. Simpson's consequent decision to take the folio for his copy-text for the plays it contains will doubtless be approved by most critics. I at least have no wish to dispute his choice.[23] Only I would point out—and here I think Dr. Simpson would agree with me—that even in

23. Simpson's procedure in taking the 1616 folio as copy-text in the case of most of the masques included, although he admits that in their case Jonson cannot be supposed to have supervised the printing, is much more questionable.

this case the procedure involves some sacrifice of individuality. For example, I notice that in the text of *Sejanus* as printed by him there are twenty-eight instances of the Jonsonian 'Apostrophus' (an apostrophe indicating the elision of a vowel that is nevertheless retained in printing) but of these only half actually appear in the folio, the rest he has introduced from the quarto. This amounts to an admission that in some respects at least the quarto preserves the formal aspect of the author's original more faithfully than the folio.

The fact is that cases of revision differ so greatly in circumstances and character that it seems impossible to lay down any hard and fast rule as to when an editor should take the original edition as his copy-text and when the revised reprint. All that can be said is that if the original be selected, then the author's corrections must be incorporated; and that if the reprint be selected, then the original reading must be restored when that of the reprint is due to unauthorized variation. Thus the editor cannot escape the responsibility of distinguishing to the best of his ability between the two categories. No juggling with copy-text will relieve him of the duty and necessity of exercizing his own judgement.

In conclusion I should like to examine this problem of revision and copy-text a little closer. In the case of a work like *Sejanus*, in which correction or revision has been slight, it would obviously be possible to take the quarto as the copy-text and introduce into it whatever authoritative alterations the folio may supply; and indeed, were one editing the play independently, this would be the natural course to pursue. But a text like that of *Every Man in his Humour* presents an entirely different problem. In the folio revision and reproduction are so blended that it would seem impossible to disentangle intentional from what may be fortuitous variation, and injudicious to make the attempt. An editor of the revised version has no choice but to take the folio as his copy-text. It would appear therefore that a reprint may in practice be forced upon an editor as copy-text by the nature of the revision itself, quite apart from the question whether or not the author exercized any supervision over its printing.

This has a bearing upon another class of texts, in which a reprint was revised, not by the author, but through comparison with some more authoritative manuscript. Instances are Shakespeare's *Richard III* and *King Lear*. Of both much the best text is supplied by the folio of 1623; but this is not a substantive text, but one set up from a copy of an earlier quarto that had been extensively corrected by collation with a manuscript preserved in the playhouse. So great and so detailed appears to have been the revision that it would be an almost impossible task to distinguish between variation due to the corrector and that due to the compositor,[24] and an editor has no choice but to take the folio as copy-text. Indeed, this would in any case be incumbent upon him for a different reason for the folio texts are in some parts connected by transcriptional continuity with the author's manuscript, whereas the quartos contain only reported texts, whose accidental characteristics can be of no authority whatever. At the same time, analogy with *Every Man in his Humour* suggests that even had the quartos of *Richard III* and *King Lear* possessed higher authority than in fact they do, the choice of copy-text must yet have been the same.

I began this discussion in the hope of clearing my own mind as well as others' on a rather obscure though not unimportant matter of editorial practice. I have done something to sort out my own ideas: others must judge for themselves. If they disagree, it is up to them to maintain some different point of view. My desire is rather to provoke discussion than to lay down the law.

---

24. Some variation is certainly due to error on the part of the folio printer, and this it is of course the business of an editor to detect and correct so far as he is able.

The Aesthetics of Textual Criticism[†]

James Thorpe

MANY PEOPLE ON occasion prefer a textual error to an authentic reading. One mistake by a compositor of Melville's *White-Jacket*—setting "soiled fish of the sea" instead of "coiled fish of the sea"—achieved an adventitious fame some years ago. Various readers have since declared themselves in favor of the error, on the grounds that "soiled fish" makes a richer, more interesting passage than the ordinary "coiled fish of the sea." In short, the error seems to them to create a better work.

The preference for one reading over another, the basic decision of textual criticism, is in this case being made on what are called aesthetic grounds. And the decision is made despite demonstrable proof that the preferred reading is a compositorial mistake. Most bibliographers, editors, and textual critics would at this point join in a chorus of denunciation of the person so ill-advised as to make such a preposterous decision.

On what grounds shall we decide which party to join? Does the wretch who hugs the error deserve denunciation because he decided on aesthetic rather than textual grounds? Because he put out the palace fire in Lilliput by improper means? Because we mistrust his taste? Because we fear lest the taste of any individual become the norm? Or because he contumaciously refused to prefer what the author wrote?

On the other hand, suppose we side with the man who chose the error. What is our reason? As a vote for value in a topsy-turvy world in

† "The Aesthetics of Textual Criticism," from *PMLA* 80.5 (December 1965): 465–82. Reprinted by permission of the Modern Language Association.

which the worse is so often preferred? As a protest against those vile mechanics, the textual bibliographers, who claim that their findings alone are logical, scientific, and irrefutable because they involve infinite pains? As a forthright preference for the best work of art?

Some choose one way and some the other. A recent writer has suggested a rearrangement of Ben Jonson's eulogy on Shakespeare by transferring lines 51–54 to a point ten lines before the place that Jonson chose to put them. The passage "would seem less awkward following the lines just quoted than where it actually occurs." The transposed passage "forms with the lines preceding and succeeding it, a perfectly coherent unit." In short, "I think," the writer says, "a good case can be made that the change is an improvement."[1] The case rests on the greater literary merit of the resulting passage. The first flowering of William Empson's genius as an anatomist of language, his *Seven Types of Ambiguity*, included discussions of several passages in which he found the authorial readings inferior to revisions which he could make. In Rupert Brooke's line about "The keen / Unpassioned beauty of a great machine," he considered "unpassioned" as "prosaic and intellectually shoddy" in comparison with his own word, "impassioned," which provided a daring and successful image. Similarly, his high evaluation of the playful dignity and rhythm of the line "Queenlily June with a rose in her hair" depended on his misreading the first word as "Queen Lily" rather than as an adverb, which made the line (he thought) ebb away "into complacence and monotony."[2]

On the other hand, writers have suggested changes which resulted, they thought, in a text of less literary merit. In his edition of Shakespeare, Samuel Johnson replaced the passage in *Hamlet* which editors had been printing as "In private to inter him" with the original reading "In hugger mugger to inter him," which had apparently been considered inelegant. "That the words now replaced are better," Johnson observed,

1. Wesley Trimpi, *Ben Jonson's Poems: A Study of the Plain Style* (Stanford, 1962), p. 151.

2. London, 1930, pp. 260–261, 83; see also p. 34. These examples were retained in the revised edition (London, 1947).

"I do not undertake to prove: it is sufficient that they are *Shakespeare's.*"
He went on to give his rationale for retaining the authorial reading in
the face of a possible improvement. "If phraseology is to be changed as
words grow uncouth by disuse, or gross by vulgarity, the history of every
language will be lost; we shall no longer have the words of any authour;
and, as these alterations will be often unskilfully made, we shall in time
have very little of his meaning."[3] In wanting to conserve the past, his
argument is basically historical.

Thus the choice in these cases seems to between the better word and
the words of the author. Such a choice was not likely to arise under an
earlier view of textual study which assumed that the authorial version
was always the "best" reading. If the power of a divine afflatus enabled
the poet to create, he could hardly be improved upon. Shelley, for example, maintained in "A Defence of Poetry" that "poetry is indeed something divine" and that verse is "the echo of the eternal music." George
Lyman Kittredge was horrified by the notion "that prompters and
proofreaders can (or could) improve Shakespeare."[4] With a less romantic
view of the act of artistic creation, one can face this possibility with
equanimity: if you happen to believe that the compositor improved on
Melville, the Great Chain of Being is not endangered.

Whether our preference lights on the better word or on the words of
the author, and whatever reason we give for our decision, we have done
more than make one elementary choice. For all textual decisions have an
aesthetic basis or are built on an aesthetic assumption, and it is idle to try to
dissociate textual grounds from aesthetic grounds as the reason for our
choice. Consequently, to make one kind of textual decision is to commit
oneself, in principle at least, to a whole series of related decisions. Before
we realize what we have done, we may have decided who should be called
the author of MacLeish's *J. B.,* whether the eighteenth-century emendations to *Comus* deserve to be incorporated into the text, and which one of
the versions of Hardy's *The Return of the Native* is the "real" novel.

3. Notes to *Hamlet* (IV.iv.84 in modern editions, IV.v in Johnson's edition).

4. Ed., *The Tragedy of Hamlet* (Boston, 1939), p. viii.

Before we make our choice, it might be useful to bring into the open at least the first aesthetic assumption which lies behind textual criticism, and to expose it to scrutiny. The basic questions are no different from those which one confronts in every form of literary study, and in the course of this essay I will discuss three assumptions about the work of art, assumptions which have a controlling effect on the practice of textual criticism. The most fundamental question is this: what is the phenomenon or aesthetic object with which textual criticism properly deals? The things which can be called aesthetic objects because they are capable of arousing an aesthetic response in us are (permit me to say) of three kinds: works of chance, works of nature, and works of art. Works of chance are any objects which are formed by random activity: a painting created when a can of paint is tipped over by the vibration of an electric fan and spills onto a canvas; a poem formed by combining an entry (selected by a throw of dice) in each column of a dictionary; a musical composition made by recording the sounds of traffic at a busy intersection; a sculpture consisting of a wastepaper basket into which an office worker has tossed the envelopes which brought the day's mail. Works of nature are any objects or effects which are formed by natural phenomena: a changing pattern of cumulus clouds against a blue sky, the sound of the wind whistling through the boughs of a tree, the smell of the blossoms of Viburnum carlesii. Since language is a human invention and not a natural phenomenon, literary works cannot by definition be works of nature. Works of art are any objects created by human agency for the purpose of arousing an aesthetic response. These are the works which satisfy our conventional ideas of the painting, the sculpture, the symphony, the poem, the play, the novel. Since the work of art is an intended aesthetic object, the idea of either a random or a natural work of art is self-contradictory. Human intelligence was purposefully engaged in the creation of the work of art, but it may not have been successful; the term "work of art" is thus descriptive rather than evaluative, and it includes failures as well as successes. The language of the literary work, whether judged a success or a failure, is a fulfillment of the author's intentions.

Having pushed all aesthetic objects into these three rooms, we cannot, however, very properly slam the doors and go on our way rejoicing. For every thing is an aesthetic object for somebody. The complex organization of some human beings will respond in aesthetic experience to the stimulus of any object, particularly if its usual scale is altered or its ordinary context is displaced. Moreover, memory stands ready, on the least hint, to supply the substance for aesthetic response. A classified ad describing a cottage for sale in Florida, with the beach on one side and an orange grove on the other, may create a response which is indistinguishable from that which derives from Marlowe's "Passionate Shepherd to His Love"; for a melancholic reader, however, the ad may be the poor man's "Dover Beach." Likewise, a random pile of beer cans may arouse a response similar to a sculpture, and so forth. These facts make the situation complicated, but we cannot simplify it by saying that people do not or should not have aesthetic experiences from such objects, or that they are all mad if they do; they do in fact have such experiences, and the invocation of madness may in these cases be the last defence of a bewildered man. Moreover, these examples do not represent clear types; there are innumerable objects which may be responded to as sculpture between the pile of beer cans on the one hand and the Pietà of Michelangelo on the other, and there is no convenient line that can be drawn which marks the limit of where the "normal" person "should" make an aesthetic response. It took "the wise men of the society of Salomon's House," in Bacon's *New Atlantis*, to be able "to discern (as far as appertaineth to the generations of men) between divine miracles, works of nature, works of art, and impostures and illusions of all sorts."

The problems of criticism become immense, even intolerable, if every object must be taken seriously as a potential source of aesthetic experience, if criticism is invited to preside over all creation. So, in self-defence, we are always on the lookout for ways to cut the area of responsibility but never in search of less authority. In the last generation or two, one tendency in criticism has been to limit attention to the aesthetic object and to move away from the complex problems associated with the artist as unpredictable personality. We have been taught, by the

French Symbolists and their followers at second and third hand, that the intentions of the artist are not to be trusted, that the intentions of the work of art are all-important, and that the task of the reader or critic is to understand the intentions of the work of art. Paul Valéry put the case sharply: "*There is no true meaning to a text*—no author's authority. Whatever he may have *wanted to say,* he has written what he has written. Once published, a text is like an apparatus that anyone may use as he will and according to his ability: it is not certain that the one who constructed it can use it better than another. Besides, if he knows well what he meant to do, this knowledge always disturbs his perception of what he has done."[5]

Though one may not like to think of art as gymnastic apparatus on which to exercise, the focus on the work of art seems manifestly sound as a way of trying to understand its intentions and its meaning. However, two secondary effects present themselves. First, we may be suspicious of anything that can be called authorial intention, for fear of committing the "intentional fallacy." Thus the authority of the author over the words which make up the text he wrote is subtly undermined by confusing it with the authority of the author over the meaning of his text. While the author cannot dictate the meaning of the text, he certainly has final authority over which words constitute the text of his literary work.

The other secondary effect is that of overturning the distinction between the aesthetic object (the genus) and the work of art (a species), of thinking that all automobiles are Fords. The fact that it generates an aesthetic response does not mean that it is a work of art. These two effects are interconnected, of course, at least under the definition I have given for the work of art, as an object created by human agency with the intention of arousing an aesthetic response. If the element of intention is minimized, the work of art tends to blend into, and be indistinguishable from, works of chance and works of nature. Indeed, these distinctions seem less important and less useful if commerce is restricted to the

5. "Concerning *Le Cimetière marin*" (1933), in Paul Valéry, *The Art of Poetry* (New York, 1958), p. 152.

aesthetic object and to the general aesthetic response of the individual. The loss of these distinctions, however, leads to confusion and (ultimately) to abandoning conceptual thinking about works of art.

The difficulties which arise from these confusions are not merely visions of theoretical possibilities or of the ineluctable deviations from ideal purity. In every art one can point to aesthetic objects which in fact blend art, chance, and nature to a significant degree. Indeterminate music, for example, combines art and chance. The composer supplies blocks of music for the performers, who are to play the sections in whatever order they fancy on a given occasion; thus the composer incorporates in the work itself a variable governed by random chance. Examples of aesthetic objects which are not primarily works of art can be multiplied: the paintings of Beauty, the chimpanzee at the Cincinnati Zoo, for whose works there has been a ready commercial market; "happenings," or unstructured episodes with characters; self-destroying machines, which are designed to follow an unpredetermined course in destroying themselves. Let me say again that each of these examples will be the occasion for aesthetic response on the part of some people, perhaps a few and perhaps a great many, and no amount of laughing at them, of saying that they are being duped by frauds, will alter the fact that they are responding to aesthetic objects.

In the literary line, there are various current examples of aesthetic objects which depend on chance. The "novel" by Marc Saporta entitled *Composition No. 1,* published by Simon and Schuster in 1963, consists of loose printed pages which are to be shuffled before reading. Many poems have been written by computer. These examples may sound familiar in their resemblance to the language frame described in the Academy of Projectors in *Gulliver's Travels*. That engine was actually a device to insure a random arrangement of words. All of the words in the language had been written on pieces of paper which were pasted on all the sides of bits of wood, which were linked together by wires. This device, twenty feet square, had forty iron handles on the sides which could be used to shake the frame and thus change the words which showed. Any groups of words which made part of a sentence were written into a book, and a rearrangement of those broken sentences was to produce the body of all arts and sciences. Swift's machine was a satire on modern learning; we are taking similar experiments in wise passiveness, perhaps because we are not sure of our grounds for responding otherwise.

The question of importance that these distinctions about aesthetic objects raise is whether criticism can deal with works of chance and nature as well as with works of art. I think that it can, but in very much more limited ways. It can give an account of affective qualities, and these reports may range from crude impressionism to elaborate psychological inquiry. It cannot ordinarily deal with those features on which criticism is most useful, matters of genre, tradition, and convention, without giving vent to a large amount of foolishness. Since textual criticism cannot traffic in works of nature, we need only distinguish between the kinds of authority it can have in dealing with works of chance and works of art. It is of course possible to establish a set of principles by which textual criticism could be applied to works of chance. In view of the random element in all works of chance, however, it is evident that an irrational variable of indefinite importance would always have to be included in the textual principles. Thus the operation of those principles would in the long run be little better than guess-work, and the results of a textual criticism established for works of chance would be about like pinning the tail on the donkey without peeking.

Let us return for a moment to the question of choosing between the "soiled fish of the sea" (the compositorial error) and the "coiled fish of the sea" (the authorial reading). What should our decision now be? Obviously we should choose the one which better fulfills our purposes. If we want to maximize our aesthetic experience by getting the biggest return from our attention, we are free to choose whichever reading satisfies that condition—with the error just as valid a choice as the authorial reading. Those readers who prefer the error—which is a simple example of a work of chance—can thus find perfectly logical grounds for their choice. It is a choice which repudiates the value of differentiating among classes of aesthetic objects, however, and the consistent application of it will, consequently, aid self-gratification on non-intellectual grounds. On the other hand, critics whose prime aesthetic interest is at that moment in works of art must choose the authorial reading whether they think it better or worse. Their main concern is to understand the literary production as a work of art, as an order of words created by the author; they cannot permit their attention to be pre-empted by any auxiliary effects, and they cannot properly set up in business as connoisseurs of all human experience. I certainly do not mean to suggest, however, that people should in general limit their aesthetic experience to works of art; it would be a sadly reduced world if we went about avoiding sunsets and other innocent forms of beauty. Only this: although one person may from time to time enjoy aesthetic experience from a wide variety of sources, he is not in a position to deal with works of nature and works of chance in his role as a textual critic; he is left, then, with literary works of art as the sole practicable subject for textual criticism.

II

Emily Dickinson's poem "I taste a liquor never brewed" was first printed, in May 1861, in the Springfield *Daily Republican*. The first stanza there reads as follows:

> I taste a liquor never brewed,
> From tankards scooped in pearl;
> Not Frankfort berries yield the sense
> Such a delicious whirl.

That was not, however, precisely what she had written. Her stanza had been more forthright and less delicate:

> I taste a liquor never brewed—
> From Tankards scooped in Pearl—
> Not all the Frankfort Berries
> Yield such an Alcohol!

The editor of the *Daily Republican* apparently thought that the stanza deserved a rhyme; he may well, like any sensible man, have objected to the logic of the third line. The version which he printed was a new stanza, produced under that power reserved by the editor to correct rhymes and alter figures of speech; he thought it (I feel sure) a notable improvement over Emily's crude work. Emily Dickinson was not at the time averse to publication; but she was, in the words of her distinguished modern editor, Thomas H. Johnson, concerned "how one can publish and at the same time preserve the integrity of one's art."[6] This is a topic which can lead into the central question, even paradox, relating to the creation of the work of art: whose intentions are being fulfilled, who can be properly called the author? The obvious answer in the present case— Emily Dickinson—is true enough, and it will serve perfectly for the manuscripts of those poems which she did not communicate to anyone. But once works of art are performed—even in elementary bardic song, or on the stage, or by a reader from copies reproduced from the author's inscription—then complex questions begin in time to arise.

In examining the nature of authorship, I am trying to inquire into what constitutes the integrity of the work of art. Whatever it is, it is apparently something which various classes of persons either do not respect or else define with such latitude that it includes their own efforts. On many magazines, for example, the editorial practice has been to alter the author's text to suit the policy or need of the magazine while retaining the author's name. The author is a tradesman, his work is a commodity which can be made more or less vendible, and the magazine is in a more favored position in the commercial hierarchy than is the author. A multitude of examples of the results can be gleaned from the pages of Frank Luther Mott's study of American magazines. When A. J. H. Duganne refused to furnish further chapters for his serial story, *The Atheist,* the editor of *Holden's* simply wrote the final chapters himself; Emerson's peculiarities were edited out of his contributions to the *Dial.*[7]

6. *The Poems of Emily Dickinson* (Cambridge, Mass., 1955), I, xxvi.

7. *A History of American Magazines 1741–1850* (New York, 1930), p. 504.

William Dean Howells acted the part of an "academic taskmaster freely blue-penciling the essays of his unhappy pupils," and he said that his proofreading "sometimes well-nigh took the character of original work, in that liberal *Atlantic* tradition of bettering the authors by editorial transposition and paraphrase, either in the form of suggestion or of absolute correction"; James Russell Lowell (the second president of the Modern Language Association) wrote to a contributor to the *North American Review* that "I shall take the liberty to make a verbal change here and there, such as I am sure you would agree to could we talk the matter over. I think, for example, you speak rather too well of young Lytton, whom I regard as both an imposter and as an antinomian heretic. Swinburne I must modify a little, as you will see, to make the *Review* consistent with itself. But you need not be afraid of not knowing your own child again."[8] Edward Bok, the editor of the *Ladies' Home Journal,* once deleted a substantial portion of a story by Mark Twain; and the editor of *Collier's* modified a story by Julian Hawthorne about a seduced maiden by inserting a secret marriage and legitimizing the child.[9] When extracts from *Huckleberry Finn* were printed in the *Century Magazine,* they were carefully altered by Richard Watson Gilder, the editor, with Twain's full consent, even though they had already been pruned both by Mrs. Clemens and by William Dean Howells; Gilder excised about a fifth of the extracts, including descriptive passages and those which (like "to be in a sweat") he thought too coarse or vulgar for his audience.[10] Examples could be multiplied indefinitely. Sometimes the editor is a famous man of letters and the author a hack, and sometimes it is the other way around; sometimes a change seems to later critics to have been improvement, and sometimes debasement.

The reflection on these facts might be simple were it not that when authors publish their periodical contributions in book form, they very

8. *A History of American Magazines 1865–1885* (Cambridge, Mass., 1938), p. 21.

9. *A History of American Magazines 1885–1905* (Cambridge, Mass., 1957), p. 37.

10. Arthur L. Scott, "The *Century Magazine* Edits *Huckleberry Finn,* 1884–1885," *AL,* XXVII (1955), 356–362.

frequently retain the changes which have been introduced by the editors. Thus, by inference, they validate the changes and give them some kind of authority. Nathaniel Hawthorne, for example, retained the changes, despite his objection to editorial meddling; at least, in the case of the four short stories for which the manuscript is extant, he seems not to have restored the original readings when the editors altered his text, in punctuation, spelling, capitalization, and diction.[11] Similarly, when Thomas Nelson Page's stories were collected by Scribner's, he did not re-introduce the omitted passages (about drink, religion, and horror) nor the original Negro dialect; the changes made by the editors of the *Century Magazine* were largely allowed to stand.[12] Charles Reade objected strenuously to the editorial pressure from *Blackwood's* on *The Woman Hater,* but he then used the serial text as copy for the book, with only a few inconsequential changes in phrasing.[13]

On the other hand, occasionally authors have restored their original readings in book publication. When Thomas Hardy's novels were first published in periodicals, the texts were considerably changed at the urging of editors. Sometimes the alterations were verbal, as the change from "lewd" to "gross," "loose" to "wicked," and "bawdy" to "sinful" in *Far from the Madding Crowd;* sometimes they were more substantial, as the omission of the seduction scene from *Tess of the D'Urbervilles* and the substitution of a mock marriage. When Hardy got his manuscripts ready for book publication, however, he restored nearly everything that the magazine editors had made him change.[14] But not always, even with Hardy. Many editorial changes were made in his manuscript for the first serial appearance, in the *Atlantic Monthly,* of *Two on a Tower.* This edited

11. Seymour L. Gross and Alfred J. Levy, "Some Remarks on the Extant Manuscripts of Hawthorne's Short Stories," *SB,* xiv (1961), 254–257.

12. John R. Roberson, "The Manuscript of Page's 'Marse Chan'," *SB,* ix (1957), 259–262.

13. Royal A. Gettman, "Henry James's Revision of *The American,*" *AL,* xvi (1945), 295.

14. Oscar Maurer, " 'My Squeamish Public': Some Problems of Victorian Magazine Publishers and Editors," *SB,* xii (1958), 21–40.

text then served, with few changes, as copy text for the first London edition, and the edited version has continued in all later editions of Hardy.[15]

In cases of these kinds, there is generally some uncertainty as to the interpretation to be put on the author's actions. Often we cannot be sure whether he makes suggested changes because of a compliant nature, whether he allows editorial alterations to stand in later editions out of laziness, whether he reverts to earlier readings out of pertinacity, or whether there is reasoned conviction in support of his actions. Once another hand helps to prepare a work of art for dissemination, it is usually difficult to distinguish with certainty which part is not by the author.

One of the most common kinds of intervention in the publication of books is made by the publisher's editor—the person whose job it is to read material before publication, to recommend acceptance or rejection, to "house style" the text, to query anything which seems inaccurate, ineffective, or offensive, and to make or suggest any changes which appeal to the editor as desirable. I suppose that almost every writer—even the lowly scholar—has found his deathless prose altered by a publisher's editor, who is sometimes an eminent man of letters and sometimes a mere slip of a girl barely out of college. Some authors blanch at the thought of any alteration, some accept any change gratefully as an improvement. There appears to be a perennial joke among editors of "educational" publishers that they completely re-write the books of some authors, reducing the text to half of its original length, and the authors never realize that any changes have been made.

Probably the most celebrated editor of this century was Maxwell E. Perkins of Charles Scribner's Sons, editor for Fitzgerald, Wolfe, Hemingway, and a dozen other writers of consequence. Perkins was rather reluctant to offer any specific suggestions to authors except about legal or libellous matters. Frequently he sent long letters or memoranda of advice to "his" authors about their manuscripts; but his suggestions were general and undemanding. He was like a kindly parent, proud of his children, always

15. Carl J. Weber, "The Manuscript of Hardy's *Two on a Tower*," *PBSA*, XL (1946), 1–21.

encouraging them to fulfill their potentialities, ready to offer a guiding hand in time of need. It was only when an author called for help that he would be party to the making of important changes in a manuscript. The most significant revisions he ever made, presumably, were his extensive cuts in Wolfe's first two manuscripts, trying to bring order out of chaos.[16] The cuts were apparently made by Perkins with Wolfe's acquiescence, and they reduced *Look Homeward, Angel* (for example) by thirty percent.[17] To mention only one more of an almost unlimited number of instances, Theodore Dreiser had the advantage—however unlikely it seems—of several editors, notably Louise Campbell. She acted as literary assistant, revised eight of his books while preparing them for publication, and even wrote character sketches for publication under his name in *Esquire*.[18] What is called ghost writing, however, goes a little beyond the usual requirements of editing.[19]

Then there are some books the final form of which (it would be accurate to say) are not so much written as constructed. Mark Twain, for example, left *The Mysterious Stranger* unfinished; Albert Bigelow Paine put it together somewhat arbitrarily and added a last chapter found separately among the author's papers. Bernard de Fallois reconstructed Marcel Proust's *Jean Santeuil,* that first rough version of *Remembrance of Things Past,* by the use of seventy notebooks and several boxes of torn and detached pages made available to him after Proust's death by Madame Gérard Mante-Proust.[20] *More Stately Mansions* was made by Karl Ragner Gierow by shortening Eugene O'Neill's partly revised script.

16. *Editor to Author: The Letters of Maxwell E. Perkins,* ed. John Hall Wheelock (New York, 1950), pp. 171–174, 175–180, 286–294, 227–230, 98–102.

17. Francis E. Skipp, "The Editing of *Look Homeward, Angel*," *PBSA,* LVII (1963), 1–13. On the basis of analyzing the material cut, Skipp is of the opinion that the changes improved the work.

18. Robert H. Elias, rev. of *Letters to Louise: Theodore Dreiser's Letters to Louise Campbell* (Philadelphia, 1959), *AL,* XXXIII (1961), 90–91.

19. For an interesting account by a noted editor (of O'Neill and Faulkner, for example) who had been a prolific ghost writer, see Saxe Commins, "Confessions of a Ghost," *PULC,* XXII (1960), 26–35.

20. Marcel Proust, *Jean Santeuil* (London, 1955), pp. ix, xxi–xxii.

Editors play an important role in the production of magazines and books, and they are often responsible for changes in the author's text. I am not trying to say whether these changes are or are not improvements, whether they are made willingly or reluctantly by the author, whether there should or should not be editors—only that textual changes for which an editor is responsible do in fact take place, frequently and regularly.

This editorial activity results in the embodiment of the editor's intentions in the work of art. In a complex way, the integrity of the work of art is thereby, in some measure, the effect of a juncture of intentions. Another major entanglement, this one mainly accidental in nature, occurs in the translation of the text from authorial to public form—the physical process of turning the author's dictated or typed or handwritten copy into print or (in earlier times) into scribal manuscript form. To speak only of printing, I suppose it is true to say that few if any books of any size have ever been printed without mistakes, even that "No book is completed until *Error* has crept in & affixed his sly Imprimatur." The usual assumption is that every printed book includes many errors, and it is easy to see why this must be: a page of type may contain from one to five thousand characters; there is only one way of getting each of them right, and many ways of getting each one wrong. No matter how experienced the compositor, he will make changes, the proofreader will fail to notice some of them, and every change is an error. The editors of the Centenary Hawthorne have sought to minimize this state of nature by having *all* proofs "read at least five times and by three or more editors."[21]

Proofreading by authors was not usual before the eighteenth century; indeed, early proofreading normally consisted of a reading (by the master printer or his assistant) of one of the first sheets printed off, without recourse to the copy, and marking any apparent errors for correction; in the meantime, of course, a certain number of uncorrected sheets would have already been printed. The fact that proof sheets were

21. *The Scarlet Letter* (Columbus, Ohio, 1962), p. xlvii.

later run off, and given to the author for correction, is certainly no guarantee that all the mistakes were caught. Careless proofreading is not uncommon, and writers differ in their interest and skill in handling such details. It has been said that F. Scott Fitzgerald's *This Side of Paradise* is an "inexcusably sloppy job, and that the blame must be distributed between author and publisher"; the first edition contained a large number of misspellings, inconsistencies, and other examples of carelessness which neither the author nor the publisher corrected—indeed, some of the errors noted by the reviewers in 1920 have not yet been corrected.[22] Even when the author and publisher both take care, there are still errors. Sinclair Lewis, for example, wrote as follows to his publisher after he had seen a list of errors and inconsistencies observed by Mr. Louis Feipel in the published version of *Babbitt:* "J. Henry! This man Feipel is a wonder—to catch all these after rather unusually careful proofreading not only by myself and my wife but also by two or three professionals!"[23] Sometimes misprints become, in effect, a permanent part of the text.[24]

Sometimes an author prefers the mistakes to his own work. Richard Ellmann has described such a preference on the part of James Joyce. It occurred while Joyce was dictating *Finnegans Wake* to Samuel Beckett. "There was a knock on the door and Joyce said, 'Come in.' Beckett, who hadn't heard the knock, by mistake wrote down 'Come in' as part of the dictated text. Afterwards he read it back to Joyce who said, 'What's that "Come in"?' 'That's what you dictated,' Beckett replied. Joyce thought for a moment, realizing that Beckett hadn't heard the knock; then he said, 'Let it stand'."[25]

22. Matthew J. Bruccoli, "A Collation of F. Scott Fitzgerald's *This Side of Paradise,*" *SB,* IX (1957), 263–265.

23. Matthew J. Bruccoli, "Textual Variants in Sinclair Lewis's *Babbitt,*" *SB,* XI (1958), 263–268.

24. M. R. Ridley, "The Perpetuated Misprint," *TLS,* 28 August 1959, p. 495.

25. "The Backgrounds of *Ulysses,*" *KR,* XVI (1954), 359–360. I have heard it said that Joyce retained some of the printer's errors in *Ulysses* because he preferred them to what he had written, but I have been unable to find any evidence for this claim.

Perhaps the play is the form of literary art in which the principles associated with the integrity of the work and the identity of the author are most visible. If the playwright wants his play to find its way onto the stage, he must accommodate his text to the financial claims of the producer, the presentational claims of the director and actors, and the undefined claims of the theatre-going public. William Gibson has given a detailed account of his struggles in revising and re-writing *Two for the Seesaw*. From the time that the first draft was completed until it opened in New York, Gibson re-wrote the entire play several times and re-cast some parts of it as many as five times. These changes were made in trying to meet objections and accommodate the text to the various claims made on it. For example, the male star did not like the character which he was to portray, and the changes made for his benefit covered a wide range: from the deletion of those speeches in which the character talked aloud to himself (since the actor "personally did not talk aloud to himself") all the way to the assurance that he would not "go onstage with one line unrewritten that he felt uncomfortable or untruthful with."

Gibson came to feel that the play as it was produced was not quite his: his collaborators had made a new play. It was a successful play, one which was (he thought) much better and more effective because of the revisions which had been forced on the writer. But not quite his. He told of visiting the studio of a painter and envying her because "she was working in a medium where she alone could ruin it. This seemed to me a definition of art." When Gibson turned over a text to his publisher, he could not bear to put his name to the final version: so he rewrote once more, using much of the stage version, restoring much of what had been surrendered, writing new bits, and ending with a composite of several versions.[26]

The rewriting of plays to meet the demands of performance has for some time been typical of theatrical practice. Oscar Wilde, for example, wrote "The Importance of Being Earnest" as a four-act play, and he did not submit it until it had passed through three stages of composition;

26. William Gibson, *The Seesaw Log: A Chronicle of the Stage Production, with the Text, of "Two for the Seesaw"* (New York, 1959), pp. 32, 37, 101, 43, 140.

when Sir George Alexander (the manager of St. James's Theatre) told him to re-cast it into three acts and to reduce the length in order to allow time for a curtain raiser, Wilde complied. It is only a few writers of strong will, fierce independence, and eminence—such as G. B. Shaw and Eugene O'Neill—who have been able to see their work performed in accordance with their own intentions, and they have had to fight for their convictions.[27] For the most part, Moss Hart's description in *Act One* (New York, 1959) of the birth of *Once in a Lifetime* is more characteristic: throughout rehearsals and try-outs the author is busily engaged in re-writing the text, adjusting it to the realities of performance, trying to make it into a show which will be a public success.

This process is by no means limited to the work of commercial experts. The conversion of Archibald MacLeish's *J. B.* is an instructive—if rather sad—example. MacLeish spent four years writing the play, which was published by Houghton Mifflin in book form in March 1958 and produced in the Yale University Theatre the next month. Alfred de Liagre, Jr., bought the play, engaged Elia Kazan as director, and brought Kazan and MacLeish together. Kazan thought the play "needed important changes for professional production," gave detailed directions, and MacLeish enthusiastically agreed. The story of the revision of the play, from July through December 1958, is one filled with demands for changes by Kazan and agreement by MacLeish. "You are right to want something from Nickles at the end of Act I," says MacLeish. "Hell, you are always right. Why should I mention it? Here is what I propose." After the Washington opening, Kazan told MacLeish that the play needed a "recognition scene," and he outlined where and why it should take place. MacLeish agreed, and in two days supplied the scene.[28]

It appears likely that the production of plays has always occasioned

---

27. "Often the rehearsals of an O'Neill play would degenerate into a series of running battles between the playwright and the producer, the director, and the actors. Invariably, O'Neill was able to stand his ground against them all." Croswell Bowen, "Rehearsing *The Iceman Cometh*," in *O'Neill and His Plays: Four Decades of Criticism,* ed. Oscar Cargill and others (New York, 1961), p. 460.

28. "The Staging of a Play," *Esquire,* LI (May 1959), 144–158.

considerable modification of the text. Undoubtedly a few dramatists at any given time have been able to stand their ground in the running battle with actors, directors, producers, and public; but usually the writer seems to have thought of his words as variable in the process of converting a text to a finished performance.[29] Thus there are, in theory at least and often in practice, two or more versions of every produced play. In Elizabethan times, the author's foul papers represent a non-produced version and the prompt book a produced version.[30] For *J. B.*, the Houghton Mifflin edition (1958) is a non-produced version, while a produced version was printed in *Theatre Arts* (February 1960) and by Samuel French, Inc.; the versions are naturally different.

In dramatic performances, collaboration on the text is greater as the non-verbal effects become more important. In a musical, for example, the author is less in control of his text than in a play, while in a musical revue the identical show is not usually repeated for two performances in succession. In the production of movies, the writer ordinarily has little control over his text, must supply changes upon demand, and may be properly listed in the credits among the chief cameraman, electrician, and sound man. In the production of "Cleopatra" (released by Twentieth Century Fox in 1963), the valuable properties were the female star and the assigna-

29. There is considerable evidence in Shakespeare's plays, for example, of revision for production. "All of the texts of the First Folio of 1623 for which there are documents for comparison show stage alteration in varying degrees, and in that fact there is a proof of the universality of stage influence on acted plays. . . . One may say that stage alteration appears in all plays that have been acted on the stage." Hardin Craig, "Textual Degeneration of Elizabethan and Stuart Plays: An Examination of Plays in Manuscript," *Rice Institute Pamphlets*, Vol. XLVI, No. 4 (1960), p. 74. See also Craig's *A New Look at Shakespeare's Quartos* (Stanford, 1961).

30. A vast amount of modern Shakespearean scholarship has been concerned with trying to infer which of these was the basis for the first printed edition of a given play. There seems to be a tacit assumption among some scholars that the earliest editors of Shakespeare were most interested in printing the words that he wrote. Alice Walker (with whom one fears to disagree) believes that Heminge and Condell "may have known that the *Lear* prompt-book better represented what Shakespeare wrote than the *Hamlet* prompt-book" (*Textual Problems of the First Folio,* Cambridge, Eng., 1953, p. 136). It seems a more plausible assumption that men of the theatre like Heminge and Condell would (unlike many modern scholars) have preferred the text which better represented the play in a good production.

tional publicity, not the text. Three distinguished writers were successively employed to provide a scenario, and most of their work was scrapped.

It can be claimed that nearly every person involved in the transmission of literary works helps, in some sense, to shape the effect that a work will have on a reader. The designer, for example, can in some measure make the experience of reading the book a little more pleasant or easy or irritating by the appropriateness of the format, paper, binding, font and size of type. His work is not usually observed consciously. In order to realize something of the range of his effect, however, one has only to imagine reading *Tom Jones* in black letter throughout, on coated art paper, with the sheets printed alternately in red and black, in a tight binding with no inner margin, with illustrations by Willem de Kooning. On the other hand, influences which shape the intentions of the artist are sometimes advantageous. Few regret, I suppose, that James T. Fields (the publisher) was successful in persuading Hawthorne to make *The Scarlet Letter* into a full-length novel rather than finishing it (as Hawthorne had planned) as a long story for publication with half a dozen shorter ones.

So far, this discussion about the integrity of the work of art has emphasized its creation and the agents who are then at work in modifying the intentions of the artist. In fact, the work of art is also subject to alteration long afterwards. For nine plays by Euripides, the earliest manuscript—and the only one with any authority—is of the thirteenth-fourteenth centuries; thus any changes made in the text in the course of that transcription, some 1,750 years after the plays were composed, would have definitively altered the intentions of the author so far as the modern reader is concerned.

Emendation may be taken as an example of that range of editorial effort which modifies the works of the past in the hope of purging corrupt readings from them. Boswell tells of Johnson confronting him with a textual problem that required an emendation for its solution. "On the 65 page of the first volume of Sir George Mackenzie's folio edition, Mr. Johnson pointed out a paragraph beginning with *Aristotle*, and told me there was an error in the text which he bid me try to discover. I hit it at once. It stands that the devil answers *even* in *engines*. I corrected it to *ever* in *enigmas*. 'Sir,' said he, 'you're a good critic. This would have been a great thing to do in the text of an ancient author'."[31] Boswell here casts himself in the role of the clever schoolboy responding to the questions of the schoolmaster, who knows all the answers. In real life, however, nobody knows the answers, and it is impossible to say "I hit it at once."

As an expression of editorial preference, emendation is the exercise of textual decision. The corrupted readings in most of the manuscripts of the authors of Greek and Latin antiquity have made their works the happy hunting ground for ingenious editors. Since any plausible reading is preferred to one which is obviously corrupt, and since there is usually no way to validate conjectural emendations beyond the tests of meter and sense, our received texts are peppered with editorial guesses which have silently become indistinguishable from what textual scholars have agreed to consider the author's intentions.

This process of reconstruction by emendation has by no means been limited to writers of classical antiquity. Even such newcomers as English and American authors have also had these benefits conferred on them. The emendations suggested by some eighteenth-century editors and critics to two lines in Milton are instructive. In the 1645 edition of Milton's *Poems,* lines 631–635 of *Comus* (the beginning of the "Haemony" passage) appear as follows:

> The leaf was darkish, and had prickles on it,
>
> But in another Countrey, as he said,
>
> Bore a bright golden flowre, but not in this soyl:
>
> Unknown, and like esteem'd, and the dull swayn
>
> Treads on it daily with his clouted shoon. . . .

31. *Boswell's Journal of A Tour to the Hebrides With Samuel Johnson, LL.D.,* ed. Frederick A. Pottle and Charles H. Bennett (New York, 1936), p. 173. Entry for Wednesday, 15 September 1773. [James Bosewell (1740–1795) was the biographer of Samuel Johnson (1709–1784), the famous lexicographer and editor of Shakespeare (1765). Sir George Mackenzie (1638?–1691) was a lawyer and politician whose collected works were published in two large volumes, in 1718 and 1722 —*Editor.*]

It is the third and fourth of these lines that were thought to require emendation. Hurd said that "the passage before us is certainly corrupt, or, at least, inaccurate; and had better, I think, been given thus . . . 'Bore a bright golden flower, *not* in this soil / Unknown, *though light* esteem'd'." Seward proposed "*but* in this soil / Unknown and *light* esteem'd." Newton suggested that no change be made beyond the omission of either "but" or "not"; thus the reading could be "*but* in this soil / Unknown and like esteem'd" or else "*not* in this soil: / Unknown, and like esteem'd." Fenton printed "*little* esteem'd" rather than "*like* esteem'd," while Warburton proposed "*light* esteem'd" as the only change.[32] No one of these emendations is now accepted. The weight of the testimony in favor of the reading with which we began is apparently so overwhelming that no one now thinks to suggest any alternative. The same reading (minor variants in orthography and punctuation aside) is to be found in the Trinity College Manuscript (in Milton's hand), in the first (1637) edition of *Comus* (which derived from the Trinity College Manuscript), in the corrected copy of the 1637 *Comus* which Milton presented to the Earl of Bridgewater, and in the 1645 *Poems*; moreover, there is no shred of evidence elsewhere that Milton's intentions were not carried out in this passage, which he reviewed so many times while he still had his sight. Each of the editorial emendations was thus (we may conclude) a temporary substitution of the intention of the editor for that of the author.

Very frequently, emendations are made in cases where there is not enough external testimony to confirm or reject them with any feeling of confidence. Sometimes they slide into the text and become the objects of our veneration on the principle that whatever is printed is right.[33] Such is the case in an indefinite number of passages in the works of writers of the past.

32. These various emendations are recorded in the notes to Henry John Todd's edition of Milton's poetical works (London, 1801, and many later editions). The most elaborate and extensive of all unnecessary emendations to Milton were undoubtedly those made by the great classical scholar Richard Bentley in his edition of *Paradise Lost* (1732).

33. See, for example, the history of the reading "mid-May" in Keats's "The Fall of Hyperion," I. 92.

Emendation offers the appeal of a puzzle and the release of creation. "The allurements of emendation are scarcely resistible," Samuel Johnson wrote. "Conjecture has all the joy and all the pride of invention, and he that has once started a happy change, is too much delighted to consider what objections may rise against it." Johnson offered a great many emendations to Shakespeare, most of them pure guesses sanctified by the supposition that Shakespeare wrote them. Unlike many critics and readers, however, he came to be aware that his own textual conjectures were likely to be mistaken; and he believed that the best any person can do is produce one of many plausible readings. He trusted conjecture less and less, and he congratulated himself on including none of his own emendations in the plays of Shakespeare that he latterly edited.[34]

Johnson put a high value on the creative aspect of emendation. He described one change by Bishop Warburton as "a noble emendation, which almost sets the critic on a level with the author."[35] One can go further than Johnson: without praising either Warburton or the emendation, one can say that the critic who adopts an emendation of his own creation, without a genuine basis for showing it to be a recovery of what the author intended to write, has indeed become co-author of this portion of the work of art—he has in fact been set on a level with the author.

This brings us to a major point about the nature of authorship and of the integrity of the work of art. The literary work is frequently the result, in a pure sense, of composite authorship. We do not have to meddle with the unconscious, the preconscious, or the race consciousness in order to hold this view. In a quite literal sense, the literary work is often

---

34. "Preface to Shakespeare," *The Works of Samuel Johnson, LL.D.* (Oxford, 1825), v, 151, 150, 149.

35. This is the "god kissing carrion" passage in *Hamlet* "For if the sun breed maggots in a dead dog, being a god kissing carrion—Have you a daughter?" (ii.ii.181–183). The folios and quartos concur in the reading "good" which Warburton emended (without any external evidence) to "god"—a reading which has been pretty generally accepted, although W. W. Greg objected, a little primly: "It is facile and plausible, but I think unnecessary. Hamlet's fancies are not always as nice as editors would have them" (*Principles of Emendation in Shakespeare,* London, 1928, p. 68). Johnson's observation appears in his edition of Shakespeare at the conclusion of his reprinting of Warburton's note to the passage.

guided or directed or controlled by other people while the author is in the process of trying to make it take shape, and it is subject to a variety of alterations throughout its history. The intentions of the person we call the author thus become entangled with the intentions of all the others who have a stake in the outcome, which is the work of art. And yet we agree to say simply *"Two for the Seesaw,* by William Gibson." Not *"Two for the Seesaw,* by William Gibson, Henry Fonda, Fred Coe, Arthur Penn, Anne Bancroft, the elevator boy, wives, friends, and others." *"Jean Santeuil,* by Marcel Proust," not "by Marcel Proust and Bernard de Fallois." *"Look Homeward, Angel,* by Thomas Wolfe," not "by Wolfe and Perkins." *"J. B.,* by MacLeish," not "by MacLeish and Kazan." Our identification of the author is partly a convention for the sake of simplicity, partly a case of the Boss being given credit, whether he wants it or not, for all the work that the office (including volunteer workers) turns out.

Whatever complexities we agree to ignore in our daily encounters with works of art, it remains a fact that the literary work is a mingling of human intentions about which distinctions should be made. Its status as a work of art is not affected by whether these intentions all belong to the titular author; even collaborative authorship does not alter that status, however much it may endanger friendships. On the other hand, the integrity of the work of art depends very much on the work being limited to those intentions which are the author's, together with those others of which he approves or in which he acquiesces. When these intentions have been fulfilled, the work of art has its final integrity or completeness. It may be aesthetically imperfect or unfinished, and it is altogether possible that an indefinite number of people may be capable of improving it. But in the authorial sense it is already finished, it is already complete, it already has that final integrity which should be the object of the critic's chief attention. This is the final integrity which it is the business of the textual critic to identify as an order of words in fulfillment of the authorial intention, the business of the literary critic to understand as an order of words in the context of all literature.

We commenced this discussion with the question, put in the mouth of Emily Dickinson, as to how one can publish and still preserve the integrity of one's art. In a pure sense it is probably impossible, but anyone who is concerned enough to ask the question will undoubtedly realize that a good deal depends on the exercise of will: one must fulfill one's own intentions rather than the conflicting intentions of others, however valuable and well-meaning. Their desire to help is praise-worthy, and altruism is all the more appealing when it is self-effacing; but the dedication of such help to the improvement of others' works of art dissipates the integrity of those works.

III

In the conclusion to *Great Expectations*, Charles Dickens thought it necessary to have a final confrontation between the hero, Pip, and the greatest of his lost expectations, Estella. They meet casually in London. Estella has married a Shropshire doctor after the death of her first husband, the cruel Drummle. She sees Pip walk by on the street while she is sitting in her carriage. They shake hands, she wrongly assumes that the boy with him is his own child, he perceives that suffering has given her an understanding heart, and the book ends. This is the "unhappy," or at least unromantic ending; in less than three hundred words these ships pass one last time, saluting each other gravely all the while. Bulwer Lytton was dissatisfied with this ending, and at his urging Dickens wrote another. This time Estella is free: she has been a widow for two years and has not remarried. They meet, not in impersonal London, but in memory's lane itself—the site of Miss Havisham's house, where they had first met, which neither has visited for some thirteen years. A silvery mist is rising, the stars are shining, and the first rays of the moon illumine the tears that course from Estella's eyes. They are full of forgiveness for one another, and understanding; they emerge from the ruins holding hands, and there is no shadow of another parting. This is the "happy," the romantic ending, accomplished in a thousand pulsing words. The ending which you read must to some degree affect your understanding of the entire novel. Which is the real *Great Expectations*?

The collection of W. H. Auden's sonnets and verse commentary which he entitled "In Time of War" concludes with these lines:

> Till they construct at last a human justice,
> The contribution of our star, within the shadow
> Of which uplifting, loving, and constraining power
> All other reasons may rejoice and operate.

It is an eloquent plea for men of good will to join together and "construct" a "human justice" for the benefit of all mankind. So the passage appeared in its first publication in 1939, in *Journey to a War.* Within a few years Auden's ideas about the right way to attain human justice—as well as his ideas about many other subjects—had changed markedly. When he came to reprint "In Time of War" in his *Collected Poetry* of 1945, he altered the concluding passage of the commentary as follows:

> Till, as the contribution of our star, we follow
> The clear instructions of that Justice, in the shadow
> Of Whose uplifting, loving, and constraining power
> All human reasons do rejoice and operate.

Instead of constructing human justice, man is now enjoined to follow Divine Justice.[36] Which is the real "In Time of War"?

Thomas Hardy printed four different versions of *The Return of the Native,* from 1878 to 1912. Between the first and second versions he made some 700 changes (of which 40 are major revisions), between the second and third about 350 changes, and between the third and

---

36. For an account of the very numerous revisions, excisions, and eliminations which Auden silently made in preparing his text for the *Collected Poetry* (New York, 1945) and *Collected Shorter Poems* (London, 1950), see Joseph Warren Beach, *The Making of the Auden Canon* (Minneapolis, 1957); his remarks on "In Time of War" are on pp. 5–10. Auden has continued to revise: the unsuspecting reader may be surprised to discover that there is a strong possibility of a significant change in any given poem reprinted in one of the "collected" volumes.

fourth about 115. These changes substantially altered the characteriza-tion and plot. In his first manuscript version, Hardy envisioned Eustacia Vye as a literal witch, a demon; by the time he had finished his revisions, she had become a passionate, unconventional beauty with a surprisingly rigid sense of morality. An example of the change in plot may be found in Eustacia's plan to run away from her husband, Clym Yeobright. In the early versions, her moral problem was whether it was right to accept assistance and financial help from Wildeve since each was married to another; in the later versions, with Wildeve more forward, her problem was whether she could avail herself of his services or whether she also had to accept him as her lover and go away with him.[37] Which is the real *Return of the Native*?

I have asked this kind of question three different times, partly because the three situations are somewhat different, partly to suggest that the prob-lem which I am now to treat is very widespread. That problem is the existence of the work of art in multiple versions, each created by the author. The principle which is involved touches the nature of composi-tion: the work in process, the work in completion, the work in re-completion. Familiar examples of authorial revision abound in all periods: there are two distinct versions of *Piers Plowman*, two of Chaucer's Pro-logue to *The Legend of Good Women* and two (possibly three) of *Troilus and Criseyde*, five of Gower's *Confessio Amantis*, two major versions of Sidney's *Arcadia*, two of Ben Jonson's *Every Man in His Humour*, several versions of Browne's *Religio Medici* and Walton's *Life of Donne*, two of Pope's *Rape of the Lock* and of *The Dunciad*, two of Keats's "La Belle Dame Sans Merci," four of FitzGerald's *Rubáiyát of Omar Khayyám*, seven of Whitman's *Leaves of Grass*, from two to five for each of Arnold's major prose works, and so on and so forth.

These are all familiar instances. To add a few other writers who have been notable revisers, within the limits (say) of nineteenth-century

---

37. See Otis B. Wheeler, "Four Versions of *The Return of the Native*," *NCF,* XIV (1959), 27–44. See also John Paterson, *The Making of "The Return of The Native"* (Berkeley, Calif., 1960), particularly for Hardy's first intentions.

poetry, one might first mention Wordsworth, who spent forty-five years in tinkering with *The Prelude,* making the 1850 version in many ways a quite different poem from the 1805 version.[38] Or Tennyson, who was a devoted, continual, and minute reviser: he worked over his manuscripts (sometimes in as many as six versions), he altered the texts in the proofs for the first and later editions, and he made marginal changes in the printed editions. Sometimes there are as many as fifteen texts, all different, each armed with the poet's authority.[39] Or Emily Dickinson, who had second and third and fourth thoughts about what she wrote, and who sometimes could not decide which was the final form of a poem. For "Blazing in Gold and quenching in Purple," in the three fair copies she sent to friends, each time one line was different in the supposed final version; "the Otter's Window" in one is "the kitchen window" in another, which is "the oriel window" in a third. She wrote them all and meant each of them to be the poem.[40]

Recent scholarly investigations have revealed that authorial revision is embodied in multiple printed versions to an extent which seems to be almost limitless. I can at least hint at the spread of these findings through the mere mention of a sampling of the subjects, naming only those to whom I have not already alluded. For the twentieth century, Joyce, Faulkner, Yeats, Conrad, Lewis, Dos Passos, Lindsay, Cozzens, and West. For the nineteenth century, James, Twain, Crane, Pater, Clough, Hawthorne, Poe, Emerson, Thoreau, Longfellow, De Quincey, Blake, and Coleridge. For the eighteenth century, Swift, Fielding, and Johnson. For the seventeenth and latter sixteenth centuries, Shakespeare, Drayton,

---

38. See Helen Darbishire's revision of Ernest de Selincourt's edition (Oxford, 1959), pp. liv–lxxiv.

39. See, for example, Edgar F. Shannon, Jr., "The History of A Poem: Tennyson's *Ode on the Death of the Duke of Wellington,*" *SB,* XIII (1960), 149–177; or Shannon, "The Proofs of *Gareth and Lynette* in the Widener Collection," *PBSA,* XLI (1947), 321–340; or W. D. Paden, "A Note on the Variants of *In Memoriam* and *Lucretius,*" *Library,* 5th ser., VIII (1953), 259–273.

40. See Thomas H. Johnson, "Emily Dickinson: Creating the Poems," *Harvard Library Bulletin,* VII (1953), 257–270; or, more comprehensively, *The Poems of Emily Dickinson,* ed. Johnson (Cambridge, Mass., 1955), esp. I, xxxiii–xxxviii and 163–165.

Daniel, Burton, Crashaw, Lee, Rochester, and Dryden. The prize for revision should probably be awarded to Philip James Bailey. He wrote seven different versions of his poem *Festus,* which was, or were, published in thirteen British (and at least forty American) editions between 1839 and 1903. In the process it grew from a modest 8,103 lines (a little shorter than *Paradise Lost*) to a monstrous 39,159 lines.[41]

The more of these scholarly studies one reads, the more one is impressed by the likelihood of authorial revision in any literary work where the writer had an opportunity to alter his work before communicating it to his public yet another time. What the scholar seems to need in order to demonstrate authorial revision in these cases is simply the good fortune to find that the evidence has not been destroyed. It seems logical to assume that revision may have taken place in other cases, wherever there was occasion for it, even though the editions, manuscripts, or letters to prove it are no longer extant.[42]

I am trying to make it clear that the examples with which I began, of works by Dickens, Auden, and Hardy, are by no means instances of authorial revision which can be dismissed because they are rare freaks. On the contrary, they seem to be examples of a fairly common phenomenon. The matters of principle which they raise will have widespread application.

When people write about literary works which exist in multiple versions, the question they commonly address is "Which is the best version?" About *Great Expectations*, for example, J. Hillis Miller writes that "the second ending is, in my opinion, the best. Not only was it, after all, the one Dickens published (would he really have acceded to Mrs. Grundy in the mask of Bulwer-Lytton without reasons of his own?), but, it seems to me, the second ending, in joining Pip and Estella, is much

41. Morse Peckham, "English Editions of Philip James Bailey's *Festus*," *PBSA,* XLIV (1950), 55–58.

42. The consideration of this possibility will, of course, complicate the reasoning of the textual critic. On the whole, it is a possibility which has usually been disregarded unless the evidence to demonstrate the fact of revision has been overwhelming.

truer to the real direction of the story."[43] On the other hand, Edgar Johnson is somewhat contemptuous of the second ending as a "tacked-on addition of a belated marriage to Estella." "Both as art and as psychology," he informs us, "it was poor counsel that Lytton gave in urging that the shaping of a lifetime in Estella be miraculously undone. Save for this, though, *Great Expectations* is the most perfectly constructed and perfectly written of all Dickens's works." Johnson then proceeds to outline a third ending, of his own imagining, which he prefers to either of those that Dickens wrote. "It should close with that misty moonlight scene in Miss Havisham's ruined garden," but the final action should be that of Pip and Estella "bidding each other a chastened farewell."[44] Personally, I do not feel greatly assisted by any of these answers The making of a choice between the versions may seem to be of a high order because it involves the exercise of taste; but it is not the first question to ask, and it turns out to be more of an innocently curious quest than a serious critical inquiry.

The first problem is to identify the work of art. The basic proposition which I submit about works created by authorial revision is that each version is, either potentially or actually, another work of art. It remains a "potential" work of art—it is in process, it is becoming—so long as the author is still giving it shape, in his mind or in successive drafts or interlineations or in whatever manner he suspends those works which he is not yet ready to release to his usual public. On the other hand, the "actual" work of art is a version in which the author feels that his intentions have been sufficiently fulfilled to communicate it to the public, as his response to whatever kinds of pressure bear on him, from within or from without, to release his work into a public domain. The distinction which I am offering is a practical (rather than idealistic) way of separating the potential from the actual, the work of art which is becoming from the work of art which is. The distinction thus turns on

43. *Charles Dickens: The World of His Novels* (Cambridge, Mass., 1958), p. 278.

44. *Charles Dickens: His Tragedy and Triumph* (New York, 1952), II, 988, 992–993.

the intentions of the artist: the work can have only such integrity, or completeness, as the author chooses to give it, and our only reasonable test of when the work has achieved integrity is his willingness to release it to his usual public. His judgment may not always be good, and he may release it too soon or too late or when (we think) he never should have; but it is his judgment not ours, his intention not ours, his work of art which he makes ours.

The nature of the public differs for different writers. For Dickens—as for most writers since the invention of printing—it was the readers of a periodical or of a book issued by publishers to whom he had turned over a text. For Emily Dickinson, however, her usual public might be her sister-in-law, Susan Dickinson, or Thomas Wentworth Higginson, or Helen Hunt Jackson. If she sent a fair copy of a poem to one of them, this action—as the equivalent of voluntary publication—can be taken as evidence that the work had achieved its integrity. For William Blake, the usual public might be anyone in the small circle of friends and kindly benefactors who accepted or purchased a copy of one of his books—written, designed, engraved, colored, and bound by Blake, with the assistance of his wife.

The application of this test is sometimes difficult, mainly when the evidence leaves obscure the question as to whether the artist intended to release the work to his public in the form in which we have it. Books which are published piratically or circulated surreptitiously are examples. Sir Thomas Browne "at leisurable houres composed" *Religio Medici,* as he says in his address "To the Reader," "for my private exercise and satisfaction"; "being communicated unto one, it became common unto many, and was by transcription successively corrupted untill it arrived in a most depraved copy at the presse. He that shall peruse that worke, and shall take notice of sundry particularities and personall expressions therein, will easily discerne *the intention was not publik.*" (I use italics to call attention to the key phrase.) There were two unauthorized editions issued anonymously in 1642, but Browne then proceeded to supply—to the same bookseller who had pirated his work—text for an authorized edition; he used a copy of one of the pirated editions, correcting some

650 errors (while overlooking many others), and adding four new sections, a dozen new passages, and many new errors.[45] However hasty and careless his alterations, *Religio Medici* was then a public work. With some writers, pirated (or even manipulated) publication has been used as an excuse to issue works (like Pope's publication of his own letters) which it might otherwise seem immodest to release to the usual public. Sometimes a writer feels that publication puts an end to his freedom to revise. Guillaume De Guileville told, in the prologue to his *Pèlerinage de la vie humaine,* of a wonderful dream he had in the year 1330 and of writing it down hastily "that I myht after, by leyser, / Correcte hyt when the day were cler." But before he had finished mending it, it was stolen from him and published abroad, "a-geyn my wyl & my plesaunce." Up to that time, he says, "fredam I hadde / To putte away, and eke to adde, / What that me lyst, lyk as I wende"; but after publication he lost that freedom. It was only after the passage of twenty-five years that he made a new version, by thorough revision, and was ready to send it forth into the world to replace the incomplete version which he had not wished published.[46]

The revisions which a writer makes while a work is in process—that is, before it becomes a version which he chooses to make public—constitute an intimate and complex view of that writer at work. "The minute changes made in their compositions by eminent writers are," in Edmond Malone's blunt dictum, "always a matter of both curiosity & instruction to literary men, however trifling and unimportant they may appear to blockheads."[47] The study of revisions can enlighten us, as Paul Valéry says, "about the secret discussion that takes place, at the time when the work is being done, between the temperament, ambition and foresight of the man, and, on the other hand, the excitements and the intellectual means of the moment. The strictness of the revisions, the number of solutions rejected, and possibilities denied, indicate the nature of the scruples, the

45. Jean-Jacques Denonain, ed., *Religio Medici* (Cambridge, Eng., 1953), pp. xxiv–xxviii.

46. EETS (Extra Series), LXXVII (1899), 6–8. (The Lydgate translation.)

47. Quoted by James M. Osborn, *John Dryden: Some Biographical Facts and Problems* (New York, 1940), p. 131.

degree of conscience, the quality of pride, and even the reserves and diverse fears that are felt in regard to the future judgment of the public." With a writer whose mind is reflective and rich in resonances, the work can only emerge "by a kind of accident which ejects it from the mind."[48] The taste for making endless revisions is, according to Valéry, an occupational disease; "in the eyes of these lovers of anxiety and perfection, a work is never *complete*—a word which to them is meaningless—but *abandoned*."[49] Other writers have less difficulty with the creative process, and some find greater satisfaction in the results they obtain.[50]

In any event, the several verbal forms in which the literary work exists while it is being written are in the private province of the writer as part of his interior dialogue with himself. When extant documents preserve these variant forms, we must remember that they provide glimpses into the creative process and not a final form. Dickens never used the first ("unhappy") ending of *Great Expectations;* he wrote it, sent it to the printer, had it set in type, and read the proofs. But he allowed his mind to be changed and wrote the second ending, which he used in the serial and book editions of the novel. The first ending was preserved by his friend and biographer, John Forster; it was never printed as part of the novel until 1937, when it was used in the Limited Editions Club version, which carried the imprimatur of an introduction by George Bernard Shaw. The Rinehart Edition prints both endings, as if each reader could choose the one he preferred. As I read the evidence, the first ending never became an integral part of the novel in a public version; only the second ending—no matter whether you think it better or worse—attained that status, and the only "real" *Great Expectations* by Charles Dickens is the one with that ending. Edgar Johnson's "third" ending, being of his own

48. "On Mallarmé" in *Selected Writings* (New York, 1950), pp. 217, 216.

49. "Concerning *Le Cimetière marin*" in *The Art of Poetry* (New York, 1958), pp. 140–141.

50. For discussion and examples of authorial revision of work in progress, see *Poets at Work,* ed. Charles D. Abbott (New York, 1948), and Robert H. Taylor and H. W. Liebert, *Authors at Work* (New York, 1957).

construction, could have status only if Johnson were considered a co-author of the novel. The work of art cannot be judged by loading it with hypotheses of what it might have been or of what it could be made to be: the work of art has a radical integrity, and we must take that integrity, once discovered, as it is. The tactic of posing self-made alternatives is one which involves tremendous risks for a doubtful advantage.

When the literary work emerges as a public version it then has the integrity of its unique authorial form. Our suspicions about the sheer decency of contemplating more than one public version of a single literary work may be allayed if we think of the versions as separated in time, with something like five years between the two versions of Auden's "In Time of War," with about thirty-four years for insulation between the first and the last *Return of the Native.*

"I cannot go back over anything I have written," said Valéry, "without thinking that I should now make something quite different of it."[51] If we consider the theory and practice of William Butler Yeats and Henry James, the status of multiple versions of a work of art will perhaps be clearer. Yeats understood, with the utmost clarity, his drive to revise. When friends objected to his habit of returning again and again to his old poems and altering them each time, he replied with these lines:

> The friends that have it I do wrong
> When ever I remake a song,
> Should know what issue is at stake:
> It is myself that I remake.[52]

Yeats was an inveterate reviser because he was, quite simply, always trying to make his poems contemporaneous with his self as a changing human being. "This volume contains what is, I hope, the final text of the poems

---

51. "Concerning *Le Cimetière marin*" in *The Art of Poetry,* p. 144.

52. Untitled poem *ss,* in *The Variorum Edition of the Poems of W. B. Yeats,* ed. Peter Allt and Russell K. Alspach (New York, 1957), p. 778. (This poem is not included in the "definitive" edition.)

of my youth," he wrote in the Preface of January 1927 to the thirteenth reprinting and revision of his *Poems* of 1895; "and yet it may not be," he added, "seeing that in it are not only the revisions from my 'Early Poems and Stories,' published last year, but quite new revisions on which my heart is greatly set." To read his prefaces to the various editions of "The Countess Cathleen," for example, is to see more clearly what is involved in the making of a new public version of a literary work.

Yeats was always re-reading his earlier poems, and always making new versions to issue to his public. He did not scruple to keep re-writing any of his previous work. Henry James, on the other hand, approached the revision of his earlier novels with anxiety, as a job that bristled with difficulties.[53] He had been at pains to dismiss his earlier work, to put it behind him, to become unacquainted with it. He was disinclined to exhume it, and very loath to start tidying it up for fear that he would become involved in expensive renovations. He had been accustomed all of his life to revising his work, it is true, to changing the periodical version for book publication, to altering the text from one edition to another; but those revision were made in warm blood while the original vision of the story was still with him. What has made his revisions of special interest was this task that he approached with such reluctance, for the Definitive New York edition. The gulf of time which separated him from most of the novels to be included made him think of the idea of re-writing them as so difficult, or even so absurd, as to be impossible; it would not be a mere matter of expression, but of somehow harmonizing the man he then was and the man he used to be.

James resolved his dilemma by discarding the idea of re-writing altogether and by taking the task of revision in its etymological sense—to see again, to look over, to re-peruse. Thus he never thought of himself as

53. The Prefaces to *Roderick Hudson* and *The Golden Bowl* (Vols. i and xxiii, respectively, in the New York edition) set forth James's central ideas on revision. In the collection of his Prefaces called *The Art of the Novel,* with an introduction by Richard P. Blackmur (New York, 1934), the passage about revision in the Preface to *Roderick Hudson* is on pp. 10–12 and the one in the Preface to *The Golden Bowl* on pp. 335–340. My exposition of James's views is based mainly on the latter passage and includes close paraphrase of what I take to be the major issues.

re-writing a novel, but of seeing it again and recording the results of that re-vision in so many close notes that the pages were made to flower. James respected his novels and their characters as having an independent existence of their own, and he wanted to keep his hands off of them. By his own application of the term "revision," he made himself believe that he had done so. I take his argument to be an innocent but necessary piece of deception to avoid facing the fact of rewriting. However James looked on his job, the revisions for the New York edition resulted in new versions of the works. He made, for example, more than two thousand revisions in *The Reverberator.*[54] Voices rise and fall as to whether James improved or debased his novels by revision, as to whether his later style is more tortuous and labored or clearer and more expressive, even as to whether the revision of a given novel makes a radical or minimal change in the effect of a certain character, like Newman in *The American*. The unarguable fact is that James supplied multiple versions of the novels which he revised.

The literary critic can afford enough detachment to observe the work of art as an historical phenomenon, as a part of the past from the moment of its creation. But few writers are able to take this view; for many of them the work continues, as for a possessive parent, a part of the self, as a child whose hair must be brushed into submission, as an adult who must be nagged into wearing more stylish clothes.

I suggested that our suspicion of multiple versions of the work of art may be allayed if we think of them as separated by long periods of time. Time is, however, only a practical convenience in envisioning why multiple versions may or must exist. No clock can measure the rate at which a man becomes different, a little, a lot. Enough might happen in a day or

---

54. See Sister Mary Brian Durkin, "Henry James's Revisions of the Style of *The Reverberator*," *AL,* xxxiii (1961), 330–349. There has been, I dare say, more extensive scholarly investigation, in books and articles and theses, of the revisions by James for the New York edition than of those by any other writer on any occasion. The three novels in which the revisions have so far been examined the most thoroughly are, probably, *The American, The Portrait of a Lady,* and *The Ambassadors.* Such fertile fields are attractive to the husband-man, and we can expect every last one of the twenty-four volumes to be harrowed in each direction.

even in a flash to require that the man rediscover his self and make a poem over in a new way.

We come back again to the questions with which we began this discussion. The problem of identifying the "real" *Great Expectations*, we found, was simplified when we insisted on respecting the public version to which Dickens gave authorial integrity. The application of this basic test will not select one or the other of Auden's "In Time of War," however, since each is a fulfillment of his intentions, and each was communicated to his usual public. From our review of what takes place in revision for private and public versions, I hope it is clear that the two versions of the Auden collection are equally "real." They stand, side by side, as two separate works, and each has every bit of the dignity and integrity with which an author can endow any work of art. So it is with Hardy, with Yeats, with James, with all multiple versions of works of art where each was given authorial integrity and communicated to the usual public.

This embarrassment of riches may make us restless to distinguish. Hence the critic asks "which is the best?" And the editor asks "which shall I print?" And the student asks "which shall I read?" Usually these three questions are the same, the latter two being applications of the first.

There is a conventional answer, made smooth by constant use. "It is generally accepted that the most authoritative edition is the last published in the author's lifetime." "The book collector may prefer to possess a first edition, however faulty the text, but an author's last revision must, as a rule, claim precedence in literature." This answer can be duplicated from the writings of most of the famous bibliographers and textual authorities, and it is also the password when one is explaining one's terms in a footnote to a textual study: "By 'best text' I mean the text that represents the poet's own final choice among variants of the poem."[55]

---

55. The first quotation is from R. W. Chapman, "The Textual Criticism of English Classics," in *English Critical Essays: Twentieth Century,* ed. Phyllis M. Jones (London, 1933), p. 274. The second is from Sir Harold Williams, *The Text of "Gulliver's Travels"* (Cambridge, Eng., 1952), p. 36. The third is from Zahava Karl Dorinson, "'I Taste a Liquor Never Brewed': A Problem in Editing," *AL,* xxxv (1963), 363, n. 1.

It is a bit puzzling to know why this dictum should for so long have passed unchallenged. For it is much like saying that an author's last poem (or novel, or play) is, as a general rule, his best one; it may be, and it may not be. This rule of thumb—whether applied to the choice among multiple versions of a work of art or among works of an author in general—is a desperate substitute for the whole process of critical understanding, which is the only sensible way of trying to arrive at a sound evaluation of anything.

IV

What is the aesthetic object with which textual criticism can deal? What constitutes the integrity of the work of art? When a literary work exists in several authorial versions, which is the real work of art?

These are the three questions which we have been addressing. The first invites us to consider the characteristics of the several types of phenomena which can be called aesthetic objects because they yield an aesthetic response. I have argued that the textual critic must limit himself to works of art: thus aesthetic objects which are the result of chance or nature are beyond his scope, however appealing or meritorious they may be, even if they improve the work of art. In being limited to the work of art, the textual critic is thereby limited to the linguistic intentions of the author. The basic goal of textual criticism is, therefore, the verification or recovery of the words which the author intended to constitute the literary work.

The second question asks us to explore the nature of authorship and of the literary work as an intricate entangling of intentions. Various forces are always at work thwarting or modifying the author's intentions. The process of preparing the work for dissemination to a public (whether that process leads to publication in printed form or production in the theatre or preparation of scribal copies) puts the work in the hands of persons who are professionals in the execution of the process. Similarly, the effort to recover a work of the past puts it in the hands of professionals known as textual critics, or editors. In all of these cases, the process must be adapted to the work at hand, and the work to the process. Sometimes through misunderstanding and sometimes through an effort to improve the work, these professionals substitute their own intentions for those of the author, who is frequently ignorant of their craft. Sometimes the author objects and sometimes not, sometimes he is pleased, sometimes he acquiesces, and sometimes he does not notice what has happened. The work of art is thus always tending toward a collaborative status, and the task of the textual critic is always to recover and preserve its integrity at that point where the authorial intentions seem to have been fulfilled.

The third question opens the nature of composition and seeks to define the authoritative quality of each work of art. Works which are in process can be called potential works of art, while the actual work of art is the one which fulfills the author's intentions. Our only practicable way of distinguishing is to observe whether the author does or does not communicate the work to his usual public. When the author provides us with multiple actual versions of what we commonly think of as a single literary work, he has in fact written separate works, among which there is no simple way to choose the best.

Throughout this discussion, the intentions of the artist have occupied a central position. It is his intentions which distinguish the work of art as an order within the class of aesthetic objects, which must be protected in order to preserve the work from becoming a collaborative enterprise, which give the integrity of completeness to the actual work of art. The inference for the textual critic is that the intentions of the artist are of controlling importance over textual work. While the textual critic should not neglect to carry out the more or less mechanical operations which his masters enjoin upon him, he must also undertake to discover all that he can, from whatever source, about the linguistic intentions of the artist. It is his interpretation of this evidence, within a consistent aesthetic, which plays the crucial role in giving his work value.

I would not wish to argue that these inferences simplify the task of the textual critic, nor that they supply him with a ready formula for solving hard cases, nor that they qualify him as a seer. They do, in fact, make his work more difficult. Whenever we deal with human motives and the operation of human intentions, we soon reach the point—if we do not have the advantage of being the omniscient author—beyond which the best we can suggest is probability, then possibility, then uncertainty. Whenever these stages are reached, the incidence of error is necessarily high. The main merit of establishing textual criticism on a consistent set of aesthetic assumptions is (I think) that it brings the real problems into the open and provides a fairer chance of producing results which will be fundamentally sound.

The Textual Event[†]

Joseph Grigely

The self-relation that forms identity is necessarily mediated by opposition to otherness.

—MARK TAYLOR,
Altarity

ONE OF THE most used, abused, and powerful words in our critical vocabularies is the word *text*. As a critical term it is enormously convenient and often seems to do when nothing else will do. If one doesn't know whether to call something a book, a word, a work, or the world, then one calls it a text because it simply sounds right, supplanting a vague uncertainty with a certain vagueness. Yet it is a word with a history (or rather histories), and by unpacking some of this history I want to examine the textual-critical tradition of seeing the text as an object, and redefine the text in an interdisciplinary format utilizing semiotics, deconstruction theory, and philosophy; that is, I want to relocate the tradition of textual studies within the larger nexus of critical theory and the philosophy of art.

THE TEXTUAL-CRITICAL TRADITION

Implicit in this effort is a more general intention of encouraging a theoretical (perhaps even metatheoretical) approach to textual philosophy—a

[†] "The Textual Event," from *Textual Editing and Literary Theory*, ed. Philip G. Cohen (xviii), (1991), pp. 167–94. Reprinted by permission of the University of Virginia Press.

kind of interdisciplinary philosophy of textuality. Until the last decade, textual "theory"—even in the work of Sir Walter Greg and Fredson Bowers—was in effect no more than a defense of textual practices; it was essentially anterior to textual study and the experience gained through what was considered the "success" and "failure" of those practices. James Thorpe, for example, describes his *Principles of Textual Criticism* as being "an effort to present . . . a discussion of the basic principles which under-lie the practice of textual criticism" (vii), and this experiential approach is typical of the cautious reserve that characterizes the discipline. Traditionally, textual studies has involved an objective of stability, a way of organizing, stabilizing, or "framing" a work of literature as an ordered set of texts. This is both useful and understandable, perhaps because criticism itself has instituted its own kind of ordering of literature in various sets and subsets that are variously classified by genre, period, author, and so on. Order, in short, seems to make things easier: it allows us to move beyond the act of ordering to other issues that build upon the distinctions we make. This is both tempting and beguiling, since it promises a certain good: it promises to deliver us from the chaos of reality—textual entrammelment—and answer our desire for such deliverance.

The ordered and organized literary signifier has thus been the desideratum of textual criticism and bibliography, but actual textual practices have not always acknowledged the implications of semiotic "order"—an order that threatens to deceive us and return to disorder. Such "order" is substantiated by the presence of a physical text, which in turn is a reflection of the Anglo-American textual tradition of seeing the text as a physical object, as a book, manuscript, a holograph, a galley proof.[1] This is partly because bibliography is acknowledged as the study of books as physical objects, but it is also because such texts are what Jerome McGann, in "*Ulysses* as a Postmodern Text," calls "determinate"

1. In contrast to the textual-critical tradition, the deconstructionist use of the term *text*, rather than closing itself on a material state of language, opens itself up to the intertextual, even metatextual, loci of language. See Roland Barthes's essay, "The Death of the Author," in *Image-Music-Text:* "a text is not a line of words releasing a single 'theological' meaning (the 'message' of an Author-God), but a multi-dimensional space in which a variety of writings, none of them original, blend and clash" (146).

representations of a work's overall instability; they provide us with specific, concrete, historical, and institutional evidence which in turn guides us toward understanding that instability (291). There is a tendency here not toward the humanistic and psychical, but towards the *physicalis* of objectivity. McGann's point is also suggested by Peter Shillingsburg, when he emphasizes that "a text is contained and stabilized by the physical form [of a document]" (49–50).[2] But it is even more emphatically stressed by William Proctor Williams and Craig S. Abbott, who explain in their *Introduction to Bibliographical and Textual Studies* that "the basic commodity for a literary scholar is the text, which is physically embodied in letters written, impressed, or transferred onto a surface" (3). This emphasis on objects, commodities even, like soybeans and pork bellies, is not unusual, particularly if we consider the etymological force of the word *literature: littera*, a letter. In another sense, however, if the business of texts and the business of literature is defined by that which gets written and printed, we are also saying—by default—that "oral literature" (which is itself a contradiction in terms) is not literature, nor can it be literature until it has written texts. Even the postmodern oral poetry is, as Jerome Rothenberg observed, mediated by print by appearing in print (*Pre-Faces 10–11, 36)*—a fact undoubtedly true for David Antin's "talk poetry" and Allen Ginsberg's tape-recorder poems. This may seem a priggish matter, but it is also a serious matter in cultures with linguistic systems that do not get written down—sign language poetry or Native American literature being good examples of what can be lost or disparaged by being different.

The idea of the text-as-an-object is, I would like to suggest, the legacy of the boundaries of the Anglo-American and German textual tradition. Both Sir Walter Greg and Ronald McKerrow, as well as Fredson Bowers and G. Thomas Tanselle, have all worked within a somewhat narrow range of literature—Anglo-American works between (roughly) 1560 and 1960—and this exposed them to a certain set of writing and publishing

---

2. For Shillingsburg a text is more particularly an immaterial representation of words and punctuation inasmuch as that order has some kind of physical representation.

conventions. Within this set of conventions they produced an admirable program of admirable approaches to the vicissitudes of textual transmission. Just as Saussure changed linguistic theory by emphasizing the synchronic study of language, the early textual scholars emphasized the synchronic activity of book production, which in turn made diachronic and typological studies more viable. In essence, textual criticism is a metachronic activity, both in time and out of time; its activity retrospective, and in many ways, canonical. We do not, for example, have a postmodern textual theory to deal with postmodern texts and genres—sound poetry, video poetry, and performance art, to cite a few—simply because textual theory is for the most part dependent on an institutional view of that canonical authority (usually for practical reasons that are also, unfortunately, economic reasons: it's easier to get a grant to edit Hawthorne than it is to get a grant to edit Johnny Rotten). The idea of the text-as-an-object is thus bound to the idea of the text-as-a-*literary*-object, and only insofar as textual theories consider texts outside canonical traditions will we arrive at a less medium-governed idea of textuality.

Such interdisciplinarity might be expanded even beyond the socio-economic conception of text production that characterizes Jerome McGann's work. For McGann a poem is not itself an object, but "a unique order of unique appearances," a network of human actions and human forces that can best be characterized as a historical event (*Beauty of Inflections* 343). Like that of his spiritual mentor, Mikhail Bakhtin, McGann's work calls for a closer look at the human element in poetry, the manner in which poetry (and literature in general) is shaped by the human condition, and the extent to which literature is a part of larger, socio-economic systems. What I have to say in the following pages might be regarded as an attempt to take this notion further by considering how human languages and the modalities of those languages (written? spoken? signed?) affect textual structures in the domain of the creative arts—poetry, painting, or performance, to name but a few.

When we theorize about "textuality" in this broader sense, we begin to realize that although texts manifest themselves as objects, they are also more than objects, and particularly more than literary objects; they are also (to take one position) signifiers, in which case we are confronted with additional questions that are less germane to textual criticism and bibliography than to semiotics and philosophy: What are the semiotic boundaries of a text? Where does a text "begin" or "end"? How is a text of a poem different from—or like—a text of a painting? Do performances have texts, or *are* they texts? Traditionally, semiotics has been understood as a kind of mediating discourse on the relationship between language and art—it informs many of the interartistic comparisons in Wendy Steiner's *Colors of Rhetoric,* for example—but in our case the arguments and answers offered by semiotics or the more nominalistic philosophy of Nelson Goodman lead us toward further questions that are not only germane to "texts" but to the very idea of literature as literature or art as art. This is the point where textual criticism becomes textual philosophy.

Given these considerations, my approach, and my critical sources, are fairly eclectic; were this essay a dinner party, one would find sitting around the table Fredson Bowers, Jerome McGann, Jacques Derrida, Nelson Goodman, and Arthur Danto—not exactly the sort of gathering that makes happy company. At times it may seem that I am unduly harsh in my criticism of textual studies (as a critical school), and at times I am. It is not that I disparage the achievements of the Anglo-American and German textual tradition; rather, I lament what seems to me the ideological closure of that tradition—a closure that is based on the consequence of decades of editing institutionally qualified, canonized works of literature. The questions I bring up are intentionally provocative; for years textual critics lamented that readers of literature take their texts for granted, and my position now is that those same textual critics might perhaps be taking their conception of textuality for granted.

ITERABILITY

In textual studies, the notion of iterability (from the Latin *iterum,* again) is present at levels that include the iterative function of language and the implied iterability of texts. We might think of "repeatability" as being a universal quality in textual studies, where efforts are made to produce or reproduce a particular text that lends itself toward a kind of scholarly utilitarianism. Even our critical discourse includes the terms *reprint* and *reissue,* although neither can be taken literally: reprints do not always reprint, inasmuch as they may include intentional or unintentional intrinsic changes, or reflect the extrinsic influence of political and economic conditions. What this suggests is that the philosophical foundations that underlie the concept of iterability in textual studies are vulnerable and open to question. Language is iterative to the extent that it is a socially shared code; but are utterances of language or units of utterances (such as texts) iterative also? In the section that follows I shall investigate (briefly) the iterability of language in literary discourse, and what I believe to be the noniterability of texts. The resources for my argument are somewhat diverse and not in a strict sense "textual" or "theoretical," if only because iterability is—at its barest—an interdisciplinary issue.

The iterability of language is presupposed by being a condition of language: it is a symbolic system comprising learnable and repeatable symbols. This is a typical feature of many semiotic systems and not in itself surprising. Repeatability allows us to formulate utterances that, as part of a shared social code, are understood within the realm of that code's usage and (if one follows Derrida on the matter in "Signature Event Context") even beyond the limits of code itself (317). It is important to remember that language is composed of units that signify in an interactive and (both) linear and nonlinear manner: the phoneme, the morpheme, the word, the phrase, the sentence: these are units that do not necessarily signify exclusively at their own level but at recombinant levels as well. Hence, we might say that the iterability of these units is essentially paradigmatic; yet it is paradigmatic only in theory, only in an ideal vacuum that is free from the actual conditions of articulation (either spoken or signed) and writing. Derrida's position—a controversial position—is that, as he says in "Signature Event Context," "A writing that was not structurally legible—iterable—beyond the death of the addressee would not be writing" (315). We can "read" an utterance

beyond the death (i.e., presence) of the addressee, but what are we reading? Or, as Robert Scholes frames the question: "We would have made a
sense *for* the marks, but would we have made sense *of* them?" (280).

What Derrida is suggesting is that although language is conceived as
being paradigmatic—like a kind of semantic Lego kit—in actual practice,
our utterances (constructions, buildings) are more properly syntagmatic.
They may survive the death of the addressee, but in a special way: they
become desyntagmatized, lifted from the context of articulation, but do
not cease to function. What happens is that the utterance—whether
written or otherwise recorded—is recontextualized, or, as Derrida says,
"grafted" (317), and such grafting is omnipresent: language deceives us as
to how its iterable presence (written words, marks, inscriptions) do not
translate to an iterable intention, or meaning. The original boundary of
an utterance—the moment of its inscription—becomes null, but not
void. We merely graft it, decontextualize it, and recontextualize it so that
the utterance gives way to its new location: it becomes, so to speak, the
resident of a particular (and new) discourse community. And so on.

What Derrida doesn't do in "Signature Event Context" is give us a
satisfactory definition of "the moment of inscription" (317); nor, for
that matter, does anyone else. "Inscription" can be taken to mean a
moment of writing by the author, the moment of publishing, or the
moment of reading—or any point in between. A moment like this
defines itself rather loosely and metaphorically as a moment of stasis.
Such a moment is not the singular representation of a work of literature
(or art even), which is instead more of a series of moments of inscription, some authorial, some not, some authorized, some not; yet all of
them are realities to the extent that are scripted, (a)scribed, and more
particularly, read. Moments like these are best characterized not by what
they say but what they do not say: they leave us with a disembodied,
decontextualized text that does not mean anything unless bound to an
agent of meaning—an interpreter.

Yet in an odd sense Derrida seems to me to be on to something quite
germane to the tradition of textual criticism. Historically, textual criticism
has tried to qualify moments of inscription according to their relative

authority, and establish a hierarchy of inscriptions according to authorial intent. It does not (from my point of view) matter whether these efforts succeed or not; indeed, there's no way to know. Nor does it matter whether the editions produced are judiciously emended texts, eclectic texts, or facsimile texts, for they constitute (and continue to constitute, as in Gabler's edition of *Ulysses*) further moments of inscription. This is where Derrida's point strikes home: a moment of inscription is no more than a moment of inscription. It may be a significantly reformulated moment, like Bowdler's 1808 edition of Shakespeare, in which case even Bowdler's moment of inscribing Shakespeare is a moment of contextual- ized presence; in essence, unique, and in its uniqueness, telling. Its "wrong- ness" is a historical argument about truth values, and such an argument cannot exist except by comparison with other moments of inscription. A play by Shakespeare (or by anyone else) cannot claim final authority because it cannot claim to be finished at any point: just as there is no con- sensus in editorial theory as to what constitutes the "final intentions" of a work, there is no consensus (as far as I know) in philosophical theory as to what constitutes a "finished" work of literature.[3] At one point Nelson Goodman asserts in *Languages of Art* that "the composer's work is done when he has written the score" (114)—but the corollary to this statement—"the poet's work is done when he has written the poem"— will not do because a work at this point is unrealized as a social commod- ity. Even if we take publication as a moment of completion, then we must also consider the fact that further publication—or even withdrawal from publication—controverts this moment but certainly does not negate it. Here I concur with the general thrust of McGann's work: instead of view- ing literature—or artworks—as finished productions, we might instead view them as works of fluxion that experience stasis, as in, say, a particular edition, or a particular exhibition space. This stasis is not so much strictly

---

3. Shillingsburg discusses four different conceptions, or "orientations," of completion: the historical ("the work of art is finished when it becomes a material artifact"); the so- ciological (a work is finished when it is ready to be distributed); the aesthetic (a work of art is never really complete); and the authorial (a work is finished when the author says so) (75–78). Although there are some holes in these orientations (particularly where they overlap), Shillingsburg's distinctions are very useful outlines.

temporal as it is contextual; that is, "spatial" within a historical context. In other words, we can say there are no final or finished works, but only final or finished texts; no final work of *Hamlet* or Keats's ode "To Autumn," but final (and particular) texts of *Hamlet* and Keats's ode. These texts redefine Derrida's original moment of inscription as a series of moments of inscription: they are utterances, "writing acts," and by the time they reach us—no matter how generous an editor is in explaining those texts—they have already, in varying degrees, broken free from those moments: they drift. A work of literature thus cannot be stabilized any more than a sculpture or a building can be stabilized: the relocation that threatened (and subsequently retextualized) Richard Serra's sculpture *Tilted Arc,* or the additions that threaten Marcel Breuer's Whitney Museum or Frank Lloyd Wright's Guggenheim Museum are not in this sense any more threatening than the next editor to face *Ulysses* or *Hamlet.* Timelessness is an illusion to the extent that there is no timeless text: a text is of a time.

The value of Derrida's argument is that it reminds us although language (*language*) is iterable, this iterability begins to rupture when applied to utterances (*parole*), even when those utterances are written. We move further and further from the moment of inscription and are attached to that moment by a small thread of words that are at once both the residue of that moment and our bond to it. Textual criticism and editorial theory do not help us here; editions imply that texts are not only repeatable but that they can be reconstructed along the lines of authorial intentions, and such reconstruction draws attention to itself as being re:construction. They are texts that are a part of the social institution of professionalized literature (again: a moment of inscription), and these texts serve all kinds of social, economic, and political purposes as much as Galignani's pirated texts ever did.[4] This may seem a harsh thing to say, but I am not trying here to apply value judgments to particular texts. I only wish to say that if two texts are different, they are essentially equal in their differences, if only because those differences—and the interpretations we bring to bear upon

4. [John Anthony Galignani (1798–1882) was a London-born Parisian printer and bookseller of Italian descent, who was responsible for the popular and inexpensive reprint series, the British Library in Verse and Prose—*Editor.*]

them—are individual in their context: one text cannot be more "individual" than another.

One possible objection to this is to say that a facsimile edition is one way to repeat a text. My response is that this too will not do, for a facsimile is at best an illusion of iterability: it draws attention to itself as something *factum simile,* as something *much like* an "original," where $X_1 \rightarrow X_2$ but $X_1 \neq X_2$. However much two texts are like each other physically or perceptually (whether real or apparent), they are not the same. What stands out particularly are the circumstances that illustrate a need or purpose for the facsimile (such as Black Letter texts), for such circumstances are a part of the event that frames the facsimile's moment of inscription. The letters and words of the facsimile may look exactly like that of its parent, but the metatextual distance between the two would be remote. Again the message is that the repeatability of language is not synonymous with the (ir)repeatability of texts.

A more nominalistic approach to literature might suggest otherwise, and Nelson Goodman is one person who might not be swayed by this argument. Goodman is one of our most important philosophers in dealing with interartistic issues, and he has a knack of asking particularly difficult questions that we otherwise might (and often do) take for granted. One of his questions that bears upon our argument goes like this: Why is it possible to make a forgery of, say, Rembrandt's *Lucretia,* but not Haydn's *London Symphony* or Gray's "Elegy"? Goodman's response is that certain fundamental differences underlie the notion of a literal, or representative iterability in the arts. He explains: "Let us speak of a work as *autographic* if and only if the distinction between original and forgery of it is significant; or better, if and only if even the most exact duplication of it thereby does not count as genuine. If a work of art is autographic, we may also call that that art autographic. Thus painting is autographic, music nonautographic, or *allographic*" *(Languages* 113). Like music, literature is described as allographic because it is "amenable to notation" (121, 207–11).[5] "Notation" in this sense suggests the presence

---

5. See also Goodman's *Of Mind and Other Matters,* 139.

of some kind of semiotic system, whether that system is primarily symbolic (as language), or symbolic and indexical (as music), or symbolic, indexical, and iconic (as dance notation). With the presence of a notation system, each "forgery" is not a forgery but merely another instance of that work. As Goodman puts it, we need only verify the spelling of a work to produce "an instance" of the work (115–16). He emphasizes the business of spelling and punctuation because, I think, he sees the printed or inscribed texts as symbolic representations of oral utterances, and in the process glosses over the gross distinctions that "literature" involves—particularly uninscribed oral genres.[6]

One response to Goodman would be to offer a clarification of the terms *work* and *text* and use the foundation of such clarification to reorient his argument. At times Goodman uses the two terms interchangeably—a habit unnerving, but not in any way unusual, for many of us are inclined to do likewise. As I discussed earlier, texts can be described along the lines of Derrida's "moment of inscription"—and such texts do not always "comply," in a strictly authorial sense, to a conception of correctness or finality. Such moments are singular, and this singularity (over time) becomes sequential. With this in mind Jerome McGann's work again offers us a clarifying perspective. I shall have rather more to say about McGann in a moment, but I would like to address here the temporal organization that McGann's work brings to textual theory. McGann's thesis in *The Beauty of Inflections* is that literature, and the act of producing literature, is a dynamic process in which the literary work is represented by a series of successive texts, each with its own historical, semantic, and aesthetic value—values that explain literature as "a dynamic event in the human experience" (108), and not, as the formalists made it, a mere aesthetic object. As McGann explained in his *Critique of Modern Textual Criticism*, this series of texts can be generically described as "a series of specific acts of production" (52). In this sense a literary work—be it a poem, a play, or a letter to

6. For an illuminating reply to Goodman on this topic, see Barbara Herrnstein Smith's *On the Margins of Discourse,* 3–13.

Auntie Em—is an assemblage of texts, a polytext.[7] This formulation can be expressed by the equation

$$W \rightarrow T_1, T_2, T_3, \ldots T_N$$

where W = work and T = text. It is important to note that the work is not equivalent to the *sum* of its texts (which would create some kind of hybridized eclectic text), but instead is an ongoing—and infinite— manifestation of textual appearances, *whether those texts are authorized or not.* Such infinity reinforces my earlier view that a work of literature cannot be "finished," just as a building is never finished: it evolves into textual states of being, in which case even ruins are an additional text along this line of time. It is thus impossible to say that the work of, say, Shakespeare's *Tempest,* exists as anything more than a Platonic form or idea. and it is ideal in its implicit acknowledgment of the impossibility of the ideal. It is a concept, but not a concept limit; a class, but not a compliance class, for its boundaries are not prescribed. It is defined by the manifestation of texts, in which case we can say there is no "text" of *The Tempest,* but only a series of texts that comprise *The Tempest*'s polytext. *The Tempest* is a work, and a copy of the First Folio represents one text of that work. Nor is it necessary to exclude performances from this formulation. Where a series of performances is based on a specific text (what Goodman might call a score), and given

$$W \rightarrow T_1, T_2, T_3, \ldots T_N$$

then we might say that

$$T_x \rightarrow P_1, P_2, P_3, \ldots P_N$$

What is important about such formulas is that they remind us we do not normally conceive a book in terms of itself as a work, but in terms of its texts, or in any case the specific texts with which we have had encounters.

7. A similar, but more finely honed point of view is shared by Shillingsburg (46–7).

We might perhaps speak of a work in terms of its extratextual myth, for works do indeed reach a stage where they are discussed as realities that we have not experienced in a more literal sense; that is, we speak *about* them, but not *of* them. Yet it seems to me that much of our critical discourse (and our "creative" discourse as well) depends upon our encounters with specific texts.

If then we consider a work as a nontangible idea represented by a sequential series of texts—whether these texts are inscribed or performed, whether they are authorized or not—then we might be able to make more out of Goodman's original question. Is it possible to make a forgery of Gray's "Elegy," or any other work of literature? The question is important because it asks us if the iterability of language is an explanation for (as Goodman sees it) the iterability of texts. Given the above discussion, my response to Goodman is two-tiered: it is not possible to make a forgery of Gray's "Elegy," but it is possible to make a forgery of a particular text of Gray's "Elegy." In this sense "literature" in the broad sense is an allographic art, but literary texts are more properly autographic in their autonomy.[8]

Suppose, for example, I wanted to forge Keats's ode "To a Nightingale" and wrote out the poem, with a pencil, on a piece of greenish paper (as I am doing now). In itself the poem I have inscribed does not purport to be any other text of the poem other than what I have written: it is simply another instance of the work, another text amongst the hundreds or thousands of such texts. In this respect Goodman is right: I cannot forge Keats's "Nightingale" ode.

Suppose, however, I wanted to make a forgery of the fair copy of Keats's poem that is in the Fitzwilliam Museum in Cambridge. Using early nineteenth-century paper and ink that were found locked in a vault beneath St. James Place, I manage to replicate Keats's admirable scrawl and (we will assume my luck is really with me) surreptiously replace Keats's

8. I leave aside for now the theoretical implications of sound poetry, as well as some *Zaum* and L=A=N=G=U=A=G=E poetry (which for the most part is intranscribable, but recordable), and some concrete poems (which are not speakable, or in some cases transcribable, but are reproducible by other means). As an oral language, the implications offered by sign language poetry would fall under the rubric posited for sound poetry, i.e., intranscribable, but recordable.

holograph with my forged transcript. Bingo. Some years later a young D.Phil. candidate at Oxford visits Cambridge and notices one of the *t*'s doesn't look quite right, and, after careful paleographic inspection using infrared photography, earlier photostats, and Robert Gittings's *The Odes of John Keats and Their Earliest Known Manuscripts*, concludes that the manuscript is a forgery. Troubled Fitzwilliam officials review their records and find that another Keats scholar had "consulted" the holograph some years back. They send out a legal posse which of course catches me, and, in court, I stammer the truth: "N–N–Nelson Goodman made me do it."

What we learn from this is that the uniqueness of texts passes for Goodman's condition of something that can be forged (he admits in *Languages of Art* that performances can be forged [113]), which more emphatically says that texts are not iterable. Such a conclusion requires us to maintain our sharp distinction between a work and a text, and this is a distinction that Goodman's otherwise thoughtful analysis overlooks. Even if we grant Goodman this distinction, his argument is caught up in what exactly he means by a "correct copy" of a poem: he would have to impose a standard of correctness, in which case a "deviant" copy—one with, say, a misplaced comma—would not be another instance of that work, but a completely new work.

Another way of looking at the question of iterability is to examine Jorge Luis Borges's story entitled "Pierre Menard, Author of the *Quixote*," which runs like this: A friend of Menard, enumerating his publications and manuscripts, notes the inclusion of the ninth and thirty-eighth chapters of the first part of *Don Quixote*, and a fragment of chapter twenty-two. Not Cervantes's *Quixote* (which was written in the seventeenth century), but Menard's (which was written in the twentieth). Menard, says his friend, "did not want to compose another *Quixote*—which is easy—but *the Quixote itself*. Needless to say, he never contemplated a mechanical transcription of the original; he did not propose to copy it. His admirable intention was to produce a few pages which would coincide—word for word and line for line—with those of Miguel de Cervantes" (39). This indeed is exactly what Menard did, and did successfully. The story proceeds:

It is a revelation to compare Menard's *Don Quixote* with Cervantes'. The latter, for example, wrote (part one, chapter nine):

> . . . truth, whose mother is history, rival of time, depository of deeds, witness of the past, exemplar and advisor to the present, and the future's counselor.

Written in the seventeenth century, written by the "lay genius" Cervantes, this enumeration is a mere rhetorical praise of history. Menard, on the other hand, writes:

> . . . truth, whose mother is history, rival of time, depository of deeds, witness of the past, exemplar and advisor to the present, and the future's counselor.

History, the *mother* of truth: the idea is astounding. Menard, a contemporary of William James, does not define history as an inquiry into reality but as its origin. Historical truth, for him, is not what has happened; it is what we have judged to have happened. The final phrases—*exemplar and advisor to the present, and the future's counselor*—are brazenly pragmatic.

The contrast in style is also vivid. The archaic style of Menard—quite foreign, after all—suffers from a certain affectation. Not so that of his forerunner, who handles with ease the current Spanish of his time. (43).

The two *Quixotes* are thus, notwithstanding their identical spelling and punctuation, quite different works—or are they? Pressed to respond to the question by his colleague Richard Wollheim, Goodman is reluctant to concede that two identically spelled inscriptions ought to be considered instances of different works (*Of Mind and Other Matters,* 140–41). It is a difficult position: for Goodman to say that they are different works, he would also be saying that two iterable inscriptions are ontologically different—and this is as he admits either untenable or an aporia. What is possible here is that the inscription is iterable, but the inscription-as-an-utterance is not. If literature (or in a broad sense human communication) boiled down to mere spellings, we would have to concede agreement with Goodman. But we can't do this because literature is not mere spellings, and Borges's story makes this its central point. The

two *Quixotes* are overtly different: Cervantes's is quite at home in its enun-
ciation of the vernacular; Menard's, in contrast, seems strangely archaic.
Cervantes's *Quixote* is rhetorically straightforward, while Menard—
contemporary of Bertrand Russell and William James—writes with a certain kind of philosophical and pragmatic reserve. Their differences arise
not from the moments of our reading (though this may be so), but from
the moments of their respective inscriptions, and only later from our
investigation of those moments. The works are ontologized—that is to
say, contextualized semantically—by the temporal history that surrounds
their composition. In an excellent discussion of the story, Arthur Danto
adds:

> It is not just that the books are written at different times by different
> authors of different nationalities and literary intentions: these facts are
> not external ones; they serve to characterize the work(s) and of course
> to individuate them for all their graphic indiscernibility. That is to say,
> the works are in part constituted by their location in the history of lit-
> erature as well as by their relationships to their authors, and as these are
> often dismissed by critics who urge us to pay attention to the work
> itself, Borges' contribution to the ontology of art is stupendous: you
> cannot isolate these factors from the work since they penetrate, so to
> speak, the *essence* of the work. (35–36)

From the discipline of philosophy, Danto's point of view seems to me
informed and right; from the angle of literary criticism he is perhaps
more naive, but certainly no less right. The critics he implicates for
extolling us to "pay attention to the work itself" are no small lot: they
constitute a tradition that began (in its most concerted form) with the
New Critics (in America) and the Prague structuralists (in Europe), and
gained momentum, as well as an inimical presence, with Euro-American
structuralism and poststructuralism. Yet in urging us (as either literary
critics or art critics) to locate the ontological "essence" of a work with
that work's history, Danto is implicitly (and I suspect unconsciously)
guiding us toward New Historicism and the work of one of structuralism's most important antagonists, Mikhail M. Bakhtin.

Bakhtin's name is hardly new to the field of textual criticism; McGann, particularly, has found it purposeful to cite from Bakhtin's work, and behind those citations is a much larger theoretical framework. The insights Bakhtin adds to textual philosophy are not only germane, but germinal as well: they constitute—in their professedly antiformalist stance—one of our first discussions on the text as a discrete social and historical utterance. A collection of Bakhtin's unfinished essays, published in English under the title *Speech Genres and Other Late Essays*, is particularly useful in that it directly confronts two of the issues I have been dragging along through this essay: the iterability of language and the illusion of iterability of texts. Bakhtin writes: "Behind each text stands a language system. Everything in the text that is repeated and reproduced, everything repeatable and reproducible, everything that can be given outside a given text (the given) conforms to this language system. But at the same time each text (as an utterance) is individual, unique, and unrepeatable, and herein lies its entire significance (its plan, the purpose for which it was created). This is the aspect of it that pertains to honesty, truth, goodness, beauty, history" (105). It seems to me that the two profound truths of this statement (that the language of a text can be repeated, but that the text as an utterance cannot) are marred by Bakhtin's attempt to claim a third truth: that the "entire significance" of a text lies within its uniqueness as a social utterance, as an act of communication. This position is illustrative of Bakhtin's inflexibility towards formalism and structuralism, and the absolutism of his historical hermeneutics also infects McGann's work (I shall have more to say about this in my conclusion). This problem is disconcerting, but not in a manner that turns one away from Bakhtin; it instead pulls us closer to the ideological edge on which his ideas move. A bit further into his essay he takes up (unknowingly) a hypothetical position vis-à-vis Nelson Goodman and the two *Quixotes*:

Two or more sentences can be absolutely identical (when they are superimposed on one another, like two geometrical figures, they coincide); moreover, we must allow that any sentence, even a complex one, in the unlimited speech flow can be repeated an unlimited number of times in completely identical form. But as an utterance (or part of an utterance) no one sentence, even if it has only one word, can ever be repeated: it is always a new utterance (even if it is a quotation). . . . The utterance as a whole is shaped as such by extralinguistic (dialogic) aspects, and it is also related to other utterances. These extralinguistic (and dialogic) aspects also pervade the utterance from within. (108–9).

Given Cervantes's and Menard's *Quixote*s, Bakhtin would, on the basis of this position, unhesitatingly pronounce them different works, and he would do so for similar reasons Danto does: they are separate utterances, tied by "dialogic relations" to their historical circumstances, and different in their relation to those circumstances. The emphasis on the extralinguistic nature of these dialogical relations also serves, to an extent, to delimit the range of those relations: Bakhtin seems perfectly willing to grant that that relationship cannot be closed ("A context," he wrote, "is potentially unfinalized; a code must be finalized" [147]). Bakhtin's inclination here brings him as close to Derrida and Barthes as he can possibly come. Why? Because the deconstructionist conception of the text as a text(ile) composed of weavings is in its own way "dialogic," but not in a manner solely exterior to language: it rather works *in* language, and between language and the world. Derrida's position is that the interweaving (*Verwebung*) of language combines both the discursive and the nondiscursive, both language and "other threads of experience" into a cloth, into a text(ile), that is inextricable and for the most part unweavable.[9] Such a text is related to social history, but it is not related to social history alone: it is related to other texts as well, and their chaotic system of interrelationships (warp, woof) undergoes (in theory) a kind of semantic fusioning and fraying. A text is thus intertextual, "caught up," as Foucault says, "in a system of references to other books, other texts, other sentences: it is a node within a network" (*The Archaeology of Knowledge* 23). In practice the textile is more controlled (Robert

9. Derrida, "Form and Meaning: A Note on the Phenomenology of Language," in *Margins of Philosophy* 160–61; see also *Positions* 26–7.

Scholes, for example, points out a kind of hermeneutic centering in Derrida's writing); but this does not seem to matter much here. Bakhtin's position is one that suggests that the utterance's singularity is protected by the utterance's volatility: we can never go back to that utterance with complete assurance, can never, literally or conceptually, conceive it in totality. Thus we face a necessity, perhaps a rule, in proclaiming a text (as a textile) is never complete. Bakhtin seems to lean in this direction when he asserts that "dialogic boundaries intersect the entire field of living human thought" (120), and as boundaries go those are pretty big. If the natural boundaries of a text can never be located (as the moment of inscription can never be recalled), by what rule or rubric do we create artificial boundaries for texts in the creative arts?

One answer is that textual boundaries are projections of our social and political identities; that they are in a sense mental conceptualizations of historical spaces. For McGann, for example, there is no such thing as a text without a context, and it is only by a combination of historical evidence and our interpretation of that evidence that this context is circumscribed. In other words, textual boundaries are not the product of reality, but of our "reading" of reality. In summarizing the work of McGann and David McKenzie, John Sutherland has written: "The force of McKenzie's critique, like McGann's is that it specifically controverts the faith of modern bibliography in the reproducibility of the 'essential' text, if only institutionally approved procedures are followed. There is, for McKenzie and McGann, no ahistorically essential text to reproduce. The task of McKenzie's 'sociology,' as he sees it, is in any case not reproduction but the reinsertion of the text into the critical moments of its historical and political existence" (586). This is a good basic overview of the situation, but I think it can be taken further. I would venture to say that not only can we not "reproduce" an "essential" text, but we cannot reproduce *any* text. To be able to reproduce a text would suggest, in Goodman's allographic terms, that a text is composed of an ahistorical, "neutral" language: it suggests that language alone constitutes a text. And it further suggests that speech events or writing events can be replicated in a manner in which a photographic negative can produce several photographs. But this won't do, either for texts or for photographs as texts, because we would in this case have to say that photographs likewise have no historical contexts, which is obviously false: as for literature, it matters how they are printed, where they are printed, how they are mounted, where they are exhibited, and where they are published.

Sutherland's use of the term *reproduce* is perhaps unavoidable; yet it is misleading. Each time we "reproduce" a text—whether we do so in an edition or in an apparatus of an edition—we do not reproduce that text at all, but rather print it in another new and different context. By changing the extralinguistic component—e.g., the publication—we change the extratextual community, and hence the interpretative strategies that are brought to bear upon that text. The audience changes; assumptions about it change. Furthermore, this applies to art and photographs as much as it applies to literature, for which reason an Anselm Kiefer painting on the wall of Marian Goodman's gallery is not the same as the identical painting on the wall of the Podunk town library. The textual-bibliographical dilemma that arises from such situations is a question—posed earlier—of what constitutes the semiotic boundary of a text; i.e., if the text is seen as a signifier, what constitutes the boundary (or boundaries) of this signifier? By arguing that the text extends beyond its physical presence in language to the context of itself as an utterance, we are saying that a text includes what is extralinguistic, even what is supposedly extratextual. In short, we are proposing a model of a text that is as radically unstable as our interpretations for that text. The free (or floating) signifieds that characterize some models of deconstruction are now matched by equally free (or floating) signifiers; and in concurrence, we find ourselves agreeing with Derrida that the "presence" of a text-as-an-object belies the absence of the text-as-an-utterance-of-another-time-and-place. That is to say, the fixedness of a text is as illusory as the fixedness of an interpretation; neither is "final," neither is "authorial." Such a proposition threatens to upset the very foundations upon which the textual-bibliographical tradition is based.

Perhaps it is just as well that this happens. Textual criticism has placed a considerable amount of (undue) faith in the idea of a definitive edition, particularly as much of this faith is placed in the textual apparatus, which is often said to allow us to "reconstruct" authoritative and collaborative versions of a work. What it doesn't do, of course, is give us the supposedly nonauthoritative, nor does it give us oral texts, nor does it give us the extralinguistic contexts of those very texts it purports to be giving. What it does give us, then, are surrogate texts that appeal to the iterability of language, but not of texts as historical events. My position here might come across to editors as unusually hard, in which case I can only say that we need to be more realistic about what an apparatus can and cannot do. Perhaps its greatest benefit is that the apparatus is indexical in its reference to, and summary of, texts; we still have the onus of chasing after them on our own. But an apparatus, or for that matter an edition, that purports to "reproduce" a text is an apparatus that lies. To reproduce is to reenact. And this won't work because the word *reenact* is an oxymoron: we can no more print the same text twice than we can step in the same stream twice. To reprint—even in facsimile—Shelley's *Adonais* merely adds another pearl onto the string of textual enactments. Bowers's Hawthorne does not reproduce or reenact Hawthorne any more than Menard's *Quixote* reenacts Cervantes's. Nor does it matter (as it seems to matter to Goodman) if two texts are alike in all physical respects, whether perceptual or inherent: their difference is instead one that is ontological.

Let me illustrate for a moment how this might be. Suppose that one should stumble upon a press operation locked away in a forgotten warehouse. Still set up in type, with original inks, paper, and binding equipment, is Ernest Hemingway's *Torrents of Spring*. Suppose now that one were to follow through on this discovery and print and bind several volumes of the book: physically they would be absolutely identical to those distributed from the initial imprint. Are they identical texts, however? My answer is that they are not. The volumes are transposed ontologically by their historical context: they are *extensions* of their discovery as texts-in-progress. That is, their stasis (or hibernation) as texts-in-progress is unbound (awakened) by their discovery. They become texts only inasmuch as they are discovered and printed. Where this historical truth is hidden, we cannot decide whether the texts are identical or not, in which case one may just as well make a killing selling them at book fairs. To borrow from (and adapt) Arthur Danto's argument in his *Transfigura-tion of the Commonplace,* we cannot vouch that holy water is holy water except by our belief as such (18). Whether the water is actually tap water or Evian water does not seem to matter so much as our belief that the water, having been blessed, is "transfigured" from a substance of quotid-ian consumption to a substance of religious signification. Chemically it is still the same stuff, just as the Hemingway printed in 1926 is materially the same as the Hemingway printed in 1989. Hence, we cannot repro-duce, reprint, or reenact a text: each act of textual production is an act of sequential (even homeostatic) production.

This brings us vis-à-vis an important—perhaps the most important—aspect of a philosophy of textuality: we can say, quite emphatically, that *a work of literature is ontologized by its texts;* it is identified as literature, or as being of a particular genre, by its particular textual manifestations. Liter-ature does not define itself as literature; it is rather we who undertake this task of defining what we come to know as the highbrow and the lowbrow, the good and the bad, the canonical and the noncanonical. One particularly good example of this surfaced quite recently in the *New Yorker.* In an extended essay on the Great Plains, Ian Frazier tells how, after a night's sleep at a truck stop, he awoke in the morning to find (as he describes it) a stock truck parked beside his car, and "on the truck's door, in big letters, a poem":

Buck Hummer

Hog Hauler (68)

Buck Hummer certainly seems real, and the poem certainly is real, but what surely isn't real is Buck's consciousness of having a poem on the door of his truck. On that door, Buck's statement is both illocutionary and perlocutionary: it advertises and solicits, and, one supposes, the stock truck's text of this poem contained an address of sorts, and perhaps even a phone number. Frazier's text of "Buck Hummer" doesn't do this, however, because it doesn't have to: it rather announces itself as a poem. If the hog hauling business picks up for Buck as a result of his truck door being reontologized in the *New Yorker,* then he's in luck. Offers to publish his future truck doors might be slow in coming, and understandably so because Buck Hummer is not the author of "Buck Hummer/Hog Hauler"; rather, Frazier is. Buck merely wrote the door; Frazier wrote the poem. What is important here is that the poem stands in relation to literature as Marcel Duchamp's "Fountain" stands in relation to art. As a readymade (or more precisely, a readywrit), the poem becomes a poem only by virtue of Frazier's transcription and his offering of it as such. We accept it as a poem just as we accept the fact that Duchamp has transfigured (to use Danto's phrase again) a urinal into an artwork. For all we know Buck Hummer might not even exist—a point that explicitly contradicts the first sentence of this paragraph. The Buck Hummer of the truck door, the Buck Hummer of *New Yorker* fame, and (presumably) the Buck Hummer of the *Yellow Pages* present different texts that are also defined by our perception of their contexts. If this is an extreme example, it has the benefit of showing us how much semantic and historical information is couched within the individual texts of a work of literature; and it emphasizes (as the two *Quixotes* emphasize) that these differences do not necessarily have something (if anything) to do with the spelling or punctuation of texts: they extend themselves to the extralinguistic, extratextual context of that text, in which case the *New Yorker* and the door of Buck's stock truck are two very different vehicles for literature—and hogs.

OBJECTS, EVENTS, OUTCOMES

Earlier I mentioned that the tradition of textual criticism and bibliography has historically sought to provide an "organizing principle" in literary studies, and this principle is normally reflected by the ideas of authority and reliability in texts and editions. Much of this authority has been found in, or contrived from, the representation of authorial intent, whether these intentions are "final" or "original" or compounded in some way. Distinguishing authority is no doubt important; and from this point on it seems to me beneficial to our interests that we qualify (but not quantify, or stratify) this authority along the notion of alterity—as differences—and seek to explain what those differences mean, and why they are there. Freed of the burden of intentionality, texts become, as we saw, radically unstable, tenuously tied to a historical context that is at best ephemeral and in many ways irrecoverable. And this is to some a problem because it controverts the faith we have invested in modern textual criticism and bibliography, particularly in editions we use and have come to rely upon. Perhaps, however, this departure, or this shaking of our faith, is precisely what we need: something that will replace textual security with textual cynicism. The idea of a physically objectified text offers a false sense of security by being advertised as "objective," and since we can hold it in our hands (say, a book or a manuscript), we find additional comfort in its tangibility. This is understandable to the extent that our Western canonical traditions treat literature as a commodity for mass consumption. Problems, however, become apparent when we realize that language (langue) is not an object, nor for that matter is speech (parole). Speech may become objectified in a recording or (in a more limited way) in a printed text, but it is not in itself a physical entity. C. S. Peirce's semiotics is grounded in the basic tenet that "a sign, or *representamen,* is something which stands to somebody in some respect or capacity" (2:135). There is no indication of physical fixedness here, nor is it present in Saussure's semiology. The sign (or signifier, as I have been calling it in accord with more widely accepted European usage), is structurally free and may or may not take any kind of permanent embodiment. It need only be, in the words of the Prague structuralist Jan Mukařovský, "a reality perceivable by sense experience" in order to have life as a signifier (5). Hence, the evanescence of speech, of gestures, or of performances poses no problems for semiotics. Logic would tell us that no art form— no poem, no painting, no dance—can exist without a "text" comprising a semiotically endowed signifier, even if the boundaries of that signifier are indeterminate. One could even argue that silence—as in John Cage's

4′ 33′—is itself a text, or in any case textual, and give further validity to his statement "silence is sound" (*Poetry in Motion*). Though Cage's work is tangential and not the norm of the canons of textual traditions, it is just the kind of thing textual critics need to begin thinking about. When Williams and Abbot argue that textual embodiment consists of "letters written, impressed, or transferred onto a surface" (3), one wants to add that not only does the surface itself matter (as in Blake), but—to take Cage's reversal seriously—so too does the white space between the letters and words, particularly when that white space has a paralinguistic function. This is a sensitive matter when typographical boundaries are subject to manipulation, as in the decollage poetry of Tom Phillips and Ronald Johnson.[10] Thus, our expansion of the description of textual "boundaries" is one that must go inward (to the tangible) as much as it must go outward (to the intangible): we need to have a description that bears signification in whatever form it appears.

Since literature by its definition (but not its etymology) includes the idea of verbal constructs (whether aesthetic or nonaesthetic, whether conceived, contrived, or appropriated), then it seems imperative that a definition for a text be able to include various modes of the literary experience: oral performances, particularly, and sign language poetry, as well as dramatic performances and the genre of performance art. Even though performance art like Karen Finley's "Yams Up My Granny's Ass" is a good long way from the Shakespearean experience, the interdisciplinary context of performance art is particularly suited to textual studies since performances by their very nature exist in different "states." As Goodman admitted, individual performances can be forged, and this establishes their autographic mode. Because performances are overtly detached from the apparent (but not real) fixedness of books, they force

10. [Tom Phillips (1937–), an English artist, and Ronald Johnson (1938–1998), an American poet, have both created new texts by radically altering previously published works. In *A Humument: A Treated Victorian Novel*, 4th ed. (London: Thames and Hudson, 2005), Phillips painted on the pages of a Victorian novel, leaving legible some words which construct a new narrative of his own. Similarly, Johnson's *Radi Os* (1977, rpt. Chicago: Flood Editions, 2005) was composed by cutting away portions of Milton's *Paradise Lost*—*Paradise Lost* —*Editor.*]

us quite directly to confront their ephemerality and describe it in a way that is part of the scheme of textual semiotics.

One way to do this is to describe a text in terms of the speech act, or perhaps more usefully, as an event. Bakhtin's idea of the text as an utterance, McGann's idea of the text as a dynamic event, and Derrida's abandoning (and reformulation) of the moment of inscription, all move in this direction, and much can be said for their positions. Paul Ricoeur, in an essay on literary ontology published in 1974, perceptively suggested that because literature consists of discourse, and since discourse occurs as an event, then literature is by consequence a "language event" (94). Such language events—like Bakhtin's theory of the utterance—retain their singularity in their (arguably) irrecoverable history, whether that history is spoken or written. In this respect the speech act is not structured in any way that is fundamentally different from the writing act: both emphasize the unboundaried "space" of the act, as well as the act's location in time—what Bakhtin calls "chronotopicity" (134).

Because such events are articulatory, their phenomenology is oriented toward the production, not the reception, of signifiers. This small point needs to be stressed. Traditional schemas for phenomenology, whether in philosophy (such as Husserl's and Merleau-Ponty's) or in literature (such as Fish's and Wolfgang Iser's) stress the perceptual aspect of the phenomenological experience: it constitutes *the moment of recognition* of the signifier / signified, a process of relational discourse in the reader's mind. Discussing Stanley Fish, for example, Stephen Mailloux wrote that a sentence is not "an object, a thing-in-itself, but an *event,* something that *happens* to, and with the participation of, the reader" (20). The event is a moment of encounter: the text meets the reader, and the reader in turn decides (or as Husserl puts it, "reduces") the text's essence. In a way the text is absolved of its textuality; it becomes absorbed by (and by default possessed by) the reader, which in turn gives rise to Fish's lemma: "The reader's response is not *to* the meaning; it *is* the meaning" (*Is There a Text in This Class?* 3). It is arguable that the realities of production and "reading" entail a more composite structure of interaction where production entails reading and reading entails production. However, such an argument is outside the scope of the present essay. The point traditional phenomenology offers us is one of contrast: it reminds us that the phenomenology of perception is paralleled by the phenomenology of text production (in a literal sense), even if reading reduces the production model to a single text.

In all of the quotations I have just cited—Ricoeur's, Searle's, and McGann's—the word *event* is pivotal. But just what is an event? This is a crucial term, and it is difficult too. Are events objects? Clearly they are not, although they can be described as objectlike, or paraobjects. We tend to objectify events (such as Christmas, the Fourth of July, or Shakespeare's birthday) giving them the religious or cultural status of objects; yet they are not physical entities. At this point we again realize that a definition of a text as an object is not going to do in the long run, however well it has served us in the past. Considered empirically, events do not consist of matter, nor are they in a conventional sense entities. Since an object suggests a kind of "retainable" entity, an event is more of what the linguist George Lakoff describes as a "conceptual" entity (542). A conceptual entity is not, as it seems to imply, an oxymoron: the space it displaces is a *mental* space, and texts—all texts, whether spoken or written—occupy such space. Although this mental space is central to critical ideology, whether that ideology belongs to Derrida or Fish, it does not normally concern textual critics and bibliographers. But perhaps it should, if only in a subconscious manner. A physical text, say, the holograph of Keats's "Nightingale" ode occupies, simultaneously, different dimensions of space: literal space, mental space, and (as we discussed earlier) historical space—and none of these locations is entirely discrete. This helps us understand how the concept of an oral text (like oral literature) fits into this paradigm; and even if the acoustic signal of the speech act is not literally an entity (how many dimensions do displaced molecules occupy?) this does not matter. What does matter is that Homer reciting the *Iliad* or Johnny Rotten ranting at Wembley are both creating and producing texts that are also events—not objects. Because events are temporarily discrete, they are finite in a useful way. Yet because events take place in space, they are in another sense infinite, since, for example, we can never know the full setting in which Homer and Rotten might have been performing, even if we ourselves are (or were) a member of the audience. The beauty of such texts is that their literal space and their historical space are largely concomitant by being an extension of the present; and as we witness them, we become a part of this extension, a part of the text itself. If such texts have a problem (some might call it an advantage) it is that they cannot be replicated; there is no "going back" to an event that, gone once, is gone forever. Since textual studies is by its nature a retrospective activity, this partly explains why oral texts and oral recordings do not find their way into editions. Occasionally they squeak into bibliographies, particularly when the recordings themselves are canonized (as in the case of Dylan Thomas). But these cases are rather exceptional. Exceptional too are critical discussions of oral textual events, perhaps because—as the artist Julian Schnabel once uttered in a rare insight—it is difficult to examine and talk about a text one cannot go back to for a second look.

Events, however, can be recorded, if only to a degree, using any of the various technologies available. Recordings are necessarily imperfect; they cannot record the speech act. Yet if the process is flawed, it is flawed only as much as *all* processes of textual transmission are inherently flawed. What is important, I think, is the denominator that links together recordings with books and manuscripts: they are objects. I would like to suggest that these objects can be more properly and usefully described as *outcomes* of events. If speech is an event, the recording of it is an outcome. If writing is an event, the recording of it (i.e., the MS, the TS, the floppy disc) is an outcome. While some events have outcomes by their very nature (writing for example), others may have deliberate outcomes (a performance that is recorded), while others do not specifically have outcomes (an unrecorded performance). The text-as-an-outcome is not necessarily better than the text-as-an-event; they are different, both physically and ontologically, and furnish their own kinds of critical playgrounds. The outcome is particularly unusual (and from the hermeneutic point of view, desirable) because it tends to recall the event that produced it, whether that event is historical (McGann), sociological (Bakhtin), or "compositional" (as in Gabler's edition of

Ulysses). Such theories constitute a nostalgia for the moment of inscription: they want to go back. Whether we can actually arrive at that point of recall, or trace it through what Barthes calls "the myth of filiation" (77) is a big question. Here, however, we move outside the critical text into critical theory—at which point the disinterested textual critic can go no further.

No further, precisely because textual theory that pretends to be critical theory betrays itself. It is an ironic way to size up the situation: is there such a thing as a disinterested critic? The notion of textuality is recessive against a foreground of critical theory: Jerome McGann stands out not as a textual theorist but as a political historicist; Hershel Parker not as a textual theorist but as a hermeneut. They may claim they are textual theorists, but only inasmuch as their textual theory serves their critical program—and it is, consequently, their critical programs that assert an institutionally political shadow over their textual work. Earlier I suggested that Bakhtin marred the persuasiveness of his argument of the text-as-an-utterance by saying that the *entire* significance of a text lay in the "dialogic relations" with its individual history. This strikes me as being unnecessarily coercive. Along nearly identical lines McGann has written in *The Beauty of Inflections:* "If we are to understand how poems mean—if we are going to gain knowledge of literary productions—we must pay attention to a variety of concrete historical particulars, and not merely to 'the poem itself' or its linguistic determination" (96). Textual studies helps one do just that: it helps reveal the complex compositional and production aspects of literature, and how these aspects are part of larger historical, political, and economic structures. But textual studies cannot necessarily tell us how language works per se, in which case McGann's light treatment of the "linguistic determination" of a poem seems to overlook abstract semantic issues as much as it is generous to concrete historical issues. If, as McGann says, we are to understand *how* poems mean, then perhaps we first need to understand how language itself means—and this is precisely where Derrida has chosen to locate himself. Linguistic determination wouldn't be such a difficult thing were we not so overwhelmed by linguistic indetermination. We can hardly be expected to make sense out of a poem if we can't make sense out of the most basic relationship between a signifier and its signified—a questionable relationship that gave Derrida the basis for grammatology, the gram as *différance* replacing the sign. It seems to me that whatever assumptions we make about texts and textual histories, our assumptions are guided by the kinds of "literary" (or even linguistic) questions we are asking. Literature after all is an art; its medium is language; language is both cognitive and social; and there is, simply, no way any one critical theory is going to tell us how all these things coalesce. Like literature itself, criticism thrives on a kind of discursiveness engendered by alterity, and explorations like McGann's, Bakhtin's, and Derrida's—explorations that have something new to say— constitute the critical discourse of the perpetual present. Literature is not a study of truths, not a study of falsities, but a study of disguises. If it were a study of truths and such like operations, we would imply that literature is also a study of closure; and this, clearly, is not the case.

We should also remember that the noniterability of texts means that textual displacement is a temporal (and hence spatial) issue: it presents the literary critic (confronted with numerous authorial and nonauthorial versions of a single work) or the art critic (with numerous re-presentations of a single work) or the performance critic (with numerous instances of a work's performance texts) with an overwhelming sense of the burden of textual history. This is daunting, and at the same time it is good: as our awareness of the numbers (and kinds) of textual states and modalities increases, so too do our interpretative possibilities. There is in fact something fundamental to how textual literacy—an awareness of the textual histories of the poems, plays, and novels we are discussing—informs literary criticism, perhaps because it makes real the endless diversity of historical spaces in which literature occurs, just as it makes real the different modalities in which language occurs. Yet these possibilities can only be the product of our own initiative. Texts do not come to us; we must go to them. The differences which texts reveal amongst themselves, and which distinguish themselves from each other, are the product of an uncentered alterity: there is no "correct" text, no "final" text, no "original" text, but only texts that are different, drifting in their like differences. By exploring, but not stratifying, these differences, we begin to understand how textual dynamics can be broken down into a phenomenology of text production, and such recognition is, I think, the beginning of a philosophy of textuality.

WORKS CITED

Bakhtin, Mikhail M. *Speech Genres and Other Late Essays*. Trans. Vern W. McGee. Ed. Caryl Emerson and Michael Holquist. Austin: U of Texas P, 1986.

Barthes, Roland. *Image-Music-Text*. 1977. Trans. Stephen Heath. New York: Hill & Wang, 1977.

Borges, Jorge Luis, "Pierre Menard, Author of the *Quixote*." In *Labyrinths*. Ed. Donald A. Yates and James E. Erby. New York: New Directions, 1964. 36–44.

Danto, Arthur. *The Transfiguration of the Commonplace*. Cambridge: Harvard UP, 1981.

Derrida, Jacques. "Signature Event Context." 1976. In *Margins of Philosophy*. Trans. Alan Bass. Chicago: U of Chicago P, 1982. 309–30.

———. *Positions*. Trans. Alan Bass. Chicago: U of Chicago P, 1981.

Fish, Stanley. *Is There a Text in This Class?* Cambridge: Harvard UP, 1980.

Foucault, Michel. *The Archaeology of Knowledge*. 1969. Trans. A. M. Sheridan Smith. New York: Pantheon, 1972.

Frazier, Ian. "A Reporter at Large: Great Plains III." *The New Yorker*, March 6, 1989, 41–68.

Goodman, Nelson. *Of Mind and Other Matters*. Cambridge: Harvard UP, 1984.

———. *Languages of Art*. 2d ed. Indianapolis: Hackett, 1976.

Lakoff, George. *Women, Fire, and Dangerous Things: What Categories Reveal about the Mind*. Chicago: U of Chicago P, 1987.

Mailloux, Stephen. *Interpretive Conventions: The Reader in the Study of American Fiction*. Ithaca: Cornell UP, 1982.

McGann, Jerome. "*Ulysses* as a Postmodern Text: The Gabler Edition." *Criticism* 27 (1985): 283–306.

———. *The Beauty of Inflections*. Oxford: Clarendon, 1985.

———. *A Critique of Modern Textual Criticism*. Chicago: U of Chicago P, 1983.

Mukařovský, Jan. "Art as a Semiotic Fact." 1936. *Semiotics of Art: Prague School Contributions*. Ed. Ladislav Matejka and Irwin R. Titunik. Cambridge: MIT P, 1976. 3–9.

Parker, Hershel. *Flawed Texts and Verbal Icons: Literary Authority in American Fiction*. Evanston: Northwestern UP, 1984.

Peirce, Charles Sanders. *Collected Papers of Charles Sanders Peirce*. Ed. Charles

Hartshorne and Paul Weiss. 1931. 6 vols. Rpt. Cambridge: Harvard UP, Belknap, 1960.

Poetry in Motion. Film. Dir. Ron Mann. 1985.

Ricoeur, Paul. "The Model of the Text: Meaningful Action Considered as Text." *New Literary History* 6 (1974): 95–110.

Rothenberg, Jerome. *Pre-Faces and Other Writings.* New York: New Directions, 1981.

Scholes, Robert. "Deconstruction and Communication." *Critical Inquiry* 14 (1988): 278–95.

Shillingsburg, Peter L. *Scholarly Editing in the Computer Age: Theory and Practice.* Athens: U of Georgia P, 1986.

Smith, Barbara Herrnstein. *On the Margins of Discourse: The Relation of Literature to Language.* Chicago: U of Chicago P, 1978.

Steiner, Wendy. *The Colors of Rhetoric.* Chicago: U of Chicago P, 1982.

Sutherland, John. "Publishing History: A Hole at the Centre of Literary Sociology." *Critical Inquiry* 14 (1988): 574–89.

Taylor, Mark C. *Altarity.* Chicago: U of Chicago P, 1987.

Thorpe, James. *Principles of Textual Criticism.* San Marino: The Huntington Library, 1972.

Williams, William Proctor, and Craig S. Abbott. *An Introduction to Bibliographical and Textual Studies.* 2d ed. New York: Modern Language Association, 1989.

The Shakespearean Editor as Shrew-Tamer[†]

Leah Marcus

WE ALL KNOW how Shakespeare's uncomfortable play *The Taming of the Shrew* ends. Kate makes a long and eloquent speech of submission to Petruchio in which she argues for the subordination of wives on legal, biological, and ethical grounds, finally offering to place her hand beneath her husband's foot if that will "do him ease." Petruchio responds with gusto, "Why, there's a wench!"[1] and after a bit more repartee, the company scatters, commenting on the miracle of Kate's taming, even though, at least as we like to read and teach the play nowadays, it is by no means clear that Kate is thoroughly converted to the system of patriarchal hegemony she advocates. Whether she is or not, there is a strong illusion of reality surrounding her speech at the end of the play: we are invited to forget that the taming of Kate by Petruchio started out as a mere play within a play performed for the delectation of one Christopher Sly, drunken tinker turned temporary aristocrat.

† "The Shakespearean Editor as Shrew-Tamer," from *English Literary Renaissance* 22: 177–200. Reprinted by permission of Blackwell Publishing.

1. *The Taming of the Shrew* 5.2.179–80, cited from the New Cambridge *The Taming of the Shrew,* ed. Ann Thompson (Cambridge, Eng., 1984). Subsequent references to the play will be to this edition and indicated by act, scene, and line number in the text.

This essay was presented at the University of Massachusetts, Amherst, as the *ELR* Lecture for 1990, now the Dan S. Collins Lecture in Renaissance Studies. The author would like to thank audiences at the University of Massachusetts, Arizona State University, Williams College, the University of Illinois at Chicago, the University of Wisconsin, and Yale University for invaluable comments and suggestions.

In actual productions of the play within the last fifteen years in London or New York, Stratford or New Haven, however, Christopher Sly is harder to forget. As often as not in recent stagings, he remains on stage and alert until almost the end of the taming plot, calling for the clown figure to come back on stage, commenting on the action, and even intervening to stop it when some of the characters appear about to be hauled off to prison.[2] When he finally does drift into sleep around the beginning of Act 5, the Lord orders him carried back to his original place and he becomes once more a drunken tinker lying in a stupor before an alehouse. Sly awakens, somewhat dazed, and concludes that the taming play he has watched has been a vivid dream, the bravest and best he has ever had. The reality of the taming plot in this version is severely undercut: it has remained "only" a play—or even a dream—throughout. Moreover, Sly's final lines compromise Kate's message even further. He lurches off, vowing to tame his own termagant wife at home now that his dream has taught him how to do it. He is unlikely to succeed, we can confidently predict, given his staggering condition and his obvious characterological distance from the charismatic stage figure Petruchio. Instead of convincing us that the inner play's wife-taming scenario is a possible one in reality, Sly's vow turns it into the wish-fulfillment fantasy of a habitual drunkard who is as likely to be punished by his wife for this night out as he has been for past transgressions. Shrew-taming becomes the compensatory fantasy of a socially underprivileged male.

It is not difficult to imagine why the Christopher Sly ending is gaining increasing popularity in theatrical productions of *The Taming of the Shrew*: it softens some of the brutality of the taming scenes, which can then be viewed as tailored to the uncultivated tastes of Sly; it distances late twentieth-century audiences from some of the most unacceptable implications of Kate's pronouncements on male sovereignty. But on what authority do directors tack the Sly episodes onto the written text as

2. For discussion of recent performances, I am indebted to Tori Haring-Smith, *From Farce to Metadrama: A Stage History of* The Taming of the Shrew, *1594–1983* (Westport, 1985), and to Graham Holderness, *Shakespeare in Performance:* The Taming of the Shrew (Manchester, Eng., 1989).

we all know it from our standard editions? To attempt to answer that question is to enter a labyrinth in which any stable sense we may have of the identity of Shakespeare and his work very quickly begins to dissolve. By examining the textual and performance history of *The Taming of the Shrew* we will gain a fresh sense of the provisionality, even the fragility, of our standard text.

II

The easy and traditional answer to the question "On what authority?" is "On no authority whatsoever." The scenes of Sly's intervention in the action and eventual return to the alehouse are, as most recent editors of the play agree, "not Shakespeare," and therefore inadmissable into the canonical text of the play and usually relegated to an appendix. These episodes featuring Sly come from *The Taming of a Shrew*, a play generally regarded by editors as artistically inferior to *The Taming of the Shrew* but viewed in its own time, for copyright purposes at least, as the same play as *The Shrew. The Taming of a Shrew* (or *A Shrew*, as it is termed to differentiate it from *The Shrew*) was published in a 1594 quarto and again in 1596 and 1607. *The Shrew* appeared in print for the first time in the 1623 First Folio of Shakespeare's works without having been entered separately in the Stationers' Register; it was reprinted in quarto form in 1631 by the printer who owned the copyright to *A Shrew*.[3] So far as we know, the earlier printed version of *A Shrew* was not republished after 1607. It was, however, closely associated with other early quarto versions of Shakespeare plays: it was, according to its 1594 title page, "sundry times acted by the Right honorable the Earle of Pembrook his servants," a company with which Shakespeare may have been briefly associated; it was sent to the printer around the same time as the quarto versions of *Henry VI Parts 2 and 3* and *Titus Andronicus,* very likely because by 1594 the Earl of Pembroke's

---

3. Thompson, pp. 1–3; the New Arden edition of *The Taming of the Shrew,* ed. Brian Morris (London, 1981), p. 3.

Men had become indigent and dissolved. A play called by Henslowe "the tamynge of A shrowe" was performed at Newington Butts in 1594 by the Lord Chamberlain's Men, a company with which Shakespeare was probably already associated by the end of that year if not earlier; other plays performed alongside it included *Titus Andronicus* and some version of *Hamlet*.[4] At the very least, *The Taming of a Shrew* was closely connected with other early plays now accepted by textual revisionists as Shakespearean.

Nevertheless, beginning with Edmond Malone in the late eighteenth century, an enormous amount of editorial energy has gone into proving—over and over again and by various ingenious strategies—that no part of *The Taming of a Shrew* can be Shakespeare. Whether consciously or not, recent editors have suppressed the degree of visibility *A Shrew* has had in the textual history of *The Shrew.* Modern editors, when they consider *A Shrew* at all, tend to state that of all Shakespeare's previous editors, only Alexander Pope admitted the Christopher Sly episodes and conclusion to his text of *The Taming of the Shrew.* That significantly understates the matter: not only Pope, but, following him, Thomas Hanmer, Lewis Theobald, Samuel Johnson, William Warburton, and Edward Capell all included some or all of the Sly materials in their editions as "Shakespeare." The eighteenth-century pattern was broken by Malone, who argued that *A Shrew* was not Shakespeare, but Shakespeare's source play for *The Shrew.*[5] Since Malone's edition of Shakespeare in the late

4. Scholarly opinion differs as to whether Shakespeare himself was a member of Pembroke's Men and whether *A Shrew* was actually performed by that company or by the Lord Chamberlain's Men at Newington Butts. There are also marked differences of opinion over which of these early *Shrews* was *A Shrew* and which may have been *The Shrew.* For representative views, see E. K. Chambers, *William Shakespeare: A Study of Facts and Problems,* 2 vols. (Oxford, 1930), 1:324–28; *The Taming of the Shrew,* ed. Sir Arthur Quiller-Couch and John Dover Wilson (Cambridge, Eng., 1928), pp. vii–xxv, 99–126; *The Taming of the Shrew,* ed. H. J. Oliver (Oxford, 1984), pp. 29–34; and David George, "Shakespeare and Pembroke's Men," *Shakespeare Quarterly,* 32 (1981), 305–23.

5. Early editions I have consulted include *The Works of Mr. William Shakespeare; In Six Volumes,* ed. Nicholas Rowe (1709); *The Works of Shakespear . . . in Six Volumes,* ed. Alexander Pope (1720–1725); *The Works of Shakespeare in Seven Volumes,* ed. Lewis Theobald (1733); *The Works of Shakespear in Six Volumes,* ed. Thomas Hanmer (1744); *The Works of Shakespear in Eight Volumes,* ed. William Warburton (1747); *The Plays of William Shakespeare, in Eight Volumes,* ed. Samuel Johnson (1765); *Mr. William Shakespeare his COMEDIES,*

eighteenth century, *The Taming of the Shrew* in printed versions has looked much as we know it in our standard editions today—with Sly dropping out early on and the taming plot opening out into "reality" at the end. In every generation there have been a few hardy souls who have argued that *A Shrew* is indeed Shakespeare—an early apprentice version of the play that later became *The Shrew.* From time to time there have also been hardy souls who have argued that their preferred text, *The Shrew,* or at least most of it, was also not written by Shakespeare. During the twentieth century, however, opinion has rigidified significantly. *The Shrew* has been generally accepted as canonical and *A Shrew* moved further and further from Shakespeare. Instead of being regarded as the source play for *The Shrew,* as it was by most editors until the 1920s, it now has lost even that status, and is generally considered instead a "vamped up" copy—a "bad quarto" of the "original" play, *The Taming of the Shrew.* Yet, curiously, *A Shrew* is not included among the other "bad quartos" in Michael J. B. Allen and Kenneth Muir's handsome facsimile edition of *Shakespeare's Plays in Quarto,* on the grounds that its text is anomalous, "longer and more coherent than the texts of the other bad quartos."[6] What gets called "Shakespeare" in the case of *A Shrew*

HISTORIES, AND TRAGEDIES, ed. Edward Capell (1768); and *The Plays and Poems of William Shakespeare in 10 Volumes,* ed. Edmond Malone (1790). Capell represents a transitional case in that the Sly materials are included in the text of his London 1768 edition but branded as non-Shakespearean in the introduction and notes of his Dublin 1771 edition, *The Plays of Shakespeare.*

6. *Shakespeare's Plays in Quarto: A Facsimile Edition of Copies Primarily from the Henry E. Huntington Library,* ed. Michael Allen and Kenneth Muir (Berkeley, 1981), p. xv; see also W. W. Greg, *The Shakespeare First Folio: Its Bibliographical and Textual History* (Oxford, 1955), pp. 210–16. For representative twentieth-century arguments about the derivative nature of *A Shrew,* see n. 23 below. For examples of dissenting opinion, to the effect that *A Shrew* is either early Shakespeare or Shakespeare's main source, see *The Taming of a Shrew,* ed. F. S. Boas (London, 1908); *The Works of Shakespeare: The Taming of the Shrew,* ed. R. Warwick Bond (Indianapolis, n. d.); *Narrative and Dramatic Sources of Shakespeare,* ed. Geoffrey Bullough, (London, 1966), l, 58; *Shakespeare's Comedy of "The Taming of the Shrew,"* ed. William J. Rolfe (New York, 1881 [new edition, 1898]); W. J. Courthope, *A History of English Poetry* (London, 1895–1910), IV, 467–74. To their credit, in *William Shakespeare: A Textual Companion* (Oxford 1987), Gary Taylor and Stanley Wells leave open the question of the relationship between *A Shrew* and *The Shrew.*

and *The Shrew* is protean and malleable, shifting over the years along with literary fashions, along with social mores, and especially—this is the part that interests me the most—along with shifting views of male violence and female subordination. "Shakespeare" is a historical construction, grounded in historical data, to be sure, but data so scanty that they can be reconfigured rather easily to support one or another hypothesis about what constitutes a genuine text.

III

In *The Taming of the Shrew* we are dealing with a particularly tricky form of marginality: what might Shakespeare have written or helped to write when he was not yet sounding like "Shakespeare"? Even though the early history of *A Shrew* so closely parallels that of *Titus Andronicus,* which now has a secure place in the canon, and that of the quarto versions of *Henry VI, Parts 2 and 3,* which are now accepted as Shakespeare by revisionist critics, *A Shrew* remains in a curious limbo. It is too regular and original to be a "bad quarto," yet somehow too derivative and uncouth to be acceptable Shakespeare. There are, I would suggest, good reasons why twentieth-century editors and critics have been particularly reluctant to associate *The Taming of a Shrew* with Shakespeare, either as source play or as Shakespeare's early version of the standard text. For traditional editors, *A Shrew* has been less acceptable than *The Shrew* at least in part because of an affinity between shrew-taming as valorized in *The Taming of the Shrew* and what editors have traditionally liked to do with texts. As an essay by Gary Taylor has recently pointed out, the editing of Shakespeare has traditionally been a gendered activity, with the editor almost always male and the text implicitly female.[7] Good texts are not supposed to be wild and unruly; to the extent that they appear so, it is the editor's job to tame them into meaning, ironing out uncouthness and

---

7. Gary Taylor, "Textual and Sexual Criticism: A Crux in *The Comedy of Errors,*" *Renaissance Drama,* n. s. 19 (1988), 195–225.

grotesqueries as a way of showing the essential elevation and refinement of "gentle Shakespeare's" creation once the disfigurements introduced by ignorant actors, copyists, and printers have been carefully cleared away. In *The Shrew,* shrew taming is explicitly associated with humanist pedagogy: Petruchio's subduing and refinement of Kate operates parallel to the purported efforts of Bianca's tutors to teach the two sisters Vergil and the art of the lute. By learning to speak the pedagogue's language of social and familial order, Kate shows herself to be a better student of standard humanist doctrine than her sister.[8] In *A Shrew,* as we shall see, the taming process is considerably less efficacious. To accept *A Shrew* as Shakespeare would be, from the standpoint of traditional editorial practice, to leave the shrew (and the text) in disorder. It would also be to lose a convenient mechanism by which the forcible suppression of female insurgency is naturalized as reality and truth.

But even for reader-critics whose views are markedly less traditional, *A Shrew* has usually been kept safely on the margins, at considerable distance from the "genuine" play, perhaps because if allowed to come into close proximity with the "correct" text, it would undermine yet another version of "gentle Shakespeare"—his time-honored reputation for unusual benignity, at least by the standards of his day, in his understanding of and sympathy for women. To the extent that they have considered *A Shrew* at all, modern editors and critics have regularly fragmented it, citing it piecemeal in order to demonstrate the superior artistry and the superior humanity of the "authentic" version. They regularly excerpt parts of Kate's speech of submission from *A Shrew,* which argues for wifely obedience on the basis of Eve's responsibility for the Fall, in order to demonstrate the vastly decreased mysogyny of Kate's arguments in Shakespeare's "authentic" version. Just as regularly, they identify as defects features of *A Shrew* which, if

8. For this point I am indebted to Margaret Downes-Gamble's paper, "The Taming-school: *The Taming of the Shrew* as Lesson in Renaissance Humanism and the Modern Humanities," *Privileging Gender in Early Modern England,* ed. Jean R. Brink (Kirksville, MO: 1993), 65–92. See also Thompson, pp. 13–14.

analyzed instead as alternate versions of the text, might make the canonical *Shrew* sound less than humane by comparison.[9] In all modern editions of the authorized text, *A Shrew* is treated not as an artistic structure with its own patterns of meaning and its own dramatic logic, but as a heap of shards thrown together by ignorant actors with no capacity for coherence. As we shall see, there has long been a radical disjunction between what passes as genuine Shakespeare in the printed text of the play and what is accepted as Shakespeare in performance,

9. See, e.g., John C. Bean, "Comic Structure and the Humanizing of Kate in *The Taming of the Shrew,*" in *The Woman's Part: Feminist Criticism of Shakespeare,* ed. Carolyn Ruth Swift Lenz, Gayle Greene, and Carol Thomas Neely (Urbana, Ill., 1980, rpt. 1983), pp. 65–78; and Peter Berek, "Text, Gender, and Genre in *The Taming of the Shrew,*" in *"Bad" Shakespeare: Revaluations of the Shakespearean Canon,* ed. Maurice Charney (London, 1988), pp. 91–104. Both essays consistently misread *A Shrew* out of a desire to demonstrate Shakespeare's greater tolerance and humanity. For use of Kate's submission speech from *A Shrew,* see Ann Thompson's fine edition (n. 1 above), pp. 28–29.

Other interpretive articles with which I may not agree but to which my own thinking is indebted include Lynda E. Boose, "Scolding Brides and Bridling Scolds: Taming the Woman's Unruly Member," *Shakespeare Quarterly,* 42 (1991), 179–213; and her essay "*The Taming of the Shrew,* Good Husbandry, and Enclosure," in *Shakespeare Reread: The Texts in New Contexts,* ed. Russ McDonald (Ithaca, 1994), 193–225; Richard A. Burt, "Charisma, Coercion, and Comic Form in *The Taming of the Shrew,*" *Criticism,* 26 (1984), 295–311; Joel Fineman, "The Turn of the Shrew," in *Shakespeare and the Question of Theory,* ed. Patricia Parker and Geoffrey Hartman (London, 1985), pp. 138–59; Thelma Nelson Greenfield, "The Transformation of Christopher Sly," *Philological Quarterly,* 33 (1954), 34–42; Robert B. Heilman, "*The Taming* Untamed, or, The Return of the Shrew," *Modern Language Quarterly,* 27 (1966), 146–61; Barbara Hodgdon's essay "Katherina Bound, or Notes on Pla(k)ating the Structures of Everyday Life," *PMLA,* 107 (1992), 538–53; Richard Hosley, "Was There a 'Dramatic Epilogue' to *The Taming of the Shrew?*" *Studies in English Literature 1500–1900,* 1 (1961), 17–34; Sears Jayne, "The Dreaming of *The Shrew,*" *Shakespeare Quarterly,* 17 (1966), 41–56; Ernest P. Kuhl, "Shakespeare's Purpose in Dropping Sly," *Modern Language Notes, 36* (1921), 321–29; Karen Newman, "Renaissance Family Politics and Shakespeare's *The Taming of the Shrew,*" *English Literary Renaissance,* 16 (1986), 86–100; Marianne L. Novy, "Patriarchy and Play in *The Taming of the Shrew,*" *English Literary Renaissance,* 9 (1979), 264–80; Marion D. Perrit, "Petruchio: The Model Wife," *Studies in English Literature 1500–1900,* 23 (1983), 223–35; Michael W. Shurgot, "From Fiction to Reality: Character and Stagecraft in *The Taming of the Shrew,*" *Theatre Journal,* 33 (1981), 327–40; Edward Tomarken's *Samuel Johnson on Shakespeare: The Discipline of Criticism* (Athens, GA, 1991); Valerie Wayne, "Refashioning the Shrew," *Shakespeare Studies,* 17 (1985), 159–87; and Karl P. Wentersdorf, "The Original Ending of *The Taming of the Shrew:* A Reconsideration," *Studies in English Literature 1500–1900,* 18 (1978), 201–15. My thanks to Lynda Boose, Edward Tomarken, and Barbara Hodgdon, who graciously shared their work in manuscript.

with performance traditions sometimes running a good half-century ahead of editorial practice. If that pattern holds, then *A Shrew,* with its heavy undercutting, through the return of Christopher Sly, of Kate's long sermon at the end about proper female subordination, may be on the verge of becoming "Shakespeare," just as it was during most of the eighteenth century and just as, since then, other suspect plays like *Titus Andronicus, King John,* and the *Henry VI* plays and their quartos have gradually been brought into the canon.

Recent poststructuralist theory positing the fundamental indeterminacy of all literary texts has shaken up most of the interpretive categories by which editors have been able to assert confidently in the matter of *A Shrew* and *The Shrew* that the latter is "Shakespeare" while the former is not. In the case of *King Lear,* many editors and bibliographers are now willing to accept the argument of Steven Urkowitz, Michael Warren, and Gary Taylor that there are not one but two authoritative versions of that play—the 1608 quarto version and the 1623 folio. Both are printed in the New Oxford Shakespeare and in Warren's *The Complete King Lear, 1608–1623* (Berkeley, 1989). Little by little, the status of the "bad quartos" of Shakespeare is rising.[10] Instead of damning them in the language of the First Folio itself as "stolne and surreptitious copies,"[11] we are beginning to regard them as valuable records of performance with their own logic and artistic merits, their own "local" identities, their own distinctive claim to critical attention. It is time to extend that attention to *A Shrew* and its undercutting of patriarchal authority.

10. See Steven Urkowitz, *Shakespeare's Revision of* King Lear (Princeton, 1980); *The Division of the Kingdoms: Shakespeare's Two Versions of* King Lear, ed. Gary Taylor and Michael Warren (Oxford, 1983); Urkowitz, "Reconsidering the Relationship of Quarto and Folio Texts of *Richard III*," *English Literary Renaissance,* 16 (1986), 442–66; Urkowitz, "Good News about 'Bad' Quartos," in *"Bad" Shakespeare: Revaluations of the Shakespeare Canon,* ed. Maurice Charney (London, 1988), pp. 189–206; Annabel Patterson, "Back by Popular Demand: The Two Versions of *Henry V,*" *Renaissance Drama,* n. s. 19 (1988). 29–62; and Leah Marcus, *Puzzling Shakespeare: Local Reading and Its Discontents* (Berkeley, 1988). The present essay appears in revised form in Leah Marcus, *Unediting the Renaissance: Shakespeare, Marlowe, Milton* (New York: Routledge, 1996).

11. *The First Folio of Shakespeare,* ed. Charlton Hinman (London, 1968), p. 7.

IV

What happens if, instead of regarding *A Shrew* as *ipse facto* a foul corruption of the "true" play, we regard it as a text in its own right, a text in which difference does not have to be read as debasement? The differences are many and striking. *A Shrew* is shorter and often simpler; the verse has many borrowings from Marlowe and is often metrically irregular, although that is occasionally true of *The Shrew* as well. More strikingly, *A Shrew* has a different setting (Athens) and different names for all the main characters except Kate. Petruchio is named Ferando. In *A Shrew,* the subplot to the taming play is quite different: Kate has two sisters instead of one and each has her own suitor, so that the rivalry of *The Shrew* for the hand of Bianca is absent. The taming plot itself is much like that of the play as we know it, except that the incidents are arranged somewhat differently, the characters are less vividly and fully drawn, Kate's motivation in accepting Petruchio is clearer, and Petruchio's in taming Kate is less clear. Editors have traditionally disparaged *A Shrew* on the grounds that its portrayal of motivation is murky, failing to notice that their generalization applies only to the male characters, not to Kate herself.[12] In *A Shrew* Kate tells the audience in an aside that she will play along with her tamer: "But yet I will consent and marry him, / For I methinks have lived too long a maid, / And match him too, or else his manhood's good."[13] That aside does not exist in *The Shrew.*

Some of the most profoundly patriarchal language of *The Shrew* is not present in *A Shrew.* Petruchio/Ferando never states that his only motive in wiving is financial, nor does he refer to Kate as one of his possessions —goods, chattels, household stuff, "My horse, my ox, my ass, my anything" (3.2.221). Indeed, *A Shrew* is remarkable for the absence of such language—none of Petruchio's most demeaning speeches in regard to female weakness and impotence exists in *A Shrew.* In *A Shrew,* as he

---

12. See, for example, *The Taming of the Shrew,* ed. Oliver, pp. 17–18.

13. *"The Taming of a Shrew" being the Original of Shakespeare's "Taming of the Shrew,"* ed. F. S. Boas (London, 1908), p. 14, lines 169–71. Subsequent quotations from this edition will be indicated by page and line number in the text.

carries Kate off after the wedding, Petruchio/Ferando even suggests that if she humors him for the present, he will do her recompense later on: "Come, Kate, stand not on terms, we will away, / This is my day; tomorrow thou shalt rule, / And I will do whatever thou commands" (p. 32, ll. 87–89). In *A Shrew*, Petruchio/Ferando's method of taming by opposites is less elaborate and cleverly psychological than in *The Shrew*, or at least less clearly articulated as such by him; on the other hand, in *A Shrew*, Kate has less far down to go in order to appear properly tame—a proper "household Kate"—and Petruchio/Ferando clearly considers some of her most flamboyant gestures of subservience to be excessive. Kate's speech of submission in *A Shrew* is very different from the parallel passage in *The Shrew*. Although the very few editors who have discussed it have, following the traditional pattern of debasing *A Shrew* in order to exalt *The Shrew*, found it *more* unredeemedly sexist than the authorized Shakespearean version, I would characterize it as offering a different kind of patriarchal argument, one that was less up-to-date in sixteenth-century terms. Whether we regard it as more or less misogynist will depend on our evaluation of different modes of patriarchy.

Kate's speech in *A Shrew* can be described as a restatement of traditional misogyny on religious grounds. Much of it is taken up with platitudes about the creation: God made the world out of chaos, a "gulf of gulfs, a body bodiless" before it was shaped by his framing hand (p. 62, l. 124). After the six days' work, he fashioned Adam, and out of his rib created woman:

> Then to His image did He make a man,
> Old Adam, and from his side asleep
> A rib was taken, of which the Lord did make
> The woe of man, so termed by Adam then
> "Wo-man," for that by her came sin to us;
> And for her sin was Adam doomed to die. (p. 62, ll. 130–35)

This interestingly inaccurate view of the fall blames woman, as usual, for the plight of humankind—she is named a "woe" by Adam before she has even had a chance to act—but it is not echoed by other elements of the play, nor does it limit the woman's sphere of action as the alternative speech in *The Shrew* does. By contrast, Kate's rationale for obedience in *The Shrew* is given a political rather than a religious base: she advocates wifely obedience in terms of a theory of sovereignty by which the household is modelled on the kingdom and wifely disobedience becomes a form of "petty treason" against her "king" and husband. "Thy husband is thy lord, thy life, thy keeper, / Thy head, thy sovereign," (5.2.146–47) "thy lord, thy king, thy governor" (5.2.138)—an authority against whom disobedience or even peevishness is (according to the doctrine of petty treason) the same crime as that of a rebellious subject against a monarch:

> Such duty as the subject owes the prince,
> Even such a woman oweth to her husband.
> And when she is froward, peevish, sullen, sour,
> And not obedient to his honest will,
> What is she but a foul contending rebel
> And graceless traitor to her loving lord? (5.2.155–60)

The machinery of state lying behind this appeal for submission is rather more awesome and immediate than the diffuse and generalized appeal for order in *A Shrew*. We will note, too, that in the two speeches, the meaning of obedience is startlingly different. In *A Shrew*, Kate appeals to wives to obey because their husbands need their assistance: "Obey them, love them, keep, and nourish them, / If they by any means do want our helps" (p. 62 ll. 137–38). In *The Shrew*, the rationale is precisely reversed: women are presented as helpless, passive, creatures of the household, who lie "warm at home, secure and safe" while their hardy lords and masters venture out into the maelstrom for their benefit (5.2.151). Kate's vision of a housewife lying safe and protected at home sounds so familiar to us that we may fail to recognize its relative newness in the Renaissance. *The Shrew*'s image of the wife as a private possession of the husband to be tucked away at home was, in England at least, only beginning to emerge as the most desirable family model for haut bourgeois households.[14]

To be sure, Kate's final gesture of submission is more extreme in *A Shrew* than in the version we are accustomed to. In *The Shrew*, she commands the wives,

> Then vail your stomachs, for it is no boot,
> And place your hands below your husband's foot.
> In token of which duty, if he please,
> My hand is ready, may it do him ease. (5.2.176–79)

Petruchio's response "Why, there's wench!" registers his approval of her extravagant gesture of submission and also, perhaps, an element of condescension. In *A Shrew*, Kate makes the same gesture, but its symbolic rationale is not articulated (and this is one of the things editors have traditionally pointed to as an indication that *A Shrew* is a borrowed and derivative text). In *A Shrew*, Kate's act becomes a piece of deliberate excess, which her husband stops instead of approving:

> Laying our hands under their feet to tread,
> If that by that we might procure their ease;
> And for a precedent I'll first begin
> And lay my hand under my husband's feet. (p. 63, ll. 139–42)

The stage direction calls for her actually to lay her hand beneath his foot. Petruchio/Ferando responds, "Enough, sweet, the wager thou hast won, /

14. See Lawrence Stone, *The Family, Sex and Marriage in England, 1500–1800* (London: Weidenfeld, 1977); Joan Kelly, "Did Women Have a Renaissance?" (1977), reprinted in *Women, History, and Theory: The Essays of Joan Kelly* (Chicago, 1984), pp. 19–50; and David Underdown's critique of Alice Clark's *Working Life of Women in the Seventeenth Century*, rev. ed. by M. Chaytor and J. Lewis (London, 1982), in Underdown's "The Taming of the Scold: The Enforcement of Patriarchal Authority in Early Modern England," in *Order and Disorder in Early Modern England*, ed. Anthony Fletcher and John Stevenson (Cambridge, Eng., 1985), pp. 116–36. Underdown accepts the theory of a general decline in the independence of women during the period, but argues that increased attention to the scold may signal increased opportunities for women in some segments of sixteenth- and seventeenth-century culture.

And they, I am sure, cannot deny the same" (p. 63, ll. 143–44), which makes her masochistic gesture something acknowledged as excessive—performed to help her husband win the bet. It is possible, of course, to make the same interpretation of her meaning in *The Shrew,* but we have to create it ourselves by reading between the lines. In *A Shrew* it is unequivocally articulated in the text.

The reaction of the other characters is also strongly contrasted in the two versions of the play. In *The Shrew,* Kate's speech silences the other women; only the men speak thereafter. In *A Shrew,* Emelia (Bianca) makes it clear that she finds Kate's speech ridiculous. After Kate and Petruchio/Ferando exit at the end, Bianca/Emelia asks Polidor (Lucentio), "How now, Polidor, in a dump? What say'st thou, man?" He retorts, "I say thou art a shrew," to which she replies, "That's better than a sheep." He responds, as though with a shrug, "Well, since 'tis done, let it go! Come, let's in" and they exit (p. 63, ll. 157–61). In this version Kate's sister is not only not silenced, it looks very much as though she has won. When she and her new spouse exit, Sly returns, and Kate's message of submission is compromised even further—contained within a series of dramatic events, rather like a nest of boxes, that narrows down its applicability and ideological impact to almost nothing.

Perhaps the most fascinating differences between *A Shrew* and *The Shrew* are metadramatic: a play is a much more limited entity in *A Shrew,* much more exalted and powerful in *The Shrew.* To imagine Shakespeare in connection with *A Shrew* is to associate The Bard with a very lowly profession. The actors in *A Shrew* are humble, ill-educated itinerants. They enter bearing packs on their backs and one of them is so ignorant that he has not mastered the classical generic terms of his trade. When the Lord asks them what they can perform for him, Sander, the actor-clown, answers, *"Marry, my lord, you may have a tragical, or a comodity, or what you will,"* and the other actor fiercely corrects him, *"A comedy, thou should'st say; souns, thou'lt shame us all"* (p. 3, ll. 59–61). In *A Shrew,* the actors and Sly inhabit the same world of hardship, and they are able to give him the entertainment he wants: he remains awake enjoying it almost to the end. In *The Shrew,* by contrast, the actors are allied with the

Lord and his household against Sly. They are urbane and well-educated, at home in the world of humanist discourse rather than alien from it. In this version, unlike the other one, Sly has never seen a play. The butt of the "comodity" joke is not an actor, but Christopher Sly himself, who queries, when offered a "pleasant comedy," "Is not a comonty a Christmas gambold or a tumbling trick?" (Induction 2.132–33). And of course the play itself is far above him: he wearies of it by the end of the first scene, " 'Tis a very excellent piece of work, madam lady. Would 'twere done!" and is never heard from again (1.1.243).

In *The Shrew* and in that version only, dramatic and pictorial art are valued for their verisimilitude: Sly is presented with sexually explicit pictures of Adonis, Cytherea, and Io "beguilèd" and ravished by Jove, "As lively painted as the deed was done" (Induction 2.52). The Lord praises one of the actors for a similar verisimilitude in a previous role: "that part / Was aptly fitted and naturally performed" (Induction 1.82–83). The same claim is made at least implicitly by the taming play itself: instead of being bounded by the reappearance of Sly, it has become independent of his narrow vision and attained, at the end, the status of "nature" rather than performance. In *The Shrew*, the Induction is also more clearly localized than its counterpart in *A Shrew*, with numerous evocations of Shakespeare's own early neighborhood in Warwickshire. In the nineteenth century, Bardolators liked to search out Slys in the Stratford area as a way of pointing to the wonderful realism of Shakespeare's art—drawn to the very life.[15]

The Shrew's more compelling aura of reality is one of the salient characteristics for which that version has been preferred over the cruder and more farcical *A Shrew*. We will note, however, that in *The Shrew* the rising status of the actors in terms of their ability to claim a kind of truth for their art is bought at the price of woman's power and autonomy, since there is nothing to qualify the "truth" of female subordination

15. F. J. Furnivall, *The New Shakespeare Society's Transactions,* Series 1, no. 1 (London, 1874), 104. See also the New Arden edition of *The Taming of the Shrew,* ed. Brian Morris (London, 1981), pp. 62–63. John Russell Brown uses the appeal to realism in *The Shrew* to build a broad argument about increasing naturalism in acting styles during the age of Shakespeare. "On the Acting of Shakespeare's Plays," (1953), rpt. in *The Seventeenth-Century Stage: A Collection of Critical Essays*, ed. G. E. Bentley (Chicago, 1968), pp. 41–54.

they offer up at the end. If we imagine the play as a relatively bounded economy, then the actors triumph by putting women down, "realizing" womanly weakness in both senses of the term through their staging of Kate's submission. In *A Shrew,* the actors are lower and stay low; the women are brought less low. John Harington's *The Metamorphosis of Ajax* (1596) referred to *A Shrew* in a way that suggested he (and other readers of the quarto) found the play's message of shrew-taming in that version to be fatally and ruefully compromised by Sly's fantasy at the end: "For the shrewd wife, read the booke of taming a shrew, which hath made a number of us so perfect, that now every one can rule a shrew in our countrey, save he that hath her."[16]

V

Given the significant ideological difference between the two versions of the play, it is relatively easy to see why modern editors and critics have been at such pains to distance the two texts from each other, or at least to go along with earlier editorial decisions to keep them apart. With the passage of the centuries, the gulf between the two has widened. In the Renaissance, as we have noted, the two *Shrews* were regarded as one in terms of copyright; in the early eighteenth century they were considered an earlier and later draft by Shakespeare. Beginning with Malone, *A Shrew* was less frequently considered early Shakespeare, more frequently identified as Shakespeare's source for *The Shrew.* In all of these hypotheses *A Shrew* comes out as the earlier play, and I have made a case for that view as well. The shifts from *A Shrew* to *The Shrew* can be seen as the articulation of "modern" ideas (for the Renaissance at least) about women's place within the household and within the absolutist state; the name of Shakespeare thus becomes identified with the rise of individualism and the development of the haut-bourgeois family model. Similarly,

16. John Harington, *The Metamorphosis of Ajax*, ed. Elizabeth Donno (London, 1962), pp. 153–54; cited in Oliver, p. 34.

the status of the actors rises considerably from *A Shrew* to *The Shrew,* running parallel to the rising status and prosperity that theatrical historians associate with the profession during Shakespeare's time and with Shakespeare's own career in particular.[17]

During the late seventeenth and eighteenth centuries, the cultural need to naturalize the story of the play was so intense that in Garrick's highly popular afterpiece *Catherine and Petruchio, The Taming of the Shrew* was whittled down to the taming story *tout seul,* a sentimentalized version of *The Shrew* with no Sly, no subplots, and a softened conclusion in which Petruchio and Kate share in the delivery of the final speech. John Lacy's *Sauny the Scot, or The Taming of the Shrew* (1667), similarly omitted the frame entirely. The Sly material was not discarded, however; it formed the basis of two farces both called *The Cobler of Preston* by Charles Johnson and Christopher Bullock respectively and both published in 1716. On the eighteenth-century stage, it would seem, the Sly plot and the taming plot were kept strictly separate so that neither could compromise the "reality" of the other. As Samuel Johnson noted scoffingly in his edition of Shakespeare, the story of the shrew and her tamer was printed as fact in *The Tatler,* passed off as a notable "transaction in Lincolnshire."[18] During the same century Kate's speech was split off from the play and published separately (with a few added lines) as a wholesome sermon on wifely duty. Eighteenth-century readers and playgoers seemingly wanted the taming story to be true, although some women readers even then found Kate's submission excessive. However, they didn't much care whether or not the story was really Shakespeare.[19]

17. See G. E. Bentley, *The Professions of Dramatist and Player in Shakespeare's Time, 1590–1642,* one-volume paperback edition (1971 and 1984, rpt. Princeton, 1986); and Muriel C. Bradbrook, "The Status Seekers: Society and the Common Player in the Reign of Elizabeth 1," 1961, rpt. in Bentley, pp. 55–69.

18. *The Plays of William Shakespeare, in Eight Volumes,* ed. Samuel Johnson (1765), III, 99. For discussion of eighteenth-century adaptations, see Haring-Smith, pp. 7–22; and *Taming,* ed. Oliver, pp. 65–69.

19. See, for an example of women's response, Marianne Novy's introduction to her *Women's Re-Visions of Shakespeare* (Urbana, 1990), p. 7.

Garrick's *Catherine and Petruchio* continued popular on the stage until almost the end of the nineteenth century. But during the same period there was a growing thirst for "authentic" Shakespeare on the part of both editors and theater-goers. The name of the exalted Bard had to be reattached to the taming story. *The Shrew* in its Folio version had been absent from the stage for two hundred years. It was revived, with the Induction but without the Sly interruptions and conclusion, in England in the 1840s, in America in the 1880s. Thereafter the "authentic" text of *The Shrew* gradually won the stage over from *Catherine and Petruchio*. In Victorian productions most directors took great care to keep Christopher Sly and the Induction from undercutting the taming story. Critics and audiences of the Victorian productions of *The Shrew* seem generally to have liked Kate's speech of submission, applauding it wildly and calling it the "choicest gem of the play." H. N. Hudson asserted that *The Shrew* was worth "All the volumes on household virtue that I know of." Even the most successful and fiery of Victorian actresses to play the part of the Shrew, Ada Rehan, saw the taming of Kate as bringing her "to the saving grace of woman." In the first British production of the "authentic" *Shrew*, one of the actors in the Induction was made up to resemble Shakespeare, then proceeded to take the role of Petruchio, brandishing the traditional whip, so that wife-taming became a Shakespearean virtue indeed.[20] "Authentic" Shakespeare for the Victorians showed the beauties of wifely acquiescence. We probably do not need to remind ourselves that the same century, through the theories of Sigmund Freud, gave us the concept of normal female masochism.

VI

Amidst all of this thirst for authenticity, there was a conceptual problem that editors had to wrestle with. If *The Shrew* was "true" Shakespeare,

---

20. For all of these and other examples, see Haring-Smith, pp. 43–64. See also Susan J. Wolfson, "Explaining to Her Sisters: Mary Lamb's *Tales from Shakespear*," in Novy, pp. 16–40, especially pp. 23–27.

then what was to be done with *A Shrew?* If *A Shrew* was also Shake-speare, then the wife-taming message was harder to associate unequivo-cally with his name. If *A Shrew* was not Shakespeare, then his originality went out the window: *The Shrew* was massively borrowed from its earlier and cruder prototype and therefore less than authentic. The problem did not come to a head until the early twentieth century, but already toward the end of the nineteenth, we find editors entertaining the idea that *A Shrew* did not precede *The Shrew,* but instead derived from it. Victorian editors of Shakespeare were generally uncomfortable with the strong, outspoken women in Shakespeare's early plays. Furnivall, for example, expressed the strong hope that Shakespeare was not responsible for "all the women's rant" in *Titus Andronicus,* the *Henry VI* trilogy, and *Richard III.*[21] To regard *A Shrew* not as a source but as a debased copy allowed them to associate the realism and patriarchy of *The Shrew* with "authentic Shakespeare." *The Shrew* and its message of wifely submission were the "original." *A Shrew,* with its freer relationship between Petruchio/Ferando and Kate, its many undercuttings of the shrew-taming moral, was, in a sub-tly sexualized language of transgression, a debased and brazen travesty of the "manly" Shakespearean original, put together in all likelihood by itin-erant actors as ignorant of dramatic art and as mean and destitute as the poor players within *A Shrew* itself.

The next stage of this editorial development is rather deliciously pre-dictable. Widespread editorial agreement with the new textual theory by which *The Shrew* was original Shakespeare, or close to it, and *A Shrew* a "vamped up" copy came in the 1920s, along with the triumph of women's suffrage. The late nineteenth- and early twentieth-century struggle for women's rights made "authentic Shakespeare" on stage in *The Taming of the Shrew* more and more uncomfortable. Increasingly, directors tried either to engage the play's topical potential directly—at least one production cast Kate as the "new woman"—or to mitigate the tensions by staging the play as farce. Reviewers commented regularly on Kate's submission as unlikely

21. *New Shakspere Society's Transactions* (1874), 95–103. See also William Benzie, *Dr. F. J. Furnivall: Victorian Scholar Adventurer* (Norman, 1983), pp. 194–96.

to commend itself, as one of them put it, "to the out-and-out feminists of the Women's Federation League or the generality of the shingled and Eton-cropped sisterhood."[22] In 1926, two years before women's suffrage in Britain, Peter Alexander wrote an influential series of articles in the *Times Literary Supplement* contending yet once more that *A Shrew* was a "later and degraded version" of Shakespeare's play and relying heavily on arguments first broached a half century before. Other editors during the 1920s and later put Shakespeare at an even greater distance, arguing that his original play was lost, and that both *A Shrew* and *The Shrew* were derivative, although the latter was more strongly Shakespearean than the former.[23] At the same time that "new women" were agitating for the vote in England, editors were burying the "vamped up" version of *A Shrew* deeper and deeper—like a shameful skeleton in the Shakespearean closet that had to be kept out of sight. Even editors who remained skeptical about Alexander's view of the relationship between the two plays displayed a nostalgia for past simplicities, as in Quiller-Couch's comment in the Cambridge edition (1928), "avoiding the present times and recalling Dickens, most fertile of inventors since Shakespeare, with Dickens's long gallery of middle-aged wives who make household life intolerable by various and odious methods, one cannot help thinking a little wistfully that the Petruchian discipline had something to say for itself."[24]

22. Thompson, p. 21.

23. See Peter Alexander, "The Taming of a Shrew," *Times Literary Supplement*, Thursday, Sept. 16, 1926, p. 614. See also his " 'II. Henry VI.' and the Copy for 'The Contention' (1594)," *Times Literary Supplement,* Oct. 9, 1924, pp. 629–30; and " '3 Henry VI' and 'Richard, Duke of York,' " *Times Literary Supplement*, Nov. 13, 1924, p. 730. For more recent refinements of the argument by which *A Shrew* is derived from *The Shrew* or from a common ancestor of both, see, e.g., Raymond A. Houk, "The Evolution of *The Taming of the Shrew*," *PMLA,* 57 (1942), 1009–38; Henry David Gray, "*The Taming of a Shrew*," *Philological Quarterly,* 20 (1941), 325–33; and G. I. Duthie, "*The Taming of a Shrew* and *The Taming of the Shrew*," *Review of English Studies*, 19 (1943), 337–56. Similar arguments are made in almost every modern single-volume edition of the play; for dissenting views, see the sources in n. 6 above.

24. *The Taming of the Shrew,* ed. Sir Arthur Quiller-Couch and John Dover Wilson (Cambridge, Eng., 1928), p. xxvi. For another similar view, see A. L. Rowse, ed., *The Annotated Shakespeare, Vol. I: The Comedies* (New York, 1978), pp. 119–21.

The textual arguments by which editors have convinced themselves (and others) that *A Shrew* is a contaminated version of *The Shrew,* or of an earlier play that was genuine Shakespeare, rest on an implicit prior ranking by which *The Shrew* is assumed to be "what Shakespeare meant," so that deviations from it are invariably read as corruptions. In the two versions we have already noted of Kate's placing her hand beneath her husband's foot, for example, the standard argument is that "the imitator, as usual, has caught something of the words of the original, which he has laboured to reproduce at a most unusual sacrifice of grammar and sense . . . he has by omitting the words 'in token of which duty' omitted the whole point of the passage."[25] I have argued earlier that the "imitator" is instead making a different point. Two other telltale passages for the derivative nature of *A Shrew* are drawn from the scene between Kate and the tailor. In the "authorized" version Grumio protests to the tailor, "Master, if ever I said 'loose-bodied gown,' sew me in the skirts of it and beat me to death with a bottom of brown thread" (4.3.131–32). The equivalent speech in *A Shrew* is, "Master, if ever I said loose body's gown, sew me in a seam and beat me to death with [a] bottom of brown thread!" (p. 44, ll. 29–31). The criticism of *A Shrew* here is that "the reporter is very close but the difference is enough to show his hand. 'Sew me in the skirts of it' has meaning whereas the variation has none."[26] The talk during the scene has been of facings, and facings quite commonly require the type of seam (although admittedly not quite the amplitude) in which a person could be sewn. Why does the idea of being sewn in a seam have no meaning? It requires no great powers of observation to recognize that facings in portraits of Elizabethan women's dresses are commonly sewn double, like what we would now call "French seams." The speech in *A Shrew* is more ludicrous than its counterpart in *The Shrew,* and also more deviously ribald if one takes the idea

25. Wilson, ed., citing, as nearly all discussions of the problem do, Samuel Hickson, "Marlowe and the Old 'Taming of a Shrew,'" *Notes and Queries,* 1 (1850), 194, 226–27, in the Cambridge ed., p. 179.

26. Wilson, ed., citing Hickson, Cambridge ed., p. 168.

of being sewn in a lady's seam as relating to her person, not her clothes. But in what way is the passage clearly derivative? Only if one has already decided what constitutes "good sense" in the text of the play, with variations representing nothing more than "rant" or "nonsense." In the second passage, which follows hard upon the first, *A Shrew* has the following exchange:

> *San.* Dost thou hear, tailor? Thou hast braved many men: brave
> not me. Thou'st faced many men—
>
> *Tailor.* Well, sir.
>
> *San.* Face not me: I'll neither be faced nor braved at thy hands, I
> can tell thee! (p. 44, ll. 37–41)

The equivalent passage in *The Shrew* reads:

> GRUMIO. Thou hast faced many things.
>
> TAILOR. I have.
>
> GRUMIO. Face not me. Thou hast braved many men; brave not
> me. I will neither be faced nor braved. (4.3.121–24)

In this case, editors argue, *A Shrew* misses the puns on "faced" and "braved" and therefore declares itself as the derivative version. But all that would be required for *A Shrew* to make as much "sense" as *The Shrew* would be for the actor to indicate through gesture that the braving and facing he has in mind are punningly linked to the tailor's trade. *A Shrew*'s version of the passage is less explicit, but would hardly be regarded as corrupt if it were allowed to stand on its own: it is editorially suspect only because it does not replicate every nuance of *The Shrew*.

Perhaps the most damning flaw of *A Shrew* in the minds of those who have argued for its derivative status is its frequent Marlovian echoes. The argument here is that the ignorant actors who patched together the pirated version of the play threw in snatches of Marlowe whenever their memories failed them, creating a pastiche with no claim to independent literary integrity. Peter Alexander characterizes the putative compiler(s) as having "a mentality very like that of ancient Pistol, and a head no more proof against the intoxication of tragic diction."[27] That *A Shrew* contains numerous passages echoing *Tamburlaine the Great* and *Doctor Faustus* is undeniable, although some of the alleged parallels are too faint to be convincing. If we grant that text the same privilege of putative intentionality that is routinely granted to *The Shrew,* however, we can regard the Marlovian passages not as mere unassimilated bombast, but as deliberate stage quotations of tragedies well known to audiences in the early 1590s—quotations designed to create a ludicrous effect of mock heroic in their new and incongruous setting. In the Induction to *A Shrew,* for example, when the nobleman and his men first enter, his grand language echoes the famous speech with which Faustus first conjures up his devils:

> *Now that the gloomy shadow of the night,*
> *Longing to view Orion's drizzling looks,*
> *Leaps from th' Antarctic world unto the sky,*
> *And dims the welkin with her pitchy breath,*
> *And darksome night o'ershads the crystal heavens* (pp. 1–2, ll. 9–13)

What the Lord conjures up, however, is not demons but the drunken, sleeping Sly. The humor can scarcely be said to be subtle, but it might have been quite funny on stage. In the corresponding scene at the end of the play, when Sly is once again lying before the alehouse, the Tapster utters a parallel passage just before stumbling upon him:

> Now that the darksome night is overpassed,
> And dawning day appears in crystal sky,
> Now must I haste abroad. But soft, who's this?
> What, Sly? (p. 64, ll. 1–4)

27. Alexander, p. 614. All editorial argument about Marlovian borrowings rests ultimately on Hickson, n. 25 above. On Marlovian borrowings, see also Boas, pp. xxx–xxxii and 91–98, and nearly every modern edition of the play. My own argument that the Marlovian passages work as successful burlesque has been anticipated in part by a few editors, most prominently Quiller-Couch, pp. xxi–xxii.

The device is doubly ludicrous the second time, and helps to underline the return of Christopher Sly: his discovery, once again, takes center stage. Marlovian echoes serve a similar comic, deflating function throughout the play, sometimes even taking the form of stage business. In the scene at Petruchio's house, *A Shrew,* unlike *The Shrew,* specifies that Petruchio/Ferando enters *"with a piece of meat upon his dagger's point,"* echoing the hideously powerful moment in *Tamburlaine the Great Part I,* 4.4 in which Tamburlaine offers food at his sword's end to the conquered Bajazeth. The many Marlovian echoes of *A Shrew* help to keep the play firmly within the realm of farce, overturning any faint whisper of the heroic about Petruchio/Ferando's campaign against the shrew, undercutting any incipient claim to realism (of the kind so prominently made in *The Shrew*) before it has a chance to develop.

VII

Barring the discovery of new historical artifacts—such as a working manuscript of one or both texts in the same hand as the passages from *Sir Thomas More* believed to be in Shakespeare's—we are unlikely ever to settle the question of which play came first, or how much of either is genuine Shakespeare. We may settle such matters to our own satisfactions, but if past editorial opinion is any guide, what pleases us as explanation may not equally please those who come after us. To the author of the present essay, *A Shrew* sounds distinctly earlier, sounds as though it could perhaps contain bits of early Shakespeare and be designed to capitalize on the public passion for Marlowe during the early 1590s. Whether or not we label *A Shrew* as Shakespeare, we need to recognize that it is a more interesting, intriguing play than its long history of suppression would suggest. But what would be the point just now of insisting on the priority of one or another version? To do so would be to revert to the old editorial mode of creating hierarchies of texts which are invariably value-laden. I would suggest instead that we start thinking of the different versions of *The Taming of the Shrew* intertextually—as a cluster of related texts which can be fruitfully read together and against each other as "Shakespeare." To do that, of course, is to give up the idea that either Shakespeare or the canon of his works is a single determinate thing. It is to carry Shakespearean textual studies out of the filiative search for a single "authentic" point of origin and into the purview of poststructuralist criticism, where the authority of the author loses its élan and the text becomes a multiple, shifting process rather than an artifact set permanently in print. In the case of *A Shrew* and *The Shrew,* it is also to interrogate the canonical version of a play we may no longer want to live with.

In twentieth-century productions of *The Shrew,* the patriarchal message of the piece has been evaded by many ingenious methods: Kate may wink at the audience even as she hoodwinks Petruchio, as in Mary Pickford's film version. Kate may be portrayed as a loveless neurotic who is cured by Petruchio through a kind of psychodrama that shows her her own excess. Quite often she abases herself out of love. Or the whole thing can be reduced to farce. At present, however, all of these methods seem to have played themselves out on stage (and film), and there are signs that the equivalent critical readings are playing themselves out as well—not only among modern feminists, who find the text too alienating to be "set right" by such strategies, but also among our students, who are increasingly unhappy with our usual readings emphasizing the mutuality of the taming and other such palliatives designed to smooth over the reality of Petruchio's domination. We can choose, of course, to remove the play quietly from the list of those we teach and discuss, as Shirley Garner and other perceptive readers have suggested we do.[28] Or we can bring back *The Shrew*'s long suppressed intertext *A Shrew,* the tactic resorted to on the modern stage.

In the eighteenth century, readers of Shakespeare got the Sly ending to the play, while theater-goers saw the play cleansed of Sly and rechristened *Catherine and Petruchio.* Now the opposite pattern prevails: theatrical

28. "*The Taming of the Shrew:* Inside or Outside of the Joke?" in *"Bad" Shakespeare,* pp. 105–19.

productions depend on the Sly framework to cast the whole patriarchal system constructed by the taming plot into doubt and unreality, while our texts banish Sly at the end and conclude with the "reality" of Kate's capitulation. If *A Shrew* comes to be accepted by editors and readers as an acceptable intertext of *The Shrew* (whether as a first draft, source, or early derivative), then several things could happen. In editions of Shakespeare that offer composite texts of other plays, *The Shrew* could also become composite. In the same way that editors have regularly inserted the mock trial scene and other brief segments from the 1608 quarto of *King Lear* into the Folio text, so editors could insert the Sly episodes from the 1594 quarto *A Shrew*—and perhaps other material as well—into *The Taming of the Shrew*. A more satisfying alternative would follow the pattern of the newest editions of *King Lear* and print both texts in their entirety, one after the other. Such a format would preserve the integrity of each early version while offering readers a dazzling, unsettling empowerment: with only a slight stretching of the traditional rationale of copytext by which the best possible text is arrived at through the combination of variant early versions, readers would be freed, if the task appealed to them, to become their own editors, to create new combinations of the two texts that are as much "Shakespeare" as the composite texts to which we are already accustomed in our standard editions of the plays.

But, it may be objected, such a procedure would be irresponsibly chaotic and ahistorical—it would take us much too far afield from the Renaissance itself, in which, whether we like it or not, patriarchy was as dominant and univocal as it is in *The Taming of the Shrew*. That is by no means clear. I have pointed to a process of naturalization by which the patriarchal ideology of *The Shrew* gradually became "reality" in terms of public expectations in the theater and readers' expectations of Shakespeare. But that process was not without its glitches, temporary reversals, and ambivalences in any period—certainly not in the Renaissance itself. The same culture that preferred *The Shrew* to *A Shrew* also made space for an antidote. In the early seventeenth century, John Fletcher continued the story of Petruchio in *The Woman's Prize, or The Tamer Tamed,* in which Kate has died and Petruchio marries a second wife, Maria, who tames him as effectively as he had earlier tamed Kate, except that Maria's methods are draconian to the point of paramilitarism. When Shakespeare's *The Shrew* and Fletcher's *The Woman's Prize* were performed within a few days of each other at the court of Charles I in 1633, Shakespeare's *The Shrew* was "liked" but Fletcher's play was "very well liked."[29] It is probably fair to say that patriarchy as a system has regularly been more consistent and orderly in the minds of historically inclined editors and readers than it has been in society at large. If we are to interrogate the canonical Shakespeare, then we need to interrogate the editorial assumptions underlying the texts by which we have come to "know" him.

29. Oliver, p. 64.

Editing without a Copy-Text[†]

G. Thomas Tanselle

IN THE HISTORY of textual criticism, as of most human affairs, a few basic viewpoints have moved through the centuries in cyclical fashion, each losing favor temporarily in one area or another and then returning to prominence in an altered form. The fields concerned with reconstructing the past, like textual criticism, constantly reverberate with alternating claims about the place of judgment in the process. At one moment, objectivity seems possible, and artifacts tell their own stories with little or no assistance; at the next moment, subjectivity is welcomed, and artifacts are a springboard for the historical imagination. In the nineteenth century, for example, the genealogical approach to biblical and classical textual criticism, now associated with the name of Karl Lachmann, emerged from a desire to minimize the role of judgment in combining readings from variant texts and was thus a reaction to the less disciplined eclecticism of many eighteenth-century editors, who often altered texts according to their personal tastes. By the early twentieth century, in turn, there were efforts—as in the work of A. E. Housman— to reinstate an open acceptance of judgment. But even Housman's brilliant advocacy of the subjective element in textual criticism did not

† This paper was presented as a Book Arts Press lecture during Rare Book School at the University of Virginia, 12 July 1993. "Editing without a Copy-Text," from *Studies in Bibliography* 47 (1994): 1–22. Reproduced by permission of *Studies in Bibliography* and the Rector and Visitors of the University of Virginia.

prevent several determined attempts in the twentieth century to develop mathematical procedures for weighing variants in ancient texts.

A distrust of subjectivity, in a different form from Lachmann's, came in the twentieth century to dominate the study of medieval writings: the procedure, which was anti-eclectic, involved selecting a "best text" and altering it only at the places that seemed obviously erroneous. Although, for post-medieval literature, the term "best text" has not been widely used, the term "copy-text" as employed by R. B. McKerrow in his 1904 edition of Thomas Nashe meant essentially the same thing. Thus the editing of Renaissance literature that proceeded alongside the "New Bibliography" emerged from this restrictive base—not unexpectedly, since what was new in the "New Bibliography" (developed by McKerrow, A. W. Pollard, W. W. Greg, and their followers) was the analysis of the physical details of books for evidence that could solve textual cruxes without the use of literary judgment (or at least limit the role of such judgment in making textual decisions). No approach to editing can totally eliminate judgment, of course; and I am less concerned here with the amount of judgment that actually entered into various editors' work than with the general avoidance or acceptance of judgment embodied in their editorial theories. McKerrow, by the end of his life in 1940, had moved toward a greater willingness to allow variants from one text to be incorporated into a chosen copy-text, as he outlined his plans for an edition of Shakespeare. But it remained for W. W. Greg in 1949 to enunciate, in his famous lecture "The Rationale of Copy-Text," a position for the editing of Renaissance drama that approached Housman's of a half-century earlier for the editing of classical literature. Greg, like Housman, elevated the role of informed judgment in choosing among variant readings.[1]

One of the most revealing facts about his rationale, however, is—as the title of his paper suggests—its retention of a concept of "copy-text," a

1. The developments summarized here are sketched more fully (with references to other accounts) in my "Classical, Biblical, and Medieval Textual Criticism and Modern Editing," *Studies in Bibliography*, 36 (1983), 21–68; reprinted in *Textual Criticism and Scholarly Editing* (1990), pp. 274–321.

basic text into which alterations (or "emendations")[2] can be incorporated. It now seems time, after another half-century, to move beyond this often useful but nevertheless inherently restrictive concept. That Greg's intention was to liberate editorial judgment is indicated by his warning against "what may be called the tyranny of the copy-text"; but his recognition that a copy-text could indeed tyrannize did not cause him to abandon the concept. He was not quite ready to carry to its logical conclusion the dominant twentieth-century English line of thinking about the textual criticism of post-medieval literature, a line that had become gradually more liberal during the first half of the century—though the position he did take certainly constituted an important extension of it. Greg's rationale has been much debated in the succeeding half-century, but the discussions have generally focused on his recommendations for selecting and emending a copy-text rather than on the necessity for designating a particular text as copy-text in the first place. To consider the latter issue is not to imply any repudiation of Greg at all; rather, living with his ideas for a considerable period has enabled us to see more clearly their essential direction and has put us in a position to understand how, paradoxically, a reduction of emphasis on "copy-text" actually builds on and completes his argument.

The first step in thinking through a new approach to the question of copy-text is to examine whether there is a future for critical editions—editions, that is, in which the editors, using their informed critical judgment, make alterations in the documentary forms of texts that have come down to us (or at least allow themselves the freedom to make such alterations, whether or not they ultimately find any changes to be necessary).

2. The term "emendation" has come to be used by editors of post-medieval literature to mean any alternation made in a copy-text by a critical editor—that is, alterations that derive from variants in other documentary texts and also alterations that originate with the editor. In the textual criticism of ancient writings, however, the term has traditionally been used to refer only to the editor's own innovations, introduced into a "recension" that resulted from an analysis of the variants in the documentary texts. This older tradition misleadingly encourages a belief that the process of recension is more objective than that of emendation (especially since the usual phrase is "conjectural emendation"), whereas the newer usage, which carries no such implication, is more realistic. This point is discussed more fully on pp. 25–27 [142–44] of the essay cited in the preceding note.

All the various "best-text" or "copy-text" theories are concerned with the process of altering documentary texts; but if a convincing argument can be made that no such process is justified, then there is no point considering critical editing further. In the continual give-and-take of arguments over subjectivity and objectivity, some scholars naturally take the position that editions presenting critical texts are less valuable (if granted any value at all) than editions containing facsimile or diplomatic (or computer "hypertext") reproductions of texts as they appear in extant documents.[3] The late twentieth century has seen an energetic resurgence of this view, springing from two seemingly contradictory premises. One—that authors do not control either the language they use or the forces that allow their work to reach the public—denigrates the significance of authorial intention and thus brings renewed attention to texts as they were published. The other premise—that the process of revision and change through which verbal works move is of more valid concern than any single final text that may be postulated—causes increased interest to be directed toward the texts of every prepublication draft and revised edition. Although the former premise tends to reject the author and the latter to concentrate exclusively on the author, both reflect disaffection with critical editing as a supposedly authoritarian imposition of stasis on inherently unstable material.[4]

These trends have therefore publicized specific programmatic reasons for the production of facsimile and diplomatic editions, besides the obvious general motivation to make widely available the texts of unique manuscripts and scarce printed editions (recognizing, of course, that no photograph or transcription can preserve all the physical evidence of the original—and that all of it may be relevant to textual study).[5] Although

3. A "diplomatic" text is one that aims to reproduce without alteration the textual features of a document (primarily the words and punctuation), but not those features that can, in the particular instance, be regarded as nontextual (such as the letterforms or the page layout). See also note 7 below.

4. I have attempted to survey recent thinking along these lines in "Textual Criticism and Literary Sociology," *SB*, 44 (1991), 83–143.

5. See my "Reproductions and Scholarship," *SB*, 42 (1989), 25–54. Cf. note 7 below.

facsimile and diplomatic editions are noncritical in that their editors' aim is to reproduce without alteration the words and punctuation of documentary texts, critical judgment is inevitably involved in deciphering handwritten (or poorly printed) texts and in deciding which documentary versions of a work to present (if all are not to be included). Because this decision-making is not intended to alter texts, however, the editions that result are usually thought of as more "objective," despite the number of subjective decisions that may have been involved; and although arguments about the relative amounts of subjectivity and objectivity in editing are normally concerned with critical editions, there is no doubt that those persons who wish to minimize subjectivity in critical editing should logically be drawn to noncritical editions. Facsimile and diplomatic editions, whatever subjectivity may underlie them, are fundamentally different in conception from editions in which the goal is to alter documentary texts according to some predetermined guideline. By not requiring such guidelines, they have seemed to need less discussion over the years than have critical editions; and their increased presence in recent methodological debates is to be welcomed as a partial redressing of the balance. There is no question that they serve an important function in the study of the past.

But any attempt to argue that they are necessarily superior to critical editions, or indeed that they constitute the only legitimate kind of edition, cannot possibly succeed. The two kinds must always coexist, for they represent two indispensable elements in approaching the past: the ordered presentation of artifactual evidence, and the creation, from that evidence, of versions of past moments that are intended to be more comprehensively faithful than the artifacts themselves—random (and perhaps damaged) survivors as they are. It is not possible, in any case, to prevent human beings from interpreting evidence; to ban critical editions would be as futile as to try to suppress any other product that reflects the natural working of the mind. Critical editions, however, are not merely inevitable; they are desirable. A text reconstructed by a person who is immersed in, and has thought deeply about, the body of surviving evidence relevant to a work, its author, and its time may well teach the rest of us something we could not have discovered for ourselves, even if the reconstruction can never be definitive—and even if, indeed, it places us in a position to criticize its own constitution. Authorially intended texts, which have been the goal of almost all critical editions in the past, cannot be expected to reside, in perfect accuracy, in surviving documents—or perhaps, for that matter, in any documents that ever existed. But the fact that they are not—and possibly never were—fully available in physical form does not deprive them of the status of historical events. (The same could of course be said of texts as intended by publishers or any of the other individuals that had a hand in the production process.)[6] Some people may not be interested in reconstructing such events, but their lack of interest cannot render the effort invalid.

There is another reason that critical editions are essential: they are demanded by the very nature of verbal works. Like musical and choreographic works—and unlike works of visual and plastic art—verbal works employ an intangible medium. Any tangible representation of such a work—as in letterforms on paper—cannot be the work itself, just as choreographic notation or traditional musical scores are not works of dance or music. The media involved—language, movement, and sound —being intangible, these works can be stored only through conversion to another form, which in effect becomes a set of instructions for reconstituting the works.[7] Any instructions—indeed, any kind of reproduction or report—may be inaccurate, and thus every attempt to reconstruct such works (or versions of works) must include a readiness to recognize

6. The difficulty of segregating the intentions of specific individuals will vary from one instance to another; but even when the difficulty seems extreme, there is no reason not to apply informed judgment to the attempt, if one is sufficiently interested.

7. Some works, of course, entail the combining (or "mixing") of media: thus there are instances in which works are partially verbal and partially visual, such as shaped or concrete poetry. The dividing line between what is textual and what is nontextual in the physical features of a document must be determined separately in each instance. Features judged to be nontextual (not part of the work) are not necessarily irrelevant as evidence for reconstructing the work; indeed, all physical characteristics of a document must be scrutinized carefully by the editor, since none can be automatically ruled out as unrelated to textual considerations. Cf. note 28 below.

textual errors in their stored forms. Understanding the difference between works and documents also enables one to see that a concern with the integrity of discrete versions is not incompatible with the adoption of variants from different documents.[8] Reconstituting works (or versions) in intangible media is a critical activity, and universal agreement about their makeup cannot be expected. But if we wish to experience the texts of works (or versions), and not simply the texts of documents, we must leave the certainty (or relative certainty) of the documentary texts for the uncertainty of our reconstructions.[9] Every act of reading is in fact an act of critical editing: we often call critical essays "readings," and critical editions are also the records of readings. The editors who produce them earn the respect of other readers to the extent that their work reflects historical learning and literary sensitivity; but no reader is likely to agree with every decision made by any other reader, even the most respected critical editor. The process of critical editing is the ineluctable, if unending, effort to surmount the limitations of artifacts in the pursuit of works from the past.

Having established the necessity of critical editions, one can then consider what procedure should be followed in making the critical judgments they entail. Some kind of guideline is required if the operation is to be disciplined and historically oriented. Otherwise, textual decisions would simply reflect the editors' own preferences, and the results, which would not necessarily be without interest, would not be an attempt at historical reconstruction. Editorial taste is indeed essential, but an edited

8. The fear of "eclecticism"—expressed often in the history of scholarly editing—is generally based on a failure to understand that versions (like works) cannot be found in the texts of specific documents. The most extended discussion of eclecticism in editing is Fredson Bowers's "Remarks on Eclectic Texts," *Proof*, 4 (1975), 31–76; reprinted in his *Essays in Bibliography, Text, and Editing* (1975), pp. 488–528.

9. For a fuller statement of the ideas outlined here, see my *A Rationale of Textual Criticism* (1989). It is surprising that some textual critics label this view of literary works "Platonic." Recognition of the intangible nature of certain media is independent of a general belief in the secondary status of the physical world. A Platonist would of course take a Platonic view of both intangible and tangible media; but the concept of intangibility is not in itself Platonic.

text should reflect, not the personal preferences of the editor, but the editor's judgments regarding the preferences of the author, or the author in conjunction with others, at a given moment. Simple as this distinction is, it has probably been the root of more textual disputes than any other single point. But since critical editing must rest on editorial judgment, a sufficient guideline would seem to be one that states the goal toward which that judgment is to be directed, perhaps indicating what ancillary information should be taken into account but without placing limits on the judgment itself: to say, for example, that an editor's literary sensitivity, informed by biographical, bibliographical, and more broadly historical research, should be employed to attempt to determine the constitution of texts at particular past moments.

The fear that encouraging editorial judgment would amount to licensing personal preference, however, has repeatedly caused textual theorists to impose restrictions on the field within which editorial judgment is allowed to operate. The "best-text" theories are one result, and they have been curiously persistent, despite the ease with which their essential illogic can be exposed. In ruling that texts can be altered only where they are obviously incorrect, this approach seems to imply, incredibly, that texts are likely to be correct wherever they are not manifestly incorrect—a patent absurdity. A. E. Housman in 1903 pointed out this flaw most memorably, in the preface to the first volume of his edition of Manilius, and he wittily added, "assuredly there is no trade on earth, excepting textual criticism, in which the name of prudence would be given to that habit of mind which in ordinary human life is called credulity."[10] Perhaps the most basic way of stating the incoherence of the "best-text" approach is to observe that it begins with a belief that documentary texts can be improved through editorial intervention (otherwise there would be no reason to allow the correction of clearcut errors) but proceeds to cast doubt on the usefulness of such intervention (otherwise

10. This preface is conveniently excerpted in Housman's *Selected Prose*, ed. John Carter (1961), pp. 23–44 (quotation from p. 43) and in *Collected Poems and Selected Prose*, ed. Christopher Ricks (1988), pp. 372–386 (quotation not included.)

it would be allowed to operate more widely). If there were a chance that editorial judgment could correct a text at places not obviously incorrect, there would seem to be no reason not to sanction the effort; and one must therefore conclude, with Housman, that these places are assumed to be correct. Actually, however, there is no point looking for an explanation of this unreasoned approach other than a reflex reaction: the belief that a restriction of judgment was required to improve on the unscholarly eclecticism of the past.

McKerrow was undoubtedly caught up in this reaction when in 1904 he chose the second edition of Nashe's *The Unfortunate Traveller* as his copy-text, to be altered only at obviously erroneous points, on the grounds that it contained some revisions by the author (2: 197). He was not happy with all the readings that this policy forced him to retain, but he felt that he had "no choice" in the matter; when he stated that an editor could not "pick and choose among the variant readings of his author's works those which he himself would prefer in writings of his own," McKerrow did not admit the possibility that choice among variants could be performed on any other basis.[11] Thirty-five years later, in his *Prolegomena for the Oxford Shakespeare* (1939), he took the significant step of recommending a limited eclecticism: he asserted that an editor could best approach the goal of reconstructing "an author's fair copy" by using as copy-text the earliest authoritative edition (which would supply spelling and punctuation closer to the author's than a later edition would be likely to contain) and inserting into it the substantive alterations from a later edition (p. 18). But once editorial judgment had determined the presence of an author's hand in a later edition, McKerrow would allow judgment to operate no further, claiming that "we must accept *all* the alterations of that edition, saving any which seem

---

11. McKerrow's sentence ends with an unexceptionable statement of one editorial goal: "to present those [the author's] works as he believes the author to have intended them to appear." But McKerrow's point is only to distinguish between the editor's own preferences and the editor's conclusions as to what the author's preferences were; he does not acknowledge the role that editorial judgment, especially as applied to every variant individually, might play in moving toward his chosen goal.

obvious blunders or misprints." He was clearly still under the spell of the "best-text" fallacy; and it was at this point that Greg stepped in to observe that alterations in a later edition may come from various sources and that it is essential to make discriminations among them.[12]

Greg's primary purpose in "The Rationale of Copy-Text" was to provide a sound argument for greater editorial freedom of choice.[13] "I am only concerned," he unambiguously proclaimed, "to uphold his [the editor's] liberty of judgment" (p. 147); at another point he called it "disastrous" to "curb the liberty of competent editors" (p. 150). He asked why, if judgment was to be admitted in distinguishing possible from impossible readings (as it was in the "best-text" approaches), "should the choice between possible readings be withdrawn from its competence?" (p. 143). The judgment of an editor, he answered, "is likely to bring us closer to what the author wrote than the enforcement of an arbitrary rule." Curiously, however, Greg's strong endorsement of editorial freedom in regard to substantive variants was not extended to what he called "accidentals" (spelling and punctuation), for it was the function of the copytext, in his view, to provide the accidentals. He made a clear distinction between the nearly automatic acceptance of copy-text accidentals and the use of judgment in dealing with substantives: "the copy-text should govern (generally) in the matter of accidentals, but . . . the choice between substantive readings belongs to the general theory of textual criticism" (p. 143). He was well aware of the fact that, if one considered it possible to evaluate the authority of accidentals, there would be no need to designate any text as a "copy-text" possessing presumptive

12. For Fredson Bowers's fuller analysis of McKerrow's illogical caution, see "McKerrow's Editorial Principles for Shakespeare Reconsidered," *Shakespeare Quarterly*, 6 (1955), 309–324. Bowers also explored some of Greg's differences from McKerrow in "McKerrow, Greg, and 'Substantive Edition,'" *Library*, 5th ser., 33 (1978), 83–107.

13. Greg's essay was first published in *SB*, 3 (1950–51), 19–36, and was reprinted in Greg's *Collected Papers*, ed. J. C. Maxwell (1966), pp. 374–391. [References in the text are to pp. 135–53 of the current volume —*Editor*.] The evolution of Greg's thought preceding this essay can be observed in his "McKerrow's Prolegomena Reconsidered," *Review of English Studies*, 17 (1941), 139–149, and in the prefaces to the first two printings of his *The Editorial Problem in Shakespeare* (1942, 1951).

authority. As he said in his sketch of the history of textual criticism at the beginning of the essay, "So long as purely eclectic methods prevailed, any preference for one manuscript over another, if it showed itself, was of course arbitrary" (p. 135). The "purely eclectic methods" he referred to were those founded on personal taste; but the point would be equally valid for any approach in which all choices among variants could be settled through the exercise of some kind of judgment. Greg's acceptance of McKerrow's idea of a copy-text, therefore, was founded on a belief that there was usually insufficient evidence for reasoning about accidentals.

It seems evident, nevertheless, that Greg was not entirely comfortable with the idea of restricting the role of judgment in any aspect of the editorial procedure. He inserted the word "generally" in his directive that "the copy-text should govern (generally) in the matter of accidentals"; and he insisted that the copy-text should not be "sacrosanct, even apart from the question of substantive variation," enumerating instances in which it is "within the discretion of an editor" to alter copy-text accidentals. He even went so far as to say that, in regard to "graphic peculiarities" (by which he meant some practices of spelling and punctuation), "the copy-text is only one among others" (p. 147). If, therefore, copy-text accidentals may be altered whenever one believes there is good reason to do so, just as copy-text substantives may certainly be, the role of the copy-text turns out to be that of supplying readings (of both substantives and accidentals) whenever there seems no other basis for deciding. Greg would never have insisted that any reading should be retained simply because it was present in the copy-text, if an editor's informed judgment pointed to a different choice; such "tyranny of the copy-text" (p. 143)[14] was what he was striving to eliminate from textual criticism.

14. In the original publication of the "Rationale," Greg did not indicate that in saying "what may be called the tyranny of the copy-text" he was not inventing the phrase himself; but in an added footnote, included in the 1966 republication of the essay, he attributed it to Paul Maas, who had used it in a review (*Review of English Studies*, 20 [1944], 76) of Greg's *The Editorial Problem in Shakespeare* when he was commenting on Greg's interest in preserving copy-text spelling.

Thus if one is to fall back on the copy-text (for accidentals as well as substantives) only when there is no other way to choose, the key element in his copy-text procedure is determining when two readings are in fact "exactly balanced" (p. 148)—or, to use the more famous term that he also employs, "completely indifferent" (p. 149). If, in an editor's view, there are no completely indifferent alternatives, then there is no need for a copy-text.[15]

Greg himself was, however, somewhat tyrannized by the *idea* of copy-text, for his essay includes this statement: "whenever there is more than one substantive text of comparable authority, then although it will still be necessary to choose one of them as copy-text, and to follow it in accidentals, this copy-text can be allowed no over-riding or even preponderant authority as far as substantive readings are concerned" (p. 146). Thus at the very moment when he emphasizes the necessity for freedom of editorial judgment in regard to substantive variants from documents of equal "extrinsic" (that is, genealogical) authority, he places a mechanical, unreasoned restriction on judgment applied to the accidentals. When the surviving texts of a work form an ancestral series and a copy-text is chosen for its position in the series, there is a justification for falling back on the copy-text when the variants seem indifferent. But when the documents do not form such a series, and when two of them seem evenly balanced in authority, there is no reason to give more

---

15. In the course of one of the more incisive analyses of Greg's position, T. H. Howard-Hill distinguishes two senses of "indifferent," one referring to the inability of an editor to judge between two readings and the other referring to the equal authority of the sources from which two readings come. In the practice of editing, however, these meanings must merge, since one's judgment of a reading takes the source of the reading into account, and one's evaluation of a source involves an analysis of its readings. See his "Modern Textual Theories and the Editing of Plays," *Library*, 6th ser., 11 (1989), 89–115; and my discussion of it in "Textual Criticism and Literary Sociology" (note 4 above), pp. 122–128 (esp. p. 123 and footnote 60). Tom Davis, in an earlier cogent discussion of Greg's rationale, also examines the crucial matter of what it means to label a variant "indifferent," suggesting that this action reinforces "the tyranny of the copy-text"; see "The CEAA and Modern Textual Editing," *Library*, 5th ser., 32 (1977), 61–74 (esp. pp. 69–71), and my comments on it in "Recent Editorial Discussion and the Central Questions of Editing," *SB*, 34 (1981), 23–65 (esp. pp. 40–42), reprinted in *Textual Criticism since Greg* (1987), pp. 65–107 (esp. pp. 82–84).

weight to the accidentals in one; the fact that there is often little basis for making decisions about accidentals does not in such an instance justify assigning authority to the accidentals that happen to be in a single document. Greg criticized editors for "abdicating" the "editorial function" if in the case of substantives "of equal extrinsic authority" they relied "on some arbitrary canon, such as the authority of the copy-text" (pp. 144–45). But he was giving them contrary advice for the accidentals.

It was after this passage, however, that he sanctioned the alteration of copy-text accidentals—presumably in both kinds of situations, both where texts can be ranked on genealogical grounds and where two or more authoritative texts appear unrankable. Thus the overriding point is the necessity for editorial judgment, which must operate regardless of the relationships among the documents; and the idea of a copy-text (feasible for ancestral series but meaningless for texts of equal authority, which offer no basis for generalizing about their readings as a whole) is not really central to the argument. Although Greg wished to warn editors about "the mesmeric influence of the copy-text" (p. 145), he did not entirely escape it himself, for his injection of the concept into his discussion ironically interfered with the full expression of a theory of editorial freedom for scholarly editing.

The voluminous commentary engendered by Greg's essay has largely been concerned with the applicability of his approach beyond the field of Renaissance drama and with the appropriateness of concentrating on final authorial intention.[16] Most commentators have spent less time scrutinizing the general principles underlying Greg's recommendations than evaluating how useful those specific recommendations seem in different contexts, and thus there has been almost no questioning of the necessity for a concept of copy-text. The basic meaning of the term "copy-text" has remained stable from McKerrow's time onward—that is, the documentary text used as the basis for a scholarly edition. But the way in which a copy-text is selected and emended has undergone a remarkable shift during the twentieth century; and when the phrase

---

16. For an evaluative survey of the commentary, see my *Textual Criticism since Greg* (1987), supplemented by the essay cited in note 4 above.

"copy-text editing" is now used it signifies not what McKerrow would have understood by it but generally something close to what Greg meant by it. Being a critic of "copy-text editing"—and there have been many such critics in recent years—is likely to mean disapproving of the elevation of texts as completed by authors over texts as they emerged from publication or theatrical production, or objecting to the preference for the author's final intention rather than an earlier intention, or indeed decrying the practice of eclectic editing itself. But criticizing "copy-text editing" has not meant attacking the *idea* of copy-text. Whether or not editors of post-medieval writings have been successful in avoiding the "tyranny of the copy-text" as envisaged by Greg, they have not escaped the tyranny of the concept of copy-text.

Perhaps the most instructive example is Fredson Bowers, since he was the most prolific and influential editor of this century in the English-speaking scholarly world. He was also the person primarily responsible for the extension of Greg's ideas to the editing of post-Renaissance literature, and therefore one might think it unreasonable to expect that he would have been critical of "copy-text." Yet he was an ardent believer in the importance of critical judgment in editing, and he did not hesitate to point out what he saw as limitations in Greg's rationale; thus his failure to question the need for a copy-text does show what Greg had called the mesmerizing power of the concept. As cases in point, one may turn to two of his essays from the 1970s, "Multiple Authority: New Problems and Concepts of Copy-Text" (1972) and "Greg's 'Rationale of Copy-Text' Revisited" (1978),[17] which are among the most trenchant analyses that Greg's ideas have received and constitute Bowers's principal reconsideration of his earlier, less measured, response to the "Rationale."

---

17. The first, a paper read before the Bibliographical Society in London, was published in the *Library*, 5th ser., 27 (1972), 81–115, and was reprinted in his *Essays in Bibliography, Text, and Editing* (1975), pp. 447–487 (the text cited here). The second paper was published in *SB*, 31 (1978), 90–161.

The first of these essays, after sketching Greg's contribution[18] and some of Bowers's own applications of Greg's rationale to later literature, takes up instances of thoroughgoing authorial revision, a subject not dealt with by Greg in much detail. In such cases, Bowers says, when "the two texts are parallel enough for a comparison of the accidentals to be pertinent," an editor "can make some essay at treating the accidentals of the revised edition on the same critical basis as its substantives" (p. 462). What the editor must not do, Bowers insists, is "to succumb to the tyranny of the copy-text." If all variants—accidentals as well as substantives—are treated critically, Bowers recognizes that "in an ideal state" the editor "would arrive at compatible results without regard for the choice of copy-text" (pp. 462–463):

> The edited text would not differ in the least, but only in apparatus. Thus I return to my original suggestion that the choice of copy-text for revised editions should actually be motivated by practical convenience, not by ideological considerations. (p. 463)

A major element in this "practical convenience" turns out to be conciseness of the apparatus. Actually the choice of copy-text would not necessarily affect the length of the apparatus, though it could frequently do so if one were using the style of apparatus Bowers generally employed. But the main point is that if a shortening of apparatus is accomplished by presenting less information (as it is in Bowers's system), one is in the odd position of claiming that the purpose of selecting a copy-text is to withhold textual evidence from the reader.[19] In fact Bowers proceeds to point

---

18. At one point (p. 459) Bowers says that before Greg the conservative position regarding the accidentals of a revised edition (essentially McKerrow's belief that they must be accepted) was "partly based on despair." Yet Greg's different recommendation—to follow the accidentals of the unrevised edition—was equally uncritical and equally a counsel of despair, founded in part—as Greg said—on "philological ignorance" (p. 147). Both positions illustrate the tendency to turn away from evaluative judgment in cases of "ignorance."

19. The kind of apparatus Bowers had in mind, as he made clear in his footnote 20, was one in which a list of emendations records all editorial alterations to the copy-text (accidentals as well as substantives) and a "historical collation" records only the substantive

out, both in a footnote on this passage and in the following paragraph, that only in an ideal world would the choice of copy-text not affect the resulting edited text—but in that case the choice is not simply "motivated by practical convenience" after all, since the text is affected by it. Yet at the end of the paragraph, Bowers comes back to the matter of convenience, saying that a revised edition should be chosen as copy-text "only in cases of the sternest necessity when to select an earlier document would pile up lists of emendations of staggering proportions" (p. 464). Exactly what function a copy-text plays is finally unclear in this discussion, but the idea that there must be a copy-text of some sort seems never in doubt.

In the second essay, six years later, Bowers gives Greg's "Rationale" a more critical reading, examines its applicability to authorially revised editions of later periods (in the light of his own further experience), and finds that he has a "serious quarrel" with Greg's belief in "the lesser authority of a revised edition in cases of doubt" (p. 123). Although he is convinced that Greg's idea of choosing a copy-text for its accidentals is "still (and no doubt invariably) sound . . . for any period" (p. 147), he concludes that the greater accuracy of compositors in periods after the Renaissance means that indifferent substantive variants in revised editions of the last three centuries may generally be regarded as more likely to be authorial than compositorial (p. 155). There is an irony here in Bowers's partial return to McKerrow's belief in the whole body of substantive variants of a revised edition. Bowers's position is more flexible, but there is considerable similarity between McKerrow's idea of adopting all the variants when some are certainly authorial and Bow-

---

variants in the collated documents. In this system, the choice of copy-text does not affect the length of the tabulation of substantive variants (since all are recorded in one list or another), but it does change the length of the listing of accidentals unless the number of required emendations of copy-text accidentals happens to be the same in any case. Bowers recognizes, at least in the instance of a revised-edition copy-text, that the unlisted first-edition variants in accidentals are of legitimate interest to the reader; and the only explanation he offers for not noting them is that it is "usually impracticable to record in the Historical Collation all rejected accidentals as well as substantives."

ers's newly formed conviction of the likelihood "that an indifferent variant in the revised text is authorial" (p. 155). Bowers even admits the possibility that this view may apply to accidentals as well as substantives (depending on one's judgment of compositorial fidelity) and thus that the revised text could become the copy-text (p. 160). But given his recognition that copy-text accidentals as well as substantives can be altered by the editor (e.g., pp. 128–129, 148–149), along with his willingness to make distinctions even among what he labels "indifferent" variants (rendering them in fact no longer indifferent),[20] one begins to wonder what is left of the concept of a copy-text as a fall-back position. That this concept is the ostensible focus of the essay reveals its tyrannizing powers, for the real subject is—as it must be in an approach that stresses judgment—the process of active decision-making. Bowers was willing—as he put it at the end of the essay—to "reverse Greg's principle for any period after the Renaissance"; but he was apparently not ready to demote the idea of denominating one text as the copy-text in every instance.

This reluctance is most dramatically revealed in his treatment of so-called "radiating texts"—texts that do not form an ancestral linear series but instead represent independent lines of descent from a common source. This kind of textual history is frequently encountered in the study of the manuscript traditions of ancient texts, but Bowers's attention was drawn to it by his editing of Stephen Crane, whose syndicated newspaper pieces provide a classically pure example of the problem: the various original newspaper texts of a piece are independently derived from (and equidistant from) the master copy supplied by the syndicate office to the subscribing newspapers. In the absence of such master copy, the syndicated appearances—"radiating" from the lost original—constitute the only evidence for reconstructing what the syndicate office sent out (which is, in turn, at least one step removed from Crane's lost

---

20. He reports that in his edition of *Tom Jones* "proportionately far more indifferent variants are inserted from the revised edition into the first-edition copy-text than in the conservatively treated *Joseph Andrews*" (p. 159).

manuscripts). In the fifth and sixth volumes of his Crane edition (*Tales of Adventure* and *Tales of War*, both 1970), Bowers first dealt with this situation extensively.[21]

His procedure, at points of variation in punctuation among the radiating texts, was generally to adopt the reading present in the largest number of them (though he recognized that not every instance could be handled on a quantitative basis); and then he selected as a copy-text the single newspaper text that contained the largest number of the readings that he had decided to adopt. As he says in discussing "The Pace of Youth," the first of the pieces in *Tales of Adventure,* the Dayton *Daily Journal* text "has been selected as copy-text for its general concurrence with majority opinion" (p. cxlii). This use of "copy-text" of course shifts the meaning of the term from what Greg (and Bowers in earlier discussions) had meant by it—for here it does not designate a text that can be accorded presumptive authority by virtue of its genealogical position, since all the radiating texts are equidistant from the copy furnished by the author. Instead of a copy-text that helps one to resolve cruxes, it is now one that is selected after the cruxes have been resolved. The problem emerges even more clearly in Bowers's account of the next piece, "One Dash—Horses," where he designates the syndicate master proof as the copy-text (even though it does not survive), because it is "the earliest recoverable archetype," and he is then driven to use the term "physical copy-text itself " for the one newspaper text that is "perhaps the closest in its accidentals to the lost master proof " (p. cxlvii). *Tales of War* also includes instances in which Bowers, after pointing out that several newspaper texts are "technically" of equal authority, chooses one as copy-text for its "convenience"—the convenience stemming from the fact that the text chosen (to quote his statement in one case) "is generally less in need of accidentals emendation" (p. cxi).[22]

21. The year before, however, in *Tales of Whilomville* (1969), he postulated that the *McClure's* and *Cornhill* texts of "His New Mittens" radiated from Crane's manuscript. But the evidence here is not conclusive, as it is with the syndicated newspaper pieces.

22. See, for example, the discussion of "A Mystery of Heroism": the six newspaper texts "are technically of equal authority," but "For convenience the *Philadelphia Press* printing

The conceptual imprecision in this shifting use of "copy-text" probably had little effect on Bowers's final text, since his copy-texts in these instances were chosen not for their authority but for the extent of their agreement with what he had already decided the text should contain. Nevertheless, the fuzziness surrounding "copy-text" here does have practical consequences for the reader, through its effect on the apparatus. Because the list of emendations provides a record of editorial alterations made in the designated copy-texts, and because the "historical collation" records only substantive variants, the variants in accidentals among the radiating texts are not fully reported. Bowers does say, in his headnote to the emendations list in both of these Crane volumes, "when as in syndicated newspaper versions a number of texts have equal claim to authority, all are noted in the Emendations listing" (5:211; 6:335). What this statement means is that a full record of variants in accidentals is normally[23] provided for each place where the designated copy-text is emended; but any variants in accidentals at places where the copy-text is not emended remain unreported. Yet the documentary authority of those variants is the same as that of the reported ones, given the genealogical equality of all the radiating texts. Thus the reader is deprived of some of the evidence from the texts that collectively form the primary authority in these cases. That Bowers himself sometimes thought of a group of radiating texts as a kind of collective copy-text is suggested by an instance in "One

---

has been selected as copy-text, since it is representative. It is reprinted here, emended as necessary by reference to the other authorities when it appears to wander whether in accidentals or in substantives from the majority view" (p. lxix). In the case of "The Clan of No-Name," the conjectural textual history "places each of the preserved documents as technically equal in authority with the others in respect to the accidentals" (p. cxix); but the "usual moderate position" of the *New York Herald* "in respect to what may be reconstructed as the accidentals of the lost typescript makes it the most satisfactory and convenient copy-text" (p. cxxiii).

23. But not always: sometimes, he asserts, "only general concurrence of the following editions is in question and exactness of detail would serve no useful purpose." In those cases he introduces a plus/minus sign to signify that the majority of the newspaper texts (but not all of them) have the cited punctuation. He adds, "If it seemed important to indicate that certain of these variant texts had such and such punctuation, then the listing would do so as most convenient." (See 6: 335–336.)

Dash—Horses" where he retains the designated copy-text's capitalization of "North" but says that it "may most properly be regarded as an emendation" (p. 199)—and then includes it (with "*stet*") in his list of emendations (p. 213). In short, the importation of a concept of copy-text into these situations is more productive of confusion than of clarity.

Bowers's primary theoretical discussion of radiating texts occurs not in the Crane edition but in the latter half of his essay on "Multiple Authority," where it constitutes his principal supplement to Greg—since it, unlike most of his other treatments of copy-text, focuses on a situation that Greg did not attempt to cover. But his discussion, pioneering as it is in many ways, is weakened by his retention of the idea of a copy-text, especially after having in effect shown why it is irrelevant. He emphasizes, quite properly, the role of critical judgment, pointing out that for radiating texts it must be applied as fully to accidentals as to substantives.[24] A statistical approach, he rightly asserts, is not sufficient, for an unconventional authorial reading might be normalized by many compositors and "preserved only by the dogged or indifferent few"; "the minority reading may sometimes need to be adopted on critical grounds" (p. 468). This cogent reasoning implies the importance of recording all the variant readings in radiating texts; and it is therefore revealing of his divided mind that he proceeds to advocate choosing a copy-text "requiring the least amount of apparatus" (p. 471).[25]

24. In making this point (p. 466), he overstates the mechanical nature of the establishment of accidentals under Greg's rationale; as Bowers elsewhere recognizes (and as Greg himself does in the "Rationale"), copy-text accidentals, like the substantives, can be emended whenever one has a basis (necessarily involving critical judgment) for doing so.

25. In a footnote Bowers acknowledges, "Paradoxically, the copy-text most faithful to the reconstructed printer's-copy conceals more information in its list of emendations by recording fewer of the multiple variants than would be the case for a copy-text less faithful." His response to this problem is not satisfactory, however, because it concentrates on a "limited" recording of additional variants and does not admit the logical necessity of a full report: "How far this concealment of the evidence on which the work was edited can be rectified by including among the substantive variants of the Historical Collation the accidentals variants rejected from the other witnesses is a procedure sometimes practicable on a limited basis." An editor who pursues this idea can, Bowers believes, "start by omitting at least the unique variants—since these will have little or no claim to

He recognizes the reasons for dispensing with the concept of copy-text altogether in such situations: if there are eight radiating texts, he says, the copy-text is "only one of eight equal witnesses, of no greater presumptive authority than the other seven" (p. 470); the choice of copy-text, then, is "theoretically indifferent" and "largely a question of convenience"; it is made only after the critical text has already been constructed (p. 471), and it is "not integral to the editing" (p. 485). He is therefore receptive to the possibility of having no copy-text; yet he maintains that a copy-text be chosen "to serve as the physical basis" (p. 471) for a critically reconstructed text, without making clear why the "physical basis" must be equated with a single document, when in fact it is a group of documents. The idea that there must be a copy-text was so firmly rooted in his mind that the only alternative he saw to selecting a single radiating text was to have a "non-extant copy-text" (p. 471), in Crane's case the lost syndicate master proofs as reconstructed from the radiating texts. To cling to a concept of "copy-text" even if it comes to mean the same thing as the scholar's reconstructed text is surely the ultimate in being tyrannized by the idea of having something called "copy-text." At the end of the essay Bowers says that to try applying Greg's rationale to radiating-text situations "would establish a real tyranny of the copy-text"; but Bowers (like Greg before him) was not able, even while warning others about this tyranny, to shake himself entirely free from its bonds.

Two years after Bowers's essay, I called attention to the inappropriateness of trying to employ in radiating-text situations the kind of apparatus that had become standard, under Bowers's influence, for use with linear genealogies. Although he recognized that Greg's "Rationale" did not apply to radiating texts, he apparently could not bring

---

authority—and then progress up the scale so far as seems practicable." But this thinking is at odds with the important point made earlier that a critical approach to variants must take precedence over a merely statistical one. (In a later volume of the edition [volume 3 but published in 1976], *The Third Violet and Active Service*, Bowers specifically notes that "a minority, or even a single newspaper, may on some very few occasions reflect more faithfully the proof than the styled majority" [p. 332].)

himself to accept fully the fact that an apparatus reflecting this rationale would not do so, either. It is noteworthy that when, in "Multiple Authority," he shrank from the notion of a "non-extant copy-text" his stated reason was not conceptual but the belief that "the problem of what form an apparatus would take for such a non-extant copy-text is acute" (p. 471). Actually, as I tried to show, there is nothing complicated in simply listing all the variants (in both substantives and accidentals) in all the radiating texts and keying this single list to the newly constructed critical text.[26] Such a list emphasizes that the critical text has been built up from the evidence of all the radiating texts and was not produced by making alterations in one of them. The only sense in which the latter operation could be said to have occurred is that some form of reproduction (xerographic, say, or photographic) of one of the texts may have been marked to produce a document that could be handed to the printer of the new scholarly text. Bowers was of course well aware, in other discussions, of the significant difference between a copy-text in

26. See "Editorial Apparatus for Radiating Texts," *Library*, 5th ser., 29 (1974), 330–337; reprinted in *Textual Criticism and Scholarly Editing* (1990), pp. 167–176 (and see my comment on p. xiii of the preface to this volume, suggesting that "the idea of editing without a copy-text, set forth briefly here in relation to one particular kind of situation, has further applications that ought to be explored"). Bowers commented on my 1974 article the following year in his "Remarks on Eclectic Texts" (see note 8 above); after saying that a copy-text selected from a group of radiating texts is "only a peg on which to hang the apparatus of variation," he refers to my "interesting proposal," which—though it seems "logically planned"—he has not "had the opportunity to test" (p. 507, footnote 26). In his 1978 essay on Greg, he repeats the idea that for radiating texts the "choice of copy-text rests on the convenience of the reader according to the ease with which he can refer to the apparatus"; then he adds, "On the other hand, if an editor chooses to adopt G. T. Tanselle's ingenious suggestions for a new kind of apparatus for radiating texts, the need for an arbitrary copy-text vanishes" (p. 149, footnote 48). (In the same footnote, Bowers suggests, without realizing it, a way in which the editorial thinking involved in a radiating-text situation could be extended to any instance of variant texts: when a statistical survey of variants determines the choice of a radiating copy-text, he says, "there should be little if any need for an editor to rely on any accidental in the copy-text simply because it occurs in the copy-text, although he may of course take that fact into account when the copy-text document seems on the whole to be relatively faithful and all other evidence is indifferent.") For a similar discussion of apparatus for radiating texts nine years later, see p. 76 of Bowers's "Mixed Texts and Multiple Authority," *Text*, 3 (1987), 63–90.

Greg's sense and a printer's copy for a scholarly edition.[27] Yet his rec-ommendation to choose a single documentary text from a group of radiating texts, and call it a "copy-text," amounts to equating "copy-text" with "printer's copy"—while at the same time elevating it unde-servedly to unique historical status by reporting its variants fully (and not those of any other text).

There is no escaping the fact that radiating texts equidistant from their common ancestor provide no text to serve as copy-text; and it is further true that this lack does not prevent an editor from constructing a critical text—as Bowers did before he chose a copy-text—or from preparing an apparatus recording all the rejected variants. Once one accepts these points, one may begin to see that the thinking involved in radiating-text situations is applicable to all critical editing. Every choice made among variants in radiating texts is an active critical choice; no reading is settled on by default, for there is no text that offers a fall-back position. When the variants in radiating texts seem "indifferent," an editor may of course choose a reading from the text that supplies the largest number of other readings; but the decision is still an active one, in which one of the factors taken into account is the apparent general reliability of a particular text. The process remains one of building up a new text rather than making changes in an old one. If this idea—that critical editing is constructive rather than emendatory—were also applied to texts in linear genealogies, the role of judgment might more clearly be seen as dominant, and any practical guideline (such as Greg's rationale) might be better recognized as an aid to judgment, not a brake on it. An editor, for example, who is following Greg in according presumptive authority to the text closest to a lost manuscript, would—following this

27. In "Mixed Texts and Multiple Authority" (see the preceding note), he includes in a footnote the explicit statement, "It is quite improper to use it [*copy-text*] as a synonym for printer's copy in general" (p. 87). For a more detailed account of this distinction, see my "The Meaning of Copy-Text: A Further Note," *SB*, 23 (1970), 191–196. When I sub-mitted this piece—which is a rejoinder to Paul Baender's "The Meaning of Copy-Text" in the previous volume of *SB* (22 [1969], 311–318)—Bowers said that he had planned (before my piece came in) to write such a response himself.

plan—speak not of "retaining" readings from that text but of "select-ing" them. The notion that wisdom supports the idea of sticking to a copy-text when two readings are indifferent places the emphasis on the preservation of a documentary text; but the idea that a critical text emerges from active choices made among the variant readings (along with, of course, the editor's own inventions, when necessary) empha-sizes editorial judgment.

The difference between the two may at first seem slight, a matter of labeling: in the former, one lets a copy-text reading stand if the variant is indifferent and there is thus no compelling argument for altering it; in the latter, two readings that might otherwise be indifferent are not actu-ally so, for the fact that one of them comes from a text of superior genealogical standing provides a reason for choosing it. But the differ-ence between these two justifications for the same decision is not super-ficial: it goes to the heart of what critical editing is. The key point is not whether an editor would make the same decision by following Greg's rationale or by designating no copy-text but still following Greg's argu-ment for the presumptive authority of the text closest to an authorial manuscript. No two editors can be expected to make the same choices by following either of these systems in any case. The important point is that the former approach places a rule above reason (as any recourse to a fall-back position must do), whereas the latter restructures the problem so that the editor's decision (even if it is the same decision) results from the positive step of taking a reasoned action.

The controlling images of the two approaches are those of initially full and initially empty sheets of paper. If one chooses a copy-text, then in effect one begins with filled sheets and proceeds to alter the text pres-ent on them; but if one has no copy-text, one begins with blank sheets, so to speak, and fills them by placing one word after another on them, drawing those readings from the relevant documents (and, on occasion, from one's own mind). I am not suggesting, of course, that an editor should actually write out a text in this way; but I do believe that an appropriate analogy for the critical editor to have in mind is the medieval scribe taking readings from various manuscripts as he prepared a new manuscript.[28] It is ironic that in classic Lachmannian textual criticism this scribal practice is called "contamination," for some such process (supplemented by the editor's own inventions) provides our only hope for rising above the limitations of individual documents. Although the followers of Lachmann may often have deluded themselves about the objectivity of their own methods, their process of "recension," with its aggregating impulse, in many cases avoided the pitfalls of the "best-text" family of approaches and therefore holds a lesson for editors of works in the modern languages.

The constructive approach I am outlining subsumes all the various points of view that can be taken toward the goal of editing. There is no reason, for example, why an editor interested in uninfluenced authorial final intention could not still follow Greg's rationale—which has proved itself effective for this purpose. But instead of treating one text as a copy-text, an editor would use the genealogical position—and thus the presumed authority—of that text as a factor in weighing each variant reading. Sometimes this factor would be decisive; sometimes other factors would be. The difference between this procedure and the conventional one is subtle but crucially significant. Genealogy is taken into account, but with judgment clearly in the dominant position. If, instead of uninfluenced authorial intention, one preferred to emphasize, say, the text that was the joint product of the author and the publisher's staff, one would then have a different attitude toward some of the first-edition readings that vary from manuscript readings (those, for instance, that seem to reflect house-styling). Or if one wished to focus on a stage that preceded a final version, the bulk of the text might be drawn from the document that provides the best evidence of the existence of such a

28. Leonard E. Boyle calls modern editors "scribe-scholars" in " 'Epistulae Venerunt Parum Dulces': The Place of Codicology in the Editing of Medieval Latin Texts," in *Editing and Editors: A Retrospect*, ed. Richard Landon (1988), pp. 29–46 (see p. 30). (This essay also provides a useful statement of the value of examining the physical "setting" in which a text has been transmitted; the examples are drawn from the study of early manuscripts, but the points made are equally applicable to the study of printed books—and have of course been made many times by analytical bibliographers.)

stage, but not without a serious weighing of the claims of variants in other documents (since versions of works cannot be equated with the texts of particular documents). What I am suggesting is not a supplement or an alternative to Greg's rationale but an overarching framework that encompasses its goal and that of other rationales as well. Obviously one could rewrite Greg so as to focus on goals other than authorial intention; but the resulting series of copy-text rationales, each aiming at a different end-product, would still not avoid the restriction on editorial judgment inherent in Greg's rationale. What is needed instead is a framework that liberates editorial judgment from the concept of copy-text while being neutral in itself as to the goal toward which that judgment should be directed.[29]

Despite the salutary emphasis of Greg and Bowers on editorial freedom, many editors are still—as Greg and Bowers were—in thrall to the notion, now about two centuries old, that responsibility in scholarly editing is, at least to some degree, incompatible with freedom of judgment. A passage in Bowers's "Multiple Authority" illustrates how inhibiting this attitude can sometimes be. Bowers claims that the evidence of the radiating newspaper texts of a Crane story enables one to attempt reconstructing the syndicate master proofs but offers no justification for pushing on back to Crane's manuscript. It is not the editor's concern, he says, "whether in their recovered form these proofs agree or disagree with Crane's habits of punctuation, spelling, and so on"; and he continues, more emphatically, to say that "it is not an editor's business to print what he may be morally certain the manuscript reading would have been when the evidence indicates strongly that the recovered proof read otherwise" (p. 473).[30] There may be good reason, of course, to be satisfied with having the text of the syndicate proofs; but if one is really interested

29. The inhibiting influence of a copy-text resembles the pressure that can also be exerted by a previous scholarly edition: Leonard Boyle has said, "the greatest threat to an editor's independence and to an unprejudiced presentation of a textual tradition is the presence of an existing edition." See " 'Epistulae Venerunt Parum Dulces' " (cited in the preceding note), p. 31.

30. Bowers makes the same point, though somewhat more moderately, in "Remarks on Eclectic Texts" (see note 8 above), pp. 522–524.

in what Crane wrote in his manuscript, and if one's knowledge and judgment make one "morally certain" of being able to reconstruct it, why should one be prevented from doing so by the fact that one is going back two or more steps behind the preserved documents rather than just a single step? The "law" of "documentary evidence," to which Bowers appeals, is surely misapplied if it outlaws the responsible use of the historical imagination. The very existence of critical editing depends on recognizing that documentary texts may legitimately be overruled by informed judgment. Whether an editor is justified in attempting to reconstruct any given stage in a text's history depends on how the task is approached, on how the editor proposes to overcome the limitations of the documents; no *a priori* ruling can decree one stage to be a valid goal for the exercise of historical judgment and another to be inappropriate.

On many other occasions, however, Bowers not only granted, but openly welcomed, the dominance of judgment—as when, in his edition of *Tom Jones* (1975), after saying that the textual situation was one in which "Greg's classic theory of copy-text must hold" (p. lxx), he declared that the operation of emendation "is a critical process almost exclusively" and that in such a process "the editor shoulders his proper responsibility" (p. lxxi). In a 1985 address he described Greg's rationale as "a discretionary principle, to be applied flexibly," and as a "liberation" from "mechanical conservatism," complaining that in America it was often used to justify "avoiding the unknown terrors of eclecticism."[31] Both Greg and Bowers unquestionably believed in the liberty of editorial judgment, but in their procedural statements they yoked this belief to a strategy that sprang ultimately from a contrary view, for they obviously carried with them just enough of an inherited distrust of judgment to make them not quite prepared for completing the long historical movement toward the full reinstatement of critical judgment in editing.

What I am proposing here is a way to take that step without abandoning the responsibilities of scholarship. It might be called "constructive

---

31. "Unfinished Business," Bowers's presidential address to the Society for Textual Scholarship, printed in *Text*, 4 (1988), 1–11 (quotations from p. 5).

critical editing" to distinguish it from an approach that emphasizes emendation. To see critical editing as an activity of rebuilding rather than repairing forces the judgment to play its central role in recovering the past. All historical reconstruction requires judgment to enable one to decide what can be accepted as facts and what can reasonably be inferred from them by an informed imagination. Experiencing verbal works as communications from the past entails this kind of reconstruction not only because they are past events but also because they employ an intangible medium, language. Reading necessarily involves the use of judgment in the extracting of a work from a document. If editors' readings, enshrined in editions, are to be exemplary, they must arise from an active embracing of judgment—which is, after all, the only thing we have to rely on.

from *The First Folio of Shakespeare*[†]

Peter W. M. Blayney

MUCH OF WHAT is now known about the printing of the First Folio is owed to the monumental study undertaken by Charlton K. Hinman. Using a special viewer that he designed and built himself, Hinman made a minutely detailed page-by-page comparison of 55 of the Folger copies. He also spent several years investigating and analyzing the patterns in which various recognizable objects reappeared throughout the book: each individual brass rule used in the box-frames around the text (identifiable by tell-tale bends and breaks); each separate setting of the running-titles used in each play; and hundreds of distinctively damaged types in the text itself. As a result, he was able to reconstruct the order in which the pages were set and printed, to identify which of several workmen set each page, and to relate many of the irregularities in the work to specific parts of other books that were being printed at the same time.

★ ★ ★

THE STRUCTURE OF THE BOOK

The Shakespeare First Folio is what is known as a 'folio in sixes'. What that means is a book made up of six-leaf sections (or 'quires'), each consisting of three sheets of paper folded together (and eventually sewn). Each sheet

---

[†] From *The First Folio of Shakespeare*. (Washington, D.C.: Folger Library Publications, 1991). By permission of the Folger Shakespeare Library.

has two pages printed on each side, so each quire contains twelve pages of text (approximately half an average play). There are, in fact, a number of 'irregular' sections in the Folio. One quire has eight leaves, another has four, three have only two, and four leaves are inserted singly. Most of the quires, however, have six leaves, and most of the exceptions are consequences of (and evidence for) irregularities in the progress of the printing.

★ ★ ★

THE ORDER OF THE PAGES

Before Hinman's study was published, it had usually been taken for granted that the text of each play had been printed from beginning to end in the 'obvious' order. Such, however, was not the case. The 12 pages in each quire are arranged in pairs on the three sheets as shown below. If the pages had been set in numerical order, the press could not have started printing any of them until the first complete pair—pages 6 and 7—had been finished. In addition to causing long delays, that system would have required a very large stock of type. No page could be distributed before pages 6 and 7 had been printed—so unless the compositors stopped work while the press was in use, they would have needed enough additional type to keep them busy until pages 6 and 7 could be distributed. Like most printers in Jacobean London, Jaggard simply did not own enough type to set eight or nine Folio pages. He therefore followed the common English practice known as 'setting by formes' (a 'forme' is a group of type-pages to be printed on one side of a sheet).

In a folio-in-sixes, pages 1 and 12 are printed on the same side of a sheet of paper.

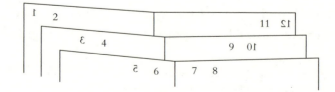

The usual method of setting a Folio quire was to begin by estimating how much text would fit in the first five pages—a process known as 'casting off' the copy. Pages 6 and 7 were the first to be set, sometimes by two men working simultaneously, but more usually by a single compositor. When those two pages (the first forme) had been made ready and given to the press, pages 5 and 8 (the next forme) were set. Those two pages were far enough apart for the copy to be physically divided between two compositors, so they were usually set by two men working simultaneously. While the press printed pages 5 and 8, the compositors distributed pages 6 and 7, and then set pages 4 and 9. After another distribution they set pages 3 and 10, then pages 2 and 11, and finally pages 1 and 12. So although the last seven pages of each quire were set in numerical order, the first five pages were set in *reverse* order.

THE IMPORTANCE OF CASTING OFF

It was not always easy to cast off manuscript copy accurately. Once pages 6 and 7 had been printed, the text assigned to pages 1–5 *had* to be fitted into those pages. If the contents of page 5 had been carelessly calculated, the compositor had a choice. He could try to follow the casting-off mark exactly, by squeezing in extra lines or by spacing out the text as appropriate. Alternatively, he could put off the problem by ignoring the mark—he could set in the usual way, make up page 5 when he had set the right number of lines, and then make a new mark of his own in the copy to show where the page had *really* started. If he then did the same with pages 4 and 3 and 2, when the time came to fit what remained into page 1, he might well find himself in difficulties.

There were several easy ways of making minor adjustments. A stage direction could be set with or without a 'white line' (a line of spaces) above it, or with another below it. Both above and below a scene-heading, there was usually a pair of white lines separated by a rule, so one or more of the white lines could be omitted if necessary. Exits were usually set against the right margin. If there was room, an exit could occupy a line by itself; if not,

The scene-heading shown below is a 'normal' one from a page in the second half of quire nn of Hamlet *(Tragedies, page 155). [The First Folio is divided into three sections, Comedies, Histories, and Tragedies, each with its own pagination —Editor.]*

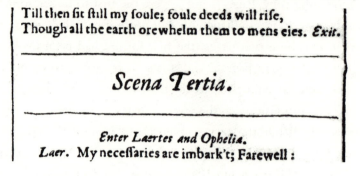

Till then fit ftill my foule; foule deeds will rife,
Though all the earth orewhelm them to mens eies. *Exit.*

Scena Tertia.

Enter Laertes and Ophelia.
Laer. My neceffaries are imbark't; Farewell :

The example below is from the first page of quire Aa in The Winter's Tale *(Comedies, page 277). A miscalculation in casting off left the compositor with too much text to fit the page, so he gained extra space by omitting all four white lines from the scene-heading.*

Arch. If the King had no Sonne, they would defire to
liue on Crutches till he had one.   *Exeunt.*
Scœna Secunda.
Enter Leontes, Hermione, Mamillius, Polixenes, Camillo.
Pol. Nine Changes of the Watry-Starre hath been

it could share a line with the end of a speech. If there was still a problem, verse could either be run together as prose or chopped into half-lines.

Sometimes, however, the measures adopted were even more extreme. *Much Ado About Nothing* ends on the first page of quire L, and whoever did the casting off left rather too much text to be crammed into that page. In this case the Folio text can be compared with the Quarto of 1600, from which it was set. Among the inevitable crop of misprints in the Folio page, one whole line of text is omitted. That omission may have been accidental, but the line was 'Heere comes the Prince and Claudio', spoken immediately before a stage direction for the entrance of those characters. A compositor in search of extra space might well have decided that the line could be sacrificed without substantial loss.

In *Antony and Cleopatra*, the first page of quire zz (Tragedies, page

The example below is from the first page of quire ss in King Lear *(Tragedies, page 305), and shows the opposite problem. The compositor did not have enough text to fill the page in the normal way, so he had to find ways of spacing it out. His methods included using a white line below the opening stage direction of this scene and setting the first two lines of verse as four half-lines.*

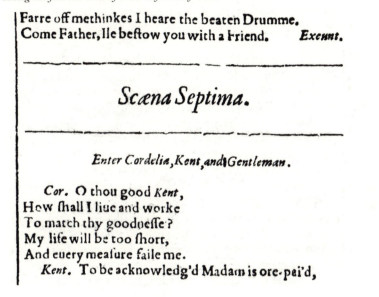

Farre off methinkes I heare the beaten Drumme.
Come Father, Ile beftow you with a Friend.   *Exeunt.*

Scæna Septima.

Enter Cordelia, Kent, and Gentleman.

Cor. O thou good *Kent*,
How fhall I liue and worke
To match thy goodneffe?
My life will be too fhort,
And euery meafure faile me.
        Kent. To be acknowledg'd Madam is ore-pai'd,

365) is another in which the text fits rather tightly. In that page the lines spoken by Proculeius immediately before and after Cleopatra is captured are printed as two consecutive speeches, each with the speech-heading, 'Pro'. It is possible that nothing has been omitted. If the speech was divided between pages of the manuscript, the 'Pro'. heading may have been repeated at the beginning of the new page. More probably, however, a stage direction describing Cleopatra's capture has been left out. That may be all—but the half-line spoken immediately before the capture is followed by a complete line when Proculeius resumes. It is therefore possible that at least one speech (perhaps a half-line spoken by Cleopatra) has also been omitted for lack of space.

By contrast, the first two pages of quire ss in *King Lear* (Tragedies, pp. 305–6) contain far less text than normal, and some lines of verse had to be broken into half-lines for the sake of filling space. The Folio text of *Lear* differs substantially from the Quarto of 1608, and the differences

Shown here is one of the most obviously crowded passages in the Folio: the end of Much Ado about Nothing, on the first page of quire L (Comedies, page 121). Among other expedients, the compositor resorted to using contractions in the first and third lines. (As is the case when the is contracted to ye, the y element in the first two contractions stands for th. The contracted words are thou and that.) He also squeezed the Messenger's entrance into the end of a line and put 'FINIS' into the 'direction line' below the text. (The L in that line is the 'signature' identifying quire L.)

> *Cla.* I had well hop'd ẙ wouldſt haue denied *Beatrice*,ẙ
> I might haue cudgel'd thee out of thy ſingle life, to make
> thee a double dealer, which out of queſtiõ thou wilt be,
> if my Couſin do not looke exceeding narrowly to thee.
>   *Bene.* Come, come, we are friends, let's haue a dance
> ere we are married, that we may lighten our own hearts,
> and our wiues heeles.
>   *Leon.* Wee'll haue dancing afterward.
>   *Bene.* Firſt, of my vvord, therfore play muſick. *Prince*,
> thou art ſad, get thee a vvife, get thee a vvife, there is no
> ſtaff more reuerend then one tipt with horn. *Enter. Meſ.*
>   *Meſſen.* My Lord, your brother *Iohn* is tane in flight,
> And brought with armed men backe to *Meſſina*.
>   *Bene.* Thinke not on him till to morrow, ile deuiſe
> thee braue puniſhments for him: ſtrike vp Pipers. *Dance.*
>   L   *FINIS.*

include numerous short insertions, one of which is found in the second column of page 305. Where the Quarto had a single verse line ('Fourescore and vpward, and to deale plainely'), the Folio has three lines of type. The Quarto line has been cut in two, and 'Not an houre more, nor lesse:' has been inserted between the two half-lines.

'Fourscore and upward' means 'over eighty'. It is anyway inappropriate to define an indefinite number of years to the nearest hour—but while 'not an hour less' makes a kind of sense, 'not an hour *more* than over eighty' makes none at all. The substance gains little from the addition, and the disrupted verse gains even less—but the line does help to fill the page. As 'evidence', that is at best only circumstantial—but it is not unreasonable to suspect that the line *may* have been made up in the printing house for the sole purpose of filling space.

★   ★   ★

Gon. No more, the text is foolish.[†]

Randall McLeod

I

σώζειν τὰ φαινόμενα

PLATO[1]

THERE ARE TWO early substantive texts of Shakespeare's drama of King Lear, *The Historie of King Lear*, published in quarto in 1608, and *The Tragedie of King Lear*, published in the Folio of 1623. All the seventeenth-century editions derived from one or other of these first two, the source in each case apparently being determined by copyright rather than by any editorial sense of the relative merits of Q and F. A different attitude toward what came to be deemed the embarrassing multiplicity of authority for *Lear* crystallized early in the eighteenth century, and still prevails two and a half centuries later: to conflate the two texts and to

† "*Gon.* No more, the text is foolish." from *The Division of the Kingdoms: Shakespeare's Two Versions of* King Lear, ed. Gary Taylor and Michael Warren (New York: Oxford University Press, 1983). Reprinted by permission of the Oxford University Press.

1. The Master Mistris of my passion is Rosalie Colie, to whose memory I dedicate this essay.
   Plato's admonition to students of astronomy 'to save the phenomena' is quoted from Simplicius's commentary on Aristotle's *de caelo* 492.30; his authority is Sosigenes, who quotes Eudemus (see also 488.23–4 and 493.3–4). My thanks to Plato scholar/business-man Ken Henwood for these references.
   I wish to thank Erindale College and the University of Toronto for granting me research leave in 1980–81 to work on problems of Shakespeare's text, and also the Social Sciences and Humanities Research Council of Canada for its research support during the leave.

create a super-*Lear* by selecting between variant readings those that are 'better'. The criteria of value seem to have been self-evident to each editor, but not to his predecessors or successors, and thus the historical collations of *Lear* editions parade before us a long historie and tragedie of 'betters'. But the more the editions changed superficially, the more profoundly they became the same—textimonials of editorial commitment to eclectic conflation. The result is that virtually no one now experiences Q and F as independent texts.

This editorial procedure began in the days when bibliographical study was in its infancy; but as it came of age, the justification of textual manipulation was felt to need to rest less on taste than on textual authority. It may have been all right for Alexander Pope, an early eighteenth-century editor, to make the best art he could from the materials available, but by the mid-twentieth century the time had come to strive to recreate editorially what Shakespeare had actually written, whether it was good or not.

Thirty years ago George Ian Duthie sought to make such an edition (*Shakespeare's 'King Lear': A Critical Edition*, Oxford, 1949), and to base it on a rationalized editorial programme that proceeded on the small scale, crux by crux, with unprecedented attention to detailed textual argument. I say 'unprecedented' because the details of Shakespeare editions are traditionally laid down by editorial fiat without explanation. Even now, Duthie's edition remains the only thorough, editorially explicit commentary on the variants between Q and F *Lear*, and the most conscientious defence of the conflationist position. (I will turn to examples of his detailed arguments in the second part of this paper.) All his arguments, however, are governed by the idea that Q and F are mere derivatives (with relatively lesser and greater fidelity) of a single, complete, historical version of greatest authority; this version, X, now lost, would, if rediscovered, render the status of Q and F non-substantive, for where they differ from X they are deemed corrupt or incomplete. Duthie's global approach to the relationship of Q and F was not entirely new, but his own detailed research into Q and questions of textual transmission, and the then recent work of Madeleine Doran and W. W. Greg, had put him in a position to speak with new objectivity.

Duthie held that Q derived from memorial reconstruction by a group of actors of their staged version.[2] Memorial reconstruction necessitates that the 'accidentals' of Q cannot bear a close relationship to those of the original prompt-book (or of the actors' part-books). Given the tricks of memory, we are to suspect many 'substantives' as well. The Folio, by contrast, is alleged to derive by scribal transmission from a prompt-book, the same prompt-book from which Q circuitously derives, or possibly a copy of it. F is thus deemed generally to have greater fidelity in both 'accidentals' and 'substantives' to the lost X than does Q. And so Duthie adopts F as his copy-text, and asserts firmly that the ideal text is virtually identical with it, and that F needs correction only when it is manifestly in error, or when comparison of it with Q's *frequently* divergent readings leads one *occasionally* to detect some otherwise unobserved problem with F (p. 18). For convenience he regards Q as a report of the F text (p. 21).

There is much fine tuning to Duthie's arguments, which I cannot detail here. But we can now draw the essentials of his textual tree (below). The dotted line is yet unexplained. Following P. A. Daniel's and W. W. Greg's discoveries, Duthie holds that the copy-text for F was an exemplar of Q marked up by Scribe E to bring it into agreement with the lost manuscript, X (or with a transcript of it, such as the prompt-book) (p. 13). Given the influence of Q press variation on the Folio text, the editor needs to allow for the possibility that through the scribe's negligence Q contaminates F elsewhere, where there is no press variation in Q to expose its influence. The corollary of this idea is one of the most

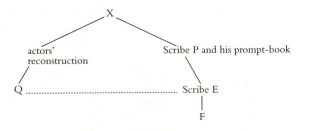

2. Duthie later retracted this explanation: see Stanley Wells's discussion in his introduction to *The Division of the Kingdoms: Shakespeare's Two Versions of* King Lear, ed. Gary Taylor and Michael Warren (New York: Oxford University Press, 1983), p. 12.

ingenious notions of *Lear* editing: that when F and Q agree anywhere, we are to be less confident of the F reading than when they disagree—even when both make sense (pp. 17–18).[3] And so, unhappy Q becomes suspect not only when it agrees with F (and has corrupted it) but also when it differs (and betrays the faulty memory of the actors).

But there is another problem which confronts the editor when he focuses on Q, and which Duthie's reconstructionism cannot face squarely. If Q is so egregiously corrupt, how can we be sure that it is a corruption of X and not of some other stage of composition, Y—with X and Y possibly related by such trees as these?[4]

Duthie spends considerable effort (pp. 19–72) arguing with detailed examples against the idea that Q represents an early draft and F a revision. But for the moment let us stay on an abstract plane. We see from the challenge posed by Y that both aspects of Duthie's twofold definition of Q are essential to his position. For (a): if Q were a *good* memorial reconstruction, then its numerous divergences from F would throw suspicion on F, or on the notion that there could exist a single substantive version of the Lear story—an X which could supersede both Q and F, and be Shakespeare's final version. And (b): if one holds Q still to be a bad text, but of *scribal* rather than memorial transmission, then one casts doubt upon the very method of transmission that is supposed to guarantee the high quality of F. Indeed, as it seems almost by definition that a

3. For when such an F reading differs from Q's, there is a strong presumption that it derives from the manuscript. But, of course, a divergent F reading can also derive from lapse or sophistication by scribe or by compositor; and for this reason the corollary cannot issue in practical editorial rules for handling specific cruxes. Its immediate practical consequence, however, is to defame Q, and to encourage editorial alteration of text.

4. The stemma on the left has actually been advanced (in a rather more complicated form) in Stone's *Textual History*: see Gary Taylor's discussion in "*King Lear*, the Date and Authorship of the Folio Version," *The Division of the Kingdoms*, p. 360.

bad scribal version cannot be as bad as a bad memorial version, respect for Q would have to increase. And if Q and F are both made respectable, their wide divergence is incompatible with the idea that they are both derivatives of the common ancestor, X, which was Shakespeare's finished version. Of course, at this point we may wish to postulate a contaminator or adapter who altered either Q copy or the prompt-book that lies behind the performance that lies behind Q. But the danger here is that Shakespeare himself might have been that contaminator or adapter. If this were true, there might be any number of Shakespearian aesthetic finalities, and the question of which finality is first in time and which last is obviously less important than what differentiates them. (Duthie does address the question of Shakespeare as abridger, but does not concede that he could have revised.[5]) And so we may come to see that 'bad' and 'memorial reconstruction' are mutually dependent attributes in Duthie's theory; together they constitute a self-fulfilling definition, which cannot be verified by external evidence (for the theory neatly deprives Q of external status).

There are some other possible definitions of Q that may drive us to doubt theoretically the existence of the X text as the final substantive version of the play. Perhaps Q and F are to be explained like this:

$$
\begin{array}{cc}
Y & X \\
| & | \\
Q & F
\end{array}
$$

—in which Y and X are independent, lost, substantive versions, the former to be reconstructed largely from Q, the latter largely from F. (If these trees were correct, we would be right to object to the phrase, so often heard, that *Lear* has *divided* authority, and assert its authority as *multiple*.) Reconstructionists might accept such trees, with the proviso that there is a radical Z (or 'transcendent X') above it all:

5. Duthie faces the obvious possibility (a position, in fact, taken by Doran) as follows: 'I do not believe that Q represents a Shakespearian first draft and F a Shakespearian revision,' adding in a footnote, 'Unless Shakespeare was concerned in the cutting which produced the F abridgement. But even if he was (and he may not have been) it cannot in my opinion be maintained that he made any revisions apart from the cutting' (p. 21).

Indeed, Z may be a necessarie letter, but even if it is, the problem is that there is no guarantee that it represents a complete play. After all, there cannot be an infinite regress of drafts, and at some point they may become scraps of speeches or scenes. The historical tree after pulling together in one trunk may branch out again as roots. Whoreson Zed may prove, to name one obvious possibility, to be a substantive version only of those scenes common to Q and F. (The scenes and episodes not common to Q and F could have been written for different runs.) If the reconstructionist were not after aesthetic unity, then his reconstruction of Z, an incomplete or unrevised draft, would pose no philosophic problem, however difficult it might be to achieve in practice. But, when we look at the rationale employed by Duthie in historical reconstruction, again and again we find that his eclectic editing depends upon faith in the aesthetic unity of X. Thus, the exaltation of X and the debasement of Q function as mutually self-constituting attributes. If the definition of either is changed, the system collapses. I reach the specific conclusion, therefore, that Duthie's postulation—that X is 'the full play'—is forced upon him; for if he allowed X to be an anterior draft he would threaten the notion of its completeness, and hence rob himself of the use of aesthetic argument in reconstruction. More generally, I fear that the editorial aesthetic serves as anaesthetic.

The direction of the next part of this essay will evolve heuristically simply from reading bits of the evidences as literary texts, without benefit of theories about their origins. I will have an eye constantly to the resistance editorial method and theory offer to such fundamental activity, for bare facts will be only as interesting to me here as the paradigms that raise them to consciousness, or that suppress them. The aim will be simply to detect whether, when we stand aside from editorial guidance, we find coherently differentiable aesthetic characteristics in Q and F. The extent to which we can bears an inverse relationship to the confidence we should owe the theory that Q is merely a corruption of X.

II

Ecce fructus myopiae[6]

Editorial commentary typically contrasts single words from Q and F in a lemma, and continues with prose commentary leading to a choice of one word and rejection of the other. The following note in Duthie's edition for the crux at I i 299 (line 303 in Riverside) is more or less typical. Before I turn to its content, I wish to comment on the format, which, I believe, prejudices discussion. I promise eventually, however, to implicate the crux in larger and larger questions of editing and dramaturgy.

In addition to the note, it will be useful to select parallel stretches of Q and F texts as contexts for discussion of these cruxes, but I do not want to retypeset the text I quote, as is traditional. As the foundations of Shakespeare editing were laid prior to photography, we have inherited formats for textual discussion that neglect iconic detail, and thereby depress visual thinking, on which textual argument must often turn. [Advances in printing technology have] recently made recovery of textual evidence *as an image* practicable, and I propose to take advantage of this photo-revolution. And so here 'photo-quoted' are the ends of the first scenes of *The Historie* and *The Tragedie*.[7] The cruxes under

6. "Behold the fruits of nearsightedness" [—*Editor*].

7. Photo-quotes of F are taken from the Yale facsimile, eds. Helge Kökeritz and Charles Tyler Prouty (New Haven, 1974). No press-variants are known in any of the F passages quoted; known press variants in Q will be detailed in the notes, where relevant. As the rules which form a conspicuous feature of the F page (see the photo-quote on p. 313) are not under discussion in this essay, they have for the most part been arbitrarily deleted. [In the parenthetical documentation for these passages, "C1" refers to the first page of signature C in the Quarto edition; "TLN" stands for "Through-Line Numbering," a system employed by Charlton Hinman in his facsimile of Shakespeare's First Folio; the third set of numbers gives traditional act, scene and line numbers for *Lear*—*Editor*.]

discussion are in the second line of each passage (C1; TLN 327–32; 1.1.302–8):

QUARTO:

> *Gono.* There is further complement of leaue taking betweene *Frauce* and him, pray lets hit together, if our Father cary autho-rity with such dispositions as he beares, this last surrender of his, will but offend vs,
>
> *Ragan.* We shall further thinke on't.
>
> *Gon.* We must doe something, and it'h heate. *Exeunt.*

FOLIO:

> *Gon.* There is further complement of leaue-taking be-tweene *France* and him, pray you let vs sit together, if our Father carry authority with such disposition as he beares, this last surrender of his will but offend vs.
>
> *Reg.* We shall further thinke of it.
>
> *Gon.* We must do something, and i'th' heate. *Exeunt.*

And here (likewise photo-quoted) is Duthie's note:*

I i 299 Q| hit   F| sit

> The F reading makes sense: see Onions's *Shakespeare Glossary*, p. 200 — '*sit*, 1, pregnantly = to sit in council, take counsel together, hold a session'. But surely this word would be more appropriate in the mouth of Regan, who says 'We shall further thinke of it', than in the mouth

SHAKESPEARE'S 'KING LEAR'

> of Goneril, who says 'We must do something, and i'th'heate'. This is an argument in favour of the Q reading; and there is another. 'Hit' meaning 'agree' is not pre-Shakespearian (see Onions, p. 106) and it is doubtful whether it would occur to a reporter, scribe, or compositor. That it is uncommon might be regarded as a possible reason for supposing that Scribe E emended it. I take it that Goneril wants the two of them to act together in agreement at once.

Let me start with the smallest details of the editor's lemma.

I i 299 Q | hit   F | sit

Duthie's note begins with roman and arabic numbers and with letters which identify not locations in the original evidences but *a* location in

---

*Duthie's note spans a page break, as evidenced by the running headline in the middle of the photo-quotation—*Editor.*

the editorial construct. Through its exclusive reference system, the ideal text may be seen to go before the debate about its nature like a fore-gone conclusion—just as the headline "SHAKESPEARE's 'KING LEAR' ", running through it, implies that there is only one Shakespearian *Lear.* I have thus spoken mistakenly hitherto of the 'crux at I i 299': at issue are the cru*xes* of Q at line 9 of page C1 and of F at page qq3, column b, line 38 (TLN 328). The editorial numbering system is a numbing system; it facilitates no access to the historical evidences, and thus effectively neutralizes whatever resistance Q and F contexts might offer to editorial manipulation, rendering the texts of their alleged cruxes submissive to the logic of eclecticism.[8]

Perhaps I may seem too concerned with irrelevant matters of convention and mechanical details; but it is interesting at the beginning of any foray into criticism to ask how certain parts of a critical text achieve uncritical status—for thus we perceive that some parts of text are more equal than others.

The next examples may seem to demonstrate more weightily that editorial reference is not neutral. The editor contrasts 'Q | hit' with 'F | sit'. But a glance at the photo-quoted cruxes shows that the modern typographic format has transformed the evidence.

hic   **ſic**

The F crux, for example, exhibits no dot over the i, and this is evidence that, as was usual in contemporary composition, a single type, a ligature in ſ and i, was set instead of a separate type for each letter. One can immediately and decisively reason that neither Q's h nor F's ſ can be a typographic error for the other.[9]

---

8. Similarly, when Duthie quotes extensive parallel passages from Q and F (pp. 32–44), he assigns no line numbers to the Q passages; but he does assign line numbers from his own edition to the F passages, with which, by virtue of the editorial relineation appropriate for an X text, they do not always correspond.

9. I have treated ligatures and other typographic details generally in 'Spellbound: Typography and the Concept of Old-Spelling Editions', *Renaissance and Reformation/Renaissance et Réforme*, NS, 3 (1979), pp. 50–65. Application of ligatures specifically to literary interpretation can be found in my 'Unemending Shakespeare's Sonnet 111', *Studies in English Literature*, 21 (1981), 75–96.

This problem does *not* have the structure, then, of the following notable cruxes which look like this in Q and F (H1ᵛ, TLN 2135; 3.7.63):

dearne   ſterne

and which are misidentified by Duthie's modernized typesetting like this:

Q | dearne   F | sterne

In the earliest known lay of the English case the compartment for the ligature in ſ and t is very near that of the d.[10] Therefore, either reading in the lemma could easily be a typo for the other, and this material observation frustrates those who automatically prefer the rarer of the two synonyms for the abstract reason that it is a 'more difficult' reading. Duthie regards the Q reading as original and the F reading as a sophistication. He cannot think, he says, that 'dearne' is 'the sort of word likely to have been substituted by reporter or compositor: reporters and compositors do not generally substitute readings more satisfactory from the literary point of view than the genuine ones' (p. 194). The problem with this line of reasoning is that if a typo is involved in either Q or F, the error does not come from a compositor's substitution of a *word* for another, but of one piece of *type* for another, and therefore need have nothing to do with literary understanding.

The perception that such a typo as is possible in the 'dearne'/'sterne' cruxes cannot be involved in the 'hit'/'sit' cruxes radically informs our knowledge of the transmissional processes of each text, and thereby refines our notions of relative probabilities of accuracy and error. If 'sit' is to be regarded as a typo, it may readily be a mis-setting of 'fit'—for fi (one of the few old ligatures still in use, as in the fount of this volume) was adjacent to the ligature in ſ and i in the old lay of the case. Conversely, if 'hit' is to be the typo, it would not be for 'sit' (or 'fit') but for a three-sort word like 'pit' (which can be ruled out as anachronistic in context) or 'wit' (which can be ruled in, in the absolute sense of the

10. Joseph Moxon's illustration of the lay in 1683 is the earliest English example. For a reproduction see my 'Unemending Shakespeare's Sonnet 111', p. 84. [For a similar illustration, see pp. 39–40, this volume —*Editor*.]

OED's 'wit', *v.* B. I. 3. c.). All this speculation does not lead us automatically to right answers, but it is surely part of an intelligent method guided by the precise typographical evidence which inheres in the text because it is text. We see here that editorial argument is biased toward literary issues to the extent that it neglects literal aspects of text. In such cases photo-quotation brings speculation immediately to heel.

So, a typo seems not to be involved. Let us shift our search for a source of supposed error to such issues as compositorial or scribal mis-hearing or mis-remembering. To understand such issues necessitates analysing a mass of detail; and a limited confrontation between Q and F in a single lemma hardly augurs adequate preparation for editorial decision. On the question of mis-hearing, however, we can quickly make some progress with a limited amount of evidence, if only in sophisticating our scepticism.

Editors habitually choose the graphically isolable word as the basis of textual citation. But the lexical divisions so rigidly part of our graphic conventions rarely coincide with pauses in speech, which are paramount in staging, and which may weigh heavily with a dramatic author with an ear for speech. What if the editor's lemma were attuned to the continuum of sound, and, contrasting Q and F like this, rendered that which the eye hath not heard?

s hit t   s fit t

Here the lexical is somewhat integrated into the phonetic context, and we are able to group it with the following, in which phonetic and graphic seem at odds:

in fight   incite

(I1ᵛ; TLN 2379; 4.4.27)

with the   we the

(L2ᵛ; TLN 3148; 5.3.186)

a dogge, fo bade in office,   a Dogg's | obey'd in Office.

(I4ᵛ; TLN 2602–3; 4.6.158–9)

If the graphic convention of h in 'hit' does not reflect aspiration in speech, as was quite possible in Shakespearian English,[11] there need have been no phonetic differentiation of 'hit' and 'sit' *in context*. This is not to say that the distinction could not have been made deliberately, but that in fast speech it might not be heard. Having argued that 'hit' and 'sit' were not then (as they are now) typographically confusable, I am arguing that in their contexts they were then (as they are not now) confusable by sound. There is thus some possibility of aural error in one text or the other, which is presumably a conclusion Duthie would be happy with (though my argument does not favour one reading more than another). But more importantly the example exposes also how strongly we are in the grip of our own graphic conventions, conventions that have no parallel in the relaxed state of English in Shakespeare's time. Much regulation of the language as we know it both in speech and writing came afterwards, and with it a shift in the relative roles of eye and ear. As the fluidity of Renaissance English was not a failure of our value system, we must not confuse pre-regular with ir-regular usage, or glean precision where it was not cultivated. The conventional modern neglect of the distinction between pre- and ir-regularity feeds quite easily in the 'hit'/'sit' cruxes into the editorial propensity to choose one reading and not the other—to choose the one because the other is a corruption of it. The present point is only indirectly related to whether Q and F derive from distinct authorial versions; I am here addressing rather an anachronistic notion of the graphic medium, one which facilitates the general idea, however it arises, that Q has suffered irregular transmission. (Paradoxically, in the present cruxes it is Q that is deemed to be right and F that is wrong.) It is true, perhaps, that irregular transmission was, as it were, regular in Renaissance

---

11. The authorities on this aspect of contemporary pronunciation are Helge Kökeritz, *Shakespeare's Pronunciation* (New Haven and London, 1953), pp. 307–9; E. J. Dobson, *English Pronunciation 1500–1700*, 2 vols. (second edn., Oxford, 1968), II, 991–2; Fausto Cercignani, *Shakespeare's Works and Elizabethan Pronunciation* (Oxford, 1981), pp. 332–6. The later work is less confident than Kökeritz of the wide distribution of loss of prevocalic *h* in stressed syllables.

texts, but these examples call in question the vocabulary and the senses through which we perceive what is regular. As Lear says to Gloucester, appealing to his insight, we must look with our ears to see how this world goes (4.6.151).[12]

Having questioned the implications of the format of the lemma, let us turn at last to the prose commentary, and proceed at a faster rate. Surprisingly, the editor concedes that both Q and F readings make sense. The prime issue for him, one he uses to justify his choice of one over the other, is that 'sit' is—not *in*appropriate to Goneril, but—*more* appropriate to Regan. To demonstrate 'appropriateness' the editor quotes a later F passage. This raises again the issue of context: Duthie suggests that subsequent speech establishes a criterion of appropriateness for prior speech, a notion that seems to deny the possibility of character development. Duthie's Goneril, it seems, is a woman of abrupt action, and 'sit' is too sedentary for her. But is it not reasonable to suppose that Goneril

12. We can also look with our eyes, or at least our minds' eyes; for in contemporary hands, especially in mixed secretarial and italic, there may be granted the possibility of confusion of letter shapes. R. B. McKerrow notes in his discussion of minuscules that the secretarial h with an unusual clockwise lower curve 'may . . . be not unlike a rather wide Italian ʃ' (*An Introduction to Bibliography for Literary Students* (Oxford, 1927), p. 347). But if his observation allows for the possibility of graphic confusability of 'hit' and 'sit' in manuscript, it does not inform us which must be the right and which the wrong version—or, indeed, whether there need be only one right version. Surely, if any of the hands involved in the transmission of the F text prior to its appearance in print offers confusion of s and h, as the general editorial rejection of 'sit' implies, then editors are obliged to scour the text for all such s/h cruxes before deciding conveniently in this instance. Not to do so is to edit impressionistically.

Another authority, W. S. B. Buck, agrees with McKerrow, but notes that secretarial h can also be confused with e, f, l, and g; and that secretarial ʃ can be confused with f, j, and st (see his 'Table of Confusibilia', in *Examples of Handwriting: 1551–1650* (Chichester, 1973), pp. 66–8). Buck thus opens the door to speculation that 'hit' and 'sit' are confusable not only with each other, but also with 'fit'. Now 'fit' was one of the readings that just loomed before us out of the darkness of the Renaissance printing house, as it could easily be mis-set as 'sit' by virtue of error of case. It is, moreover, a literarily defensible reading. As soon as editors reject the reading of the respected Folio, then (as editors like Duthie, who trust in the badness of the quarto, continually argue) they are under no compulsion to discover right readings in the doubted quarto. Hence, 'fit' emerges as a reading as good as either 'sit' or 'hit'—if the fact of the variance of Q and F is taken to indicate corruption of F. Editorial argument that appeals to precise feature of lost manuscripts inevitably is a two-edged sword.

finally calls for action in the heat precisely because she is moved thither by Regan's hesitation even to 'sit' together? Duthie depends here on static notions of character; but as soon as characters interact the notion of appropriateness must become dynamic.

Furthermore, the quotations do not prove his point merely as words on the page. If, for example, when Regan says, 'We shall further thinke of it', her 'we' is royal, the editor's argument is supported; but if it is merely plural, and if she stresses 'shall', then he is contradicted. If when Goneril responds, 'We must do something', she stresses 'do' against her sister's 'thinke', Duthie is suppported; but if Regan stresses 'shall' and Goneril stresses 'must' or 'something', then Regan is quite eye to eye with her sister. By his neglect of the ambiguity inherent in the graphic medium, the editor gives evidence that he has his own way of reading, stressing and delimiting the meanings of text—in short, he has his own mental production of the play, which silently identifies *an* optional reading as *the* reading.[13]

I will conclude discussion of Duthie's note by analysing its second point. The editor offers another argument 'in favour of the Q reading'—by which curious phrase he must mean 'in favour of rejecting the F reading'. (But of course, praise of Q is not in itself a reason for dispraising the reading of another text. The issue of aesthetics is being irrationally crossed with that of textual authority.) The editor proceeds to imply that 'hit' here means 'agree', defending his choice by citing Onions's *A Shakespeare Glossary*. This reference work was created to 'supply definitions and illustrations of words or senses of words now obsolete or surviving only in provincial or archaic use' (Oxford, 1911; repr. 1941, p. iii). Onions in fact quotes the present F crux, and it is he who provides the convoluted epithet 'not pre-S[hakespearian]'. This phrase subtly implies that Shakespeare invented this usage—and we must be very hard-hearted if we would reject a Shakespearian neologism for plain old 'sit'. But that no use of 'hit' in this sense is recorded in the *OED* prior to Shakespeare does not really mean he gave the word this meaning—or even that it is

13. Not all editors hide the influence of production on their texts. Kenneth Muir, the new Arden editor, reveals, for example, that his text is a revision of one he used in an amateur production before he became an editor of the play for publication (rev. edn., 1972, p. ix).

new.[14] (Indeed, the *OED* gives a transitive usage from 1580 (*hit*, 15).) But more to the point, how can Duthie, Onions, or the *OED*, the ultimate source of the definition, prove that 'hit' here means only 'agree'? Why cannot 'hit' mean or also mean 'strike', as the *OED* says it has since 1205? One wonders whether the attractiveness to most[15] editors of 'hit' over 'sit' is the violence of this editorially unacknowledged definition—'strike'.

But Duthie's argument is being directed not toward the content but toward the unfamiliarity of the word in this sense to 'reporter, scribe, or compositor' behind Q and to the scribe behind F, so that the former group could not have invented it, and the Folio scribe could plausibly have altered or 'emended' the reading of his copy, 'hit', to a more familiar word. Such an argument is suspicious. Why, for example, did the unfamiliarly defined 'hit' survive transmission in early times (1607–8) through the alleged reporter, scribe, and compositor (all of whom are taken to be unreliable), then survive the compositor of Q2 in 1619, and then *not* survive the single agent, Scribe E, who worked well after 1608

14. For the limits on *OED*'s reliability in identifying first usages see Jürgen Schäfer's *Documentation in the O.E.D.: Shakespeare and Nashe as Test Cases* (Oxford, 1980).

15. Most editors adopt F as their basic text, and all but six of the fifty editors who had access to Q—I am therefore excluding Rowe—whose editions are collated in the Furness Variorum edition, chose the Q reading here (Philadelphia, 1880; repr. New York, 1963, p. 41). The tradition also has a theatrical basis. The Smock Alley prompt-book known as 'Lear 1' (in Charles H. Shattuck, *The Shakespeare Promptbooks*, Urbana and London, 1965, p. 206), and which he dates from the 1670s, and therefore *before the editorial tradition of conflation*, is a Third Folio that has been annotated with many Q readings, especially early in the text. It too deletes 'Sit' and substitutes 'hit'. (It does not, however, insert the 'not' from Q in Gonerill's 'the obser-/vation we have made of it hath been little'.) In her discussion of this crux Alice Walker begins, 'If we reject, as of course we must, the Folio's "sit together" . . . for the quarto's "hit together" . . .' (*Textual Problems of the First Folio*, Cambridge, 1953, p. 63). Walker's theory of Q's derivation has special relevance to this paper: 'I have put forward briefly elsewhere what the evidence suggests to me: that the quarto was not based on an acting version of the play but on the foul papers and that these were surreptitiously dictated to a scribe by an actor who, for some reason we can only guess at (haste, over-confidence, laziness, inattention), relied on his memory instead of his script for dialogue with which he was familiar. The contaminating actor-reader was, I judge, a small-part actor, probably the boy who played Goneril. The scribe may have been an actor too. The memorial contamination is certainly heaviest in scenes involving both Goneril and Regan, and it is in scenes where contamination is most marked that we must look for the actor, or actors, responsible for the quarto text' (p. 41).

(when the alleged sense of 'hit' would have been better known, and when 'hit' was before him in both documents he collated, Q and the manuscript)—especially when Scribe E is considered a more competent workman than any behind the Q transmission? We should not trust an argument based on the strangeness of definition of 'hit' to justify its presence in Q and absence from F (as Duthie defines these two editions). It seems that the argument is worked backwards from the decision to eliminate divergent readings, and not forward from the evidence itself, which in this case offers no convincing rationale for selection even if it seems to offer one for preference, as Duthie feels, or for aural confusion in context, as I have suggested.

Let us come back to context. The editor's comment on 'hit' and 'sit', with which we began, might have been forced to take a different turn if he had argued from his lemma at the bottom of p. 216. Here is the relevant reading in the critical text for I i 299, and below it is the lemma.

pray you let vs hit

299 pray . . . hit] pray you let vs sit F.   pray lets hit Q.

If Duthie's note had discussed 'hit' and 'sit' in the contexts quoted in this lemma (instead of merely in that of F or of his critical edition), he would have had to deal with the obvious possibility that the verbal differences in the contrasted Q and F phrases were co-ordinate. One would want to know the relative distribution of vocative pronouns in imperatives (like 'pray you') or of contractions ('lets') in and between both texts. One would then wonder whether the laconic diction of the Q phrase connotes haste or impetuousness (and therefore suits the editor's concept of appropriateness, and suits 'hit'). But one might also feel that the slower pace of the whole F phrase is appropriate to 'sit'. And if so, how could the editor justify choosing the word but not the phrase? Contextualized lemmata would throw appropriately frustrating obstacles in the way of haste.

The last paragraph brought us to the notion of co-ordinate differentiation of Q and F, a particularly useful form of contextualizing, because it
is open to structural considerations in ways impossible to atomized,
single-word citations in a lemma, and because it opens itself to potentially
relevant contexts. Of course, criticism could scarcely proceed with the
ideal co-ordination—simply of all of Q with all of F; but practical criticism can still function by attending to the patterns of its own contexting,
and so not be blind to the collational format and its implicit values. The
literary-critical questions are unbegged then, as the textual critic continually searches out the bias of contextualizing. (I'll try to do it as I go.)

The idea of co-ordinate differentiation of Q and F may be sketched
now by working back into their first scenes as far, say, as Lear's exit (B4ᵛ;
TLN 291; 1.1.266), and investigating the variations in all the speeches of
Goneril and all those of Regan. As soon as we begin such a task with the
photo-quotations before us, we realize that our criterion for designating
the fields of comparison is suspicious. First of all, 'Goneril' and 'Regan'
are names used in Duthie's commentary (and in most modern texts); but
in Q we find 'Gonorill' and sometimes 'Ragan', whereas the Folio offers
'Gonerill' and 'Regan'. From here on, therefore, I will use the synthetic
rather than the analytical terms, 'Ragan' instead of 'Regan in Q'
(though with some awkwardness, I admit), in order not to allow the
modern abstraction to eclipse the evidences, and to throw appropriately
frustrating obstacles in the way of my own haste. In actuality the spelling
of names varies within each text. In Q, for example, in 1.1 the shift in
spelling 'Regan'/'Ragan' coincides with the end of a page (B4ᵛ), and
one habitually suspects a change of compositor at such a point. If I were
aiming at greater subtlety, my spelling of the names should vary as I dealt
with text of various pages or speeches; but let me limit myself to a
milder form of confusion in this essay. If Duthie's note employed such
awkwordness he would be driven to frame the concept of appropriateness in terms not only of the different diction of Q and F speeches, but
also of the differently spelled names of the speakers.

Indeed, one could go farther than that, for look at these speech assignments (B4ᵛ; TLN 301–5; 1.1.276–9):

QUARTO

> *Gonorill.* Prefcribe not vs our duties ?
> *Regan.* Let your ftudy be to content your Lord,
> Who hath receaued you at Fortunes almes,
> You haue obedience fcanted,
> And well are worth the worth that you haue wanted.

FOLIO:

> *Regn.* Prefcribe not vs our dutie.
> *Gon.* Let your ftudy
> Be to content your Lord, who hath receiu'd you
> At Fortunes almes, you haue obedience fcanted,
> And well are worth the want that you haue wanted.

One can proffer different kinds of explanation for the varying speech assignments. For example, if we consider the end of the scene, we see that in Q Gonorill and Ragan each have at least one long speech. Perhaps the distribution of long speeches between sisters serves to balance their stage presences in this episode. Perhaps, to state another kind of explanation for Q's distribution, the short burst in reply to Cordelia serves to characterize Gonorill's aggression. (And we note that Gonorill's speech 'hits off', as it were.) But in the Folio episode it is Regan who speaks in short phrases; it is she who flies at Cordelia with her second-person negative imperative ('Prescribe not'), whereas Gonerill 'sits' back with a third-(im)personal positive imperative ('Let . . . be.'), and is always more long-spoken in this episode. (In this explanation consistently contrasted characterization outweighs balancing.) However we figure it, such co-ordinations of differentiation immediately explode the idea that there is a simple Goneril and Regan to whom a simple notion of appropriateness can be simply applied.

Co-ordinate with the different ascriptions are differences in diction; Gonorill's 'Prescribe not vs our duties' (Q) contrasts with Regan's 'Prescribe not vs our dutie' (F). To my ear the former speech, with its plural 'duties', reads most easily as a speech on behalf of both the older sisters; if so, 'vs' is a simple plural form, though it could also be the royal 'us'. The royal 'us' is more the tone of Regan's 'vs', as I hear it, perhaps because of the singular 'dutie' in her version of the speech.[16] But I am also looking ahead to another way of contexting this crux, by comparing its (invariant) personal pronouns with those of the next speeches by these sisters, directly after Cordelia's exit.

QUARTO:

> *Gonor.* Sifter, it is not a little I haue to fay,
> Of what moft neerely appertaines to vs both,
> I thinke our father will hence to night.
> *Reg.* Thats moft certaine, and with you, next mon eth with vs

FOLIO:

> *Gon.* Sifter, it is not little I haue to fay,
> Of what moft neerely appertaines to vs both,
> I thinke our Father will hence to night.   (with vs.
> *Reg.* That's moft certaine, and with you: next moneth

It is quite possible to read this and all of Ragan's and Regan's remaining speeches in this episode as employing the royal distancing 'vs' in contrast to her sister's 'vs both'. Each text has its own range of ambiguity here; but I wish to suggest that in addition there is a differential structure for the ambiguity of each text that arises from 'reading between the texts'. We should hold back on the notions of appropriateness of characters until these differential structures are clearer.

Of course, I do not expect that every difference between the texts is either explicable or Shakespearian; but if, as we proceed with larger and larger ranges of text, we find more and more thematic consistency to the co-ordinate variation, we will naturally decrease our suspicion of accidents and agents of transmission, and have to speculate in earnest about purposeful differentation of Q and F.

There is another variant in this episode which the editor comments on, and which is of interest if we are contexting on the basis of all of

---

16. Of course this variant might be due to compositorial error: Compositor E, who set this page of Folio *Lear*, was particularly prone to omission or addition of terminal *s*. (See Paul Werstine's discussion in "Folio Editors, Folio Compositors, and the Folio Text of *King Lear*" in *The Division of the Kingdoms*, pp. 263–64.)

Gonorill's and Gonerill's speeches. Look in the second lines (B4ᵛ; TLN 315; 1.1.289):

QUARTO:

> *Gon.* You fee how full of changes his age is the obferuation we haue made of it hath not bin little; hee alwaies loued our fifter moft, and with what poore iudgement hee hath now caft her off, appeares too groffe.

FOLIO:

> *Gon.* You fee how full of changes his age is, the ob-fcruation we haue made of it hath beene little;he alwaies lou'd our Sifter moft,and with what poore iudgement he hath now caft her off,appeares too groffely.

It is worth while again to devote a moment to criticizing Duthie's lemma.

I i 286 Q | not   F | om.

If F made good sense Q's 'not' would be easily explicable as a repetition from line 281. Schmidt accepts F, extracting from it the meaning—'All our observation in the past is little in comparison with what we may expect in the future, to judge from Lear's treatment of Cordelia' (see Furness's note).[17] We might accept F and say that in the past Goneril and Regan have not observed Lear's inconstancy much, though now they have striking evidence of it: but this is surely inconsistent with the fact that the sisters are able to make the statements, 'he hath euer but slenderly knowne himselfe' and 'The best and soundest of his time hath bin but rash'. It seems more likely that the F compositor has accidentally omitted 'not'.

(p. 169)

'F/om.' must mean the Folio version has left something out which ought to be there. But, before we have seen the evidence, this is a prejudicial statement. It would be foolish to say, for example, that a man *omits* a womb.

17. Alexander Schmidt edited *King Lear* in 1879. Horace Howard Furness edited a variorum edition of *King Lear* in 1980. See note 15, above [—*Editor*].

Closer to home, it would be wrong to say that *The Tragedie* omits Macbeth's speech 'Out, out breefe Candle'; for *Macbeth* and *Lear* are not trying to be the same play. And how do we know that *The Historie* is trying to be *The Tragedie*—or some hybrid of them both? Duthie does use 'omit' properly (though incorrectly, I think) at the end of his note, where he hypothesizes that the 'not' was left out of F by compositorial accident. It is true that the negative adverb has statistically a higher chance of coming and going during textual transmission than do nouns and verbs, the omission of which often conspicuously disrupts sense. (There are those seventeenth-century worldly-wise Bibles, for example, one of which commands,

Thou shalt commit adultery

—and another of which prophesies,

the unrighteous shall inherit
the Kingdom of God.)[18]

But we can reduce the plausibility of the suggestion that F omits 'not' here simply by exposing a contradiction in Duthie's argument; for he confuses Lear's inconstancy with both his lack of self-knowledge and his rashness, with neither of which it is logically identified or even associated. A person can be precipitous and self-ignorant, and yet be constant. Moreover, in their next speeches Gonorill and Gonerill say that the addition specifically of 'way-wardnesse' to Lear's 'long ingraffed' (or 'long ingrafted') 'condition' is something of his *age* (TLN 322–3; C1; 1.1.297–8).

18. Arthur Freeman, 'Inaccuracy and Castigation: The Lessons of Error', in Anne Lancashire, ed., *Editing Renaissance Dramatic Texts. English, Italian and Spanish: Papers given at the eleventh annual Conference on Editorial Problems, University of Toronto . . . 1975* (New York and London, 1976), p. 105, where Freeman cites A. S. Herbert, ed., T. H. Darlow and H. F. Moule, *Historical Catalogue of Printed Editions of the English Bible, 1525–1961* (London and New York, 1962), p. 162, and notes that a German Bible of 1731 is supposed to sanction the same licence in the seventh commandment as the 1631 English Bible; the Corinthians reading is from a Bible of 1651.

This observation throws up before us a differential reading in the same speeches that might otherwise go unnoticed. Gonorill says that their observation of Lear's 'poore iudgement' 'appeares too grosse', but Gonerill says it 'appeares too grossely'. Q uses an adjective, F an adverb. F emphasizes that because the observation of Lear's inconstancy 'hath been little' it appears 'grossely' now. But in Q, where the observation 'hath not bin little', Lear's poor judgement appears 'grosse' among lesser examples to date. The subtle difference of adverb and adjective in these parallel passages may be seen to be coordinate with the differentiated interpretation of the sisters that arose from the previous divergent readings in Q and F.[19]

Duthie says that 'If F made good sense Q's "not" [in 286] would be easily explicable as a repetition from line 281' ('*Gonor.* Sister, it is not a little I haue to say'). As F has been shown to make good sense, might not Q's 'not' be wrong indeed, against Duthie's judgement? But if Q is wrong here, might it not be co-ordinately wrong in the 'grosse' that 'hits' with it? Again and again eclectic editing seems to proceed on the selective projection of error into the primary evidence whenever it is various, which editing then aims to 'correct' by elimination of variation.

We can now add these recent co-ordinate variants to the pictures presented by those considered earlier, and conclude discussion of this scene. In Q the imperious Gonorill comes out fighting and proceeds in the initial crux to 'hit'. The Q picture is consistently augmented by her observation in the last discussed crux of how her father's age has been and continues to be full of changes—the last being too gross. She appears to have premeditated her present scheme for power from consistent obser-

---

19. A word of caution. The contrasted passages could have registered as more synonymous than they do now. But they could also, I gather, have evoked the precise contrast they do for us, depending on the inflection of the respective sentences. See E. A. Abbott, *A Shakespearian Grammar*, third ed. (1870), § 1: 'Adjectives are freely used as Adverbs.' The reverse is also possible: 'It is characteristic of the unsettled nature of the Elizabethan language that, while . . . adjectives were freely used as adverbs without the termination *ly*, on the other hand *ly* was occasionally added to words from which we have rejected it' (§ 23).

vation. But in F Gonerill is more reserved (in sharper contrast with pug-
nacious and perhaps haughty and aloof Regan), and she asks merely to
'sit' together with her in open discussion, without stipulating that they
must agree or must strike. The latest co-ordinate variation shows Gonerill off balance, thinking on her feet in an attempt to grasp an unprecedented situation, which has erupted before her grossly and without
notice. Regan's alleged delay in embracing Gonerill's plan could now be
understood in F as a function not only of the general haughtiness and
self-absorption I thought to attribute to her in that text, but also of the
specific novelty of the problem for her and her sister.

Such subtleties of interpretation can scarcely come to us from the
conflated *Lear.* Neither are they likely to occur to us from reading either
text in isolation. They can reveal themselves readily, however, if we
engage in differential reading of whole texts, if we bypass the atomized
lemmata of the editorial tradition and the eclecticism they implicitly
inculcate. And they seem to lead us to a startling, if tentative, conclusion:
in the first scene Gonerill need not be such a bitch after all, though
Gonorill may be.

To obtain an external fix on this question we might seek out co-
ordinate variants in speeches to or about the sisters, such as those in
Cordelia's first (and only) speech to them, just after Lear's exit and just
before her own. Here in Q she bids them 'vse well our Father',
whereas in F she bids them 'Loue' him well (B4^v; TLN 296; 1.1.271).
True, the different diction may reflect co-ordinate differentiation of
Cordelia between Q and F, which would have to be detected by
expanding the contexting of her speech and of speeches to her. (For
example, Lear's first mention of 'his ioy' in Q (B2; 1.1.83) is as 'the
last not least in our deere loue;' but in F (TLN 89) she is simply 'our
last and least'.) The variants in her speech to her sisters suggest that in
F, at least, they may indeed be capable of loving Lear—if Cordelia is
any judge of character. But, of course, she may not be a good judge of
character. Our disposition to think of her so may depend on questions we should not yet have answered, but whose answers may have
come to us unbidden from our experience of the eclectic tradition in

which we all first learned *Lear*. Citing the variant 'vse'/'Loue' in Cordelia's speeches, Duthie finds occasion to demonstrate Q's memorial confusion (with a much later passage) and to show that its reading is unsuitable to 'the context'; then he argues that it also has no claim to be the reading of a 'Shakespearian first draft', and that F's 'Loue' is the point of the line 'as initially conceived'. These extraordinary claims, especially the last, are not atypical of the editor's frequent assertions of the author's original intent. (It seems sometimes that 'original intent' and 'final draft' are synonymous in this edition—an equation which neatly excludes the possibility of intermediate drafts.) Here is Duthie's analysis (pp. 55–6):

I i 269 F | Loue well our Father:

     Q | vse well our Father,

  Cf. I v 14—

     F | Shalt see thy other Daughter will vse thee kindly,

     Q | Shalt see thy other daughter will vse thee kindly,

The earlier and later passages could easily be confused in the memory: both concern the treatment of Lear by Goneril and Regan after the distribution of the kingdom. And it can be said quite confidently that in I i 269 the F reading is appropriate to the context while that of Q is not. The next line makes this clear—'To your professed bosomes I commit him,' (the wording is the same in both texts). Cordelia is in effect saying to Goneril and Regan, 'You have said that you love our father—do so'. As Greg says (*Editorial Problem*, p. 93), 'she had yet no ground for supposing they would use the old man ill'. The person responsible for the Q reading was thinking ahead. (The fact that the Q reading is unsuited to the context militates, of course, against the theory that 'vse' is the reading of a Shakespearian first draft and 'Loue' that of a revision. The use of 'professed' in the next line shows quite definitely that the point of line 269 as initially conceived lay in the word 'Loue'.)

In general this argument makes the frequent editorial mistake of neglecting staging, which creates a 'context' for Cordelia's reaction, just as surely as does the dialogue. If to the audience the sisters have looked insincere or hypocritical, Cordelia will seem to have every justification to act as if they are so. But Duthie's argument can be more convincingly challenged here from philology, simply by observing that he neglects the irony that is part and parcel of the definition of 'professed' from well before Shakespeare's time. This example of his textual argument shows how editorial clairvoyance about the lost precursors can arise from not looking clearly at the present evidence.

However the variations relating to Cordelia impinge on previous discussion, we can observe that the initial presentation of Gonerill may be like that of Edmund and Edmond in both texts. Only after the Bastard's first appearance does the audience rethink him, gradually—and not necessarily until after his witty defence of bastardy—withdrawing sympathy and respect. That in both plays the elder sisters and the bastards are finally more sinning than sinned against is not in doubt; but the co-ordinate variation of the beginning of the texts suggests that F offers a vision of somewhat greater moral ambiguity than does Q, a subtlety that does not survive eclectic conflation.

At this point I wish to change scale again: instead of expanding the kinds of contexting, I shall sketch rapidly forward into the texts the contexting already begun. If the differentiation of Gonerill and Gonorill and the consequent slight shift of the moral tone of the tragedy is more than accident, we might search for a point where F and Q draw back together. If this comes as soon as the next scene, it will be hard to convince anyone that the small differences cited are more than accidental. But if the differentiation continues for some while, we will have to reconsider whether the tragic visions of *The Historie* and *The Tragedie* are the same.

Here with some contexts clinging to them are the third scenes of the plays (C3; TLN 502–32: 1.2.182–1.4.2).

QUARTO:

> My praſtiſes ride eaſie, I ſee the buſines,
> Let me if not by birth, haue lands by wit,
> All with me's meete, that I can faſhion fit.   *Exit.*
>   *Enter Gonorill and Gentleman.*
> *Gon.* Did my Father ſtrike my gentleman for chiding of his
> foole?,
> *Gent.* Yes Madam.
> *Gon.* By day and night he wrongs me,
> Euery houre he flaſhes into one groſſe crime or other
> That ſets vs all at ods, ile not indure it,
> His Knights grow ryotous, and him ſelfe obrayds vs,
> On euery trifell when he returnes from hunting,
> I will not ſpeake with him, ſay I am ſicke,
> If you come ſlacke of former ſeruice s,
> You ſhall doe well, the fault of it ile anſwere,
> *Gent.* Hee's coming Madam, I heare him.
> *Gon.* Put on what wearie negligence you pleaſe, you and your
> fellow ſeruants, i'de haue it come in queſtion, if he diſlike it, let
> him to our ſiſter, whoſe mind and mine I know in that are one,
> not to be ouerruld; idle old man that ſtill would manage thoſe
> authorities that hee hath giuen away, now by my life old fooles
> are babes again, & muſt be vs'd with checkes as flatteries, when
> they are ſeené abuſd, remember what I tell you.
> *Gent.* Very well Madam.
> *Gon.* And let his Knights haue colder looks among you, what
> growes of it no matter, aduiſe your fellowes ſo. I would breed
> from hence occaſions, and I ſhall, that I may ſpeake, ile write
> ſtraight to my ſiſter to hould my very courſe, goe prepare for
> dinner.   *Exit.*
>   *Enter Kent.*
> *Kent.* If but as well I other accents borrow, that can my ſpeech
>   **C 3**   deſuſe,

The contexts of the quoted scenes—the concluding lines of the Bastard's and of Edmund's speeches, and the opening lines of Kent's—show that both groups of three scenes are concerned with dissimulations. To catch the right tones of each we would surely have to consider widely. But it may be enough to say (putting the theatrical appeal of the different characters aside) that, since Bastard Edmund has sounded a very low moral note, Gonorill and Gonerill would have to behave most wickedly not to shine relatively. The opening texts of the Q and F scenes show that if she thought to act in

FOLIO:

My practifes ride eafie : I fee the bufineffe.
Let me, if not by birth, haue lands by wit,
All with me's meete, that I can fafhion fit.   *Exit.*

Scena Tertia.

Enter Gonerill, and Steward.

Gon. Did my Father ftrike my Gentleman for chi-
ding of his Foole ?
Ste. I Madam,
Gon. By day and night, he wrongs me, euery howre
He flafhes into one groffe crime, or other,
That fets vs all at ods : Ile not endure it ;
His Knights grow riotous, and himfelfe vpbraides vs
On euery trifle. When he returnes fromhunting,
I will not fpeake with him, fay I am ficke,
If you come flacke of former feruices,
You fhall do well , the fault of it Ile anfwer.
Ste. He's comming Madam, I heare him.
Gon. Put on what weary negligence you pleafe,
You and your Fellowes: I'de haue it come to queftion;
If he diftafte it, let him to my Sifter,
Whofe mind and mine I know in that are one,
Remember what I haue faid.
Ste. Well Madam.
Gon. And let his Knights haue colder lookes among
you : what growes of it no matter, aduife your fellowes
fo, Ile write ftraight to my Sifter to hold my courfe; pre-
pare for dinner.   *Exeunt.*

Scena Quarta.

Enter Kent.

Kent. If but as will I other accents borrow,

the heat (her last word), she has missed her cue—for Lear is a jump ahead of her. Unlike the Bastard, the Duchess is on the defensive; the attack on her Gentleman challenges both propriety and her own authority.

When John Keats read *Lear*, toward the end of the second decade of the nineteenth century, he left extensive underlinings, markings and annotations in his text. In the first scene he marked dozens of lines, including Gonerill's speech to Cordelia so assigned in F only ('Let your study | Be to content your Lord'), and he underlined the one in which she declares, in F only, that their observation of their father's changes has been little. When Keats came to the third scene, by contrast, he underlined only one phrase—'weary negligence' (at the start of Goneril's third speech). The paucity of his underlining here is consonant with the fact that Keats's text was a facsimile of the First Folio;[20] there Gonerill's response to the report of Lear's violence to her gentleman is measured, and her behaviour is in keeping with the Gonerill whose speeches he had marked earlier. In Q, however, a different woman was appearing than the one Keats was heeding, as we see if we contrast the Duchess's last two speeches in the Q and F scenes; for Gonorill shrilly calls her father 'idle old man', and regards him as one among the old fools that turn babes again. There is, of course, more than a grain of truth in her charges, but her tone invites invidious comparison—in Q only—with her professed love for her father—'Dearer then eye-sight, space or libertie' (B1^v; TLN 61; 1.1.56). Her hypocrisy in Q seems appropriate to the Gonorill who claimed in the first scene that she had observed many examples of her father's changes, and who asked Ragan to 'hit together' with her. Of this hypocrisy Keats's Folio revealed nothing; his noting of Gonorill's weary negligence in that text is indicative of Keats's eye not only for romantic idiom, but also (and unconsciously, I think) for the Folio characterization of the Duchess.

If we read either Q or F in isolation, we see in both that the Duchess is heading intentionally for confrontation with her father. As soon as we contrast the texts, however, we see that the plan to slack service in F is

20. Keats's 1804 'type' facsimile is now at Keats House, Hampstead. I discuss Keats's experience of *The Tragedie* extensively in 'UN*Editing* Shak-speare,' *Sub-Stance*, 33/34 (1982), 26–55. Keats did not, by the way, mark Gonerill's speech in 1.1 that contains the 'sit' crux.

relatively cool; it reads like the reasoned tit for tat of a woman who is conscious of propriety and principle, and who responds to provocation slowly and in proportion. The Q Duchess by contrast seems to have lost her grip on herself, and her Q-only vituperations seem to offer an inner glimpse of a woman so insecure about the 'authorities that hee hath giuen away' that she is impelled to force his hand by 'breed[ing] from hence occasions'. When we contrast Q and F it seems that Gonerill the Bitch has yet to appear in *The Tragedie*; in *The Historie*, however, Gonorill is now taking on monstrous dimensions.

All the variants considered till now seem consistent with this conclusion, and suggest the hypothesis that there is purposeful differentiation of *Historie* and *Tragedie*. Duthie's policy is to conflate, adding the Q-only passages to the F text. This makes Gonerill more like Gonorill, as does the editor's adoption of 'not' and 'hit' in the first scene. The editor's Goneril is certainly a unified synthesis, but if we ground our notions of appropriateness in historical evidence, and read her against Gonorill and Gonerill, she seems schizoid, and the editorial *Lear* takes on the shape of a *cadavre exquis*.[21]

In the next, the fourth scenes, the numerous variations need not concern us until well past Goneril's frowning entrance, in which, provoked, the daughter demands that Lear lessen his train. Speaking of the infection of 'this our court', she compares it with an inn (D2; TLN 753–65; 1.4.244–55):

QUARTO:

The Hiſtorie of King Lear.

like a riotous Inne, epicuriſme, and luſt make more like a tauerne or brothell, then a great pallace, the ſhame it ſelfe deth ſpeake for inſtant remedie, be thou deſired by her, that elſe will take the thing ſhee begs, a little to diſquantitie your traine, and the remainder that ſhall ſtill depend, to bee ſuch men as may beſort your age, that know themſelues and you.

Lear. Darkenes and Deuils! ſaddle my horſes, call my traine together, degenerate baſtard, ile not trouble thee, yet haue I left a daughter.

21. "Exquisite corpse" (French), a collective literary (or graphic) work assembled by collaborators taking turns adding to the work [—*Editor*].

FOLIO:

> Shewes like a riotous Inne ; Epicurifme and Luft
> Makes it more like a Tauerne, or a Brothell,
> Then a grac'd Pallace. The fhame it felfe doth fpeake
> For inftant remedy. Be then defir'd
> By her, that elfe will take the thing fhe begges,
> A little to difquantity your Traine,
> And the remainders that fhall ftill depend,
> To be fuch men as may befort your Age,
> Which know themfelues, and you.
>   *Lear.* Darkneffe, and Diuels.
> Saddle my horfes : call my Traine together.
> Degenerate Baftard, Ile not trouble thee ;
> Yet haue I left a daughter.

That Gonorill should speak of a 'great pallace' but Gonerill of a 'grac'd Pallace' is consistent with the differentiations noted thus far; and so is her 'be thou desired' in Q as opposed to her 'be then desired' in F. One must admit the ease of phonetically or graphically confusing 'grac'd' and 'great', 'thou' and 'then', but the issue is whether one need postulate error in either text. Her thouing her father here in Q is the first such address to him in the play, and immediately precedes his first 'thee' to her, which it may be thought to provoke. In retrospect, her vaunting of herself, '*our* court', is as high as her 'thee' to Lear is low. We are impressed with how authority and its abuse continue to weigh on her mind. By contrast the 'then' in F may be interpreted as 'consequently', and thus may serve as an element of reasoning from evidence and allegations to conclusions, showing as before Gonerill's commitment to the rationale of her position, whereas Gonorill's interest seems to lie merely in her position. A corollary of these differences is that Lear's 'thee' to Gonerill registers as an aggressive escalation in F, not as the counter response of Q. Duthie follows F here completely and produces from his sources a milder Goneril than he had before.

After Lear's exit Albany begins to remonstrate with his wife. The stage business is much more complex in F, where his wife interrupts him with a speech addressing first him, then the Fool and her steward in rapid succession.[22] Though she seems generally more agitated in *The Tragedie*, her tone specifically to her husband, as Duthie also notes (p. 35), is softer and more respectful than in Q: 'Pray you content' rather than 'Come sir no more' (TLN 833; D2ᵛ; 1.4.312). Duthie holds that the Q reading is 'inappropriate in this context'—by which he means his own editorial context rather than those of Q and F. His Goneril speaks 'soothingly and in a conciliatory manner. Her attitude to Albany at this stage of the play is certainly not such as to warrant her being so rude as to say "Come sir no more" to him. Consequently, [he concludes,] I do not believe that Q gives the version of a first draft here' (I iv 298 in his edition, 313 in Riverside). I rather think that Duthie's eclecticism in the third scene *has* prepared us for 'rudeness without warrant', and that his assessment of Goneril is truer of F than of his own edition. But my main point is that the differences of Q and F continue to be appropriate to what we have observed in differential reading. The conclusion of Duthie's remarks is typical of his repeated assertions about the derivation of Q: a credo.

Of greatest interest in this scene is Gonerill's explosion when the Fool has followed Lear off stage, thirteen lines that occur only in *The Tragedie* (D2ᵛ; TLN 841–61; 1.4.321–38).

QUARTO:

>   followes after.
>   *Gon.* What *Ofwald,* ho.   *Ofwald.* Here Madam,
>   *Gon.* What haue you writ this letter to my fifter?
>   *Ofw.* Yes Madam.
>   *Gon.* Take you fome company, and away to horfe, informe
>   her full of my particular feares, and thereto add fuch reafons of

FOLIO:

>   So the Foole followes after.   *Exit*
>   *Gon.* This man hath had good Counfell,
>   A hundred Knights?
>   'Tis politike, and fafe to let him keepe
>   At point a hundred Knights: yes, that on euerie dreame,

22. For detailed discussion see Steven Urkowitz, *Shakespeare's Revision of* King Lear (Princeton: Princeton University Press, 1980), pp. 44–46.

Each buz, each fancie, each complaint, dislike,
He may enguard his dotage with their powres,
And ho'd our liues in mercy. *Oswald*, I say.
  Alb. Well you may feare too farre.
  Gon. Safer then trust too farre;
Let me still take away the harmes I feare,
Not feare still to be taken. I know his heart,
What he hath vtter'd I haue writ my Sister:
If she sustaine him, and his hundred Knights
When I haue shew'd th'vnfitnesse.

       Enter Steward.

How now *Oswald?*
What haue you writ that Letter to my Sister?
  Stew. I Madam.
  Gon. Take you some company, and away to horse,
Informe her full of my particular feare,

These thirteen lines show her wrought in the extreme. At first she argues ironically for Lear's cause, but then, naming names, speaks—as she did earlier in this scene in both Q and F—of Lear's dotage (D2; TLN 805; 1.4.293), and comes at last to her fear, that he will hold their lives in jeopardy. (Here she is not using the royal singular 'our' as 'liues' shows, but seems to be including her husband.) Whether this speech testifies to paranoia, deceptive rhetoric, or recognition of a real danger, I will not argue; but differential reading is clear on one thing. If we compare the lines unique to Q in Scene Three, when Gonorill reacted to the striking of her gentleman, and the lines unique to F here in the fourth scene, we see that the latter lines show her wrought up, appropriately, only after the event, and even then self-possessed in her emotional extremity, trenchant in irony and rational in argumentation. This is not to judge her cause, of course, but it is to suggest that, unlike Gonorill, she is coming to the boil slowly.

That *The Historie* offers no address to the Duke corresponding to the F lines does not mean that there is a lack of information about Gonorill at this point. The fact that she exploded upon her father's striking merely her gentleman, but, now that he has cursed her, has absolutely nothing personal to say, merely turning to execute the next item of business, suggests a most perverse psychology: her response runs contrary to stimulus. Duthie, by adopting the Q-only lines in the third scene and the F-only lines in this scene, renders her continually volatile. He thus is true neither to the slow build in F nor to the 'manic depressive' alternation of Q.[23]

In the last variant to consider here, her address to Oswald, she refers to her 'particular feares' in Q but her 'particular feare' in F. These differences are minute but not necessarily trivial; like so many of the small details accumulated in this differential reading, they are consistent with Goner-ill's self-control and the specificity of her grievance with her father in *The Tragedie*, and with Gonorill's general wildness in *The Historie*.

The next major variants arise in the scene in which the united sisters strip Lear of his retainers. We first hear of Gonorill and Gonerill from her sister; she counsels Lear to be patient and think better of his eldest daughter. In both versions Regan has received her sister's letter inform-ing her, as Regan says, of the 'ryotous knights' (D4ᵛ; TLN 1033; 2.1.94), on which advice she decided not to be at home if they came to sojourn with her. She has also read Lear's letter. As we have read neither, we have no reason to account Regan's behaviour as sinister *per se* in either text. Certainly in F she can scarcely be seen as a hypocrite in this particular instance, for she reveals to Lear (in F only) that she knows Gonerill 'restrained the Riots' of his followers (F1; TLN 1416–25; 2.4.138–46).

QUARTO:

> *Reg.* I pray fir take patience, I haue hope
> You leſſe know how to value her defert,
> Then ſhe to ſlacke her dutie.
> *Lear.* My curſſes on her.

---

23. W. D. Moriarty, 'The Bearing on Dramatic Sequence of the Varia in *Richard the Third* and *King Lear*', *Modern Philology*, 10 (1913), 451–71, was convinced of a 'causal relation-ship between the principle of dramatic sequence and the varia in . . . *King Lear*'. He held that the older Shakespeare was willing to cut characterizations of inner conflict (in Q) to expedite plot (in F). 'Two varia are produced when the folio (I, iv, 323–34) has Goneril explain to Albany instead of to her steward, as the quarto makes her in I, iii, 17–21, the pretended grounds upon which she treats her father as she does' (p. 457); and related to this, in Q 'Goneril explains to Oswald in vindictive fashion her theory of governing her father, but the folio omits this explanation and has Goneril use it expanded and more speciously stated in defending to Albany her actions toward her father' (pp. 452–3).

FOLIO:

> *Reg.* I pray you Sir, take patience, I haue hope
> You leſſe know how to value her deſert,
> Then ſhe to ſcant her dutie.
> *Lear,* Say ? How is that ?
> *Reg.* I cannot thinke my Siſter in the leaſt
> Would faile her Obligation. If Sir perchance
> She haue reſtrained the Riots of your Followres,
> Tis on ſuch ground, and to ſuch wholeſome end,
> As cleeres her from all blame,
> *Lear.* My curſes on her.

Now, neither Q nor F makes me think that I could ever see behind Regan's politic mask (as I feel I do behind Gonorill's in the Q-only lines in the third scene); but Regan's second F speech mitigates the bluntness of the first (her only one in Q), and so may render us less sympathetic to Lear's repetition of his curse on Gonerill, which it postpones.

When eventually Goneril enters, the texts vary strikingly. At the beginning and end of both the following quotations Lear demands to know who stocked his servant, as he has twice earlier in the scene (E3ᵛ, F1ᵛ, TLN 1286–8, 1467; 2.4.11–12, 182). And after Gonerill's entrance in F (in the middle of the excerpt), he asks again. But in Q the diction of the speech is different, and it is spoken by Gonorill, not by her father (F1ᵛ; TLN 1467–90; 2.4.182–98).[24]

QUARTO:

> *Lear.* Who put my man i'th ſtockes ?
> *Duke.* What trumpets that ?   *Enter Steward.*
> *Reg.* I know t my ſiſters, this approues her letters,
> That ſhe would ſoone be here, is your Lady come ?
> *L. sr.* This is a ſlaue, whoſe eaſie borrowed pride
> Dwels in the fickle grace of her, a followes,
> Out varlet, from my ſight.
> *Duke.* What meanes your Grace ?   *Enter Gon.*
> *Gon.* Who ſtruck my ſeruant, *Regan* I haue good hope
> Thou didſt not know ant.

24. See Urkowitz, *Revision*, pp. 36–8.

Lear. Who comes here ? O heauens !
If you doe loue old men, if you fweet fway allow
Obedience, if your felues are old, make it your caufe,
Send downe and take my part,
Art not afham'd to looke vpon this beard?
O *Regan* wilt thou take her by the hand ?

   Gon. Why not by the hand fir, how haue I offended?
Als not offence that indifcretion finds,
And dotage tearmes fo.

   Lear. O fides you are too tough,
Will you yet hold ? how came my man it'h ftockes ?

FOLIO:

   Lear. Who put my man i'th'Stockes ?
         Enter Steward.|
   Corn. What Trumpet's that ?.
   Reg. I know't, my Sifters : this approues her Letter,
That fhe would foone be heere. Is your Lady come ?

   Lear. This is a Slaue, whofe eafie borrowed pride
Dwels in the fickly grace of her he followes.
Out Varlet, from my fight.

   Corn. What meanes your Grace?
         Enter Gonerill.
   Lear. Who ftockt my Seruant? *Regan,* I haue good hope
Thou did'ft not know on't.
Who comes here ? O Heauens !
If you do loue old men, if your fweet fway
Allow Obedience : if you your felues are old,
Make it your caufe : Send downe, and take my part.
Art not afham'd to looke vpon this Beard ?
O *Regan,* will you take her by the hand ?

   Gon. Why not by'th'hand Sir? How haue I offended?
All's not offence that indifcretion findes,
And dotage termes fo.

   Lear. O fides, you are too tough !
Will you yet hold ?
How came my man i'th'Stockes ?

In *The Historie* Gonorill strides in on the offensive, not even greeting her father, but demanding explanation of the wrong done her. She is harping on the same theme as in the third scene, the affront to her retinue. When in

Q Ragan takes her sister's hand, she is seen by Lear, who thous her, and perhaps by us, to close ranks aggressively with a co-aggressor. In F, however, Gonerill, silent, may seem, by virtue of Lear's attempt at shaming her, to enter on the defensive; and we can thus easily read Regan as coming impulsively to her embattled sister's aid. Lear's respect for Regan seems to continue, as he yous her. The subsequent lines, leading up to Lear's distracted exit for the heath and the storm, are not themselves greatly differentiated. But these contrasting lines that initiate that confrontation can strongly swing our sympathies and horrors in different directions as we head into it. My main point is simply that F, by not having Gonerill press again the matter of her servant, by having Lear harp again and again on his servant, and by having Gonerill take Lear's abuse silently, argues her restraint relative to Gonorill's, in a way consonant with the earlier differential readings.

Duthie regards Q as corrupt here. His allegation of scribal error is one of his most convoluted and fantastic editorial flights, and makes interesting reading (in [footnote]) against the simple, contrasting drama of the Q and F lines.[25]

The next variant concerns Lear on the heath; he arraigns his elder daughters—but only in the mad trial scene unique to Q (G3ᵛ–G4;

---

25. These notes are from pp. 88 and 392–3. *Caveat scriba. Caveat lector.*

At II iv 184–5 the two texts run as follows:

Q| *Enter Gon.*
  Gon. Who struck my seruant, *Reagan* I haue good hope
        Thou didst not know ant.
  Lear. Who comes here? O heauens!

F| *Enter Gonerill.*
  Lear. Who stockt my Seruant? *Regan,* I haue good hope
        Thou did'st not know on't.
        Who comes here? O Heauens!

The reconstructing actors may have given the text correctly as it appears in F. The scribe, looking over his work subsequently, may have misread his own 'stockt' as 'struck', and, remembering that Oswald had been struck, altered the speech-heading from '*Lear.*' to '*Gon.*', writing in '*Lear.*' in front of 'Who comes here? . . .' He may, going over his manuscript, have read 'stockt' correctly, but, remembering Oswald's being struck, and noticing that Goneril had just come on, he may have made the two alterations in speech-heading and dialogue on his own responsibility. Again, it is possible that the actor of Lear's part, dictating, pro-

3.6.17–56). Its fantastic visions of Gonorill—as a 'ioyne stoole' and as one who 'kickt the poore king her father'—offer us at this point a mad reminder (in Q only) of her agency in driving her father to distraction. After this, both Q and F mention Regan, and in the context of an anatomy of her heart. In Q we can see the initial trial metaphor as modulating into one of dissection; but I suspect most readers of Q (or of the conflation) see the anatomy as a continuation of the trial; in F, however, it cannot be a metaphor of trial, and must be taken literally. Perhaps to the reader of F the anatomical violence against Regan at this point becomes paired with the memory of Lear's curse of Gonerill in the fourth scene, when he invoked Nature to dry up her organs of increase. But in Q we link the anatomy of Ragan most readily with the immediately preceding arraignment of her sister. These different interpretative strategies can be spelled out theoretically: in the context of non-parallel portions of Q and F, portions of Q and F that do run parallel need not have the same meaning. This, I think, is the critical principle that invalidates Duthie's argument, widely echoed since by conflationists, that F is somehow incoherent because its 'omission' of the trial scene 'renders pointless the words "Then let them Anatomize *Regan:*" which it retains at III vi 74' (p. 8). Such the-

---

nounced 'stockt' as 'stuckt', that his '-t' was indistinct, that the scribe thought he was saying 'struck', took that down, and subsequently, looking over the manuscript, altered the speech-heading to conform with 'struck'. At any rate, I do not think it necessary to suppose that the reconstructing actors were responsible for the misassignation of the speech. (88)

184 Q *Gon.*   See p. 88. As regards the suggestion of misreading, it is quite possible
    Q struck   that 'stockt' was misread as 'struke' (i.e. 'struck'). Misreading of 'o' as 'r' is found elsewhere in Q—cf. III iv 6, where Q uncorr. has 'crulentious', a misreading of 'contentious' (F) (see Greg, *Variants*, p. 164). There are also examples of 'e' misread as 't': cf. III iv 115, where Q uncorr. has 'harte', Q corr. 'hare' (the compositor misread 'hare' as 'hart' and set up 'harte'), and IV ii 56, where Q uncorr. has 'noystles', Q corr. 'noyseles'. Examples of 't' misread as 'e' occur elsewhere: e.g. *Hamlet*, III ii 310, where Q2 has 'stare' for 'start', and *Othello*, I i 48, where Q1 has 'noughe' for 'nought'. Misreading of 'c' as 'u' is also possible: at I ii 130, where F reads 'my Cue', Q has 'mine', which does not make sense: this reading 'mine' may well be the result of the Q compositor having misread 'my cu' as 'myne' (cf. III iv 199, Q uncorr. 'thu', Q corr. 'the'): and if 'c' could be misread as 'n' it could also be misread as 'u', since 'n' and 'u' are frequently confused. (392–3)

oretical questions of literary interpretation aside, the main points for this analysis are clear. Q adds to our stock of extreme pictures of Gonorill already culled from differential reading, and reminds us at the depths of Lear's madness of her responsibility. But F ignores Gonerill here to dwell on her sister, as if to give Regan her turn for Lear's wrath. Differential reading continues our sense that F presents a relatively less extreme picture of Gonerill's behaviour and of her perception by others than does Q.

I said 'relatively less extreme', as it would be perverse to hide the fact that by this point in the play any hope we might have had in Gonerill as a force for moderation has blown away in the great storm that closes Act Two. It is true that she does not, like her sister, participate in the actual blinding of Gloucester (3.7), but her grimly prophetic (or instigating) 'Plucke out his eyes' (G4^v; TLN 2064; 3.7.5) brands her.

The next scene of strongly differentiated dialogue concerning Goneril, from the Q version of which the title of this essay is drawn, opens with a further damning revelation—of her adultery with the Bastard. Upon the exit of her lover and entrance of her husband, the two texts diverge widely. In Q Albany directs at his wife some thirty lines of thrilling denunciation not found in F (H3^v–H4; TLN 2301–13; 4.2.29–71).[26]

QUARTO:

> *Alb.* O *Gonoril,*you are hot worth the dult which the
> Blowes in your face,I feare your difpofition
> That nature which contemnes ith origin
> Cannot be bordered certaine in it felfe,
> She that her felfe will fliuer and disbranch
> From her materiall fap, perforce muft wither,
> And come to deadly vfe.
>   *Gon.* No more, the text is foolifh.
>   *Alb.* Wifedome and goodnes,to the vild feeme vild,
> Filths fauor but themfelues, what haue you done ?
> Tigers, not daughters, what haue you perform'd ?
> A father,and a gracious aged man
>   Whofe

26. See Urkowitz, *Revision*, pp. 88–93. In the Folio, the 'seemes' in Albany's second speech agrees with the reading of the first state of Q1, which contains a number of press variants in this passage. Other variants affect the dialogue unique to Q, here reproduced in its second state. The first state reads 'it origin' for 'ith origin', 'beniflicted' for 'benifited', 'the vild' for 'this vild', 'Humanly' for 'Humanity', 'selfe' for 'self ', 'know'st fools', for 'know'st, fools', 'noystles' for 'noyseles', 'slayer begin threats' for 'state begins thereat', 'Whil's' for 'Whil'st', 'horid' for 'horrid', and 'now' for 'mew'.

The Hiſtorie of King Lear.

Whoſe reuerence euen the head-lugd beare would lick.
Moſt barbarous, moſt degenerate haue you madded,
Could my good brother ſuffer you to doe it?
A man, a Prince, by him ſo benifited,
If that the heauens doe not their viſible ſpirits (come
Send quickly downe to tame this vild offences, it will
Humanity muſt perforce pray on it ſelf like monſters of
   Gon. Milke liuerd man   (the deepe.
That beareſt a cheeke for bloes, a head for wrongs,
Who haſt not in thy browes an eye deſeruing thine honour,
From thy ſuffering, that not know'ſt, fools do thoſe vilains pitty
Who are puniſht ere they haue done their miſchiefe,
Wher's thy drum? *France* ſpreds his banners in our noyſeles land,
With plumed helme, thy ſtate begins thereat
Whil'ſt thou a morall foole ſits ſtill and cries
Alack why does he ſo?
   Alb. See thy ſelfe deuill, proper deformity ſhewes not in the
fiend, ſo horrid as in woman.
   Gon. O vaine foole!
   Alb. Thou changed, and ſelfe-couerd thing for ſhame
Be-monſter not thy feature, wer't my fitnes
To let theſe hands obay my bloud,
They are apt enough to diſlecate and teare
Thy fleſh and bones, how ere thou art a fiend,
A womans ſhape doth ſhield thee.
   Gon. Marry your manhood mew---
   Alb. What newes.   *Enter a Gentleman.*
   Gent. O my good Lord the Duke of *Cornwals* dead, ſlaine by

FOLIO:

   Alb. Oh *Generill,*
You are not worth the duſt which the rude winde
Blowes in your face.
   Gon. Milke-Liuer'd man,
That bear'ſt a cheeke for blowes, a head for wrongs,
Who haſt not in thy browes an eye-diſcerning
Thine Honor, from thy ſuffering.
   Alb. See thy ſelfe diuell:
Proper deformitie ſeemes not in the Fiend
So horrid as in woman.
   Gon. Oh vaine Foole.
        Enter a Meſſenger.
   Meſ. Oh my good Lord, the Duke of *Cornwals* dead,

Albany's speeches in Q form an impassioned catalogue of the Duchess's sins, and signal a major turn in the moral dynamic of *The Historie*. Lear, of course, has himself been able to anatomize his daughter's sins, but Gonorill's husband is a more impartial (and sane) spokesman than her father. Curiously the scene is written so as to inform us of Gonorill's adultery immediately before Albany's tirade; this juxtaposition drives home all the more strongly Albany's impartiality. If he knew of the adultery he would have the greatest personal reason to speak to her in the tone he now adopts; Albany's condemnation of her, however, is not as a husband, but as a moral man—and hence her pejorative 'morall foole'. She joins this barb to a taunt against his manhood and his patriotism, for French troops are landed. Her criticism sticks, of course (though it hardly justifies her savage reaction to Gloucester's 'treason'). In any case, Q documents the rising of moral indignation in Albany at this point as a deeply true but deeply non-practical response. Albany's truth may remind us somewhat of the wildly idealistic truth-telling of Cordelia or Kent. Moreover, we see him from some ironic distance, no matter how strongly we yearn for his attack: for he does not seem to see the horns on his own head.

What a contrast is *The Tragedie*. The short exchange between Gonerill and Albany barely hints his future strength. We see his indignation aroused, but at what? He has relatively so little to say about her, before the messenger's entrance and his wife cut him off, that the audience's great relief in Q to find her monstrosity named can find no parallel in F, just as her arraignment in the mad trial found no parallel in F. He is so undefined by his own words here that our dominant sense of him may tend towards pity, as his cuckoldry bulks proportionately larger than it does in Q. Thus, through its first two acts, F seems to retard both the coming of our convictions of Gonerill's evil, and, thereafter, through the present scene, the cry of indignation against her; but Q speeds both along. As I commented at the end of discussion of the first scene, so in this present scene F offers a greater vision of moral ambiguity than does Q, and this subtlety does not survive conflation. The conflated version absorbs the Q-only lines into F and thus forces a turning of the moral tide before that text, in its own integrity, has revealed it. F continues to present relatively less extreme and irrational behaviour by Gonerill and perceptions of her than does Q.[27]

The variants do not stop here. From this point to the end of the play one's impression of Gonerill is that she is ever more self-possessed than her Quarto counterpart, but that her comparable perversity is paradoxically both more chilling and theatrically attractive—as was Edmund's—by virtue of wit. This element of Gonerill's characterization emerges quite late. When in 1.2.134 the Bastard wittily characterized his brother's approach— 'out hee comes like the Catastrophe of the old Co-|medy' (C2ᵛ, TLN 464)—he seemed almost to be a spectator of the play, like ourselves, rather than merely a character in it. So Gonerill's Folio-only line, 'An enterlude' (TLN 3035; 5.3.89), in which she tries to laugh off the allegation of adultery in Albany's speech to Regan, suggests a comparable (though less successful) manipulation of her opponent, by pretending that she is real, but he fictitious. Here she interrupts her husband (TLN 3033–6; 5.3.88–90):

> If you will marry, make your loues to me,
> My Lady is befpoke.
> *Gon.* An enterlude.
> *Alb.* Thou art armed *Glefter,*

By contrast, Gonorill's silence in the Quarto (L1; 5.3.88–90)—

> If you will mary, make your loue to me,
> My Lady is befpoke, thou art arm'd *Glofter,*

—eloquently points up her vulnerability, and even perhaps her being wounded by her husband's charge. (I argued above in discussion of 1.4 that Gonorill's dark silence in response to her father's curse showed how

27. The treatment of Albany is taken up by M. Warren, 'Albany and Edgar', pp. 98–101, 105. Concerning Albany's tirade against Goneril in Act Four, Moriarty felt that 'The length of the speeches in the bombastic interchange of personality by Albany and Goneril in Act IV might indeed be considered as needlessly interfering with the rapid development of plot' ('The Bearing on Dramatic Sequence,' p. 459). The Q-only passages were 'evidently intended in the quarto version not merely to furnish mouth-filling lines, but to foreshadow the bitterness of the conflict and to prepare for Albany's final stand' (p. 460). Also, the foreshadowing of Albany's final stand against Goneril is discarded from F because it partakes 'too much of melodramatic declamation to produce the truest effect of tragedy' (p. 459).

deeply he had affected her.) Ironically, it is Gonorill's speaking here in 5.1, two scenes earlier, that reveals (as did her Quarto-only lines in 1.3) her continuing inner turmoil and anxiety in *The Historie* (K3; 5.1.16–20).

> *Baſt.* Feare me not, ſhee and the Duke her husband.
>   *Enter Albany and Gonorill with troupes,*
> *Gono.* I had rather looſe the battaile, then that ſiſter ſhould
> loofen him and mee.
> *Alb.* Our very louing ſiſter well be-met

Her silence in F at this point (TLN 2863–5; 5.1.16–20)

> *Baſt.* Feare not, ſhe and the Duke her husband.
>
> *Enter with Drum and Colours, Albany, Gonerill, Soldiers.*
>
> *Alb.* Our very louing Siſter, well be-met:

—allows us to fix the strong image we have developed of her to the end of 4.2 in that version of the play, where she was unscathed by Albany's minimal challenge to her.

In the Folio, at 5.3 again, her wit reappears in variants in this aside; Q reads as mere villainy (L1; 5.3.95–6):

> *Reg.* Sicke, ô ſieke.
> *Gon.* If not, ile nere truſt poyſon.

By contrast, F reads as a villainous joke (TLN 3043–4; 5.3.95–6)—

> *Reg.* Sicke, O ſicke.
> *Gon.* If not, Ile nere truſt medicine.

—for 'medicine' was (and is) both a synonym and an antonym of 'poyson'. The full wit of her diction in F is to be detected by contrasting not merely Q with F 5.3, but also QF 5.3 with QF 4.7. For the word 'medicine' occurs there in its only other use in *Lear*, when Cordelia exhorts Restoration to hang its medicine on her lips, and to let her kiss repair the violent harms her sisters had made in Lear's reverence (K2; TLN 2776–9; 4.7.25–8). Gonerill's ambiguous 'medicine' in F 5.3 is the middle ground, in *The Tragedie* only, that connects the

lips of restoration and the swollen lips of the corpse Lear exclaims
upon as he dies. Of course, Gonerill's wit here makes its impact upon
the audience in ways we cannot attribute to her intent, as she did not
hear Cordelia's reference to medicine, and will not live to see her dead;
but we in the audience hear the echo, and sound its ironic depths. As
differential reading of her speech in 5.3 leads us to see the sophisticated
ambiguity of her *Tragedie*-only diction, the wit seems to redound (irrationally) to her credit.

Whether or not we detect an infusion of wit in Gonerill's character at
the end of *The Tragedie*, there is a very clear differentiation of Gonorill
and Gonerill around her final exit. This exit is implicated in a variant,
like that discussed in 2.4.188, which is made complex by virtue of differently assigned speeches (L2; TLN 3112–20).[28]

QUARTO:

> *Alb.* Stop your mouth dame, or with this paper fhall I ftople
> it, thou worfe then any thing, reade thine owne euill, nay no
> tearing Lady, I perceiue you know't.   (me for't.
> *Gon.* Say if I do, the lawes are mine not thine, who fhal atraine
> *Alb.* Moft monftrous know'ft thou this paper?
> *Gon.* Aske me not what I know.   *Exit. Gonorill.*
> *Alb.* Go after her, fhee's defperate, gouerne her.

FOLIO:

> *Alb.* Shut your mouth Dame,
> Or with this papet fhall I ftop it : hold Sir,
> Thou worfe then any name, reade thine owne euill :
> No tearing Lady, I perceiue you know it.
> *Gon.* Say if I do, the Lawes are mine not thine,
> Who can araigne me for't ?   *Exit.*
> *Alb.* Moft monftrous ! O, know'ft thou this paper?
> *Baft.* Aske me not what I know.
> *Alb.* Go after her, fhe's defperate, gouerne her.

In F, it is true, Gonerill leaves the stage challenged, but she is in a position
of strength, and asserts that she is above the law—even as her dismissive
'An enterlude' asserted that she was real while her husband was role-
playing in a farce. Exactly what Gonerill will do after her exit eventually

28. See Urkowitz, *Revision*, pp. 112–14.

proves pitiful, of course; but at the moment the unknown is part of her strength. Seemingly about her defence, she exits with threats and taunts; she is still the owner of her face. Only when her suicide is announced, and the 'trifle' of her corpse revealed, do we fathom her bluff. In Q, however, Gonorill leaves the stage already defeated and shamefaced. Having claimed at first to stand above the law, she ultimately implies her guilt; not denying her husband's charge, she attempts merely to suppress it and run away from it. Her exit in defeat and her suicide, when it is revealed, do not contradict each other, as they do in *The Tragedie.*

What functions as Gonorill's weak exit line in Q ('Ask me not what I know.') is assigned to the Bastard in F, where, ironically, it serves him as a strong line; for all of what he knows (and we know too) counterpoises the mere carnal knowledge that weighs so heavily in Albany's scale of justice. It is the carnage that Edmund knows, that great thing of Albany forgot—the fate of Cordelia and Lear, whom Gonerill's accomplice in the ranks of death has sent to execution. The different speech assignments give us two very strong impressions of evil in F; two weaker ones in Q.

But enough. As Goneril's variants impinge on those of her husband and her lover, and as Q and F seem to be offering us distinct dramatic and moral visions, analysis of Goneril's variants in isolation becomes less compelling. Anyway, myopia yields to strabismus.

III

The essay began by questioning abstractly the editorial tendency to exalt by debasing—to enlarge its own freedoms at the expense of the evidence; to make a problem, in the case of *Lear*—and not of *Lear* alone—of textual variation. But the proof of such scepticism has to come—if it does come for the reader—in the close readings of my second section. Fraught with both the dead and the living weight of textual tradition, we need to ask rigorously how and what we read—I mean *exactly*. What are the physical objects—never mind the abstraction 'text'—that one's eyes perceive? Are we to look as low as a ligature, are we to see with our ears? And how is our awareness to arise from this basis?

Of course, I did not look at every variant relating to Goneril—this long paper is far too short for that; the reader will have to determine whether my selection has been fair. As the evidence seemed to point away from random differentiation, however, I saw growing something of great constancy, and thought to provide Theseus with the rational argument he may need. As the integral calculus for all the differentiation should have become apparent as I went along, I will not repeat here what separates Gonorill and Gonerill. Moreover, as the other characters we measure them against are also in flux, the attempt at a final statement is premature. But I will give a hard sell for the method that raised the question. Editors have had something of a free hand with *Lear* because they have controlled access to the rare evidence through their collations. But seeing is believing. Photography, by holding the mirror up to the copy-text, has ended their status as an elite, and a more appropriate role for them now is as commentators on the icon of the text rather than as atomizers of it, and as manipulators of its fragments.

By manipulating text, the editorial tradition has put supposed essence before known existences. When taste is the editors' motive, I cannot object to improving Shakespeare—if only the editors would state before their own names on the title pages (as I recently saw brazenly trumpeted in an eighteenth-century edition) 'SHAKESPEARE *as adapted for the stage by. . .*' . But when the historicism of the eighteenth, nineteenth, and twentieth centuries culminates in the same *Lear* as that of the tradition of taste, we are in the sleep of a settled idea, one that has enslaved rather than saved the phenomena. In so doing, the tradition may be said to have created great, but not likely Shakespearian, plays. By conflating contents, it has neglected form. If the difference between Q and F is the result of authorial revision, then the neglect of form for content is like the spurning of architecture for bricklaying. And if the difference stems from an adapter who is not Shakespeare, then the time has come to celebrate his artistic abilities, and not to meld them with another author's.

The editorial *Lear* of tradition has grown in Duthie's edition to be complexly simplistic: complex in the inordinate number of epicycles it requires to pull the evidences into the orbit of Truth; simplistic in its faith that this is the way of Art. As Blake says in his 'Proverbs of Hell' (*The Marriage of Heaven and Hell*, 10):

Improvent makes strait roads, but the crooked roads without Improvement, are roads of Genius.

Producing Manuscripts and Editions†

Ralph Hanna, Jr.

In some measure this volume, *Crux and Controversy*, testifies to a considerable disruption in the life of Middle English textual critics, the appearance of George Kane and E. Talbot Donaldson's edition, *'Piers Plowman': The B Version*.[1] This volume has caused an important coming to consciousness on the part of readers: they can no longer avoid noticing that mediation which editorial activity always performs. But predictably enough, in the normal mystifications under which textual criticism operates, such coming to consciousness is a delayed and often anguished one. Fifteen years have elapsed between *The B Version* and this volume, and my own intervention in the following pages has in many ways been forestalled.[2]

But this volume might be seen to involve yet further delays. For the responses which *'Piers Plowman': The B Version* has provoked are essentially objections to what already existed as a fully formed method of textual attack in Kane's 1960 edition of the A Text of *Piers*.[3] In fact, the

---

† "Producing Manuscripts and Editions," from *Crux and Controversy in Middle English Textual Criticism*, ed. A. J. Minnis and Charlotte Brewer (Cambridge: D. S. Brewer, 1992). Reprinted by permission of Boydell and Brewer Ltd.

1. *'Piers Plowman': The B Version* (London, 1975).

2. Largely by Lee Patterson, 'The Logic of Textual Criticism and the Way of Genius: The Kane-Donaldson *Piers Plowman* in Historical Perspective', in *Negotiating the Past* (Madison, Wisconsin, 1987), pp. 77–113, the most recent revision of an essay originally delivered and published elsewhere.

3. *'Piers Plowman': The A Version* (London, 1960; 2nd edn. London 1988, my citation text). However, cf. note 49 below for an important distinction I would make between the editions of A and B.

method only became controversial when applied to the canonical B text, that form of the poem publicly revered—even through a nineteenth-century edition which users have frequently recognized as inadequate.[4] It required unsettled responses—predicated upon a text already presumed fixed and stable, even if inadequately—to create both crux and controversy. This state of affairs surely testifies to a certain naïveté about the editorial process: it is hard to envision—in an age of reprints—a new edition unless it radically innovates, rewrites its predecessors.[5]

But such an identification of the innovative immediately identifies the site of controversy. For if a standard edition might be completely and radically re-done on the basis of identical source materials, the issue of editorial certitude, the truth-claims of the text presented, obviously becomes very pressing indeed. 'Piers Plowman': The B Version forces this problem on any reader by offering itself frankly as the product of modern editorial acumen alone. In doing so, this edition, of course, impolitely displays what might be considered establishment standards (largely, I fear, claims set for editors by bemused literary critics) as the emperor's new clothes. Editors are supposed to present misreadable and mystificatory editions—ones which purport to offer, or can be construed as offering, unific and universally 'correct' texts. But those who have edited—and Kane and Donaldson might well be lauded for their clarity in this regard[6]—know otherwise: they know only too well that the task

4. This is, of course, Walter W. Skeat's great edition *The Vision of William Concerning Piers the Plowman*, 2 vols. (London, 1886).

5. Merely as one example of this anguish, see Charlotte Brewer, 'The Textual Principles of Kane's A Text', *YLS* 3 (1989): 67–90. This essay laudably attempts to come to terms with Kane's editorial behavior, but is marked both by conspicuous illogicality and by a general ignorance of the longstanding conversation among textual critics over several centuries and concerning texts in several different languages. (A great many of Kane's 'innovations' have been the metier of classicists since at least the eighteenth century, for example.) Of this conversation, especially as it concerns discrimination among variant readings, Kane and Patterson seem to me conspicuously aware: see 'Piers Plowman': The A Version, pp. 53–54, note 3; and 'Way of Genius', pp. 97–110.

6. Although clarity rather frequently becomes obscured, particularly in Kane's post-1975 writings, by claims for the editorial power to recognize intuitively what is Langlandian. Such claims seem to me hyperbole (although a hyperbole Patterson accepts and analyses at length) not borne out by practice. If nothing else, the laborious introductions

they perform is an interpretative act, not especially different from the critical act.[7] The controversy in which Kane and Donaldson then embroil their readers might thus be rephrased in the terms of Ivan Karamazov's Grand Inquisitor: if some transcendently objective text is not possible, are any and all editorial acts permissible?

Two versions of this question seem to recur in various responses to the Athlone editions. One line of argument would direct attention toward failure, to a vast area of textual indeterminacy which the editors do not resolve. It thus finds the procedure inherently limited in ways which preclude its use.[8] On the other hand, attacks on the overexuberance of Kane and Donaldson's recuperation of Langland are, of course, legion and go back to the very earliest reviews. Most such readers wish to settle for a 'document', for the apparent certainty provided by a recorded manuscript version.

It is with this second area of complaint that I take up my argument, by presenting a writing almost overly familiar, one which all my readers will recognize:

Tempest þe nouȝt al croked to redresse

Tempest (A[1] C Cov El Eg Ph)] Restreyne A[4], Peyne A[6] Co Cx F[1] F[2] H[4] Hat Kk Lam Ld Leyd Nott P R[2-1] R[2-2] S[1] S[2]; Ne study Cp. þe] om.

---

to both *'Piers Plowman': The A Version* and *'Piers Plowman': The B Version* show the Athlone editors striving to localize, not the author, but variant classes, varieties of readings, which might be identified as transmissional. Identifying these, for the most part created by scribal inadvertences (not necessaily 'stupidities'), with a recognized variant type will presuppose that another variant must be logically prior, the reading either of archetype or author.

7. And, I would insist, this process partakes of that very chicken-and-egg problem which always defines 'the hermeneutic circle'. (How do we know one variant is prior? because it explains the others in terms of a recognizable class. How does it explain the others? because it is prior.)

8. This is the less frequent case, but see *SB* 41 (1988): 191–93. Such authors might well be directed to the basic study, Walter W. Greg, 'The Rationale of Copy-Text', *SB* 3 (1950): 19–36. [Reprinted in this volume, pp. 135–53—*Editor.*] Minute detail is never fully recoverable, even in the most modern instances.

Cp. al] euery A^4, eche Cp Cx F^1 F^2 Ld Leyd P S^1. croked] crokis Ph.
to redresse] to redes A^4; for to redresse R$^{2-2}$.^{9}

Obviously enough, this is a textual display—in this case, a line of Middle English poetry (Chaucer, *Truth* 8), accompanied by what is usually referred to as 'all the evidence' for those readings editorially adopted. But although I would not, at some level, question such an evidentiary showing, I'm intrigued by the ways such a display renders a substantial amount of 'evidence' about Chaucer's work and its transmission unrecoverable. All my readers will know, for example, that each letter form, each sigil, represents a manuscript (in two cases, F and R^2, two copies within the same manuscript). But from the information which I supply, a collation or *corpus lectionum*, we find nothing about these objects (in the edition I am quoting, the editors, at pp. 52–53, do indicate the folios they quote and the approximate date of the hands which wrote them). But we know nothing else about these evidentiary objects, except that they have been here rejected as valid evidence for Chaucer's text (in the case of the first lemma, unusually—because a major crux where the witnesses divide—manuscripts with the reading identified as correct do get listed). But in every case, the editors' sigla refer to material objects, books; from this edition, we can find nothing about such objects—not their contents (either gross or immediate), nor how they were put together (in this edition not even whether made of parchment or paper), when (script) and where (dialect), what sort of decoration (or other guides to textual consumption) they include.

Moreover, one cannot exactly reconstitute the poem as it appears in any single book: 'by convention', rejected lections are virtually uncoverable. For example, A^4 can be reconstructed to read '*Restreyne* þe nouȝt *euery* croked *to redes*', and from the display, one can be certain that only the words I italicize in fact have the cited form in the manuscript.

---

9. Adopted from George B. Pace and Alfred David (eds.), *Geoffrey Chaucer, Volume V, The Minor Poems, Part One* (Norman, 1982), p. 61. Because I use this as merely an illustrative example, I forbear linking sigla with shelfmarks.

(Moreover, this is an unusually full report, since the arbitarily assigned sigil A^4 occurs early in the alphabet; *Leyd*, for example, remains completely closed to a reader, since 'by convention' the corpus only tells one that this book provides what may be construed as the same word as that cited following the lemma.) The notion of evidence enshrined here is quite peculiar: it serves to alienate one from a material survival of a complex series of (fifteenth-century) labors. They range from those of the shepherd boy (or rag gatherer) and collector of oak-galls through those of butchers and parchmyners to that of a scribe or scriveyn to those of a great English poet.

On the other hand, having presented this material as evidence in this way is equally an act of material labour—although obviously very differently constituted from what it presents. This is our academic labour—in this instance, labour of a highly hegemonic sort—offered in the service of a canonized poet, and because canonized, deemed of great cultural centrality. Only that centrality—and the need to read Chaucer to validate it—requires the care which produces this textual display.

This second labour, textual criticism, is an act of cultural recuperation. It attempts to effect an historical bridge between a lost productive past and a consuming present. But as a bridging gesture, such activity needs constantly to be aware of its own historicity. In the English tradition, at least, such historicist activity reflects, not the site of manuscript production, but a print world. Within this alien culture, Middle English works have been accommodated to foreign norms of textual presentation which preexisted any effort at editing the medieval—norms developed to present the classics and a tradition of English authors imitating the classics (notably Ben Jonson). Significantly, Middle English texts in such a format began to appear in the 1710s and 1720s; such editorial ministrations are precisely contemporary with the invention in English of the idea of authorial property with Pope.[10] And this idea is predicated upon

10. Cf. Anne Hudson's identification of Thomas Hearne's *Robert of Gloucester* as the first modern edition, 'Middle English', in A.G. Rigg (ed.), *Editing Medieval Texts: French, English, and Latin Written in England*, 12th Toronto Conference on Editorial Problems

the eighteenth-century author's need to address an anonymous general audience which will pay for the privilege of private reading (thus making profit a possibility and, consequently, property a necessity).

In contrast to this modern situation, we might consider one portion of a medieval production history, that of Trevisa's *Polychronicon*.[11] I give a particularly gross and externalized version of this history, without attention to the details of codicology or dispersed readings.

In spite of its enormous bulk, Trevisa's *Polychronicon* resembles a huge range of medieval English texts in being, first, occasional, bound to a specific, personalized historical situation, and, second, not primarily 'artistic' in any way which makes sense in post-Romantic terms. If one believes the representation in the 'Dialogue' and 'Epistle' which Trevisa prefaced to the work, the whole enterprise originated in a personal relationship, a command of the Lord Thomas Berkeley IV to his dependent cleric, the vicar of his parish church; and the Lord's public-spirited impulse was designed to inform, to have produced in English an authoritative body of historical knowledge. This claim, that the cleric Trevisa was coerced into performing a service for his lord, is a complimentary representation, and the rhetorical claim involved enacts a patronal imperative, deference to the Lord's superior wisdom and social presen/cience.[12] Further, the domestic

---

(New York, 1977), pp. 34–57, at p. 35. One could further cite Urry's Chaucer. For other examples and comments on the inexactness with which these editors imitated the classical model, see A.S.G. Edwards, 'Observations on the History of Middle English Editing', in Derek Pearsall (ed.), *Manuscripts and Texts: Editorial Problems in Later Middle English Literature* (Cambridge, 1987), pp. 34–48, at pp. 40–42. The importance of Pope, and of his battles against publishers who pirated his works, to the conception of literary property is an idea I owe to Mark Rose.

11. I expand upon a history I first outlined in 'Sir Thomas Berkeley and His Patronage', *Speculum* 64 (1989): 878–916, at pp. 891–92, 894–96, 909–13. I am acutely conscious of the difficulties which attend the typology I will offer: one can only discuss textual traditions one knows, yet simultaneously one knows that every text involves certain unique transmissional features.

12. Trevisa is far more likely to have known the *Polychronicon* in any form than is Berkley. John Taylor, *The 'Universal Chronicle' of Ranulf Higden* (Oxford, 1966), pp. 105–09, 152–59, indicates that the visible circulation of the Latin original passed through conventional clerical channels. And a minimal number of surviving copies show any sign of medieval lay ownership, the most contemporary example being the civil and canon

service component of this labor appears in Trevisa's renting rooms at Queen's College, Oxford for an extended period in the mid-1380s, in all probability to consult a copy of the source-text. Such a protracted absence, as well as the money for room-rental (and any supplies necessary for making the translation), would have required Berkeley's releasing Trevisa from local duties as Vicar of Berkeley (and very likely as a member of the household clerical staff) and possibly subsidizing his vacation.

Upon completion of his translation (dated in the text 18 April 1387), Trevisa would presumably have given some variety of fair-copy to the lord/patron who had stimulated and underwritten his efforts. (The 'Epistle', after all, is addressed to him and claims that the work exists as a service to him and for his personal use.) In the case of the *Polychronicon*, no evidence survives as to whether (a) any in-progress drafts were handed round the Berkeley household, in the form of patronal circulation or circulation among a coterie;[13] or whether (b) any object so formal as a 'presentation copy' ever existed. Moreover, as an act of domestic service, so far as we can tell, Trevisa's work was essentially unremunerated (if one discounts the delights of spending several years in college).[14] This disparity from the modern situation in which we consume the

---

lawyer Adam of Usk's British Library, MS Additional 10104 (see Taylor, pp. 129–30); a copy now lost belonged to Henry IV (see Carol Meale, in Jeremy Griffiths and Derek Pearsall (eds.), *Book Production and Publishing in Britain 1375–1475* (Cambridge, 1989), p. 203). In contrast, in the late 1370s, Trevisa and others were accused of removing from Queen's College, Oxford, *inter alia*, twenty-four books, including a *Polychronicon*; see David C. Fowler, 'John Trevisa and the English Bible', *Modern Philology* 58 (1960): 81–98, item 11 in the list on p. 94. Moreover, Trevisa's renting rooms at Queen's (see A.B. Emden, *BRUO* 3: 1903) suggests that neither he nor his patron had access to a copy for translation at Berkeley.

13. I have suggested that such documents lie behind the Hengwrt *Canterbury Tales* in 'The Hengwrt Manuscript and the Canon of the *Canterbury Tales*', *English Manuscript Studies 1100–1700* 1 (1989): 64–84.

14. Although it is at least possible that Trevisa's strongarm efforts at asserting title to a canonry in the college at Westbury on Trym in 1388–89 reflect some effort by his patron to reward him (perhaps including the patron's provision of an esquire from his retinue to aid Trevisa). See Fowler, 'New Light on John Trevisa', *Traditio* 18 (1962): 289–317, at pp. 311–13; and Nigel Saul, *Knights and Esquires: The Gloucestershire Gentry in the Fourteenth Century* (Oxford, 1981), p. 166.

Polychronicon is worth insisting upon, since at every later stage of this text's production, someone profited, always someone other than Trevisa, whom we might identify from a firmly modernist perspective as the primary literary producer. (At a minimum, such beneficiaries included the booktrade individuals—butchers, parchmyners, scriveyns, rubricators, limners who sold their skills to manufacture the product, manuscripts of the text.) But at the point at which Trevisa's service ended, the work appears to have passed into his patron's control—just like the fruits of all Berkeley's other servants' diverse labors.[15]

The absence of authorial property in the work may be paralleled by a very significant non-congruency of hand-written and typeset situations in their possible definition of the work's immediate audience. The modern typographic situation, especially in the last two centuries, usually presupposes an anonymous mass public comprised of private readers. And the very idea of preparing an edited text equally assumes such an audience—a group of largely passive recipients of something produced, a group which assumes it reads from a universally available identical copy (that is, after all, the whole purpose of edited texts, and mass print culture has in fact created the interest in having such a profession as editor). In contrast, the immediate medieval audience needs to be situated in the patron's coterie, in the absolutely personal relationship. Moreover, in terms of these audience relations, medieval authorship may even be construed as 'present' in a nearly Derridian sense: the work hovers between oral and written, inasmuch as its consumption may be supervised by authorial reading and/or conversational commentary.[16] The situation

15. See further *Speculum* 64 (1989): 892–94, 914–15 (full reference in note 11 above).

16. Cf. H. Marshall Leicester Jr.'s discussion, ' "Oure Tonges *Difference*:" Textuality and Deconstruction in Chaucer', which emphasizes Chaucer's representation of his chagrin at being *read* in his absence, without his supervisory comment as to intention, in Laurie A. Finke and Martin B. Schichtman (eds.), *Medieval Texts and Contemporary Readers* (Ithaca, 1987), pp. 15–26, esp. pp. 19–20. Instructively, this Chaucerian self-representation is virtually contemporary with a moment important for general literary history, the point at which official cognizance of the power and danger of the freely circulating *written* English word first occurs, 30 March 1388. See H.G. Richardson, 'Heresy and the Lay Power Under Richard II', *English Historical Review* 51 (1936): 1–28.

approaches the modern complicity of authors and producers only in the very occasional evidence for supervised copying (perhaps with Gower and Capgrave, and alluded to in Chaucer's stanza to 'Adam Scriveyn').[17]

Medieval literary workmanship differs from the model known and available in English since at least Ben Jonson in another way. In addition to the different social situation described in the last paragraph, authorship is non-professionalized. This status does not simply reflect a pre-copyright culture but again is imbricated in social structure. The literary worker presents his text as almost an unremunerated 'gift'. His remuneration comes from the coterie to which he offers the work (not of course, 'his' but the patron's): payment is predicated, not on literary work but other patronal services. In effect, remuneration is the product of a 'real profession', usually a function of or support to the workman's coterie standing.[18]

Although the very earliest stages of the *Polychronicon*'s circulation are hidden, one can talk about immediate dispersal outside the coterie. Three surviving copies retain dialectical forms congruent with local copying in Berkeley or the immediate area, in two instances probably during Trevisa's lifetime: they presumably testify to efforts by Berkeley or his coterie at insuring circulation of the book in the neighbourhood. Two of these copies, London, British Library, *MS* Cotton Tiberius D. vii and British Library, *MS* Stowe 65, look, from the quality of their text, as if derived from something like Trevisa's holograph or his presentation copy or a

---

17. The traditional view of Gower's supervision was laid out in large measure by Macaulay and Fisher; but now see Peter Nicholson, 'Gower's Revisions in the *Confessio Amantis*', *ChR* 19 (1984): 123–43; and 'Poet and Scribe in the Manuscripts of Gower's *Confessio Amantis*', in *Manuscripts and Texts*, pp. 130–42. Peter J. Lucas has written extensively about the Capgrave scriptorium; for his original study in the area, see 'John Capgrave, O.S.A. (1393–1464), Scribe and "Publisher"', *Transactions of the Cambridge Bibiliographical Society* 5, i (1969): 1–35.

18. Consider the number of poets so supported: Chaucer's numerous administrative posts; Hoccleve's office in the Privy Seal; Langland's patronage, according to Kane-Donaldson, *'Piers Plowman':The B Version*, p. 122 and note 47 (cf. the possible reference to Wille/Langland as legal scribe at A 8.43). Later 'professional authors', like Lydgate and Capgrave, had substantial support from the clerical organizations of which they were members.

carefully corrected faircopy.[19] But the third of these codices, Manchester, Chetham's Library, *MS* 11379, was of other origins: given what the other two survivors imply, a notable success at this localized 'publication' enterprise, the Chetham manuscript seems to represent a second exemplar prepared to facilitate further copying in the face of some demand. And in fact, either the Chetham manuscript, its source, or one of its immediate derivatives was to become the source of virtually all other copies of the *Polychronicon*[20]—it served the purpose for which it was prepared. Whatever form Trevisa's original copy had, it appears to have been retained by his patron or the Berkeley household coterie, while the archetype prepared to facilitate wider publication was made generally available for other users.

Dispersed circulation of the Chetham text occurred at a very early date (at the very outside, pre-1420) in London, at least initially under Berkeley auspices. Four copies, the first three by the same known London scribe[21]—British Library, MS Additional 24194; Cambridge, St. John's College, MS H.1; Princeton University Library, MS Garrett 151; *olim* Boies Penrose (which last changed hands at Sotheby's, London, 6 December 1988, as lot 45)—reflect this stage of dispersal, ultimately the source of nearly all surviving non-Berkeley copies of the *Polychronicon*. With the exception of the first named (and probably oldest) of these copies, directly associable with Berkeley, since it was prepared for the patron's son-in-law, Richard Beauchamp, earl of Warwick, each was made for a separate client, a new patron who wanted his/her own copy of Trevisa's text. Inferentially, given the total output of the London

19. The provenance of Stowe may perhaps be specifiable: the book initia constantly include, among other decorative features, wiverns, some with human heads, perhaps a badge. The manuscript also contains a note suggesting Norwich ownership *c.* 1557.

20. Two further copies represent later dispersed derivatives of the Berkeley tradition: Princeton University Library, Taylor MS (the London hooked g scribe, s. xv$^{3/4}$) and Glasgow, University Library, *MS* Hunterian 367.

21. See A.I. Doyle and Malcolm B. Parkes, 'The Production of Copies of the Canterbury Tales and the Confessio Amantis in the Early Fifteenth Century', in Parkes and Andrew G. Watson (eds.), *Medieval Scribes, Manuscripts and Libraries: Essays Presented to N.R. Ker* (London, 1978), pp. 163–210, at p. 206.

scribe delta and his identifiable contemporaries, these were persons like Berkeley and Beauchamp, aristocratic (whether rural lord or London oligarch) clients also engaged in patronizing copies of Chaucer and Gower.[22]

To this dispersed London circulation, Berkeley—the current proprietor of the text—contributed only his archetype. By this act, he fulfilled both those altruistic designs with which Trevisa credits him in the 'Dialogue'—socially dispersed historical information in English—and, more importantly, his longing for what every medieval lordly patron most desired, social prestige: Look what I can get my servant(s) to do. But at this point, having through the Chetham archetype made possible the social dispersal of his text, and perhaps his name, his property in the work was, like his servant's, ended. The *Polychronicon* had now entered the public domain, become shared out among book-trade individuals (who may actually at this point have possessed the Chetham archetype) and their individual patrons, the persons who would commission them to produce new copies, usually to their narrow individual specifications.

Such passage of patronage—from the patron/coterie who commissions the initial literary work to a second, plural set of patrons who commission that work's public dispersal—constitutes the 'bespoke book-trade', which typifies English production until well into the third quarter of the fifteenth century.[23] Such a trade functions through private patronal use of someone else's work; this the new patron takes as his/her own, and for it s/he creates

22. One should contrast the circulation of Trevisa's *De Proprietatibus Rerum,* known only from dispersed scribal treatment, the earliest copy London, British Library, MS Additional 27944, prepared in London; see Doyle-Parkes, 'Production', pp. 177, 195–96. Possible local circulation of *Properties* may be indicated by paraphrased excerpts in Oxford, Magdalen College, MS lat. 182, in the hand of a monk of Muchelney (Somerset) *c.* 1440, a reference I owe to S.J. Ogilvie-Thomson and A.S.G. Edwards.

23. Graham Pollard argued that such bespoke trade, rather than the standing stock we associate with print-era publishers, was the fifteenth-century norm; see 'The Company of Stationers before 1557', *Library* 4 ser. 18 (1937): 1–38, at pp. 15–18. The most recent surveys of the situation only vindicate this as the normal state of affairs until the third quarter of the fifteenth century; see Griffiths-Pearsall, *Book Production,* pp. 2–7 (Pearsall), 14 (Roderick Lyall), 110 (Doyle), 183 (Kate Harris), 220 (Meale), 259–60 and 264–66 (Edwards and Pearsall).

a new audience. In this process, a work originally occasional becomes adopted for a new occasion, a new personalized use. Moreover, in such a trade, scribal book-production markets skills (writing, limning, etc.), but it does not market demand. Book-trade individuals make a living in a variety of other ways, e.g. through preparation of non-English manuscripts, especially liturgical and legal ones, and secondhand sales. In this context, virtually all English books must be seen as special orders, a state of affairs which implies that buyers know the text they want in advance and that such foreknowledge stimulates the desire to own a copy. This prior familiarity, almost necessarily, implies something like 'reading knowledge' of at least part of the work; and in turn, such familiarity must be predicated—as Trevisa's literary service had been—upon a nonliterary social connection, comradeship, which allows access to a pre-existing copy, necessarily someone else's property. Moreover, special ordering within the bespoke trade presupposes the uniqueness of every copy: each reflects some specific negotiations as to standards, for example, type of script and level of decoration. Obviously enough, in this situation of uniqueness, negotiations may address the quality of the text as well. Such features deserve to be insisted upon because of certain peculiar features of the entry of the *Polychronicon* into the bespoke trade, that of new, non-Berkeley patrons.

One gauge of this second level of patronal behavior concerns a single (and notorious) error in the text of the *Polychronicon*. Apparently that version of the Chetham archetype available to scribe delta on his first copying, Additional 24194, lacked a quire, and the scribe simply lost a substantial block of text. But in his second (and all subsequent copyings), this same scribe was able, at least in part, to remedy this deficiency. Either the scribe or the patron noted an archetypal omission (it would be readily signalled on a quick check of the available archetype by failure either of consecutive capitulation or of consecutive quire signatures or of both), decided that textual continuity and completeness were desirable, and inserted a different bit of translation (perhaps produced for the occasion from a text of the Latin source) to fill the gap. Within certain limits (on the evidence of the Berkeley texts, the translation included in the St. John's, Garrett, and Penrose manuscripts was not Trevisa's final version), scribe delta and/or the patron managed to improve a text which had become defective by accident.[24]

Moreover, such a meliorative effort with the *Polychronicon* in this situation of dispersed patronage was not unique. In the three manuscripts which contain the supplied translation, the passage differs distinctly from the surrounding text. A second group of bespoke copies within this dispersed arena was able to improve upon scribe delta and his/her patron(s): the production-team behind London, British Library, MS Harley 1900 (and through them the producer of Huntington Library, MS HM 28561 and Caxton, in his *editio princeps*) retrieved what had been lost in the Additional copy and retrieved it in a form congruent (although in detail not identical) with the *Polychronicon* as it appears in the Berkeley copies.[25]

In context, this step appears part of a massive research effort stimulated by a patron who wished, to a degree not even scribe delta's second patron did, to restore the literary worker Trevisa and his original patron to the text.[26] For behind the Harley manuscript and its derivatives is an

24. The locution 'not Trevisa's final version' is my equivocation; I think the supply entirely book-trade activity, but Ronald Waldron argues that the production team was able to access Trevisan draft; see 'John Trevisa and the Use of English', *Proceedings of the British Academy* 74 (1988): 171–202, at pp. 192–98, 200–01. Waldron's explanation would suggest that scribe delta's production team retained some links with the Berkeley coterie, but raises a most instructive paradox: in the process of 'improving' the text, correcting it, there is implicit an absence of interest in correctness. Given the nature of the supplied translation, the coterie source Waldron presupposes would no longer have recognized (and perhaps would not have cared) that at this moment three different forms of text were circulating from Berkeley—the Tiberius version, the Chetham version, and the draft version supplied for the London manuscripts. Obviously, our print-book demands for scrupulous editorial accuracy differ markedly from a more fluid medieval construction of 'the accurate'.

25. I.e. their recourse was not to the original Berkeley version but to a descendant copy prepared for bespoke use, like the Chetham manuscript.

26. The Harley manuscript (which includes a note reflecting Chester ownership *c.* 1448) was produced roughly contemporaneously with what may be the earliest effort to present Trevisa explicitly as *auctor* (along with Chaucer, Edward, Duke of York, and Lydgate). This deliberately canonizing procedure occurs in the poem John Shirley affixed to London, British Library, MS Additional 16165, probably in the late 1420s. See Eleanor Prescott Hammond, *English Verse between Chaucer and Surrey* (Durham, 1927), pp. 194–96, esp. lines 35–44, 93–95; and for discussion, Seth Lerer, 'Textual Criticism and Literary Theory: Chaucer and His Readers', *Exemplaria* 2, i (Spring 1990): 329–45.

effort to see the *Polychronicon* in a way which had not occurred since Trevisa's lifetime (and has not been repeated since), not as an isolated quasi-canonical Great Work but as the center of a series of Trevisan texts.[27] The patron—for in this case, given that it involved textual extension, a larger and more expensive book, it must be his/her initiative which is at issue—not only saw to it that a Trevisan text was restored within the work, but set the work within a full Trevisan context, not isolated but as part of an extensive anthology. S/he did not simply insure that the *Polychronicon* read as the best available Berkeley sources indicated it should. S/he also acquired two texts unknown outside the Berkeley circulation of the work, the 'Dialogue' and 'Epistle' which emphatically mark the text as Trevisan and done to patronal order.[28] And s/he further resuscitated two texts known to scribe delta but never considered integral to the presentation of the *Polychronicon* (they occur in scribe delta's Additional and St. John's manuscripts, but not in his/her Garrett or the contemporary London Penrose; in the Berkeley Stowe and Chetham, but not Tiberius)—Trevisa's translations of Pseudo-Ockham's *Dialogus* and FitzRalph's *Defensio*. And this patron's acquisition procedures went further, to include what may be a unique Trevisan text otherwise unknown, the translation of Pseudo-

27. Over the last century plus, the three groups of texts I mention below have been dispersed and presented separately from one another—*Polychronicon* facing Higden's Latin in the nine-volume Rolls Series edition of 1865–86, the shorter translations in Aaron James Perry's *Dialogus* (E.E.T.S. 167), the 'Dialogue' and 'Epistle' in pre-Renaissance form only in Ronald Waldron's edition, in Edward Donald Kennedy, Waldron, and Joseph J. Wittig (eds.), *Middle English Studies Presented to George Kane* (Woodbridge, 1988), pp. 285–99. Such presentation, especially the chronological ordering of the publications, reflects a feature of modern canonicity in which book-length texts have priority over oddments.

28. They elsewhere occur only in the Tiberius and Stowe manuscripts, fragmentarily (one bobbed text each) in their two descendants, the Taylor and Hunter manuscripts. The Chetham archetype may have contained them—in which case they were suppressed as irrelevant local details in the new patronal situation of London copying (even by the family member Richard Beauchamp). Only two leaves from quire 4 of Chetham 11379 survive, and it is uncertain whether those lost would have contained the texts.

Methodius which follows the other brief texts in both the Harley and Huntington manuscripts.[29]

This example, however extended, should indicate the profound difference between the textual mediations of manuscript and print culture. And, as a narrative, it provides some context for considering that uniqueness of manuscripts, with which textual criticism must deal. Analysing the *Polychronicon* is useful, both because of the fullness of the early record and because it suggests a general typological range of situations within which medieval book-production proceeded.

There are obvious analogies between the history I have sketched and the model of genetic/stemmatic editorial studies. Such efforts to construct stemmata diagramming a work's dispersal presuppose a three- or four-level model: what such an editor calls O ('authorial holograph') could be identified with the coterie/presentation text; what s/he calls O[1] ('the archetype of all surviving copies'—and perhaps also alpha/beta/gamma) with the patron's text prepared to market a servant production; alpha/beta/gamma ('archetypes of individual families', if different from the preceding) with the lost representatives of the early stages of such marketing; A, B, C, . . . Z with the surviving manuscripts derived from the preceding steps, the product of the bespoke trade, a new dispersed patronage.

But a stemmatic model overlooks two important aspects of the textual process which this Trevisan narrative should highlight. First, because stemmatics forms a retrospective historicism which begins with surviving manuscripts, as a procedure it may in fact be profoundly misrepresentative. Its model action is to reverse history, not analyze it; but any textual tradition is a progressive historical development, potentially

29. Perry rejects the text as apocryphal; see E.E.T.S. 167: cxi–cxv. And a copy of the work may have been commissioned in this place as an editorial addition quite apart from Trevisan enthusiasm. The Methodius would complete Higden's universal history by treating the accepted *termini* 'the beginning of worldes and the end of worlds'. The codicology of Harley 1900 would support a source different from that of the Trevisan materials: fols. 22–23, which include the Methodius, appear to have been ruled to hold the *Polychronicon* contents table, rather than a text, a sign of a mid-production adjustment of contents.

localizable in time and space, which runs from early to late and must always be seen as such, as a series of ordered representations of a work. Thus, the Tiberius and Stowe manuscripts of the *Polychronicon* in stemmatic terms would have to be seen retrospectively as initial representatives of a family alpha, whereas the historical evidence may indicate that, in their possible derivation from holograph, they in fact predate what would be in stemmatic terms O^1, a generally available scribal copy; similarly, the Chetham manuscript, rather than the earliest descendant of a family beta, may in fact be equivalent either to O^1 or to beta itself, as Ronald Waldron suggests.[30]

Second, stemmatics presupposes the constancy of degeneration as a product of dissemination. In some general way, this seems an inarguable truth, although one never clearly true for any individual instance, the lemma. For individual acts of production can improve the text, as I have just shown two sets of *Polychronicon* book-producers attempting. Thus, the very goal of stemmatics, to use isolated shared errors to signal deviant textual versions which can then be rejected *in toto*, proves fundamentally misbegotten: no manuscript or reading can *a priori* be ignored.[31]

The linearity of stemmatic diagrams does, however, suggest one important fact: the general uniqueness of each productive moment in manuscript culture. Although individual copies may be of more than one source (as London copies of the *Polychronicon* after the Additional and Harley manuscripts, in different ways, surely are), each is produced in a situation of finite availability. Unlike the print world to which we are accustomed, no medieval work can be assumed to have universal social distribution, to be everywhere and always available; and in particular it can never be assumed to be universally available in all of its stages of

30. In his unpublished article 'The Manuscripts of Trevisa's Translation of the *Polychronicon*'. I am very grateful to Waldron for sharing his views with me.

31. A point I have touched upon previously, in discussing Chaucer's 'Truth' at *SAC* 10 (1988): 34–35 and *The Siege of Jerusalem* reproduced in Lambeth Palace, MS 491 at *SB* 42 (1989): 125–26.

distribution. A manuscript work is at any given moment always socially single (or, perhaps better, to take conflation into account, limited): it may, within the bespoke trade, be memorially conflated, contain both the available exemplar and what the scribe can remember of the version which stimulated his copying—which may not be from the same exemplar. (This possibility is especially likely where patron and producer are identical.) But overall the work is simply whatever is known to the individual patron and producer—which is not the whole tradition as known to the modern scholar.

The uniqueness associated with the individual manuscript's productive moment limits the effectiveness of several recent efforts to retheorize the editing of medieval texts. In many ways, these efforts begin with a point to which I will return, the peculiar manner in which textual 'authority' is dispersed within medieval culture. But in attaching this premise to various (post)modernist conceptions of literary work, such theorising manages to misrepresent the medieval literary situation. One powerful source of such views, Jerome J. McGann, has been subjected to particularly devastating misappropriation.[32] McGann's arguments appear relevant to the medieval situation because he insists, against Fredson Bowers and Thomas Tanselle, upon the constant complicity of authors and book-trade individuals in textual production. But, as McGann always asserts, the 'modern scripture' which he discusses differs from that of earlier eras because of a superfluity of authority, an irreducible plethora of authorially sanctioned versions, whereas with earlier texts the problem is, as it has always been posed, the difficulty of finding any authority at all. Moreover, McGann can scarcely, either in his volumes critiquing modern textual criticism or in his practice as an editor of Byron, be described as opposed to editorial activity. He does revise the editorial construction he has received: he carefully argues the representative nature of the one textual version he chooses to present in terms of that authorial contact with a public which it effects (thus rejecting the

32. See *A Critique of Modern Textual Criticism* (Chicago, 1983).

'rule of final intentions'); and he dispenses with a great deal of the impedimenta associated with Bowers's versions of copy-text.

A more recent theorization, in many ways not far removed from the traditional conception of an 'oral text', is that of Bernard Cerquiglini.[33] He argues, on the basis of deconstructive theory, that medieval writing forms the ultimate postmodern *texte*: the individual work automatically dissolves into the plurality of all its variants, and its meaning resides precisely in such *mouvance* or *variance*. From such a perspective, the best edition will merely set variants adrift, allow them to generate collisions one with another (as in the unrestrained puns of which Howard Bloch is so fond). But however strongly Cerquiglini's formulation may appeal to our situation, it remains ultimately detached from that history it purports to explain. For to create his infinitely generating *texte*, Cerquiglini must presuppose the simultaneous social ubiquity of all textual forms, whatever their temporal or spatial disparities. In doing so, he assumes a literary community like that of centralized modern print culture and ignores the strongest evidence for the medieval situation—precanonical, personalized and limited.[34]

On the basis of these thoughts, I think one can conceive some imperatives for editors. Surviving manuscripts, what we consider 'the evidence'

33. See *Eloge de la variante: Histoire critique de la philologie* (Paris, 1989). For an example of Howard Bloch, to whom I refer below, at work, see 'New Philology and Old French,' *Speculum* 65 (1990): 38–58.

34. The text of Hollywood film perhaps provides a better modern analogy—an example suggested to me by Philip Gaskell's provocative lecture at the Clark Library, Los Angeles, 8 February 1985. Film texts have proved notoriously unstable, since they are subjected to a wide variety of modern entrepreneurial uses (possible analogues to medieval dispersed patronal use?). Directors' final cuts are frequently subjected to studio revision before general release; theatre versions may vary (e.g. the responses of preview audiences may motivate textual alterations); and non-theatrical versions—those shown on airflights, available for videotape rental, or recut for television presentation (not just to fit variable advertising and time-slot requirements but recast to convert a 70 mm image into the 35 mm dimensions of the small screen)—show further variations. But one who has seen any one version has 'seen the film' and will not discover s/he has not save by chance—a second viewing which turns out to be another version. However, there are immediate limits to the analogy, e.g. (a) film is a ubiquitously dispersed vehicle of modern popular culture; (b) its production represents corporate activity, like the drama, in which 'authorship' is not simply shared but fractured.

—reduced to apparently equivalent rejected readings each flagged by a neat letter—testify to a variety greater than the number of all surviving copies (since each copy embeds a usually indeterminate number of prior archetypes). Such variety does not clearly signal the apparent equivalents of our collations, but noncommensurate situations, substantially different social sitings: autographs, supervised copies, patronal/coterie copies, copies from bespoke (dispersed patronal) situations. Manuscript versions of a work do not, as their uniform sigil status suggests, provide equivalent information, but information reflective of different historical and potentially historicizable situations. Or in editorial terms, 'authority' is quite intentionally dispersed in unique ways, most of the time not the property of an individual we identify as the literary workman today: variation does not simply inhere naturally in a literary text *per se* (as is the case with print compositors ostensibly engaged in accurate *ad litteram* reproduction) but is also the product of work done under a specific mode of production, a set of material circumstances, a specific confluence between a piece of writing, a patron, and a variety of manual tasks.

Viewed in these terms, 'the editorial issue' should become: what varieties of mediation can modern textual consumption allow so as to address its public constituency, with its desire to canonize medieval works in forms consonant with those customary for presenting 'modern scripture' while still remaining in palpable contact with the extraordinary evidential plurality of manuscript culture? Most modern readers require the singularity of A Text and, indeed, as I've noted elsewhere, canonicity in some measure demands one.[35] But the manuscript situation in an equally absolute way requires some greater access to 'the evidence' than standard formats based on collation forms derived from print-books allows: the text is only a series of human products, every bit as mediated in their own differing ways as the standard modern edition, each historically situated and incapable of being understood outside that situation.

---

35. See 'Presenting Chaucer as Author', in Tim William Machan (ed.), *Medieval Literature, Texts and Interpretation* (Binghamton, NY, 1991), pp. 17–39.

One can thus visualize, not An Edition, but a range of use- or interest-driven possible editions. Such plurality becomes justified because it will approximate, through diversity of approach and method, that plurality which is a property of its subject, texts in manuscript. And such plurality will prove especially helpful for manuscript works which have been produced through active bespoke assimilations. In such cases, the uses to which medieval patrons have wished to subject a work usually have been denatured by the modern desire for a single text. Two typical situations might suggest potential options open to future editors.

One neat example typifies what is often perceived as the 'uneditability' of medieval romance, but a feature in fact endemic to a variety of manuscript versions of a great many texts (e.g. work of the producers of London, British Library, MS Arundel 286, a collection of religious tracts in prose). In the well-known version of *Sir Orfeo* in British Library, MS Harley 3810,[36] the producers of two small loose quires objected to what modern readers of the poem (always read in the form of the Auchinleck manuscript) have seen as one of its brilliances—its insistence, not simply on Orfeo's ability to retrieve his wife from faeryland, but also on the fidelity he has inspired in his steward. This latter material the Harley manuscript simply excises; it thus presents a work radically different from that customarily read. Such a work deserves, indeed requires for any appreciation, a presentation outside a standard collation format; a text parallel to that of Auchinleck is the only ready solution. Yet simultaneously one must recognize that many Harley lines are functionally equivalent to those of Auchinleck, although they obviously include variations. These might well, whatever the form of presentation, deserve some deeper interrogation than the term 'variant'

---

36. Best seen in A. J. Bliss (ed)., *Sir Orfeo* (2nd edn.; London, 1966), an edition which gives the most useful way for handling this text (and that here seconded) but which is objectionable on other grounds hinted in my paragraph's closing queries. Cf. the thoroughly inadequate statements motivating Bliss's textual presentation on pp. xv–xvii. Cf. Derek Pearsall's discussion of the paradox that 'the manuscript the editor must reject is always the most interesting', in 'Texts, Textual Criticism, and Fifteenth Century Manuscript Production', in Robert F. Yeager (ed.), *Fifteenth-Century Studies* (Hamden, 1984), pp. 121–36, at p. 128.

implies: to what extent do these record motivated support for a patron's decisions about the kind of poem the Harley *Orfeo* was designed to be?[37] To what extent do they in fact retain, at a very great temporal remove, readings not transmitted by the Auchinleck team and putatively part of its archetype?

A second and similar situation concerns intertextuality. Modern critical editions always reify separate works. In doing so, they divorce their chosen works utterly from manuscript context and thus fail to see that the motivated desires of medieval patrons, rather than some internal literary or scribal dynamics, may exercise a determining factor upon the form a text can take. For example, modern medievalists know *The Siege of Jerusalem* only in the isolated canonical form enshrined in Kölbing and Day's edition (E.E.T.S. 188). But in fact, no known medieval reading of *The Siege* was devoid of contextualizing gestures (and ones very different from the modern print in its binding standardized to fit within an extensive series of volumes): the work never occurs alone in manuscript.

Moreover, the manuscript versions display highly individualistic contextual determinants quite foreign to the modern scholarly sense that the work participates in a single canon (alliterative poetry). Some copies, e.g. Oxford, Bodleian Library, MS Laud Misc. 656; Princeton University Library, Taylor MS; London, Lambeth Palace, MS 491; present *The Siege* in a context where it should read as a quasi-Scriptural narrative, a pendant to the Passion (a reading which accords with one of author's sources, a *Vindicta salvatoris* derivative). Another, the second booklet of Robert Thornton's British Library, MS Additional 31042, combines this interest with one in specifically crusader poetry. Another associates *The Siege* with romance (British Library, MS Cotton Caligula A.ii). And Cambridge, University Library, MS Mm.v.12 apparently takes

---

37. I thus, in passing, reject the contention that objectivity has any role to play in the editorial process: editors must know in absolute thoroughness what their texts mean literarily, and the only 'editorial' situation in which this is not desirable, diplomatic, is no more than transcription.

the poem as learned classical history, a story of Roman conquest (a reading in accord with other sources of the work, the *Polychronicon* and Josephus's *Bellum Iudaicum*). To what extent in any copy does such generic placement motivate variation? And to what extent does it change what *The Siege* 'is'?[38]

One can thus conceive of another type of edition, designed to highlight intertextual connections. Such a volume might present a coherent group of works (for example, the contents of a single 'booklet') or all the works found in a particular codex. Although the texts presented might well stop short of full critical apparatus—perhaps a corrected transcript only—the highlighting of the intertextual collocations should demand comparative work. Only thus can one demonstrate the specific historical (in this case medieval) mediations at work in tailoring the group of texts for presentation to the patron who has commissioned the volume. And only thus can one have any idea of whether there is such a concept as an 'individual scribe's copying practice'.[39]

But among such endeavours, the critical edition or something that does the same work seems to me an indispensible center and grounding. Suppose one contends that only objectively correctible errors deserve emendation and that such variation is trivial and uninteresting (essentially

38. And what of the one truly aberrant text, Huntington Library, MS HM 128, like Harley 3810 redacted, but in this case on a painstaking line-by-line basis in a manuscript characterized by elaborate editorial correction? See George Kane in John A. Alford (ed.), *A Companion to 'Piers Plowman'* (Berkeley, 1988), p. 187; quite typically of single work-centered editorial concerns, Kane shuts the scribal handling in one portion of the manuscript off from that in another and has not examined this text of *The Siege* (admittedly not the work of the *Piers Plowman* scribes). He thus may not offer the final word on such activities. Instructively, of witnesses to *The Siege*, only the Caligula manuscript has really been perceived as aberrant—and that because of difficult stemmatic affiliations: in fact, strikingly in a text collected as a romance, the patron responsible for this manuscript appears to have decided, after copying had already begun, to strive for an accurate text and, for the duration, to have allowed producers line-by-line choice between the 'best readings' offered by two sources.

39. Cf. the variety of studies of Robert Thornton's scribal behaviour which centre on *Morte Arthure* and ignore the kind of comparative evidence illustrated in Hoyt N. Duggan, 'Alliterative Patterning as a Basis for Emendation in Middle English Alliterative Poetry', *SAC* 8 (1986): 73–105.

senseless *lapsus calami*).[40] Such a view raises, implicitly, the problem of purposeful and interesting variation. But in so doing, it evokes a task which only a critically conceived edition can perform. Essentially, one knows variation only on the basis of a transmission history: while 'variation' need not imply some positive pole, as 'error' surely does, it does imply some standard of comparison from which difference is perceptible, a Read Text.[41] Thus, the most provocative suggestions for the use of single manuscripts, whether from the point of view of a 'scribal literary criticism'[42] or of 'authorial recomposition and revision', always presuppose the basic tasks of editing. For one cannot distinguish 'intelligent, meddling, and improving scribes' without some knowledge of their archetypes, without in fact full collation and construction of a stemma. For only through such means might one decide that such variation constituted a motivated commentary, what we would call 'criticism'. And similarly, discussions of authorial activities require some traditional editorial consideration of manuscript variation, some theorization which might distinguish the 'authorial' from any other evidence which a manu-

40. Kane's introduction to *'Piers Plowman': The A Version,* esp. pp. 115–63, probably demolishes this point of view by argumentative action. For, as described there, Kane's development of *durior lectio* as an editorial technique began when he considered what appeared palpable errors—unique variants in a poem of wide dispersal. Ultimately, Kane could find such readings pellucidly erroneous only through a consideration of their genesis, through an effort to explain their occurrence.

41. A lesson from the practice of deconstruction, which constantly must presuppose and then construct an Ur-text before it can find an intention which it can show to be vitiated by the activities of language languaging. But this is a lesson only: as those who have read deconstructive criticism will note, my subsequent move validates work and human intentions, not the domain of the linguistic.

42. The quotation-marks in this paragraph surround phrases I have lifted from my notes to a presentation by Derek Pearsall at the University of California, Los Angeles, 17 May 1991. Pearsall, of course, in many ways animates my discussion every bit as much as do Kane and Donaldson: his insistence upon the importance of manuscripts and their textual versions, delivered in a series of papers over more than a decade, has stimulated a new palaeography/philology now disciplinarily central. For Pearsall's most recent essays in this regard, see his review of the Brewer facsimile, *The Vernon Manuscript*, in *Speculum* 65 (1990): 773–74; and the volume of essays on that codex which he edited, *Studies in the Vernon Manuscript* (Cambridge, 1990). On scribal criticism, see Barry Windeatt, 'The Scribes as Chaucer's Early Critics', *SAC* 1 (1979): 119–41.

script provides. But, sticking to the situation of the single work, in these terms, to be of interest, variation must be variation *from* and minimally implies the full history, so far as it is recoverable, of a text's distribution.

A wide range of works exist as models for such an endeavor at recording textual histories. They would include such editorial efforts as Root's or Windeatt's *Troilus*, Kane's *'Piers Plowman': The A Version* and Kane-Donaldson's *'Piers Plowman': The B Version*, Manly-Rickert's *Canterbury Tales*, Kölbing-Day's *Siege of Jerusalem*. I would contend that the term 'critical' which defines such works describes, not a technique of textual handling, but something more important, a quality of scrutiny. And it is such scrutiny, the product of judgement and not of facticity, which validates the procedures and insures the usefulness of such editions, however various these may be. Although editors always deal with an oppressive mass of detail, and must deal with it on detail-by-detail basis, what is more important than local choices is the open presentation of the process of choice itself, the degree of reasoned explanatory detail the editor offers.[43]

Such scrutiny and openness reveals itself in what can be seen as common to these works, those features which make critical editions repositories of information central to the discussion of any medieval work. I would identify in these treatments four common features. First, fundamental to them all is full evidentiary display: all of them provide full collations of the relevant materials.[44] In doing so, they open for inspection the basis for any other work they have done, as well as at least suggesting to others, within what I have already described as the overly constrained limits of substantive citation, kinds of work which might need to be done. The collations, for example, make it possible to identify patronally

43. This seems to me an area in which Kane-Donaldson's *'Piers Plowman': The B Version* might most strongly be faulted, both because of its dispersal of explanation and of its collation—which does not provide the information often most relevant to the B text as printed, readings, not of individual B manuscripts, but of *Piers* A, C, and AC.

44. Root's edition proper does not actually fill this requirement, but he had discussed virtually all agreements of two texts in error quite extensively elsewhere; see *The Textual Tradition of Chaucer's 'Troilus'* (Chaucer Soc. 1st ser. 99).

assimilated textual forms requiring fuller treatment, perhaps only in other contexts, and to establish new tasks for readers.

Secondly, in none of these volumes does the evidentiary display stand without some critique. All such volumes—Manly-Rickert perhaps most notoriously—contain quite elaborate (but never, as I have argued above, quite elaborate enough) descriptions of the available witnesses and such information as can be gleaned of their history and provenance. More importantly, all contain some extensive analysis of what the recorded evidence demonstrates to have been the historical generation of the text. Every edition offers evidence toward the construction of a *stemma codicum*, an identification, at the minimum, of manuscript relations and of copies which share the same archetype. This is true even of Kane-Donaldson's *'Piers Plowman': The B Version*, although the editors trenchantly dispute the value of a *stemma* every step of the way.[45]

As I indicate earlier, most of these efforts at genetic analysis for me stop too soon. While I concur with Kane-Donaldson that no constructed *stemma* can edit a text, no other method provides a way to historicize textual generation and to link this behaviour to specific human work. And Kane-Donaldson's total rejection of the value of attestation—the stemmatic discovery that multitudinous shared readings may represent in the last analysis only a single, historicizable production decision—seems to me less than compelling. Not only do they reject as impossible any historically plausible construction of the evidence by attending to potential vertical descent of readings, but they surrender any interest in the historical development of the text and thus tend to remove it from history altogether.

Thirdly, all the critical editions I outline share a norm of textual presentation. They are fundamentally editions predicated on the rule of 'copy-text'. Each chooses, often with an elaborate rationale for so doing, a single textual version designed to provide the format in which the text

45. See *'Piers Plowman'; The B Version*, pp. 17–20; the rejection of attestation I mention in the next paragraph occurs at p. 63.

will be consumed, often a format chosen to accord with some specific authorial norm.[46]

The choice of copy-text presentation is intimately linked to the fourth feature all critical editions share—the practice of intervention into the text. Following 'the rule of copy-text' as it has been conceived since Greg, the editors all view the forms of the presented textual basis only as forms ('accidentals') and not as universally sacrosanct. As a corollary to whatever historical interest the editions show, their editors presume the recuperability of history, the possibility of explanation (although the varying terms in which they conceive this task clearly render this a highly contentious topic), and they universally choose to mark the text itself with such explanations. Thus, all the editors conceive their tasks as explanatory and include, in either introductions or textual notes, often elaborate discussions of the generation of individual lemmata, in some cases centers of intervention, in others not.[47]

The fundamental issue here seems to me not the degree to which intervention occurs—if it occurs at all, the text has already been irradiated with modern mediations[48]—but the editor's theorization of mediation. Following my previous analysis, I perceive what occurs in such editions as an effort to privilege some moment in the ongoing historical

46. See further the important recent discussion by D.C. Greetham, 'The Place of Fredson Bowers in Mediaeval Editing', *PBSA* 82 (1988): 53–69.

47. Greg's rule of copy-text (see note 8 above) should govern what is printed, with irresolvable base readings retained (cf. Kane, *'Piers Plowman': The A Version*, pp. 147, and 441 [5.69n], 448 [7.160n], 449 [7.231n]). The term 'irresolvable', however, is again a contentious one, as responses to Kane-Donaldson's *'Piers Plowman': The B Version* would indicate (and cf. *'Piers Plowman': The A Version*, pp. 148, 152–54).

48. The possibility of some unmediated contact with The Medieval seems to me a foolish nostalgia and longing for what cannot be attained; cf. Louise O. Fradenburg, ' "Voice Memorial": Loss and Reparation in Chaucer's Poetry', *Exemplaria* 2, i (Spring 1990): 169–202, esp. pp. 172–77. Further, the notion that a manuscript provides some unmediated contact is, as I have suggested in my *Polychronicon* narrative above, quite simply unsustainable. And the claim that a facsimile or diplomatic presentation allows such direct contact with the past ignores rather different mediations—a facsimile does not mean in modern book culture what the manuscript would have meant in fifteenth-century book culture, for example.

process which has produced the extant witnesses; once such a privileged moment is identified, the edition may be given over to constructing the text as it existed at that moment and other editorial choices will follow with utter inevitability. Thus the form and extent of intervention actually follows from a prior, frequently untheorized, decision.

In the critical editions I have mentioned, two moments of privilege have canonical status. Manly-Rickert represent one of these decisions well: the editors identify the object to be privileged as O^1, 'the archetype of all surviving manuscripts', the scribal copy which has generated all the surviving evidence. This decision commits Manly-Rickert to intervention in a copy-text, but in virtually all cases to choice among and emendation from readings within the recorded tradition; conjecture has no place in the edition proper (but frequently appears in textual notes where the editors acknowledge dissatisfaction with the text they print). Nonetheless, the procedure rests on judgement, not some transcendent objectivity, and is subjected to elaborate explanatory annotation in the textual notes.

In contrast, Kane-Donaldson (like Root and, implicitly, the laconic Kölbing-Day *Siege*) identify the privileged textual moment as O, the author's holograph manuscript.[49] Their procedure is thus fully interventionist. While not inherently or necessarily more searching than the activity by which any editor strives to reconstruct an archetype (although more so in actual practice), Kane-Donaldson willingly interrogate, seek to explain, and remove (often through conjecture) a variety of widely attested readings. Although these may be archetypal, the goal of the edition is to pass beyond that stage of transmission, and the editors thus have no qualms about rejecting the totality of the visible evidence. But again, although Kane-Donaldson's explanation is dispersed, their edition displays a persistent effort at explaining the textual history of the B text of *Piers Plowman*, usually on a lemma by lemma basis.

---

49. Kane's *'Piers Plowman': The A Version*, so far as I can ascertain, is, like the Manly-Rickert *Canterbury Tales*, an O^1 text; see, for example, the fragmentary form in which Kane prints A 7.5 and his explanatory note, p. 446.

A final form of critical presentation, which I would call 'responsible best textism', has yet to be attempted but deserves consideration. Such an alternative has at least entered the editorial conversation of medievalists, if only as a recognition of Manly-Rickert's implicit best-textism, their edition's overreliance on the Hengwrt manuscript of Chaucer's *Canterbury Tales*. Such a view would privilege the best example of the extant manuscript tradition.[50] But in doing so, it would have to examine its preconceptions, to lay bare for readers the logic (and limits) of its designation 'best', and to perform various steps in order to achieve the same variety of display and scrutiny which other modes of critical edition routinely offer. Specifically, such an edition would have explicitly to recognize (a) that a best manuscript is, by definition, not a perfect one and thus always potentially open to intervention; (b) (a restatement) that a manuscript is best in aggregate and never clearly so in any individual reading; and (c) that 'best' is a judgement made on quality of readings and that that claim must be re-enunciated for every lemma through an explanation which demonstrates the adequacy of this manuscript within the context of the historical development indicated by remaining copies. To expand upon category (c): such an edition must include copious analytical notes which explain the retention of contested lemmata as a plausible state of the evidence, for the concept of 'best text in aggregate' adds a further restraint to that initially imposed by copy-text editing.[51]

While I expend much time on its properties, I see the 'critical edition' as only one among a range of options. The notion of 'edition' could well gain from a particularly medieval polysemousness and take considerably

50. The Oklahoma Chaucer Variorum perhaps attempts to actualize such principles, but to my mind is not a responsible endeavour—it falls under the strictures I implicitly place upon that oxymoronic beast 'best diplomatic edition' in note 37 above: a mindless defense of a single version through thick and thin—usually thin in major controversial readings. See further my discussion. 'The Chaucer Variorum', *Analytical and Enumerative Bibliography* 8 (1984): 184–97.

51. One can imagine alternative editions of the same general stripe, subject to the same constraints; e.g. an oldest text edition; or a socially central text edition (perhaps a version of the intertextual edition I discuss above).

greater advantage of the plurality of the recorded evidence. I have tried
to indicate some possible range of productive situations from which
Middle English works enter our ken, and I see no reason why editors
cannot be interested in all of them, so long as they remain aware which
they are dealing with and how. In particular, I remain open to variant
texts as objects of editorial inquiry, an inquiry in the service of literary
history.

This is so, because we medievalists know comparatively little about
the literary history of our period, and because nearly all we are going to
discover will be from the bearers of texts, books themselves, which consequently we cannot afford to leave merely as errors already rejected.
Texts most editors would frankly want to suppress from a 'critical
edition' point of view have immense interest as objects of *Rezeptionsäs-
thetik*. Similarly, as someone who has developed a penchant for dis-
membering manuscript production procedures, I remain fascinated by
the power of the codex to generate meaning: many late medieval book-
producers create highly idiosyncratic individual canons and, in effect,
'read' their texts as they insert them into developing volumes.[52] Further,
the effects of codicological aesthetics have scarcely been considered:
medieval book-producers, in every case, had to devise a format in order
to present a text, had to plan out a *mise en page*, an apparatus, a decorative
system. These choices, again, provide particularly provocative 'readings'.
And finally, even fields with such modest claims as dialectology and traditional palaeography provide vital information: they ground individual
books in time and space, offer data useful in creating networks of literary
relationship.

Thus, as an editor, I finally situate myself as a historically-bound
medium for historical understanding. Editions exist, not simply as vehicles for modern hegemonic usages, but precisely as always mediated

---

52. See in this regard my essays 'Booklets in Medieval Manuscripts: Further Considera-
tions', *SB* 39 (1986): 100–11; and 'The Origins and Production of Westminster School
MS 3', *SB* 41 (1988): 197–218; and the very provocative comments in Griffiths-Pearsall,
Book Production, pp. 302 (Julia Boffey and John Thompson) and pp. 324–26 (Vincent
Gillespie).

activities of historical construction. Such construction has about it very little which is objective, and it needs to be equally aware that its documentary resources probably lack that objectivity as well. The various moves of my paper are designed to construct a theoretical context in which to discuss such issues, to illustrate simple—and apparently for medievalists, troubling—dicta: that editing texts is a concern in all domains of literary study, that it is a major feature of post-Renaissance cultural practice (and undissociable from that practice), and that an editor's medium is precisely and only consciousness. To expand upon the last: editors need to come to awareness of those forces which impell their activity (and which are never just the pristine mediation of data) and to recognize that their effort is to comprehend those past forms of consciousness which have provided the opportunity to read the past.[53]

53. I owe particular thanks to Tim William Machan for allowing me to read a rather different version of these ideas—entitled 'The Mark of Kane(-Donaldson): Textual Criticism in Disarray' at a session he organized for the Medieval Academy of America, Madison, 14 April 1989; and to David Lawton, for customarily trenchant comments on a somewhat different draft version.

Texts in Search of an Editor: Reflections on *The Frankenstein Notebooks* and on Editorial Authority†

Charles E. Robinson

Every novel exists in a plurality of texts, and none dramatizes this fact more than Mary Shelley's *Frankenstein*, the Draft and Fair-Copy Notebooks of which I have recently edited for Garland Press.[1] My editorial labors on this famous novel have made me painfully aware of how it developed through its various texts, from its original conception on ?17 June 1816 through its gestation, quickening, lightening, birth, and development into the novel (or novels) that so many of us now read. I here take the liberty of applying a creative metaphor to describe this developmental process because the novel itself concerns creativity and because both Mary Shelley and her persona Robert Walton took nine months to write their narratives: Robert Walton wrote his series of letters and journals over a period of 276 days between 11 December 17[96] and 12 September 17[97]; and, although Mary Shelley took eleven months between conceiving the story and finishing the Fair Copy (?17 June 1816 through 10/13 May 1817), it appears that the first two months were spent in writing the ur-text of the novel and that

† "Texts in Search of an Editor: Reflections on *The Frankenstein Notebooks* and on Editorial Authority," from *Textual Studies and the Common Reader: Essays on Editing Novels and Novelists*, ed. Alexander Pettit (Athens, GA: University of Georgia Press, 2000), pp. 91–110. Reprinted by permission of the University of Georgia Press.

1. *The Frankenstein Notebooks: A Facsimile of Mary Shelley's Manuscript Novel, 1816–17 (with alterations in the hand of Percy Bysshe Shelley) as it survives in Draft and Fair Copy deposited by Lord Abinger in the Bodleian Library, Oxford (Dep. c. 477/1 and Dep. c. 534/1–2)*, ed. Charles E. Robinson, parts 1 and 2 (New York: Garland, 1996); hereafter cited as *1816–17 Robinson.*

she therefore devoted the next nine months to expanding, drafting, and fair-copying her novel. What happened in the novel, therefore, can be seen to parallel or "figure" what happened outside of the novel.[2]

It would be fair to say further that Walton's writing *in* the novel and Mary Shelley's writing *of* the novel are also "figured" by the creative work of Victor Frankenstein himself. Victor's assembling of disparate body parts into his monster is not that different from Walton's assembling his discrete notes about Victor into a narrative; and both these creative acts may be compared to Mary Shelley's esemplastic fusing of words and images and symbols and punctuation into the text of her novel. Mary Shelley herself encouraged this kind of comparison when she bade her novel, her "hideous progeny," to "go forth and prosper," suggesting that her monster was a metaphor for her novel and that both creations would be altered by their experiences in the world.[3] Because of these alterations, it would also be fair to say that the monster and the text were not only "authored" but also "edited"—both words in their etymologies denote a bringing forth, a giving birth to something new.

If we pursue the editing metaphor further, we encounter another collaborator who assisted in the development of *Frankenstein*, namely, the midwife Percy Bysshe Shelley who helped bring Mary Shelley's novel to its full term and then helped present it to an audience on publication day, 1 January 1818. This assistance, as evidenced by his no fewer than 4,000 words in this 72,000-word novel, resulted from his correcting and augmenting portions of the Draft and the Fair Copy (and the proofs and the revises) of the novel. The nature of his editorial labors, which are made manifest in my edition of *The Frankenstein Notebooks*, will be briefly discussed below, but for the moment I wish to draw one more parallel

2. It can even be argued that Walton's dates of writing from 11 December 17[96] to 12 September 17[97] (the years arrived at with the help of a perpetual calendar) are very close to the dates when Mary Shelley was conceived and born; see *1816–17 Robinson*, 1:lxv–lxvi and nn.

3. [Mary W. Shelley], *Frankenstein: or, The Modern Prometheus*, rev. ed. (London: Henry Colburn and Richard Bentley, 1831), xii; hereafter cited as *1831*. Other editions will be similarly cited in this essay: thus, for example, *1818* provides a shorthand for *Frankenstein; or, The Modern Prometheus*, 3 vols. (London: Lackington, Hughes, Harding, Mavor & Jones, 1818).

between the actions inside and outside the novel: what Percy Shelley did to (or for) the novel is "figured" by both Walton and Victor Frankenstein serving as editors of each other's narratives. Indeed, the more we look at the novel, the more we are led to the conclusion that *Frankenstein* is a series of texts in search of an editor, one who will ultimately give form and shape to the novel.

Frankenstein is a frame tale and, as such, is very much about the question of authorial and editorial control. That is, the device of a frame tale enabled Mary Shelley to write as if she were Robert Walton writing the narrative of Victor Frankenstein, in which was embedded the story of the monster who recounted not only his adventures but also those of the De Laceys and the Arabian Safie. These interlocked narratives seem to make Mary Shelley's the dominant voice until we realize that Walton is her persona, and it is his voice we hear. After explaining to his sister Margaret that Victor "would commence his narrative the next day" on 20 August 17[97], Walton described how he would serve as both amanuensis and editor for Victor's words:

> I have resolved every night, when I am not engaged, to record, as nearly as possible in his own words, what he has related during the day. If I should be engaged, I will at least make notes. This manuscript will doubtless afford you the greatest pleasure: but to me, who know him, and who hear it from his own lips, with what interest and sympathy shall I read it in some future day! (*1818*, 1:37–38)

We as readers, of course, are the ones who are destined for the "greatest pleasure" if, like Margaret, we read Victor's narration as edited by Walton. But was Walton the editor who brought forth Victor's tale? It is equally valid to argue that Victor Frankenstein edited the "notes" that Walton made about Victor's history of Victor:

> Frankenstein discovered that I made notes concerning his history: he asked to see them, and then himself corrected and augmented them in many places; but principally in giving the life and spirit to the conversations he held with his enemy. "Since you have preserved my

narration," said he, "I would not that a mutilated one should go down to posterity." (*1818*, 3:157)

Victor, it seems, expressed greater concern for his text than he did for his monster. And although it appears that Victor had the last word in his own novel about himself, it was Walton who ultimately voiced Victor's concern for editorial authority. If, however, we privilege author over character and claim that Mary Shelley was the ultimate authority here, the manuscript versions of this passage reveal that Mary Shelley miscopied a phrase when she transcribed the Draft into the Fair Copy and that the error required a later correction by a hand that seems different from that of either of the Shelleys.[4]

The question of editorial authority in this novel gets even more complex if we ask in what form we read Victor's story as edited by Walton edited by Victor edited by Walton—because the question of form potentially introduces yet another collaborator in the editorial process. Do we read the manuscript written out by Walton for Margaret's eyes only—or do we read a version of that manuscript that his sister Margaret received and then edited for the press? Mary Shelley provides no answer to this question, but in either case Margaret acts as a surrogate for the reader. But is Margaret Walton Saville a surrogate only for the reader— or do her initials, MWS, force us to read her as a surrogate for Mary Wollstonecraft Shelley? If these initials are purposeful, then we have a novel written by MWS as if she were Walton writing to MWS—and the silent MWS stands in the corner of this narrative, teasing us to see her as both author and reader (and author and editor) of her own work.

If the questions of editorial authority inside the novel tease us out of thought, even more complex and teasing questions await us outside the novel as we encounter no fewer than ten texts that go into the making of *Frankenstein*, texts that have been edited by Mary Shelley herself (more than once), Percy Shelley (more than once), William Godwin, various publishers' readers and printers, and then the long list of nineteenth- and

---

4. See *1816–17 Robinson*, 2:606–7, 2:736–37, 2:806.

twentieth-century scholars who have printed and edited and otherwise disseminated the novel to millions of readers, each of whom may be said to "edit" the text while assembling and re-assembling the ideas, words, and punctuation that make up the spirit and matter of the thing we call a novel (which exists, as Percy Shelley would have it, only as it is perceived by the reader).[5] When I was invited to join this editorial procession, I anticipated doing little more than creating a useful "diplomatic" edition of *The Frankenstein Notebooks*, one that would faithfully represent the text of the extant Draft and Fair Copy by reproducing photographs of the manuscript pages, each of which would be faced by a type facsimile of the manuscript of that page. I was familiar with Mary Shelley's hand, having published a similar albeit simpler edition of the Fair Copies of her mythological dramas *Proserpine* and *Midas*,[6] I could recognize Percy Shelley's hand in the manuscript, and I planned somehow to distinguish his hand from that of Mary Shelley. In short, I would serve the scholarly community by bringing empirical and hard evidence into the various debates on Mary Shelley's most famous novel. What I did not anticipate was how much the editing of these Notebooks would force me to contextualize the extant manuscripts by reference to other manuscripts, proofs, revises, printed texts, and editions of *Frankenstein*.

My first step down that road of contextualization resulted from three circumstances that determined the character of my edition: a Garland policy (worked out in collaboration with Donald H. Reiman and the Bodleian Library) to reproduce in photofacsimile all extant manuscript pages, each of which would be faced by a type facsimile of the manuscript; a set of *Frankenstein* manuscripts in which Mary Shelley wrote fewer than ten words in each line; and Garland's predetermined nine-by-

5. Percy Shelley more than once remarked that "all things exist as they are perceived"; see, for example, "A Defence of Poetry," in *Shelley's Poetry and Prose: Authoritative Texts, Criticism*, ed. Donald H. Reiman and Sharon B. Powers (New York: Norton, 1977), 505; see also "nothing exists but as it is perceived" (Percy Shelley, "On Life," in *Shelley's Poetry and Prose*, 476).

6. Mary Shelley, *Mythological Dramas: Proserpine and Midas, Bodleian* MS. *Shelley d.* 2, ed. Charles E. Robinson (New York: Garland, 1992).

twelve-inch format that enabled me to print on each recto not only the type facsimile of the manuscript (with different fonts to distinguish Mary Shelley's hand from Percy Shelley's) but also, in tandem with the manuscript, a literal transcript of the 1818 first edition (all glossed by footnotes at the bottom of each page).[7] On one page, the reader could see what Mary Shelley originally wrote, then what she and Percy Shelley corrected, then what was printed a few months later, and finally the footnotes that addressed not only anomalies in the manuscript but also errors in the text of *1818*. These anomalies and errors forced me to extend my study of the transmission of the text in two directions: backward from *1818* through revises and proofs and Fair Copy and Draft to the ur-text that I hypothetically reconstructed; and forward from the first edition of 1818 through to the third and revised edition of 1831 (and also through to some recent critical editions of the novel). New discoveries about the meaning and form of the novel awaited me at every step in this sequence of texts, the interrelations of which I have discussed in the introduction, chronology, and footnotes in *The Frankenstein Notebooks*. Here, however, I will rely on the following outline to indicate how one text leads directly to another between the years of 1816 and 1831. The two exceptions to this direct sequence are *1818 Thomas* and [*1826*], both of which have been indented to allow the stemma arrows to pass by them.

THE TEXTS OF *FRANKENSTEIN*

1816 **Ur-text:** A novella-length narrative written between ?17 June and
        ?August 1816—not extant: certainly in the hand of Mary Shelley, but no
↓   evidence one way or the other of Percy Shelley's direct involvement.

1816–17 **Draft:** A two-volume novel in two hard-cover notebooks written
        between ?August 1816 and 17 April 1817—most of the now disbound
        Notebooks A and B survive in 152 leaves (with text on 301 pages)
        together with three insert leaves and two insert slips (with text on a total
        of eight pages), all of which are reproduced in *The Frankenstein Notebooks*

---

7. The terms "photofacsimile," "type facsimile," and "literal transcript" are adapted from D. C. Greetham, *Textual Scholarship: An Introduction* (New York: Garland, 1994), 350.

and account for approximately 87 percent of the *1818* text: in the hand of
↓   Mary Shelley, with alterations in the hand of Percy Shelley.

1817 **Fair Copy:** A three-volume novel in ?eleven soft-cover notebooks written between 18 April and 10/13 May 1817—parts of now disbound
Notebooks c1 and c2 survive in twenty-nine leaves (with text on fifty-
eight pages) together with one insert leaf (with text on one page) as well
as one substitute leaf (with text on two pages), all of which are reproduced in *The Frankenstein Notebooks* and contain approximately 12 percent of the *1818* text: in the hand of Mary Shelley, with the last twelve
and three-quarters pages of Notebook c2 in the hand of Percy Shelley.
There is additional evidence that Percy Shelley corrected other parts of
↓   the Fair Copy.

Proofs: A three-volume novel issued between ?23 September and ?3 November
1817—not extant, but there is evidence that both Shelleys read and corrected the proofs and that Mary and/or Percy made three major additions
↓   to the text, one in September and two in October.

Revises: Three or more sheets of revised proofs printed between ?23 September and ?20 November 1817—not extant, but the three major additions
to the proofs would certainly have resulted in revises that Mary and/or
↓   Percy Shelley would have read.

1818: A three-volume novel (1st ed.) published anonymously on 1 January
1818 in 500 copies by Lackington, Hughes, Harding, Mavor, & Jones.

    1818 Thomas: Copy of first edition (*1818*) corrected by Mary Shel-
ley and given to a Mrs. Thomas in Genoa by July 1823—survives at the
↓   Pierpont Morgan Library in New York City.

1823: A two-volume novel (2nd ed.) published on 11 August 1823 in an
unknown number of copies by G. and W. B. Whittaker (set from *1818*
rather than from *1818 Thomas*)—William Godwin rather than Mary
Shelley made the arrangements for this edition, the copy-text for which
would have been either *1818* or a proof copy that Godwin may have
possessed. Godwin, it appears, was the one responsible for the 123 substantive variants introduced into this edition, almost all of which were
carried over to *1831*, suggesting that *1823* was used as the copy-text for
1831 and that Mary Shelley no longer possessed a copy of *1818* to use
for this purpose.

    [*1826*]: [?Re-issue of 2nd ed. (*1823*)] "published" on 4 April 1826 by
Henry Colburn. Because no copy of an *1826* edition has ever been
located or described, Colburn appears to have purchased and offered for
sale the unsold sheets of *1823* without printing a new title page, but no
collation of multiple copies of *1823* has been done to determine if there
↓   was in fact a distinct *1826* re-issue of *1823*.

1831: A one-volume novel (3rd or revised ed.) published on 31 October 1831 in 4,020 stereotyped copies by Henry Colburn and Richard Bentley in the "Standard Novels" series: Mary Shelley was responsible for the substantial changes made to the text, and she apparently used *1823* as copy-text.

This brief outline of the texts of *Frankenstein* should suggest that there were at least three major editorial hands (of the two Shelleys and of Godwin) in the versioning of the novel between the time it was "finished" and fair-copied for the publisher and printer in April/May 1817 and the time it was revised in 1831; this of course does not count the publishers and their readers, or the printers and their compositors, who also exercised some influence on the text. A glance at the extant Fair Copy (which was also printer's copy), for example, will show that more than one unidentified hand made small alterations to the text that had been transcribed by Mary and Percy Shelley.

All these interventions should help to dispel the still-persistent myth of the solitary artist who has total control over a text. Granted, Mary Shelley was responsible for the novel's first words ("It was on a dreary night of November . . ."; see *1831*, xi), and she apparently had the last word when she prepared her revised edition of *1831*—or did she? Wherein lies governance of her text? In 1816, she ruled the margins of Notebook A only to allow her husband-to-be to make alterations, and in 1816 and 1817, Percy Shelley did in fact read, edit, and alter the text in both Draft Notebooks. In April and May 1817, Mary Shelley accepted most of his alterations when she transcribed the Draft into the Fair Copy; and in May 1817, Percy Shelley further changed the text when he fair-copied the last few pages of the novel, and Mary shortly thereafter recopied his transcription and retained nearly all his embellishments. In September 1817, she gave Percy "carte blanche" to make alterations to at least one section of the proofs,[8] and in late October 1817, not long before the novel was published on 1 January 1818, he was probably responsible

8. *The Letters of Mary Wollstonecraft Shelley*, ed. Betty T. Bennett, 3 vols. (Baltimore: Johns Hopkins University Press, 1980–88), 1:42.

for one of two major additions to the text. Mary Shelley herself was involved in editing her own prose during all this time, and then a year later in December 1818 she began to correct a copy of *1818*, but we are uncertain whether those corrections actually survived. In all likelihood, however, the copy corrected was the one given to Mrs. Thomas in 1823. Although we have the benefit of the editorial changes in *1818 Thomas*, they do not seem to have affected the received text, for Mary Shelley apparently did not keep a copy of these corrections. Then in the summer of 1823, Mary Shelley's father William Godwin introduced new words into the text of *1823*. Finally, in 1831, Mary Shelley redacted *1823* into *1831*, a text that is substantially different from *1818*.

And then came the scores of "professional" editors who looked back and woefully simplified (or willfully ignored) the textual history of the novel by first privileging *1831*, the text that was reprinted in most editions of the novel until James Rieger's groundbreaking edition of *1818* that not only printed the holograph corrections and additions that Mary Shelley made in *1818 Thomas* but also collated *1818* with *1831*.[9] Mary Shelley scholarship was revolutionized by that edition, for it gave evidence of an artist at work: the "Thomas" corrections showed the care that Mary Shelley took with her prose, and the collations with *1831* (all in one fell swoop in an appendix) demonstrated that she was interested in further emphasizing character and theme. Until now, however, the critical debate has focused primarily on the two published texts, *1818* and *1831*. Now, with the evidence and the arguments made available by *The Frankenstein Notebooks*, other aspects of Mary Shelley's artistry can be studied—particularly the ways in which she expanded one text into another.

---

9. Mary Shelley, *Frankenstein or The Modern Prometheus: The 1818 Text*, ed. James Rieger (Chicago: University of Chicago Press, 1982), includes variant readings, an introduction, and notes; hereafter cited as *1818 Rieger*. This important edition was first published in 1974 in the Library of Literature (Indianapolis: Bobbs-Merrill), and reprinted in 1976 (with different pagination and lineation) by Pocket Books (New York). The 1982 Chicago reprint, however, is to be preferred because it corrects "minor errors in the introduction and apparatus" and lists "some additional 1818/1831 variants at the end of the volume" (x).

One of the most important discoveries made during the editing of *The Frankenstein Notebooks* is suggested by the very title of the edition—namely, that Mary Shelley drafted her novel in two bound, hardcover notebooks, a fact that was not known until this edition was undertaken and until Bruce Barker-Benfield of the Bodleian Library (where the manuscripts owned by Lord Abinger are housed) made the initial discovery. It had formerly been assumed that the now loose sheets had some kind of common source. But only upon inspection of the sewing holes, glue residue, torn edges, offset ink blots, and original foliation and pagination of the individual leaves did it became clear that Mary Shelley actually drafted her novel in bound notebooks, providing incontrovertible evidence that most of the text was drafted in the sequence of the narrative as we have it and as it is paginated in the notebooks. (And exceptions could be clearly identified because of distinct insert leaves, some of which had been cannibalized from later quires in the notebooks.) In fact, the entire quiring sequences of the original notebooks could be reconstructed, thereby providing evidence about the number of missing pages resulting from revisions that were made to the Draft (or resulting from the Fair-Copy pages that were apparently lost during the printing of the novel). The very "look" of Notebooks A and B gives further evidence that what Mary Shelley actually wrote was an "intermediate" Draft, one that was in part copied from another source. Some pages are cluttered by Percy Shelley's additions to the text at that point, but most are almost "clean" enough to go to a printer as Fair Copy.

The manuscript evidence suggesting that Mary Shelley in the Draft was in fact copying from (and expanding upon) an earlier text is further supported by mistakes in the Draft that are best explained as copying errors. These mistakes suggest that Mary Shelley miscopied from her ur-text, sometimes jumping ahead of herself, canceling the error, returning to the ur-text at the proper place, and then beginning again so she could correctly copy what she had miscopied and then canceled. The most persuasive evidence for the existence of an ur-text from which Mary Shelley copied is to be found in her twice writing "Myrtella" for Elizabeth in passages drafted well into the narrative after Elizabeth's name had been written numerous times. In fact, there is considerable evidence in the Draft to suggest that in the ur-text Victor Frankenstein grew up not with Elizabeth and Clerval but with Myrtella and Carignan—and that Victor's mother was Caroline Beaumont rather than Caroline Beaufort. (These and other name changes in the Draft will enable more precise study of the artistic functions of names in *Frankenstein* and Mary Shelley's other fictions.)

The existence of an ur-text is also supported by other evidence. We have always known that Mary Shelley began a "short tale" in June 1816, that Percy Shelley encouraged her that summer to "develope the idea at greater length," and that Percy and Mary "talk[ed] about [the] story" on 21 August 1816.[10] But it is only with the publication of *The Frankenstein Notebooks* that we have been able to speculate that Mary Shelley during that summer wrote something more like a novella than a story—and that it probably contained in one form or another all the major incidents of the narrative (for example, Justine's trial and possibly even part of the story of the De Laceys). The two missing sections of the Draft, however, suggest that Mary Shelley's task in copying and expanding the ur-text into the Draft also involved adding two substantial parts to her narrative: Walton's outermost frame and Safie's innermost tale. What eventually became Walton's four introductory letters to his sister Margaret Walton Saville are now missing with the first forty pages of the Draft, suggesting that these notebook pages were in fact more like a rough draft, discarded after they were copied into some kind of intermediate state that is also now lost. A similar lacuna involving part of Safie's story (together with other manuscript evidence and statements in Mary Shelley's letters and journals) strongly indicates that Mary Shelley did not even conceive the Safie story until late November or early December 1816, at the point in the novel when the monster learned language while overhearing the De Laceys teach French to the Arab Safie. The manuscript evidence that

---

10. See *1831*, xi, and *The Journals of Mary Shelley, 1814–1844*, ed. Paula R. Feldman and Diana Scott-Kilvert, 2 vols. (Oxford: Clarendon, 1987), 1:130; see also *1816–17 Robinson*, 1:xxxi.

yokes these two parts of *Frankenstein* suggests further relations between the two women in these narratives: "Saville" pronounced as a French name is strongly echoed by "Safie," and it is quite possible that Mary Shelley decided on both names as late as March/April 1817, during her final editing and correcting of the Draft. (In the first versioning of the tale in December 1816, Safie had been called Maimouna and then Amina.) If the names were intended to be homophonic, then we would have added reason to read Safie, as we did Margaret Walton Saville, as a "figure" for Mary Shelley (and Safie's dead mother as a "figure" for Mary Wollstonecraft).

As Mary Shelley expanded her ur-text into a novel, she set in motion a very peculiar symmetry in the text as it developed from 1816 through 1831. The *1816* ur-text would have been one volume at most (and in published form would have most likely shared covers with another text); the *1816–17* Draft was a two-volume novel; the *1817* Fair Copy was a three-volume novel; the *1818* first edition was a three-volume novel; the *1823* edition was a two-volume novel; and the *1831* revised edition returns us full circle to a one-volume edition (which *Frankenstein* shared with volume 1 of Schiller's two-volume *The Ghost-Seer*). None of these versions is identical to another (even with regard to the words therein), and in fact there are very striking differences among them. The aesthetic implications of all these differences (indeed, the very differences themselves), especially the differing formats that occasion different arrangements to the chapters, have never been studied, and I propose at least to outline the relations among these texts in the remainder of this essay.

When Mary Shelley expanded her *1816* ur-text into the *1816–17* Draft, she not only added the outermost and innermost narratives, she consciously divided her text (in the very process of drafting it) into two separate volumes. (This two-volume division was completely independent of the two Notebooks A and B that she used; that is, volume 2 of her novel began well before she finished using Notebook A for her draft.) Volume 1 of the Draft novel consists of chapters numbered 1 to 14 (actually fifteen chapters because of two separate chapters that are numbered "7") that are preceded by what appears to have been Walton's four introductory letters to his sister Margaret (the first forty pages of the Draft are missing, but there are four letters in *1818* dated 11 December 17[96], and 28 March, 7 July, and 5 August 17[97], this last letter extending into a journal with additional dates of 13 August and 19 August). Volume 2 consists of chapters numbered 1 to 18, the last containing or eliding into Walton's final remarks to his sister that are dated in Draft as 13 August 17[97] (26 August 17[97] in Fair Copy and in *1818*), 31 August (2 September in *1818*), 6 September (5 September in *1818*), 7 September (7 September in *1818*), and 12 September (12 September in *1818*).

The textual evidence suggests that as Mary Shelley drafted her novel, she clearly had in mind a two-volume novel with a special structure: after Walton's letters, volume 1 (drafted from August or September until late November 1816) consisted of Victor's narrative of his childhood through the creation of the monster, the death of William, and the trial of Justine— all ending with the Frankenstein family journeying to Chamounix and the dramatic moment of Victor meeting his monster for the first time on the Mer de Glace, which he traversed between Montanvert and Mont Blanc. Percy Shelley himself was privileged in this final chapter of volume 1, because it contained two stanzas from his poem "Mutability" that had been recently published in the *Alastor* volume (1816). And volume 2 (drafted from late November or early December until mid-April 1817) opened with an equally dramatic moment, the beginning words of the monster's narrative ("It is with difficulty that I remember the aera of my being" [*1816–17 Robinson*, 1:271]), and it contained the monster's entire narrative (chapters 1 though 8), the monster's demand for a female mate, the remainder of Victor's narrative until he was taken aboard Walton's ship, and finally Walton's "continuation" that recounted the death of Victor and the encounter with the monster on the ship.

By the time that Mary Shelley finished the Draft of her novel in two volumes in early April 1817 and then corrected it between 10 and 17 April, she had decided to transform her two-volume narrative into a three-volume work. Were it not for the Fair Copy that gives evidence of being in three volumes, I might have conjectured that Mary Shelley's original idea for a two-volume novel was compromised by the commercial interests of a publisher who wished to inflate the price by selling a three-volume rather than a two-volume novel.[11] But the Fair-Copy evidence is unequivocal—and there is further evidence in the Draft that both Shelleys helped to transform the two-volume Draft into a three-volume Fair Copy. That evidence, a series of marginal sums, was baffling to me until I realized that the Shelleys were estimating the number of pages that the Draft would occupy in three volumes. The imbalance of a fifteen-chapter volume 1 and an eighteen-chapter volume 2—together with a novel that may have become longer than Mary Shelley initially envisaged—is a possible reason why Mary and/or Percy decided to make the alteration, but an argument could still be made that the dramatically structured two-volume Draft version was sacrificed to the expediency of expectations and finances in the commercial world of publishing that influenced the Shelleys' decision.

When Mary Shelley transformed her novel into a three-volume Fair Copy, the existing thirty-three chapters of the two-volume Draft had to be reconfigured. The net result in the Fair Copy and in *1818* was twenty-three differently arranged chapters: seven each in volumes 1 and 3, and nine in volume 2. This new structure, occasioned in part because of the Walton letters that began and ended the novel, was not quite matched by the pages in each volume in *1818*: volume 1, chapters 1–7, pages 1–181; volume 2, chapters 1–9, pages 1–156; volume 3, chapters 1–7, pages 1–192.[12] And it could be argued that the new chapters in three volumes were in fact arbitrary, not quite fulfilling Mary Shelley's design in the earlier Draft—especially because she cut into existing chapters as she restructured her novel, as is revealed by the following outline:

11. The really inflated pricing of triple-deckers was perhaps a decade away, when novels sold at a guinea and a half—that is, 31s.6d. Mary Shelley's *1818* novel, one of the shortest triple-deckers on record, sold for 16s.6d. in boards.

12. Because the extant Fair Copy reveals that Mary Shelley's transcriptions were written to rule, producing leaves with fourteen lines on one side and nineteen lines on the other (with an average of 285 words per leaf), and because these pages run in almost exact tandem with *1818* (where there are approximately 285 words per leaf), I have argued that the Fair Copy itself would have had approximately the same number of pages as *1818*. For more on this complicated issue, see *1816–17 Robinson*, 1:lxii–lxv.

Draft	1818
Volume 1	**Volume 1**
chapters 1–2	= chapter 1
chapters 3–4	= chapter 2
chapters 5–6	= chapter 3
chapters 7a–part of 7b	= chapter 4
chapters part of 7b–8	= chapter 5
chapters 9–10–part of 11	= chapter 6
chapters part of 11–12	= chapter 7
	Volume 2
chapter 13	= chapter 1
chapter 14	= chapter 2
Volume 2	
chapters 1–part of 2	= chapter 3
chapters part of 2–3[13]	= chapter 4
chapter [?4]	= chapter 5
"another chapter"	= chapter 6
chapters [6][14]–part of 7	= chapter 7
chapters part of 7–8	= chapter 8
chapter 9	= chapter 9
	Volume 3
chapter 10	= chapter 1
chapters 11–part of 12	= chapter 2
chapters part of 12–13	= chapter 3
chapters 14–part of 15	= chapter 4
chapters part of 15–16	= chapter 5
chapter 17	= chapter 6
chapter 18	= chapter 7

13. The concluding Draft pages for chapter 3 are missing, as are the Draft pages for what eventually became chapter 5 in *1818*—the "trauma" in the text at this point concerns the intersections of Notebook A (continental blue paper) and Notebook B (English white paper).

14. Although unnumbered, this "chapter" beginning Notebook B (with the monster's words, "Such was the history of my beloved cottagers") precedes "Chap. 7th."

That Mary Shelley herself determined at least some if not all these restructurings is suggested by her holograph in the Draft: "Finish Chap. 2 here" (*1816–17 Robinson*, 1:472). The note appears in volume 2 of the Draft, one-third of the way through chapter 12, at the point where in the *1818* text (and therefore in the Fair Copy, which is missing at this point) chapter 2 does in fact end and chapter 3 begins. This particular alteration does not drastically change Mary Shelley's original chapter divisions: her Draft chapter 12 originally consisted of Victor journeying from Edinburgh to the Orkney Islands, starting to create a female for the monster, then deciding to destroy this half-finished creation, and finally confronting the companionless monster who promised to retaliate by being with Victor on his "marriage night." Her *1818* chapter 2 ends with Victor's early work on the female, and chapter 3 begins with Victor deciding to destroy the female creature, proceeds through the monster's threat about the "wedding-night," and then (embracing all of Draft chapter 13) continues through Victor's sinking of the female creature's parts in the sea and his subsequent apprehension by the Irish, who suspected him of having murdered Clerval. There are other places where the new *1818* chapter divisions take greater liberties with the flow of the original narrative, and a study of the aesthetic implications of all of the alterations needs to be undertaken to determine if Mary Shelley herself compromised the original design of a novel in two volumes.

Of course, such changes as a text moves toward publication are not that unusual, especially to those who have studied the relations among drafts, fair copies, and first editions. And if we had the proofs and revises that intervened between the Fair Copy and *1818*, then we might be able to determine if other changes to the text were made by publishers' readers and/or compositors. But even without these proofs and revises, we can deduce in the case of *Frankenstein* that the Shelleys made at least three substantive changes to the text, the most significant occurring in *1818*, volume 3, chapter 1, pages 17–19, where what appears to have been a two-hundred-word description of Holland (which the Shelleys also used in their collaborative *History of a Six Weeks' Tour* [1817]) was replaced by an important and longer passage in which Victor reflected on Clerval's "wild and enthusiastic imagination," "the sensibility of his heart," and the survival of his "mind" and "spirit" after death—together with quotations from Leigh Hunt's *The Story of Rimini* (1816) and William Wordsworth's "Tintern Abbey" (1798). This important passage, added so late to the novel, reveals that the Shelleys continued to refine the text they were both preparing for publication.

Mary Shelley continued her own editorial improvements in December 1818 when she began to "Correct Frankenstein,"[15] possibly in the very copy of *1818* that she eventually gave to Mrs. Thomas in 1823. In *1818 Thomas* she noted that she wanted to "re-write [the] two first chapters [in volume 1]. The incidents are tame and ill arranged—the language sometimes childish—. They are unworthy of the rest of the . . . narration"; she also noted that Elizabeth's letter to Victor in chapter 5 "ought to be re-written."[16] But she did not comment one way or the other about structuring her novel in two or three volumes. The first to introduce that restructuring was her father, William Godwin, who in 1823 arranged for the publisher Whittaker to publish the novel in two volumes, requiring a resetting of the three-volume *1818* (in 529 pages) into the two-volume *1823* (in 529 pages). The twenty-three chapters in *1818* are translated into *1823* as follows: volume 1, chapters 1–11, pages 1–249; and volume 2, chapters 1–12, pages 1–280, the first chapter of volume 2 opening with the monster's continuing narrative of the De Lacey family, thus indicating that the two-volume *1823* is quite unlike the two-volume Draft that opened with the beginning of the monster's narrative. Although Godwin's two-volume edition has no authority, the 123 substantive changes that he also made to (or oversaw in) *1823* do eventually gain a degree of authority, for Mary Shelley appears to have used *1823* as copy-text for the revised *1831* edition. In doing so, she accepted (perhaps unknowingly) the word changes that Godwin had initiated.

15. *Journals of Mary Shelley*, 1:245.

16. Qtd. in *1818 Rieger*, 43n., 62n.

Mary Shelley's final editing of her novel resulted from an opportunity to republish *Frankenstein* in the Standard Novels series that was started by the publishers Henry Colburn and Richard Bentley—a series that encouraged authors to make alterations to their texts. The full extent of the revisions that Mary Shelley made in *1831* may be found in *1818 Rieger* and now in *1818 Crook*,[17] and *1818 Butler* offers a convenient summary of the types of changes made in *1831*.[18] Those who have compared the two texts will remember, among the many changes, that Elizabeth was Victor's first cousin in *1818* but a foundling in *1831*, that the doppelgänger theme became more prominent in *1831*, and that Mary Shelley expanded her description of Victor's early life with Elizabeth and Clerval in Geneva, thereby requiring an additional chapter—so the twenty-three chapters of the three-volume *1818* became twenty-four chapters in the one-volume *1831* novel, the last version of *Frankenstein* that Mary Shelley prepared during her lifetime. However, she did attempt to make at least one more alteration: in a letter to Bentley's assistant Charles Ollier, probably written in February 1833, she inquired, "if there is another real <introd> edition of Frankenstein—that is if it goes to the press again—will you remember that I have a short passage to add to the introduction. Do not fail me with regard to this—it will only be a few lines—& those not disagreable to C. & B. [the publishers Colburn

17. Mary Shelley, *Frankenstein or The Modern Prometheus*, ed. Nora Crook, in vol. 1 of *The Novels and Selected Works of Mary Shelley*, ed. Crook, introduced by Betty T. Bennett (London: Pickering & Chatto, 1996). Crook provides four valuable "Endnotes": "Textual Variants" (182–227), in which she prints Mary Shelley's autograph corrections in *1818 Thomas* and the substantive variants in *1823* and *1831*; "A Note on Spelling Variants in *1818, 1823* and *1831*" (228); "Unauthorized Variants" (229), in which she indicates that *1831 Joseph* introduced six textual errors and that *1818 Macdonald* incorrectly listed these errors as *1831* variants of the *1818* text; and "Silent Corrections" (230–31). For full bibliographical information on *1831 Joseph, 1818 Macdonald*, and other frequently used editions, see "Short Titles" in *1816–17 Robinson*, 1:xv–xvii.

18. Mary Shelley, *Frankenstein or The Modern Prometheus: The 1818 Text*, ed. Marilyn Butler (London: Pickering, 1993), 199–201. Butler's edition was reprinted in paper as part of Oxford University Press's series The World's Classics (1994). Both the original and the reprint have an appendix in which Butler prints "The Third Edition (1831): Substantive Changes" together with "Collation of the Texts of 1818 and 1831," but the collations are not complete.

and Bentley]—but the contrary."[19] We can only conjecture what Mary Shelley might have added, but it could have been a quotation from Percy Shelley's review of *Frankenstein* that had recently been published in the *Athenaeum* (10 Nov. 1832).

In the preceding paragraphs I have attempted to contextualize the editing of *The Frankenstein Notebooks* and thereby raise serious questions about the text of the novel that we read. The more I read in and about Mary Shelley's most famous novel, the more I am humbled by the richness and complexity of the issues that it raises. The complexity is sometimes daunting, as it was the first time that I unsuccessfully attempted to explain my new edition at a talk at the annual meeting of the Modern Language Association (MLA) in December 1995, at which time I had neither conceived nor written my introduction to the edition. When I did write that introduction in the summer of 1996, it ultimately grew to 110 printed pages and offered what I judge to be a series of useful glosses on *Frankenstein*: (1) an annotated list of short titles that includes an efficient means to name and order the texts of the novel; (2) an analysis of the physical makeup of the four extant notebooks together with quiring charts and beta-radiographs of the watermarks—all this evidence enabling a reconstruction of the sequence in which the novel was drafted; (3) reflections on "naming" in the novel; (4) hypothetical reconstructions of both the ur-text and the Fair Copy; (5) remarks on the significance of numbers and dates in *The Frankenstein Notebooks*; (6) a discussion of the collaboration between the two Shelleys; and (7) a thirty-page, single-spaced chronology that provides in one place the important dates, facts, and quotations from letters, journals, and contemporary documents that deal with *Frankenstein*—so that the reader can experience in much greater detail (with all the proper citations) what went into the making of Mary Shelley's monster.

19. *The Letters of Mary Wollstonecraft Shelley*, 2:129, where the letter is conjecturally dated [?February–10 March 1831] and where the angle brackets indicate a restored deletion. I have redated this letter because it seems to refer to the already published introduction of *1831* and to anticipate a resetting of the introduction ("if it goes to press again") in another "real" edition rather than the stereotyped reissue of *1831* in 1832. For more on this, see *1816–17 Robinson*, 1:cv.

Since publishing *The Frankenstein Notebooks* with its introduction and chronology, I have given a more thoughtful talk at the MLA meeting of December 1996 as well as other presentations at some of the bicentennial conferences in such places as Bristol, New York, Calgary, Cambridge, and Bologna, where Mary Shelley's birth in 1797 and her exceptional creative life were being celebrated. What this edition has taught me most is that much work yet remains to be undertaken on *Frankenstein*, and I hope that my editorial labors will provide others the means for more precise and accurate explorations of the novel, especially with regard to the collaboration between the two Shelleys, the differences between *1818* and *1831* and other versions of the novel, and the new discoveries that are made possible by studying the manuscript evidence in the context of a detailed chronology. Consider, for example, that we now know that Mary Shelley was reading her mother's *Vindication of the Rights of Woman* at the same time she was writing the chapters that concerned Safie's education by her mother.[20] Or consider that a portion of Victor's Draft description of his boat trip with Elizabeth on their wedding night was taken word-for-word from Percy Shelley's journal description of his boat trip with Byron on Lake Geneva in June 1816, at a time when Mary Shelley was beginning to write her ur-text of the novel (see *1816–17 Robinson*, 1:lxxix, 2:560–61). Even after Mary Shelley appropriated Percy Shelley's text for her Draft, Percy made an editorial change to the text, thereby drawing attention to the intimate nature of their collaboration and suggesting that the inner- and intertextuality of this novel is so complex that it would be impossible ever to purge Percy Shelley's prose or voice from this novel—even given the Draft by which we can now identify his specific alterations.

One final reflection: does the manuscript evidence give us the means for a new edition of *Frankenstein* that would somehow conflate all that

20. Mary Shelley read *Vindication* in December 1816: see entries for 6–9 December in *Journals of Mary Shelley*, 1:149; see also Charles E. Robinson, "A Mother's Daughter: An Intersection of Mary Shelley's *Frankenstein* and Mary Wollstonecraft's *A Vindication of the Rights of Woman*, in *Mary Wollstonecraft and Mary Shelley: Writing Lives*, ed. Helen M. Buss, D. L. Macdonald, and Anne McWhir (Waterloo: Wilfrid Laurier University Press, 2001), 131, 134–36.

was judged "best" from the different versions? At least one recent edition has conflated the revised text of *1831* with the three-volume structure of *1818*,[21] creating a new kind of monster that has no validity, in my judgment. It would be much more defensible to reconstruct hypothetically the revises, the proofs, and the entire Fair Copy, all of which could then be used to filter *1818* back to the two-volume structure of the Draft. Or would we all be better served by merely making available for study the edited and corrected versions of the two-volume Draft and the three-volume *1818* (which has up to 100 textual errors) and the one-volume *1831*—and treat them much as we do William Wordsworth's two-part *Prelude* of 1799, his thirteen-book *Prelude* of 1805, and his fourteen-book *Prelude* of 1850? If the study of the transmission of these texts can teach us more about the creative process, do we then have an added obligation in this electronic age to link all these texts hypertextually in formats being developed by such places as the Electronic Text Center at the University of Virginia? If we exploit the latest electrical, electronic, and scientific technologies, then readers of the future will have all the parts of all the extant texts and thereby be able to assemble their own *Frankensteins*! In effect, these future readers will become authors or at least editors of their own texts of Mary Shelley's novel—with, of course, the threat that a web of undisciplined texts about a monster might produce texts more monstrous than we already have as this novel lumbers toward its own two-hundredth birthday in 2016—or should that be that 2017—or 2018—or 2023—or 2026—or 2031?

21. Mary Shelley, *Frankenstein or The Modern Prometheus*, ed. Maurice Hindle (London: Penguin, 1992).

PART THREE

Working with Editions

from *Mansfield Park*†

Jane Austen

Jane Austen, author of *Emma, Pride and Prejudice,* and *Persuasion,* among other novels, revised *Mansfield Park* slightly between first (1814) and second (1816) publication. The text and notes below, from Claudia L. Johnson's edition of the novel, provide a good exercise in working backward through the notes to the witnesses upon which the critical edition is based. Asterisks indicate that the editor has supplied a textual note.

† From *Mansfield Park,* Norton Critical Edition, ed. Claudia L. Johnson (New York: W. W. Norton, 1998). Notes from *Mansfield Park,* Norton Critical Edition by Jane Austen, edited by Claudia L. Johnson. Copyright © 1998 by W. W. Norton & Company, Inc. used by permission of W. W. Norton & Company, Inc.

from Claudia L. Johnson's Norton Critical Edition, including her textual note

be off for Spithead by six, so you had better go with him. I have been to Turner's[4] about your mess[5]*; it is all in a way to be done. I should not wonder if you had your orders to-morrow; but you cannot sail with this wind, if you are to cruize to the westward; and Captain Walsh thinks you will certainly have a cruize to the westward, with the Elephant. By G—, I wish you may. But old Scholey was saying just now, that he thought you would be sent first to the Texel.[6] Well, well, we are ready, whatever happens. But by G—, you lost a fine sight by not being here in the morning to see the Thrush go out of harbour. I would not have been out of the way for a thousand pounds. Old Scholey ran in at breakfast time, to say she had slipped her moorings and was coming out. I jumped up, and made but two steps to the platform.[7] If ever there was a perfect beauty afloat, she is one; and there she lays at Spithead, and anybody in England would take her for an eight-and-twenty.[8] I was upon the platform two hours this afternoon, looking at her. She lays close to the Endymion, between her and the Cleopatra,[9] just to the eastward of the sheer hulk."*[1]

"Ha!" cried William, "*that's* just where I should have put her myself. It's the best birth at Spithead.* But here is my sister, Sir, here is Fanny," turning and leading her forward;—"it is so dark you do not see her."

With an acknowledgment that he had quite forgot her, Mr. Price now received his daughter; and, having given her a cordial hug, and observed that she was grown into a woman, and he supposed would be wanting a husband soon, seemed very much inclined to forget her again.

Fanny shrunk back to her seat, with feelings sadly pained by his language and his smell of spirits; and he talked on only to his son, and only of the Thrush, though William, warmly interested, as he was, in that subject, more than once tried to make his father think of Fanny, and her long absence and long journey.

After sitting some time longer, a candle was obtained; but, as there was still no appearance of tea, nor, from Betsey's reports from the kitchen, much hope of any under a considerable period, William determined to go and change his dress, and make the necessary prepa-

---

4. A naval supplier or agent whose shop was at 85 High Street. Austen mentions Turner's twice in her letters, in both cases relative to her sailor brothers.
5. Provisions.
6. The channel between the Dutch mainland and the Dutch island of Texel, through which ships could enter from the North Sea. Because Napoleon held the Netherlands during this time, the Texel was the site of British naval blockades.
7. The Saluting Platform, overlooking the harbor, built in the 1490s.
8. A frigate with twenty-eight guns. William's ship, the *Thrush*, was a modern sloop built in 1806, which is why the proud Mr. Price says it could be mistaken for a twenty-eight-gun frigate, even though sloops are smaller, differently rigged, and generally mount fewer guns.
9. Actual ships on which Austen's brother Charles served.
1. The hull of an old ship, fitted up with devices for the maintenance and repair of other ships; i.e., a floating dockyard.

VOLUME III: CHAPTER VII 259

rations for his removal on board directly, that he might have his tea in comfort afterwards.

As he left the room, two rosy-faced boys, ragged and dirty, about eight and nine years old, rushed into it just released from school, and coming eagerly to see their sister, and tell that the Thrush was gone out of harbour; Tom and Charles: Charles had been born since Fanny's going away, but Tom she had often helped to nurse, and now felt a particular pleasure in seeing again. Both were kissed very tenderly, but Tom she wanted to keep by her, to try to trace the features of the baby she had loved, and talked to,* of his infant preference of herself. Tom, however, had no mind for such treatment: he came home, not to stand and be talked to, but to run about and make a noise; and both boys had soon burst away from her, and slammed the parlour door till her temples ached.

She had now seen all that were at home; there remained only two brothers between herself and Susan, one of whom was a clerk in a public office in London, and the other midshipman on board an Indiaman.[2] But though she had *seen* all the members of the family, she had not yet *heard* all the noise they could make. Another quarter of an hour brought her a great deal more. William was soon calling out from the landing-place of the second story, for his mother and for Rebecca. He was in distress for something that he had left there, and did not find again. A key was mislaid, Betsey accused of having got at his new hat, and some slight, but essential alteration of his uniform waist-coat, which he had been promised to have done for him, entirely neglected.

Mrs. Price, Rebecca, and Betsey, all went up to defend themselves, all talking together, but Rebecca loudest, and the job was to be done, as well as it could, in a great hurry; William trying in vain to send Betsey down again, or keep her from being troublesome where she was; the whole of which, as almost every door in the house was open, could be plainly distinguished in the parlour, except when drowned at intervals by the superior noise of Sam, Tom, and Charles chasing each other up and down stairs, and tumbling about and hallooing.

Fanny was almost stunned. The smallness of the house, and thinness of the walls, brought every thing so close to her, that, added to the fatigue of her journey, and all her recent agitation, she hardly knew how to bear it. *Within* the room all was tranquil enough, for Susan having disappeared with the others, there were soon only her father and herself remaining; and he taking out a newspaper—the accustomary loan[3] of a neighbour, applied himself to studying it, without seeming to recollect her existence. The solitary candle was held between himself and the paper, without any reference to her possible convenience; but

2. A ship of large tonnage belonging to the East India Company.
3. Being very expensive, newspapers were often shared among friends.

Textual Notes

A = First Edition of *Mansfield Park*, 1814
B = Second Edition of *Mansfield Park*, 1816

THE TEXT OF this edition of *Mansfield Park* was arrived at by collating copies of the first and second editions held by Cornell University and Princeton University. Austen's second edition (1816) is the basis for this text, as it is for all modern editions of the novel. This edition, however, strives to make editorial intervention explicit and to allow those inconsistencies that cannot be adjudicated on the basis of known information about the text to stand.

These textual notes, and my discussion in the Introduction (pp. xvi–xxi), record the evidence for my decisions. The notes detail the instances where *A*'s readings are improved by those in *B*, but include only examples of *A*'s significant errors in word choice, grammar, and punctuation, rather than of *A*'s minor grammatical errors, frequent typographical mistakes, and inconsequential spelling differences against *B*. Such infelicities in *A* are usually corrected by *B*. Similarly, errors at this level that remain in *B* or, as is rarely the case, are introduced by *B*, I have silently corrected.

All instances where *A*'s reading is to be preferred to *B*'s are listed. In each case where *A* and *B* err independently or jointly and I have had, thus, to emend the text, their readings are noted.

These notes do not contain an exhaustive account of the differences between the Chapman edition (1923; revised Mary Lascelles, 1966) and *AB*, although the character of Chapman's edition is discussed in my Introduction (pp. xx–xxi). Nevertheless, as an aid to the reader, Chapman's editorial decisions and comments are noted whenever the passage offers interpretative difficulties.

* * *

III.vii.258: *mess] things A*

III.vii.258: *Old Scholey . . . sheer hulk"] Old Scholey ran in at break-fast time, to say that she was under weigh. I jumped up, and made but two steps to the point. If ever there was a perfect beauty afloat, she is one; and there she lays at Spithead, and anybody in England would take her for an eight-and-twenty. I was upon the platform two hours this afternoon, looking at her. She lays just astern of the Endymion, with the Cleopatra to larboard." A*

III.vii.258: *It's the best birth at Spithead.] omitted in A*

III.vii.259: *talk to, of his infant] AB (Chapman considers this a crux, emending it to talk to him. AB make adequate sense if we suppose that Fanny is saying that she used to soothe and talk to Tom when he was an infant, a possibility Chapman finds illogical. Given that this is a section Austen seemed to have revised with some care, it is hard to imagine that she would let stand an obscurity of the magnitude Chapman supposes.)*

* * *

from *Moll Flanders*†

Daniel Defoe

Daniel Defoe, perhaps best known for *Robinson Crusoe*, first published *The Fortunes and Misfortunes of the Famous Moll Flanders* in 1722, even though some title pages read 1721. The second and third editions, published in the same year, show significant revision, apparently not by the author, reducing the length of the text. Editors now believe that the first edition preserves a record of one of Defoe's revisions of the novel in manuscript, namely two passages that describe the same event and that contradict one another.

This example allows for practice in reconstructing salient features of the witnesses from the notes, but other exercises are possible with it as well. One might start by collating the first edition against the critical edition to see what features of an early modern book a modern edition does not report, or what sorts of changes the editor does not record. By collating the third edition against the first one can begin to investigate the large and small ways that the text changes between these two significant editions. What accounts for these changes? What are their implications for questions of authorship, intention, or other matters of textual studies?

Hands, and brought me back an Answer from her in writing; and when he gave me the Answer, gave me the Shilling again, *there*, says he, there's your Shilling again too, for I deliver'd the Letter my self; I could not tell what to say, I was so surpris'd at the thing; but after some Pause, *I said*, Sir you are too kind, it had been but Reasonable that you had paid yourself Coach hire then.

No, no, *says he*, I am over paid: What is the Gentlewoman your Sister?

No, SIR, *said I*, she is no Relation to me, but she is a dear Friend, and all the Friends I have in the World: well, *says he*, there are few such Friends in the World: why she cryes after you like a Child, Ay, *says I again*, she would give a Hundred Pound, I believe, to deliver me from this dreadful Condition I am in.

WOULD she so? *says he*, for half the Money I believe, I cou'd put you in a way how to deliver yourself, but this he spoke softly that no Body cou'd hear.

Alas! SIR, *said I*, but then that must be such a Deliverance as if I should be taken again, would cost me my Life; Nay, *said he*, if you were once out of the Ship you must look to yourself afterwards, that I can say nothing to; so we drop'd the Discourse for that time.

IN the mean time my Governess faithful to the last Moment, convey'd my Letter to the Prison to my Husband, and got an Answer to it, and the next Day came down herself to the Ship, bringing me in the first Place a *Sea-Bed* as they call it, and all its Furniture, such as was convenient, but not to let the People think it was extraordinary; she brought with her a *Sea-Chest*, that is a Chest, such as are made for Seamen with all the Conveniences in it, and fill'd with every thing almost that I could want; and in one of the corners of the Chest, where there was a Private Drawer was my Bank of Money, *that is to say*, so much of it as I had resolv'd to carry with me; for I order'd a part of my Stock to be left behind me, to be sent afterwards in such Goods as I should want when I came to settle; for Money in that Country is not of much use where all things are bought for Tobacco, much more is it a great loss to carry it from Hence.[3]

BUT my Case was particular; it was by no Means proper to me to go thither without Money or Goods, and for a poor Convict that was to be sold as soon as I came on Shore, to carry with me a Cargo of Goods would be to have Notice taken of it, and perhaps to have them seiz'd by the Publick; so I took part of my Stock with me thus, and left the other part with my Governess.

MY Governess brought me a great many other things, but it was not proper for me to look too well provided in the Ship, at least, till I knew what kind of a Captain we should have. When she came into

---

3. I.e., England. Tobacco, rather than money, was the standard for trade in Maryland and Virginia.

the Ship, I thought she would have died indeed; her Heart sunk at
the sight of me, and at the thoughts of parting with me in that Condition, and she cry'd so intolerably, I cou'd not for a long time have
any talk with her.

I TOOK that time to read my fellow Prisoners Letter, which however greatly perplex'd me; he told me he was determin'd to go, but
found it would be impossible for him to be Discharg'd time enough
for going in the same Ship, and which was more than all, he began
to question whether they would give him leave to go in what Ship
he pleas'd, tho' he did voluntarily Transport himself; but that they
would see him put on Board such a Ship as they should direct, and
that he would be charg'd upon the Captain as other convict Prisoners
were; so that he began to be in dispair of seeing me till he came to
Virginia, which made him almost desperate; seeing that on the other
Hand, if I should not be there, if any Accident of the Sea, or of
Mortality should take me away, he should be the most undone Creature there in the World.

THIS was very perplexing, and I knew not what Course to take; I
told my Governess the Story of the Boatswain, and she was mighty
eager with me to treat with him; but I had no mind to it, till I heard
whether my Husband, or fellow Prisoner, *so she call'd him*, cou'd be
at liberty to go with me or no; at last I was forc'd to let her into the
whole matter, except only, that of his being my Husband; I told her
I had made a positive Bargain or Agreement with him to go, if he
could get the liberty of going in the same Ship, and that I found he
had Money.[4]

IN this Condition I lay for three Weeks in the Ship, not knowing
whether I should have my Husband with me or no; and therefore
not resolving how, or in what manner to receive the honest Boatswain's proposal, which indeed he thought a little strange at first.

AT the End of this time, behold my Husband came on Board; he
look'd with a dejected angry Countenance, his great Heart was
swell'd with Rage and Disdain; to be drag'd along with three Keepers
of *Newgate*, and put on Board like a Convict, when he had not so
much as been brought to a Tryal; he made loud complaints of it by
his Friends, for it seems he had some interest;[5] but his Friends got
some Checque in their Application, and were told he had had *Favour
enough*, and that they had receiv'd such an Account of him since the
last Grant of his Transportation, that he ought to think himself very
well treated that he was not prosecuted a new. This answer quieted
him at once, for he knew too much what might have happen'd, and

---

4. In the first edition, the next two paragraphs appear before the paragraph beginning "The
Ship began now to fill. . . ." (p. 387). For the two paragraphs appearing at this point in
the first edition, and an explanation of this emendation, see pp. 269–72 below.
5. Influence (because of well-connected people working on his behalf to advance his "interest"). *With*: By. *Keepers*: Guardians, wardens.

what he had room to expect; and now he saw the goodness of the Advice to him, which prevail'd with him to accept of the offer of a voluntary Transportation, and after his chagrine at these Hell Hounds, *as he call'd them*, was a little over; he look'd a little compos'd, began to be chearful, and as I was telling him how glad I was to have him once more out of their Hands, took me in his Arms, and acknowledg'd with great Tenderness, that I had given him the best Advice possible, *My Dear*, says he, *Thou hast twice sav'd my Life, from hence forward it shall be all employ'd for you, and I'll always take your Advice*.

OUR first business was to compare our Stock: He was very honest to me, and told me his Stock was pretty good when he came into the Prison, but the living there as he did in a Figure like a Gentleman, *and which was ten times as much*, the making of Friends, and soliciting his Case, had been very Expensive; and in a Word, all his Stock that he had left was an Hundred and Eight Pounds, which he had about him all in Gold.

I GAVE him an Account of my Stock as faithfully, that is to say of what I had taken to carry with me, for I was resolv'd what ever should happen, to keep what I had left with my Governess, in Reserve; that in Case I should die, what I had with me was enough to give him, and that which was left in my Governess Hands would be her own, which she had well deserv'd of me indeed.

MY Stock which I had with me was two Hundred forty six Pounds, some odd Shillings; so that we had three Hundred and fifty four Pound between us, but a worse gotten Estate was scarce ever put together to begin the World with.

OUR greatest Misfortune as to our Stock, was that it was all in Money, which every one knows is an unprofitable Cargoe to be carryed to the Plantations; I believe his was really all he had left in the World, as he told me it was; but I who had between seven and eight Hundred Pounds in Bank when this Disaster befel me, and who had one of the faithfulest Friends in the World to manage it for me, considering she was a Woman of no manner of Religious Principles, had still Three Hundred Pounds left in her Hand, which I reserv'd, as above, besides some very valuable things, as particularly two gold Watches, some small Peices of Plate, and some Rings; all stolen Goods; the Plate, Rings and Watches were put up in my Chest with the Money, and with this Fortune, and in the Sixty first Year of my Age, I launch'd out into a new World, as I may call it, in the Condition (as to what appear'd) only of a poor nak'd Convict, order'd to be Transported in respite from the Gallows, my Cloaths were poor and mean, but not ragged or dirty, and none knew in the whole Ship that I had any thing of value about me.

HOWEVER, as I had a great many very good Cloaths, and Linnen in abundance, which I had order'd to be pack'd up in two great Boxes, I had them Shipp'd on Board, not as my Goods, but as consign'd to my real Name in *Virginia*; and had the Bills of Loading sign'd by a Captain in my Pocket; and in these Boxes was my Plate and Watches, and every thing of value except my Money, which I kept by itself in a private Drawer in my Chest, which cou'd not be found, or open'd if found, without splitting the Chest to peices.

THE Ship began now to fill, several Passengers came on Board, who were embark'd on no Criminal account, and these had Accommodations assign'd them in the great Cabbin, and other Parts of the Ship, whereas we *as Convicts* were thrust down below, I know not where; but when my Husband came on Board, I spoke to the Boatswain, who had so early given me Hints of his Friendship in carrying my Letter; I told him he had befriended me in many things, and I had not made any suitable Return to him, and with that I put a Guinea into his Hands; I told him that my Husband was now come on Board, that tho' we were both under the present Misfortunes, yet we had been Persons of a differing Character from the wretched Crew that we came with, and desir'd to know of him, whether the Captain might not be mov'd, to admit us to some Conveniences in the Ship, for which we would make him what Satisfaction he pleas'd, and that we would gratifie him for his Pains in procuring this for us. He took the Guinea as I cou'd see with great Satisfaction, and assur'd me of his Assistance.

THEN he told us, he did not doubt but that the Captain, who was one of the best humour'd Gentlemen in the World, would be easily brought to Accommodate us, as well as we cou'd desire, and to make me easie, told me he would go up the next Tide on purpose to speak to the Captain about it. The next Morning happening to sleep a little longer than ordinary, when I got up, and began to look Abroad, I saw the Boatswain among the Men in his ordinary Business; I was a little melancholly at seeing him there, and going forwards to speak to him, he saw me, and came towards me, but not giving him time to speak first, I said smiling, *I doubt, Sir, you have forgot us,* for I see you are very busy; he return'd presently,[6] come along with me, and you shall see, so he took me into the great Cabbin, and there sat a good sort of a Gentlemanly Man for a Seaman writing, and with a great many Papers before him.

HERE says the Boatswain to him that was a writing, is the Gentlewoman that the Captain spoke to you of, and turning to me, he said, I have been so far from forgetting your Business, that I have been up at the Captain's House, and have represented faithfully to the Captain what you said, relating to your being furnished with better

---

6. Answered immediately.

A Textual Problem in *Moll Flanders*

THIS EXCERPT FROM the first edition of *Moll Flanders* (pp. 383–87)* contains a textual problem, first noted by J. Paul Hunter in his edition of the novel (Crowell, 1970). Briefly, two contradictory passages, of approximately the same length, appear at this point in the narrative. The contradictions are even more pronounced in the second edition, which prints both passages consecutively. In Hunter's view, the printer of the first edition was supposed to replace one passage with the other but, for some reason, ended up printing both. Believing that Defoe had revised his manuscript to make the role of the governess more prominent, Hunter retained the first passage ("Then I read a long Lecture . . . but by Directions") and deleted the second ("In this Condition . . . *always take your Advice*"), relegating it to an appendix. Two years later, Rodney M. Baine argued that, while Hunter was certainly right in suggesting that one passage was meant to replace the other, the second passage is actually the revision because it fits in better with the surrounding context and the ensuing events in the novel. In short, Hunter had canceled the wrong passage in his edition. After examining the evidence and discussing the matter with Hunter, who now agrees with Baine's assessment, I have corrected the text of

---

* See pages 402–06, this volume—*Editor.*

Moll Flanders to eliminate this apparent compositor's error. I reprint the original text here so that both passages may be read as they initially appeared.

* * *

THIS was very perplexing, and I knew not what Course to take; I told my Governess the Story of the Boatswain, and she was mighty eager with me to treat with him; but I had no mind to it, till I heard whether my Husband, or fellow Prisoner, *so she call'd him*, cou'd be at liberty to go with me or no; at last I was forc'd to let her into the whole matter, except only, that of his being my Husband; I told her I had made a positive Bargain or Agreement with him to go, if he could get the liberty of going in the same Ship, and that I found he had Money.

THEN I read a long Lecture to her of what I propos'd to do when we came there, how we could Plant, Settle; and in short, grow Rich without any more Adventures, and as a great Secret, I told her that we were to Marry as soon as he came on Board.

SHE soon agreed chearfully to my going, when she heard this, and she made it her business from that time to get him out of the Prison in time, so that he might go in the same Ship with me, which at last was brought to pass tho' with great difficulty, and not without all the Forms of a Transported Prisoner *Convict*, which he really was not yet, for he had not been try'd, and which was a great Mortification to him. As our Fate was now determin'd, and we were both on Board, actually bound to *Virginia*, in the despicable Quality of Transported Convicts destin'd to be sold for Slaves, I for five Year, and he under Bonds and Security not to return to *England* any more, as long as he liv'd; he was very much dejected and cast down; the Mortification of being brought on Board, as he was like a Prisoner, piqu'd him very much, since it was first told him he should Transport himself, and so that he might go as a Gentleman at liberty; it is true he was not order'd to be sold when he came there, as we were, and for that Reason he was oblig'd to pay for his

Passage to the Captain, which we were not; as to the rest, he was as much at a loss as a Child what to do with himself, or with what he had, but by Directions.

Our first business was to compare our Stock: He was very honest to me, and told me his Stock was pretty good when he came into the Prison, but the living there as he did in a Figure like a Gentleman, *and which was ten times as much,* the making of Friends, and soliciting his Case, had been very Expensive; and in a Word, all his Stock that he had left was an Hundred and Eight Pounds, which he had about him all in Gold.

I Gave him an Account of my Stock as faithfully, that is to say of what I had taken to carry with me, for I was resolv'd what ever should happen, to keep what I had left with my Governess, in Reserve; that in Case I should die, what I had with me was enough to give him, and that which was left in my Governess Hands would be her own, which she had well deserv'd of me indeed.

My Stock which I had with me was two Hundred forty six Pounds, some odd Shillings; so that we had three Hundred and fifty four Pound between us, but a worse gotten Estate was scarce ever put together to begin the World with.

Our greatest Misfortune as to our Stock, was that it was all in Money, which every one knows is an unprofitable Cargoe to be carryed to the Plantations; I believe his was really all he had left in the World, as he told me it was; but I who had between seven and eight Hundred Pounds in Bank when this Disaster befel me, and who had one of the faithfulest Friends in the World to manage it for me, considering she was a Woman of no manner of Religious Principles, had still Three Hundred Pounds left in her Hand, which I reserv'd, as above, besides some very valuable things, as particularly two gold Watches, some small Peices of Plate, and some Rings; all stolen Goods; the Plate, Rings and Watches were put up in my Chest with the Money, and with this Fortune, and in the Sixty first Year of my Age, I launch'd out into a new World, as I may call it in the Condition (as to what appear'd) only of a poor nak'd Convict, order'd to be Transported in respite from the Gallows; my Cloaths were poor and mean, but not ragged or dirty, and none knew in the whole Ship that I had any thing of value about me.

HOWEVER, as I had a great many very good Cloaths, and Linnen in abundance, which I had order'd to be pack'd up in two great Boxes, I had them Shipp'd on Board, not as my Goods, but as consign'd to my real Name in *Virginia*; and had the Bills of Loading sign'd by a Captain in my Pocket; and in these Boxes was my Plate and Watches, and every thing of value except my Money, which I kept by itself in a private Drawer in my Chest, which cou'd not be found, or open'd if found, without splitting the Chest to peices.

IN this Condition I lay for three Weeks in the Ship, not knowing whether I should have my Husband with me or no; and therefore not resolving how, or in what manner to receive the honest Boatswain's proposal, which indeed he thought a little strange at first.

AT the End of this time, behold my Husband came on Board; he look'd with a dejected angry Countenance, his great Heart was swell'd with Rage and Disdain; to be drag'd along with three Keepers of *Newgate,* and put on Board like a Convict, when he had not so much as been brought to a Tryal; he made loud complaints of it by his Friends, for it seems he had some interest; but his Friends got some Checque in their Application, and were told he had had *Favour enough,* and that they had receiv'd such an Account of him since the last Grant of his Transportation, that he ought to think himself very well treated that he was not prosecuted a new. This answer quieted him at once, for he knew too much what might have happen'd, and what he had room to expect; and now he saw the goodness of the Advice to him, which prevail'd with him to accept of the offer of a voluntary Transportation, and after his chagrine at these Hell Hounds, *as he call'd them,* was a little over; he look'd a little compos'd, began to be chearful, and as I was telling him how glad I was to have him once more out of their Hands, took me in his Arms, and acknowledg'd with great Tenderness, that I had given him the best Advice possible, *My Dear*, says he, *Thou hast twice sav'd my Life; from hence forward it shall be all employ'd for you, and I'll always take your Advice.*

THE Ship began now to fill, several Passengers came on Board, who were embark'd on no Criminal account, and these had Accommodations assign'd them in the great Cabbin, and other Parts of the Ship, whereas we *as Convicts* were thrust down below, I know not where; but when my Husband came on Board, I spoke to the Boatswain, who had so early given me Hints of his Friendship in carrying my Letter; I told him he had befriended me in many things, and I had not made any suitable Return to him, and with that I put a Guinea into his Hands; I told him that my Husband was now come on Board, that tho' we were both under the present Misfortunes, yet we had been Persons of a differing Character from the wretched Crew that we came with, and desir'd to know of him, whether the Captain might not be mov'd, to admit us to some Conveniences in the Ship, for which we would make him what Satisfaction he pleas'd, and that we would gratifie him for his Pains in procuring this for us. He took the Guinea as I cou'd see with great Satisfaction, and assur'd me of his Assistance.

* * *

(383)

ther Hand, if I fhould not be there, if any Accident of the Sea, or of Mortality fhould take me a-
way, he fhould be the moft undone Creature there
in the World.

THIS was very perplexing, and I knew not
what Courfe to take ; I told my Governefs the
Story of the Boatfwain, and fhe was mighty eager with me to treat with him ; but I had no
mind to it, till I heard whether my Husband, or
fellow Prifoner, *fo fhe call'd him*, cou'd be at liberty to go with me or no ; at laft I was forc'd to
let her into the whole matter, except only, that
of his being my Husband ; I told her I had made
a pofitive Bargain or Agreement with him to go,
if he could get the liberty of going in the fame
Ship, and that I found he had Money.

THEN I read a long Lecture to her of what I
propos'd to do when we came there, how we could
Plant, Settle ; and in fhort, grow Rich without
any more Adventures, and as a great Secret, I
told her that we were to Marry as foon as he came
on Board.

SHE foon agreed chearfully to my going, when
fhe heard this, and fhe made it her bufinefs from
that time to get him out of the Prifon in time, fo
that he might go in the fame Ship with me,
which at laft was brought to pafs tho' with great
difficulty, and not without all the Forms of a
Tranfported Prifoner *Convict*, which he really was
not yet, for he had not been try'd, and which
was a great Mortification to him. As our Fate was
now determin'd, and we were both on Board,
actually bound to *Virginia*, in the defpicable Quality of Tranfported Convicts deftin'd to be fold
for Slaves, I for five Year, and he under Bonds
and Security not to return to *England* any more,
                                                            as

(384)

as long as he liv'd; he was very much dejected and cast down; the Mortification of being brought on Board, as he was like a Prisoner, piqu'd him very much, since it was first told him he should Transport himself, and so that he might go as a Gentleman at liberty; it is true he was not order'd to be sold when he came there, as we were, and for that Reason he was oblig'd to pay for his Passage to the Captain, which we were not; as to the rest, he was as much at a loss as a Child what to do with himself, or with what he had, but by Directions.

Our first business was to compare our Stock: He was very honest to me, and told me his Stock was pretty good when he came into the Prison, but the living there as he did in a Figure like a Gentleman, *and which was ten times as much*, the making of Friends, and soliciting his Case, had been very Expensive; and in a Word, all his Stock that he had left was an Hundred and Eight Pounds, which he had about him all in Gold.

I Gave him an Account of my Stock as faithfully, that is to say of what I had taken to carry with me, for I was resolv'd what ever should happen, to keep what I had left with my Governess, in Reserve; that in Case I should die, what I had with me was enough to give him, and that which was left in my Governess Hands would be her own, which she had well deserv'd of me indeed.

My Stock which I had with me was two Hundred forty six Pounds, some odd Shillings; so that we had three Hundred and fifty four Pound between us, but a worse gotten Estate was scarce ever put together to begin the World with.

Our

(385)

OUR greateſt Misfortune as to our Stock, was
that it was all in Money, which every one knows
is an unprofitable Cargoe to be carryed to the
Plantations ; I believe his was really all he had
left in the World, as he told me it was ; but I
who had between ſeven and eight Hundred Pounds
in Bank when this Diſaſter befel me, and who had
one of the faithfuleſt Friends in the World to
manage it for me, conſidering ſhe was a Woman
of no manner of Religious Principles, had ſtill
Three Hundred Pounds left in her Hand, which I
reſerv'd, as above, beſides ſome very valuable
things, as particularly two gold Watches, ſome
ſmall Peices of Plate, and ſome Rings ; all ſtolen
Goods ; the Plate, Rings and Watches were put
up in my Cheſt with the Money, and with this
Fortune, and in the Sixty firſt Year of my Age,
I launch'd out into a new World, as I may call
it in the Condition (as to what appear'd) only of
a poor nak'd Convict, order'd to be Traſported in
reſpite from the Gallows , my Cloaths were poor
and mean, but not ragged or dirty, and none knew
in the whole Ship that I had any thing of value
about me.

HOWEVER, as I had a great many very good
Cloaths, and Linnen in abundance, which I had
order'd to be pack'd up in two great Boxes, I had
them Shipp'd on Board, not as my Goods, but as
conſign'd to my real Name in *Virginia* ; and had
the Bills of Loading ſign'd by a Captain in my
Pocket ; and in theſe Boxes was my Plate and
Watches, and every thing of value except my
Money, which I kept by itſelf in a private
Drawer in my Cheſt, which cou'd not be found,
or open'd if found, without ſplitting the Cheſt to
peices.

C c   IN

(386)

I N this Condition I lay for three Weeks in the Ship, not knowing whether I should have my Husband with me or no ; and therefore not resolving how, or in what manner to receive the honest Boatswain's proposal, which indeed he thought a little strange at first.

A T the End of this time, behold my Husband came on Board ; he look'd with a dejected angry Countenance, his great Heart was swell'd with Rage and Disdain ; to be drag'd along with three Keepers of *Newgate*, and put on Board like a Convict, when he had not so much as been brought to a Tryal ; he made loud complaints of it by his Friends, for it seems he had some interest ; but his Friends got some Checque in their Application, and were told he had had *Favour enough*, and that they had receiv'd such an Account of him since the last Grant of his Transportation, that he ought to think himself very well treated that he was not prosecuted a new. This answer quieted him at once, for he knew too much what might have happen'd, and what he had room to expect ; and now he saw the goodness of the Advice to him, which prevail'd with him to accept of the offer of a voluntary Transportation, and after his chagrine at these Hell Hounds, *as he call'd them,* was a little over; he look'd a little compos'd, began to be chearful, and as I was telling him how glad I was to have him once more out of their Hands, took me in his Arms, and acknowledg'd with great Tenderness, that I had given him the best Advice possible, *My Dear,* says he, *Thou hast twice sav'd my Life, from hence forward it shall be all employ'd for you, and I'll always take your Advice.*

T H E

(387)

THE Ship began now to fill, feveral Paffengers came on Board, who were embark'd on no
Criminal account, and thefe had Accommodations affign'd them in the great Cabbin, and other
Parts of the Ship, whereas we *as Convicts* were
thruft down below, I know not where; but when
my Husband came on Board, I fpoke to the Boatfwain, who had fo early given me Hints of his
Friendfhip in carrying my Letter; I told him
he had befriended me in many things, and I
had not made any fuitable Return to him, and
with that I put a Guinea into his Hands; I told
him that my Husband was now come on Board,
that tho' we were both under the prefent Misfortunes, yet we had been Perfons of a differing
Character from the wretched Crew that we came
with, and defir'd to know of him, whether the
Captain might not be mov'd, to admit us to fome
Conveniences in the Ship, for which we would
make him what Satisfaction he pleas'd, and that
we would gratifie him for his Pains in procuring
this for us. He took the Guinea as I cou'd fee
with great Satisfaction, and affur'd me of his Affiftance.

THEN he told us, he did not doubt but that
the Captain who was one of the beft humour'd
Gentlemen in the World, would be eafily brought
to Accommodate us, as well as we cou'd defire,
and to make me eafie, told me he would go up the
next Tide on purpofe to fpeak to the Captain a-
bout it. The next Morning happening to fleep
a little longer than ordinary, when I got up, and
began to look Abroad, I faw the Boatfwain a-
mong the Men in his ordinary Bufinefs; I was a
little melancholly at feeing him there, and going forwards to fpeak to him, he faw me, and

C c 2   came

(328)

when I came to fettle ; for Money in that Country, is not of much Ufe where all things are bought for Tobacco, much more is it a great Lofs to carry it from Hence.

But my Cafe was particular ; it was by no Means proper for me to go without Money or Goods, and for a poor Convict that was to be fold as foon as I came on Shore, to carry a Cargo of Goods would be to have Notice taken of it, and perhaps to have them feiz'd ; fo I took part of my Stock with me thus, and left the reft with my Governefs.

My Governefs brought me a great many other things, but it was not proper for me to appear too Well, at leaft, till I knew what kind of a Captain we fhould have : When fhe came into the Ship, I thought fhe would have died indeed ; her Heart funk at the Sight of me, and at the Thoughts of parting with me in that Condition, and fhe cry'd fo intolerably, I could not for a long time have any talk with her.

I Took that time to read my fellow Prifoner's Letter, which greatly perplex'd me ; he told me it would be impoffible for him to be difcharg'd time enough for going in the fame Ship, and which was more than all, he began to queftion whether they would give him leave to go in what Ship he pleas'd, tho' he did voluntarily tranfport himfelf ; but that they would fee him put on Board fuch a Ship as they fhould direct, and that he would be charg'd upon the Captain as other convict Prifoners were ; fo that he began to be in Difpair of feeing me 'till he came to *Virginia*, which made him almoft defperate ; feeing that on the other Hand, if I fhould not be there, if any Accident of the Sea, or of Mortality fhould take me away, he fhould be the moft undone Creature in the World.

This was very perplexing, and I knew not what Courfe to take ; I told my Governefs the Story of the

(329)

the Boatſwain, and ſhe was mighty eager with me to treat with him ; but I had no mind to it, till I heard whether my Husband or fellow Priſoner, *ſo ſhe call'd him*, cou'd be at liberty to go with me or no ; at laſt I was forc'd to let her into the whole matter, except only, that of his being my Husband ; I told her that I had made a poſitive Agreement with him to go, if he could get the liberty of going in the ſame Ship, and I found he had Money.

THEN I told her what I propos'd to do when we came there, how we could Plant, Settle ; and in ſhort, grow Rich without any more Adventures, and as a great Secret, I told her we were to Marry as ſoon as he came on Board.

SHE ſoon agreed chearfully to my going, when ſhe heard this, and ſhe made it her buſineſs from that time to get him deliver'd in time, ſo that he might go in the ſame Ship with me, which at laſt was brought to paſs, tho' with great difficulty, and not without all the Forms of a Tranſported *Convict*, which he really was not, for he had not been try'd, and which was a great Mortification to him : As our Fate was now determin'd, and we were both on Board, actually bound to *Virginia*, in the deſpicable Quality of Tranſported Convicts, deſtin'd to be ſold for Slaves, I for five Year, and he under Bonds and Security not to return to *England* any more, as long as he liv'd ; he was very much dejected and caſt down ; the Mortification of being brought on Board as he was, like a Priſoner, piqu'd him very much, ſince it was firſt told him he ſhould Tranſport himſelf, ſo that he might go as a Gentleman at liberty ; it is true he was not order'd to be ſold when he came there, as we were, and for that Reaſon he was oblig'd to pay for his Paſſage to the Captain, which we were not ; as to the reſt, he was as much at a loſs as a Child what to do with himſelf, but by Directions.

How-

(330)

However, I lay in an uncertain Condition full three Weeks not knowing whether I fhould have my Husband with me or no; and therefore not refolv'd how, or in what manner to receive the honeft Boat-fwain's Propofal, which indeed he thought a little ftrange.

At the End of this time, behold my Husband came on Board; he look'd with a dejected angry Countenance, his great Heart was fwell'd with Rage and Difdain; to be drag'd along with three Keepers of *Newgate*, and put on Board like a Convict, when he had not fo much as been brought to a Try-al; he made loud complaints of it by his Friends, for it feems had fome Intereft; but they got fome Checque in their Application, and were told he had had *Favour cnough*, and that they had receiv'd fuch an Account of him fince the laft Grant of his Tranfportation, that he ought to think himfelf very well treated, that he was not profecuted a new: This anfwer quieted him, for he knew too much what might have happen'd, and what he had room to ex-pect; and now he faw the goodnefs of that Advice to him, which prevail'd with him to accept of the offer of Tranfportation, and after his chagrin at thefe Hell Hounds, *as he call'd them*, was a little over, he look'd more compos'd, began to be chear-ful, and as I was telling im how glad I was to have him once more out of their Hands, he took me in his Arms, and acknowledg'd with great Tendernefs, that I had given him the beft Advice poffible: *My Dear*, fays he, *Thou haft twice fav'd my Life, from hence forward it fhall be employ'd for you, and I'll al-ways take Your Advice.*

Our firft bufinefs was to compare our Stock: He was very honeft to me, and told me his Stock was pretty good when he came into the Prifon, but that living there as he did like a Gentleman, and, *which was much more*, the making of Friends, and foliciting his Cafe, had been very Expenfive; and in a

Word

(331)

Word, all his Stock left was an Hundred and Eight Pounds, which he had about him in Gold.

I G A V E him an Account of my Stock as faithfully, that is to fay what I had taken with me ; for I was refolv'd what ever fhould happen, to keep what I had left in Referve; that in Cafe I fhould die, what I had was enough to give him, and what was left in my Governefs Hands would be her own, which fhe had well deferv'd of me indeed.

MY Stock which I had with me was two Hundred forty fix Pounds, fome odd Shillings; fo that we had three Hundred fifty four Pound between us, but a worfe gotten Eftate was never put together, to begin the World with.

OUR greateft Misfortune as to our Stock, was that it was in Money, an unprofitable Cargoe to be carryed to the Plantations; I believe his was really all he had left in the World, as he told me it was; But I who had between feven and eight Hundred Pounds in Bank when this Diffafter befel me, and who had one of the faithfuleft Friends in the World to manage it for me, confidering fhe was a Woman of no Principles, had ftill Three Hundred Pounds left in her Hand, which I had referv'd, as above; befides I had fome very valuable things with me, as particularly two gold Watches, fome fmall Peicts of Plate, and fome Rings; all ftolen Goods; with this Fortune, and in the Sixty firft Year of my Age, I launch'd out into a new World, as I may call it, in the Condition only of a poor Convict, order'd to be Tranfported in refpite from the Gallows; my Cloaths were poor and mean, but not ragg'd or dirty, and none knew in the whole Ship that I had any thing of value about me.

HO WE V E R, as I had a great many very good Cloaths, and Linnen in abundance, which I had order'd to be pack'd up in two great Boxes, I had them Shipp'd on Board, not as my Goods, but as confign'd

to

(332)

to my real Name in *Virginia* ; and had the Bills of Loading in my Pocket ; and in thefe Boxes was my Plate and Watches, and every thing of value, except my Money, which I kept by itfelf in a private Drawer in my Cheft, and which cou'd not be found, or open'd if found without fplitting the Cheft to peices.

THE Ship began now to fill, feveral Paffengers came on Board, who were embark'd on no Criminal account, and thefe had Accommodations affign'd them in the great Cabbin, and other Parts of the Ship, whereas we *as Convicts* were thruft down below, I know not where ; but when my Husband came on Board, I fpoke to the Boatfwain, who had fo early given me Hints of his Friendfhip ; I told him he had befriended me in many things, and I had not made any fuitable Return to him, and with that I put a Guinea into his Hand ; I told him that my Husband was now come on Board, that tho' we were under the prefent Misfortunes, yet we had been Perfons of a differing Character from the wretch'd Crew that we came with, and defir'd to know whether the Captain might not be mov'd, to admit us to fome Conveniences in the Ship, for which we would make him what Satisfaction he pleas'd, and that we would gratifie him for his Pains in procuring this for us. He took the Guinea as I cou'd fee with great Satisfaction, and affur'd me of his Affiftance.

THEN he told us, he did not doubt but that the Captain who was one of the beft humour'd Gentlemen in the World, would be eafily brought to Accommodate us, as well as we cou'd defire, and to make me eafie, told me he would go up the next Tide on purpofe to fpeak to him about it : The next Morning happening to fleep a little longer than ordinary, when I got up, and began to look Abroad, I faw the Boatfwain among the Men in his ordinary Bufinefs ; I was a little melancholly at feeing him there,

Art

Herman Melville

After the novels for which he is famous, Herman Melville turned to composing poetry, pursuing it with care but without much critical success. John Bryant's 2001 edition of selections from Melville's works includes the poem "Art," emphasizing compositional process and revisions over a fixed, final text. His editorial "revisions narratives" refuse to hide the interrelatedness of editing and interpretation. In short, Bryant's is a kind of genetic edition. How else might one present Bryant's data—Melville's notes and drafts?

from John Bryant's Critical Edition[†]

"ART" IS MELVILLE'S most frequently anthologized poem. Along with "Dupont's Round Fight" and the posthumously published Camoëns poems, among others, "Art" examines the creative process, claiming for it here a fiery mating and mystic fusing of "unlike things," comparable to the mythic and sensual struggle between Jacob and Angel in the Old Testament. Readers know the poem almost exclusively in its printed version, but it also exists in manuscript, which bears evidence of at least six stages of revision, each constituting an early version of the poem. Thus, "Art" is not only *about* the making of a poem; its successive manuscript versions *enact* the making of a poem. By inspecting all versions of this fluid text, readers may determine to what degree Melville's writing practice corresponds to his vision of the creative process.

Melville may have begun "Art" in the 1870s, about the time he was composing *Clarel*, and bits of phrasing scattered throughout Melville's epic ("nervous energies," "thought's extremes agree," "brave schemes") are echoed in the poem. In content, "Art" resembles Washington Allston's sonnet "Art" with its fiery transcendentalism and final Hebraic imagery. But in structure, it is more of a "truncated sonnet" (see the Camoëns poems). Although its sound, development, and startling final couplet make it sonnet-like, its deliberately imperfect rhyme scheme and only eleven four-beat lines make it shorter in all dimensions than the traditional pentameter sonnet. Melville's strategic resistance to this poetic convention is also revealed in his incessant revision.

The surviving documents for "Art" consist of four working draft leaves (pinned to each other) and a fair copy. Each of the four draft leaves is a fragment of the poem representing a stage of development in the composition of the poem, but each fragment also bears considerable revision, suggesting additional substages. The six versions of "Art"

† "Introduction," by John Bryant, copyright © 2002 by John Bryant, from *Tales, Poems, and Other Writings* by Herman Melville, edited by John Bryant. Used by permission of Modern Library, a division of Random House, Inc.

reproduced here are a good guess at what Melville might have done as he revised his poem. The Revision Narratives explain each hypothetical step and the specific revisions italicized in each text.

VERSION 1: EPIGRAM

– " –

Hard to grapple and upsweep
One dripping trophy from the deep.

– " –

In him who would evoke—create,
Contraries must meet and mate;
Flames that burn, and winds that freeze;

VERSION 2: EXPANSION

In him who would evoke—create,
Contraries must meet and mate;
Flames that burn, and winds that freeze;
Sad patience—joyous energies;
Humility, and pride, and scorn;
Reverence; love and hate twin-born;
Instinct and culture; era meet

REVISION NARRATIVE, VERSIONS 1 AND 2

The earliest surviving manuscript indicates that Melville first conceived of his poem as one of two epigrams of two to maybe four lines, defining creation as the meeting and mating of contraries. But the two epigrams grew into separate poems, the first with its "dripping trophy" becoming "In a Garret," and the second becoming "Art." In Version 1, Melville transcribes only three lines of his "meet and mate" epigram, waiting, it seems, for an inspired fourth line to be added later. But that line was not forthcoming. Perhaps because of some inadequacy of its abstract flame/wind image, Melville inevitably expanded his epigram by adding one set upon another of more concrete paired contraries to create Version 2.

VERSION 3: RESHAPING

Art

_ " _

In him who would evoke—create,
What extremes must meet and mate;
Flame that burns,—a wind to freeze;
Sad patience—joyous energies;
Humility, *yet* pride, and scorn;
Audacity—reverence; love and hate
Instinct and culture. *These must mate*
With more than Even Jacob's heart

REVISION NARRATIVE, VERSION 3

With the epigrammatic concision undermined by so many paired contraries, Melville worked in Version 3 toward a more shapely structure for his longer poem, giving it a title, pairing "Audacity" with "reverence," and inserting the first crystallization of the poem's concluding image of Jacob's heart. In line 2, Melville also vacillated between "contraries" and "extremes" (actually settling back to "contraries"). He was modulating on the mating of opposites, a notion of bipolarity he would eventually drop altogether in Version 5. Finally, by removing "twin-born" from "love and hate," Melville breaks his couplet's rhyme, thus consciously leaving "scorn" in line 6 the only unrhymed end-of-line word. Melville keeps this innovation throughout all subsequent versions, thus giving his "truncated sonnet," its unconventional "ragged edge."

VERSION 4: REVISED ENDING

In him who would evoke—create,
What extremes must meet and mate;
Flame that burns,—a wind to freeze;
Sad patience—joyous energies;
Humility, yet pride, and scorn;
Instinct and study; love and hate;
Audacity—reverence; these must mate—
With much of mystic Jacob's heart
To wrestle with that angel—Art.

VERSION 5: REVISED OPENING

In placid hours we easy dream
Of many a bright unbodied scheme.
But forms to give, true life create
What unlike things must meet and mate;
A flame to melt—a wind to freeze;
Sad patience,—joyous energies;
Humility, yet pride, and scorn;
Instinct and study; love and hate;
Audacity—reverence. These must mate—
And fuse with Jacob's mystic heart
To wrestle with *the* angel—Art.

REVISION NARRATIVE, VERSION 4

In line 6, Melville revises "culture" to "study" to give the paired contrary "Instinct and study," which along with the removal of "era" in Version 3 eradicates an apparent reference to Matthew Arnold's *Culture and Anarchy*. At the same time he repositions "Instinct and study" so that "Audacity—reverence" becomes the dramatic culmination of his paired contraries. In addition, Melville enhances the Hebraism of his final Jacob image by adding the images of mysticism and angelic struggle.

VERSION 6: FAIR COPY

Art

In placid hours *well pleased we* dream
Of many a *brave* unbodied scheme.
But *form to lend, pulsed* life create,
What unlike things must meet and mate;
A flame to melt—a wind to freeze;
Sad patience—joyous energies;
Humility—yet pride and scorn;
Instinct and study; love and hate;
Audacity—reverence. These must mate,
And fuse with Jacob's mystic heart,
To wrestle with the angel—*Art*.

REVISION NARRATIVE, VERSIONS 5 AND 6

In Version 5, Melville develops a new opening. Because the startling leap of "angel—Art" introduced in the last line of Version 4 too closely mirrors "evoke—create" in line 1, he reconceives the opening altogether to establish a Wordsworthian placidity of inspiration, which intensifies the contrast to come of the more fiery, less transcendental, process of the actual creation of "true life" in art. In line 4, the conversion of "extremes" to "unlike things" unhinges the bipolar contraries from idealized antithesis and redefines them more concretely in terms of the natural dissimilitude of material objects, or for that matter gender and sexuality, which in the "meet and mate" phrasing, present in all versions, has been the poem's implied force of creativity. This hidden sensuality is augmented by the revision of "burns" to "melt" (line 5) and the insertion of "fuse" (line 10). In Version 6, the fair copy and final print text of "Art" add to this sensualizing process, especially with the revision of "true life" to "pulsed life" in line 3. By altering "easy" to "well pleased" and "bright" to "brave," Melville further heightens the contrast between the mental conception of an idea and the actual expression or embodiment of that idea in words.

from *King Lear* and *Othello*

William Shakespeare

For a long time the popular line about Shakespeare's writing was that he did not revise; indeed, as Jonson quotes his fellow player's praise of Shakespeare, he "never blotted out a line." But since the 1980s scholars have been reading the early printed editions of many of Shakespeare's plays for evidence of revision, the popular tragedies *Hamlet*, *King Lear*, and *Othello* perhaps chief among them. *Hamlet* is perhaps the most studied textually and may be the most complicated textually, as it survives in three remarkably different but interrelated early printed editions. But *King Lear* and *Othello* are also quite complex, as each exists in two early editions that have surprising and meaningful variants. The following selections illustrate not only some of the evidence of this revision but also the degree to which a critical edition allows one to work backward through its notes to the witnesses on which it is based in order to read for possible revision.

Borrowing their text (but not always all features of it) from the Oxford critical edition, the editors of *The Norton Shakespeare* present three different versions of *King Lear*. The first two, *The History of King Lear*, based on the first printing, Q1 in 1608, and *The Tragedy of King Lear*, based on the second, F1 in 1623, are printed in facing pages. The notes that follow these versions are keyed to the

Tragedy's act, scene, and line numbers, but they record the witnesses' readings for emendations made to both texts. After these two versions, the editors also print a conflation of the two texts. The excerpt here is what the conflation calls Act 4, scene 7 (scene 21 in *History* and Act 4, scene 6 in *Tragedy*), in which Lear and Cordelia are reunited. When readers first encounter facing-page editions, they sometimes find their reading processes disrupted or slowed, as one must skip a page of print in order to read continuously, and the layout encourages readers to collate the two texts as they as they read. But a collation of these two versions will be incomplete without referring to the textual notes, since both versions have been emended with reference to one another. Can one reconstruct editorial principles from the choices the editors have made in each of the three texts? Are there what we might call editorial contradictions? In what ways might a conflation risk disguising one or another source more than incorporating it?

For the selection from Act 4, scene 2 of *Othello*, one might compare the text and textual notes from *The Norton Shakespeare* (again, based on the Oxford edition) with the fuller information from the *Textual Companion*, which reports emendations and readings not reported in the first. To these one can then compare the facsimiles of the two primary witnesses for Othello, the Quarto from 1622 and the Folio, printed a year later. To what extent do the sets of notes allow one to arrive at the two versions on which the modern text is based?

from Stephen Greenblatt's (et al.) three-text edition of *King Lear: The History* (1608) and *The Tragedy* (1623) in facing pages

Scene 21

[Soft music.] Enter CORDELIA, *and* KENT *[disguised]*

CORDELIA O thou good Kent,
How shall I live and work to match thy goodness?
My life will be too short, and every measure° fail me.   *attempt*
KENT   To be acknowledged, madam, is o'erpaid.°   *is more than enough*
5   All my reports go¹ with the modest truth,
Nor more, nor clipped, but so.²
CORDELIA   Be better suited.°   *attired*
These weeds° are memories of those worser hours.   *clothes*
I prithee put them off.
KENT   Pardon me, dear madam.
Yet to be known shortens my made intent.³
10   My boon I make it⁴ that you know° me not   *acknowledge*
Till time and I think meet.°   *suitable*
CORDELIA   Then be't so, my good lord.
[Enter DOCTOR *and* FIRST GENTLEMAN]
How does the King?
DOCTOR   Madam, sleeps still.
CORDELIA   O you kind gods,
Cure this great breach in his abusèd nature;
The untuned and hurrying senses O wind up⁵
Of this child-changèd⁶ father!
15   DOCTOR   So please your majesty
That we may wake the King? He hath slept long.
CORDELIA   Be governed by your knowledge, and proceed
I'th' sway° of your own will. Is he arrayed?°   *By the authority / clothed*
FIRST GENTLEMAN   Ay, madam. In the heaviness of his sleep
20   We put fresh garments on him.
DOCTOR   Good madam, be by when we do awake him.
I doubt not of his temperance.°   *calmness*
CORDELIA   Very well.
DOCTOR   Please you draw near. Louder the music there!
*[*LEAR *is discovered° asleep]*   *revealed*
CORDELIA   O my dear father, restoration hang
25   Thy medicine on my lips, and let this kiss
Repair those violent harms that my two sisters
Have in thy reverence° made!   *aged dignity*
KENT   Kind and dear princess!
CORDELIA   Had you not⁷ been their father, these white flakes°   *locks of hair*
Had challenged° pity of them. Was this a face   *Would have provoked*
30   To be exposed against the warring winds,
To stand against the deep dread-bolted thunder
In the most terrible and nimble stroke
Of quick cross-lightning, to watch°—poor *perdu*⁸—   *to stand guard*

Scene 21 Location: The French camp at Dover.
1. May all accounts of me agree.
2. Not greater or less, but exactly the modest amount I deserve.
3. Revealing myself now would abort my designs.
4. The reward I beg is.
5. *The . . . up*: Reorder his confused and delirious mind.

The image is of tightening the strings of a lute.
6. Changed by his children; changed into a child; playing on a musical key change.
7. Even if you had not.
8. Lost one; in military terms, a dangerously exposed sentry.

4.6

Enter CORDELIA, KENT *[disguised], and [the* FIRST*]* GEN-
TLEMAN

CORDELIA O thou good Kent, how shall I live and work
 To match thy goodness? My life will be too short,
 And every measure° fail me.   *attempt*
KENT To be acknowledged, madam, is o'erpaid.°   *is more than enough*
5 All my reports go[1] with the modest truth,
 Nor more, nor clipped, but so.[2]
CORDELIA   Be better suited.°   *attired*
 These weeds° are memories of those worser hours.   *clothes*
 I prithee put them off.
KENT   Pardon, dear madam.
 Yet to be known shortens my made intent.[3]
10 My boon I make it[4] that you know° me not   *acknowledge*
 Till time and I think meet.°   *suitable*
CORDELIA   Then be't so, my good lord. —
 How does the King?
FIRST GENTLEMAN Madam, sleeps still.
CORDELIA   O you kind gods,
 Cure this great breach in his abusèd nature;
 Th'untuned and jarring senses O wind up[5]
 Of this child-changèd[6] father!
15 FIRST GENTLEMAN   So please your majesty
 That we may wake the King? He hath slept long.
CORDELIA Be governed by your knowledge, and proceed
 I'th' sway° of your own will. Is he arrayed?°   *By the authority / clothed*
FIRST GENTLEMAN Ay, madam. In the heaviness of sleep
20 We put fresh garments on him.
    Enter LEAR *[asleep,] in a chair carried by servants*
 Be by, good madam, when we do awake him.
 I doubt not of his temperance.°   *calmness*
CORDELIA O my dear father, restoration hang
 Thy medicine on my lips, and let this kiss
25 Repair those violent harms that my two sisters
 Have in thy reverence° made!   *aged dignity*
KENT   Kind and dear princess!
CORDELIA Had you not[7] been their father, these white flakes° *locks of hair*
 Did challenge° pity of them. Was this a face   *Would have provoked*
 To be opposed against the warring winds?

4.6 Location: The French camp at Dover.
1. May all accounts of me agree.
2. Not greater or less, but exactly the modest amount I
deserve.
3. Revealing myself now would abort my designs.
4. The reward I beg is.

5. *Th'untuned . . . up:* Reorder his confused and delirious
mind. The image is of tightening the strings of a lute.
6. Changed by his children; changed into a child; playing on a musical key change.
7. Even if you had not.

With this thin helm?° Mine injurer's mean'st dog,   *helmet (of hair)*
35   Though he had bit me, should have stood that night
Against my fire. And wast thou fain,° poor father,   *glad*
To hovel thee with swine and rogues forlorn
In short° and musty straw? Alack, alack,   *scant; broken*
'Tis wonder that thy life and wits at once
40   Had not concluded all!° [*To* DOCTOR] He wakes. Speak to him.   *altogether*
DOCTOR   Madam, do you; 'tis fittest.
CORDELIA [*to* LEAR]   How does my royal lord? How fares your majesty?
LEAR   You do me wrong to take me out o'th' grave.
Thou art a soul in bliss, but I am bound
45   Upon a wheel of fire, that mine own tears
Do scald like molten lead.[9]
CORDELIA   Sir, know me.
LEAR   You're a spirit, I know. Where did you die?
CORDELIA [*to the* DOCTOR]   Still, still far wide!°   *unbalanced*
DOCTOR   He's scarce awake. Let him alone a while.
50   LEAR   Where have I been? Where am I? Fair daylight?
I am mightily abused.° I should e'en die with pity   *wronged; deceived*
To see another thus. I know not what to say.
I will not swear these are my hands. Let's see:
I feel this pin prick. Would I were assured
Of my condition.
55   CORDELIA [*kneeling*]   O look upon me, sir,
And hold your hands in benediction o'er me.
No, sir, you must not kneel.
LEAR   Pray do not mock.
I am a very foolish, fond° old man,   *silly*
Fourscore and upward, and to deal plainly,
60   I fear I am not in my perfect mind.
Methinks I should know you, and know this man;
Yet I am doubtful, for I am mainly° ignorant   *entirely*
What place this is; and all the skill I have
Remembers not these garments; nor I know not
65   Where I did lodge last night. Do not laugh at me,
For as I am a man, I think this lady
To be my child, Cordelia.
CORDELIA   And so I am.
LEAR   Be your tears wet?[1] Yes, faith. I pray, weep not.
If you have poison for me, I will drink it.
70   I know you do not love me; for your sisters
Have, as I do remember, done me wrong.
You have some cause; they have not.
CORDELIA   No cause, no cause.

---

9. *but I . . . lead:* Lear puts himself in either hell or purgatory, both places of such punishment in medieval accounts.

1. Are your tears real?; is this really happening?

30   Mine enemy's dog, though he had bit me, should have stood
    That night against my fire. And wast thou fain,° poor father,   *glad*
    To hovel thee with swine and rogues forlorn
    In short° and musty straw? Alack, alack,   *scant; broken*
    'Tis wonder that thy life and wits at once
35   Had not concluded all!° [*To the* GENTLEMAN] He wakes. Speak   *altogether*
      to him.
FIRST GENTLEMAN   Madam, do you; 'tis fittest.
CORDELIA [*to* LEAR]   How does my royal lord? How fares your majesty?
LEAR   You do me wrong to take me out o'th' grave.
    Thou art a soul in bliss, but I am bound
40   Upon a wheel of fire, that mine own tears
    Do scald like molten lead.[8]
CORDELIA   Sir, do you know me?
LEAR   You are a spirit, I know. Where did you die?
CORDELIA [*to the* GENTLEMAN]   Still, still far wide!°   *unbalanced*
FIRST GENTLEMAN   He's scarce awake. Let him alone a while.
45 LEAR   Where have I been? Where am I? Fair daylight?
    I am mightily abused.° I should ev'n die with pity   *wronged; deceived*
    To see another thus. I know not what to say.
    I will not swear these are my hands. Let's see:
    I feel this pin prick. Would I were assured
    Of my condition.
50 CORDELIA [*kneeling*]   O look upon me, sir,
    And hold your hands in benediction o'er me.
    You must not kneel.
LEAR   Pray do not mock.
    I am a very foolish, fond° old man,   *silly*
    Fourscore and upward,
55   Not an hour more nor less; and to deal plainly,
    I fear I am not in my perfect mind.
    Methinks I should know you, and know this man;
    Yet I am doubtful, for I am mainly° ignorant   *entirely*
    What place this is; and all the skill I have
60   Remembers not these garments; nor I know not
    Where I did lodge last night. Do not laugh at me,
    For as I am a man, I think this lady
    To be my child, Cordelia.
CORDELIA   And so I am, I am.
LEAR   Be your tears wet?[9] Yes, faith. I pray, weep not.
65   If you have poison for me, I will drink it.
    I know you do not love me; for your sisters
    Have, as I do remember, done me wrong.
    You have some cause; they have not.
CORDELIA   No cause, no cause.

---

8. *but I . . . lead*: Lear puts himself in either hell or purgatory, both places of such punishment in medieval

accounts.
9. Are your tears real?; is this really happening?

678 ✦ The History of King Lear / Scene 21

LEAR Am I in France?
KENT In your own kingdom, sir.
75 LEAR Do not abuse° me.   *deceive; mock*
DOCTOR Be comforted, good madam. The great rage
    You see is cured in him, and yet it is danger
    To make him even o'er° the time he has lost.   *go over*
    Desire him to go in; trouble him no more
80   Till further settling.°   *Until his mind eases*
CORDELIA [*to* LEAR] Will't please your highness walk?
LEAR You must bear with me.
    Pray now, forget and forgive. I am old
    And foolish.   *Exeunt. Manent*° KENT *and* [FIRST] GENTLEMAN   *Remain*
FIRST GENTLEMAN Holds it true, sir, that the Duke
    Of Cornwall was so slain?
85 KENT   Most certain, sir.
FIRST GENTLEMAN Who is conductor° of his people?   *commander*
KENT   As 'tis said,
    The bastard son of Gloucester.
FIRST GENTLEMAN   They say Edgar,
    His banished son, is with the Earl of Kent
    In Germany.
KENT   Report° is changeable.   *Rumor*
90 'Tis time to look about.° The powers of the kingdom   *prepare defenses*
    Approach apace.
FIRST GENTLEMAN The arbitrement° is   *encounter*
    Like to be bloody. Fare you well, sir.   [*Exit*]
KENT My point and period[2] will be throughly wrought,
    Or° well or ill, as this day's battle's fought.   *Exit*   *For*

Scene 22
Enter EDMUND, REGAN, *and their powers*
EDMUND Know° of the Duke if his last purpose hold,[1]   *Inquire*
    Or whether since he is advised by aught[2]
    To change the course. He's full of abdication[3]
    And self-reproving. Bring his constant pleasure.°   *his settled intent*
                        [*Exit one or more*]
5 REGAN Our sister's man is certainly miscarried.[4]
EDMUND 'Tis to be doubted,° madam.   *feared*
REGAN   Now, sweet lord,
    You know the goodness I intend upon you.
    Tell me but truly—but then speak the truth—
    Do you not love my sister?
EDMUND   Ay: honoured° love.   *honorable*
10 REGAN But have you never found my brother's way
    To the forfended[5] place?

---

2. The purpose and end of my life; literally, the full stop.
Scene 22 Location: The British camp near Dover.
1. If his previous intention (to wage war) remains firm.
2. Since then anything has persuaded him.

3. A tendency to give up his intentions or put aside his responsibilities.
4. Has surely come to grief by some accident.
5. Forbidden (to Edmund, because it is adulterous).

LEAR   Am I in France?
70   KENT   In your own kingdom, sir.
  LEAR   Do not abuse° me.   *deceive; mock*
  FIRST GENTLEMAN   Be comforted, good madam. The great rage
    You see is killed in him. Desire him to go in.
    Trouble him no more till further settling.°   *until his mind eases*
75   CORDELIA *[to* LEAR*]*   Will't please your highness walk?
  LEAR   You must bear with me. Pray you now, forget
    And forgive. I am old and foolish.   *Exeunt*

from *The Norton Shakespeare*, Textual Notes to *King Lear*, "Textual Variants: Tragedy"

4.6 *Scaena Septima* **22 not of** [Q] of **29 warring** [Q] iarring **51 your hands** [Q] yours hand [Fa] your hand [Fb] **52 mock** [Q1] mocke me

from Stephen Greenblatt's (et al.) three-text edition of
King Lear: The Tragedy (Conflated Text)

EDGAR I know thee well: a serviceable° villain;   *an officious*
As duteous to the vices of thy mistress
As badness would desire.
GLOUCESTER   What, is he dead?
250 EDGAR Sit you down, father; rest you.
Let's see his pockets; the letters that he speaks of
May be my friends. He's dead; I am only sorry
He had no other death'sman.° Let us see.   *executioner*
Leave,° gentle wax;[9] and, manners blame us not.   *By your leave*
255 To know our enemies' minds, we'd rip their hearts;
Their° papers, is more lawful.   *To rip their*
(*Reads*) "Let our reciprocal vows be remembered. You have
many opportunities to cut him off. If your will want° not, time   *lacks*
and place will be fruitfully offered. There is nothing done,° if   *accomplished*
260 he return the conqueror. Then am I the prisoner, and his bed
 . my jail; from the loathed warmth whereof deliver me, and sup-
ply° the place for your labor.[1]   *fill*
                Your—wife, so I would say—
                Affectionate servant,
265   Goneril."
O undistinguished space of woman's will![2]
A plot upon her virtuous husband's life;
And the exchange° my brother! Here, in the sands,   *substitute*
Thee I'll rake up,° the post unsanctified°   *cover up / unholy messenger*
270 Of murderous lechers; and in the mature time°   *when the time is ripe*
With this ungracious° paper strike the sight   *ungodly*
Of the death-practiced duke.[3] For him 'tis well
That of thy death and business I can tell.
GLOUCESTER The king is mad. How stiff is my vile sense,[4]
275 That I stand up, and have ingenious feeling[5]
Of my huge sorrows! Better I were distract;°   *mad*
So should my thoughts be severed from my griefs,
And woes by wrong° imaginations lose   *false*
The knowledge of themselves.
          Drum afar off
EDGAR   Give me your hand.
280 Far off, methinks, I hear the beaten drum.
Come, father, I'll bestow° you with a friend.   *Exeunt*   *lodge*

4.7
Enter CORDELIA, KENT, DOCTOR, *and a* GENTLEMAN
CORDELIA O thou good Kent, how shall I live and work,
To match thy goodness? My life will be too short,
And every measure° fail me.   *attempt*
KENT To be acknowledged, madam, is o'erpaid.°   *is more than enough*
5 All my reports go[1] with the modest truth;
Nor more nor clipped, but so.[2]
CORDELIA   Be better suited.°   *attired*
These weeds° are memories of those worser hours.   *clothes*
I prithee, put them off.

---

9. The wax seal on the letter.
1. *for your labor:* as a reward for your endeavors, and for further sexual exertion.
2. Limitless extent of woman's wilfullness. As with "hell" in line 124, "will" might also refer to a woman's genitals.
3. Of the Duke whose death is plotted.
4. How obstinate is my unwanted power of reason.

5. That I remain upright and firm in my sanity and have rational perceptions.
4.7 Location: The French camp at Dover.
1. May all accounts of me agree.
2. Not greater or less, but exactly the modest amount I deserve.

KENT   Pardon me, dear madam;
   Yet to be known shortens my made intent.[3]
10   My boon I make it,[4] that you know° me not   *acknowledge*
   Till time and I think meet.°   *suitable*
CORDELIA   Then be 't so, my good lord. (*To the* DOCTOR) How
   does the king?
DOCTOR   Madam, sleeps still.
CORDELIA   O you kind gods,
15   Cure this great breach in his abuséd nature!
   The untuned and jarring senses, O, wind up[5]
   Of this child-changéd[6] father!
DOCTOR   So please your majesty
   That we may wake the king? He hath slept long.
CORDELIA   Be governed by your knowledge, and proceed
20   I' the sway° of your own will. Is he arrayed?°   *By the authority / clothed*
   Enter LEAR *in a chair carried by servants*
GENTLEMAN   Aye, madam. In the heaviness of his sleep
   We put fresh garments on him.
DOCTOR   Be by, good madam, when we do awake him;
   I doubt not of his temperance.°   *calmness*
CORDELIA   Very well.
   Music
25   DOCTOR   Please you, draw near. Louder the music there!
CORDELIA   O my dear father! Restoration hang
   Thy medicine on my lips; and let this kiss
   Repair those violent harms that my two sisters
   Have in thy reverence° made!   *aged dignity*
KENT   Kind and dear princess!
30   CORDELIA   Had you not[7] been their father, these white flakes°   *locks of hair*
   Had challenged° pity of them. Was this a face   *Would have provoked*
   To be opposed against the warring winds?
   To stand against the deep dread-bolted thunder?
   In the most terrible and nimble stroke
35   Of quick, cross lightning? to watch°—poor perdu![8]—   *to stand guard*
   With this thin helm?° Mine enemy's dog,   *helmet (of hair)*
   Though he had bit me, should have stood that night
   Against my fire; and wast thou fain,° poor father,   *glad*
   To hovel thee with swine, and rogues forlorn,
40   In short° and musty straw? Alack, alack!   *scant; broken*
   'Tis wonder that thy life and wits at once
   Had not concluded all.° He wakes; speak to him.   *altogether*
DOCTOR   Madam, do you; 'tis fittest.
CORDELIA   How does my royal lord? How fares your majesty?
45   LEAR   You do me wrong to take me out o' the grave.
   Thou art a soul in bliss; but I am bound
   Upon a wheel of fire, that mine own tears
   Do scald like molten lead.[9]
CORDELIA   Sir, do you know me?
LEAR   You are a spirit, I know. When did you die?
50   CORDELIA   Still, still, far wide!°   *unbalanced*

3. Revealing myself now would abort my designs.
4. The reward I beg is.
5. *The . . . up:* Reorder his confused and delirious mind. The image is of tightening the strings of a lute.
6. Changed by his children; changed into a child; playing on a musical key change.
7. Even if you had not.
8. Lost one; in military terms, a dangerously exposed sentry.
9. *but I . . . lead:* Lear puts himself in either hell or purgatory, both places of such punishment in medieval accounts.

DOCTOR   He's scarce awake. Let him alone awhile.

LEAR   Where have I been? Where am I? Fair daylight?
　I am mightily abused.° I should e'en die with pity,   *wronged; deceived*
　To see another thus. I know not what to say.
55　I will not swear these are my hands. Let's see.
　I feel this pin prick. Would I were assured
　Of my condition!

CORDELIA　　　　　　O, look upon me, sir,
　And hold your hands in benediction o'er me:
　No, sir, you must not kneel.

60 LEAR   Pray, do not mock me.
　I am a very foolish fond° old man,   *silly*
　Fourscore and upward, not an hour more nor less;
　And, to deal plainly,
　I fear I am not in my perfect mind.
65　Methinks I should know you, and know this man;
　Yet I am doubtful; for I am mainly° ignorant   *entirely*
　What place this is; and all the skill I have
　Remembers not these garments; nor I know not
　Where I did lodge last night. Do not laugh at me;
70　For, as I am a man, I think this lady
　To be my child Cordelia.

CORDELIA　　　　　　And so I am, I am.

LEAR   Be your tears wet?[1] Yes, faith. I pray, weep not.
　If you have poison for me, I will drink it.
　I know you do not love me; for your sisters
75　Have, as I do remember, done me wrong.
　You have some cause, they have not.

CORDELIA　　　　　　　　　　No cause, no, cause.

LEAR   Am I in France?

KENT　　　　　　In your own kingdom, sir.

LEAR   Do not abuse° me.   *deceive; mock*

DOCTOR   Be comforted, good madam. The great rage,
80　You see, is killed in him; and yet it is danger
　To make him even o'er° the time he has lost.   *go over*
　Desire him to go in. Trouble him no more
　Till further settling.°   *Until his mind eases*

CORDELIA   Will't please your highness walk?

LEAR　　　　　　　　　You must bear with me:
85　Pray you now, forget and forgive. I am old and foolish.
　　　　　　　　Exeunt all but KENT *and* GENTLEMAN

GENTLEMAN   Holds it true, sir, that the Duke of Cornwall was so
　slain?

KENT   Most certain, sir.

GENTLEMAN   Who is conductor° of his people?   *commander*

90 KENT   As 'tis said, the bastard son of Gloucester.

GENTLEMAN   They say Edgar, his banished son, is with the Earl
　of Kent in Germany.

KENT   Report° is changeable. 'Tis time to look about.° The pow-   *Rumor / prepare defenses*
　ers of the kingdom approach apace.

95 GENTLEMAN   The arbitrement° is like to be bloody. Fare you   *encounter*
　well, sir.　　　　　　　　　　　　　*Exit*

KENT   My point and period[2] will be throughly wrought,
　Or° well or ill, as this day's battle's fought.　　*Exit*   *For*

---

1. Are your tears real?; is this really happening?　　2. The purpose and end of my life; literally, the full stop.

from Stephen Greenblatt's (et al.) edition of *Othello*

	I understand a fury in your words,	
	But not the words.	
35	OTHELLO Why, what art thou?	
	DESDEMONA Your wife, my lord, your true and loyal wife.	
	OTHELLO Come, swear it, damn thyself,	
	Lest, being° like one of heaven, the devils themselves	*appearing*
	Should fear to seize thee. Therefore be double-damned:	
	Swear thou art honest.	
40	DESDEMONA Heaven doth truly know it.	
	OTHELLO Heaven truly knows that thou art false as hell.	
	DESDEMONA To whom, my lord? With whom? How am I false?	
	OTHELLO [*weeping*] Ah, Desdemon, away, away, away!	
	DESDEMONA Alas, the heavy day! Why do you weep?	
45	Am I the motive of these tears, my lord?	
	If haply° you my father do suspect	*perhaps*
	An instrument of this your calling back,	
	Lay not your blame on me. If you have lost him,	
	I have lost him too.	
	OTHELLO Had it pleased God	
50	To try me with affliction; had He rained	
	All kind of sores and shames on my bare head,	
	Steeped me in poverty to the very lips,	
	Given to captivity me and my utmost hopes,	
	I should have found in some place of my soul	
55	A drop of patience. But, alas, to make me	
	The fixèd figure for the time of scorn	
	To point his slow and moving finger at[4]—	
	Yet could I bear that too, well, very well.	
	But there where I have garnered° up my heart,	*stored*
60	Where either I must live or bear no life,	
	The fountain[5] from the which my current runs	
	Or else dries up—to be discarded thence,	
	Or keep it as a cistern for foul toads	
	To knot and gender° in! Turn thy complexion there,	*To couple and engender*
65	Patience,[6] thou young and rose-lipped cherubin,	
	Ay, here look grim as hell.	
	DESDEMONA I hope my noble lord esteems me honest.	
	OTHELLO O, ay—as summer flies are in the shambles,°	*slaughterhouse*
	That quicken even with blowing.[7] O thou weed,	
70	Who art so lovely fair, and smell'st so sweet,	
	That the sense aches at thee—would thou hadst ne'er been born!	
	DESDEMONA Alas, what ignorant sin have I committed?	
	OTHELLO Was this fair paper, this most goodly book,	
	Made to write 'whore' upon? What committed?	
75	Committed?[8] O thou public commoner,°	*prostitute*
	I should make very forges of my cheeks,	
	That would to cinders burn up modesty,	
	Did I but speak thy deeds. What committed?	

---

4. *The fixed . . . at:* The designated object of scorn for this scornful time to point (as on a clock face) its slowly moving hand at.
5. Spring. The language here imagines Desdemona as the source of Othello's potential offspring.
6. *Turn . . . / Patience:* Change color at the thought of that, Patience. Or perhaps Patience and the "cherubin"

(end of line) are Desdemona, whom Othello directs to gaze at his own face or a mirror.
7. Who come to life (or bring their offspring to life and hence make the meat foul) as soon as the eggs are deposited. The point seems to be the speed of breeding, inferred from Desdemona's supposed infidelity.
8. Lines 75–78 do not appear in Q.

Heaven stops the nose at it, and the moon winks;° | *closes its eyes*
80 The bawdy° wind, that kisses all it meets, | *promiscuous*
Is hushed within the hollow mine of earth° | *within a cave*
And will not hear't. What committed?
DESDEMONA   By heaven, you do me wrong.
OTHELLO   Are not you a strumpet?
85 DESDEMONA   No, as I am a Christian.
If to preserve this vessel for my lord
From any other foul unlawful touch
Be not to be a strumpet, I am none.
OTHELLO   What, not a whore?
DESDEMONA   No, as I shall be saved.
90 OTHELLO   Is't possible?
DESDEMONA   O heaven forgive us!
OTHELLO   I cry you mercy° then. | *I beg your pardon*
I took you for that cunning whore of Venice
That married with Othello. [*Calling*] You, mistress,
95 That have the office opposite to Saint Peter
And keeps the gate of hell,
          Enter EMILIA
                              you, you, ay, you.
We ha' done our course.° [*Giving money*] There's money for your pains. | *business*
I pray you, turn the key and keep our counsel.   *Exit*
EMILIA   Alas, what does this gentleman conceive?° | *believe*
100 How do you, madam? How do you, my good lady?
DESDEMONA   Faith, half asleep.
EMILIA   Good madam, what's the matter with my lord?
DESDEMONA   With who?
EMILIA   Why, with my lord, madam.
DESDEMONA   Who is thy lord?
EMILIA   He that is yours, sweet lady.
105 DESDEMONA   I ha' none. Do not talk to me, Emilia.
I cannot weep, nor answers have I none
But what should go by water.° Prithee tonight | *appear in tears*
Lay on my bed my wedding sheets, remember.
And call thy husband hither.
EMILIA   Here's a change indeed.   *Exit*
110 DESDEMONA   'Tis meet° I should be used so, very meet. | *fitting*
How have I been behaved, that he might stick
The small'st opinion on my least misuse?[9]
          Enter IAGO *and* EMILIA
IAGO   What is your pleasure, madam? How is't with you?
DESDEMONA   I cannot tell. Those that do teach young babes
115 Do it with gentle means and easy tasks.
He might ha' chid me so, for, in good faith,
I am a child to chiding.
IAGO   What is the matter, lady?
EMILIA   Alas, Iago, my lord hath so bewhored her,° | *called her whore*
Thrown such despite° and heavy terms upon her, | *spite*
120 That true hearts cannot bear it.
DESDEMONA   Am I that name, Iago?
IAGO   What name, fair lady?
DESDEMONA   Such as she said my lord did say I was.

9. *that . . . misuse:* perhaps, which would cause him to suspect even slightly the least fault.

from *The Norton Shakespeare*, Textual Notes to *Othello*, "Textual Variants"

4.2.5 'em [Q] them **16 ha'** [Q] haue **24 ha'** [Q] haue **32 nay** [Q] May **33 knees** [Q] knee **35 But not the words** [Q; not in F] 49 God Heauen 50 **He** [Q] they **71 ne'er** [Q] neuer **97 ha'** [Q] haue **105 ha'** [Q] haue **116 ha'** [Q] haue **120 hearts** [Fb] heart [Fa] **145 heaven** [Q] Heauens **152** O God O Good [Q] Alas **159 them in** them: or **171 And he does chide with you** [Q; not in F] 186 Faith [Q; not in F] **I have heard too much, for your words, and** [Q] And hell gnaw his bones, [Fa] I haue heard too much: and your words and [Fb] **192 'em** [Q] them **224 takes** [Q] taketh **228 of** [Q; not in **F**]

from *William Shakespeare: A Textual Companion*, ed. S. Wells and G. Taylor†

★4.2.3/2414   Yes,] Yes, and
★4.2.8/2419   o'th'] o'the
★4.2.10/2421   her gloues, her mask] (Gloues . . . Mask); her mask, her gloues
★4.2.17/2428   heauen] (Heauen); heauens
★4.2.19/2430   their Wiues] her Sex
★4.2.25/2436   you] *not in* Q
★4.2.33/2444   doth] does
★4.2.43/2454   Ah] O
★4.2.43/2454   *Desdemon*] *Deſdemona*
★4.2.45/2456   motiue of these] occaſion of thoſe
4.2.48–9/2459–60   lost . . . lost] left . . . left
★4.2.49/2460   I] Why I
4.2.50/2461   rain'd] ram'd
★4.2.51/2462   kind] kindes
★4.2.53/2464   vtmost] *not in* Q

† From *William Shakespeare: A Textual Companion*, ed. Stanley Wells, Gary Taylor, John Jowett, and William Montgomery (New York: Oxford University Press, 1987). Reprinted by permission of the Oxford University Press.

*4.2.54/2465   place] part

*4.2.56/2467   The] A

*4.2.57/2468   finger] fingers

*4.2.57/2468   at—] (at.); at – – oh, oh,

4.2.65/2476   thou] thy

*4.2.68/2479   as summer] (as Sommer Fb; as a Sommer Fa); as ſummers

*4.2.69/2480   thou] thou blacke

*4.2.70/2481   Who . . . faire,] why . . . faire?

*4.2.70/2481   and] Thou

*4.2.74/2485   vpon] on

*4.2.75–8/2486–9   Committed? . . . deedes. What commited?] *not in* Q

4.2.81/2492   hollow] hallow

*4.2.82/2493   committed?] (commited); committed, impudent ſtrumpet.

*4.2.87/2498   other] hated

*4.2.91/2502   forgiue vs] forgiueneſe Q

*4.2.92/2503   then] *not in* Q

*4.2.96/2507   gate of] gates in

*4.2.96/2507   you, you: I you] (You,); I, you, you, you

*4.2.104/2515   DESDEMONA. Who is . . . Lady.] *not in* Q

*4.2.106/2517   answeres] anſwer

*4.2.108/2519   my] our

*4.2.109/2520   Here's] (Heere's); Here is

*4.2.110/2521   very meete] very well

4.2.112/2523   small'st] F; ſmalleſt

*4.2.112/2523   least misvse] Fc; miſe vſe Fa; mſvſe Fb; greateſt abufe Q

*4.2.117/2528   to] at

*4.2.120/2531   That] As

*4.2.120/2531   beare it] beare

*4.2.123/2534   said] ſayes

4.2.129/2540   Hath] Has

*4.2.130/2541   and her friends] (And); all her friends

*4.2.132/2543   for't] for it

*4.2.134/2545   I will] I'le

4.2.142/2553   forme] (Forme); for me

*4.2.143/2554   most villanous] outragious

*4.2.147/2558   rascalls] (Raſcalls); raſcall

4.2.148/2559   th'west] the Weſt

*4.2.148/2559   dore] (doore); dores

*4.2.149/2560   them] him

*4.2.155–68/2566–79   Here I kneele . . . make me.] (Heere); *not in* Q

*4.2.173/2584   It is] Tis

4.2.173/2584   warrant] warrant you

4.2.174/2585   summon] ſummon you

*4.2.175/2586   The . . . The meate.] (Venice); And the great
   Meſengers of *Venice* ſtay,

*4.2.182/2592   me now,] me, thou

*4.2.182/2592   keep'st] keepetſ

*4.2.188/2599   performances] (Performances); performance

*4.2.190/2601   With naught but truth:] *not in* Q

*4.2.191/2602   my meanes] meanes

*4.2.192/2603   deliuer] deliuer to

4.2.193/2604   hath] has

*4.2.194/2605   expectations] expectation

*4.2.195/2606   acquaintance] acquittance

*4.2.196/2607   well] good

*4.2.197–8/2608   nor tis] it is

*4.2.198/2609   nay I think it is] (Nay); by this hand, I ſay tis very. F
   may be a conscious expurgation.

*4.2.201/2612   I tell you, 'tis] I ſay it is

*4.2.203/2614   I will] I'le

*4.2.207/2618   and said] and I haue ſaid

*4.2.210/2621   instant] time

*4.2.212/2623   exception] conception

*4.2.213/2624   affaire] (Affaire); affaires

*4.2.217/2628   in] within

*4.2.220/2631   enjoy] enjoyeſt

*4.2.223/2634   what is it? Is] is

*4.2.225/2636   commission] (commiſſion); command

*4.2.237/2648   I:if] I, and if

*4.2.237/2648   a right] right

*4.2.238/2649   harlotry] (Harlotry); harlot

The Tragedy of Othello

70

Oth. Let me see your eyes - - looke in my face.

Def. What horrible fancy's this ?

Oth. Some of your function miftriffe,
Leaue procreants alone, and fhut the dore,
Coffe, or cry hem, if any body come,
Your miftery, your miftery : nay difpatch.   *Exit* Em.

   Def. Vpon my knees, what does your fpeech import ?
I vnderftand a fury in your words,
But not the words.

   Oth. Why, what art thou ?

   Def. Your wife my Lord, your true and loyall wife.

   Oth. Come, fweare it, dam thy felfe,
Leaft being like one of heauen, the diuells themfelues
Should feare to ceafe thee, therefore be double dambd,
Sweare thou art honeft.

   Def. Heauen doth truely know it.

   Oth. Heauen truely knowes, that thou art falfe as hell.

   Def. To whom, my Lord, with whom ? how am I falfe?

   Oth. O *Defdemona*, away, away, away.

   Def. Alas the heauy day, why do you weepe ?
Am I the occafion of thofe teares my Lord ?
If haply you my father doe fufpect,
An Inftrument of this your calling backe,
Lay not your blame on me ; if you haue left him,
Why I haue left him too.

   Oth. Had it pleas'd heauen
To try me with affliction, had he ram'd
All kindes of fores, and fhames on my bare head,
Steep'd me in pouerty, to the very lips,
Giuen to captiuity, me and my hopes,
I fhould haue found in fome part of my foule
A drop of patience; but alas, to make me
A fixed figure, for the time of fcorne,
To point his flow vnmouing fingers at - - oh, oh,
Yet could I beare that too, well, very well.
But there : where I haue garner'd vp my heart,
Where either I muft liue, or beare no life,

                                   The

The Moore of Venice.   71

The fountaine, from the which my currant runnes,
Or else dryes vp , to be discarded thence,
Or keepe it as a Cesterne, for foule Toades
To knot and gender in : turne thy complexion there,
Patience thy young and rose-lip'd Cherubin,
I here looke grim as Hell.

   Des. I hope my noble Lord esteemes me honest.
   Oth. O I, as summers flies, are in the shambles,
That quicken euen with blowing :
O thou blacke weede, why art so louely faire ?
Thou smell'st so sweete, that the sence akes at thee,
Would thou hadst ne're bin borne.

   Des. Alas, what ignorant sinne haue I committed?
   Oth. Was this faire paper, this most goodly booke,
Made to write whore on ? --- What, committed ?
Heauen stops the nose at it, and the Moone winkes,
The bawdy wind, that kisses all it meetes,
Is husht within the hallow mine of earth,
And will not hear't : -- what committed, - impudent strumpet,

   Des. By heauen you doe me wrong.
   Oth. Are not you a strumpet ?
   Des. No, as I am a Christian :
If to preserue this vessell for my Lord,
From any hated foule vnlawfull touch,
Be not to be a strumpet, I am none.

   Oth. What, not a whore ?
   Des. No, as I shall be saued.   *Enter* Emillia.
   Oth. Ist possible ?
   Des. O heauen forgiuenesse.
   Oth. I cry you mercy,
I tooke you for that cunning whore of *Venice*,
That married with *Othello* : you mistrisse,
That haue the office opposite to S. *Peter*,
And keepes the gates in hell, I, you, you, you;
We ha done our course; there's money for your paines,
I pray you turne the key, and keepe our counsell.   *Exit.*

   Em. Alas, what does this Gentleman conceiue ?

          K 4   How

72 *The Tragedy of* Othello

How doe you Madam, how doe you my good Lady?

Def. Faith halfe afleepe.

Em. Good Madam, what's the matter with my Lord?

Def. With who?

Em. Why with my Lord Madam.

Def. I ha none, doe not talke to me *Emillia,*
I cannot weepe, nor anfwer haue I none,
But what fhould goe by water: preethee to night
Lay on my bed our wedding fheetes, remember,
And call thy husband hither.

Em. Here is a change indeed.   *Exit.*

Def. Tis meete I fhould be vfde fo, very well;
How haue I bin behau'd, that he might fticke
The fmalleft opinion, on my greateft abufe.

Iag. What is your pleafure Madam,   *Enter* Iago.
How ift with you?   *and* Emillia.

Def. I cannot tell: thofe that doe teach young babes
Doe it with gentle meanes, and eafie taskes,
He might ha chid me fo, for in good faith,
I am a child at chiding.

Iag. What is the matter Lady?

Em. Alas *Iago,* my Lord hath fo bewhor'd her,
Throwne fuch defpite, and heauy termes vpon her,
As true hearts cannot beare.

Def. Am I that name *Iago*?

Iag. What name faire Lady?

Def. Such as fhe fayes my Lord did fay I was?

Em. He call'd her whore: A begger in his drinke,
Could not haue layed fuch tearmes vpon his Callet.

Iag. Why did he fo?

Def. I doe not know, I am fure I am none fuch.

Iag. Doe not weepe, doe not weepe: alas the day.

Em. Has fhe forfooke fo many noble matches,
Her Father, and her Countrey, all her friends,
To be cald whore? would it not make one weepe?

Def. It is my wretched fortune.

Iag. Befhrew him for it; how comes this tricke vpon him?

                                                    Defd.

The Moore of Venice. 73

Def. Nay, heauen doth know.

Em. I will be hang'd, if some eternall viliaine,
Some busie and insinuating rogue,
Some cogging, cousening slaue, to get some office,
Haue not deuisde this slander, I'le be hang'd else.

Iag. Fie, there is no such man, it is impossible.

Def. If any such there be, heauen pardon him.

Em. A halter pardon him, and hell gnaw his bones:
Why should he call her whore? who keepes her company?
What place, what time, what for me, what likelihood?
The Moore's abus'd by some outragious knaue:
Some base notorious knaue, some scuruy fellow,
O heauen, that such companions thoudst vnfold,
And put in euery honest hand a whip,
To lash the rascall naked through the world,
Euen from the East to the West.

Iag. Speake within dores.

Em. O fie vpon him; some such squire he was,
That turnd your wit, the seamy side without,
And made you to suspect me with the Moore.

Iag. You are a foole, goe to.

Def. O Good *Iago,*
VVhat shall I doe to win my Lord againe?
Good friend goe to him, for by this light of heauen,
I know not how I lost him.

Iag. I pray you be content, tis but his humour,
The businesse of the State does him offence,
And he does chide with you.

Def. If t'were no other.

Iag. Tis but so, I warrant you,
Harke how these Instruments summon you to supper,
And the great Messengers of *Venice* stay,
Goe in, and weepe not, all things shall be well.   *Exit women.*
How now *Roderigo?*   *Enter* Roderigo.

Rod. I doe not finde that thou dealst iustly with me.

Iag. VVhat in the contrary?

Rod. Euery day, thou dofttst me, with some deuise *Iago;*

from the First Folio of *Othello*, F1 (1623)

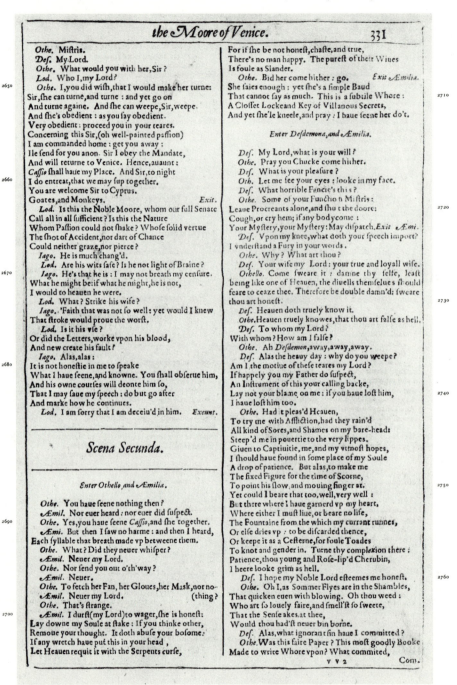

Othe. Miftris.

Def. My Lord.

Othe. What would you with her, Sir?

Lod. Who I, my Lord?

Othe. I, you did wifh, that I would make her turne:
Sir, fhe can turne, and turne : and yet go on
And turne againe. And fhe can weepe, Sir, weepe.
And fhe's obedient : as you fay obedient.
Very obedient : proceed you in your teares.
Concerning this Sir, (oh well-painted paffion)
I am commanded home : get you away :
Ile fend for you anon. Sir I obey the Mandate,
And will returne to Venice. Hence, auaunt :
Caffio fhall haue my Place. And Sir, to night
I do entreat, that we may fup together.
You are welcome Sir to Cyprus.
Goates, and Monkeys.   *Exit.*

Lod. Is this the Noble Moore, whom our full Senate
Call all in all fufficient? Is this the Nature
Whom Paffion could not fhake? Whofe folid vertue
The fhot of Accident, nor dart of Chance
Could neither graze, nor pierce?

Iago. He is much chang'd.

Lod. Are his wits fafe? Is he not light of Braine?

Iago. He's that he is : I may not breath my cenfure.
What he might be : if what he might, he is not,
I would to heauen he were.

Lod. What? Strike his wife?

Iago. 'Faith that was not fo well : yet would I knew
That ftroke would proue the worft.

Lod. Is it his vfe?
Or did the Letters, worke vpon his blood,
And new create his fault?

Iago. Alas, alas :
It is not honeftie in me to fpeake
What I haue feene, and knowne. You fhall obferue him,
And his owne courfes will deonte him fo,
That I may faue my fpeech : do but go after
And marke how he continues.

Lod. I am forry that I am deceiu'd in him.   *Exeunt.*

Scena Secunda.

Enter Othello, and Æmilia.

Othe. You haue feene nothing then?

Æmil. Nor euer heard : nor euer did fufpe&.

Othe. Yes, you haue feene *Caffio*, and fhe together.

Æmi. But then I faw no harme : and then I heard,
Each fyllable that breath made vp betweene them.

Othe. What? Did they neuer whifper?

Æmil. Neuer my Lord.

Othe. Nor fend you out o'th'way?

Æmil. Neuer.

Othe. To fetch her Fan, her Gloues, her Mask, nor no-

Æmil. Neuer my Lord.   (thing?

Othe. That's ftrange.

Æmi. I durft (my Lord) to wager, fhe is honeft:
Lay downe my Soule at ftake : If you thinke other,
Remoue your thought. It doth abufe your bofome.
If any wretch haue put this in your head,
Let Heauen requit it with the Serpents curfe,

For if fhe be not honeft, chafte, and true,
There's no man happy. The pureft of their Wiues
Is foule as Slander.

Othe. Bid her come hither : go.   *Exit Æmilia.*
She faies enough : yet fhe's a fimple Baud
That cannot fay as much. This is a fubtile Whore :
A Cloffet Locke and Key of Villanous Secrets,
And yet fhe'le kneele, and pray : I haue feene her do't.

Enter Defdemona, and Æmilia.

Def. My Lord, what is your will?

Othe. Pray you Chucke come hither.

Def. What is your pleafure?

Oth. Let me fee your eyes : looke in my face.

Def. What horrible Fancie's this?

Othe. Some of your Fun&io n Miftris :
Leaue Procreants alone, and fhu t the doore :
Cough, or cry hem; if any body come :
Your Myftery, your Myftery : May difpatch. *Exit Æmi.*

Def. Vpon my knee, what doth your fpeech import?
I vnderftand a Fury in your words.

Othe. Why? What art thou?

Def. Your wife my Lord : your true and loyall wife.

Othello. Come fweare it : damne thy felfe, leaft
being like one of Heauen, the diuells themfelues fhould
feare to ceaze thee. Therefore be double damn'd : fweare
thou art honeft.

Def. Heauen doth truely know it.

Othe. Heauen truely knowes, that thou art falfe as hell.

Def. To whom my Lord?
With whom? How am I falfe?

Othe. Ah *Defdemon*, away, away, away.

Def. Alas the heauy day : why do you weepe?
Am I the motiue of thefe teares my Lord?
If happely you my Father do fufpe&,
An Inftrument of this your calling backe,
Lay not your blame on me : if you haue loft him,
I haue loft him too.

Othe. Had it pleas'd Heauen,
To try me with Affli&ion, had they rain'd
All kind of Sores, and Shames on my bare-head :
Steep'd me in pouertie to the very lippes,
Giuen to Captiuitie, me, and my vtmoft hopes,
I fhould haue found in fome place of my Soule
A drop of patience. But alas, to make me
The fixed Figure for the time of Scorne,
To point his flow, and mouing finger at.
Yet could I beare that too, well, very well :
But there where I haue garnerd vp my heart,
Where either I muft liue, or beare no life,
The Fountaine from the which my currant runnes,
Or elfe dries vp : to be difcarded thence,
Or keepe it as a Cefterne, for foule Toades
To knot and gender in. Turne thy complexion there :
Patience, thou young and Rofe-lip'd Cherubin,
I heere looke grim as hell.

Def. I hope my Noble Lord efteemes me honeft.

Othe. Oh I, as Sommer Flyes are in the Shambles,
That quicken euen with blowing. Oh thou weed :
Who art fo louely faire, and fmell'ft fo fweete,
That the Senfe akes, at thee,
Would thou had'ft neuer bin borne.

Def. Alas, what ignorant fin haue I committed?

Othe. Was this faire Paper? This moft goodly Booke
Made to write Whore vpon? What commited,

y v 2   *Com.*

332   *The Tragedie of Othello*

Committed? Oh, thou publicke Commoner,
I should make very Forges of my cheekes,
That would to Cynders burne vp Modestie,
Did I but speake thy deedes. What commited?
Heauen stoppes the Nose at it, and the Moone winks:
The baudy winde that kisses all it meetes,
Is hush'd within the hollow Myne of Earth
And will not hear't. What commited?

Def. By Heauen you do me wrong.

Othe. Are not you a Strumpet?

Def. No, as I am a Christian.
If to preserue this vesseil for my Lord,
From any other foule vnlawfull touch
Be not to be a Strumpet, I am none.

Othe. What, not a Whore?

Def. No, as I shall be sau'd.

Othe. Is't possible?

Def. Oh Heauen forgiue vs.

Othe. I cry you mercy then.
I tooke you for that cunning Whore of Venice,
That married with *Othello.* You Mistris,

Enter Æmilia.

That haue the office opposite to Saint *Peter,*
And keepes the gate of hell. You, you: I you.
We haue done our course: there's money for your paines:
I pray you turne the key, and keepe our counsaile. *Exit.*

Æmil. Alas, what do's this Gentleman conceiue?
How do you Madam? how do you my good Lady?

Def. Faith, halfe a sleepe.

Æmi. Good Madam,
What's the matter with my Lord?

Def. With who?

Æmil. Why, with my Lord, Madam?

Def. Who is thy Lord?

Æmil. He that is yours, sweet Lady.

Def. I haue none: do not talke to me *Æmilia,*
I cannot weepe: nor answeres haue I none,
But what should go by water. Prythee to night,
Lay on my bed my wedding sheetes, remember,
And call thy husband hither.

Æmil. Heere's a change indeed. *Exit.*

Def. 'Tis meete I should be vs'd so: very meete.
How haue I bin behau'd, that he might sticke
The smal'st opinion on my least misvse?

Enter Iago, and Æmilia.

Iago. What is your pleasure Madam?
How is't with you?

Def. I cannot tell: those that do teach yong Babes
Do it with gentle meanes, and easie taskes.
He might haue chid me so: for in good faith
I am a Child to chiding.

Iago. What is the matter Lady?

Æmil. Alas (*Iago*) my Lord hath so bewhor'd her,
Throwne such dispight, and heauy termes vpon her
That true hearts cannot beare it.

Def. Am I that name, *Iago?*

Iago. What name (faire Lady?)

Def. Such as she said my Lord did say I was.

Æmil. He call'd her whore: a Begger in his drinke:
Could not haue laid such termes vpon his Callet.

Iago. Why did he so?

Def. I do not know: I am sure I am none such.

Iago. Do not weepe, do not weepe: alas the day.

Æmil. Hath she forsooke so many Noble Matches?
Her Father? And her Country? And her Friends?

To be call'd Whore? Would it not make one weepe?

Def. It is my wretched Fortune.

Iago. Beshrew him for't:
How comes this Tricke vpon him?

Def. Nay, Heauen doth know.

Æmi. I will be hang'd, if some eternall Villaine,
Some busie and insinuating Rogue,
Some cogging, cozening Slaue, to get some Office,
Haue not deuis'd this Slander: I will be hang'd else.

Iago. Fie, there is no such man: it is impossible.

Def. If any such there be, Heauen pardon him.

Æmil. A halter pardon him:
And hell gnaw his bones.
Why should he call her Whore?
Who keepes her companie?
What Place? What Time?
What Forme? What liklyhood?
The Moore's abus'd by some most villanous Knaue,
Some base notorious Knaue, some scuruy Fellow.
Oh Heauens, that such companions thou'd'st vnfold,
And put in euery honest hand a whip
To lash the Rascalls naked through the world,
Euen from the East to th'West.

Iago. Speake within doore.

Æmil. Oh fie vpon them: some such Squire he was
That turn'd your wit, the seamy-side without,
And made you to suspect me with the Moore.

Iago. You are a Foole: go too.

Def. Alas Iago,
What shall I do to win my Lord againe?
Good Friend, go to him: for by this light of Heauen,
I know not how I lost him. Heere I kneele:
If ere my will did trespasse 'gainst his Loue,
Either in discourse of thought, or actuall deed,
Or that mine Eyes, mine Eares, or any Sence
Delighted them: or any other Forme,
Or that I do not yet, and euer did,
And euer will, (though he do shake me off
To beggerly diuorcement) Loue him deerely,
Comfort forsweare me. Vnkindnesse may do much,
And his vnkindnesse may defeat my life,
But neuer taynt my Loue. I cannot say Whore,
It do's abhorre me now I speake the word,
To do the Act, that might the addition earne,
Not the worlds Masse of vanitie could make me.

Iago. I pray you be content: 'tis but his humour:
The businesse of the State do's him offence.

Def. If 'twere no other.

Iago. It is but so, I warrant,
Hearke how these Instruments summon to supper:
The Messengers of Venice staies the meate,
Go in, and weepe not: all things shall be well.

Exeunt Desdemona and Æmilia.

Enter Rodorigo.

How now *Rodorigo?*

Rod. I do not finde
That thou deal'st iustly with me.

Iago. What in the contrarie?

Rodori. Euery day thou dafts me with some deuise
Iago, and rather, as it seemes to me now, keep'st from
me all conueniencie, then suppliest me with the least ad-
uantage of hope: I will indeed no longer endure it. Nor
am I yet perswaded to put vp in peace, what already I
haue foolishly suffred.

Iago. Will you heare me *Rodorigo?*

Rodori. I

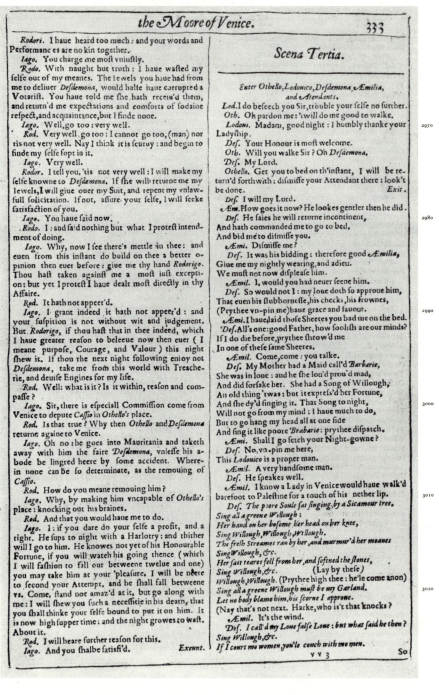

Rodori. I haue heard too much: and your words and Performances are no kin together.

Iago. You charge me most vniustly.

Rodo. With naught but truth: I haue wasted my selfe out of my meanes. The Iewels you haue had from me to deliuer *Desdemona*, would halfe haue corrupted a Votarist. You haue told me she hath receiu'd them, and return'd me expectations and comforts of sodaine respect, and acquaintance, but I finde none.

Iago. Well, go too: very well.

Rod. Very well, go too: I cannot go too, (man) nor tis not very well. Nay I think it is scuruy: and begin to finde my selfe fopt in it.

Iago. Very well.

Rodor. I tell you, 'tis not very well: I will make my selfe knowne to *Desdemona*. If she will returne me my Iewels, I will giue ouer my Suit, and repent my vnlawfull solicitation. If not, assure your selfe, I will seeke satisfaction of you.

Iago. You haue said now.

Rodo. I : and said nothing but what I protest intendment of doing.

Iago. Why, now I see there's mettle in thee: and euen from this instant do build on thee a better opinion then euer before : giue me thy hand *Rodorigo*. Thou hast taken against me a most iust exception : but yet I protest I haue dealt most directly in thy Affaire.

Rod. It hath not appeer'd.

Iago. I grant indeed it hath not appeer'd : and your suspition is not without wit and judgement. But *Rodorigo*, if thou hast that in thee indeed, which I haue greater reason to beleeue now then euer (I meane purpose, Courage, and Valour) this night shew it. If thou the next night following enioy not *Desdemona*, take me from this world with Treacherie, and deuise Engines for my life.

Rod. Well: what is it? Is it within, reason and compasse?

Iago. Sir, there is especiall Commission come from Venice to depute *Cassio* in *Othello's* place.

Rod. Is that true? Why then *Othello* and *Desdemona* returne againe to Venice.

Iago. Oh no: he goes into Mauritania and taketh away with him the faire *Desdemona*, vnlesse his abode be lingred heere by some accident. Wherein none can be so determinate, as the remouing of *Cassio*.

Rod. How do you meane remouing him?

Iago. Why, by making him vncapable of *Othello's* place: knocking out his braines.

Rod. And that you would haue me to do.

Iago. I : if you dare do your selfe a profit, and a right. He sups to night with a Harlotry: and thither will I go to him. He knowes not yet of his Honourable Fortune, if you will watch his going thence (which I will fashion to fall out betweene twelue and one) you may take him at your pleasure. I will be neere to second your Attempt, and he shall fall betweene vs. Come, stand not amaz'd at it, but go along with me: I will shew you such a necessitie in his death, that you shall thinke your selfe bound to put it on him. It is now high supper time: and the night growes to wast. About it.

Rod. I will heare further reason for this.

Iago. And you shalbe satisfi'd.   *Exeunt.*

Scena Tertia.

Enter Othello, Lodouico, Desdemona, Æmilia, and Attendants.

Lod. I do beseech you Sir, trouble your selfe no further.

Oth. Oh pardon me: 'twill do me good to walke.

Lodou. Madam, good night: I humbly thanke your Ladyship.

Des. Your Honour is most welcome.

Oth. Will you walke Sir? Oh *Desdemona*.

Des. My Lord.

Othello. Get you to bed on th'instant, I will be return'd forthwith: dismisse your Attendant there : look't be done.   *Exit.*

Des. I will my Lord.

Æm. How goes it now? He lookes gentler then he did.

Des. He saies he will returne incontinent, And hath commanded me to go to bed, And bid me to dismisse you.

Æmi. Dismisse me?

Des. It was his bidding: therefore good *Æmilia*, Giue me my nightly wearing, and adieu. We must not now displease him.

Æmil. I, would you had neuer seene him.

Des. So would not I: my loue doth so approue him, That euen his stubbornesse, his checks, his frownes, (Prythee vn-pin me)haue grace and fauour.

Æmi. I haue laid those Sheetes you bad me on the bed.

Des. All's one: good Father, how foolish are our minds? If I do die before, prythee shrow'd me In one of these same Sheetes.

Æmil. Come, come: you talke.

Des. My Mother had a Maid call'd *Barbarie*, She was in loue: and he she lou'd prou'd mad, And did forsake her. She had a Song of Willough, An old thing 'twas: but it exprest'd her Fortune, And she dy'd singing it. That Song to night, Will not go from my mind: I haue much to do, But to go hang my head all at one side And sing it like poore *Brabarie*: prythee dispatch.

Æmi. Shall I go fetch your Night-gowne?

Des. No, vn-pin me here, This *Lodouico* is a proper man.

Æmil. A very handsome man.

Des. He speakes well.

Æmil. I know a Lady in Venice would haue walk'd barefoot to Palestine for a touch of his nether lip.

Des. The poore Soule sat singing, by a Sicamour tree. Sing all a greene Willough:
Her hand on her bosome her head on her knee,
Sing Willough, Willough, Willough.
The fresh Streames ran by her, and murmur'd her moanes
Sing Willough, &c.
Her salt teares fell from her, and softned the stones,
Sing Willough, &c.   (Lay by these)
Willough, Willough. (Prythee high thee: he'le come anon)
Sing all a greene Willough must be my Garland.
Let no body blame him, his scorne I approue.
(Nay that's not next. Harke, who is't that knocks?

Æmil. It's the wind.

Des. I call'd my Loue false Loue: but what said he then? Sing Willough, &c.
If I court mo women, yow'le couch with mo men.

VV 3   So

[Safe in their alabaster chambers]

Emily Dickinson

Emily Dickinson clearly thought of her poetry in terms of publication, though not in the ways that we are most familiar with. She gathered and carefully ordered (and apparently carefully copied) her poems into manuscript booklets, called *fascicles*, and may have circulated some of them (or earlier versions of them) among friends. She also often included poems in her letters to friends and family. All but a few of her poems, however, were first printed only after her death in collections edited by Mabel Loomis Todd and T. W. Higginson, who felt that her idiosyncratic manuscript presentations—and perhaps some of her word choices—needed adjustments for a general audience. Critical editors have twice returned to her manuscripts, working to reconstruct those that were damaged by previous editors, and have recorded both the forms that Dickinson gave to her poems and her fascicles and the forms that these poems saw in wider circulation. The following selections illustrate different editorial philosophies with one well-known poem.

from *Poems*, edited by Mabel Loomis Todd and T. W. Higginson

Preface

THE VERSES OF Emily Dickinson belong emphatically to what Emerson long since called "the Poetry of the Portfolio,"—something produced absolutely without the thought of publication, and solely by way of expression of the writer's own mind. Such verse must inevitably forfeit whatever advantage lies in the discipline of public criticism and the enforced conformity to accepted ways. On the other hand, it may often gain something through the habit of freedom and the unconventional utterance of daring thoughts. In the case of the present author, there was absolutely no choice in the matter; she must write thus, or not at all. A recluse by temperament and habit, literally spending years without setting her foot beyond the doorstep, and many more years during which her walks were strictly limited to her father's grounds, she habitually concealed her mind, like her person, from all but a very few friends; and it was with great difficulty that she was persuaded to print, during her lifetime, three or four poems. Yet she wrote verses in great abundance; and though curiously indifferent to all conventional rules, had yet a rigorous literary standard of her own, and often altered a word many times to suit an ear which had its own tenacious fastidiousness.

Miss Dickinson was born in Amherst, Mass., Dec. 10, 1830, and died there May 15, 1886. Her father, Hon. Edward Dickinson, was the leading lawyer of Amherst, and was treasurer of the well-known college there situated. It was his custom once a year to hold a large reception at

From *Poems*, ed. Mabel Loomis Todd and T. W. Higginson (Boston: Roberts Brothers, 1891).

his house, attended by all the families connected with the institution and by the leading people of the town. On these occasions his daughter Emily emerged from her wonted retirement and did her part as gracious hostess; nor would any one have known from her manner, I have been told, that this was not a daily occurrence. The annual occasion once past, she withdrew again into her seclusion, and except for a very few friends was as invisible to the world as if she had dwelt in a nunnery. For myself, although I had corresponded with her for many years, I saw her but twice face to face, and brought away the impression of something as unique and remote as Undine or Mignon or Thekla.

This selection from her poems is published to meet the desire of her personal friends, and especially of her surviving sister. It is believed that the thoughtful reader will find in these pages a quality more suggestive of the poetry of William Blake than of anything to be elsewhere found,—flashes of wholly original and profound insight into nature and life; words and phrases exhibiting an extraordinary vividness of descriptive and imaginative power, yet often set in a seemingly whimsical or even rugged frame. They are here published as they were written, with very few and superficial changes; although it is fair to say that the titles have been assigned, almost invariably, by the editors. In many cases these verses will seem to the reader like poetry torn up by the roots, with rain and dew and earth still clinging to them, giving a freshness and a fragrance not otherwise to be conveyed. In other cases, as in the few poems of shipwreck or of mental conflict, we can only wonder at the gift of vivid imagination by which this recluse woman can delineate, by a few touches, the very crises of physical or mental conflict. And sometimes again we catch glimpses of a lyric strain, sustained perhaps but for a line or two at a time, and making the reader regret its sudden cessation. But the main quality of these poems is that of extraordinary grasp and insight, uttered with an uneven vigor sometimes exasperating, seemingly wayward, but really unsought and inevitable. After all, when a thought takes one's breath away, a lesson on grammar seems an impertinence. As Ruskin wrote in his earlier and better days, "No weight nor mass nor beauty of execution can outweigh one grain or fragment of thought."

THOMAS WENTWORTH HIGGINSON.

I V.

Safe in their alabaster chambers,
Untouched by morning and untouched by noon,
Sleep the meek members of the resurrection,
Rafter of satin, and roof of stone.

Light laughs the breeze in her castle of sunshine;
Babbles the bee in a stolid ear;
Pipe the sweet birds in ignorant cadence,—
Ah, what sagacity perished here!

Grand go the years in the crescent above them;
Worlds scoop their arcs, and firmaments row,
Diadems drop and Doges surrender,
Soundless as dots on a disk of snow.

from *The Poems of Emily Dickinson, including variant readings critically compared with all known manuscripts,* edited by Thomas H. Johnson[†]

Notes on the Present Text

AT THE TIME of her death in 1886, Emily Dickinson left in manuscript a body of verse far more extensive than anyone imagined. Of the seven poems known to have been published in her lifetime, all were anonymous and most were issued surreptitiously. Today seventeen hundred seventy-five poems may be attributed to her. All except forty-one have been previously published. Of those unpublished, nineteen are holograph copies; the larger part survive in transcripts for the most part made by Susan Gilbert Dickinson, presumably of copies which Emily sent her, now lost.

There are one hundred twenty-three published poems for which no autograph is known. Some were incorporated in letters that have been destroyed. Some may yet be recovered, though patient search has not yet located them. Nothing at all is known about the rest, which survive in the fifty-three transcripts made by Mabel Loomis Todd, and the sixty-one transcripts made by Susan Dickinson. Mrs. Todd made transcripts of many hundreds of poems at the time she was editing them. Since it was her practice to return the autographs to Lavinia Dickinson when her transcriptions had been made, one must assume that those fifty-three missing autographs

† From *The Poems of Emily Dickinson, including variant readings critically compared with all known manuscripts,* ed. Thomas H. Johnson. Reprinted by permission of the publishers and Trustees of Amherst College from *The Poems of Emily Dickinson,* Thomas H. Johnson, ed., pp. lxi–lxii, 152–155, Cambridge, Mass.: The Belknap Press of Harvard University Press, Copyright © 1951, 1955, 1979, 1983 by the President and Fellows of Harvard College.

disappeared after they were returned. Throughout her life, Emily sent copies of her poems to Susan, and a very large number of those autographs are extant. One supposes that the missing originals of Susan's sixty-one transcripts were at one time in her possession. The fact remains that all trace of these one hundred eleven holograph copies has vanished.[1]

The purpose of this edition is to establish an accurate text of the poems and to give them as far as possible a chronology. Such of course can be done when holographs survive. The date (but not the literatim text) can be established when missing poems have been published in letters that can be dated from internal evidence. In all instances where holographs are wanting, the text derives from the most authentic source.[2] When no other source is known, the earliest published text is reproduced together with a record of later alterations if such were made.[3] The poems have been given a chronological arrangement even though at best it is but an approximation. Since very few poems can be given exact dates, any chronology must be considered relative.

1. There is some reason to suspect that the copies sent to Susan Dickinson were missing before her death in 1913. Her daughter Martha Dickinson Bianchi published *The Single Hounds* (1914), a volume of 143 poems, from copies in her possession. Holographs of 40 are missing today, but the texts of all but two of the 40 can be collated with surviving transcripts made by her mother. The reason for thinking the text of those 38 poems derived from Susan Dickinson's transcripts lies in the nature of certain printed errors. Susan's stylized handwriting is especially difficult to decipher. The following misreadings bear a striking resemblance to the form of the letters misread:

    no. 1677: acre] area
        rocks] reeks
    no. 1682: At *most*] *Almost*
    no. 1684: in] to
        there] *Then*
    no. 1701: their] this
        Untumbled] Untroubled
    no. 1703: more] mere

2. There are instances where the absence of holographs requires speculation whether the text of a published poem reproduces a lost variant or is merely a misreading. A case in point is discussed in the notes to "Away from home are some and I" (no. 821).

3. Transcripts made by Mabel Loomis Todd (referred to as TT) supply the text for 53 poems; transcripts made by Susan Gilbert Dickinson (referred to as ST) do so for 61. A detailed identification of all missing poems is in Appendix 11: "Distribution of Missing Autographs."

Where there is choice among texts for principal representation, the earliest fair copy is selected. Such a rule has exceptions. Within a given year the arrangement is in the following order:

(a) fair copies to recipients
(b) other fair copies
(c) semifinal drafts—but where the packet priority can be reasonably determined, the order of both (b) and (c) is subdivided in conformity with such priority
(d) worksheet drafts

If a poem seems to achieve its final version at a date later than that of earlier fair copies, it is placed among poems written during the later year. Texts which derive from undatable transcripts or published sources are perforce grouped together following all chronologically arranged poems and their order is alphabetical by first lines. Such are the final one hundred twenty-seven poems, numbered 1649–1775.

★ ★ ★

2 1 6

Safe in their Alabaster Chambers—
Untouched by Morning
And untouched by Noon—
Sleep the meek members of the Resurrection—
Rafter of satin,
And Roof of stone.

Light laughs the breeze
In her Castle above them—
Babbles the Bee in a stolid Ear,
Pipe the Sweet Birds in ignorant cadence—
Ah, what sagacity perished here!

version of 1859

Safe in their Alabaster Chambers—
Untouched by Morning—
And untouched by Noon—
Lie the meek members of the Resurrection—
Rafter of Satin—and Roof of Stone!

Grand go the Years—in the Crescent—above them—
Worlds scoop their Arcs—
And Firmaments—row—
Diadems—drop—and Doges—surrender—
Soundless as dots—on a Disc of Snow—

version of 1861

MANUSCRIPTS: It is unlikely that ED ever completed this poem in a version that entirely satisfied her. The earlier version she copied into packet 3 (H 11c) sometime in 1859.[1] The later version she copied into packet 37 (H 203c) in early summer, 1861. The story of how she labored in 1861 to create a finished poem unfolds in an exchange of notes with Sue, who evidently had not approved the earlier version when ED had asked her opinion. The first note (H B 74a), in pencil, reads thus:

Safe in their Alabaster Chambers,
Untouched by Morning—
And untouched by Noon—
Lie the meek members of the Resurrection—
Rafter of Satin—and Roof of Stone—

Grand go the Years—in the Crescent—above them—
Worlds scoop their Arcs—
And Firmaments—row—
Diadems—drop—and Doges—surrender—
Soundless as dots—on a Disc of Snow—

1. Abbreviations for witnesses and previous editions are roughly the same as those for the next selection; see pp. 457 and 460–62 [—*Editor*].

Perhaps this verse would please you better—Sue—

Emily—

This new version at first must have seemed satisfactory to ED, since she copied it into packet 37 (identical in text and form with the above except that the first stanza is concluded with an exclamation point). One conjectures that the transcript she made for Sue was copied down at the same time and dispatched to the house next door. Sue replied (in art): (H B 74b):

I am not suited dear Emily with the second verse—It is remarkable as the chain lightening that blinds us hot nights in the Southern sky but it does not go with the ghostly shimmer of the first verse as well as the other one—It just occurs to me that the first verse is complete in itself it needs no other, and can't be coupled—Strange things always go alone—as there is only one Gabriel and one Sun—You never made a peer for that verse, and I *guess* you[r] kingdom does'nt hold one—I always go to the fire and get warm after thinking of it, but I never *can* again— . . .

Sue—

Pony Express

Evidently ED, having received Sue's "Pony Express," again attempted a second stanza, for immediately following the second version, in packet 37, are these variant trial substitutes:

> Springs—shake the sills—
> But—the Echoes—stiffen—
> Hoar—is the window—
> And numb the door—
> Tribes—of Eclipse—in Tents—of Marble—
> Staples—of Ages—have buckled—there—

> ————————

> Springs—shake the Seals—
> But the silence—stiffens—
> Frosts unhook—in the Northern Zones—

> Icicles—crawl from Polar Caverns—
> Midnight in Marble—Refutes—the Suns—

Having pondered her choice, she selected the first of the two and dispatched this note to Sue. (H B 74c):

Is *this frostier?*

> Springs—shake the Sills—
> But—the Echoes—stiffen—
> Hoar—is the window—and numb—the Door—
> Tribes of Eclipse—in Tents of Marble—
> Staples of Ages—have buckled there—

> Dear Sue—
> Your praise is good—to me—because I *know*
> it *knows*—and *suppose* it *means*—
> Could I make you and Austin—proud—
> sometime—a great way off—'twould give me
> taller feet— . . .
>
> Emily

She "supposes" those from whom she seeks advice mean to help and she yearns to give them reason to respect her art. But here the matter ends.

One conjectures that ED had sought advice from Sue in an attempt to comply with a request from Samuel Bowles to publish the poem in his newspaper: it is very possible that she had incorporated the original version in a recent letter to him. In any event, it is the original version (with "cadence" altered to "cadences") that appeared anonymously in the *Springfield Daily Republican* on Saturday, 1 March 1862:

> The Sleeping
> Safe in their alabaster chambers,
> Untouched by morning,

And untouched by noon,

Sleep the meek members of the Resurrection,

Rafter of satin, and roof of stone.

Light laughs the breeze

In her castle above them,

Babbles the bee in a stolid ear,

Pipe the sweet birds in ignorant cadences:

Ah! what sagacity perished here!

Pelham Hill, June 1861.

ED had an especial fondness for the Pelham hills, and viewing them she may have remembered a visit to an old burying ground there. A clue to the puzzling dating of the lines perhaps lay in the letter to Bowles which presumably accompanied the copy she sent him.

When ED initiated her correspondence with T. W. Higginson on 15 April, six weeks after "The Sleeping" had appeared in the *SDR*, she enclosed four poems for his critical assessment. Among them was a copy of the second version of this poem (BPL Higg 4), given a new line arrangement:

Safe in their Alabaster Chambers—

Untouched by Morning—

And untouched by Noon—

Sleep the meek members of the Resurrection,

Rafter of Satin—and Roof of Stone—

Grand go the Years,

In the Crescent above them—

Worlds scoop their Arcs—

And Firmaments—row—

Diadems—drop—

And Doges—surrender—

> Soundless as Dots,
>
> On a Disc of Snow.

Higginson's reply does not survive, but from her next letter to him there is no reason to suppose that he singled the poem out for special comment. What ED's final thoughts about these versions may have been are not known. She seems never to have referred to the poem again, and there is no later copy in any version or arrangement.

PUBLICATION: The *SDR* publication is discussed above. The packet copy version of 1859 was one of fourteen poems selected for publication in an article contributed by T. W. Higginson to the *Christian Union*, XLII (25 September 1890), 393. The text is arranged as two quatrains but is not otherwise altered. Higginson comments on it:

> This is the form in which she finally left these lines, but as she sent them to me, years ago, the following took the place of the second verse, and it seems to me that, with all its too daring condensation, it strikes a note too fine to be lost.

He then quotes the second stanza from the copy that ED had sent to him. The text issued in *Poems* (1890), 113, without title, is a reconstruction of the two versions arranged as three stanzas, and in this form has persisted in all editions. The version of 1859 furnished the text for stanzas 1 and 2; the second stanza of the version of 1861 becomes stanza 3, and the lines are arranged as three quatrains. One phrase is altered:

> caste above them] castle of sunshine

Portions of the correspondence with Sue and of the unused stanza ("Springs shake . . .") are in *LL* (1924), 78, and *FF* (1932), 164. A facsimile of the copy sent to Higginson is reproduced in T. W. Higginson and H. W. Boynton, *A Reader's History of American Literature*, Boston, 1903, pages 130–131.

from *The Poems of Emily Dickinson: Variorum Edition,* edited by R. W. Franklin†

Introduction

★ ★ ★

THIS EDITION IS the third editing from manuscript for most of the poems. Like its predecessors, it takes license to make public what Dickinson herself never did, honoring the interests of history over her reticence. Although she complained only once, censuring a question mark in "A narrow fellow in the grass," she invested no direct authority in any text published in her lifetime. An editor's task therefore is to turn to her manuscripts and against criteria that were never explicitly hers prepare texts for the public. The criteria can vary, as they have throughout the publishing history. The altered versions of the nineteenth century were immensely successful, as were the editions of Martha Dickinson Bianchi and Millicent Todd Bingham in the twentieth. All of them are historical and of interest, for the contemporaneous culture absorbed Dickinson's work in those forms—alterations, misreadings, and all. For most of his career, Robert Frost knew Dickinson's work only in this way. What he knew was collaboration, Dickinson-Todd-Higginson in the nineteenth century and other combinations in the twentieth. While involvement is inevitable—all editors exercise judgment—some Dickinson editors have been more innovative than others, though the course of events has brought increasing

† From *The Poems of Emily Dickinson: Variorum Edition*, ed. R. W. Franklin (Cambridge, MA: The Belknap Press of Harvard University Press, 1998), pp. 17–47. Reprinted by permission of the publishers and Trustees of Amherst College from *The Poems of Emily Dickinson*, Ralph W. Franklin, ed., pp. 27–47, Cambridge, Mass.: The Belknap Press of Harvard University Press, copyright © 1998 by the president and Fellows of Harvard College, copyright © 1951, 1955, 1979, 1983 by the president and Fellows of Harvard College.

fidelity to what Dickinson wrote. This edition, affirming this direction, which reached distinction in the Johnson edition of 1955, seeks to intrude minimally and therefore turns again to the manuscripts, accepting them as their own standard, almost the only record we have of her intentions.

Like every previous appearance of Dickinson's poems, beginning with "Sic transit gloria mundi" (2) in 1852, this edition is based on the assumption that a literary work is separable from its artifact, as Dickinson herself demonstrated as she moved her poems from one piece of paper to another. Even the fascicles, her most formal organization of her work, were the source for further copies. There can be many manifestations of a literary work. Hers was manuscript, this one is typographical. Others, like *The Manuscript Books of Emily Dickinson,* are in facsimile or, like *The Master Letters of Emily Dickinson,* in facsimile and type. Although this edition is a printed codex, it has an electronic database—the poems are in bits and bytes; other outputs are possible, including other printed editions, organized or presented differently. Dickinson and Hypertext may be well matched, and images are particularly useful with an unpublished poet who left her poems unprepared for others. Whatever the ongoing course of Dickinson editing, standard typography will have continuing utility. Even with digital images, where the poems are in pixels, an editor will need typography to explain the relationship of images and to transcribe the texts, confirming what the eye sees but may not understand and disclosing what the eye, unaided, cannot detect.

Included in this edition are the poems found in Dickinson's possession at her death as well as those sent separately to others, enclosed with letters, or incorporated into letters as poetry. The intent is to present a separate text for each known manuscript. Dickinson invested individual manuscripts with identities of their own, even if, for all their variance, she thought of them as representing a single poem. "Morns like these we parted" was sent to the Norcross cousins and to her sister-in-law as well as copied for Fascicle 1, the only record Dickinson retained after destroying the draft from which all three manuscripts derived. The result was three fair copies with separate histories, including two that passed beyond her control. She preserved hers, as did her sister-in-law, while the Norcross cousins, closely protective, apparently had theirs destroyed. As her stemmata suggest, Dickinson handled "Morns like these we parted" as a single poem, maintaining relationships among manuscripts while creating and destroying manuscripts herself. Since nearly every text differs in some respect from all others, each has been presented individually, gathered within a single entry. A poem as extensively revised as "Two butterflies went out at noon" is treated as one poem having two variant manuscripts.

For the 1,789 poems, there are nearly 2,500 texts, but the number of Dickinson's manuscripts was much greater. Fascicle 1, for example, contains twenty-seven poems, with twelve more manuscripts known from other sources, bringing the total represented in this edition to thirty-nine. Another twenty-six certainly existed at one time, for Dickinson did not compose onto the fascicle sheets, and only one of the extant manuscripts is a working draft ("If those I loved were lost"). It is certain that there were at least sixty-five manuscripts for these twenty-seven poems. There could have been as many as ninety-two, if Dickinson had also made an intermediate draft for each of them. She may not have needed one for short poems such as "To him who keeps an orchis' heart," and during her intense push from mid-1862 to early 1864, some of the poems in fascicles appear to have come directly from worksheets, bypassing intermediate drafts. A third of her poems are not in a fascicle or set, while some of the late poems never progressed beyond an initial draft. One cannot say exactly how many manuscripts she produced for these 1,789 poems, but the number may have been twice what we know, as many as 5,000 manuscripts, instead of 2,500.

When there is more than one text for a poem, no principal representation has been made. Dickinson did not do so in her workshop, not even in the fascicles, where unfinished texts—those with alternatives pending—can follow fair copies sent to friends, all of them deriving from the same working draft. The latest documents for a poem may be incomplete or shaped to specific occasions, and her copies to friends have individual histories with claims of their own. Principal representation implies choice for a particular purpose: an edition of the fascicles would have to choose those manuscripts, an edition of poems sent to a particular recipient, those. The aim of this edition is a comprehensive account, not a selection for a specific end. Within individual entries, the texts are presented without priority, sequenced chronologically. When sequence is not clear, as when manuscripts are missing and the text incomplete, convenience of presentation may be followed instead.

★ ★ ★

With Dickinson's custom as the standard for representing her texts, this edition follows her spelling and, within the capacity of standard type, her capitalization and punctuation. Although some genetic information is reported, as well as some physical characteristics of the manuscripts, the aim is to present the multiple texts of poems, not their documents or artifacts, as the reuniting of words divided by end-line hyphenation, part of the larger restoration of broken lines, indicates. To maintain a clear text, the record of lineation, including word division, appears as part of the apparatus, not as part of the text itself. The record of division is separate from the record of emendation, a term used for substantive changes, and a few of punctuation and indentation, introduced by the editor and similarly recorded in the apparatus for a text.

For six damaged holographs, readings have been supplied from other sources, creating a critical text, but for most incomplete documents, where the loss is larger or indeterminate, the text has been presented only to the extent that the source permits, sometimes only a line, as in the Norcross lists. Holographs have been emended to correct miswritings (*appal, Bargmen, Bavest, bemumbed, beyoned,* etc.) and other readings inconsistent with her custom, again creating a text that is not identical with any surviving document. One holograph, here emended, begins "The Life we have is verg great" (1178):

The Life we have is very great

Emendation   I very] verg

The supplied omissions, which only occasionally are a letter or a word, include opening or closing quotation marks and apostrophes in contractions (*hadst, Youll*) and possessives (*Eternitys, Loves*). Secondary sources—

transcripts by various hands or published texts—reflect the habits, style, and errors of the copyist or publishing house. They have been emended to conform with Dickinson's practice, including her spelling, which changed over the years. Her form, for example, was *extasy* until 1873, *opon* until 1880, *etherial, Savior, show,* and *shown* until the end. The emendations have been gathered into Appendix II.

★ ★ ★

Texts deriving from fascicles or sets are identified to the right of the first lines, with their position in the fascicles indicated after the period (F23.4). Position is not so indicated in the sets, where internal order, if any, is unknown (s5).

The entries have two sections: Manuscripts and Publication. Following a summary of their number, date, and condition, the manuscripts are presented individually and chronologically. They may be assumed to be in ink, unless otherwise noted. Locations are given, including certain numbers assigned to Dickinson papers at the Amherst College Library, the Boston Public Library, and the Houghton Library of Harvard University, prefixed by A, BPL, and H respectively (as in A 291, BPL 25, H 220). The individual texts are given as fully as possible from the available documents, even if only in part, not cited or summarized as in *Poems* (1955). They are enumerated alphabetically, with those deriving from secondary sources indicated by placing the alphabetic character in brackets. The three sources for "Morns like these we parted"—a Norcross transcript and two holographs—are thus identified as [A], B, and C. When two secondary sources represent a single holograph, they are identified in the manner of [A. 1] and [A.2].

When page breaks divide texts in this edition, the texts may be assumed to continue without a stanza break, unless indicated otherwise by the symbol □ at the foot of the page.

The texts may be followed by alternative readings, aspects of the inscription, or both. Multiple alternative readings for a lemma are separated by a bullet (•). When a line number is followed by a bracket, the entire line constitutes the lemma.

With the austerer sweet –   4

4 the] an – • this –   4] With this sufficient Sweet   4 With]
the W *over* <T>

Angled brackets enclose canceled readings. Any text, including the alternatives, was subject to revision, as in Dickinson's change of a line in
"The wind begun to rock the grass" (796).

The Cattle flung to Barns –   14

Revision   14 flung] *canceled;* fled *interlined above*

Unless otherwise noted, revision was in pencil. There follows, as applicable, an account of line and page division and of emendation, labeled
Division and *Emendation* respectively. When texts of a poem vary substantively among themselves, the variants are summarized in a statement
or table.

From the information given, it is possible to quote texts in several
ways—in their emended or unemended state, with or without their
physical line breaks, as first written on the document or as later revised:

The Life we have is very great

The Life we
have is very great

The Life we have is verg great

The Life we
have is verg great

The Cattle flung to Barns –

The Cattle

flung to Barns—

The Cattle fled to Barns –

The Cattle

fled to Barns –

★   ★   ★

The publication information includes appearances in the primary editions as well as first printings elsewhere. Cited from the early publication history are the three nineteenth-century *Poems* (1890, 1891, 1896) and the three early twentieth-century volumes: *The Single Hound* (1914), *Further Poems* (1929), and *Unpublished Poems* (1935). Not cited, unless required by special circumstances, are the Bianchi collections that followed each of the last three: *Complete Poems* (1924), *Poems* (1930), and *Poems* (1937). The publication history continues through *Poems* (1955) and *Complete Poems* (1960), whose poem numbers—(J132), for example—are given at the end of the descriptions and are indexed separately. Later editions, to 1997, are also cited if they are substantially based on primary materials. The editorial selection among alternatives that produced a given text is noted, along with variations in line or stanza arrangement.

Following the publishing history is an account of variants in the published texts, including alterations, misreadings, and some differing editorial judgments. Changes in spelling, capitalization, and punctuation, along with evident typographical errors, are passed over, unless they create different substantives or, in a few instances, are in texts intended to be literal.

A   7 Where] When *AM29 FP29 P30 P37*   7 dye] die *AM29 FP29 P30 P37 P55 CP60*   8 Hemlocks] hundreds *AM29 FP29 P30 P37*

The codes are mnemonic, as in these for *Further Poems of Emily Dickinson* (*FP29*) and the collected editions of *Poems* that appeared in 1930 and 1937 (*P30 P37*). A list of short titles for the principal editions and a table of their codes follow. Other codes may be readily inferred, as in *AM29*, which refers to "*Atlantic Monthly*, 143 (March 1929), 329" in the publication information.

Symbols have been used to identify the principal institutions holding Dickinson material. Other institutions and individuals are cited briefly in the text.

LOCATION SYMBOLS

A   Amherst College Library. Emily Dickinson Collections

           To—Mabel Todd editorial material
           Tr—transcripts by Mabel Todd and others
           1896PC—the printer's copy for *Poems* (1896)

           Also available are guide sheets by Jay Leyda, who prepared the materials received from Millicent Todd Bingham, which included part of Emily Dickinson's papers.

BPL   Boston Public Library. Thomas Wentworth Higginson Papers

H   Houghton Library, Harvard University. Emily Dickinson Collections

           B - poems with special association for Martha Dickinson Bianchi
           H - poems and letters sent to Elizabeth and Josiah Gilbert Holland
           L - letters with special association for Martha Dickinson Bianchi
           ST - transcripts by Susan Dickinson

           In addition to part of Emily Dickinson's papers, some of the holographs sent to others, including ones to

Mary Haven, Thomas Wentworth Higginson, and Maria Whitney, are available at the Houghton Library, as well as editorial materials of Martha Dickinson Bianchi and Alfred Leete Hampson and the photostats of Dickinson's poems and letters used by Thomas H. Johnson in preparing his editions.

Y–BRBL   Beinecke Rare Book and Manuscript Library, Yale University

Y–MSSA   Manuscripts and Archives, Sterling Memorial Library, Yale University

MLT–Mabel Loomis Todd Papers
MTB–Millicent Todd Bingham Papers

EDITORIAL SYMBOLS

< >   to enclose canceled readings
     <world->

•   to separate multiple alternative readings
     disperse-] dissolve - • withdraw - • retire -

| to indicate physical line divisions
     this |
     bewildered] bewil -| dered

no| to indicate no physical line division occurs
     lost, *no*|

|| to indicate page or column breaks
     sublime ||
     preferred] pre -|| ferred

/   to mark line endings of poems

    when bewildered -/ bore

        his riddle in –

▫   to indicate a stanza break at a page break

    Oh fraud that cannot cheat the Bee.

    Almost thy plausibility

    Induces my belief,   ▫

SHORT TITLES FOR EDITIONS

Poems (1890)	*Poems by Emily Dickinson.* Boston, 1890.
Poems (1891)	*Poems by Emily Dickinson.* Boston, 1891.
Letters (1894)	*Letters of Emily Dickinson.* Boston, 1894.
Poems (1896)	*Poems by Emily Dickinson.* Boston, 1896.
SH (1914)	*The Single Hound.* Boston, 1914.
LL (1924)	Bianchi. *The Life and Letters of Emily Dickinson.* Boston, 1924.
CP (1924)	*The Complete Poems of Emily Dickinson.* Boston, 1924.
FP (1929)	*Further Poems of Emily Dickinson.* Boston, 1929.
Poems (1930)	*The Poems of Emily Dickinson.* Boston, 1930.
Letters (1931)	*Letters of Emily Dickinson.* New York, 1931.
UP (1935)	*Unpublished Poems of Emily Dickinson.* Boston, 1935.
Poems (1937)	*The Poems of Emily Dickinson.* Boston, 1937.
BM (1945)	*Bolts of Melody.* New York, 1945.
LH (1951)	*Letters to Dr. and Mrs. Josiah Gilbert Holland.* Cambridge, 1951.
Poems (1955)	*The Poems of Emily Dickinson.* Cambridge, 1955.
Letters (1958)	*The Letters of Emily Dickinson.* Cambridge, 1958.
CP (1960)	*The Complete Poems of Emily Dickinson.* Boston, 1960.
MB (1981)	*The Manuscript Books of Emily Dickinson.* Cambridge, 1981.

RELATED WORKS

FF (1932)	Bianchi. *Emily Dickinson Face to Face.* Boston, 1932.
AB (1945)	Bingham. *Ancestors' Brocades.* New York, 1945.

CODES FOR EDITIONS

Poems

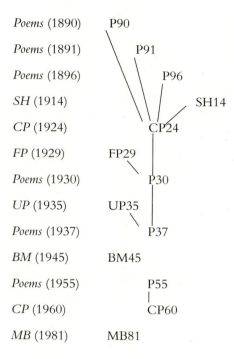

Poems (1890)	P90
Poems (1891)	P91
Poems (1896)	P96
SH (1914)	SH14
CP (1924)	CP24
FP (1929)	FP29
Poems (1930)	P30
UP (1935)	UP35
Poems (1937)	P37
BM (1945)	BM45
Poems (1955)	P55
CP (1960)	CP60
MB (1981)	MB81

Letters

Letters (1894)	L94
LL (1924)	LL24
Letters (1931)	L31
LH (1951)	LH51
Letters (1958)	L58

Related Works

FF (1932)	FF32
AB (1945)	AB45

★ ★ ★

1 2 4 SAFE IN THEIR
ALABASTER CHAMBERS

MANUSCRIPTS: Six (one lost) or seven (two lost), variant, about 1859, 1861, and 1862. There are versions from 1859 and 1861, two further attempts on the second stanza in 1861, and an 1862 holograph of the 1861 version.

The lost manuscript, sent to Susan Dickinson, presumably about late 1859, appears to have been the source for publication of the poem in the *Springfield Daily Republican* (1 March 1862), there titled "The Sleeping" and dated "*Pelham Hill, June*, 1861."

[A]   Safe in their alabaster chambers,
           Untouched by morning,
           And untouched by noon,
           Sleep the meek members of the Resurrection,
           Rafter of satin, and roof of stone.   5

           Light laughs the breeze
           In her castle above them,
           Babbles the bee in a stolid ear,
           Pipe the sweet birds in ignorant cadence:
           Ah! what sagacity perished here!   10

Emendation   3, 5, 8, 10] *indented*   9 cadence] cadences

The lost manuscript was still in Susan's possession in December 1890, when she marked out a phrase in her copy of *Poems* (1890) (Y-BRBL), interlining another:

castle <of sunshine> above them

The canceled reading was an editorial alteration in the 1890 text, which derived from the fascicle, already in other editorial hands. The authentic reading there, as in Susan's manuscript and the *Republican*, was "castle above them"; no other source has this variant.

The *Republican* text is substantively identical to the fascicle, except for line 9 in the newspaper, which has "cadences" instead of "cadence." Since Susan did not mark this word when annotating the 1890 text, which also has the singular form, one may conjecture that "cadence" appeared in her manuscript and that the plural form in the *Republican* was alteration or error.

When Samuel Bowles visited Amherst in June 1861, he may have acquired from Susan a copy of the early version: on 1 March 1862 it was published in the *Republican* curiously dated "*Pelham Hill, June, 1861.*" Pelham Hill, according to the *Republican* itself (6 July 1861, in a passage that Bowles may have written), was about two miles east of Amherst, the site of a new water-cure hotel named the Orient. This area is now called Mount Orient and Orient Springs, while the center of the town of Pelham, then known as Pelham Heights, has become known as Pelham Hill.

The record copy in Fascicle 6 is the earliest extant holograph, transcribed about late 1859 (H II).

B   Safe in their Alabaster Chambers –   F6.12
      Untouched by morning
      And untouched by noon –
      Sleep the meek members of the Resurrection –
      Rafter of satin,   5
      And Roof of stone.

      Light laughs the breeze
      In her Castle above them –
      Babbles the Bee in a stolid Ear,
      Pipe the sweet Birds in ignorant cadence –   10
      Ah, what sagacity perished here!

About 1861, perhaps as a consequence of Bowles's visit, a literary exchange with Susan Dickinson took this early version as the starting point. To Susan's criticism of the second stanza, ED responded with a new version: the familiar first stanza (but variant in line 4: "Lie" for "Sleep") followed by a new one. She concluded the manuscript (H B74a), which is written in pencil and signed "Emily," with a note:

Perhaps this verse would please you better - Sue -

C   Safe in their Alabaster Chambers,
              Untouched by morning -
              And untouched by noon -
              Lie the meek members of the Resurrection -
              Rafter of satin - and Roof of stone -   5

              Grand go the Years - in the Crescent - above them -
              Worlds scoop their Arcs -
              And Firmaments - row -
              Diadems - drop - and Doges - surrender -
              Soundless as dots - on a Disc of snow -   10

Division   4 of | 5 Roof of | 6 in the | 9 Doges - | 10 a |

Susan liked the new stanza less than the earlier one and renewed her criticism by "Pony Express" (H B74b).

I am not suited dear Emily with the second verse - It is remarkable as the chain lightening that blinds us hot nights in the Southern sky but it does not go with the ghostly shimmer of the first verse as well as the other one - It just occurs to me that the first verse is complete in itself it needs no other, and can't be coupled - Strange things always go alone - as there is only one Gabriel and one Sun - You never made a peer for that verse, and I *guess* you[r] kingdom does'nt hold one - I always go to the fire and get warm after thinking of it, but I never *can* again.

ED tried her hand at two more versions of the second stanza, dispatching one next door with a question and a final note to the exchange (H B74c).

Is *this frostier?*

D   Springs – shake the Sills –

      But – the Echoes – stiffen –

      Hoar – is the Window – and numb – the Door –

      Tribes of Eclipse – in Tents of Marble –

      Staples of Ages – have buckled – there –   5

      Division 3 and | 4 Tents | 5 have |

Her note; which follows the poem, begins with the passage:

Dear Sue –

 Your praise is good – to me – because I *know* it *knows* – and *suppose* it *means* –

Could I make you and Austin – proud – sometime – a great way off – 'twould give me taller feet –

In the second half of 1861, ED copied the revised portions of the poem onto a sheet of stationery (H 203), which she bound up as part of Fascicle 10. It was a complete record of the new attempts, including the stanza she had not sent to Susan.

E   Safe in their Alabaster chambers –

      Untouched by Morning –

      And untouched by Noon –

      Lie the meek members of the Resurrection –

      Rafter of Satin – and Roof of Stone!   5

      Grand go the Years – in the Crescent – above them –

      Worlds scoop their Arcs –

And Firmaments – row –

Diadems – drop – and Doges – surrender –

Soundless as dots – on a Disc of snow –   10

6–10]

Springs – shake the sills –

But – the Echoes – stiffen –

Hoar – is the window –

And – numb – the door –

Tribes – of Eclipse – in Tents – of Marble –

Staples – of Ages – have buckled – there –

•

Springs – shake the seals –

But the silence – stiffens –

Frosts unhook – in the Northern Zones –

Icicles – crawl from polar Caverns –

Midnight in Marble –

Refutes – the Suns –

Division 1 Alabaster | 4 of | 6 in the | 9 Doges—| 10 a | *alt*
6–10 window—|| *alt* 6–10 Tents—| *alt* 6–10 have | *alt* 6–10 in the |
alt 6–10 polar |

When ED sent her first letter to T. W. Higginson on 15 April 1862, six weeks after the early version of "Safe in their alabaster chambers" had appeared in the *Republican*, she enclosed a copy of the later version (BPL 2), one of four poems sent for his critical assessment. It is substantively identical with the copy in Fascicle 10, except for a return to "Sleep" in line 3.

F   Safe in their Alabaster Chambers –

Untouched by Morning –

And untouched by noon –
Sleep the meek members of the Resurrection,
Rafter of Satin and Roof of Stone –   5

Grand go the Years,
In the Crescent above them –
Worlds scoop their Arcs –
And Firmaments – row –
Diadems – drop –
And Doges – surrender –   10
Soundless as Dots,
On a Disc of Snow.

Division   1 Alabaster] Alabas – | ter   4 members] mem – | bers | 5 and
| 7 above | 9 row – ||

A transcript of the first stanza in an unidentified hand (A Tr 69) may
derive from another holograph now lost. The nature of the variants suggests the text to have been recalled, unreliably, from memory.

[G]   Deep in their alabaster chambers,
                 Untouched by morn and untouched by noon,
                 Sleep the mute members of the Resurrection
                 Roof of satin and rafter of stone,

                 Emendation 2 and] &   4 and] &

Each of the four lines, cited with the line numbering of the transcript,
differs from all other sources:

	Republican, Fascicles, Susan, Higginson	Transcript
1	Safe	Deep
2	morning	morn
3	meek	mute
4	Rafter of satin	Roof of satin
4	roof of stone	rafter of stone

Where the other sources vary in line 3, the transcript agrees with three of them:

	SDR, Fascicle 6, Higginson, Transcript	Susan, Fascicle 10
3	Sleep	Lie

PUBLICATION: *Springfield Daily Republican* (1 March 1862), 2, apparently from the lost copy to Susan Dickinson ([A]). Higginson, *Christian Union*, 42 (25 September 1890), 393, the complete poem from the early version in Fascicle 6 (B) and, separately, the second stanza of the later version that had been sent to him (F). Higginson explained that the separate stanza struck "a note too fine to be lost." *Poems* (1890), 113, combined these elements, arranged as three quatrains, with the early fascicle version (B) as stanzas 1 and 2 and the second stanza of the later version, apparently from Higginson's copy (F), as stanza 3. A facsimile of Higginson's copy was printed in Higginson and Boynton, *A Reader's History of American Literature* (1903), 130–31. *LL* (1924), 78, the second stanza of the second version to Susan (C) and the third version of the stanza to her (D). Bingham, *AB* (1945), 383n, the first alternative version for the second stanza, as a quatrain, from Fascicle 10 (E). *Poems* (1955), 151–55 ([A] as possibly sent to Bowles, B principal, C, D, E principal, F; without [G]); *CP* (1960), 100 (B, E). *Letters* (1958), 379–80 (B as if sent to Susan, C, D). Higgins, *American Literature*, 38 (March 1966), 21, from the unidentified transcript ([G]). *MB* (1981), 103 (B) and 193–94 (E), in facsimile. (J216)

[A]   *Title* The Sleeping *SDR62*   9 cadence] cadences *SDR62*

B   8 above them] of sunshine *P90 CP24 P30 P37*   *after 11*] *the second stanza of F P90 CP24 P30 P37*

C   1–5] *omitted LL24*   8 row] bow *LL24*

D   1 the] their *LL24*

from *The Norton Anthology of Poetry*, 5th ed., edited by Margaret Ferguson, Mary J. Salter, and John Stallworthy[†]

124 (216), FIRST VERSION[1]

Safe in their Alabaster[2] Chambers -
Untouched by morning
And untouched by noon -
Sleep the meek members of the Resurrection -
Rafter of satin,
And Roof of stone.

Light laughs the breeze
In her Castle above them -

† From *The Norton Anthology of Poetry*, Fifth Edition, ed. Margaret Ferguson, Mary J. Salter, and John Stallworthy (New York: W. W. Norton, 2005). Reprinted by permission of the publishers and Trustees of Amherst College from *The Poems of Emily Dickinson*, Thomas H. Johnson, ed., pp. lxi–lxii, 152–155, Cambridge, Mass.: The Belknap Press of Harvard University Press, Copyright © 1951, 1955, 1979, 1983 by the President and Fellows of Harvard College.

Notes: From *The Norton Anthology of Poetry*, 5th edition, edited by Margaret Ferguson, Mary Jo Salter, Jon Stallworthy. Copyright © 2005, 1996, 1983, 1975, 1970 by W. W. Norton & Company, Inc. Used by permission of W. W. Norton & Company, Inc.

1. This poem is one of many that exist in varying versions and illustrate wholesale revision. Dickinson sent the 1859 version to her sister-in-law, Sue Dickinson, whose suggestions prompted substantial changes. The first version here, the earliest extant, was one of the few poems Dickinson published (in a magazine). In correspondence in 1862 with Thomas W. Higginson, the literary critic who would help publish her poems posthumously, Dickinson sent a modified version, the basis of the second version here.

2. Translucent white material.

Babbles the Bee in a stolid Ear,
Pipe the sweet Birds in ignorant cadence –
Ah, what sagacity perished here!

1859[3]   1862

1 2 4 (2 1 6) , SECOND VERSION

Safe in their Alabaster Chambers –
Untouched by Morning –
And untouched by noon –
Sleep the meek members of the Resurrection,
Rafter of Satin and Roof of Stone –

Grand go the Years,
In the Crescent above them –
Worlds scoop their Arcs –
And Firmaments – row –
Diadems° – drop –   *crowns*
And Doges[4] – surrender –
Soundless as Dots,
On a Disc of Snow.

1862   1890

3. The first date indicates the date of composition; the second indicates the date of first publication [—*Editor*].

4. Chief magistrates in the republics of Venice and Genoa from the eleventh through the sixteenth centuries.

Working with Documents

from *The Tragedie of Mariam,*
the Faire Queene of Jewry

Elizabeth Cary

Elizabeth Cary's tragedy, the first published drama (1613) to have been written by an Englishwoman, is a closet drama, not intended for the stage but for non-professionals to read aloud privately. Cary seems to have provided the printer with the copy, but the printing has many typographical errors. What other editorial issues arise as one works with this passage?

Actus primus.   Scœna prima.

Mariam sola.

HOw oft haue I with publike voyce runne on?
To censure *Romes* last *Hero* for deceit :
   Because he wept when *Pompeie* life was gone,
Yet when he liu'd, hee thought his Name too great.
But now I doe recant , and *Roman* Lord
Excuse too rash a judgement in a woman :
My Sexe pleads pardon, pardon then afford,
Mistaking is with vs, but too too common.
Now doe I finde by selfe Experience taught,
One Object yeelds both griefe and ioy :
You wept indeed , when on his worth you thought,
But ioyd that slaughter did your Foe destroy .
So at his death your Eyes true droppes did raine,
Whom dead, you did not wish aliue againe.
When *Herod* liu'd, that now is done to death,
Oft haue I wisht that I from him were free :
Oft haue I wisht that he might lose his breath,
Oft haue I wisht his Carkas dead to see.
Then Rage and Scorne had put my loue to flight,
That Loue which once on him was firmely set :
Hate hid his true affection from my sight,
And kept my heart from paying him his debt.
And blame me not, for *Herods* Iealousie
Had power euen constancie it selfe to change :
For hee by barring me from libertie,
To shunne my ranging , taught me first to range.
But yet too chast a Scholler was my hart,
To learne to loue another then my Lord :
To leaue his Loue, my lessons former part,

A 3   I

THE TRAGEDIE

I quickly learn'd, the other I abhord.
But now his death to memorie doth call,
The tender loue, that he to *Mariam* bare:
And mine to him, this makes those riuers fall,
Which by an other thought vnmoiſtned are.
For *Ariſtobolus* the lowlyeſt youth
That euer did in Angels ſhape appeare :
The cruell *Herod* was not mou'd to ruth,
Then why grieues *Mariam Herods* death to heare?
Why ioy I not the tongue no more ſhall ſpeake,
That yeelded forth my brothers lateſt dome:
Both youth and beautie might thy furie breake,
And both in him did ill befit a Tombe.
And worthy Grandſire ill did he requite,
His high Aſſent alone by thee procur'd,
Except he murdred thee to free the ſpright
Which ſtili he thought on earth too long immur'd.
How happie was it that *Sohemus* maide
Was mou'd to pittie my diſtreſt eſtate?
Might *Herods* life a truſtie ſeruant finde,
My death to his had bene vnſeparate.   (beare,
Theſe thoughts haue power, his death to make me
Nay more, to wiſh the newes may firmely hold:
Yet cannot this repulſe ſome falling teare,
That will againſt my will ſome griefe vnfold.
And more I owe him for his loue to me,
The deepeſt loue that euer yet was ſeene:
Yet had I rather much a milke-maide bee,
Then be the Monarke of *Iudeas* Queene.
It was for nought but loue, he wiſht his end
Might to my death, but the vaunt-currier proue:
But I had rather ſtill be foe then friend,
To him that ſaues for hate, and kills for loue.
Hard-hearted *Mariam*, at thy diſcontent,
What flouds of teares haue drencht his manly face ?
How canſt thou then ſo faintly now lament,
Thy trueſt louers death, a deaths diſgrace :
I now mine eyes you do begin to right

Th

OF MARIAM.

The wrongs of your admirer. And my Lord,
Long since you should haue put your smiles to flight,
Ill doth a widowed eye with ioy accord.
Why now me thinkes the loue I bare him then,
When virgin freedome left me vnrestraind:
Doth to my heart begin to creepe agen,
My passion now is far from being faind.
But teares flie-backe, and hide you in your bankes,
You must not be to *Alexandra* seene:
For if my mone be spide, but little thankes
Shall *Mariam* haue, from that incensed Queene.

Actus primus : Scœna Secunda.

Mariam. Alexandra.

Alex :   (mistake,

WHat meanes these teares ? my *Mariam* doth
    The newes we heard did tell the *Tyrants* end:
What weepst thou for thy brothers murthers sake,
Will euer wight a teare for *Herod* spend?
My curse pursue his breathles trunke and spirit,
Base *Edomite* the damned *Esaus* heire:
Must he ere *Iacobs* child the crowne inherit ?
Must he vile wretch be set in *Dauids* chaire ?
No *Dauids* soule within the bosome plac'te,
Of our forefather *Abram* was asham'd :
To see his seat with such a toade disgrac'te,
That seat that hath by *Iudas* race bene fain'd.
Thou fatall enemie to royall blood,
Did not the murther of my boy suffice,
To stop thy cruell mouth that gaping stood?
But must thou dim the milde *Hercanus* eyes?
My gratious father, whose too readie hand
Did lift this *Idumean* from the dust :
And he vngratefull catiffe did withstand,
The man that did in him most friendly trust.
What kingdomes right could cruell *Herod* claime,
Was he not *Esaus* Issue, heyre of hell?
Then what succession can he haue but shame ?
Did not his Ancestor his birth-right sell ?

O

THE TRAGEDIE

O yes,he doth from *Edoms* name deriue,
His cruell nature which with blood is fed :
That made him me of Sire and sonne depriue,
He euer thirsts for blood, and blood is red.
Weepst thou because his loue to thee was bent?
And readst thou loue in crimson caracters?
Slew he thy friends to worke thy hearts content?
No : hate may Iustly call that action hers.
He gaue the sacred Priesthood for thy sake,
To *Aristobolus*. Yet doomde him dead:
Before his backe the *Ephod* warme could make,
And ere the *Myter* setled on his head.
Oh had he giuen my boy no lesse then right,
The double oyle should to his forehead bring :
A double honour, shining doubly bright,
His birth annoynted him both Priest and King.
And say my father, and my sonne he slewe,
To royalize by right your Prince borne breath:
Was loue the cause, can *Mariam* deeme it true,
That *Mariam* gaue commandment for her death?
I know by fits, he shewd some signes of loue,
And yet not loue, but raging lunacie:
And this his hate to thee may iustly proue,
That sure he hates *Hercanus* familie.
Who knowes if he vnconstant wauering Lord,
His loue to *Doris* had renew'd againe?
And that he might his bed to her afford,
Perchance he wisht that *Mariam* might be slaine.

Ma: ~~Alex.~~ *Doris*, Alas her time of loue was past,
Those coales were rakte in embers long agoe :
If *Mariams* loue and she was now disgrast,
Nor did I glorie in her ouerthrowe.
He not a whit his first borne sonne esteem'd,
Because as well as his he was not mine:
My children onely for his owne he deem'd,
These boyes that did descend from royall line.
These did he stile his heyres to *Dauids* throne,
My *Alexander* if he liue, shall sit

In

OF MARIAM.

In the Maiesticke seat of *Salamon*,
To will it so, did *Herod* thinke it fit.

   Alex. Why? who can claime from *Alexanders* brood
That Gold adorned Lyon-guarded Chaire?
Was *Alexander* not of *Dauids* blood?
And was not *Mariam Alexanders* heire?
What more then right could *Herod* then bestow,
And who will thinke except for more then right,
He did not raise them, for they were not low,
But borne to weare the Crowne in his despight:
Then send those teares away that are not sent
To thee by reason, but by passions power:
Thine eyes to cheere, thy cheekes to smiles be bent,
And entertaine with ioy this happy houre.
Felicitie, if when shee comes, she findes
A mourning habite, and a cheerlesse looke,
Will thinke she is not welcome to thy minde,
And so perchance her lodging will not brooke.
Oh keepe her whilest thou hast her, if she goe
She will not easily returne againe:
Full many a yeere haue I indur'd in woe,
Yet still haue sude her presence to obtaine:
And did not I to her as presents send
A Table, that best Art did beautifie
Of two, to whom Heauen did best feature lend,
To woe her loue by winning *Anthony*:
For when a Princes fauour we doe craue,
We first their Mynions loues do seeke to winne:
So I, that sought Felicitie to haue,
Did with her Mynion *Anthony* beginne,
With double slight I sought to captiuate
The warlike louer, but I did not right:
For if my gift had borne but halfe the rate,
The *Roman* had beene ouer-taken quite.
But now he fared like a hungry guest,
That to some plenteous festiuall is gone,
Now this, now that, hee deemes to eate were best,
Such choice doth make him let them all alone.

        B   The

THE TRAGEDIE

The boyes large forehead first did fayrest seeme,
Then glaunst his eye vpon my *Mariams* cheeke:
And that without comparison did deeme,
VVhat was in eyther but he most did seeke.
And thus distracted, eythers beauties might
VVithin the others excellence was drown'd:
Too much delight did bare him from delight,
For eithers loue, the others did confound.
VVhere if thy portraiture had onely gone,
His life from *Herod, Anthony* had taken:
He would haue loued thee, and thee alone,
And left the browne *Egyptian* cleane forsaken.
And *Cleopatra* then to seeke had bene,
So firme a louer of her wayned face :
Then great *Anthonius* fall we had not seene,
By her that fled to haue him holde the chase.
Then *Mariam* in a *Romans* Chariot set,
In place of *Cleopatra* might haue showne :
A mart of Beauties in her visage met,
And part in this, that they were all her owne.
  Ma. Not to be Emprise of aspiring *Rome*,
Would *Mariam* like to *Cleopatra* liue:
With purest body will I presse my Toome,
And wish no fauours *Anthony* could giue.
  Alex. Let vs retire vs, that we may resolue
How now to deale in this reuersed state :
Great are th'affaires that we must now reuolue,
And great affaires must not be taken late.

Actus primus. Scœna tertia.

Mariam, Alexandra. Salome.

Salome.

MOre plotting yet? Why? now you haue the thing
For which so oft you spent your supliant breath:
  And *Mariam* hopes to haue another King,
Her eyes doe sparkle ioy for *Herods* death.

Alex.

OF MARIAM.

Alex. If she desir'd another King to haue,
She might before she came in *Herods* bed
Haue had her wish. More Kings then one did craue,
For leaue to set a Crowne vpon her head.
I thinke with more then reason she laments,
That she is freed from such a sad annoy :
Who ist will weepe to part from discontent,
And if she ioy, she did not causelesse ioy.

Sal. You durst not thus haue giuen your tongue the
If noble *Herod* still remaind in life :   (raine,
Your daughters betters farre I dare maintaine,
Might haue reioyc'd to be my brothers wife.

Mar. My betters farre, base woman t'is vntrue,
You scarce haue euer my superiors seene :
For *Mariams* seruants were as good as you,
Before she came to be *Iudeas* Queene.

Sal. Now stirs the tongue that is so quickly mou'd,
But more then once your collor haue I borne :
Your fumish words are sooner sayd then prou'd,
And *Salomes* reply is onely scorne.

Mar. Scorne those that are for thy companions
Though I thy brothers face had neuer seene,   (held,
My birth, thy baser birth so farre exceld,
I had to both of you the Princesse bene.
Thou party Iew, and party Edomite,
Thou Mongrell : issu'd from reiected race,
Thy Ancestors against the Heauens did fight,
And thou like them wilt heauenly birth disgrace.

Sal. Still twit you me with nothing but my birth,
What ods betwixt your ancestors and mine ?
Both borne of *Adam*, both were made of Earth,
And both did come from holy *Abrahams* line.

Mar. I fauour thee when nothing else *I* say,
VVith thy blacke acts ile not pollute my breath :
Else to thy charge *I* might full iustly lay
A shamefull life, besides a husbands death.

Sal. Tis true indeed, *I* did the plots reueale,
That past betwixt your fauorites and you :
I ment not *I*, a traytor to conceale.

                    B 2   *Thus*

THE TRAGEDIE

Thus *Salome* your Mynion *Ioseph* slue.

    Mar. Heauen, dost thou meane this Infamy to smo-
Let slandred *Mariam* ope thy closed eare :   (ther?
Selfe guilt hath euer bene suspitious mother,
And therefore I this speech with patience beare.
No, had not *Salomes* vnstedfast heart,
In *Iosephus* stead her *Constabarus* plast,
To free her selfe, she had not vsde the art,
To slander haplesse *Mariam* for vnchast.

    Alex. Come *Mariam*, let vs goe: it is no boote
To let the head contend against the foote.

Actus primus. Scœna quarta.

Salome, Sola.

Liues *Salome*, to get so base a stile
   As foote, to the proud *Mariam Herods* spirit :
    In happy time for her endured exile,
For did he liue she should not misse her merit:
But he is dead : and though he were my Brother,
His death such store of Cinders cannot cast
My Coales of loue to quench : for though they smo-
The flames a while, yet will they out at last.   (ther
Oh blest *Arabia*, in best climate plast,
I by the Fruit will censure of the Tree :
Tis not in vaine, thy happy name thou hast,
If all *Arabians* like *Silleus* bee :
Had not my Fate bene too too contrary,
When I on *Constabarus* first did gaze,
Silleus had beene obiect to mine eye :
Whose lookes and personage must allyes amaze.
But now ill Fated *Salome*, thy tongue
To *Constabarus* by it selfe is tide:
And now except I doe the Ebrew wrong
I cannot be the faire *Arabian* Bride :
What childish lets are these? Why stand I now
On honourable points? Tis long agoe

                     Since

OF MARIAM.

Since shame was written on my tainted brow:
And certaine tis, that shame is honours foe.
Had I vpon my reputation stood,
Had I affected an vnspotted life,
Iosephus vaines had still bene stuft with blood,
And I to him had liu'd a sober wife.
Then had I neuer cast an eye of loue,
On *Constabarus* now detested face,
Then had I kept my thoughts without remoue
And blusht at motion of the least disgrace :
But shame is gone, and honour wipt away,
And Impudencie on my forehead sits :
She bids me worke my will without delay,
And for my will I will imploy my wits.
He loues, I loue; what then can be the cause,
Keepes me for being the *Arabians* wife?
It is the principles of *Moses* lawes,
For *Contabarus* still remaines in life,
If he to me did beare as Earnest hate,
As I to him, for him there were an ease,
A separating bill might free his fate:
From such a yoke that did so much displease.
Why should such priuiledge to man be giuen ?
Or giuen to them, why bard from women then ?
Are men then we in greater grace with Heauen ?
Or cannot women hate as well as men?
Ile be the custome-breaker : and beginne
To shew my Sexe the way to freedomes doore,
And with an offring will I purge my sinne,
The lawe was made for none but who are poore.
If *Herod* had liu'd, I might to him accuse
My present Lord. But for the futures sake
Then would I tell the King he did refuse
The sonnes of *Baba* in his power to take.
But now I must diuorse him from my bed,
That my *Silleus* may possesse his roome:
Had I not begd his life he had bene dead,
I curse my tongue the hindrer of his doome,

B 3

But

On the Death of the Reverend Dr. Sewell

Phillis Wheatley

Brought to Boston as a slave when she was about seven years old, Phillis Wheatley surprised her owners by learning to compose sophisticated verse, such as this poem about the death of her pastor, Joseph Sewell. Dedicated to Selina Hastings, Countess of Huntingdon, a leader in the Methodist movement, Wheatley's poetry saw two editions, one in England in 1773, a second in the United States in 1786. But she also circulated her poems in manuscript, revising between sending copies to friends and to people she admired. Below are all the witnesses to this poem that have been discovered to date. It should be noted that one of Wheatley's editors, William Robinson, reported that the Countess of Huntingdon's papers in the Cheshunt Foundation Archives at Westminster College, Cambridge, holds not only the holograph manuscript printed below, but a second manuscript, one that differs in punctuation and does not contain lines 36–37. This information was repeated by Vincent Carretta in his edition of Phillis Wheatley's works.[1] But this manuscript seems to be what bibliographers and librarians call a *ghost*, a document that may in fact have existed but for which no physical evidence now remains. In fact, the Cheshunt Foundation Archives has no record that a second manuscript ever existed.

1. See William H. Robinson, *Phillis Wheatley and Her Writings* (New York: Garland Press, 1984), 365, and *Phillis Wheatley, Complete Writings*, ed. Vincent Carretta (New York: Penguin, 2001), 109.

from the first edition, 1773

VARIOUS SUBJECTS.   19

On the Death of the Rev. Dr. SEWELL,
1769.

ERE yet the morn its lovely bluſhes ſpread,
  See *Sewell* number'd with the happy dead.
Hail, holy man, arriv'd th' immortal ſhore,
Though we ſhall hear thy warning voice no more.
Come, let us all behold with wiſhful eyes   5
The ſaint aſcending to his native ſkies;
From hence the prophet wing'd his rapt'rous way
To the bleſt manſions in eternal day.
Then begging for the Spirit of our God,
And panting eager for the ſame abode,   10
Come, let us all with the ſame vigour riſe,
And take a proſpect of the bliſsful ſkies;
While on our minds *Chriſt's* image is impreſt,
And the dear Saviour glows in ev'ry breaſt.
Thrice happy ſaint! to find thy heav'n at laſt, 15
What compenſation for the evils paſt!

            C 2   Great

Great God, incomprehenſible, unknown
By ſenſe, we bow at thine exalted throne.
O, while we beg thine excellence to feel,
Thy ſacred Spirit to our hearts reveal,   20
And give us of that mercy to partake,
Which thou haſt promis'd for the *Saviour's* ſake!

  " *Sewell* is dead."   Swift-pinion'd *Fame* thus
      cry'd.
  " Is *Sewell* dead," my trembling tongue reply'd,
O what a bleſſing in his flight deny'd !   25
How oft for us the holy prophet pray'd !
How oft to us the Word of Life convey'd !
By duty urg'd my mournful verſe to cloſe,
I for his tomb this epitaph compoſe.

  " Lo, here a man, redeem'd by *Jeſus'* blood, 30
  " A ſinner once, but now a ſaint with God ;
  " Behold ye rich, ye poor, ye fools, ye wiſe,
  " Nor let his monument your heart ſurprize ;
  " 'Twill tell you what this holy man has done,
  " Which gives him brighter luſtre than the ſun.
                              " Liſten,

VARIOUS SUBJECTS. 21

" Liften, ye happy, from your feats above.
" I fpeak fincerely, while I fpeak and love,
" He fought the paths of piety and truth,
" By thefe made happy from his early youth !
" In blooming years that grace divine he felt,   40
" Which refcues finners from the chains of guilt.
" Mourn him, ye indigent, whom he has fed,
" And henceforth feek, like him, for living bread ;
" Ev'n *Chrift*, the bread defcending from above,
" And afk an int'reft in his faving love.   45
" Mourn him, ye youth, to whom he oft has told
" God's gracious wonders from the times of old.
" I, too have caufe this mighty lofs to mourn,
" For he my monitor will not return.
" O when fhall we to his bleft ftate arrive ?   50
" When the fame graces in our bofoms thrive."

On

from the second edition, 1786

14 POEMS ON

On the Death of the Rev. Dr. SEWELL,
1769.

ERE yet the morn its lovely blushes spread,
See *Sewell* number'd with the happy dead.
Hail, holy man, arriv'd th' immortal shore,
Though we shall hear thy warning voice no more.
Come, let us all behold with wishful eyes   5
The saint ascending to his native skies;
From hence the prophet wing'd his rapt'rous way
To the blest mansions in eternal day.
Then begging for the Spirit of our God,
And panting eager for the same abode,   10
Come, let us all with the same vigour rise,
And take a prospect of the blissful skies;
While on our minds *Christ*'s image is imprest,
And the dear Saviour glows in ev'ry breast.
Thrice happy saint! to find thy heav'n at last,   15
What compensation for the evils past!
   Great God, incomprehensible, unknown
By sense, we bow at thine exalted throne.
O, while we beg thine excellence to feel,
Thy sacred Spirit to our hearts reveal,   20
And give us of that mercy to partake,
Which thou hast promis'd for the *Saviour*'s sake!
   " *Sewell* is dead." Swift-pinion'd *Fame* thus cry'd.
" Is *Sewell* dead," my trembling tongue reply'd,
O what a blessing in his flight deny'd!   25
How oft for us the holy prophet pray'd!
How oft to us the Word of Life convey'd!
By duty urg'd my mournful verse to close,
I for his tomb this epitaph compose.
   " Lo, here a man, redeem'd by *Jesus*'s blood,   30
" A sinner once, but now a saint with God;
" Behold ye rich, ye poor, ye fools, ye wise,
" Nor let his monument your heart surprise;
                                            " 'Twill

VARIOUS SUBJECTS. 15

" 'Twill tell you what this holy man has done,
" Which gives him brighter luftre than the fun.   35
" Liften, ye happy, from your feats above.
" I fpeak fincerely, while I fpeak and love,
" He fought the paths of piety and truth,
" By thefe made happy from his early youth;
" In blooming years that grace divine he felt,   40
" Which refcues finners from the chains of guilt.
" Mourn him, ye indigent, whom he has fed,
" And henceforth feek, like him, for living bread;
" Ev'n *Chrift*, the bread defcending from above,
" And afk an int'reft in his faving love.   45
" Mourn him, ye youth, to whom he oft has told
" God's gracious wonders from the times of old.
" I too have caufe this mighty lofs to mourn,
" For he my monitor will not return.
" O when fhall we to his bleft ftate arrive?   50
" When the fame graces in our bofoms thrive."

On the Death of the Rev. Mr. GEORGE
WHITEFIELD. 1770.

HAIL, happy faint, on thine immortal throne,
     Poffeft of glory, life, and blifs unknown;
We hear no more the mufic of thy tongue,
Thy wonted auditories ceafe to throng.
Thy fermons in unequall'd accents flow'd,   5
And ev'ry bofom with devotion glow'd;
Thou didft in ftrains of eloquence refin'd
Inflame the heart, and captivate the mind.
Unhappy we the fetting fun deplore,
So glorious once, but ah! it fhines no more.   10
  Behold the prophet in his tow'ring flight!
He leaves the earth for heav'n's unmeafur'd height, ⎫
And worlds unknown receive him from our fight.   ⎬
                                                    ⎭
                                              There

from the Dartmouth College Library, MS Ticknor 769940.2

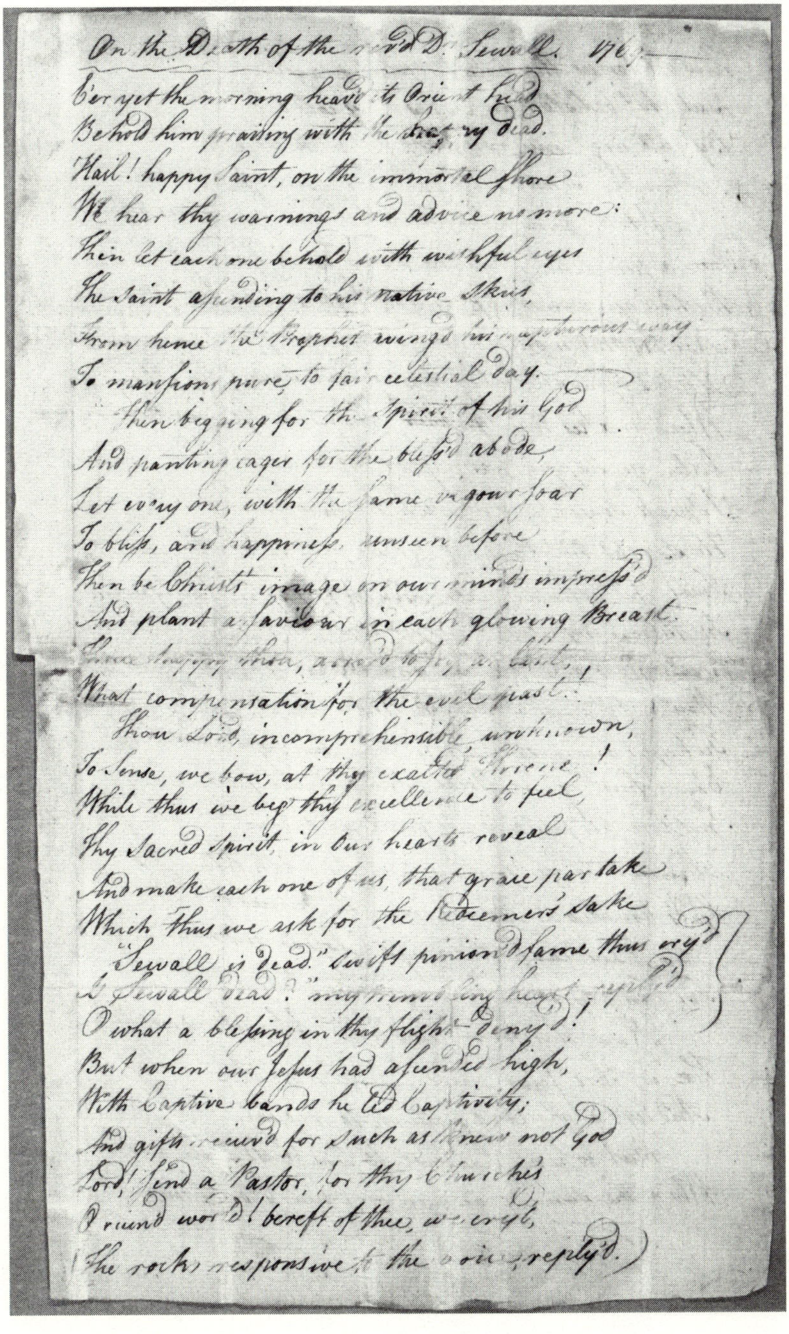

Behold ye rich and poor and fools and wise
Nor let this monitor your hearts surprize
I'll tell you all what this great saint has done
That makes him Brighter than the Glorious sun
Listen ye happy from the seats above
I speak sincerely and with truth and Love
He sought the paths of virtue and of truth
Twas this, that made him happy in his youth
In Blooming years he found that grace divine
That gives admittance to the sacred shrine —
Mourn him ye Indigent whom he has fed
Seek yet more earnest for the living bread
E'n Christ your bread descend from above
Implore his pity and his grace and Love
Mourn him ye youth whom he has often told
Gods bounteous mercy from the times of Old
I too, have cause this heavy loss to mourn:
Because my monitor will not return
Now this faint semblance of his complete:
He is thro' Jesus made divinely great
And set a Glorious Pattern to repeat
But when shall we to this bless'd state arrive?
When the same graces in our hearts do thrive

Phillis Wheatley

On the Decease of the rev'd Dr. Sewell ⸺

Er yet the morning heav'd its orient head
Behold him praising with the happy dead;
Hail happy Saint on the Immortal shore
We hear thy warnings, and twice no more
Then let each one, behold with wistful eyes
The saint ascending to his native skies
From hence the Prophet wing'd his rapturous way
To mansions pure, to fair celestial day ⸺
Then longing for the Spirit of this soul
And panting eager for the blest abode
Let every one with the same ardour soar
To bliss and happiness unseen before
Then be christ's image on our minds imprest
And blant a favour in each glowing breast
Thrice happy thou arriv'd to joy at last
What compensation for the evil past ⸺
Thou Lord incomprehensible unknown,
By sense ⸺ we bow at thy exalted throne
While thus we beg thy excellence to feel
Thy Sacred Spirit in our hearts reveal
To make each one of us thy grace partake
Which thus we beg for the Redeemer's sake
Sewell is dead swift pinion'd fame this cry'd
Is Sewell dead, my trembling heart reply'd
Behold to us, a benefit deny'd ⸺
But when our Jesus had ascended high
With captive bands he led captivity
And gifts receiv'd for such as knew not God
Lord and a Pastor for thy Churches good;
 Ruin'd world, my mournful thots reply'd
And ruin'd continent the echo cry'd
How oft for us the holy Prophet pray'd
But now behold him in his clay cold bed
By duty urg'd my weeping verse to close
I'll on his tomb an Epitaph compose
Here lies a man bought with christ's precious blood
Once a poor Sinner, now a saint with God

Behold ye rich and poor and fools and wise
Nor let this monitor your heart surprize
I'll tell you all, what this great saint has done
That makes him brighter than the glorious sun
Listen ye happy, from the seats above
I speak sincerely and with truth and love
He sought the paths of virtue and of truth
'Twas this that made him happy in his youth
In blooming years he found that grace divine
That gives admittance to the sacred shrine
Mourn him ye indigent, whom he has fed
Seek yet more earnest for the living bread
Even Christ, your bread that cometh from above
Implore his pity and his grace and love
Mourn him ye youth whom he hath often told
Gods bounteous mercies from the times of Old
I too have cause this heavy loss to mourn
For this my monitor will not return
Now this faint resemblance of his life complete
He is thro' Jesus made divinely great
And set a glorious pattern to repeat ____
But when shall we to this bless'd state arrive
When the same graces in our hearts do thrive

Phillis Wheatley

from the American Antiquarian Society, Worcester, Massachusetts: MSS Dept., Miscellaneous MSS boxes "W"

How oft for us this holy Prophet pray'd:
But ah! behold him in his Clay-cold bed
By duty urg'd my weary Eyes to close
On his Tomb, an Epitaph compose.

Lo' here; a man bought with Christ's precious blood
Once a poor Sinner, now a Saint with God.
Behold ye rich and poor, and fools and wises;
Nor let this monitor your hearts surprize
I'll tell you all, what this great Saint has done
Which makes him brighter than the Glorious Sun.
Listen ye happy, from your seats above
I speak sincerely and with truth and Love.
He sought the Paths of virtue and of Truth
'Twas this which made him happy in his Youth.
In blooming year he found that grace divine
Which gives admittance to the sacred shrine.
Mourn him, ye Indigent, whom he has fed,
Seek yet more earnest for the living Bread.
Ev'n Christ your Bread, who cometh from above
Implore his pity and his grace and Love.
Mourn him ye Youth, whom he hath often told
Gods bounteous Mercy from the times of Old.
I too, have cause this mighty loss to mourn
For this my monitor will ne'er return.
Now this faint semblance of his life complete
He is, thro' Jesus, made divinely great.
And left a glorious pattern to repeat.
But when shall we, to this bless'd State arrive?
When the same grace in our hearts do thrive.

from *Frankenstein*

Mary Wollstonecraft Shelley

Frankenstein was for a long time known mainly in editions derived from the 1831 version, which is, in fact, the third edition of the novel. First printed in 1818, *Frankenstein, or the Modern Prometheus* was published again in 1823, in an edition prepared by Shelley's father, William Godwin, while she was out of the country. Meanwhile, Shelley gave a copy of the 1818 edition with pen revisions to a friend of hers in Genoa, a copy that has come to be known as the Thomas Copy. When Shelley extensively revised her novel for the 1831 edition, she seems to have worked from a copy of 1823, not 1818, so that her revisions in the Thomas Copy were not published in her lifetime. The large portions of the manuscript of *Frankenstein* that still survive show that her husband, Percy Bysshe Shelley, extensively revised her prose and even contributed ideas to the plot. Unfortunately, the manuscript is missing for the selection reprinted here.

from the 1818 edition, with the author's pen
corrections in the Pierpont Morgan Library, New York
("the Thomas Copy")

happy to have possessed as the brother
of my heart.

I shall continue my journal concerning the stranger at intervals, should I
have any fresh incidents to record.

August 13th, 17—.

My affection for my guest increases
every day. He excites at once my admiration and my pity to an astonishing
degree. How can I see so noble a
creature destroyed by misery without
feeling the most poignant grief? He is
so gentle, yet so wise; his mind is so *in his nature*
cultivated; and when he speaks, although *language*
his words are culled with the choicest *which is*
art, yet they flow with rapidity and un- *French,*
paralleled eloquence.

He is now much recovered from his
illness, and is continually on the deck,
apparently watching for the sledge that
preceded his own. Yet, although un-

c 4

32   FRANKENSTEIN; OR,

happy, he is not so utterly occupied by his own misery, but that he interests himself deeply in the employments of others. He has asked me many questions concerning my design; and I have related my little history frankly to him. He appeared pleased with the confidence, and suggested several alterations in my plan, which I shall find exceedingly useful. There is no pedantry in his manner; but all he does appears to spring solely from the interest he instinctively takes in the welfare of those who surround him. He is often overcome by ^a gloom, ~~and then~~ *Which veils his countenance like deep night - he neither speaks or notices any thing around* ~~he sits by himself,~~ and tries to overcome all that is sullen or unsocial in his humour. These paroxysms pass from him like a cloud from before the sun, *him, but if try on again will gaze on the rear* though his dejection never leaves him. I have endeavoured to win his confidence; and I trust that I have suc- dence; and I trust that I have suc-

and I have sometimes observed his dark eyelash wet with a tear which falls ~~silently~~ silently in the deep. This unobtrusive sorrow excites in me the most painful interest, and he will at times reward my sympathy by throwing aside this veil of mortal woe, and then his ardent looks, his deep toned voice and powerful eloquence entrance me with delight

ceeded. One day I mentioned to him
the desire I had always felt of finding
a friend who might sympathize with
me, and direct me by his counsel. I
said, I did not belong to that class of
men who are offended by advice. " I am
self-educated, and perhaps I hardly rely
sufficiently upon my own powers. I wish
therefore that my companion should
be wiser and more experienced than
myself, to confirm and support me;
nor have I believed it impossible to
find a true friend."

" I agree with you," replied the stranger, " in believing that friendship is
not only a desirable, but a possible acquisition. I once had a friend, the
most noble of human creatures, and am
entitled, therefore, to judge respecting
friendship. You have hope, and the
world before you, and have no cause
for despair. But I——I have lost

c 5

34   FRANKENSTEIN; OR,

every thing, and cannot begin life
anew."

As he said this, his countenance became expressive of a calm settled grief,
that touched me to the heart.   But
he was silent, and presently retired to
his cabin.

Even broken in spirit as he is, no-
one can feel more deeply than he does
the beauties of nature.   The starry
sky, the sea, and every sight afforded
by these wonderful regions, seems still
to have the power of elevating his soul
from earth.   Such a man has a double
existence: he may suffer misery, and
be overwhelmed by disappointments;
yet when he has retired into himself, he
will be like a celestial spirit, that has
a halo around him, within whose circle
no grief or folly ventures.

Will you laugh at the enthusiasm I
express concerning this divine wan-

THE MODERN PROMETHEUS. 35

derer? If you do, you must have certainly lost that simplicity which was once your characteristic charm. Yet, if you will, smile at the warmth of my expressions, while I find every day new causes for repeating them.

August 19th, 17—.

Yesterday the stranger said to me, " You may easily perceive, Captain Walton, that I have suffered great and unparalleled misfortunes. I had determined, once, that the memory of these evils should die with me; but you have won me to alter my determination. You seek for knowledge and wisdom, as I once did; and I ardently hope that the gratification of your wishes may not be a serpent to sting you, as mine has been. I do not know that the relation of my misfortunes will be useful to you, yet, if you are inclined, listen to my tale. I believe that the strange incidents connected with it will afford a view of nature, which may enlarge your faculties and understanding. You will hear of powers and occurrences, such as you have been accustomed to believe impossible: but I do not doubt that my tale conveys in its series internal evidence of the truth of the events of which it is composed."

You may easily conceive that I was much gratified by the offered communication; yet I could not endure that he should renew his grief by a recital of his misfortunes. I felt the greatest eagerness to hear the promised narrative, partly from curiosity, and partly from a strong desire to ameliorate his fate, if it were in my power. I expressed these feelings in my answer.

"I thank you," he replied, "for

your sympathy, but it is useless; my
fate is nearly fulfilled. I wait but for
one event, and then I shall repose in
peace. I understand your feeling,"
continued he, perceiving that I wished
to interrupt him ; " but you are mistaken, my friend, if thus you will allow
me to name you ; nothing can alter my
destiny : listen to my history, and you
will perceive how irrevocably it is determined.

He then told me, that he would commence his narrative the next day when
I should be at leisure. This promise
drew from me the warmest thanks. I
have resolved every night, when I am
not engaged, to record, as nearly as
possible in his own words, what he has
related during the day. If I should
be engaged, I will at least make notes.
This manuscript will doubtless afford
you the greatest pleasure : but to me,

38   FRANKENSTEIN; OR,

who know him, and who hear it from
his own lips, with what interest and
sympathy shall I read it in some future
day!

from the 1831 edition

14   FRANKENSTEIN ; OR,

" And yet you rescued me from a strange and perilous situation ; you have benevolently restored me to life."

Soon after this he enquired if I thought that the breaking up of the ice had destroyed the other sledge ? I replied, that I could not answer with any degree of certainty ; for the ice had not broken until near midnight, and the traveller might have arrived at a place of safety before that time ; but of this I could not judge.

From this time a new spirit of life animated the decaying frame of the stranger. He manifested the greatest eagerness to be upon deck, to watch for the sledge which had before appeared ; but I have persuaded him to remain in the cabin, for he is far too weak to sustain the rawness of the atmosphere. I have promised that some one should watch for him, and give him instant notice if any new object should appear in sight.

Such is my journal of what relates to this strange occurrence up to the present day. The stranger has gradually improved in health, but is very silent, and appears uneasy when any one except myself enters his cabin. Yet his manners are so conciliating and gentle, that the sailors are all interested in him, although they have had very little communication with him. For my own part, I begin to love him as a brother ; and his constant and deep grief fills me with sympathy and compassion. He must have been a noble creature in his better days, being even now in wreck so attractive and amiable.

I said in one of my letters, my dear Margaret, that I should find no friend on the wide ocean ; yet I have found a man who, before his spirit had been broken by misery, I should have been happy to have possessed as the brother of my heart.

I shall continue my journal concerning the stranger at intervals, should I have any fresh incidents to record.

August 13th, 17—.

My affection for my guest increases every day. He excites at once my admiration and my pity to an astonishing degree. How can I see so noble a creature destroyed by misery, without feeling the most poignant grief ? He is so gentle, yet so wise; his mind is so cultivated; and when he speaks, although his words are culled with the choicest art, yet they flow with rapidity and unparalleled eloquence.

He is now much recovered from his illness, and is continually on the deck, apparently watching for the sledge that preceded his own. Yet, although unhappy, he is not so utterly occupied by his own misery, but that he interests himself deeply in the projects of others. He has frequently conversed with me on mine, which I have communicated to him without disguise. He entered attentively into all my arguments in favour of my eventual success, and into every minute detail of the measures I had taken to secure it. I was easily led by the sympathy which he evinced, to use the language of my heart; to give utterance to the burning ardour of my soul; and to say, with all the fervour that warmed me, how gladly I would sacrifice my fortune, my existence, my every hope, to the furtherance of my enterprise. One man's life or death were but a small price to pay for the acquirement of the knowledge which I sought; for the dominion I should acquire and transmit over the elemental foes of our race. As I spoke, a dark gloom spread over my listener's countenance. At first I perceived that he tried to suppress his emotion; he placed his hands before his eyes; and my voice quivered and failed me, as I beheld tears trickle fast from between his fingers,—a groan burst from his heaving breast. I paused;—at length he spoke, in broken accents:—"Unhappy man! Do you share my madness? Have you drank also of the intoxicating draught? Hear me,—let me reveal my tale, and you will dash the cup from your lips!"

Such words, you may imagine, strongly excited my curiosity; but the paroxysm of grief that had seized the stranger overcame his weakened powers, and many hours of repose and tranquil conversation were necessary to restore his composure.

Having conquered the violence of his feelings, he appeared to despise himself for being the slave of passion; and quelling the dark tyranny of despair, he led me again to converse concerning myself personally. He asked me the history of my earlier years. The tale was quickly told:

16   FRANKENSTEIN; OR,

but it awakened various trains of reflection. I spoke of my
desire of finding a friend — of my thirst for a more intimate
sympathy with a fellow mind than had ever fallen to my
lot ; and expressed my conviction that a man could boast
of little happiness, who did not enjoy this blessing.

" I agree with you," replied the stranger ; " we are
unfashioned creatures, but half made up, if one wiser, better,
dearer than ourselves — such a friend ought to be — do not
lend his aid to perfectionate our weak and faulty natures.
I once had a friend, the most noble of human creatures,
and am entitled, therefore, to judge respecting friendship.
You have hope, and the world before you, and have no
cause for despair. But I — I have lost every thing, and
cannot begin life anew."

As he said this, his countenance became expressive of a
calm settled grief, that touched me to the heart. But he
was silent, and presently retired to his cabin.

Even broken in spirit as he is, no one can feel more
deeply than he does the beauties of nature. The starry
sky, the sea, and every sight afforded by these wonderful
regions, seems still to have the power of elevating his soul
from earth. Such a man has a double existence : he may
suffer misery, and be overwhelmed by disappointments ;
yet, when he has retired into himself, he will be like a
celestial spirit, that has a halo around him, within whose
circle no grief or folly ventures.

Will you smile at the enthusiasm I express concerning
this divine wanderer ? You would not, if you saw him.
You have been tutored and refined by books and retirement
from the world, and you are, therefore, somewhat fastidious ;
but this only renders you the more fit to appreciate the
extraordinary merits of this wonderful man. Sometimes I
have endeavoured to discover what quality it is which he
possesses, that elevates him so immeasurably above any
other person I ever knew. I believe it to be an intuitive
discernment ; a quick but never-failing power of judgment ; a penetration into the causes of things, unequalled
for clearness and precision ; add to this a facility of expression, and a voice whose varied intonations are soul-sub-
duing music.

August 19. 17—.

Yesterday the stranger said to me, " You may easily perceive, Captain Walton, that I have suffered great and unparalleled misfortunes. I had determined, at one time, that the memory of these evils should die with me ; but you have won me to alter my determination. You seek for knowledge and wisdom, as I once did ; and I ardently hope that the gratification of your wishes may not be a serpent to sting you, as mine has been. I do not know that the relation of my disasters will be useful to you ; yet, when I reflect that you are pursuing the same course, exposing yourself to the same dangers which have rendered me what I am, I imagine that you may deduce an apt moral from my tale ; one that may direct you if you succeed in your undertaking, and console you in case of failure. Prepare to hear of occurrences which are usually deemed marvellous. Were we among the tamer scenes of nature, I might fear to encounter your unbelief, perhaps your ridicule ; but many things will appear possible in these wild and mysterious regions, which would provoke the laughter of those unacquainted with the ever-varied powers of nature : — nor can I doubt but that my tale conveys in its series internal evidence of the truth of the events of which it is composed."

You may easily imagine that I was much gratified by the offered communication ; yet I could not endure that he should renew his grief by a recital of his misfortunes. I felt the greatest eagerness to hear the promised narrative, partly from curiosity, and partly from a strong desire to ameliorate his fate, if it were in my power. I expressed these feelings in my answer.

" I thank you," he replied, " for your sympathy, but it is useless ; my fate is nearly fulfilled. I wait but for one event, and then I shall repose in peace. I understand your feeling," continued he, perceiving that I wished to interrupt him ; " but you are mistaken, my friend, if thus you will allow me to name you ; nothing can alter my destiny : listen to my history, and you will perceive how irrevocably it is determined."

c

18   FRANKENSTEIN ; OR,

' He then told me, that he would commence his narrative
the next day when I should be at leisure. This promise
drew from me the warmest thanks. I have resolved every
night, when I am not imperatively occupied by my duties,
to record, as nearly as possible in his own words, what he
has related during the day. If I should be engaged, I will
at least make notes. This manuscript will doubtless afford
you the greatest pleasure : but to me, who know him, and
who hear it from his own lips, with what interest and
sympathy shall I read it in some future day ! Even now,
as I commence my task, his full-toned voice swells in my
ears ; his lustrous eyes dwell on me with all their melan-
choly sweetness ; I see his thin hand raised in animation,
while the lineaments of his face are irradiated by the soul
within. Strange and harrowing must be his story ; frightful
the storm which embraced the gallant vessel on its course,
and wrecked it — thus !

CHAPTER I.

I AM by birth a Genevese; and my family is one of the
most distinguished of that republic. My ancestors had
been for many years counsellors and syndics; and my father
had filled several public situations with honour and reputation. He was respected by all who knew him, for his
integrity and indefatigable attention to public business. He
passed his younger days perpetually occupied by the affairs
of his country ; a variety of circumstances had prevented
his marrying early, nor was it until the decline of life that
he became a husband and the father of a family.

As the circumstances of his marriage illustrate his character, I cannot refrain from relating them. One of his
most intimate friends was a merchant, who, from a flou-
rishing state, fell, through numerous mischances, into poverty. This man, whose name was Beaufort, was of a
proud and unbending disposition, and could not bear to
live in poverty and oblivion in the same country where he
had formerly been distinguished for his rank and magni-

Truth

Geoffrey Chaucer

Chaucer's poem known as "Truth" was his most popular lyric, as the number of witnesses indicate. The poem survives in twenty-two early manuscripts, two of which have two copies each; one of these manuscripts is in fact a transcript from after 1721 (made by William Thomas) of a manuscript that perished in the Cotton Library fire that so damaged the *Beowulf* manuscript in 1731. The poem also survives in six printed editions, beginning with William Caxton's in 1477, that are early enough to have perhaps preserved a text with some claim to authority. Printed here are all thirty of these traditional witnesses.

In the 1860s Cambridge University Librarian Henry Bradshaw was at work on a Chaucer edition that he later abandoned. Included among his papers at King's College, Cambridge, are transcriptions and collations of the poem "Truth," among which is one copy in Bradshaw's hand that may be from an unidentified and now lost manuscript. This copy is printed here for the first time.

Only one witness, the first in the list, contains a fourth stanza, the envoy, but it has been preferred as the best witness by almost all editors since its discovery in the late nineteenth century. It was copied (probably before the middle of the fifteenth century) at the end of an early-fifteenth-century manuscript of Chaucer's translation of Boethius's *Consolation of Philosophy*. In the next column, the same scribe has copied a version of the portrait of the Parson from the General Prologue of Chaucer's *Canterbury Tales*. Enterprising students who collate this text with that in any edition of *The Canterbury Tales* will discover immediately how deficient it is. This situation raises the question all modern editors of "Truth" have had to address: how much can we trust the only manuscript with a fourth stanza?

British Library, London, Add 10340, fol. 41r
(early fifteenth century)

British Library, London, Add 22139, fol. 138r (before 1450)

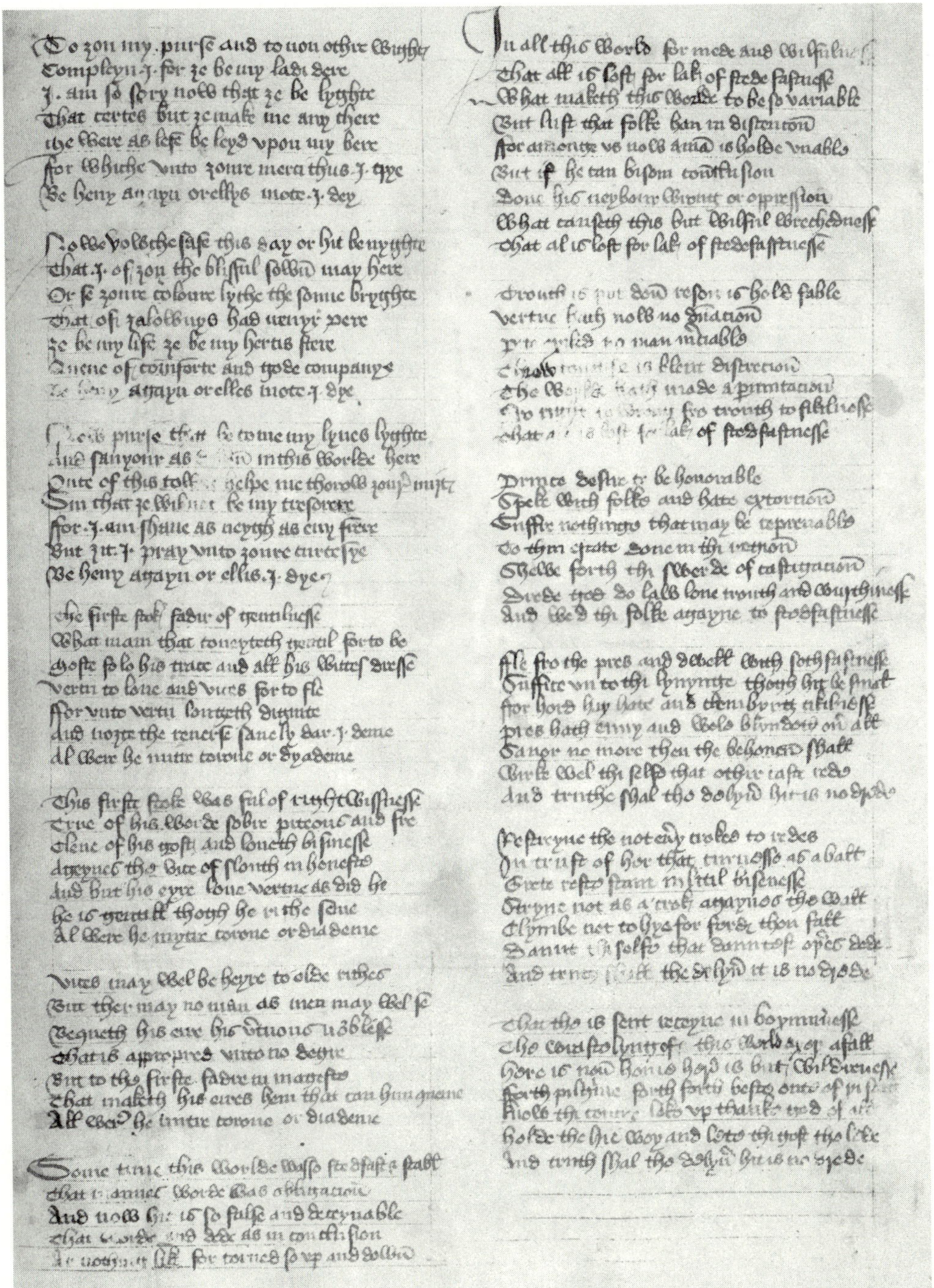

British Library, London, Add 36983, fol. 262r (before 1450)

Fle ffrom the prees and dwell w' sothfastnesse
Suffyse vnto thi gode though it be smalle
ffor hope hathe hate and clymbyng tykilnes
Pres hathe envye and wele is blent on all
Sauonye nomore thenne the behove schalt
Do wele thy selfe that other ffolks canst rede
And trouthe the schall delyue it is no drede

Peyne the nat all croked to redresse
In tryst of hir that tryneth as a balle
Grete rest stant in litell besinesse
Bewaye also to spryne a yenst an all
Stryve nat as dothe the crokk w' the walle
Daunte thy selfe þ dauntest otheys dede
And trouthe the schall delyue it is no drede

That the is sent receyve in buxumnesse
The wrastelyng of this wolde axeth a falle
Here is none home here is butt wildynes
fforthe pilgryme forthe fforthe best oute of thy stalle
loke vp on high and thank thy god of all
Wayfe thy lust and lete thy gost the lede
And trouthe the schall delyue it is no drede

glendor / n r'

A knyght that is hardy as a lyon
Ner a squyer that is amerons
Ner a coshawke that ffleeth for the heron
Ner a spanyelde on bryddes corageons
Ner he that ffor to stryne is desyrons
None of all these I do yow well assure
Off trewely lyght may no while endure

British Library, London, Cotton Cleopatra D.VII, fol. 189r–v (early fifteenth century)

British Library, London, Cotton Cleopatra D.VII, fol. 189r–v (early fifteenth century)

British Library, London, Cotton Otho A xviii

(fifteenth century, but from a transcript by William Thomas, after p. 548 in BL 643.m.4, a copy of Urry's 1721 edition)

otho A.18. A Balade by Geffrey Chaucer vppon his dethe bedde
lyenge in thes his Grete Anguysse.

p.548

Flee from the prees and wonne wt sothefastnesse
Suffice vnto thy goode though hit be smalle
For horde hathe hate and kymblynge tikelnesse
Prece hath Envie and wele is blent over alle
Savo no more thanne he behove shalle
Do wele thy selfe that other folkes canste rede
And trouithe the schalle delyue it is no drede

Peyne the noughte alle crokyd to redresse
In truste off hir that turneth as a balle
Grete reste stondeth yn litell besynesse
Be ware alle so to spurne agenst an alle
Stryveth noughte as dothe the Crocke wt the walle
Daunte ay thy selfe that dauntest otheres dede
And trouithe the schalle delyu it is no drede

That he is sent receyue in buxumnesse
The wrastlynge of this worled axith a falle
Here is no more home here is but wildvennesse
Forthe pylgryme forthe beste oute of thy stalle
Loke vpp: An hye thank god of alle
Distreyne thy luste and lete thy goste the lede
And trouith the schalle delyu it is no drede

Balade Ryalle made by Poetacall Chaucer
A Ganfrede

Sometyme this worled was so stedefaste and stable
That mannes wurde was obligacion
And now it is so false and deceyable
That wurde and dede as yn conclusion
Is no thynge oon for turned vppe so down
Is alle this worled for mede and wilfulnesse
That alle is loste for lacke of stedefastnesse

Whate maketh this worled to be vary able
But luste that folke haue in discencione
Amonges vs nowe a man is holde vnable
But yf he can by some collusione
Do his neyghborough wronge & oppressione
Whate causith this but wilfefull wreucheddnesse
That alle is loste for lacke of stedefastnesse

British Library, London, Harley 7333, fol. 147v (after 1450)

British Library, London, Lansdowne 699, fols. 82v–83r (late fifteenth century)

So excercion / of the mageste
that al pruereth / of he nightbisynesse
that same thyng / ffortune I clepe ye
ye blynd beestis / ful of rudenesse
the henene hath proprite of skynnesse
this world hath euer / restles trauaile
the last day / is eende of my mistresse
in genal / this rewle may nat faile

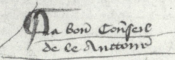

A bon conseil
de le Auttorr

fflee from the prees / & dwell w' sothfastnesse
suffise to thi good / thouh it be smal
for hoorde hath hate / & clymbyng tikilnesse
prees hath enuie / & wele is blent ouiall
sauour no more / that the behove shall
rewle thi self / that other folk canst reede
& trouth the shal / deliuer it is no drede

peyn the nat / eche crokid to redresse
in trust of hire that turneth as a ball
gret rest stant in litel besynesse
bewar also / to spurne ageyn a wall
striue nat as doth / a crokke a yeis a wall
daunt thi self / that dauntist othris deede
and trouth the shal deliuer it is no drede

British Library, London, Lansdowne 699, fols. 82v–83r (late fifteenth century)

that the is fant/ receibe m empunesse
the wrestlyng of this world/ axith a fall
heer is noon room/ heer is but wildirnesse
forth pilgrym forth/ forth beest out of thi stalle
look vpon high & thank god of all
waive thi lust & lat thi gost the leede
an trouthe the shal delyver it is no dreade

Et optim' tractatus
de ffortuna

Incipit ffabecia vocat
Stans puer ad mensam

Wylte thou than make / A statute on thy quene .
That I shall be ay at thyne ordynaunce .
Thow borne arte in my reygne of varyaunce :
Aboute the whele with other must thou dryue .
my lore is better than thy wycked gouernaunce .
And eke thou hast thy best frende alyue .

Pauptas ad fortunam .

Thy lore I dampne . it is aduersyte .
my frende mayst thou not rene blynde goddes
And that I frendes knewe I thanke it the .
Take them agayne let them go lye on presse .
The negardes kepynge theyre ryches .
Pronostyke is her toure thou wylt assayle .
Wyckede appetyte cometh a before sykenesse .
In generall this rule may not fayle .

Fortuna ad pauptatem .

Thow pynchest at my mutabilite .
For I the lente a droppe of my rychesse .
And nowe me lykethe to withdrawe me .
Why sholdest thou my ryalte oppresse .
The se may ebbe and flowe more and lesse .
The skye hathe myght to shyne rayne and hayll .
Right so may I stowe my brytylnesse .
In generall this rule may not fayll .

Paupertas ad fortunam .

So execucion of the mageste .
That all puruayeth of his ryghtwysnes .
That same thynge fortune clepe ye .
ye blynde bestes full of rudenesse .
The heuen hathe properte of sykernesse .
this worlde hathe euer restles trauayll .
Thy last day is ende of myne intresse .
In generall this rule may not fayle .

Fines .

Ecce bonu consiliu galfridi chaucere ytra fortuna
Le from the presse dwell with sothfastnes .
Suffyse vnto thy god thoughe it be small .
For horde hathe hate & clymbynge tykilnes .
Prece hathe enuye & welle is blent ou all .

Bodleian Library, Oxford, Arch. Selden B.10, fols. 201v–202r (first quarter of the sixteenth century)

Sauoure no more than the behoue shall.
Rule thy selfe that other folke canst rede.
And trouthe the shall delyuer it is no drede.

Payne the not eche croked to redresse.
In truste of her that turneth as a ball.
Grete rest stonde in litill besynes.
Beware also to sporne agaynst a wall.
Stryue not as dothe a crocke with a wall.
Daunt thy self that dauntest other dede.
And trouthe the shall delyuer it is no drede.

That the is sente receyue it in buxumnes.
The wrasttynge of this worlde asketh a fall.
Here is non home here is but wyldernes.
Forthe pylgrym forthe the beste oute of the stall.
Loke vp on hye the an thanke oure lorde of all.
Weye thy luste and let thy goste the lede.
And trouthe shall the delyuer it is no drede.

He vnsure gladnes p̄ ioye transytory.
The vnstable surenes p̄ trismutacions.
The gloury brightnes p̄ fals eclipsed gloye.
Of erthly prynces which haue possesshyons.
And monarchyes and dominacyons.
Their sodeyne chaunge declareth to vs all.
Theyre pompous fygures meynt with bitter gall.

This blynde goddes in her consystoure.
Withe her pleasaunce medleth dyscencyons.
After tryumphes conqueste and victoure.
Reueth fro prynces theyre sceptres p̄ theyr crounes.
And troubleth the people withe fals rebellyounes.
Syth by these dukes whiche from her whele be fal.
All worldly suger is meynt with bitter gall.

This tragedye maketh a memorye.
Of dukes twayne and of theyre hye renownes.
And of theyre lawe wryte a grete hystorye.
And how they conquered dyuers renyownes.
Gouerned cytees countrees and eke townes.

Bodleian Library, Oxford, Arch. Selden B.24, fol. 119r (late fifteenth to early sixteenth century)

Bodleian Library, Oxford, Fairfax 16, fol. 40r
(second quarter of the fifteenth century)

fle fro the prees and dwelle with sothfastnesse
suffice the thy good thogh hit be smale
for horde hath hate and clymbyng tikelnesse
prees hath envye and wele is blent over alle
savour no mor then the be hove shalle
So wel thy self that other folke canst rede
and trouthe the shal delyner hit ys no drede

Tempe the not ech croked to redresse
In trust of hir that turneth as a balle
grete rest stant in litil besynesse
be war also to spurne ayeyn an walle
stryve not as doth a crok with a walle
Daunte thy selfe that dauntest otheres dede
and trouthe the shal delyner hit is no drede

That the ys sent receyve in buxumnesse
the wrastlyng of this world asketh a falle
her is no home her is but wyldyrnesse
forth pilgryme forth best out of thy stalle
loke vp an hye and thonke god of alle
weyve thy lust and let thy goste the lede
and trouthe shal the delyner hit is no drede

Explicit Le bon counseill'
De. G. Chaucer.

Va Cupidinis dei amatoris directa subditis
suis amatoribz Goddesse

Cupido vnto whos comaundement
the gentil kynrede of goddis an hy
and pepill infernal ben obedient
and al mortel folke sorwen besech
of the goddesse sone Sythera only
to al thes that to owre deyte
ben suggetis herty gretyng sende we

Bodleian Library, Oxford, Fairfax 16, fol. 201r
(second copy in same hand)

Bodleian Library, Oxford, Hatton 73, fol. 118v
(mid-fifteenth century)

Cam. xxiii. How our lady was purified

Cam. xxiiii. How Symeon made Nunc Dimittis

Cam. xxv. How Anna doughter of Phanuel ioyede of Crist

Cam. xxvi. Of the appurtees of the turtle & the dowue

Cam. xxvii. How candelmasse day toke first his name

Good conseytt

Fle fro the prees and dwelle with sothfastnesse
Suffise unto thi good though it be smal
For hoord hath hate and clymbynge tykulnesse
Prees hath enbye and wele is blent over al
Savour no more than the bihove shal
Do wele thi self that other folk canst yede
And trouthe the shal delyver it is no drede

Peyne the nat alle crokede to redyesse
In truste of hir that turneth as a bal
Gret yeste stondeth in litel bisinesse
Be war also to spurne agenst an al
Stryf nat as doth the crok with the wal
Daunte thi self that dauntest others dede
And trouthe the shal delyver it is no drede

That the is sent receyve in buxumnesse
The wrastlynge with the world axeth a fal
Her is non home her is but wildernesse
Forth pilgryme forth forth beest out of thi stal
Loke up an hie and thank god of al
Weyve thi luste and lete thi goost the lede
And trouthe the shal delyve it is no drede

Cambridge University Library, Gg.4.27, fol. 8v
(before 1450)

Scogan þᵗ knelist at þe wellis hed   r wpnisþoie

Of grace of alle honour and worþinesse

In þe ende of which strem I am dul as ded

ffouȝete in solitarie wildirnes   r a Frenedwych

Ȝit Scogan ythinȝ oñ tullius kyndenes

Mynewe þyn frend þe it may fructifie

ffarewel & loke þᵘ neue eft loue defye

Balade de   Fle fro þe pres & dwelle wᵗ soþfastnesse   **bone couseyl**

Suffise unto þyn þyinȝ þoȝ it be smal

ffor hord haþ hate & chymbyinȝ tekilnesse

Pres haþ enuye & wele blyndyþ oual

Sauoie no more þan þe behoue sthal

Werke wel þyn self þᵗ oþir folk canst rede

And trouthe sthal deluerye it is no drede

Tempest þe nouȝt al crokyd to redresse

In trust of hire þᵗ turnyþ as a bal

Gret reste stant in litil besinesse

And ek be war to sporne aȝeyns an al

Stryue not as doþ þe crokke wᵗ þe wal

Daunte þyn self þᵗ dauntyst oþis dede

And trouthe sthal delyuere it is no drede

Þat þe is sent recepue in buysinesse

Þe wrastelynȝ for þis world axeþ a fal

Here nis non home here nis but wildirnesse

fforth pilgrym forth forth beste out of þi stal

knowe þyn cuntre loke up þank god of al

Hold þe hepe wey & lat þyn gost þe lede

And trouthe sthal delyure it is no drede

u may whan euy herte is lyȝt

And flouris frosschely spiede & spryinȝe

And phebz wᵗ hise beinys briȝte

Was in þe bole so cler sthynyinȝe

þᵗ sesyn in a morwenynȝe

unyn for for spyȝhte to doū socour

Cambridge University Library, Kk.1.5, part 6, fols. 4v–5r (late fifteenth century)

Cambridge University Library, Kk.1.5, part 6, fol. 4v–5r (late fifteenth century)

Corpus Christi College Library, Oxford, MS 203, pp. 22–23 (second half of the fifteenth century)

Corpus Christi College Library, Oxford, MS 203, pp. 22–23 (second half of the fifteenth century)

Coventry City Record Office, MS Accesssion 325, fol. 76v (mid-fifteenth century)

Huntington Library, San Marino, Ellesmere MS,
fol. viiir (mid-fifteenth century)

Huntington Library, San Marino, HM140
(used to be Phillips 8299), fols. 83v–84r (after 1450)

Huntington Library, San Marino, HM140
(used to be Phillips 8299), fol. 84v (after 1450)

Lambeth Palace Library, London, MS 344, fol. 10v
(late fifteenth century)

Lambeth Palace Library MS 344 is too fragile and bound too tightly to photograph perfectly, so that some of the text is lost in the gutter. What follows is a transcription of this witness, checked against that done by Henry Noble McCracken (See "Notes Suggested by a Chaucer Codex," *Modern Language Notes* 23.7 [1908]: 212–14.)

Goode Counselle

Fle fro the prees & dwell wyth sothefastnese
Suffyce vnto thy good thought it[1] be small
For hoorde hathe hate and clymbyng tykelnese
Prees hath envye and wele ys blent ouer all
Saveour no more than the be hove shalle   5
Do well thy self that other folk canst rede
And trowthe[2] shall the dylyuere yt ys no drede

Peyne the not alle crokede to redresse
In trust of here that turneth as a[3] balle
Gret reest stondeth yn lytell besynesse   10
Be war also to spurne ageynst analle
Stryf nat as doth the croked[4] wyth the walle
Daunt thy self that dauntest others dede
And trowthe the shal[5] dylyuere yt ys no drede

That ys sent reseyue hyt yn [ ][6] buxvmnesse[7]   15
The wrastylige wyth the wor[ ]le axeth afall
Here ys non home here ys byt wyldernesse
Forth pylgryme forth beest oute of thy stall
Loke vp ann[8] hye and thanke god[9] of alle
Weye thy lust and lete thy gost the lede   20
And trowyth the shall dylyver yt ys no drede

1. it] *written above line.*

2. trowthe] *originally* trowthes *(?); final letter, probably an s, has been erased.*

3. a] *originally* as; *the s has been erased.*

4. croked] *McCracken reads* crokes. *Cf.* crokede *in line 8 and as earlier in this line.*

5. shal] *originally* shalt; *the t has been erased.*

6. *A hole in the parchment disrupts lines 15–16 here. No text seems to have been lost.*

7. buxvmnesse] *McCracken reads* buxsumnesse, *but the letter after the x is plainly a v (cf.* Saveour *in line 5) not an s (cf.* ys *earlier in this line), and there are not enough minims after it to make up* umn.

8. ann] an *with a nasal suspension (a line that loops back up over the n), meaning to double the n. Cf.* passyoun *in the previous poem on the page (line 7).*

9. god] d *written above line.*

Leyden University Library, Vossius GG.qv.9, p. 191
(late fifteenth century)

Nottingham University Library, MS Me LM 1, fol. 2r (after 1450)

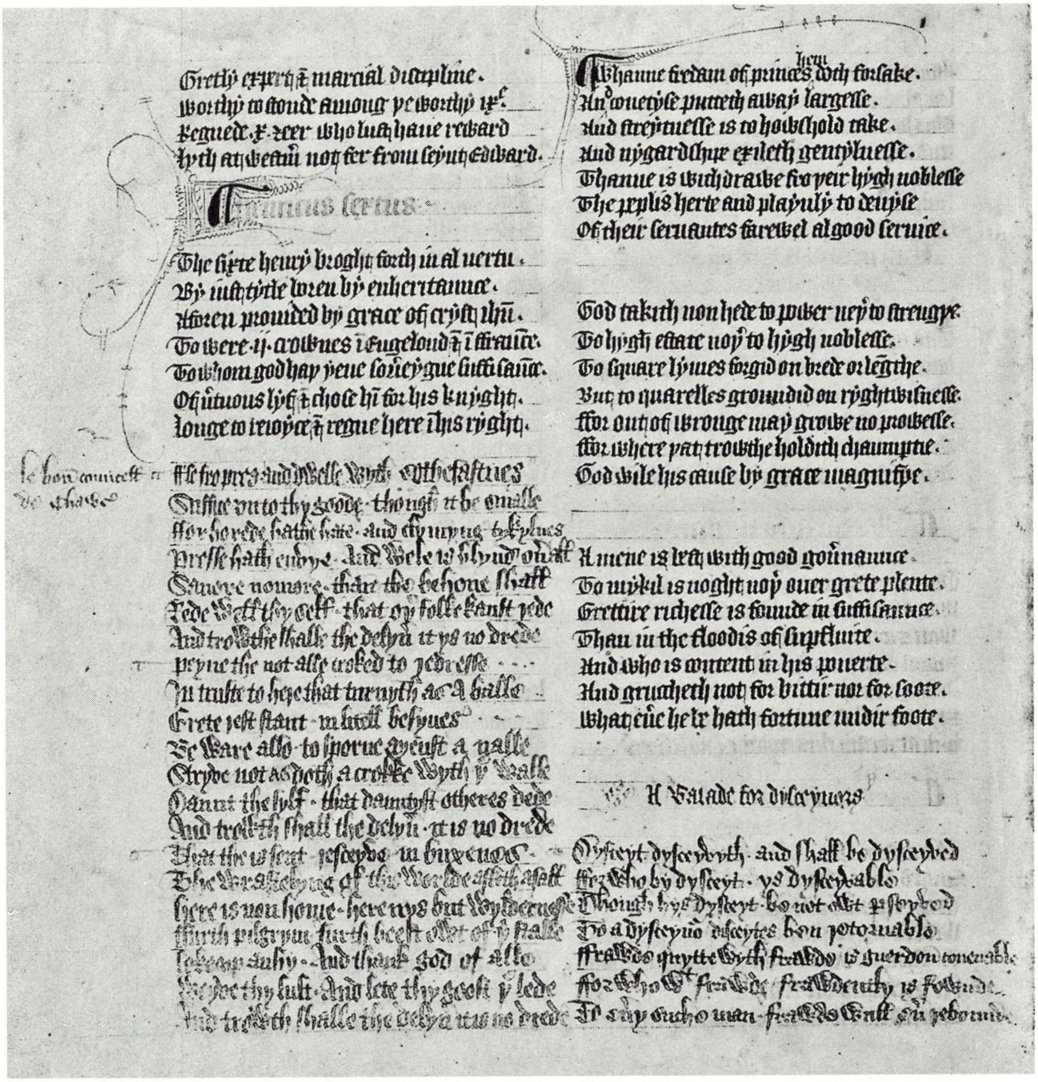

Magdalene College Library, Cambridge, Pepys 2006, pp. 389–90 (late fifteenth century)

389·

ye be my liff ye be my herte stere
Quene of comfort and of gode compaignye
Be heuy agayn or ell mot I dye

Now purs that ben to me my lynes light
And sauyour as doun in this world here
Out of this toun help me thorogh your myght
Syn that ye will not be my tresorere
for I am shaue as nygh as any frere
But yet I pray onto your curtesye
Be heuy agayn or ell mot I dye

Lenuoy
O conquerour o Brutes Albion
Which that be lyne and free election
Been they kynge this to yow I send
that and ye mowe alle Harmes Amende
Haue mynde on my supplicacioun

le bon counsell ———— De chaucer

Flee fro the prees And dwelle with sothfastnesse
Suffise vnto thy gode though it be small
ffor horde hath hate and clymbynge tikilnesse
Prees hath enuye and wele is blent oueral
Sauonye no more than bihoue shall
Rule thy self that other folk canst rede
And trouth the shall delyuer it is no drede

Peyn the not all croked to redresse
In trust of here that turneth as a ball
Grete reste stant in lytell besynesse
Be ware also to spurn ageyn a all
Stryue not as doth a crokke with a wall
Daunte thy self that dauntest others dede
And trouthe the shall delyuer it is no drede

Magdalene College Library, Cambridge, Pepys 2006,
pp. 389–90 (late fifteenth century)

Balade ryale ⁘ By Chaucer

This worlde hath euermore / restlesse trauayle
My latter dayes to spende / of myne mercesse
In generall me vile / may no wyse fayle
⸿ On London or la request de fortune

⸿ Prynces I prey yow of yowre gentylesse
Let not this man this on the ouer and pleyne
And I shal glorye yelde vnto yowre lownesse
Þat this poore lyfe releue him of his peyne
Preyere his best frend of his noblesse this
Þat to some better estate / he may atteyne

⸿ Balade þat Chaucer made on his deth bedde

⸿ Flee fro þe prees and dwelle with sothfastnesse
Suffyse vnto thy good / though hit be smal
For hord hath hate / and clymbyng tikelnesse
Prees hath enuye / and wele blent ouer al
Sauour namore / than the byhoue shal
Do wele thy self / that other folke canst rede
And trouthe the shal delyuer / hit is no drede

⸿ Peyne the not eche croked / al croked to redresse
In trust of hir / that turneth as a bal
Gret reste stant / in litel bosynesse
Beware also / to sporne agenst an al
Stryue not as doth / the crokke with the wal
Daunte wele thy self / that dauntest others dede
And trouthe the shal delyuer / hit is no drede

⸿ That the is sent / receyue in buxumnesse
The wrastlyng of the worlde / axeth a fal
Here is non home / here is but wildernesse
Forth pilgryme forth / forth beste out of thy stal
Loke vp on hye / and thanke god of al
Weyue thy lust / and let thy gost the lede
And trouthe the shal delyuer / hit is no drede

¶ Chaucer

¶ Thoughe couetyse is blent discrecion /
þe worlde haþ made a permutacioun
ffrome right to wrong / frome trouth to fikilnesse /
þat al is lost for lacke of stedfastnesse /

¶ Lenuoye to kyng Richard þe seconde /

¶ O prynce desyre / for to bee honurable
Cherisshe þy folke and hate extorcioun
Suffre no thing / þt may bee reprochable
To þyne estate / doon in þy Regioun
Chewe forþe þe swerde of castigacioun
Drede god / do lawe / loue trouth and worþynesse
And wedde þy people ageine to stedfastnesse

¶ Balade by Chaucier on his deth bede

Flee frome þe prees / and dwelle wt soþefastnesse
Suffice vn to þy goode þaughe it bee smal /
ffor horde haþ hate / and clymbing tikilnesse
prees haþ enuye / and wele is blent ouer al
Sauoure na more / þanne þe behoue shal
Do wele þy selff / þat oþer folke canst rede
And trouthe þe shal delyuer it is no drede

¶ Peyne þe nought / al crooked to redresse
In trust of hir þat tornethe as a bal
Gret rest standeþ in litel besynesse
Bewar alsoo to sporne agaynst an al
Stryue nought as doþe þe crooke wt þe wal
Daunte þy selff / þat dauntest oþere dede
And trouth þe shal delyuer it is no drede

Trinity College Library, Cambridge, R.3.20, p. 358
(second copy in same hand)

STC 5091 Caxton, 1477, fol. 21v–22r, Cambridge University Library: Inc.5.J.1.1[3485]

The best is to chese as I gesse
But do as ye list / I me excuse expresse
I Wil be sory / yf that ye me myschese
God conforme you / in Vertuous goodnes
So that thurgh necligence / no thing ye lese

Thus endeth the traytye Whiche Iohn
Skogan sent to the lordes and esta
tes of the kynges hous +

Wyth empty honde men may no hawkes lure
Bye yf thou maye / for al is for to selle
Lytyl Wit suffyseth With good aventure
And alWay as the Wide standeth set thy melle
The heuene to heuens lord / z feend to helle
May to the World ptede / z thou shal streche
And Bere thy self be noght / z be a Breche

The good councel of chaucer

STC 5091 Caxton, 1477, fol. 21v–22r, Cambridge University Library: Inc.5.J.1.1[3485]

Fle ye fro þ prees ⁊ dwelle with sothfastnes
Suffyse vnto the good yf it be smal
For horde hath hate / ⁊ clymyng tikelnes
Prese hath enuye / ⁊ Wele is blent ouer al
Sauoure nomore / than the behoue shal
Rede Wel thy self that other folk rede
And trouthe the shal delyue / it is no drede

Payne the not eche croked to redresse
In trust of her / that torneth as a balle
Grete reste standith in litil besynesse
BeWare also to spurne agayn an alle
Stryue not as doth a crock With a Wall
Deme thy self / that demest others dede
And troutthe þ shal deliue it is no drede

That the is sent / resceyue in buxomnes
The Wrastlyng of this World axith a fall
Here is no home / here is but Wildernes
Forth pylgrym / forth best out of thy stall
Loke vpon high / and thank god of all
Weyue thy lust / and late thy gost the lede
And troutthe the shal delyuer / it is no dred

STC 17027 de Worde, 1520, A3v–A4r, Huntington: 31325

The see may ebbe & flowe moze and lesse

The skye hath myght to shyne / rayne and hayle

Ryght so may I flowe my bryttylnesse

In generall this rule may not fayle

¶ Paupertas ad fortuna.

So execucyon of the mageste

That all puruayeth of his ryght wysnesse

That same thyng fortune clepe ye

ye blynde beestes / full of rudenesse

The heuen hathe pzoperte of sykernesse

This wozlde hathe euer / restles trauayll

Thy laste daye is ende of myn interesse

In generall I this rule may not fayll

¶ finis.

¶ Ecce bonu consiliu galfridi chaucers cotra fortuna.

Fle from the prece & dwell with sothefastnesse
Suffyse vnto thy good though it be small

For hoorde hathe hate / & clymbynge tykylnesse

Prece hath enuye / and wele is blente ouer all

Sauoure no moze than the behoue shall

Rule thy selfe that other folke canst reede

And trouthe the shall delyuer it is no dzede

Payne the not eche croked to redzesse

In truste of her that turneth as a ball

Grete reste stande in lytell besynesse

Beware also to spozne agaynst a wall

Stryue not as dothe a cocle with a whall

Daunt thy selfe that dauntest other dede

And trouth the shall delyuer it is no dzede

That the is sente receyue it in busumnesse

The wzastlynge of this wozlde asketh a fall

STC 17027 de Worde, 1520, A3v,
Huntington: 31325

Here is none home/here is but wyldernesse
Forth pylgrym forth/forth beest out of the stall
Loke vpon hyghe/and thanke our lorde of all
Weye thy lust/& let thy ghoost the lede
And trouthe the shall delyuer it is no drede

The vnsure gladnesse the Joye transytory
The vnstable surenes the transmutacyons
The gloury bryghtnes/the false eclypsed glorye
Of erthly pryncess whiche haue possessyons
And monarchyes and domynacyons
Theyr sodayne chaunge declareth to vs all
Theyr pompous fygures meynt with bytter gall

This blynd goddesse in her consystour
With her pleasaunce medleth dysceneyons
After tryumphes conquest and vyctour
Reueth fro pryncess theyr sceptres & theyr crownes
And troubleth the people with fals rebellyownes
Syth by these dukes whiche from her whele be fall
All worldly suger is meynt with bytter gall

This tragedye maketh a memorye
Of dukes twayne & of theyr hye renownes
And of theyr lawe wryte a grete hystorye
And how they conquered dyuers regyownes
Gouerned cytees/countrees and eke townes
Tyll fortune theyr prowesse dyde appall
To theyr suger was meynt with bytter gall

Pryncess pryncesses seeth how deceptour
Ben all these worldly reuolucyons
And how fortune in her reclinatour
With her tryacle tempreth false poysons
So merueylous ben her confeccyons

STC 5088 Pynson, 1526, e4, Harvard University, Houghton Library: HEW 5.11.8 F

STC 5068 Thynne, 1532, Vvv4r–v, Huntington Library, San Marino

of the kynges house. fo. CCC. lxxxi.

Nowe seeth there ayenst howe vtuous nobles
Roted i youth with good pseuerauce (nesse
Dryueth away al vyces and wretchednesse
As slogardrie/ rpote/ and distaunce
Seeth eke howe Vertue causeth suffysaunce
Seeth eke howe Vertue voydeth al Vyce
And who so hath Vertue/hath al habundaunce
Of wele/as ferre as reason can deuyse

Taketh hede of Tullius Hostylius
That fro pouert came to hygh degre
Through Vertue/redeth eke of Iulius
The conquerour/howe poore a man was he
yet through his Vertue and his humylite
Of many countrey had he gouernaunce
Thus Vertue bryngeth a man to great degre
Eche wight that lust to do hym entendaunce

Rede here ayenst nowe of Nero Vertulees
Taketh hede also of proude Balthasare
They hated Vertue/equpte and pees
And loke howe Antyochus fyl fro his chare
That he his skyn and bones al to tare
Loke what mischaunce they had for her Vyces
Who so wol not by these signes beware
I dare wel say infortunate and nyce is

I can no more nowe say/but herby may ye se
Howe Vertue causeth perfyte sykernesse
And Vyces eyplen al prosperyte
The best is eche man to chose as I gesse
Dothe as you lyst/ I me eycuse eypresse
I wolde be right sory if that ye mischese
God consyrme you in Vertuous noblesse
So that through neglygence ye not it lese.
℧ Eyplicit.

Somtyme y worlde so stedfast was & stable
That mannes worlde was an obsygacioun
And nowe it is so false and disceyuable
That worde and dede as in conclusyoun
Is nothyng lyke/for turned is vp so doun
Al the worlde/through mede and sykelnesse
That al is loste for lacke of stedfastnesse

What maketh the worlde to be so varyable
But lust that men haue in discensyon

for amonge vs a man is holde vnable
But if he can vp some collusyon
Do his neyghbour wronge and oppressyon
What causeth this but wylful wretchydnesse
That al is loste for lacke of stedfastnesse

Trouthe is put downe/ reason is holde fable
Vertue hath nowe no dompnation
Pyte is eypled/no man is merciable
Through couetyse is blente discretion
The worlde hath made a permutation
fro right to wronge/ fro trouth to fykelnesse
That al is lost for lacke of stedfastnesse

℧ Lenuoye.
Prince desyre to be honourable
Cherisshe thy folke/and hate eytorcyon
Suffre nothyng that may be reprouable
To thyne estate done in thy regyon
Shewe forthe the yerde of castygacion
Drede god/do lawe/ loue trouth & worthynes
And wedde thy folke ayen to stedfastnesse.
℧ Eyplicit.

℧ Good counsayle of Chaucer.

flye ye fro y prease & dwel wt sothfastnesse
Suffyse vnto the good if it be smal
for horde hath hate/and clymbyng tykelnesse
Preace hath enuye/and wele is blent ouer al
Sauour no more than the behoue shal
Rede wel thy selfe that other folke shal rede
And trouthe the shal delyuer it is no drede,

Payne the not eche croked to redresse
In truste of her that turneth as a balle
Great rest stondeth in lytel besynesse
Beware also to spurne agayne a nalle
Stryue not as dothe a crocke with a walle
Deme thy selfe that demest others dede
And trouth the shal delyuer it is no drede

That the is sent receyue in buyomnesse
The wrastlyng of this worlde asketh a fal
Here is no home/here is but wyldernesse
forthe pylgrym/forthe beest out of thy stal
Loke vp on highe and thanke god of al
Deyue

STC 5068 Thynne, 1532, Vvv4r–v, Huntington Library, San Marino

Balades.

Weyue thy luste and lette thy gost the lede
And trouthe the shal delyuer it is no drede.
℣ Explicit.
℣ Balade of the Vyllage without payntyng.

Playntyfe to fortune.
This wretched worldes transmutation
As wele and wo/ nowe poore & nowe honour
Without order or dewe discretion
Gouerned is by fortunes errour.
But nathelesse the lacke of her fauour
Ne may nat do me syng though that I dye
Iay tout pardu mon temps et labour
For fynally fortune I defye

Yet is me lefte the syght of my reasoun
To knowe frende fro foe in thy myrrour
So moche hath yet thy tournyng vp & doun
Itaught me to knowen in an hour
But trewly no force of thy reddour
To him that ouer him selfe hath maistry
My suffysaunce shalbe my socour
For finally fortune I defye

O Socrates thou stedfast champion
She myght neuer be thy turmentour
Thou neuer dreddest her oppressyon
Ne in her chere founde thou no fauour
Thou knewe the disceyte of her colour
And that her most worship is for to lye
I knowe her eke a false dissymulour
For finally fortune I defye

The answer of fortune.
No man is wretched but him selfe it wene
He that hath him selfe hath suffysaunce
Why sayst thou than I am to the so kene
That hast thy selfe out of my gouernaunce
Say thus/ graütmercy of thyne habundaüce
That thou hast lent or this/ ý shalt nat stryue
What wost thou yet howe I the wol auaunce
And eke thou hast thy best frende a lyue

I haue the taught deuysion bytwene
Frende of effecte/ and frende of countenaüce
The nedeth nat the galle of an hyne
That cureth eyen derke for her penaunce

Nowe seest thou clere that were in ignoraüce
yet holt thyne anker/ & yet thou mayst aryue
There bounte bereth the key of my substaüce
And eke thou haste thy best frende a lyue

Howe many haue I refused to sustene
Sithe I haue the fostred in thy plesaunce
Wolte thou than make a statute on thy quene
That I shalbe aye at thyne ordynaunce
Thou borne arte in my reigne of Varyaunce
About the whele with other must thou dryue
My lore is bette/ than wicke is thy greuaunce
And eke thou haste thy best frende a lyue

The answere to fortune.
Thy lore I dampne/ it is aduersyte
My frende mayst ý nat reue blynde goddesse
That I thy frendes knowe I thanke it the
Take hem agayne / lette hem go lye a presse
The nygardes in kepyng her rychesse
Pronostyke is thou wolte her toure assayle
Wicke appetyte cometh aye before sicknesse
In general this rule maye nat fayle

℣ Fortune.
Thou pynchest at my mutabylyte
For I the lent a droppe of my rychesse
And nowe me lyketh to withdrawe me
Why shuldest thou my royalte oppresse
The see may ebbe and flowe more and lesse
The welken hath myzt to shyne/ rayn/ & hayle
Right so must I kythe my brotylnesse
In general this rule may nat fayle

The playntyfe.
Lo/ the execution of the maieste
That al purueyeth of his rightwysenesse
That same thynge fortune clepen ye
ye blynde beestes ful of leudnesse
The heuen hath properte of sykernesse
This worlde hath euer restlesse trauayle
The laste day is ende of myne entresse
In general this rule may nat fayle

Thenuoye of fortune.
Princes I pray you of your gentylnesse
Lette nat this man on me thus crye & playne
And I shal quyte you this besynesse
And if ye lyst releue him of his payne
Pray ye his best frende of his noblesse
That to some better estate he may attayne
℣ Explicit.   Lenuoye

STC 13861 Tottel, 1557, fol. 82r, Huntington Library, San Marino: 59482

and Sonettes.   Fo.82.

To leade a vertuous and honest life.

Flee fro the prease and dwell with sothfastnes,
Suffise to thee thy good though it be small,
For horde hath hate, and climing tickleness,
Praise hath enuy, and weall is blinde in all,
Fauour no more, then thee behoue shall.
Rede well thy selfe that others well canst rede,
And trouth shall thee deliuer, it is no drede.

Paine thee not eche croked to redresse,
In hope of her that turneth as a ball,
Great rest standeth in litle businesse,
Beware also to spurne against a nall,
Striue not as doth a crocke against a wall,
Deme first thy selfe, that demest others dede,
And truth shall thee deliuer, it is no drede.

That thee is sent, receiue in buxomnesse,
The wrestling of this world asketh a fall:
Here is no home, here is but wildernesse.
Forth pilgryme forth, forth beast out of thy stall,
Looke vp on hye, geue thankes to God of all:
Weane well thy lust, and honest life ay leade,
So trouth shall thee deliuer, it is no dreade.

The wounded louer determineth to make sute to his lady for his recure.

Sins Mars first moued warre or stirred men to strife,
Was neuer sene so scarce a fight, I scarce could scape with life.
Resist so long I did, till death approched so nye,
To saue my selfe I thought it best, with spede away to flye.
In daunger still I fled, by flight I thought to scape
From my dere foe, it vailed not, alas it was to late.
For Venus from her campe brought Cupide with his bronde,
Who sayd now yelde, or els desire shall chace thee in euery londe.
Yet would I not straight yelde, till fansy fiercely stroke,
Who fro my will did cut the raines & charged me with this yoke.

K.ii.   Then

STC 5075 Stowe, 1561, Ooo5v–6r,
Folger Shakespeare Library

To the lordes and gentilmen.

Driueth vp and doun without gouernaunce
Wenyng that calme would laste yere by yere
Right so fare thei for very ignoraunce.

For berie shame know we thei not by reason
that after an eb there cometh a flood ful rage
In thesame wise whe youth passeth his seaso
Cometh croked and vnweldie palled age
And sone after comen the Kalendes of dotage
And if ý her youth haue no vertue prouided
All men woll saie fie on her vassalage
Thus hath her sloth fro worship hem deuided

Boecius the clerk, as men maie rede and se
Saieth in his booke of Consolacion
What man desireth of vine or tree
Plenteous fruict in reapyng season
Must euer escue to doe oppression
Vnto the roote while it is yong and grene
Thus maie ye see well by that inclusion
That youth vertulesse doeth moche tene.
                                        (nesse
Now seeth there ayenst how vertuous noble-
Rooted in youth with good parseueraunce
Driueth awaie all vices and wretchednesse
Is slogardrie, riote, and distaunce
Seeth eke how vertue causeth suffisaunce
Seeth eke how vertue voideth all vice
And who so hath vertue, hath al habundauce
Of wele, as ferre as reason can deuise.

Taketh hede of Tullius Hostilius
That fro pouert came to high degree
Through vertue, redeth eke of Julius
The conquerour, how poore a man was he
Yet through his vertue and his humilitee
Of many countrey had he in gouernaunce
Thus vertue bringeth a man to great degree
Eche wight that lust to do hym entendaunce

Rede here ayenst now of Nero vertulees
Taketh hede also of proude Balthasare
Thei hated vertue, equitie and pees
And looke how Antiochus fill fro his chare
That he his shin and bones all to tare
Loke what mischaunce thei had for her vices
Who so woll not by these signes beware
I dare well saie infortunate and nice is.

I can no more now saie, but hereby maie ye se
How vertue causeth perfite sikernesse
And vices exilen all prosperitee
The best is eche man'to chose as I gesse
Doeth as you list, I me excuse expresse
I would be right sorie if that ye mischese

God confirme you in vertuous noblesse
So that through negligence ye not it lese.

Explicit.

Omtyme the worlde so stedfast
was and stable
That mannes woorde was an
Obligacioun
And now it is so false and dis-
ceiuable
That worde and deede as in conclusioun
Is nothyng like, for tourned is vp so doun
All the worlde, through mede and fikelnesse
That all is loste for lacke of stedfastnesse.

What maketh the worlde to be so variable
But lust that men haue in discension
For emong vs a man is holde vnable
But if he can by some collusion
Doe his neighbour wrong and oppression
What causeth this but wilfull wretchednesse
That all is loste for lacke of stedfastnesse.

Trouthe is put doune, reason is holde fable
Vertue hath now no dominacion
Pitie is exiled, no man is merciable
Through couetise is blente discrecion
The worlde hath made a permutacion
Fro right to wrong, fro trouthe to fikelnesse
That is all loste for lacke of stedfastnesse.

Lenuoye.

Prince desire to be honourable
Cherishe thy folke, and hate extorcion
Suffre nothyng that maie be reprouable
To thine estate doen in thy region
Shewe forthe the yerde of castigacion
Drede God, do law, loue trouth & worthines
And wedde thy folke ayen to stedfastnesse.

Explicit.

Good counsaile of Chaucer.

Flie fro the prease and
dwell with sothfastnesse
Suffise vnto thy good
though it bee small
For horde hath hate, and
climbyng tikelnesse
Preace hath enuie, & wele
it blent ouer all
Sauour no more then thee behoue shall
Rede well thy self that other folke canst rede
                                        And

STC 5075 Stowe, 1561, Ooo5v–6r,
Folger Shakespeare Library

Ballade. Fol.cccrrrbj.

And trouthe thee shall deliuer it is no drede.

Paine thee not eche croked to redresse
In trust of her that tourneth as a balle
Greate rest standeth in little businesse
Beware also to spurne again a naile
Striue not as doeth a crocke with a walle
Deme thy self that demest others dede
And trouthe thee shall deliuer it is no drede.

That thee is sent receiue in buxomnesse
The wrastlyng of this worlde asketh a fall
Here is no home, here is but wildernesse
Forthe pilgrim, forthe beast out of thy stall
Looke vp on high and thanke God of all
Weiue thy luste and let thy ghost thee lede
And trouthe thee shall deliuer it is no drede.

Explicit.

Balade of the

village without paintyng.

Plaintife to Fortune.

His wretched worldes
transmutacion
Is weale and wo, nowe
poore and now honour
without ordre or due dis-
crecion
Gouerned is by fortunes
errour
But nathelesse the lacke of her fauour
Ne maie not doe me syng though, that I die
l'ay tout pardu mon temps & labour
For finally fortune I defie.

Yet is me left the light of my reasoun
To knowe frende fro foe in thy mirrour
So moche hath yet thy tournyng vp & doun
Itaught me to knowen in an hour
But truly no force of thy reddour
To hym that ouer hymself hath maistrie
My suffisaunce shal be my succour
For finally fortune I defie

O Socrates thou stedfast champion
She might neuer be thy turmentour
Thou neuer dreddest her oppression
Ne in her chere founde thou no fauour
Thou knewe the disceipt of her colour
And that her moste worship is for to lie

I knowe her eke a false dissimulour
For finally fortune I defie

The answere of Fortune.

No man is wretched but hymself it wene
He that hath hymself hath suffisaunce
Why saiest thou then I am to thee so kene
That hast thy self out of my gouernaunce
Saie thus, grauntmercie of thin habundance
That y hast lent or this, thou shalt not striue
What wolt thou yet how I thee woll auance
And eke thou hast thy best frende a liue.

I haue thee taught deuision betwene
Frende of effecte, and frende of countenaunce
Thee nedeth not the galle of an Hine
That cureth iyen darke for her penaunce
Now seest thou clere that wer in ignoraunce
Yet holt thine anker, & yet thou maiest ariue
There bountie beareth y kep of my substaunce
And eke thou hast thy best frende a liue.

How many haue I refused to sustene
Sith I haue thee fostred in thy pleasaunce
Wolt thou then make a statute on thy quene
That I shall be aie at thine ordinaunce
Thou borne art in my reigne of variaunce
About the whele with other must thou driue
My lore is bet, then wicke is thy greuaunce
And eke thou hast thy best frende a liue.

The answere to Fortune.

Thy lore I dampne, it is aduersitie
My frend maist thou not reue blind goddesse
That I thy frendes knowe I thanke it thee
Take hem again, let them go lie a presse
The nigardes in keppyng her richesse
Pronostike is thou wolt her toure assaile
Wicke appetite cometh aie before sickenesse
In generall this rule maie not faile.

Fortune.

Thou pinchest at my mutabilitie
For I thee lent a droppe of my richesse
And now my liketh to withdrawe me
Why shouldest thou my roialtie oppresse
The sea maie ebbe and flowe more and lesse
The welke hath mizt to shene, rain, and haile
Right so must I kithe my brotilnesse
In generall this rule maie not faile

The plaintife.

Lo.

King's College Archives, Cambridge, BRA/1/1, file 1
(copy made in the late nineteenth century)

Trewthe.

1.

Flee from the pres and dwelle with soothfastnesse
Suffyse unto thy good though it be smal
For hord hath hate and clymbing tikelnesse
Pres hath envye and wele blyndeth overal
Savoure no more than thee behove shal
Werke wel thyself that other folk canst rede
And trewthe thee shal delivere it is no drede.

2.

Tempeste thee nought al crooked to redresse
In trust of here that turneth as a bal
Gret reste stant in litel besinesse
And eke be war to sporne azeynst an al
Stryve not as doth the crokke with the wal
Daunte thy self that daunbest otheres dede
And trewthe thee shal delivere it is no drede.

3.

That thee is sent receyve in buxomnesse
That wrastling for this world axeth a fal
Here nis non home here nis but wildernesse
Forth pilgrim forth forth beste oute of thy stal
Knowe thy countree looke up thanke god of al
Holde the hye way and let thy gost thee lede
And trewthe thee shal delivere it is no drede.

Poetry

Marianne Moore

This often-anthologized poem is justly famous not only among readers of twentieth-century poetry but also among textual critics. First published in *Others*, an avant-grade literary journal, in 1919, the poem was instantly popular, and almost as instantly revised by the author for the journal's anthology in 1920. Moore shocked many when she cut the poem from the well-known twenty-nine-line version (which had been in print since, roughly, 1935) to only three lines in 1967, five years before her death. She allowed her editor to place this longer version in the notes at the back (mis-leadingly called the "the original version" until 1981, when the note began calling it, still somewhat misleadingly, "the longer version"). Moore's drastic revision may have been less of a shock to some had they known more about the poem's textual history. The selections below offer a beginning for that history. Of special note is the reproduction of the 1921 edition, from a copy presented by Moore to poet and translator Jean Starr Untermeyer, containing revisions not entirely accounted for in later editions.

from *Others* (1919)

OTHERS   *Marianne Moore*   Page 5

POETRY

I too, dislike it: there are things that are important
                 beyond all this fiddle.
   Reading it, however, with a perfect contempt for it,
               one discovers that there is in
it after all, a place for the genuine.
     Hands that can grasp, eyes
       that can dilate, hair that can rise
          if it must, these things are important not because a

high sounding interpretation can be put upon them
                 but because they are
   useful; when they become so derivative as to
               become unintelligible, the
same thing may be said for all of us—that we
     do not admire what
     we cannot understand. The bat,
       holding on upside down or in quest of something to

eat, elephants pushing, a wild horse taking a roll,
              a tireless wolf under
   a tree, the immovable critic twinkling his skin like a
             horse that feels a flea, the base-
ball fan, the statistician—case after case
     could be cited did
     one wish it; nor it is valid
       to discriminate against "business documents and

school-books"; all these phenomena are important.
              One must make a distinction
   however: when dragged into prominence by half poets,
            the result is not poetry,
nor till the autocrats among us can be
   "literalists of
     the imagination"—above
       insolence and triviality and can present

for inspection, imaginary gardens with real toads
             in them, shall we have
   it. In the meantime, if you demand on one hand,
           in defiance of their opinion—
the raw material of poetry in
   all its rawness and
   that which is on the other hand,
     genuine then you are interested in poetry.

from *Others for 1919,* 1920

POETRY

I, too, dislike it: there are things that are important
    beyond all this fiddle.
Reading it, however, with a perfect contempt for it,
    one discovers that there is in
it after all, a place for the genuine.
    Hands that can grasp, eyes
    that can dilate, hair that can rise
      if it must, these things are important not be-
      cause a

high sounding interpretation can be put upon them
    but because they are
useful; when they became so derivative as to
    become unintelligible, the
same thing may be said for all of us — that we
    do not admire what
    we cannot understand. The bat,
      holding on upside down or in quest of some-
      thing to

eat, elephants pushing, a wild horse taking a roll,
    a tireless wolf under
a tree, the immovable critic twinkling his skin like a
    horse that feels a flea, the base-
ball fan, the statistician — case after case
    could be cited did

132   *MARIANNE MOORE*

one wish it; nor it is valid
        to discriminate against " business documents
    and

school-books "; all these phenomena are important.
        One must make a distinction
however: when dragged into prominence by half
            poets,
        the result is not poetry,
nor till the autocrats among use can be
    " literalists of
    the imagination " — above
        insolence and triviality and can present

for inspection, imaginary gardens with real toads
        in them, shall we have
    it.   In the meantime, if you demand on one hand,
            in defiance of their opinion —
    the raw material of poetry in
all its rawness, and
that which is on the other hand,
        genuine, then you are interested in poetry.

from *Poems* (1921),
Jean Starr Untermeyer's copy

POEMS BY MARIANNE MOORE

POETRY

I too, dislike it: there are things that are important beyond all this fiddle.
    Reading it, however, with a perfect contempt for it, one discovers that there
        is in
    it after all, a place for the genuine.
        Hands that can grasp, eyes
        that can dilate, hair that can rise
            if it must, these things are important not because a

high sounding interpretation can be put upon them but because they are
    useful; when they become so derivative as to become unintelligible, the
    same thing may be said for all of us—that we
        do not admire what
        we cannot understand. The bat,
            holding on upside down or in quest of something to

eat, elephants pushing, a wild horse taking a roll, a tireless wolf under
    a tree, the immovable critic twinkling his skin like a horse that feels a flea,
        the base-
    ball fan, the statistician—case after case
        could be cited did
        one wish it; nor is it valid
            to discriminate against "business documents and

school-books"; all these phenomena are important. One must make a distinction
    however: when dragged into prominence by half poets, the result is not
        poetry,
    nor till the autocrats among us can be *not until poets can be*
        "literalists of
        the imagination"—above
        insolence and triviality and can present

for inspection, imaginary gardens with real toads in them, shall we have
    it. In the meantime, if you demand on one hand, in defiance of their opinion—
    the raw material of poetry in
        all its rawness and
        that which is, on the other hand,
        genuine then you are interested in poetry.

From *Poems* (London: Egoist Press, 1921), p. 22. Kind permission from Marianne Craig Moore, Executor of the Estate of Marianne Moore for the right to reproduce the facsimile of the 1921 version of "Poetry" and the Beinecke Rare Books and Manuscripts Library, Yale University.

from *Observations,* 1924

POETRY

I TOO, dislike it: there are things that are important be-
　　　yond all this fiddle.
　Reading it, however, with a perfect contempt for it, one
　　　　discovers that there is in
it after all, a place for the genuine.
　　Hands that can grasp, eyes
　　　that can dilate, hair that can rise
　　　　if it must, these things are important not because a

high sounding interpretation can be put upon them but be-
　　　cause they are
　useful; when they become so derivative as to become un-
　　　intelligible,
　the same thing may be said for all of us, that we
　　do not admire what
　　we cannot understand: the bat,
　　　holding on upside down or in quest of something to

eat, elephants pushing, a wild horse taking a roll, a tireless
　　　wolf under
　a tree, the immovable critic twitching his skin like a horse
　　　that feels a flea, the base-
　ball fan, the statistician—
　　nor is it valid
　　　to discriminate against "business documents and

school-books"; all these phenomena are important. One
　　　must make a distinction
　however: when dragged into prominence by half poets,
　　　the result is not poetry,
　nor till the poets among us can be
　　"literalists of
　　　the imagination"—above
　　　　insolence and triviality and can present

30

POETRY

for inspection, imaginary gardens with real toads in them,
        shall we have
it. In the meantime, if you demand on one hand,
the raw material of poetry in
        all its rawness and
        that which is on the other hand
            genuine, then you are interested in poetry.

from *Observations*, 1925

POETRY

I too, dislike it:
　there are things that are important beyond all this fiddle.
The bat, upside down; the elephant pushing,
a tireless wolf under a tree,
the base-ball fan, the statistician—
"business documents and schoolbooks"—
these phenomena are pleasing,
but when they have been fashioned
into that which is unknowable,
we are not entertained.
It may be said of all of us
that we do not admire what we cannot understand;
enigmas are not poetry.

from *The New Poetry* (1932)

POETRY

I too, dislike it; there are things
   that are important beyond all this fiddle. Reading it,
      however, with a perfect contempt for it,
         one discovers that there is in it, after all, a place for the
            genuine:
            hands that can grasp, eyes that can dilate, hair that
               can rise if it must,

the bat holding on upside down,
   an elephant pushing, a tireless wolf under a tree,
      the immovable critic twitching his skin
         like a horse that feels a fly, the base-ball fan, the statis-
            tician—nor is it
               valid to discriminate against business documents,
               school-books,

MARIANNE MOORE   415

trade reports—these phenomena
   are important; but dragged into conscious oddity by
      half poets, the result is not poetry.
         This we know. In a liking for the raw material in all
            its rawness,
               and for that which is genuine, there is liking for poetry.

from *Selected Poems* (1935)

POETRY

I, too, dislike it: there are things that are important beyond all
        this fiddle.
    Reading it, however, with a perfect contempt for it, one dis-
        covers in
    it after all, a place for the genuine.
        Hands that can grasp, eyes
        that can dilate, hair that can rise
            if it must, these things are important not because a

high-sounding interpretation can be put upon them but because
        they are
    useful. When they become so derivative as to become un-
        intelligible,
    the same thing may be said for all of us, that we
        do not admire what
        we cannot understand: the bat
            holding on upside down or in quest of something to

eat, elephants pushing, a wild horse taking a roll, a tireless wolf
        under
    a tree, the immovable critic twitching his skin like a horse that
        feels a flea, the base-
    ball fan, the statistician—
        nor is it valid
            to discriminate against 'business documents and

school-books'; all these phenomena are important. One must make
        a distinction
    however: when dragged into prominence by half poets, the
        result is not poetry,

[36]

nor till the poets among us can be
    'literalists of
    the imagination'—above
       insolence and triviality and can present

for inspection, imaginary gardens with real toads in them, shall
       we have
  it. In the meantime, if you demand on the one hand,
  the raw material of poetry in
    all its rawness and
    that which is on the other hand
       genuine, then you are interested in poetry.

[37]

from *The Complete Poems of Marianne Moore* (1967)

POETRY

I, too, dislike it.

Reading it, however, with a perfect contempt for it, one discovers in
it, after all, a place for the genuine.

[Thus the poem appeared on page 36 of the 1967 edition. Turning to
the back of the volume, one finds in the notes to the poems the
following on pages 266–67—Editor.]

POETRY

ORIGINAL VERSION:

I, too, dislike it: there are things that are important beyond all this fiddle.

Reading it, however, with a perfect contempt for it, one discovers in
it after all, a place for the genuine.

Hands that can grasp, eyes
that can dilate, hair that can rise
if it must, these things are important not because a

high-sounding interpretation can be put upon them but because they are
useful. When they become so derivative as to become unintelligible,
the same thing may be said for all of us, that we
do not admire what
we cannot understand: the bat
holding on upside down or in quest of something to
eat, elephants pushing, a wild horse taking a roll, a tireless wolf under

a tree, the immovable critic twitching his skin like a horse that feels a flea,

the base-

ball fan, the statistician—
    nor is it valid
        to discriminate against "business documents and

school-books"; all these phenomena are important. One must make a

distinction

however: when dragged into prominence by half poets, the result is not

poetry,

nor till the poets among us can be
    "literalists of
    the imagination"—above
        insolence and triviality and can present

for inspection, "imaginary gardens with real toads in them," shall we have
    it. In the meantime, if you demand on the one hand,
    the raw material of poetry in
        all its rawness and
        that which is on the other hand
            genuine, you are interested in poetry.

Diary of Tolstoy, p. 84: "Where the boundary between prose and poetry lies, I shall never be able to understand. The question is raised in manuals of style, yet the answer to it lies beyond me. Poetry is verse: prose is not verse. Or else poetry is everything with the exception of business documents and school books."

"Literalists of the imagination." Yeats, *Ideas of Good and Evil* (A. H. Bullen, 1903), p. 182. "The limitation of his view was from the very intensity of his vision; he was a too literal realist of imagination, as others are of nature; and because he believed that the figures seen by the mind's eye, when exalted by inspiration, were 'eternal existences,' symbols of divine essences, he hated every grace of style that might obscure their lineaments."

GLOSSARY

accidental   Any element in a *text* that is not *substantive*, that is, whose *variation* does not affect meaning; traditionally includes spelling, punctuation, and capitalization.

apparatus   Elements of a *critical edition* that support the *text*, such as the *textual introduction, textual notes,* and lists of *variants*.

archetype   The single (usually lost) *document* from which all surviving *witnesses* of a *work* ultimately derive, not necessarily synonymous with an author's *fair copy*.

authority   A relative value assigned to a particular *text* or to a particular *reading*, usually but not always indicating how certain it is that the text or reading derives from an author.

autograph   See *holograph*.

best-text editing   An editorial approach that (using various criteria) chooses one *document* as the least corrupted, and reproduces its *text* as closely as possible.

bibliography   The study of books as objects, with an eye toward listing and distinguishing (or enumerating) them, describing their physical properties (such as typography or *format*), reconstructing the histories of their production, and their contents. Textual bibliography is another term for *textual criticism*. See also *codicology* and *paleography*.

bifolia   (singular is *bifolium*) A *sheet* with a single fold, producing two leaves sharing a spine, usually nested in other bifolia to form a *quire* or *gathering*.

cancel   A portion of a *text* that has been marked for deletion; also a portion of a book, usually a leaf or more, that has been inserted to replace a portion that has either been removed or marked for replacement.

cast off   To mark a *manuscript* for *printing by formes*, estimating how many words will fit per printed page and marking approximate page breaks in the manuscript.

cladistics   A computer-assisted version of *stemmatics* with methods borrowed from the biological sciences, in which the most parsimonious *stemma*, i.e., trees with the fewest branches, are developed to explain the development of a manuscript tradition; see *genealogical edition*.

clear-text edition   A *critical edition* in which the *apparatus* is kept separate from the *text*, which is presented with as little editorial interruption as possible. In a clear-text edition, the *textual notes* are not printed at the bottom of each page of text, for instance, but are reserved for the end of the volume or even for another volume entirely.

codex   (plural is *codexes* or *codices*) A *manuscript*; more specifically a book having a form differentiated from the *scroll*, that is, with leaves joined at a spine.

codicology   A branch of *bibliography* attending to *manuscripts*.

collation   In *textual criticism*, the close comparison of two or more *texts* in order to list their shared *readings* and their *variants*; also the list so produced.

composing stick   Also *compositor's stick*, or, more simply, *stick*; a small, hand-held shelf that can be adjusted to a selected line length, in which the compositor assembles the pieces of type from the *type cases* into a handful of lines before assembling lines as a page.

compositor   A typesetter, especially one in a hand-press operation.

conflated text   A *text* pieced together from two or more distinct *versions* of a *work*.

conjecture   An *emendation* not deriving from a *reading* found in any *witness*.

conjunction   *Readings* about which two or more *texts* agree; see *disjunction*.

content notes   Also called *explanatory notes*, and distinguished from *textual notes*, they are notes which supply background information, definitions, etymologies, interpretations, etc.

copy   The *document* that provides the *compositor* the *text* to be set into type; in *manuscript* production, such a document is called an *exemplar*.

copyright   Exclusive legal right to publish a given *work* and to approve or deny such license to others.

copy-text   The *text* upon which an *edition* is based, especially in *eclectic editions*.

coterie   A small group of people, usually with shared interests, among whom an author might circulate a *work*, usually in *manuscript*.

critical edition   An *edition* based upon an examination and evaluation of the available *witnesses* of a *work*.

crux   A passage that has been the subject of discussion and disagreement among textual scholars; a problem in the *text*.

deep editing   See *eclectic edition*.

definitive edition   The *edition* that sets the standard for the *text* of a particular *work* or works, generally to be preferred for scholarship; also called the *standard edition*.

diplomatic edition   An *edition* based on a diplomatic *transcript*, a transcript that reports the *text* of a *document* as exactly as possible, without *emendation*; also called *documentary edition*.

direct editing   See *eclectic edition*.

disjunction   *Readings* in which two or more *texts* disagree; used with *conjunction* to group witnesses into families.

distribute   To disassemble pages and sort pieces of type to their boxes in the *type cases*; pieces of type are occasionally returned to the wrong place during distribution, resulting in "foul cases," which can lead to typographical errors when the type is next used.

dittography   Repetition of a portion of *text*.

divinatio   In the *Lachmannian* method, the process of making *emendations* to a *text* when other processes (see *emendatio*) do not produce acceptable results.

document   The physical object—such as a *manuscript*—in which a *text* can be found, to be distinguished from *work*.

documentary edition   See *diplomatic edition*.

duodecimo   A small-sized book, smaller than *octavo*, made from *sheets* folded in such a way to form *gatherings* of twelve leaves, twenty-four pages; also written *twelvemo*, *12°*, or *12mo*.

eclectic edition   An *edition* based upon more than one *text*, usually with one serving as a *copy-text*, with other texts occasionally supplying *variant readings*.

edition   In *bibliography*, all copies of a book printed (for the most part) from a single setting of type; more generally, any printed *version* of a *work*.

editio princeps   The first printed *edition* of a *work*.

eliminatio codicum descriptorum   A *manuscript* that can be proven to have been copied directly from another surviving manuscript, and therefore of no *authority*; also the process by which such manuscripts are discovered.

emendatio   The process in *Lachmannian editing* of correcting the *texts* of a *witness* group in order to reconstruct the *hyparchetype* and, ultimately, the *archetype*.

emendation   A change made to a *text* by an editor; if not recorded in the *apparatus*, it is a *silent emendation*.

exemplar   The *manuscript* from which another manuscript is copied; in printing, such a document is called *copy*.

eyeskip   An omission of letters, words, and even whole lines, resulting from the copyist's, *compositor's*, or typesetter's eye "skipping" ahead too far when returning to the *exemplar* or *copy* and picking up with a similar or repeated word. See *haplography*.

facsimile   An *edition* or portion of an edition that reproduces a particular *document*'s *text* and non-textual features, usually by photography but sometimes by another means, such as type.

fair copy   A clean *manuscript version* of a *work* made either by the author or by a scribe commissioned by the author; see *foul papers*.

folio   A large-size book made from *sheets* folded only once, forming two leaves, four pages; usually nested within other such sheets to form a folio-in-fours or a folio-in-sixes; abbreviated as *F*, *fol.*, or *2°*. Also any leaf from a book numbered by folios, so that each leaf (rather than each page) is given a number, the sides of which are designated by the abbreviations for *recto* (*r*) or *verso* (*v*), as in *fol. 41ʳ* or *fols. 22v–23r.*

format The structure of a book, such as *folio* or *octavo*, indicating the way in which a *sheet* is folded after having been printed, thus determining the layout of type pages in the *forme*.

forme The wooden or metal frame in which type pages are locked up for printing; also the pages so locked up in a forme or printed from the forme. If the forme includes the first page (the *recto* of the first leaf) of a gathering, it is the outer forme; if it includes the second page (the *verso* of the first leaf), it is the inner forme.

foul papers An author's rough draft, usually reserved for *manuscript* copies.

gathering a collection of *bifolia*, each nested within the next to form a single spine, forming one section (called a *signature*) of a book. See also *quire*.

genealogical edition Not to be confused with *genetic edition*, an edition that reconstructs a lost *text* by determining the "family" relationships among surviving *witnesses*; see *stemmatics*, *Lachmannian*, and *cladistics*.

genetic edition Not to be confused with *genealogical edition*, an *edition* that records and displays the development of a *text* over time, sometimes restricted to a single *document*, such as an author's rough draft.

gloss A note, sometimes written between lines of *text*, sometimes in the margin, providing an explanation or translation of a word, phrase, or passage.

haplography The accidental elimination of repeated letters, words or phrases, and so on; *eyeskip* is one form.

holograph A *manuscript* in an author's own handwriting.

horizontal contamination The result of a *text* having been copied from more than one *exemplar* or *copy*, that is, introducing *readings* from more than one family of the *manuscript* tradition. Horizontal contamination complicates and sometimes precludes determining family trees, or *stemmas*, for a *genealogical edition*.

hyparchetype   The single *manuscript* (usually lost) from which a sub-group of surviving *witnesses* of a *work* descend; in a *genealogical edition* the hyparchetypes are reconstructed from the surviving witnesses, and the *archetype* from comparison of the hyparchetypes.

justify   To adjust the type, spacing, and (in early printing) the spelling of a line of prose, perhaps hyphenating a word, so that the right margin is even.

Lachmannian   A *genealogical edition* or editorial approach, based on principles developed in part by German philologist Karl Lachmann (1793–1851).

lectio dificilior potior   "The harder reading is to be preferred," a princi-ple of *textual criticism* that holds that copyists will generally simplify texts when they encounter something that puzzles them, such as words they do not know, so that, when an editor must choose between two or more *readings*, the one more likely to cause errors is to be preferred.

lection   See *reading*.

lemma   (pl. *lemmata*) The first part of a *textual note*, that is, the heading, the word or passage quoted from the *text* on which the rest of the note is a commentary.

manuscript   Any handwritten *document*; more specifically, a handwrit-ten book; abbreviated *MS* (singular) and *MSS* (plural). See also *typescript*.

minim   A short vertical stroke in handwriting, forming the basis of many letters, such as *i*, *m*, *n*, and *u*. In certain medieval hands, the ways minims are joined with one another can make it difficult to distinguish these characters from one another.

modernization   A kind of *regularization* and *normalization*, making an older *text* conform to current practices of, say, spelling and punctu-ation.

normalization A kind of *regularization*, making a *text*'s variations in spelling, punctuation, capitalization, etc., conform to the practice of a given authority (such as *The Chicago Manual of Style*, or the *MLA Style Manual*).

octavo A small-sized book made of *sheets* folded three times to form *gatherings* of eight leaves, sixteen pages.

paleography The study of old handwriting.

palimpsest A *manuscript* in which some early text has been erased and a second text has been copied over, with the first text sometimes still partially legible.

parallel-text edition An edition which places two or more versions of the same work side-by-side, either in columns or in facing pages.

perfect (pronounced *per-féct*) To print the second side of a *sheet* which has already had the first side printed.

proofs Pages of a text printed so that corrections can be made to the text or layout.

public domain Describes a work not protected by *copyright*.

quarto (abbreviated Q or 4°) A book size and format, larger than *octavo* but smaller than *folio*, made from *sheets* folded twice to form *quires* of four leaves, eight pages, and sometimes nested one within another to form a quarto-in-eights.

quire A group of nested *bifolia*, originally one of four leaves, eight pages, deriving from a single, folded *sheet* of paper or parchment, later becoming roughly synonymous with *gathering*. See also *signature*.

reading The wording of a passage in question.

received text The *text* that had the widest circulation and acceptance, often the *editio princeps*; the standard *version* of a work.

recensio The analysis by which a *genealogical edition* determines the family relationships among *witnesses*.

recto The right-hand-side page of any opening in a book; that is, the front side of a leaf; see *verso*.

regularization Reducing variations in spelling, punctuation, or capitalization so that they accord to a rule, without necessarily conforming to the practice of any particular authority or period; *normalization* and *modernization* are stricter forms.

scholarly edition   Any *edition* that bases its *text* on a critical evaluation of the *witnesses* of a *work*.

scrolls   An ancient form of book, in contrast to the *codex*, consisting of rolls of either parchment or papyrus, with the *text* generally written in short columns across the width of the scroll.

seriatim   A method of setting type by following the order of pages in which they will be read; compare with *setting by formes*.

setting by formes   Setting type by the order in which pages would be printed, rather than by the order in which they would be read. Pages that will appear together in a single *forme* would be set at a single time. The process required the *compositor* to *cast off* the *copy*, but was a more efficient use of type than setting type *seriatim*.

sheet   a piece of paper (less often parchment) that can be printed and then folded to a determined *format*.

siglum   (pl. *sigla*) An abbreviated code or symbol standing for a *document* or *witness;* often an abbreviation of the library or collection that holds the *manuscript*, or an abbreviation of the printer's, publisher's or editor's name for printed texts; in early modern printed books, sometimes its *format*, followed by its sequence in the printing of that format, as so: *F1, F2, Q1, Q2*, etc.

signature   A *gathering* or section of a printed book distinguished from other sections by a symbol (usually a letter or series of letters), placed at the foot of the first page of the *gathering* and often on several (but not all) *recto* pages thereafter, with a number added to indicate the leaf of the signature. Signatures guide binders in properly folding sheets and putting *gatherings* in the proper order. In early printed books, printed page or *folio* numbers are occasionally faulty, but signatures rarely are, so that scholars prefer to cite pages in early printed books by signatures, as follows: *A3^r–B2^v*

silent emendation   An *emendation* not recorded in the notes; editors will often categorize in the *textual introduction* the elements of a *text* that have been silently emended.

standard edition   The *edition*, usually a *critical edition*, that the scholarly community generally agrees provides the best *version* or *text* of a given *work* or body of works.

stemma   (or *stemma codicum*) A family tree for a reconstructed *text* or a *work*, sometimes graphical, indicating relationships among *witnesses*, *hyparchetypes*, and the *archetype*.

stemmatic reading   That part of a *textual note* that follows a *lemma*, the *reading* of a witness for a particular lemma.

stop-press corrections   Corrections made in the type in the midst of a print run rather than prior to the run, so that some copies of an *edition* will contain uncorrected pages.

substantive   Any element in a *text* that is not *accidental*, that is, whose variation can affect meaning; traditionally, the wording of a *text* rather than its punctuation or orthography.

text   An arrangement of words; in *textual criticism*, not to be confused with *work* or *document*.

textual criticism   The critical examination and evaluation of the *text* of a *work*.

textual introduction   That part of the *apparatus* that explains the methods and reasoning behind the preparation of a *critical edition*.

textual notes   That part of the *apparatus* that details editorial decisions for individual *lemmata* and that often records significant *variants* for the *critical edition*.

textus receptus   The *received text*.

transcript   A copy of the *text* of a *document* by someone other than its author.

type case   A shallow, open box with sufficient subdivisions for storing pieces of type. A divided lay or divided case (common until the end of nineteenth century) consists of two such boxes, normally positioned one above another on angled shelves, so that capital letters are in the upper case, while small letters are in the lower case (hence the terms *uppercase* and *lowercase*).

typescript   In contrast to *manuscript*, a *document* produced by a typewriter or word processor. Abbreviated *TS* (singular) and *TSS* (plural).

variant   A *reading* in the *text* of one *document* that differs from that in the text of another document of the same *work*; also used to describe a document that contains variants, as in *a variant manuscript*.

variorum   an *edition*—not necessarily *critical*—that presents commentary and/or *variant readings* from *witnesses* or from previous editions.

version   A *text* that differs substantially from another text of the same *work*, due, for instance, to revision.

verso   The left-hand page in any opening in a book; the back of a leaf or *folio*.

witness   The *text* of a *document* used to provide evidence about the text of a *work*.

work   Traditionally, any discrete verbal production, such as a poem or play; more specifically, a work is a mental construct, which, though real and composed of words, may take many physical forms, such as a *manuscript*, printed book, or audio recording; to be distinguished from *document* and *text*.

SELECTED BIBLIOGRAPHY

GENERAL

The grandfather of guidebooks to bibliography and textual scholarship is McKerrow's, whose effort was updated and supplanted by Gaskell's. Williams and Abbott's more succinct *Introduction* is better for the beginner. Each of these has in some senses been superseded by Greetham's monumental textbook, *Textual Scholarship*. McKenzie's lecture offers the best short argument for the interconnectedness of all fields of textual study.

Altick, Richard D. *The Scholar Adventures*. Columbus: Ohio State UP, 1987.

Altick, Richard D., and John J. Fenstermaker. *The Art of Literary Research*. 4th ed. New York: W. W. Norton & Company, 1993.

Gaskell, Philip. *A New Introduction to Bibliography*. New York: Oxford UP, 1972.

Glaister, Geoffrey Ashall. *Encyclopedia of the Book*. 2nd ed. New Castle, Del.: Oak Knoll Press, 1996.

Greetham, D. C. *Textual Scholarship: An Introduction*. Rev. ed. New York: Garland, 1994.

McKenzie, D. F. *Bibliography and the Sociology of Texts*. London: British Library, 1986.

McKerrow, Ronald B. *An Introduction to Bibliography for Literary Students*. Oxford: Clarendon, 1928.

Williams, William Proctor, and Craig S. Abbott. *An Introduction to Bibliographical and Textual Studies*. 3rd ed. New York: MLA, 1999.

JOURNALS

The following journals offer the richest sources of discussions for textual and bibliographical matters. The entire *Studies in Bibliography* series is available online without subscription.

Documentary Editing. Association for Documentary Editing. 1979–.

The Library: Transactions of the Bibliographical Society. The Bibliographical Society. 1892–. (Now in its seventh series.)

Papers of the Bibliographical Society of America. Bibliographical Society of America. 1906–.

Studies in Bibliography. Bibliographical Society of the University of Virginia. 1948–. Website: etext.virginia.edu/bsuva/sb/.

Text: Transactions of the Society for Textual Scholarship. Society for Textual Scholarship. 1984–2005. Continued by *Textual Cultures*.

Textual Cultures. The Society for Textual Scholarship. 2006–.

Variants. The European Society for Textual Scholarship. 2001–.

BOOK HISTORY

Textual criticism and textual editing are best understood within the larger field of Book History, most ably introduced by Finkelstein and McCleery's collection. The classic texts are by Febvre and Martin and by Eisenstein.

Barthes, Roland. "From Work to Text." *Image, Music, Text*. Trans. Stephen Heath. New York: Hill and Wang, 1977. 155–64.

Eisenstein, Elizabeth L. *The Printing Press as an Agent of Change*. New York: Cambridge UP, 1979.

Febvre, Lucien, and Henri-Jean Martin. *The Coming of the Book: The Impact of Printing, 1450–1800*. Trans. David Gerard., ed. Geoffrey Nowell-Smith and David Wooton. Atlantic Highlands, N.J.: Humanities, 1976.

Finkelstein, David, and Alistair McCleery. *An Introduction to Book History*. London: Routledge, 2005.

———, eds. *The Book History Reader*. 2nd ed. London: Routledge, 2006.

BIBLIOGRAPHY AND CODICOLOGY

After Gaskell's and Greetham's introductions, above, interested students might wish to explore works with a more narrow focus. The selections below suggest the breadth this field possesses. Moxon's book, written and illustrated by a printer himself, is a treasury of information on how printing was carried out in the hand-press era. Nickell's richly illustrated book details writing instruments, with an emphasis on the nineteenth and twentieth centuries.

Davison, Peter, ed. *The Book Encompassed: Studies in Twentieth-Century Bibliography*. New York: Cambridge UP, 1992.

King, Katie. "Bibliography and a Feminist Apparatus for Literary Production." *Text* 5 (1991): 91–104.

Legros, Lucien Alfonse and John Cameron Grant. *Typographical Printing-Surfaces: The Technology and Mechanism of Their Production*. 1916, rpt. New York: Garland, 1980.

McKenzie, D. F. "Printers of the Mind: Some Notes on Bibliographical Theories and Printing House Practices." *Studies in Bibliography* 22 (1969): 1–75.

Morrisson, Stanley. *The Typographic Book, 1450–1935*. Chicago: Chicago UP, 1963.

Moxon, Joseph. *Mechanick Exercises on the Whole Art of Printing*. 1683–84. 2nd ed. Ed. Herbert Davis and Harry Carter. New York: Dover, 1962.

Nickell, Joe. *Pen, Ink, and Evidence: A Study of Writing and Writing Materials for the Penman, Collector, and Document Detective*. Lexington: UP of Kentucky, 1990.

Pollard, A. W. *Shakespeare Folios and Quartos: A Study in the Bibliography of Shakespeare's Plays, 1594–1685*. London: Methuen, 1909.

Richards, Mary P., ed. *Anglo-Saxon Manuscripts: Basic Readings*. London: Routledge, 1994.

Tanselle, G. Thomas. *Selected Studies in Bibliography*. Charlottesville: UP of Virginia, 1979.

PALEOGRAPHY

Brown's *Guide* and Preston and Yeandle's *English Handwriting* are good places for beginners to dip into the complications and details of paleogrpaphy.

Bischoff, Bernhard. *Latin Palaeography: Antiquity and the Middle Ages.* Trans. Daibhí Ó Cróinín and David Ganz. Cambridge: Cambridge UP, 1990.

Brown, Michelle P. *A Guide to Western Historical Scripts from Antiquity to 1600.* Toronto: U of Toronto P, 1990.

Croft, P. J. *Autograph Poetry in the English Language: Facsimiles of Original Manuscripts from the Fourteenth to the Twentieth Centuries.* 2 vols. London: Cassell, 1973.

Denholm-Young, Noel. *Handwriting in England and Wales.* Cardiff: U of Wales P, 1964.

Derolez, Albert. *The Paleography of Gothic Manuscript Books, from the Twelfth to the Early Sixteenth Century.* Cambridge: Cambridge UP, 2003.

Mooney, Linne R. "Chaucer's Scribe." *Speculum* 81.1 (2006): 97–138.

Parkes, Malcolm B. *English Cursive Book Hands, 1250–1500.* Berkeley: U of California P, 1980.

———. *Scribes, Scripts, and Readers.* London: Hambledon, 1991.

Preston, Jean F., and Laetitia Yeandle. *English Handwriting, 1400–1650.* Binghamton: Medieval and Renaissance Texts and Studies, 1992.

Tannenbaum, S. A. *The Handwriting of the Renaissance; Being the Development and Characteristics of the Script of Shakspere's Time.* New York: Columbia UP, 1930.

Whalley, J. I. *English Handwriting, 1540–1853: An Illustrated Survey.* London: HMSO, 1969.

TEXTUAL CRITICISM AND EDITING

After Greetham's *Textual Scholarship*, students might turn to Tanselle's *Textual Criticism Since Greg* for a history of recent debates and trends in textual criticism. Kline and Johanson's *Guide* is the standard for documentary editing, while Maas's *Textual Criticism* is the modern source for genealogical approaches.

Barney, Stephen, ed. *Annotation and Its Texts.* New York: Oxford UP, 1991.

Bennett, Betty T. "Feminism and Editing Mary Wollstonecraft Shelley: The Editor And?/Or? the Text." *Palimpsest: Editorial Theory in the Humanities.* Ed. George Bornstein and Ralph Williams. Ann Arbor: U of Michigan P, 1993. 67–96.

Blayney, Peter W. M. *The Texts of* King Lear *and Their Origins, vol. 1: Nicholas Okes and the First Quarto.* New York: Cambridge UP, 1982.

Bornstein, George, and Ralph Williams, eds. *Palimpsest: Editorial Theory in the Humanities.* Ann Arbor: U of Michigan P, 1993.

Bornstein, George, ed. *Representing Modernist Texts: Editing as Interpretation.* Ann Arbor: U of Michigan P, 1991.

Bowers, Fredson. "Authorial Intention and Editorial Problems," *Text* 5 (1991): 49–62.

———. *Bibliography and Textual Criticism.* Oxford: Clarendon, 1964.

———. "Current Theories of Copy-Text with an Illustration from Dryden." *Modern Philology* 68 (1950): 12–20.

———. *Essays in Bibliography, Text, and Editing.* Charlottesville: UP of Virginia, 1975.

———. "Greg's 'Rationale of Copy-Text' Revisited." *Studies in Bibliography* 31 (1970): 90–161.

———. "Mixed Texts and Multiple Authority," *Text* 3 (1987): 63–90.

———. "Practical Texts and Definitive Editions." *Two Lectures on Editing: Shakespeare and Hawthorne.* Ed. Charlton Hinman and Fredson Bowers. Columbus: Ohio State UP, 1969. 21–70.

———. "Some Principles for Scholarly Editions of Nineteenth-Century American Authors." *Studies in Bibliography* 17 (1964): 223–28.

———. *Textual and Literary Criticism.* Cambridge: Cambridge UP, 1966.

———. "Textual Criticism." *The Aims and Methods of Scholarship in Modern Languages and Literatures.* 2nd ed. Ed. James Thorpe. New York: MLA, 1970.

Brack, O. M., Jr., and Warner Barnes, eds. *Bibliography and Textual Criticism: English and American Literature, 1700 to the Present.* Chicago: U of Chicago P, 1969.

Burnard, Lou, Katherine O'Brien O'Keefe, and John Unsworth, eds., *Electronic Textual Editing.* New York: MLA, 2006.

Cohen, Philip, ed. *Devils and Angels: Textual Editing and Literary Theory.* Charlottesville: UP of Virginia, 1991.

Dagenais, John. "That Bothersome Residue: Towards a Theory of the Physical Text." *Vox Intexta: Orality and Textuality in the Middle Ages.* Ed. A. N. Doane and Carol Braun Pasternack. Madison: U of Wisconsin P, 1991. 246–59.

De Grazia, Margareta. "What Is a Work? What Is a Document?" *New Ways of Looking at Old Texts: Papers of the Renaissance English Text Society, 1985–1991.* Ed. W. Speed Hill. Binghamton: Medeival and Renaissance Texts and Studies, 1993. 199–208.

Dearing, Vinton. "Concepts of Copy-Text Old and New." *The Library* 5th ser., 28 (1973): 281–93.

———. *Principles and Practice of Textual Analysis.* Berkeley: U of California P, 1974.

Donaldson, E. Talbot. "The Psychology of Editors of Middle English Texts." *Speaking of Chaucer.* New York: Norton, 1972. 102–18.

Edel, Leon. "The Text of the *Ambassadors*." *Harvard Library Bulletin* 14 (1960): 453–60.

Gabler, Hans Walter, George Bornstein, and Gillian Pierce, eds. *Contemporary German Editorial Theory*. Ann Arbor: U of Michigan P, 1995.

Gaskell, Philip. *From Writer to Reader: Studies in Editorial Method*. Oxford: Clarendon, 1978.

Gottesman, Ronald, and Scott Bennett, eds. *Art and Error: Modern Textual Editing*. Bloomington: Indiana UP, 1970.

Greetham, D. C., ed. *The Margins of the Text*. Ann Arbor: U of Michigan P, 1997.

———, ed. *Scholarly Editing: A Guide to Research*. New York: MLA, 1995.

———. "[Textual] Criticism and Deconstruction." *Studies in Bibliography* 44 (1991): 1–30.

———. "Textual and Literary Theory: Redrawing the Matrix." *Studies in Bibliography* 42 (199): 1–24.

———. "Textual Scholarship." *Introduction to Literary Scholarship in the Modern Languages and Literatures*. 2nd ed. Ed. Joseph Gibaldi. New York: MLA, 1991.

———. *Theories of the Text*. Oxford: Clarendon, 1999.

Greg. W. W. *The Calculus of Variants*. Oxford: Clarendon, 1927.

———. *Collected Papers*. Ed. J. C. Maxwell. Oxford: Clarendon, 1966.

Hall, Donald. "Robert Frost Corrupted." *The Weather for Poetry: Essays, Reviews, and Notes on Poetry, 1971–1981*. Ann Arbor: U of Michigan P, 1982. 140–59.

Halpenny, Francess G., ed. *Editing Twentieth-Century Texts*. Toronto: U of Toronto P, 1972.

Hill, W. Speed, ed. *New Ways of Looking at Old Texts: Papers of the Renaissance English Text Society, 1985–1991*. Binghamton: Medieval and Renaissance Texts and Studies, 1993.

Hinman, Charlton. *The Printing and Proof-reading of the First Folio of Shakespeare*. 2 vols. Oxford: Clarendon, 1963.

Kappel, Andrew J. "Complete with Omissions: The Text of Marianne Moore's Complete Poems." *Representing Modernist Texts: Editing and Interpretation*. Ed. George Bornstein. Ann Arbor: U of Michigan P, 1991. 125–56.

Kline, Mary-Jo, and Linda Johanson. *A Guide to Documentary Editing*. 2nd ed. Baltimore: Johns Hopkins UP, 1998.

Lancashire, Anne, ed. *Editing Renaissance Dramatic Texts: English, Italian, and Spanish*. New York: Garland, 1976.

Lancashire, Ian. "Renaissance Electronic Texts: Encoding Guidelines." *Renaissance Electronic Texts Supplementary Studies* 1 (1994).

Luey, Beth. *Editing Documents and Texts: An Annotated Bibliography*. Madison: Madison House, 1990.

Maas, Paul. *Textual Criticism*. Trans. Barbara Flower. Oxford: Clarendon, 1958.

Machan, Tim William. "Editing, Orality, and Late Middle English Texts." *Vox Intexta: Orality and Textuality in the Middle Ages*. Ed. A. N. Doane and Carol Braun Pasternack. Madison: U of Wisconsin P, 1991. 229–45.

————. *Textual Criticism and Middle English Texts*. Charlottesville: UP of Virginia, 1994.

Madden, David, and Richard Powers. *Writer's Revisions: An Annotated Bibliography of Articles and Books about Writer's Revisions and Their Comments on the Creative Process*. Metuchen: Scarecrow, 1991.

Maguire, Laurie E., and Thomas L. Berger, eds. *Textual Formations and Reformations*. Newark: U of Delaware P, 1998.

Marcus, Leah. "Textual Scholarship." *Introduction to Scholarship in Modern Languages and Literatures*. 3rd ed. Ed. David G. Nicholls. New York: MLA, 2007.

McCarren, Vincent, and Douglas Moffat, eds. *A Guide to Editing Middle English*. Ann Arbor: U of Michigan P, 1998.

McGann, Jerome J. *The Beauty of Inflections: Literary Investigations in Historical Method and Theory*. Oxford: Clarendon, 1988.

————. "The Case of *The Ambassadors* and the Textual Condition." *Palimpsest: Editorial Theory in the Humanities*. Ed. George Bornstein and Ralph Williams. Ann Arbor: U of Michigan P, 1993. 151–66.

————. *A Critique of Modern Textual Criticism* (Chicago: U of Chicago P, 1983).

————. "The Monks and the Giants: Textual and Bibliographical Studies and the Interpretation of Literary Works." *Textual Criticism and Literary Interpretation*. Chicago: University of Chicago Press, 1982. 180–99.

————. "A Note on the Current State of Humanities Scholarship." *Critical Inquiry* 30.2 (2004): 409–13.

————. *The Textual Condition*. Princeton: Princeton UP, 1991.

————, ed. *Textual Criticism and Literary Interpretation*. Chicago: U of Chicago P, 1985.

————. "What Is Critical Editing?" *The Textual Condition*. Princeton: Princeton UP, 1991. 48–68.

McKerrow, Ronald B. *Prolegomena for the Oxford Shakespeare: A Study in Editorial Method*. Oxford: Clarendon, 1939.

McLeod, Randall (as Random Cloud). "The Psychopathology of Everyday Art." *The Elizabethan Theatre* 9 (1986): 100–68.

————. "Information upon Information." *Text* 5 (1991): 241–86.

————. "Spellbound." *Play-Texts in Old Spelling*. Ed. G. B. Shand and Raymond C. Shady. New York: AMS, 1984. 81–96.

Minnis, A. J. and Charlotte Brewer, eds. *Crux and Controversy in Middle English Textual Criticism*. Cambridge: Brewer, 1992.

MLA. *Professional Standards and American Editions: A Response to Edmund Wilson*. New York: MLA, 1969.

MLA Center for Editions of American Authors. *Statement of Editorial Principles and Procedures*. Rev. ed. New York: MLA, 1972.

MLA Committee for Scholarly Editions. "Guidelines for Editors of Scholarly Editions." *Electronic Textual Editing*. Ed. Lou Burnard, Katherine O'Brien O'Keeffe, and John Unsworth. New York: MLA, 2006.

Monteiro, George. "To Point or Not to Point: Frost's 'Stopping by Woods.'" *ANQ* 16.1 (2003): 38–40.

Oliphant, Dave and Robin Bradford, eds. *New Directions in Textual Studies*. Austin: Harry Ransom Humanities Research Center, 1990.

Parker, Hershel. *Flawed Texts and Verbal Icons: Literary Authority in American Fiction*. Evanston: Northwestern UP, 1984.

———. "Regularizing Accidentals: The Latest Form of Infidelity." *Proof: Yearbook of American Bibliographical and Textual Studies* 3 (1973): 1–20.

Parkes, Malcolm B. *Pause and Effect: An Introduction to the History of Punctuation in the West*. Berkeley: U of California P, 1993.

Poirier, Richard. *Robert Frost: The Work of Knowing*. New York: Oxford UP, 1977.

Reiman, Donald H. *Romantic Texts and Contexts*. Columbia: U of Missouri P, 1987.

———. "Rogers's Oxford Shelley," *Romantic Texts and Contexts*. Columbia: U of Missouri P, 1987. 41–54.

———. *The Study of Modern Manuscripts: Public, Confidential, and Private*. Baltimore: Johns Hopkins UP, 1993:

———. "'Versioning': The Presentation of Multiple Texts." *Romantic Texts and Contexts*. Columbia: U of Missouri P, 1987. 167–80.

Shawcross, John T. "Scholarly Editions: Composite Editorial Principles of Single Copy-Texts, Multiple Copy-Texts, Edited Copy-Texts." *Text* 4 (1988): 297–318.

Shillingsburg, Peter. *Scholarly Editing in the Computer Age: Theory and Practice*. 3rd ed. Ann Arbor: U of Michigan P, 1996.

Stillinger, Jack. *Multiple Authorship and the Myth of Solitary Genius*. New York: Oxford UP, 1991.

———. "Multiple Authorship and the Question of Authority." *Text* 5 (1991): 285–96.

———. "Who Wrote J. S. Mill's *Autobiography*?" *Victorian Studies* 27.1 (1983): 7–23.

Tanselle, G. Thomas. "Greg's Theory of Copy-Text and the Editing of American Literature." *Studies in Bibliography* 28 (1975): 167–229.

———. *Literature and Artifacts*. Charlottesville: UP of Virginia, 1998.

———. *A Rationale of Textual Criticism*. Philadelphia: U of Pennsylvania P, 1989.

———. "Textual Criticism and Deconstruction." *Studies in Bibliography* 43 (1990): 1–33.

———. *Textual Criticism and Scholarly Editing*. Charlottesville: UP of Virginia, 1990.

———. *Textual Criticism Since Greg: A Chronicle, 1950–1985*. Charlottesville: UP of Virginia, 1987.

———. "Textual Scholarship." *Introduction to Literary Scholarship in the Modern Languages and Literatures*. Ed. Joseph Gibaldi. New York: MLA, 1981.

Taylor, Gary, and Michael Warren, eds. *The Division of the Kingdoms: Shakespeare's Two Versions of* King Lear. Oxford: Oxford UP, 1983.

Thompson, Ann. "Feminist Theory and the Editing of Shakespeare: *The Taming of the Shrew* Revisited." *Margins of the Text*. Ed. D. C. Greetham. Ann Arbor: U of Michigan P, 1997. 83–103.

Thorpe, James. *Principles of Textual Criticism*. San Marino: Huntington Library, 1972.

Urkowitz, Stephen. *Shakespeare's Revision of* King Lear. Princeton: Princeton UP, 1980.

Van Hulle, Dirk, "Annotated Bibliography: Key Works in the Theory of Textual Editing," commissioned by the MLA Committee on Scholarly Editions, www.mla.org/resources/documents/rep_scholarly/cse_bibliography.

Walker, Alice. *Textual Problems of the First Folio*. Cambridge: Cambridge UP, 1953.

Weisenburger, Steven C. "Errant Narrative and *The Color Purple*." *Journal of Narrative Technique* 19.3 (1989): 257–75.

Wells, Stanley. *Modernizing Shakespeare's Spelling*. Oxford: Clarendon, 1979.

West, James L. W., III. "Fair Copy, Authorial Intention, and 'Versioning.'" *Text* 6 (1993): 81–92.

———. *Textual Criticism and Editorial Technique Applicable to Greek and Latin Texts*. Stuttgart: Teubner, 1973.

White, Patricia S. "Black and White and Read All Over: A Meditation on Footnotes." *Text* 5 (1991): 81–90.

Willker, Wieland. *A Textual Commentary on the Greek Gospels*, vol. 4b, The *Pericope de Adultera*: Jo 7:53–8:11 (*Jesus and the Adultress*). 3rd ed. 2005 (www-user.uni-bremen.de/~wie/TCG/TC-John-PA.pdf).

Willis, James. "The Science of Blunders: Confessions of a Textual Critic." *Text* 6 (1993): 63–80.

Wilson, Edmund. "The Fruits of the MLA: I. 'Their Wedding Journey.'" *New York Review of Books* 26 Sept. 1968: 7–10.

———. "The Fruits of the MLA: II. Mark Twain." *New York Review of Books* 10 Oct. 1968: 6–14.

Zeller, Hans. "A New Approach to the Critical Constitution of Literary Texts." *Studies in Bibliography* 28 (1975): 231–64.

EDITIONS

The list of editions below gives a variety of approaches and degrees of editorial intervention. When the neoscholastic arguments and the details of critical editing seem to become madness, the reader is urged to turn to Vladimir Nabokov's *Pale Fire*, a parody of critical and scholarly editions. The novel purports to be an edition of a poem by a fictional poet, but its notes instead narrate a perhaps delusional autobiography of its fictional editor.

Austen, Jane. *The Novels of Jane Austen: The Text Based on Collation of the Early Editions*. 3rd ed. 5 vols. Ed. R. W. Chapman. Oxford: Oxford UP, 1933.

Bandel, Betty. *An Officer and a Lady: The World War II Letters of Lt. Col. Betty Bandel, Women's Army Corps*. Ed. Sylvia J. Bugbee. Hanover, NH: UP of New England, 2004.

Blake, William. *The Complete Poetry and Prose*. Rev. ed. Ed. David V. Erdman. Berkeley: U of California P, 1982.

Bradstreet, Anne. *The Works of Anne Bradstreet*. Ed. Jeannine Hensley. Cambridge: Harvard UP, 1967.

Burney, Fanny. *Evelina, or the History of a Young Lady's Entrance into the World*. Ed. Edward A. Bloom and Lilian D. Bloom. Oxford: Oxford UP, 1968.

Byron, George Gordon, Lord. *Lord Byron: The Complete Poetical Works*. 7 vols. Ed. Jerome J. McGann. Oxford: Clarendon, 1980–1993.

Chaucer, Geoffrey. *The Canterbury Tales: A Facsimile and Transcription of the Hengwrt Manuscript with Variants from the Ellesmere Manuscript*. Ed. Paul G. Ruggiers, et al. Norman: U of Oklahoma P, 1979.

———. *The General Prologue on CD-ROM*. Ed. Elizabeth Solopova. New York: Cambridge UP, 2000.

———. *The Hengwrt Chaucer Digital Facsimile*. Research Ed. Birmingham: SDE, 2000.

———. *The Riverside Chaucer*. Ed. Larry D. Benson, et al. Boston: Houghton Mifflin, 1986.

———. *The Text of* The Canterbury Tales. 8 vols. Eds. J. M. Manly and Edith Rickert. Chicago: U of Chicago P, 1940.

Crane, Stephen. *The Works of Stephen Crane*. 10 vols. Ed. Fredson Bowers. Charlottesville: UP of Virginia, 1969–75.

Dickinson, Emily. *The Manuscript Books of Emily Dickinson: A Facsimile Edition*. Ed. Ralph Franklin. Cambridge: Harvard UP, 1981.

Donne, John. *The Poems of John Donne*. Ed. H. J. C. Grierson. Oxford: Clarendon, 1912.

Eliot, T. S. *The Waste Land: A Facsimile and Transcript.* Ed. Valerie Eliot. New York: Harcourt, 1971.

Emerson, Ralph Waldo. *Journals and Miscellaneous Notebooks of Ralph Waldo Emerson.* 16 vols. Ed. William H. Gilman. Cambridge: Harvard UP, 1969–82.

Fitzgerald, F. Scott. *The Last Tycoon.* New York: Scribner, 1941.

———. *The Love of the Last Tycoon.* Ed. Matthew J. Bruccoli. New York: Simon and Schuster, 1995.

Franklin, Benjamin. *The Autobiography of Benjamin Franklin: A Genetic Text.* Eds. J. A. Leo Lemay and P. M. Zall. Knoxville: U of Tennessee P, 1981.

Frost, Robert. *New Hampshire.* New York: Holt, 1923.

———. *The Poetry of Robert Frost.* Ed. Edward Connery Lathem. New York: Holt, 1969.

Hoccleve, Thomas. *Thomas Hoccleve's Complaint and Dialogue.* Ed. J. A. Burrow. Early English Text Society, O. S. 313. Oxford: Oxford UP, 1999.

James, Henry. *The Ambassadors.* 2nd ed. Ed. S. P. Rosenbaum. New York: W. W. Norton & Company, 1994.

Jonson, Benjamin. *Ben Jonson.* 11 vols. Ed. C. H. Herford, Percy Simpson, and Evelyn Simpson. Oxford: Clarendon, 1925–52.

———. *Every Man in His Humour: A Parallel-Text Edition of the 1601 Quarto and the 1616 Folio.* Ed. J. W. Lever. Lincoln: U of Nebraska P, 1971.

Joyce, James. *Ulysses: A Critical and Synoptic Edition.* 3 vols. Ed. Hans Walter Gabler. New York: Garland, 1984.

Keats, John. *The Poems of John Keats.* Ed. Jack Stillinger. Cambridge: Harvard UP, 1978.

Langland, William. *The Vision of William Concerning Piers the Plowman, in Three Parallel Texts, Together with Richard the Redeless.* 2 vols. Ed. W. W. Skeat. Oxford: Clarendon, 1886.

———. *Piers Plowman: The B Version.* Ed. George Kane and E. Talbot Donaldson. London: Athlone, 1975.

Lowell, Amy. *Selected Poems.* Ed. Honor Moore. New York: Library of America, 2004.

Melville, Herman. *The Writings of Herman Melville.* 15 vols. Ed. Harrison Hayford, Hershel Parker, and G. Thomas Tanselle. Evanston: Northwestern UP, and Chicago: The Newberry Library, 1968–90.

Moore, Marianne. *Becoming Marianne Moore: The Early Poems, 1907–1924.* Ed. Robin G. Schulze. Berkeley: U of California P, 2002.

Nashe, Thomas. *The Works of Thomas Nashe.* Ed. R. B. McKerrow. London: Bullen, 1904–10.

Nabokov, Vladimir. *Pale Fire.* New York: Vintage, 1962.

Poe, Edgar Allan. *The Complete Works of Edgar Allan Poe.* Ed. James A. Harrison (1902).

————. *The Works of Edgar Allan Poe*. Ed. John Henry Ingram (1874).

————. *The Works of Edgar Allan Poe: Newly Collected and Edited, with a Memoir, Critical Introductions, and Notes*. Ed. Edmund Clarence Stedman and George Edward Woodberry (1894).

————. *The Works of the Late Edgar Allan Poe: With Notices of His Life and Genius*. Ed. Rufus W. Griswold, N. P. Willis, and James Russell Lowell (1856).

Rossetti, Dante Gabriel. *The Rossetti Archive*. Ed. Jerome J. McGann. Website: www.rossettiarchive.org/index.html.

Shakespeare, William. *The Complete Works*. Modern Spelling Edition. Ed. Stanley Wells and Gary Taylor. Oxford: Clarendon, 1986.

————. *The Complete Works*. Original Spelling Edition. Ed. Stanley Wells and Gary Taylor. Oxford: Clarendon, 1986.

————. *The First Folio of Shakespeare: The Norton Facsimile*. Ed. Charlton Hinman. New York: W. W. Norton, 1968.

————. *Mr. William Shakespeare's Comedies, Histories, & Tragedies: A photographic facsimile of the First Folio edition*. Ed. Helge Kökeritz and Charles Tyler Prouty. New Haven: Yale UP, 1954.

————. *The Norton Shakespeare*. Ed. Stephen Greenblatt, et al. New York: W. W. Norton Company, 1997.

————. *The Riverside Shakespeare*. 2nd ed. Ed. G. Blakemore Evans. Boston: Houghton Mifflin, 1997.

Shelley, Percy Bysshe. *The Complete Poetical Works of Percy Bysshe Shelley*. 2 vols. Ed. Neville Rogers. Oxford: Clarendon Press, 1972.

————. *The Complete Poetry of Percy Bysshe Shelley*. 2 vols. Ed. Donald H. Reiman and Neil Fraistat. Baltimore: Johns Hopkins University Press, 2000, 2004.

Suggs, M. Jack, Katharine Doob Sakenfeld, and James R. Mueller, eds. *The Oxford Study Bible, Revised English Bible with the Apocrypha*. New York: Oxford UP, 1992.

Wharton, Edith. *Fast and Loose and The Buccaneers*. Ed. Viola Hopkins Winner. Charlottesville: UP of Virginia, 1993.

Woolf, Virginia. *To the Lighthouse*. Ed. Mark Hussey. Orlando: Harcourt, 2005.

CREDITS

WORKING WITH DOCUMENTS

pp. 474–82 From *The Tragedie of Mariam, the Faire Queene of Jewry*. STC 4613.2. By permission of the Folger Shakespeare Library.

pp. 484–86 Courtesy of the Special Collections Department, University of Kentucky Libraries.

pp. 487–89 Courtesy of the American Antiquarian Society.

p. 490 MS Ticknor 769940.2. Courtesy of Dartmouth College Library.

pp. 491–92 Cheshunt Foundation Archives, Westminster College, Cambridge, MS A3/1/29. Reproduced by permission of The Cheshunt Foundation, Westminster College, Cambridge.

pp. 493–94 Courtesy of the American Antiquarian Society.

pp. 496–503 The Pierpont Morgan Library, New York. PML 16799.

pp. 504–08 Courtesy of the Special Collections Department, University of Kentucky Libraries.

p. 510 © British Library Board. All Rights Reserved. Add 10340, fol. 41r.

p. 511 © British Library Board. All Rights Reserved. Add 22139, fol. 138r.

p. 512 © British Library Board. All Rights Reserved. Add 36983, fol. 262r.

p. 513–14 © British Library Board. All Rights Reserved. Cotton Cleopatra D.VII, fol. 189r-v.

p. 515 © British Library Board. All Rights Reserved. Cotton Otho A xviii.

p. 516 © British Library Board. All Rights Reserved. Harley 7333, fol. 147v.

pp. 517–18 © British Library Board. All Rights Reserved. Lansdowne 699, fols. 82v-83r.

pp. 519–20 The Bodleian Library, University of Oxford, MS. Arch. Selden B.10, fols. 201v-202r.

p. 521 The Bodleian Library, University of Oxford, MS. Arch. Selden B.24, fol. 119r.

p. 522 The Bodleian Library, University of Oxford, MS. Fairfax 16, fol. 40r.

p. 523 The Bodleian Library, University of Oxford, MS. Fairfax 16, fol. 201r.

p. 524 The Bodleian Library, University of Oxford, MS. Hatton 73, fol. 118v.

p. 525 Cambridge University Library Gg.4.27, fol. 8v. Courtesy of Cambridge University Library.

pp. 526–27 Cambridge University Library Kk.1.5, part 6, fol. 4v–5r. Courtesy of Cambridge University Library.

pp. 528–29 By permission of the President and Fellows of Corpus Christi College, Oxford, CCC MS 203, pp. 22–23.

p. 530 Coventry City Record Office MS Accesssion 325, fol. 76v. By permission of the Coventry Archives.

p. 531 Ellesmere MS, 26 C9 f. viiir. Reproduced by permission of the Huntington Library, San Marino, California.

INDEX